LITERATURE
of Yesterday and To-day

THE HEART OF MIDLOTHIAN

LITERATURE OF YESTERDAY AND TO-DAY

COMPLETE TEXTS

P. L. ANDERSON *With the Eagles*

ANTHOLOGIES *A Century of English Essays · The Golden Book of Modern English Poetry · The Golden Treasury (Palgrave) · The Golden Treasury of Longer Poems · Plays for Boys and Girls · A Poetry Book for Boys and Girls · A Story Book for Boys and Girls*

RICHARD ARMSTRONG *Sea Change · Sabotage at the Forge · The Whinstone Drift · Danger Rock*

JANE AUSTEN *Emma · Mansfield Park · Persuasion · Pride and Prejudice · Sense and Sensibility*

KITTY BARNE *Bracken, My Dog · She Shall Have Music · Family Footlights · Barbie*

VIOLA BAYLEY *The Dark Lantern · Paris Adventure · Storm on the Marsh*

H. BEST *Garram, the Hunter*

CHARLOTTE BRONTË *Jane Eyre · Shirley · Villette · The Professor*

EMILY BRONTË *Wuthering Heights*

PATRICIA BROOKS *The Treasure of the Mountain*

FRANCES BROWNE *Granny's Wonderful Chair*

T. BULFINCH *The Age of Fable*

JOHN BUNYAN *The Pilgrim's Progress*

ARTHUR CATHERALL *Ten Fathoms Deep*

RICHARD CHURCH *The Cave*

JULIA CLARK *Crab Village*

WILKIE COLLINS *The Moonstone*

'C. COLLODI' *Pinocchio*

JOSEPH CONRAD *Lord Jim · The Mirror of the Sea · The Rover · Typhoon and Amy Foster*

F. CONVERSE *Long Will*

H. C. CREW *The Trojan Boy*

P. CUMMING *No Place for Ponies*

MURIEL DENISON *Susannah of the Mounties · Susannah of the Yukon*

CHARLES DICKENS *Barnaby Rudge · Great Expectations · Hard Times*

GEORGE ELIOT *Adam Bede · The Mill on the Floss*

MARGARET GOVAN *The Trail of the Red Canoe*

G. & W. GROSSMITH *The Diary of a Nobody*

P. HILL *Wind and Weather Permitting*

M. D. HILLYARD *Minikin's Visit*

ANTHONY HOPE *The Prisoner of Zenda · Rupert of Hentzau*

W. H. HUDSON *Far Away and Long Ago · Nature in Downland and An Old Thorn · A Shepherd's Life*

THOMAS HUGHES *Tom Brown's Schooldays*

JEROME K. JEROME *Three Men in a Boat · Three Men on the Bummel*

CHARLES KINGSLEY *Hereward the Wake · Westward Ho!*

FRED KITCHEN *Brother to the Ox · Jesse and his Friends*

BRIGID KNIGHT *Anne-Marie and the Pale Pink Frock*

CHARLES LAMB *Essays and Last Essays of Elia · Tales from Shakespeare*

W. M. LEVICK *Dry River Farm*

PATRICIA LYNCH *The Turf-Cutter's Donkey · The Turf-Cutter's Donkey goes Visiting*

ROBERT LYND *Further Essays · Things One Hears*

M. R. MITFORD *Our Village*

MARY NORTON *The Borrowers*

CAROLA OMAN *Alfred, King of the English · Robin Hood*

NICOLAI POLIAKOFF *Coco the Clown*

SIR A. T. QUILLER-COUCH *The Blue Pavilions · Shorter Stories · Troy Town*

CHARLES READE *The Cloister and the Hearth*

J. REASON *Bran, the Bronze-Smith · The Mad Miller of Wareham · 'Prentices and Clubs · Red Pennons Flying · The Secret Fortress*

SIR WALTER SCOTT *Guy Mannering · The Heart of Midlothian · Ivanhoe · Kenilworth · Old Mortality · Quentin Durward · Redgauntlet · Rob Roy · The Talisman*

DAVID SMITH *No Rain in those Clouds*

JOHANNA SPYRI *Heidi*

R. L. STEVENSON *The Master of Ballantrae and Weir of Hermiston · Virginibus Puerisque and Familiar Studies*

NOEL STREATFEILD *Ballet Shoes · The Circus is Coming · The House in Cornwall · Tennis Shoes*

JONATHAN SWIFT *Gulliver's Travels* (School Edition)

A. P. TERHUNE *Lad: a Dog*

W. M. THACKERAY *Henry Esmond*

ANTHONY TROLLOPE *Barchester Towers · The Small House at Allington · The Warden*

JOYCE WEST *Drovers Road*

LORNA WOOD *The People in the Garden*

ALISON WRIGHT *The Blakes*

THE HEART OF MIDLOTHIAN

Sir Walter Scott

J. M. DENT AND SONS LTD

BEDFORD ST LONDON W.C.2

PREFACE

THE first six Waverley Novels had shown a rise and fall, like that of a temperature chart, in Scott's creative powers. With the seventh, *The Heart of Midlothian*, Scott's genius soared to an Everest of achievement. It was in September 1817 that he entered into treaty with Archibald Constable, the publisher, for the four-volume work, the prospective publication of which was to be kept absolutely secret. During the first stages of the negotiation he wrote to him on 10th November: 'These will be the best volumes which have appeared. I pique myself on . . . *The Heart of Midlothian*.' *Rob Roy* was off his hands by the end of December, and he started on the new novel in a few days' time. Early in 1818 Constable was informed that the work proceeded in force.[1]

As *Tales of My Landlord*, Second Series, *The Heart of Midlothian* appeared on 4th June 1818. Naturally, as the theme concerned an important period in the history of the Scottish capital, its effect in Edinburgh was phenomenal, receiving an enthusiasm, Lockhart tells us, 'such as I never witnessed there on the appearance of any other literary novelty.' It was translated into French (1818), German (1821), Italian (1824), Swedish (1824), Spanish (1831), Portuguese (1844), Dutch (1872), and Danish (no date). To Daniel Terry, his actor friend who dramatized several of the Waverleys, Scott wrote on 16th May 1818: 'I think we could hammer a neat *comédie bourgeoise* out of *The Heart of Mid-Lothian*.' On 12th April 1819 Terry informed him of the progress of his stage version, the manuscript of which he had sent to Abbotsford for Scott's perusal. The adaptation, with occasional music by Bishop, was produced at Covent Garden on 17th April when Terry himself was the first actor to play David Deans. It ran for only fifteen performances. By 7th June Terry reported: '*The Heart of Mid-Lothian* goes on but I cannot say with that vigour of effect and power of attraction that could have been wished.' Replying on 15th June, Scott remarked: 'I am sorry, not surprised, that the *H. of M. L.* has done but

[1] *Letters of Sir Walter Scott*, vol. i (1932), pp. 516–17, 519, and vol. v (1933), pp. 13, 37, 101.

so-so—better luck another time.' [1]   There have been other
plays, under the novel's title; one by T. J. Dibdin which had
170 performances (1819), and another by W. H. Murray at the
Edinburgh Theatre Royal (1824).   A play called *Jeanie Deans*
by D. L. Boucicault had fifty-four performances in New York
(1860) and was given later in London (1863).   The novel was
also the basis of two opera versions.   *La Prison d'Édimbourg*,
with a libretto by Scribe and Planard and music by M. E. Carafa,
had twenty-two performances at the Paris Opéra Comique in
1833, and the opera, *Jeanie Deans*, with a libretto by Joseph
Bennett and music by Hamish MacCunn, had its *première* at
the Edinburgh Theatre Royal in 1894.   The latter, considered
MacCunn's best work, was revived at Daly's Theatre in 1896,
the Shaftesbury Theatre in 1918, and at Edinburgh in 1934.

The novel takes its title from Edinburgh's Old Tolbooth
or prison, known as 'the heart of Midlothian.' [2]   It opens
with the account of the Porteous Riot of 1736.   Captain John
Porteous, commander of the City Guard, had unjustifiably
caused the deaths of several citizens by ordering his force to
fire, and himself had fired, on the crowd assembled at the
hanging of a convicted robber, one Wilson.   The latter had
been sentenced to death but had been reprieved, whereupon
some of the incensed mob, headed by one Robertson, the
associate of Wilson, broke into the Tolbooth, carried Porteous
out, and hanged him.

With these authentic historical events Scott linked the
story of Jeanie and Effie Deans.   Robertson, whose real name
is George Staunton, a reckless character, is the lover of Effie,
imprisoned in the Tolbooth on a charge of child-murder,
from which she is unable to clear herself.   She refuses to
escape.   When she is tried, her devoted half-sister Jeanie
refuses to give the false evidence that would secure her ac-
quittal, and Effie is sentenced to death.   As an expression
of her deep devotion for Effie, the redoubtable Jeanie goes
on foot to London to get a pardon from the king through the
influence of John, Duke of Argyll.   He obtains an interview
for her with Queen Caroline, and by Jeanie's moving and
dignified pleading Effie is pardoned.

---

[1] *Letters of Sir Walter Scott*, vol. v (1933), pp. 148, 361 note 1, 396 note,
397.
[2] The Old Tolbooth door was presented to Scott by the Edinburgh
Magistrates after it was pulled down in 1817.   It is set into an upper wall
of Abbotsford House, where pilgrims of that literary shrine are shown it
as one of the treasured relics.

By the duke's favour Jeanie is also able to marry her lover, Reuben Butler, a Presbyterian minister, and her stern Cameronian father, 'Douce Davie Deans,' settles in a farm on the duke's estate. Meanwhile, Effie has eloped with, and married, George Staunton, eventually becoming Lady Staunton. It is now revealed that her child, whom she was accused of murdering, is actually alive. He had been carried off by Madge Wildfire, the insane daughter of Margaret Murdockson (who had charge of Effie during her confinement), and given over to some vagabonds. In his efforts to recover his son, Sir George Staunton is shot by him in the affray. Lady Staunton, overcome by the tragedy, retires to a convent in France and dies there. Jeanie's husband is given a good parish by the Duke of Argyll, whom Jeanie's heroism made a friend for life.

The earliest, and perhaps the most penetrating, analytical criticism, a remarkable epitome of the book, came from Lady Louisa Stuart, who wrote on 1st and 11th August 1818, to Scott, who was at Drumlanrig Castle on his way to visit his friend Morritt at Rokeby. 'I have got no farther than the death of Porteous,' ran her first letter, 'but can perceive in that scene the same hand, the same way of working up circumstances, which I know of old; nothing weakened or impaired.' And in the second letter from Sheffield Place: 'I am in a house where everybody is tearing it [the novel] out of each other's hands and talking of nothing else. So much for its success. The more flattering because it overcomes a prejudice. People were beginning to say the author would wear himself out, it was going on too long in the same key, and no striking notes could possibly be produced. On the contrary, I think the interest is stronger here than in any of the former ones (always excepting my first love Waverley) and one may congratulate you upon having effected what many have tried to do and nobody yet succeeded in, making the perfectly good character the most interesting. . . .

'Had this very story been conducted by a common hand, Effie would have attracted all our concern and sympathy, Jeanie only cold approbation. Whereas, Jeanie, without youth, beauty, genius, warm passions, or any other novel-perfection, is here our object from beginning to end. This is "enlisting the affections in the cause of virtue" ten times more than ever Richardson did; for whose male and female pedants, all-excelling as they are, I never could care half so much as I found myself inclined to do for Jeanie before I finished the first volume.'

But, finding Scott's Edinburgh legal characters tiresome, Lady Louisa thought they would not entertain English readers. Then she made a very shrewd observation. 'The latter part of the fourth volume unavoidably flags to a certain degree; after Jeanie is happily settled at Roseneath, we have no more to wish for.' Nevertheless, on the credit side, she asserted that 'Carlisle and Corby castles in Waverley did not affect me more deeply than the prison and trial scenes. The end of poor Madge Wildfire is also most pathetic. The meeting at Muschat's cairn most tremendous. . . . I shall own that my old family prejudices were secretly gratified by the light in which you place Uncle John of Argyle. . . . You have drawn him to the very life. I heard so much of him in my youth, so many anecdotes, so often "as the Duke of Argyle used to say," that I really believe I am almost as good a judge as if I had seen and lived with him. . . . My beloved mother [1] has told me that when she married (in 1737, the very time) he was still remarkably handsome; with manners more graceful and engaging than she ever saw in anyone else; the most agreeable person in conversation, the best teller of a story. When fifty-seven captivates eighteen, the natural powers of pleasing must be extraordinary. You have likewise coloured Queen Caroline exactly right, but I was bred up in another creed about Lady Suffolk, of whom, as a very old deaf woman, I have some faint recollection. My mother knew her intimately, and never would allow she had been the King's mistress, though she owned it was currently believed. She said he had just enough liking for her to make the Queen very civil to her, and very jealous and spiteful . . . I dare swear many of your readers never heard of the Duke of Argyle before.' [2]

In Jeanie Deans, Scott's own favourite among his heroines —'the lass kept tugging at my heartstrings,' he said—Lady Louisa perceived certain marked traits of her and Scott's deceased friend, Frances, Lady Douglas (the sister of Henry, 3rd Duke of Buccleuch). Shortly after that lady's death Lady Louisa had written to Scott on 27th January 1818,

---

[1] She was Mary Wortley Montagu (later Baroness Mount Stuart of Wortley), the wife of John Stuart, 3rd Earl of Bute. Lady Louisa was their youngest daughter.
[2] MS. 3889, ff. 161, 167, National Library of Scotland.

Preface ix

suggesting that he might introduce into prose some picture of her character. 'If *you* excel in any thing, it is in setting human beings as they are before our eyes; you possibly might at some time or other weave such a representation into something that would last. . . . You must have tasted the peculiar *raciness* there was *there*; and I have often and often thought that you could form an image we should recognize. Yet perhaps I might quarrel with it when you had done and think a thousand traits wanting.'[1]

She now seems to discern in Jeanie's character Scott's attempt to model her on the lady in question. 'Is it possible that you had at all in your eye what my wishes pointed to when I wrote to you last winter? If not, you will think the question strange yet with all the differences of situation, improvement, refinement, etc., nay with all the power to charm and dazzle, there was a strong likeness of character: the same steady attachment to rectitude, the same simplicity and singleness of heart, the same inward humility, the same forgetfulness of self, the same strong, plain, straightforward understanding, always hitting exactly right. . . . Let me dream that you designed this resemblance, whether you did or not; I would rather be indulged in the thought than set right, and I should like it the better for being so veiled by circumstances that the rest of the world would pass it without observation.'

It was, however, on Helen Walker of Cluden in Kirkcudbrightshire, whose life story he received from Mrs Thomas Goldie, that Scott based his heroine.[2] As he himself gives an account of this in his Introduction and Postscript, it is needless here to dilate further on the prototype, in whose memory, and to fulfil Mrs Goldie's desire, Scott arranged for the erecting of an inscribed (his own inscription) stone in 1831 in Kirkpatrick-Irongray churchyard where Helen was buried.

In addition to the general Shakespearean spaciousness which suffuses *The Heart of Midlothian*, there is also a Shakespearean quality in that Scottish Ophelia, Madge Wildfire (kinswoman in madness to Meg Merrilies), whose song, that incomparable lyric, 'Proud Maisie,' possesses an Elizabethan magic. And we should have to resort to the Elizabethan tragic dramatists like Webster or Ford to match the dark

---

[1] MS. 3889, f. 10, National Library of Scotland.
[2] In 1918 A. M. Bell contended that Scott's Jeanie Deans was taken from one Isabel Alison.
* 134

grandeur and terrifying vision of Muschat's Cairn when
Madge hints at invoking Ailie Muschat 'and she and I will
hae a grand bouking-washing, and bleach our claise in the
beams of the bonny Lady Moon. . . . But the moon, and the
dew, and the night-wind, they are just like a caller kail-blade
laid on my brow; and whiles I think the moon just shines on
purpose to pleasure me, when naebody sees her but mysell'
(chap. xvii, p. 191). Madge was modelled on a weak-minded
vagrant, Feckless Fannie, who roamed the country at the end
of the eighteenth century. Joseph Train supplied Scott with
all available information concerning her. According to the
late Dr W. S. Crockett, another possible original of Madge
was Whirlybet Meg (Betty Grahamslaw), a harmless maniac
who lived in the Melrose district.

I do not agree with those critics who disparage the sub-
sidiary characters such as the Saddletrees, whose racy comments not only give an added vitality to the bustling scene of
the Porteous mob but provide humorous relief to the novel's
tense main theme. Scott makes them speak in that rich
Doric which, when used in his masterly fashion, one would
not wish away. The shrewd, commonsensical Mrs Saddletree; the knowledgeable, self-esteemed Saddletree; the grasping, good-natured Dumbiedikes; the courageous but irascible
Captain of Knockdunder; the ingratiating turnkey, James
Ratcliffe, not to mention others, are an assemblage from the
teeming cornucopia of Scott's imagination hard to beat. No
wonder he was 'in great glee' over this novel and felt himself
'very strong.'

These minor characters reveal themselves, and are dif-
ferentiated, as much by their remarks as by their actions.
Take, for instance, Mrs Saddletree's droll comments on her
husband's prentice boy Willie: 'He was in rags when his
mother died; and the blue polonie that Effie made for him
out of an auld mantle of my ain, was the first decent dress the
bairn ever had on' (chap. v, p. 60). Or Ratcliffe's remarks
on conscience: 'A'body has a conscience, though it may be ill
wunnin at it. I think mine's as weel out o' the gate as maist
folk's are; and yet it's just like the noop of my elbow, it
whiles gets a bit dirl on a corner' (chap. xvii, p. 185). Even
Mrs Dolly Dutton, the Duke of Argyll's dairymaid, contributes her mite to this wealth of characterization. When she
apologizes to Knockdunder for arriving late at breakfast,
she is ready with the nonchalant remark: 'As we say in

Cheshire . . . I was like the Mayor of Altringham, who lies in bed while his breeches are mending, etc.' (chap. xlv, p. 459). As we survey this great concourse of characters we are, indeed, moved to echo Dryden's words on Chaucer: 'Here is God's plenty.'

The topographical background of the novel requires no speculation. Apart from London, Richmond, and Roseneath, the localities in and near Edinburgh (Scott's 'own romantic town') are easily recognized. Beyond the west door of the Church of St Giles there is a heart-shaped design in the cause-way which marks the site of 'the heart of Midlothian' of the romance. Other locales are mainly in the Arthur's Seat neighbourhood. Close to the Queen's Park is Muschat's Cairn, where Jeanie met Robertson. On the Park's south-west boundary is St Leonard's Hill with the little cottage supposed to have been Davie Deans's abode. About half way up the north-west side of Arthur's Seat is St Anthony's Chapel, among the ruins of which Robertson eluded the pursuit of Sharpitlaw. The Hunter's Bog surrounds all that side of the hill, and from the bottom of a precipice there springs St Anthony's Well, the whole situation being well adapted for a hermitage.

In this masterpiece Scott proved himself once more a con-summate builder of character but a weak architect in plot construction. The design is loose, and the latter part of the narrative, as Lady Louisa so early pointed out, is conventional, and rather melodramatic, anticlimax, although John Buchan, defending it, maintained that 'the conception of the Rose-neath chapters is right. Scott was always social historian as well as novelist, and he wanted to show Scottish life passing into a mellower phase. . . . Artistically, too, the instinct was sound.' [1]

Most contemporary critics, however, took exception to these later chapters. *Blackwood's Magazine* (August 1818), while praising the story of the Porteous mob as being almost his-torically accurate, considered the fourth volume superfluous. The *Monthly Review* (December 1818) thought the beginning of the novel was as excellent as the conclusion was 'lame and impotent.' Nassau Senior, discussing, in the *Quarterly Review* (October 1822), the Waverleys to date and asserting that *The Heart of Midlothian* was, so far, the most perfect, yet thought that almost all the fourth volume might have

[1] *Sir Walter Scott* (1932), p. 188.

been suppressed as 'it has the effect of a farce after a tragedy.'
Narrative prolixity throughout the book was deprecated by
the *Monthly Review*, and, much later, by Georg Brandes, the
Danish critic, who considered the finest scene, the trial, was
spoiled by its diffuseness. Again, the *Quarterly* withheld
praise for Jeanie's interview with the queen because 'Jeanie's
pleading appears to us much too rhetorical for the person
and for the occasion; and the queen's answer, supposing her
to have been overpowered by Jeanie's entreaties, "This is
eloquence," is still worse.'

For Jeanie herself, Scott's supreme triumph in the novel,
there was, with one or two exceptions, a chorus of praise.
Blackwood's, however, expressed a rather snobbish attitude
to this somewhat new kind of fiction character. 'Perhaps
there is a little too much of it [the character], as even with
persons not very aristocratical, the attention may appear to
be too long, and too diffusely called to the concerns of a cowfeeder and his daughter.' Walter Bagehot felt reluctant to
give Jeanie full marks as she was not essentially feminine in
the qualities that attracted readers to her. On the other
hand, in the *Edinburgh Review* (January 1820) even that
most exacting critic Jeffrey, though finding the novel comparatively languid, could not praise sufficiently one of Scott's
greatest figures, the moulding of which 'is superior to anything we can recollect in the history of invention . . . a remarkable triumph over the greatest of all difficulties in the
conduct of a fictitious narrative,' Jeanie is 'in the highest
degree both pathetic and sublime; and yet she never says or
does anything that the daughter of a Scotch cowfeeder might
not be supposed to say. . . . She is never sentimental, nor
refined, nor elegant; and though acting always, and in very
difficult situations, with the greatest judgment and propriety,
never seems to exert more than that downright and obvious
good sense which is so often found to rule the conduct of
persons of her condition.' Senior in the *Quarterly* also discovered in Jeanie 'a splendid exception to the insipidity of
perfect characters, and she excites and retains the reader's
deepest interest without possessing the advantage of a single
fault.' In 1833 a writer asked where should we seek for
Jeanie's prototype 'but among the well-educated and well-
principled peasantry of "dear Caledonia"?' And then in
July 1840 the critic in the *New York Review* declared that the
elevation of Jeanie to heroic rank is made in itself a kind of

moral inspiration and victory. As for Madge Wildfire, while *Blackwood's* saw nothing but exaggeration in her madness, the *Quarterly* noted a resemblance between her warning Robertson by her songs that an enemy was near and 'the incident in *The Lady of the Lake* where FitzJames is warned of the ambush by the song of the maniac Blanche.'

First and foremost, *The Heart of Midlothian* is a national epic, as national as one of Shakespeare's English historical plays, and it is noteworthy that three critics compared Scott's quality with that of Shakespeare. John Leycester Adolphus thought that the first interview of Jeanie with her imprisoned sister was 'a piece of writing which alone might entitle its author to sit down at the feet of Shakespeare.' [1] Edward Bulwer Lytton, in Colburn's *New Monthly Magazine* (1st October 1832) went even farther. Shakespeare, he argued, had not invoked our sympathy for ordinary men and women like Scott. 'Shakespeare paints the follies of the mob with a strong and unfriendly hand. Where, in Shakespeare, is there a Jeanie Deans?'

Discussing Scott's style in general, Professor Oliver Elton has pointed out how the writing in *The Heart of Midlothian*, as soon as Scott gets his bearings and becomes concrete, 'ceases to lumber and becomes easy, classical, and strong,' and Lord David Cecil has been impressed by the great force of biblical language in the novel. Comparison with other novelists has entered into one or two criticisms of the work. A hostile critic, D. F. Hannigan, translator of French novels into English, condescended to suggest that but for its ending *The Heart of Midlothian* might compare with Fielding and George Eliot, if not with Balzac or Flaubert, while Sir Hugh Walpole, referring to modern preoccupation with psychology, asks if there is anything of that nature 'more truly discerned than the Bennet family in *Pride and Prejudice* and the contrasted Jeanie and Effie Deans in *The Heart of Midlothian*?'

Three distinguished literary critics have voiced the general praise of Scott's masterpiece with authority. 'In at least passages, and those very large ones, of *The Heart of Midlothian*,' wrote Saintsbury, 'Scott went as high as he ever had done, or ever did thereafter. . . . Abundant as are the good things afterwards, I do not know that Scott ever showed his actual original genius, his faculty of creation and combination,

---

[1] *Letters to Richard Heber*, by J. L. Adolphus (1821), p. 76. In this book Adolphus was about the first critic to detect Scott in his novels.

to such an extent and in such proportion again.' [1] Benedetto
Croce was inclined to regard this work 'as the best of his
[Scott's] novels, because it is compacted of goodness, not
only in certain details, but in the very web of the narrative
itself.' [2] But let Hazlitt have the last word in a brief, pithy
sentence that seems to summarize the feelings of all true
lovers of this romance. He addressed himself to Scott, who
was then still alive: 'Were thou to live a thousand years and
write a thousand novels, thou wouldst never, old True-penny,
beat thy own *Heart of Midlothian*!'

The manuscript of *The Heart of Midlothian*, of which some
leaves are missing, is in the National Library of Scotland,
Edinburgh. It was presented in 1935 by Miss J. G. C. Top-
ham, M.B.E., of Middleham House, Yorkshire, a great-
granddaughter of Alexander Cowan of Valleyfield Mills,
Penicuik, paper-maker, to whom it was presented by the
creditors of Scott's publishers, Archibald Constable & Co.,
in appreciation of his services as their Trustee.

1956.   W. M. PARKER.

SELECT BIBLIOGRAPHY

POETRY. Collected editions: *The Poetical Works of Sir Walter Scott*, ed.
J. G. Lockhart, in any edition.

Separate Works: *The Chase, and William and Helen* (from the German
of G. A. Bürger), 1796; *Goetz of Berlichingen* (from the German of Goethe),
1799; *The Eve of St John*, 1800; *The Lay of the Last Minstrel*, 1805; *Ballads
and Lyrical Pieces*, 1806; *Marmion; a Tale of Flodden Field*, 1808; *The
Lady of the Lake; a Poem*, 1810; *The Vision of Don Roderick*, 1811; *Rokeby;
a Poem*, 1813; *The Bridal of Triermain, or The Vale of St John*, 1813; *The
Lord of the Isles; a Poem*, 1815; *The Field of Waterloo; a Poem*, 1815;
Harold the Dauntless; a Poem, 1817: *Halidon Hill; a Dramatic Sketch*, 1822;
The Doom of Devorgoil, A Melodrama, 1830; *Auchindrane, or, The Ayrshire
Tragedy*, 1830; *New Love Poems by Sir Walter Scott*, ed. D. Cook, 1932.

NOVELS AND TALES. Collected editions: *Waverley Novels* (Everyman's
Library), 25 vols., 1906, etc.; Oxford edition, 24 vols., 1914, etc.

Separate Works: *Waverley, or 'Tis Sixty Years Since*, 1814; *Guy Mannering, or The Astrologer*, 1815; *The Antiquary*, 1816; *Tales of My Landlord*
(first series, *The Black Dwarf* and *Old Mortality*), 1816; *Tales of My Landlord* (second series, *The Heart of Midlothian*), 1818; *Rob Roy*, 1817; *Tales of*

---

[1] *Sir Walter Scott* (1897), pp. 87, 88.
[2] *European Literature in the Nineteenth Century*, translated from the
Italian by Douglas Ainslie (1924), p. 75.

Select Bibliography

My Landlord (third series, *The Bride of Lammermoor* and *A Legend of Montrose*), 1819; *Ivanhoe, a Romance*, 1820; *The Monastery, a Romance*, 1820; *The Abbot*, 1820; *Kenilworth, a Romance*, 1821; *The Pirate*, 1822; *The Fortunes of Nigel*, 1822; *Peveril of the Peak*, 1822; *Quentin Durward*, 1823; *St Ronan's Well*, 1824; *Redgauntlet; a tale of the eighteenth century*, 1824; *Tales of the Crusaders* (*The Betrothed* and *The Talisman*), 1825; *Woodstock: or, The Cavalier*, 1826; *Chronicles of the Canongate* (first series, *The Highland Widow, The Two Drovers*, and *The Surgeon's Daughter*), 1827; *My Aunt Margaret's Mirror, The Tapestried Chamber*, and *The Laird's Jock* (in *The Keepsake*), 1828; *Chronicles of the Canongate* (second series, *St Valentine's Day: or The Fair Maid of Perth*), 1828; *Anne of Geierstein: or The Maiden of the Mist*, 1829; *Tales of My Landlord* (fourth series, *Count Robert of Paris* and *Castle Dangerous*), 1832.

MISCELLANEOUS PROSE WORKS. Collected edition: *The Miscellaneous Prose Works of Sir Walter Scott*, 28 vols., 1834–6.

Separate Works: Contributions to *Edinburgh Review, Quarterly Review*, and *Foreign Quarterly Review* (details in Lockhart's *Life*); *Biographical Memoir of John Leyden, M.D.* (*Edinburgh Annual Register* for 1811); *The Eyrbiggia Saga* (in *Illustrations of Northern Antiquities*), 1814; articles 'Chivalry' and 'Drama' in *Encyclopaedia Britannica*, 1814; review of Jane Austen's *Emma* (*Quarterly Review*, Oct. 1815); *Historical Sketches* (*Edinburgh Annual Register*) 1814–15; *Paul's Letters to his Kinsfolk*, 1816; *Provincial Antiquities of Scotland*, 1819–26; *Description of the Regalia of Scotland*, 1819; *Account of the Coronation of George IV*, 1821; *Lives of the Novelists* (prefixed to Ballantyne's Novelists' Library), 1821–4; (Everyman's Library) 1910; article 'Romance' in *Encyclopaedia Britannica*, 1822; *Character of the late Lord Byron* (in *The Pamphleteer*, vol. xxiv), 1824; *Thoughts on the Proposed Change of Currency* from Malachi Malagrowther, 1826; *Character of Frederick, Duke of York* (subjoined to *An Account of The Death of Frederick, Duke of York*, by J. Sykes), 1827; *The Life of Napoleon Buonaparte*, 9 vols., 1827; *Religious Discourses, By a Layman*, 1828; *Tales of a Grandfather* (four series, 1828–31); *History of Scotland* (in Lardner's *Cabinet Cyclopaedia*), 1829–30; *Letters on Demonology and Witchcraft*, 1830; *Essays on Chivalry, Romance, and the Drama*, 1868.

LETTERS. Edited by H. J. C. Grierson, W. M. Parker, and others, 12 vols., 1932–7.

JOURNAL. Edited by D. Douglas, 2 vols., 1890; re-edited by J. G. Tait and W. M. Parker, 3 vols., 1939–46; 1 vol., 1950.

Besides editing *Minstrelsy of the Scottish Border* (1802–3; ed. T. Henderson, 1931), and many other works, Sir Walter Scott contributed Lives to the *Works of John Dryden* (18 vols., 1808) and to the *Works of Jonathan Swift* (19 vols., 1814); also an edition of Somers's *Tracts*, 13 vols., 1809–15.

BIOGRAPHY. J. Hogg: *Domestic Manners and Private Life of Sir W. Scott*, 1834; 3rd ed., 1909; J. G. Lockhart: *Memoirs of The Life of Sir Walter Scott*, 7 vols., 1837–8; 10 vols., 1839; Everyman's Library, 1906; G. Saintsbury: *Sir Walter Scott*, 1897; John Buchan: *Sir Walter Scott*, 1932; E. A. Baker: *History of the English Novel*, VI, 1935; H. J. C. Grierson: *Sir Walter Scott, a new Life*, 1938; Dame Una Pope Hennessy: *The Laird of Abbotsford*, 1932.

BIBLIOGRAPHY. W. Ruff: *A Bibliography of the Poetical Works of Sir Walter Scott, 1796–1832*, 1938; J. C. Corson: *Bibliography of Sir Walter Scott*, 1943.

CONTENTS

THE HEART OF MID-LOTHIAN

Hear, Land o' Cakes and brither Scots,
Frae Maidenkirk to Johnny Groat's,
If there's a hole in a' your coats,
          I rede ye tent it;
A chiel's amang you takin' notes,
             And, faith, he'll prent it!
                    BURNS.

Ahora bien, dixo il Cura, traedme, señor huésped, aquesos libros, que los quiero ver. Que me place, respondió el, y entrando, en su aposento, sacó dél una maletilla vieja cerrada con una cadenilla, y abriéndola, halló en ella tres libros grandes y unos papeles de muy buena letra escritos de mano.—DON QUIXOTE, Parte I. Capitulo 32.

It is mighty well, said the priest ; pray, landlord, bring me those books, for I have a mind to see them. With all my heart, answered the host ; and going to his chamber, he brought out a little old cloke-bag, with a padlock and chain to it, and pening it, he took out three large volumes, and some manuscript papers written in a fine character.—JARVIS'S *Translation.*

INTRODUCTION

THE author has stated in the preface to the Chronicles of the Canongate, 1827, that he received from an anonymous correspondent an account of the incident upon which the following story is founded. He is now at liberty to say, that the information was conveyed to him by a late amiable and ingenious lady, whose wit and power of remarking and judging of character still survive in the memory of her friends. Her maiden name was Miss Helen Lawson, of Girthhead, and she was wife of Thomas Goldie, Esq., of Craigmuie, Commissary of Dumfries.

Her communication was in these words:

"I had taken for summer lodgings a cottage near the old Abbey of Lincluden. It had formerly been inhabited by a lady who had pleasure in embellishing cottages, which she found perhaps homely and even poor enough; mine therefore possessed many marks of taste and elegance unusual in this species of habitation in Scotland, where a cottage is literally what its name declares.

"From my cottage door I had a partial view of the old Abbey before mentioned; some of the highest arches were seen over, and some through, the trees scattered along a lane which led down to the ruin, and the strange fantastic shapes of almost all those old ashes accorded wonderfully well with the building they at once shaded and ornamented.

"The Abbey itself from my door was almost on a level with the cottage; but on coming to the end of the lane, it was discovered to be situated on a high perpendicular bank, at the foot of which run the clear waters of the Cluden, where they hasten to join the sweeping Nith,

'Whose distant roaring swells and fa's.'

As my kitchen and parlour were not very far distant, I one day went in to purchase some chickens from a person I heard offering them for sale. It was a little, rather stout-looking woman, who seemed to be between seventy and eighty years of age; she was almost covered with a tartan plaid, and her cap had over it a black silk hood, tied under the chin, a piece of dress still much in use among elderly women of that rank of life in Scotland; her eyes were dark, and remarkably lively and intelligent; I entered into conversation with her, and began by asking how she maintained herself, &c.

3

"She said that in winter she footed stockings, that is, knit feet to countrypeople's stockings, which bears about the same relation to stocking-knitting that cobbling does to shoemaking, and is of course both less profitable and less dignified ; she likewise taught a few children to read, and in summer she whiles reared a few chickens.

"I said I could venture to guess from her face she had never been married. She laughed heartily at this, and said, 'I maun hae the queerest face that ever was seen, that ye could guess that. Now, do tell me, madam, how ye cam to think sae ?' I told her it was from her cheerful disengaged countenance. She said, 'Mem, have ye na far mair reason to be happy than me, wi' a gude husband and a fine family o' bairns, and plenty o' everything? for me, I'm the puirest o' a' puir bodies, and can hardly contrive to keep mysell alive in a' the wee bits o' ways I hae tell't ye.' After some more conversation, during which I was more and more pleased with the old woman's sensible conversation, and the *naïveté* of her remarks, she rose to go away, when I asked her name. Her countenance suddenly clouded, and she said gravely, rather colouring, 'My name is Helen Walker ; but your husband kens weel about me.'

"In the evening I related how much I had been pleased, and inquired what was extraordinary in the history of the poor woman. Mr. —— said, there were perhaps few more remarkable people than Helen Walker. She had been left an orphan, with the charge of a sister considerably younger than herself, and who was educated and maintained by her exertions. Attached to her by so many ties, therefore, it will not be easy to conceive her feelings, when she found that this only sister must be tried by the laws of her country for child-murder, and upon being called as principal witness against her. The counsel for the prisoner told Helen, that if she could declare that her sister had made any preparations, however slight, or had given her any intimation on the subject, that such a statement would save her sister's life, as she was the principal witness against her. Helen said, 'It is impossible for me to swear to a falsehood ; and, whatever may be the consequence, I will give my oath according to my conscience.'

"The trial came on, and the sister was found guilty and condemned ; but, in Scotland, six weeks must elapse between the sentence and the execution, and Helen Walker availed herself of it. The very day of her sister's condemnation, she got a petition drawn up, stating the peculiar circumstances of the case, and that very night set out on foot to London.

"Without introduction or recommendation, with her simple (perhaps ill-expressed) petition, drawn up by some inferior clerk of the court, she presented herself, in her tartan plaid and country attire, to the late Duke of Argyle, who immediately procured the pardon she petitioned for, and Helen returned with it, on foot, just in time to save her sister.

"I was so strongly interested by this narrative, that I determined immediately to prosecute my acquaintance with Helen Walker; but as I was to leave the country next day, I was obliged to defer it till my return in spring, when the first walk I took was to Helen Walker's cottage.

"She had died a short time before. My regret was extreme, and I endeavoured to obtain some account of Helen from an old woman who inhabited the other end of her cottage. I inquired if Helen ever spoke of her past history, her journey to London, &c. 'Na,' the old woman said, 'Helen was a wily body, and whene'er ony o' the neebors asked anything about it, she aye turned the conversation.'

"In short, every answer I received only tended to increase my regret, and raise my opinion of Helen Walker, who could unite so much prudence with so much heroic virtue."

This narrative was enclosed in the following letter to the author, without date or signature:—

"SIR,—The occurrence just related happened to me 26 years ago. Helen Walker lies buried in the churchyard of Irongray, about six miles from Dumfries. I once proposed that a small monument should have been erected to commemorate so remarkable a character, but I now prefer leaving it to you to perpetuate her memory in a more durable manner."

The reader is now able to judge how far the author has improved upon, or fallen short of, the pleasing and interesting sketch of high principle and steady affection displayed by Helen Walker, the prototype of the fictitious Jeanie Deans. Mrs. Goldie was unfortunately dead before the author had given his name to these volumes, so he lost all opportunity of thanking that lady for her highly valuable communication. But her daughter, Miss Goldie, obliged him with the following additional information.

"Mrs. Goldie endeavoured to collect further particulars of Helen Walker, particularly concerning her journey to London, but found this nearly impossible; as the natural dignity of her character, and a high sense of family respectability, made her so indissolubly connect her sister's disgrace with her own exertions, that none of her neighbours durst ever question her upon the subject. One old woman, a distant relation of Helen's, and who is still living, says she worked an harvest with her, but that she never ventured to ask her about her sister's trial, or her journey to London; 'Helen,' she added, 'was a lofty body, and used a high style o' language.' The same old woman says, that every year Helen received a cheese from her sister, who lived at Whitehaven, and that she always sent a liberal portion of it to herself or to her father's family. This fact, though trivial in itself, strongly marks the affection subsisting between the two sisters, and the complete conviction on the mind of the criminal, that her sister had acted solely from high principle, not from any want of feeling, which another small but characteristic trait will further illustrate. A gentleman, a relation of Mrs. Goldie's, who happened to be travelling in the North of England, on coming to a small inn, was shown into the parlour by a female servant, who, after cautiously shutting the door, said, 'Sir, I'm Nelly Walker's sister.' Thus practically showing that she considered her sister as better known by her high conduct, than even herself by a different kind of celebrity.

"Mrs. Goldie was extremely anxious to have a tombstone and an inscription upon it, erected in Irongray churchyard; and if Sir Walter Scott will condescend to write the last, a little subscription could be easily raised in the immediate neighbourhood, and Mrs. Goldie's wish be thus fulfilled."

It is scarcely necessary to add, that the request of Miss Goldie will be most willingly complied with, and without the necessity of any tax on the public. Nor is there much occasion to repeat how much the author conceives himself obliged to his unknown correspondent, who thus supplied him with a theme affording such a pleasing view of the moral dignity of virtue, though unaided by birth, beauty, or talent. If the picture has suffered in the execution, it is from the failure of the author's powers to present in detail the same simple and striking portrait, exhibited in Mrs. Goldie's letter.

ABBOTSFORD, *April* 1, 1830.

POSTSCRIPT

ALTHOUGH it would be impossible to add much to Mrs. Goldie's picturesque and most interesting account of Helen Walker, the prototype of the imaginary Jeanie Deans, the Editor may be pardoned for introducing two or three anecdotes respecting that excellent person, which he has collected from a volume entitled, "Sketches from Nature, by John M'Diarmid," a gentleman who conducts an able provincial paper in the town of Dumfries.

Helen was the daughter of a small farmer in a place called Dalwhairn, in the parish of Irongray; where, after the death of her father, she continued, with the unassuming piety of a Scottish peasant, to support her mother by her own unremitted labour and privations; a case so common, that even yet, I am proud to say, few of my countrywomen would shrink from the duty.

Helen Walker was held among her equals *pensy*, that is, proud or conceited; but the facts brought to prove this accusation seem only to evince a strength of character superior to those around her. Thus it was remarked, that when it thundered, she went with her work and her Bible to the front of the cottage, alleging that the Almighty could smite in the city as well as in the field.

Mr. M'Diarmid mentions more particularly the misfortune of her sister, which he supposes to have taken place previous to 1736. Helen Walker, declining every proposal of saving her relation's life at the expense of truth, borrowed a sum of money sufficient for her journey, walked the whole distance to London barefoot, and made her way to John Duke of Argyle. She was heard to say, that, by the Almighty's strength, she had been enabled to meet the Duke at the most critical moment, which, if lost, would have caused the inevitable forfeiture of her sister's life.

Isabella, or Tibby Walker, saved from the fate which impended over her, was married by the person who had wronged her (named Waugh), and lived happily for great part of a century, uniformly acknowledging the extraordinary affection to which she owed her preservation.

7

8 Postscript

Helen Walker died about the end of the year 1791, and her remains are interred in the churchyard of her native parish of Irongray, in a romantic cemetery on the banks of the Cairn. That a character so distinguished for her undaunted love of virtue, lived and died in poverty, if not want, serves only to show us how insignificant, in the sight of Heaven, are our principal objects of ambition upon earth.

A PLEASED AND INDULGENT READER

JEDEDIAH CLEISHBOTHAM

WISHES HEALTH, AND INCREASE, AND CONTENTMENT

COURTEOUS READER,—If ingratitude comprehendeth every vice, surely so foul a stain worst of all beseemeth him whose life has been devoted to instructing youth in virtue and in humane letters. Therefore have I chosen, in this prolegomenon, to unload my burden of thanks at thy feet, for the favour with which thou hast kindly entertained the Tales of my Landlord. Certes, if thou hast chuckled over their facetious and festivous descriptions, or hast thy mind filled with pleasure at the strange and pleasant turns of fortune which they record, verily, I have also simpered when I beheld a second story with attics, that has arisen on the basis of my small domicile at Gandercleugh, the walls having been afore-hand pronounced by Deacon Barrow to be capable of endur-ing such an elevation. Nor has it been without delectation, that I have endued a new coat (snuff-brown, and with metal buttons), having all nether garments corresponding thereto. We do therefore lie, in respect of each other, under a recipro-cation of benefits, whereof those received by me being the most solid (in respect that a new house and a new coat are better than a new tale and an old song), it is meet that my gratitude should be expressed with the louder voice and more preponderating vehemence. And how should it be so ex-pressed?—Certainly not in words only, but in act and deed. It is with this sole purpose, and disclaiming all intention of purchasing that pendicle or poffle of land called the Carlines-croft, lying adjacent to my garden, and measuring seven acres, three roods, and four perches, that I have committed to the eyes of those who thought well of the former tomes, these four additional volumes of the Tales of my Landlord. Not the less, if Peter Prayfort be minded to sell the said poffle, it is at his own choice to say so; and, peradventure he may meet with a purchaser: unless (gentle reader) the pleasing pour-traictures of Peter Pattieson, now given unto thee in particular, and unto the public in general, shall have lost their favour in thine eyes, whereof I am no way distrustful. And so much confidence do I repose in thy continued favour, that, should thy lawful occasions call thee to the town of Gander-cleugh, a place frequented by most at one time or other in their lives, I will enrich thine eyes with a sight of those precious manuscripts whence thou hast derived so much delectation, thy nose with a snuff from my mull, and thy palate with a dram from my bottle of strong waters, called, by the learned of Gandercleugh, the Dominie's Dribble o' Drink.

It is there, O highly esteemed and beloved reader, thou wilt be able to bear testimony, through the medium of thine own senses, against the children of vanity, who have sought to identify thy friend and servant with I know not what inditer of vain fables; who hath cumbered the world with his devices, but shrunken from the responsibility thereof. Truly, this hath been well termed a generation hard of faith; since what can a man do to assert his property in a printed tome, saving to put his name in the title-page thereof, with his description, or designation, as the lawyers term it, and place of abode? Of a surety I would have such sceptics consider how they themselves would brook to have their works ascribed to others, their names and professions imputed as forgeries, and their very existence brought into question; even although, per-adventure, it may be it is of little consequence to any but themselves, not only whether they are living or dead, but even whether they ever lived or no. Yet have my maligners carried their uncharitable censures still farther.

These cavillers have not only doubted mine identity, although thus plainly proved, but they have impeached my veracity and the authenticity of my historical narratives! Verily, I can only say in answer, that I have been cautelous in quoting mine authorities. It is true, indeed, that if I had hearkened with only one ear, I might have rehearsed my tale with more acceptation from those who love to hear but half the truth. It is, it may hap, not altogether to the discredit of our kindly nation of Scotland, that we are apt to take an interest, warm, yea partial, in the deeds and sentiments of our forefathers. He whom his adversaries describe as a perjured prelatist, is desirous that his predecessors should be held moderate in their power, and just in their execution of its privileges, when, truly, the unimpassioned peruser of the Annals of those times shall deem them sanguinary, violent, and tyrannical. Again, the representatives of the suffering non-conformists desire that their ancestors, the Cameronians, shall be represented not simply as honest enthusiasts, oppressed for conscience-sake, but persons of fine breeding, and valiant heroes. Truly, the historian cannot gratify these predilections. He must needs describe the cavaliers as proud and high-spirited, cruel, remorseless, and vindictive; the suffering party as honourably tenacious of their opinions under persecution; their own tempers being, however, sullen, fierce, and rude; their opinions absurd and extravagant, and their whole course of conduct that of persons whom hellebore would better have suited than prosecutions unto death for high-treason. Natheless, while such and so preposterous were the opinions on either side, they were, it cannot be doubted, men of virtue and worth on both, to entitle either party to claim merit from its martyrs. It has been demanded of me, Jedediah Cleishbotham, by what right I am entitled to constitute myself an impartial judge of their discrepancies of opinions, seeing (as it is stated) that I must necessarily have descended from one or other of the contending parties, and be, of course, wedded for better or for worse, according to the reasonable practice of Scotland, to its dogmata, or opinions, and bound, as it were, by the tie matrimonial, or, to speak without metaphor, *ex jure sanguinis*, to maintain them in preference to all others.

But, nothing denying the nationality of all the rule, which calls on all now living to rule their political and religious opinions by those of their great-grandfathers, and inevitable as seems the one or the other horn of the dilemma betwixt which my adversaries conceive they have pinned me to the wall, I yet spy some means of refuge, and claim a privilege to write and speak of both parties with impartiality. For, O ye powers of logic! when the Prelatists and Presbyterians of old times went together by the ears in this unlucky country, my ancestor (venerated be his memory!) was one of the people called Quakers, and suffered severe handling from either side, even to the extenuation of his purse and the incarceration of his person.

Craving thy pardon, gentle Reader, for these few words

concerning me and mine, I rest, as above expressed, thy sure
and obligated friend,[1]   J. C.

GANDERCLEUGH,
this 1st of April, 1818.

[1] It is an old proverb, that "many a true word is spoken in jest." The
existence of Walter Scott, third son of Sir William Scott of Harden, is instructed, as it is called, by a charter under the great seal, Domino Willielmo
Scott de Harden Militi, et Waltero Scott suo filio legitimo tertio genito,
terrarum de Roberton.* The munificent old gentleman left all his four sons
considerable estates, and settled those of Eilrig and Raeburn, together with
valuable possessions around Lessudden, upon Walter, his third son, who is
ancestor of the Scotts of Raeburn, and of the Author of Waverley. He
appears to have become a convert to the doctrine of the Quakers, or Friends,
and a great assertor of their peculiar tenets. This was probably at the time
when George Fox, the celebrated apostle of the sect, made an expedition into
the south of Scotland about 1657, on which occasion he boasts, that "as he
first set his horse's feet upon Scottish ground, he felt the seed of grace to
sparkle about him like innumerable sparks of fire." Upon the same occasion,
probably, Sir Gideon Scott of Highchester, second son of Sir William, immediate elder brother of Walter, and ancestor of the author's friend and kinsman, the present representative of the family of Harden, also embraced the
tenets of Quakerism. This last convert, Gideon, entered into a controversy
with the Rev. James Kirkton, author of "The Secret and True History of the
Church of Scotland," which is noticed by my ingenious friend Mr. Charles
Kirkpatricke Sharpe, in his valuable and curious edition of that work, 4to,
1817. Sir William Scott, eldest of the brothers, remained, amid the defection
of his two younger brethren, an orthodox member of the Presbyterian Church,
and used such means for reclaiming Walter of Raeburn from his heresy, as
savoured far more of persecution than persuasion. In this he was assisted by
MacDougal of Makerston, brother to Isabella MacDougal, the wife of the said
Walter, and who, like her husband, had conformed to the Quaker tenets.

The interest possessed by Sir William Scott and Makerston was powerful
enough to procure the two following acts of the Privy Council of Scotland,
directed against Walter of Raeburn as an heretic and convert to Quakerism,
appointing him to be imprisoned first in Edinburgh jail, and then in that of
Jedburgh ; and his children to be taken by force from the society and direction
of their parents, and educated at a distance from them, besides the assignment
of a sum for their maintenance, sufficient in those times to be burdensome to
a moderate Scottish estate.

"*Apud Edin. vigesimo Junii* 1665.

"The Lords of his Majesty's Privy Council having receaved information
that Scott of Raeburn, and Isobel Mackdougall, his wife, being infected with
the error of Quakerism, doe endeavour to breid and traine up William, Walter,
and Isobel Scotts, their children, in the same profession, doe therefore give
order and command to Sir William Scott of Harden, the said Raeburn's
brother, to seperat and take away the saids children from the custody and
society of the saids parents, and to cause educat and bring them up in his
owne house, or any other convenient place, and ordaines letters to be direct at
the said Sir William's instance against Raeburn, for a maintenance to the
saids children, and that the said Sir Wm. give ane account of his diligence
with all conveniency."

"*Edinburgh, 5th July* 1666.

"Anent a petition presented be Sir Wm. Scott of Harden, for himself and
in name and behalf of the three children of Walter Scott of Raeburn, his

* See Douglas's Baronage, page 215.

brother, showing that the Lords of Councill, by ane act of the 22nd day of Junii 1665, did grant power and warrand to the petitioner, to separat and take away Raeburn's children, from his family and education, and to breed them in some convenient place, where they might be free from all infection in their younger years, from the principalls of Quakerism, and, for maintenance of the saids children, did ordain letters to be direct against Raeburn; and, seeing the Petitioner, in obedience to the said order, did take away the saids children, being two sonnes and a daughter, and after some paines taken upon them in his owne family, hes sent them to the city of Glasgow, to be bread at schooles, and there to be principled with the knowledge of the true religion, and that it is necessary the Councill determine what shall be the maintenance for which Raeburn's three children may be charged, as likewise that Raeburn himself, being now in the Tolbooth of Edinburgh, where he dayley converses with all the Quakers who are prisoners there, and others who daily resort to them, whereby he is hardened in his pernitious opinions and principles, without all hope of recovery, unlesse he be separat from such pernitious company, humbly therefore, desyring that the Councell might determine upon the soume of money to be payed be Raeburn, for the education of his children, to the petitioner, who will be countable therefore; and that, in order to his conversion, the place of his imprisonment may be changed. The Lords of his Maj. Privy Councell having at length heard and considered the foresaid petition, doe modifie the soume of two thousand pounds Scots, to be payed yearly at the terme of Whitsunday be the said Walter Scott of Raeburn, furth of his estate to the petitioner, for the entertainment and education of the said children, beginning the first termes payment thereof at Whitsunday last for the half year preceding, and so furth yearly, at the said terme of Whitsunday in tym comeing till furder orders; and ordaines the said Walter Scott of Raeburn to be transported from the tolbooth of Edinburgh to the prison of Jedburgh, where his friends and others may have occasion to convert him. And to the effect he may be secured from the practice of other Quakers, the said Lords doe hereby discharge the magistrates of Jedburgh to suffer any persons suspect of these principles to have access to him; and in case any contraveen, that they secure ther persons till they be therfore puneist; and ordaines letters to be direct heirupon in form, as effeirs."

Both the sons, thus harshly separated from their father, proved good scholars. The eldest, William, who carried on the line of Raeburn, was, like his father, a deep Orientalist; the younger, Walter, became a good classical scholar, a great friend and correspondent of the celebrated Dr. Pitcairn, and a Jacobite so distinguished for zeal, that he made a vow never to shave his beard till the restoration of the exiled family. This last Walter Scott was the author's great-grandfather.

There is yet another link betwixt the author and the simple-minded and excellent Society of Friends, through a proselyte of much more importance than Walter Scott of Raeburn. The celebrated John Swinton of Swinton, nineteenth baron in descent of that ancient and once powerful family, was, with Sir William Lockhart of Lee, the person whom Cromwell chiefly trusted in the management of the Scottish affairs during his usurpation. After the Restoration, Swinton was devoted as a victim to the new order of things, and was brought down in the same vessel which conveyed the Marquis of Argyle to Edinburgh, where that nobleman was tried and executed. Swinton was destined to the same fate. He had assumed the habit, and entered into the society of the Quakers, and appeared as one of their number before the Parliament of Scotland. He renounced all legal defence, though several pleas were open to him, and answered, in conformity to the principles of his sect, that at the time these crimes were imputed to him, he was in the gall of bitterness and bond of iniquity; but that God Almighty having since called him to the light, he saw and acknowledged these errors, and did not refuse to pay the forfeit of them, even though, in the judgment of the Parliament, it should extend to life itself. Respect to fallen greatness, and to the patience and calm resignation with which a man once in high power expressed himself under such a change of fortune, found Swinton friends; family connections, and some interested considerations of Middleton the Commissioner, joined to procure his safety, and he was dismissed, but after a long imprisonment, and much dilapidation of his estates. It is said, that Swinton's admonitions, while confined in the Castle of Edinburgh, had a considerable share in converting to the tenets of the Friends Colonel David Barclay, then lying there in garrison. This was the father of Robert Barclay, author of the celebrated Apology for the Quakers. It may be observed among the inconsistencies of human nature, that Kirkton, Wodrow, and other Presbyterian authors, who have detailed the sufferings of their own sect for non-conformity with the established church, censure the government of the time for not exerting the civil power against the peaceful enthusiasts we have treated of, and some express particular chagrin at the escape of Swinton. Whatever might be his motives for assuming the tenets of the Friends, the old man retained them faithfully till the close of his life.

Jean Swinton, grand-daughter of Sir John Swinton, son of Judge Swinton, as the Quaker was usually termed, was mother of Anne Rutherford, the author's mother.

And thus, as in the play of the Anti-Jacobin, the ghost of the author's grandmother having arisen to speak the Epilogue, it is full time to conclude, lest the reader should remonstrate that his desire to know the Author of Waverley never included a wish to be acquainted with his whole ancestry.

CHAPTER I

BEING INTRODUCTORY

So down thy hill, romantic Ashbourn, glides
The Derby dilly, carrying six insides.
                                                    FRERE.

THE times have changed in nothing more (we follow as we
were wont the manuscript of Peter Pattieson) than in the rapid
conveyance of intelligence and communication betwixt one part
of Scotland and another.   It is not above twenty or thirty
years, according to the evidence of many credible witnesses
now alive, since a little miserable horse-cart, performing with
difficulty a journey of thirty miles *per diem*, carried our mails
from the capital of Scotland to its extremity.   Nor was Scotland much more deficient in these accommodations than our
richer sister had been about eighty years before.   Fielding, in
his Tom Jones, and Farquhar, in a little farce called The
Stage-Coach, have ridiculed the slowness of these vehicles
of public accommodation.   According to the latter authority,
the highest bribe could only induce the coachman to promise
to anticipate by half-an-hour the usual time of his arrival at the
Bull and Mouth.

But in both countries these ancient, slow, and sure modes
of conveyance, are now alike unknown; mail-coach races
against mail-coach, and high-flyer against high-flyer, through
the most remote districts of Britain.   And in our village alone,
three post-coaches, and four coaches with men armed, and in
scarlet cassocks, thunder through the streets each day, and
rival in brilliancy and noise the invention of the celebrated
tyrant :—

> *Demens, qui nimbos et non imitabile fulmen,*
> *Ære et cornipedum pulsu, simularat, equorum.*

Now and then, to complete the resemblance, and to correct
the presumption of the venturous charioteers, it does happen
that the career of these dashing rivals of Salmoneus meets
with as undesirable and violent a termination as that of their

prototype. It is on such occasions that the Insides and Outsides, to use the appropriate vehicular phrases, have reason to rue the exchange of the slow and safe motion of the ancient Fly-coaches, which, compared with the chariots of Mr. Palmer, so ill deserve the name. The ancient vehicle used to settle quietly down, like a ship scuttled and left to sink by the gradual influx of the waters, while the modern is smashed to pieces with the velocity of the same vessel hurled against breakers, or rather with the fury of a bomb bursting at the conclusion of its career through the air. The late ingenious Mr. Pennant, whose humour it was to set his face in stern opposition to these speedy conveyances, had collected, I have heard, a formidable list of such casualties, which, joined to the imposition of innkeepers, whose charges the passengers had no time to dispute, the sauciness of the coachman, and the uncontrolled and despotic authority of the tyrant called the Guard, held forth a picture of horror, to which murder, theft, fraud, and peculation lent all their dark colouring. But that which gratifies the impatience of the human disposition will be practised in the teeth of danger, and in defiance of admonition; and, in despite of the Cambrian antiquary, mail-coaches not only roll their thunders around the base of Penman-Maur and Cader Edris, but

> Frighted Skiddaw hears afar
> The rattling of the unscythed car.

And perhaps the echoes of Ben Nevis may soon be awakened by the bugle, not of a warlike chieftain, but of the guard of a mail-coach.

It was a fine summer day, and our little school had obtained a half holiday. by the intercession of a good-humoured visitor.[1] I expected by the coach a new number of an interesting periodical publication, and walked forward on the highway to meet it, with the patience which Cowper has described as actuating the resident in the country when longing for intelligence from the mart of news :—

> ————The grand debate.
> The popular harangue,—the tart reply,—
> The logic, and the wisdom, and the wit,
> And the loud laugh,—I long to know them all;—
> I burn to set the imprison'd wranglers free,
> And give them voice and utterance again.

---

[1] His honour Gilbert Goslinn of Gandercleugh; for I love to be precise in matters of importance.—J. C.

It was with such feelings that I eyed the approach of the new coach, lately established on our road, and known by the name of the Somerset, which, to say truth, possesses some interest for me, even when it conveys no such important information. The distant tremulous sound of its wheels was heard just as I gained the summit of the gentle ascent, called the Goslin-brae, from which you command an extensive view down the valley of the river Gander. The public road, which comes up the side of that stream, and crosses it at a bridge about a quarter of a mile from the place where I was standing, runs partly through enclosures and plantations, and partly through open pasture land. It is a childish amusement perhaps,—but my life has been spent with children, and why should not my pleasures be like theirs?—childish as it is then, I must own I have had great pleasure in watching the approach of the carriage, where the openings of the road permit it to be seen. The gay glancing of the equipage, its diminished and toy-like appearance at a distance, contrasted with the rapidity of its motion, its appearance and disappearance at intervals, and the progressively increasing sounds that announce its nearer approach, have all to the idle and listless spectator, who has nothing more important to attend to, something of awakening interest. The ridicule may attach to me, which is flung upon many an honest citizen, who watches from the window of his villa the passage of the stage-coach; but it is a very natural source of amusement, notwithstanding, and many of those who join in the laugh are perhaps not unused to resort to it in secret.

On the present occasion, however, fate had decreed that I should not enjoy the consummation of the amusement by seeing the coach rattle past me as I sat on the turf, and hearing the hoarse grating voice of the guard as he skimmed forth for my grasp the expected packet, without the carriage checking its course for an instant. I had seen the vehicle thunder down the hill that leads to the bridge with more than its usual impetuosity, glittering all the while by flashes from a cloudy tabernacle of the dust which it had raised, and leaving a train behind it on the road resembling a wreath of summer mist. But it did not appear on the top of the nearer bank within the usual space of three minutes, which frequent observation had enabled me to ascertain was the medium time for crossing the bridge and mounting the ascent. When double that space had elapsed, I became alarmed, and walked hastily forward. As I came in sight of the bridge, the cause of delay was too manifest, for the Somerset had made a summerset in good earnest, and overturned so completely, that it was literally resting upon the ground, with the roof undermost, and the four wheels in the air. The "exertions of the guard and coachman," both of whom were gratefully commemorated in the newspapers, having succeeded in disentangling the horses by cutting the harness, were now proceeding to extricate the *insides* by a sort of summary and Cæsarean process of delivery, forcing the hinges from one of the doors which they could not open otherwise. In this manner were two disconsolate damsels set at liberty from the womb of the leathern conveniency. As they immediately began to settle their clothes, which were a little deranged, as may be presumed, I concluded they had received no injury, and did not venture to obtrude my services at their toilette, for which, I understand, I have since been reflected upon by the fair sufferers. The *outsides*, who must have been discharged from their elevated situation by a shock resembling the springing of a mine, escaped, nevertheless, with the usual allowance of scratches and bruises, excepting three, who, having been pitched into the river Gander, were dimly seen contending with the tide, like the relics of Æneas's shipwreck—

Rari apparent nantes in gurgite vasto.

I applied my poor exertions where they seemed to be most needed, and with the assistance of one or two of the company who had escaped unhurt, easily succeeded in fishing out two of the unfortunate passengers, who were stout active young fellows ; and but for the preposterous length of their greatcoats, and the equally fashionable latitude and longitude of their Wellington trousers, would have required little assistance from any one. The third was sickly and elderly, and might have perished but for the efforts used to preserve him.

When the two great-coated gentlemen had extricated themselves from the river, and shaken their ears like huge water-dogs, a violent altercation ensued betwixt them and the coachman and guard, concerning the cause of their overthrow. In the course of the squabble, I observed that both my new acquaintances belonged to the law, and that their professional sharpness was likely to prove an overmatch for the surly and official tone of the guardians of the vehicle. The dispute ended in the guard assuring the passengers that they should have seats in a heavy coach which would pass that spot in less than half-an-hour, providing it were not full. Chance seemed to favour this arrangement, for when the expected vehicle arrived, there were only two places occupied in a carriage which professed to carry six. The two ladies who had been disinterred out of the fallen vehicle were readily admitted, but positive objections were stated by those previously in possession to the admittance of the two lawyers, whose wetted garments being much of the nature of well-soaked sponges, there was every reason to believe they would refund a considerable part of the water they had collected, to the inconvenience of their fellow-passengers. On the other hand, the lawyers rejected a seat on the roof, alleging that they had only taken that station for pleasure for one stage, but were entitled in all respects to free egress and regress from the interior, to which their contract positively referred. After some altercation, in which something was said upon the edict, *Nautæ, caupones, stabularii*, the coach went off, leaving the learn d gentlemen to abide by their action of damages.

They immediately applied to me to guide them to the next village and the best inn ; and from the account I gave them of the Wallace Head, declared they were much better pleased to stop there than to go forward upon the terms of that impudent scoundrel the guard of the Somerset. All that they now wanted was a lad to carry their travelling-bags, who was easily procured from an adjoining cottage ; and they prepared to walk forward, when they found there was another passenger in the same deserted situation as themselves. This was the elderly and sickly-lo king person, who had been precipitated into the river along with the two young lawyers. He, it seems, had been too modest to push his own plea against the coachman when he saw that of his betters rejected, and now remained behind with a look of timid anxiety, plainly intimating that he was deficient in those means of recommendation which are necessary passports to the hospitality of an inn.

I ventured to call the attention of the two dashing young blades, for such they seemed, to the desolate condition of their fellow-traveller. They took the hint with ready good nature.

" Oh, true, Mr. Dunover," said one of the youngsters, " you must not remain on the pavé here ; you must go and have some dinner with us—Halkit and I must have a post-chaise to go on, at all events, and we will set you down wherever suits you best."

The poor man, for such his dress, as well as his diffidence, bespoke him, made the sort of acknowledging bow by which says a Scotchman, "It's too much honour for the like of me;" and followed humbly behind his gay patrons, all three besprinkling the dusty road as they walked along with the moisture of their drenched garments, and exhibiting the singular and somewhat ridiculous appearance of three persons suffering from the opposite extreme of humidity, while the summer sun was at its height, and everything else around them had the expression of heat and drought. The ridicule did not escape the young gentlemen themselves, and they had made what might be received as one or two tolerable jests on the subject before they had advanced far on their peregrination.

"We cannot complain, like Cowley," said one of them, "that Gideon's fleece remains dry, while all around is moist; this is the reverse of the miracle."

"We ought to be received with gratitude in this good town; we bring a supply of what they seem to need most," said Halkit.

"And distribute it with unparalleled generosity," replied his companion; "performing the part of three water-carts for the benefit of their dusty roads."

"We come before them, too," said Halkit, "in full professional force—counsel and agent——"

"And client," said the young advocate, looking behind him. And then added, lowering his voice, "that looks as if he had kept such dangerous company too long."

It was, indeed, too true, that the humble follower of the gay young men had the threadbare appearance of a worn-out litigant, and I could not but smile at the conceit, though anxious to conceal my mirth from the object of it.

When we arrived at the Wallace Inn, the elder of the Edinburgh gentlemen, and whom I understood to be a barrister, insisted that I should remain and take part of their dinner; and their inquiries and demands speedily put my landlord and his whole family in motion to produce the best cheer which the larder and cellar afforded, and proceed to cook it to the best advantage, a science in which our entertainers seemed to be admirably skilled. In other respects they were lively young men, in the heyday of youth and good spirits, playing the part which is common to the higher classes of the law at Edinburgh, and which nearly resembles that of the young templars in the days of Steele and Addison. An air of giddy gaiety mingled with the good sense, taste, and information which their conversation exhibited;

and it seemed to be their object to unite the character of men
of fashion and lovers of the polite arts. A fine gentleman,
bred up in the thorough idleness and inanity of pursuit, which
I understand is absolutely necessary to the character in per-
fection, might in all probability have traced a tinge of professional pedantry which marked the barrister in spite of his
efforts, and something of active bustle in his companion, and
would certainly have detected more than a fashionable mixture
of information and animated interest in the language of both.
But to me, who had no pretensions to be so critical, my
companions seemed to form a very happy mixture of good-
breeding and liberal information, with a disposition to lively
rattle, pun, and jest, amusing to a grave man, because it is
what he himself can least easily command.

The thin pale-faced man, whom their good-nature had
brought into their society, looked out of place as well as out
of spirits; sate on the edge of his seat, and kept the chair at
two feet distance from the table; thus incommoding himself
considerably in conveying the victuals to his mouth, as if by
way of penance for partaking of them in the company of his
superiors. A short time after dinner, declining all entreaty to
partake of the wine, which circulated freely round, he informed
himself of the hour when the chaise had been ordered to
attend; and saying he would be in readiness, modestly withdrew from the apartment.

"Jack," said the barrister to his companion, "I remember
that poor fellow's face; you spoke more truly than you were
aware of; he really is one of my clients, poor man."

"Poor man!" echoed Halkit—"I suppose you mean he is
your one and only client?"

"That's not my fault, Jack," replied the other, whose name
I discovered was Hardie. "You are to give me all your
business, you know; and if you have none, the learned gentleman here knows nothing can come of nothing."

"You seem to have brought something to nothing though,
in the case of that honest man. He looks as if he were
just about to honour with his residence the HEART OF MID-
LOTHIAN."

"You are mistaken—he is just delivered from it.—Our
friend here looks for an explanation. Pray, Mr. Pattieson,
have you been in Edinburgh?"

I answered in the affirmative.

"Then you must have passed, occasionally at least, though

probably not so faithfully as I am doomed to do, through a
narrow intricate passage, leading out of the north-west corner
of the Parliament Square, and passing by a high and antique
building, with turrets and iron grates—

> Making good the saying odd,
> 'Near the church and far from God——'"

Mr. Halkit broke in upon his learned counsel, to contribute
his moiety to the riddle—" Having at the door the sign of the
Red Man——"

"And being on the whole," resumed the counsellor, interrupting his friend in his turn, "a sort of place where misfortune is happily confounded with guilt, where all who are in
wish to get out——"

"And where none who have the good luck to be out, wish
to get in," added his companion.

"I conceive you, gentlemen," replied I; "you mean the
prison."

"The prison," added the young lawyer—"You have hit it
—the very reverend Tolbooth itself; and let me tell you, you
are obliged to us for describing it with so much modesty and
brevity; for with whatever amplifications we might have chosen
to decorate the subject, you lay entirely at our mercy, since
the Fathers Conscript of our city have decreed, that the venerable edifice itself shall not remain in existence to confirm or
to confute us."

"Then the Tolbooth of Edinburgh is called the Heart of
Mid-Lothian?" said I.

"So termed and reputed, I assure you."

"I think," said I, with the bashful diffidence with which a
man lets slip a pun in presence of his superiors, "the metro-
politan county may, in that case, be said to have a sad heart."

"Right as my glove, Mr. Pattieson," added Mr. Hardie;
"and a close heart, and a hard heart—Keep it up, Jack."

"And a wicked heart, and a poor heart," answered Halkit,
doing his best.

"And yet it may be called in some sort a strong heart, and
a high heart," rejoined the advocate. "You see I can put
you both out of heart."

"I have played all my hearts," said the younger gentleman.

"Then we'll have another lead," answered his companion.—
"And as to the old and condemned Tolbooth, what pity the
same honour cannot be done to it as has been done to many

of its inmates. Why should not the Tolbooth have its 'Last Speech, Confession, and Dying Words'? The old stones would be just as conscious of the honour as many a poor devil who has dangled like a tassel at the west end of it, while the hawkers were shouting a confession the culprit had never heard of."

"I am afraid," said I, "if I might presume to give my opinion, it would be a tale of unvaried sorrow and guilt."

"Not entirely, my friend," said Hardie; "a prison is a world within itself, and has its own business, griefs, and joys, peculiar to its circle. Its inmates are sometimes short-lived, but so are soldiers on service; they are poor relatively to the world without, but there are degrees of wealth and poverty among them, and so some are relatively rich also. They cannot stir abroad, but neither can the garrison of a besieged fort, or the crew of a ship at sea; and they are not under a dispensation quite so desperate as either, for they may have as much food as they have money to buy, and are not obliged to work whether they have food or not."

"But what variety of incident," said I (not without a secret view to my present task), "could possibly be derived from such a work as you are pleased to talk of?"

"Infinite," replied the young advocate. "Whatever of guilt, crime, imposture, folly, unheard-of misfortunes, and un-looked-for change of fortune, can be found to chequer life, my Last Speech of the Tolbooth should illustrate with examples sufficient to gorge even the public's all-devouring appetite for the wonderful and horrible. The inventor of fictitious narratives has to rack his brains for means to diversify his tale, and after all can hardly hit upon characters or incidents which have not been used again and again, until they are familiar to the eye of the reader, so that the development, *enlèvement,* the desperate wound of which the hero never dies, the burning fever from which the heroine is sure to recover, become a mere matter of course. I join with my honest friend Crabbe, and have an unlucky propensity to hope when hope is lost, and to rely upon the cork-jacket, which carries the heroes of romance safe through all the billows of affliction." He then declaimed the following passage, rather with too much than too little emphasis:

> "'Much have I fear'd, but am no more afraid,
> When some chaste beauty, by some wretch betray'd
> Is drawn away with such distracted speed,
> That she anticipates a dreadful deed.

> Not so do I—Let solid walls impound
> The captive fair, and dig a moat around;
> Let there be brazen locks and bars of steel,
> And keepers cruel, such as never feel;
> With not a single note the purse supply,
> And when she begs, let men and maids deny;
> Be windows there from which she dares not fall,
> And help so distant, 'tis in vain to call;
> Still means of freedom will some Power devise,
> And from the baffled ruffian snatch his prize.'

"The end of uncertainty," he concluded, "is the death of interest; and hence it happens that no one now reads novels."

"Hear him, ye gods!" returned his companion. "I assure you, Mr. Pattieson, you will hardly visit this learned gentleman, but you are likely to find the new novel most in repute lying on his table, — snugly intrenched, however, beneath Stair's Institutes, or an open volume of Morrison's Decisions."

"Do I deny it?" said the hopeful jurisconsult, "or wherefore should I, since it is well known these Dalilahs seduce my wisers and my betters? May they not be found lurking amidst the multiplied memorials of our most distinguished counsel, and even peeping from under the cushion of a judge's arm-chair? Our seniors at the bar, within the bar, and even on the bench, read novels; and, if not belied, some of them have written novels into the bargain. I only say, that I read from habit and from indolence, not from real interest; that, like Ancient Pistol devouring his leek, I read and swear till I get to the end of the narrative. But not so in the real records of human vagaries—not so in the State Trials, or in the Books of Adjournal, where every now and then you read new pages of the human heart, and turns of fortune far beyond what the boldest novelist ever attempted to produce from the coinage of his brain."

"And for such narratives," I asked, "you suppose the History of the Prison of Edinburgh might afford appropriate materials?"

"In a degree unusually ample, my dear sir," said Hardie— "Fill your glass, however, in the meanwhile. Was it not for many years the place in which the Scottish Parliament met? Was it not James's place of refuge, when the mob, inflamed by a seditious preacher, broke forth on him with the cries of 'The sword of the Lord and of Gideon—bring forth the wicked

Haman'? Since that time how many hearts have throbbed within these walls, as the tolling of the neighbouring bell announced to them how fast the sands of their life were ebbing; how many must have sunk at the sound—how many were supported by stubborn pride and dogged resolution—how many by the consolations of religion? Have there not been some, who, looking back on the motives of their crimes, were scarce able to understand how they should have had such temptation as to seduce them from virtue? and have there not, perhaps, been others, who, sensible of their innocence, were divided between indignation at the undeserved doom which they were to undergo, consciousness that they had not deserved it, and racking anxiety to discover some way in which they might yet vindicate themselves? Do you suppose any of these deep, powerful, and agitating feelings, can be recorded and perused without exciting a corresponding depth of deep, powerful, and agitating interest?—Oh! do but wait till I publish the *Causes Célèbres* of Caledonia, and you will find no want of a novel or a tragedy for some time to come. The true thing will triumph over the brightest inventions of the most ardent imagination. *Magna est veritas, et prævalebit.*"

"I have understood," said I, encouraged by the affability of my rattling entertainer, "that less of this interest must attach to Scottish jurisprudence than to that of any other country. The general morality of our people, their sober and prudent habits——"

"Secure them," said the barrister, "against any great increase of professional thieves and depredators, but not against wild and wayward starts of fancy and passion, producing crimes of an extraordinary description, which are precisely those to the detail of which we listen with thrilling interest. England has been much longer a highly civilised country; her subjects have been very strictly amenable to laws administered without fear or favour, a complete division of labour has taken place among her subjects, and the very thieves and robbers form a distinct class in society, subdivided among themselves according to the subject of their depredations, and the mode in which they carry them on, acting upon regular habits and principles, which can be calculated and anticipated at Bow Street, Hatton Garden, or the Old Bailey. Our sister kingdom is like a cultivated field,—the farmer expects that, in spite of all his care, a certain number of weeds will rise with the corn, and can tell you beforehand their names and appearance. But Scotland is like one of her own Highland glens, and the moralist who reads the records of her criminal jurisprudence, will find as many curious anomalous facts in the history of mind, as the botanist will detect rare specimens among her dingles and cliffs."

"And that's all the good you have obtained from three perusals of the Commentaries on Scottish Criminal Jurisprudence?" said his companion. "I suppose the learned author very little thinks that the facts which his erudition and acuteness have accumulated for the illustration of legal doctrines, might be so arranged as to form a sort of appendix to the half-bound and slipshod volumes of the circulating library."

"I'll bet you a pint of claret," said the elder lawyer, "that he will not feel sore at the comparison. But as we say at the bar, 'I beg I may not be interrupted'; I have much more to say upon my Scottish collection of *Causes Célèbres*. You will please recollect the scope and motive given for the contrivance and execution of many extraordinary and daring crimes, by the long civil dissensions of Scotland—by the hereditary jurisdictions, which, until 1748, rested the investigation of crimes in judges, ignorant, partial, or interested—by the habits of the gentry, shut up in their distant and solitary mansion-houses, nursing their revengeful passions just to keep their blood from stagnating—not to mention that amiable national qualification, called the *perfervidum ingenium Scotorum*, which our lawyers join in alleging as a reason for the severity of some of our enactments. When I come to treat of matters so mysterious, deep, and dangerous, as these circumstances have given rise to, the blood of each reader shall be curdled, and his epidermis crisped into goose skin.— But, hist!—here comes the landlord, with tidings, I suppose, that the chaise is ready."

It was no such thing—the tidings bore, that no chaise could be had that evening, for Sir Peter Plyem had carried forward my landlord's two pairs of horses that morning to the ancient royal borough of Bubbleburgh, to look after his interest there. But as Bubbleburgh is only one of a set of five boroughs which club their shares for a member of parliament, Sir Peter's adversary had judiciously watched his departure, in order to commence a canvass in the no less royal borough of Bitem, which, as all the world knows, lies at the very termination of Sir Peter's avenue, and has been held in leading-strings by him and his ancestors for time immemorial. Now Sir Peter was thus placed in the situation of an ambitious monarch, who, after having commenced a daring inroad into his enemies' territories, is suddenly recalled by an invasion of his own hereditary dominions. He was obliged in consequence to return from the half-won borough of Bubbleburgh, to look after the half-lost borough of Bitem, and the two pairs of horses which had carried him that morning to Bubbleburgh, were now forcibly detained to transport him, his agent, his valet, his jester, and his hard-drinker, across the country to Bitem. The cause of this detention, which to me was of as little consequence as it may be to the reader, was important enough to my companions to reconcile them to the delay. Like eagles, they smelled the battle afar off, ordered a magnum of claret and beds at the Wallace, and entered at full career into the Bubbleburgh and Bitem politics, with all the probable "petitions and complaints" to which they were likely to give rise.

In the midst of an anxious, animated, and, to me, most unintelligible discussion, concerning provosts, bailies, deacons, sets of boroughs, leets, town-clerks, burgesses resident and non-resident, all of a sudden the lawyer recollected himself. "Poor Dunover, we must not forget him;" and the landlord was despatched in quest of the *pauvre honteux*, with an earnestly civil invitation to him for the rest of the evening. I could not help asking the young gentlemen if they knew the history of this poor man; and the counsellor applied himself to his pocket to recover the memorial or brief from which he had stated his cause.

"He has been a candidate for our *remedium miserabile*," said Mr. Hardie, "commonly called a *cessio bonorum*. As there are divines who have doubted the eternity of future punishments, so the Scotch lawyers seem to have thought that the crime of poverty might be atoned for by something short of perpetual imprisonment. After a month's confinement, you must know, a prisoner for debt is entitled, on a sufficient statement to our Supreme Court, setting forth the amount of his funds, and the nature of his misfortunes, and surrendering all his effects to his creditors, to claim to be discharged from prison."

"I had heard," I replied, "of such a humane regulation."

"Yes," said Halkit, "and the beauty of it is, as the foreign fellow said, you may get the *cessio* when the *bonorums* are all spent—But what, are you puzzling in your pockets to seek your only memorial among old play-bills, letters requesting a meeting of the Faculty, rules of the Speculative Society, syllabus' of lectures—all the miscellaneous contents of a young advocate's pocket, which contains everything but briefs and bank notes? Can you not state a case of *cessio* without your memorial? Why, it is done every Saturday. The events follow each other as regularly as clock-work, and one form of condescendence might suit every one of them."

"This is very unlike the variety of distress which this gentleman stated to fall under the consideration of your judges," said I.

"True," replied Halkit; "but Hardie spoke of criminal jurisprudence, and this business is purely civil. I could plead a *cessio* myself without the inspiring honours of a gown and three-tailed periwig — Listen. — My client was bred a journeyman weaver—made some little money—took a farm— (for conducting a farm, like driving a gig, comes by nature)— late severe times—induced to sign bills with a friend, for which he received no value—landlord sequestrates—creditors accept a composition—pursuer sets up a public-house—fails a second time—is incarcerated for a debt of ten pounds, seven shillings and sixpence—his debts amount to blank— his losses to blank—his funds to blank—leaving a balance of blank in his favour. There is no opposition; your lordships will please grant commission to take his oath."

Hardie now renounced this ineffectual search, in which there was perhaps a little affectation, and told us the tale of poor Dunover's distresses, with a tone in which a degree of feeling, which he seemed ashamed of as unprofessional, mingled with his attempts at wit, and did him more honour. It was one of those tales which seem to argue a sort of ill-luck or fatality attached to the hero. A well-informed, industrious, and blameless, but poor and bashful man, had in vain essayed all the usual means by which others acquire independence, yet had never succeeded beyond the attainment of bare subsistence. During a brief gleam of hope, rather than of actual prosperity, he had added a wife and family to his cares, but the dawn was speedily overcast. Everything retrograded with him towards the verge of the miry Slough of Despond, which yawns for insolvent debtors;

and after catching at each twig, and experiencing the protracted agony of feeling them one by one elude his grasp,
he actually sunk into the miry pit whence he had been extricated by the professional exertions of Hardie.

"And, I suppose, now you have dragged this poor devil
ashore, you will leave him half naked on the beach to
provide for himself?" said Halkit. "Hark ye,"—and he
whispered something in his ear, of which the penetrating
and insinuating words, "Interest with my Lord," alone
reached mine.

"It is *pessimi exempli*," said Hardie, laughing, "to provide
for a ruined client; but I was thinking of what you mention,
provided it can be managed—But hush! here he comes."

The recent relation of the poor man's misfortunes had
given him, I was pleased to observe, a claim to the attention
and respect of the young men, who treated him with great
civility, and gradually engaged him in a conversation, which,
much to my satisfaction, again turned upon the *Causes Célèbres*
of Scotland. Emboldened by the kindness with which he
was treated, Mr. Dunover began to contribute his share to
the amusement of the evening. Jails, like other places, have
their ancient traditions, known only to the inhabitants, and
handed down from one set of the melancholy lodgers to the
next who occupy their cells. Some of these, which Dunover
mentioned, were interesting, and served to illustrate the
narratives of remarkable trials, which Hardie had at his
finger ends, and which his companion was also well skilled
in. This sort of conversation passed away the evening till
the early hour when Mr. Dunover chose to retire to rest,
and I also retreated to take down memorandums of what
I had learned, in order to add another narrative to those
which it had been my chief amusement to collect, and to
write out in detail. The two young men ordered a broiled
bone, Madeira negus, and a pack of cards, and commenced a
game at picquet.

Next morning the travellers left Gandercleugh. I afterwards learned from the papers that both have been since
engaged in the great political cause of Bubbleburgh and
Bitem, a summary case, and entitled to particular despatch;
but which, it is thought, nevertheless, may outlast the duration
of the parliament to which the contest refers. Mr. Halkit,
as the newspapers informed me, acts as agent or solicitor;
and Mr. Hardie opened for Sir Peter Plyem with singular

ability, and to such good purpose, that I understand he has since had fewer play-bills and more briefs in his pocket. And both the young gentlemen deserve their good fortune; for I learned from Dunover, who called on me some weeks afterwards, and communicated the intelligence with tears in his eyes, that their interest had availed to obtain him a small office for the decent maintenance of his family; and that, after a train of constant and uninterrupted misfortune, he could trace a dawn of prosperity to his having the good fortune to be flung from the top of a mail-coach into the river Gander, in company with an advocate and a writer to the signet. The reader will not perhaps deem himself equally obliged to the accident, since it brings upon him the following narrative, founded upon the conversation of the evening.

CHAPTER II

> Whoe-er's been at Paris must needs know the Grève,
> The fatal retreat of the unfortunate brave,
> Where honour and justice most oddly contribute,
> To ease heroes' pains by an halter and gibbet.
>
> There death breaks the shackles which force had put on,
> And the hangman completes what the judge but began;
> There the squire of the poet, and knight of the post,
> Find their pains no more baulk'd, and their hopes no more cross'd.
>
> PRIOR.

IN former times, England had her Tyburn, to which the devoted victims of justice were conducted in solemn procession up what is now called Oxford Road. In Edinburgh, a large open street, or rather oblong square, surrounded by high houses, called the Grassmarket, was used for the same melancholy purpose. It was not ill chosen for such a scene, being of considerable extent, and therefore fit to accommodate a great number of spectators, such as are usually assembled by this melancholy spectacle. On the other hand, few of the houses which surround it were, even in early times, inhabited by persons of fashion; so that those likely to be offended or over deeply affected by such unpleasant exhibitions were not in the way of having their quiet disturbed by them. The houses in the Grassmarket are, generally speaking, of a mean description; yet the place is not without some features of grandeur, being overhung by the southern side of the huge rock on which the castle stands, and by the moss-grown battlements and turreted walls of that ancient fortress.

It was the custom, until within these thirty years, or thereabouts, to use this esplanade for the scene of public executions. The fatal day was announced to the public, by the appearance of a huge black gallows-tree towards the eastern end of the Grassmarket. This ill-omened apparition was of great height, with a scaffold surrounding it, and a double ladder placed against it, for the ascent of the unhappy criminal and the executioner. As this apparatus was always arranged before dawn, it seemed as if the gallows had grown out of the earth in the course of one night, like the production of some foul demon; and I well remember the fright with which the schoolboys, when I was one of their number, used to regard these ominous signs of deadly preparation. On the night after the execution the gallows again disappeared, and was conveyed in silence and darkness to the place where it was usually deposited, which was one of the vaults under the Parliament House, or courts of justice. This mode of execution is now exchanged for one similar to that in front of Newgate,—with what beneficial effect is uncertain. The mental sufferings of the convict are indeed shortened. He no longer stalks between the attendant clergymen, dressed in his grave-clothes, through a considerable part of the city, looking like a moving and walking corpse, while yet an inhabitant of this world; but, as the ultimate purpose of punishment has in view the prevention of crimes, it may at least be doubted, whether, in abridging the melancholy ceremony, we have not in part diminished that appalling effect upon the spectators which is the useful end of all such inflictions, and in consideration of which alone, unless in very particular cases, capital sentences can be altogether justified.

On the 7th day of September 1736, these ominous preparations for execution were descried in the place we have described, and at an early hour the space around began to be occupied by several groups, who gazed on the scaffold and gibbet with a stern and vindictive show of satisfaction very seldom testified by the populace, whose good-nature, in most cases, forgets the crime of the condemned person, and dwells only on his misery. But the act of which the expected culprit had been convicted was of a description calculated nearly and closely to awaken and irritate the resentful feelings

of the multitude. The tale is well known ; yet it is necessary
to recapitulate its leading circumstances, for the better understanding what is to follow ; and the narrative may prove long,
but I trust not uninteresting, even to those who have heard
its general issue. At any rate, some detail is necessary, in
order to render intelligible the subsequent events of our
narrative.

Contraband trade, though it strikes at the root of legitimate
government, by encroaching on its revenues,—though it
injures the fair trader, and debauches the minds of those
engaged in it,—is not usually looked upon, either by the
vulgar or by their betters, in a very heinous point of view.
On the contrary, in those counties where it prevails, the
cleverest, boldest, and most intelligent of the peasantry, are
uniformly engaged in illicit transactions, and very often with
the sanction of the farmers and inferior gentry. Smuggling
was almost universal in Scotland in the reigns of George I.
and II. ; for the people, unaccustomed to imposts, and regarding them as an unjust aggression upon their ancient
liberties, made no scruple to elude them whenever it was
possible to do so.

The county of Fife, bounded by the two firths on the south
and north, and by the sea on the east, and having a number
of small seaports, was long famed for maintaining successfully
a contraband trade ; and, as there were many seafaring men
residing there, who had been pirates and buccaneers in their
youth, there were not wanting a sufficient number of daring
men to carry it on. Among these, a fellow, called Andrew
Wilson, originally a baker in the village of Pathhead, was
particularly obnoxious to the revenue officers. He was
possessed of great personal strength, courage, and cunning,
—was perfectly acquainted with the coast, and capable of
conducting the most desperate enterprises. On several
occasions he succeeded in baffling the pursuit and researches
of the king's officers ; but he became so much the object
of their suspicious and watchful attention, that at length he
was totally ruined by repeated seizures. The man became
desperate. He considered himself as robbed and plundered ;
and took it into his head that he had a right to make
reprisals, as he could find opportunity. Where the heart
is prepared for evil, opportunity is seldom long wanting.
This Wilson learned, that the Collector of the Customs at
Kirkcaldy had come to Pittenweem, in the course of his

official round of duty, with a considerable sum of public money in his custody. As the amount was greatly within the value of the goods which had been seized from him, Wilson felt no scruple of conscience in resolving to reimburse himself for his losses, at the expense of the Collector and the revenue. He associated with himself one Robertson, and two other idle young men, whom, having been concerned in the same illicit trade, he persuaded to view the transaction in the same justifiable light in which he himself considered it. They watched the motions of the Collector; they broke forcibly into the house where he lodged,—Wilson, with two of his associates, entering the Collector's apartment, while Robertson, the fourth, kept watch at the door with a drawn cutlass in his hand. The officer of the customs, conceiving his life in danger, escaped out of his bedroom window, and fled in his shirt, so that the plunderers, with much ease, possessed themselves of about two hundred pounds of public money. This robbery was committed in a very audacious manner, for several persons were passing in the street at the time. But Robertson, representing the noise they heard as a dispute or fray betwixt the Collector and the people of the house, the worthy citizens of Pittenweem felt themselves no way called on to interfere in behalf of the obnoxious revenue officer; so, satisfying themselves with this very superficial account of the matter, like the Levite in the parable, they passed on the opposite side of the way. An alarm was at length given, military were called in, the depredators were pursued, the booty recovered, and Wilson and Robertson tried and condemned to death, chiefly on the evidence of an accomplice.

Many thought, that, in consideration of the men's erroneous opinion of the nature of the action they had committed, justice might have been satisfied with a less forfeiture than that of two lives. On the other hand, from the audacity of the fact, a severe example was judged necessary; and such was the opinion of the government. When it became apparent that the sentence of death was to be executed, files, and other implements necessary for their escape, were transmitted secretly to the culprits by a friend from without. By these means they sawed a bar out of one of the prison-windows, and might have made their escape. but for the obstinacy of Wilson who, as he was daringly resolute, was doggedly pertinacious of his opinion. His comrade. Robertson, a young and slender man, proposed to make the experiment of passing the foremost through the gap they had made, and enlarging it from the outside, if necessary, to allow Wilson free passage. Wilson, however, insisted on making the first experiment, and being a robust and lusty man, he not only found it impossible to get through betwixt the bars, but, by his struggles, he jammed himself so fast, that he was unable to draw his body back again. In these circumstances discovery became unavoidable, and sufficient precautions were taken by the jailor to prevent any repetition of the same attempt. Robertson uttered not a word of reflection on his companion for the consequences of his obstinacy; but it appeared from the sequel, that Wilson's mind was deeply impressed with the recollection, that, but for him, his comrade, over whose mind he exercised considerable influence, would not have engaged in the criminal enterprise which had terminated thus fatally; and that now he had become his destroyer a second time, since, but for his obstinacy, Robertson might have effected his escape. Minds like Wilson's, even when exercised in evil practices, sometimes retain the power of thinking and resolving with enthusiastic generosity. His whole thoughts were now bent on the possibility of saving Robertson's life, without the least respect to his own. The resolution which he adopted, and the manner in which he carried it into effect, were striking and unusual.

Adjacent to the tolbooth or city jail of Edinburgh, is one of three churches into which the cathedral of St. Giles is now divided, called, from its vicinity, the Tolbooth Church. It was the custom, that criminals under sentence of death were brought to this church, with a sufficient guard, to hear and join in public worship on the Sabbath before execution. It was supposed that the hearts of these unfortunate persons, however hardened before against feelings of devotion, could not but be accessible to them upon uniting their thoughts and voices, for the last time, along with their fellow-mortals, in addressing their Creator. And to the rest of the congregation, it was thought it could not but be impressive and affecting, to find their devotions mingling with those, who, sent by the doom of an earthly tribunal to appear where the whole earth is judged, might be considered as beings trembling on the verge of eternity. The practice, however edifying, has been discontinued, in consequence of the incident we are about to detail.

The clergyman, whose duty it was to officiate in the Tolbooth Church, had concluded an affecting discourse, part of which was particularly directed to the unfortunate men, Wilson and Robertson, who were in the pew set apart for the persons in their unhappy situation, each secured betwixt two soldiers of the city guard. The clergyman had reminded them, that the next congregation they must join would be that of the just, or of the unjust: that the psalms they now heard must be exchanged, in the space of two brief days, for eternal hallelujahs, or eternal lamentations; and that this fearful alternative must depend upon the state to which they might be able to bring their minds before the moment of awful preparation: that they should not despair on account of the suddenness of the summons, but rather to feel this comfort in their misery, that, though all who now lifted the voice, or bent the knee in conjunction with them, lay under the same sentence of certain death, *they* only had the advantage of knowing the precise moment at which it should be executed upon them. "Therefore," urged the good man, his voice trembling with emotion, "redeem the time, my unhappy brethren, which is yet left; and remember, that, with the grace of Him to whom space and time are but as nothing, salvation may yet be assured, even in the pittance of delay which the laws of your country afford you."

Robertson was observed to weep at these words; but Wilson seemed as one whose brain had not entirely received their meaning, or whose thoughts were deeply impressed with some different subject;—an expression so natural to a person in his situation, that it excited neither suspicion nor surprise.

The benediction was pronounced as usual, and the congregation was dismissed, many lingering to indulge their curiosity with a more fixed look at the two criminals, who now, as well as their guards, rose up, as if to depart when the crowd should permit them. A murmur ot compassion was heard to pervade the spectators, the more general, perhaps, on account of the alleviating circumstances of the case; when all at once, Wilson, who, as we have already noticed, was a very strong man, seized two of the soldiers, one with each hand, and calling at the same time to his companion, "Run, Geordie, run!" threw himself on a third, and fastened his teeth on the collar of his coat. Robertson stood for a second as if thunderstruck, and unable to avail himself of the opportunity of escape; but the cry of "Run, run!" being echoed from many around, whose feelings surprised them into a very natural interest in his behalf, he shook off the grasp of the remaining soldier, threw himself over the pew, mixed with the dispersing congregation, none of whom felt inclined to stop a poor wretch taking this last chance for his life, gained the door of the church, and was lost to all pursuit.

The generous intrepidity which Wilson had displayed on this occasion augmented the feeling of compassion which attended his fate. The public, where their own prejudices are not concerned, are easily engaged on the side of disinterestedness and humanity, admired Wilson's behaviour, and rejoiced in Robertson's escape. This general feeling was so great, that it excited a vague report that Wilson would be rescued at the place of execution, either by the mob or by some of his old associates, or by some second extraordinary and unexpected exertion of strength and courage on his own part. The magistrates thought it their duty to provide against the possibility of disturbance. They ordered out, for protection of the execution of the sentence, the greater part of their own City Guard, under the command of Captain Porteous, a man whose name became too memorable from the melancholy circumstances of the day, and subsequent events. It may be necessary to say a word about this person, and the corps which he commanded. But the subject is of importance sufficient to deserve another chapter.

CHAPTER III

And thou, great god of aqua-vitæ!
Wha sways the empire of this city,
(When fou we're sometimes capernoity,)
Be thou prepared,
To save us frae that black banditti,
The City Guard!
FERGUSON'S *Daft Days.*

CAPTAIN JOHN PORTEOUS, a name memorable in the traditions of Edinburgh, as well as in the records of criminal jurisprudence, was the son of a citizen of Edinburgh, who endeavoured to breed him up to his own mechanical trade of a tailor. The youth, however, had a wild and irreclaimable propensity to dissipation, which finally sent him to serve in the corps long maintained in the service of the States of Holland, and called the Scotch Dutch. Here he learned military discipline; and, returning afterwards, in the course

of an idle and wandering life, to his native city, his services
were required by the magistrates of Edinburgh in the disturbed year 1715, for disciplining their City Guard, in which
he shortly afterwards received a captain's commission. It
was only by his military skill, and an alert and resolute character as an officer of police, that he merited this promotion,
for he is said to have been a man of profligate habits, an
unnatural son, and a brutal husband. He was, however,
useful in his station, and his harsh and fierce habits rendered
him formidable to rioters or disturbers of the public peace.

The corps in which he held his command is, or perhaps we
should rather say *was*, a body of about one hundred and
twenty soldiers, divided into three companies, and regularly
armed, clothed, and embodied. They were chiefly veterans
who enlisted in this corps, having the benefit of working at
their trades when they were off duty. These men had the
charge of preserving public order, repressing riots and street
robberies, acting, in short, as an armed police, and attending
on all public occasions where confusion or popular disturbance might be expected.[1] Poor Ferguson, whose irregularities
sometimes led him into unpleasant rencontres with these military conservators of public order, and who mentions them
so often that he may be termed their poet laureate, thus
admonishes his readers, warned doubtless by his own experience:

> "Gude folk, as ye come frae the fair,
>   Bide yont frae this black squad;
> There's nae sic savages elsewhere
>   Allow'd to wear cockad."

In fact, the soldiers of the City Guard, being, as we have
said, in general discharged veterans, who had strength enough
remaining for this municipal duty, and being, moreover, for
the greater part, Highlanders, were neither by birth, education, or former habits, trained to endure with much patience
the insults of the rabble, or the provoking petulance of truant
schoolboys, and idle debauchees of all descriptions, with whom
their occupation brought them into contact. On the contrary,
the tempers of the poor old fellows were soured by the indignities with which the mob distinguished them on many occa-

---

[1] The Lord Provost was ex-officio commander and colonel of the corps,
which might be increased to three hundred men when the times required it.
No other drum but theirs was allowed to sound on the High Street between
the Luckenbooths and the Netherbow.

sions, and frequently might have required the soothing strains of the poet we have just quoted—

> " O soldiers ! for your ain dear sakes,
> For Scotland's love, the Land o' Cakes,
> Gie not her bairns sic deadly paiks,
>   Nor be sae rude,
> Wi' firelock or Lochaber-axe,
>   As spill their bluid ! "

On all occasions when a holyday licensed some riot and irregularity, a skirmish with these veterans was a favourite recreation with the rabble of Edinburgh. These pages may perhaps see the light when many have in fresh recollection such onsets as we allude to. But the venerable corps, with whom the contention was held, may now be considered as totally extinct. Of late the gradual diminution of these civic soldiers, reminds one of the abatement of King Lear's hundred knights. The edicts of each succeeding set of magistrates have, like those of Goneril and Regan, diminished this venerable band with the similar question, " What need we five-and-twenty?—ten?—or five?" And it is now nearly come to, "What need one?" A spectre may indeed here and there still be seen, of an old grey-headed and grey-bearded Highlander, with war-worn features, but bent double by age; dressed in an old-fashioned cocked hat, bound with white tape instead of silver lace; and in coat, waistcoat, and breeches of a muddy-coloured red, bearing in his withered hand an ancient weapon, called a Lochaber-axe; a long pole, namely, with an axe at the extremity, and a hook at the back of the hatchet.[1] Such a phantom of former days still creeps, I have been informed, round the statue of Charles the Second, in the Parliament Square, as if the image of a Stewart were the last refuge for any memorial of our ancient manners; and one or two others are supposed to glide around the door of the guard house assigned to them in the Luckenbooths, when their ancient refuge in the High Street was laid low.[2] But the fate of manuscripts bequeathed to friends and executors

[1] This hook was to enable the bearer of the Lochaber-axe to scale a gateway, by grappling the top of the door, and swinging himself up by the staff of his weapon.

[2] This ancient corps is now entirely disbanded. Their last march to do duty at Hallow-fair, had something in it affecting. Their drums and fifes had been wont on better days to play, on this joyous occasion, the lively tune of

" Jockey to the fair;"

but on this final occasion the afflicted veterans moved slowly to the dirge of

"The last time I came ower the muir."

is so uncertain, that the narrative containing these frail memorials of the old Town-Guard of Edinburgh, who, with their grim and valiant corporal, John Dhu (the fiercest-looking fellow I ever saw), were, in my boyhood, the alternate terror and derision of the petulant brood of the High School, may, perhaps, only come to light when all memory of the institution has faded away, and then serve as an illustration of Kay's caricatures, who has preserved the features of some of their heroes. In the preceding generation, when there was a perpetual alarm for the plots and activity of the Jacobites, some pains were taken by the magistrates of Edinburgh to keep this corps, though composed always of such materials as we have noticed, in a more effective state than was afterwards judged necessary, when their most dangerous service was to skirmish with the rabble on the king's birthday. They were, therefore, more the objects of hatred, and less that of scorn, than they were afterwards accounted.

To Captain John Porteous, the honour of his command and of his corps seems to have been a matter of high interest and importance. He was exceedingly incensed against Wilson for the affront which he construed him to have put upon his soldiers, in the effort he made for the liberation of his companion, and expressed himself most ardently on the subject. He was no less indignant at the report, that there was an intention to rescue Wilson himself from the gallows, and uttered many threats and imprecations upon that subject, which were afterwards remembered to his disadvantage. In fact, if a good deal of determination and promptitude rendered Porteous, in one respect, fit to command guards designed to suppress popular commotion, he seems, on the other, to have been disqualified for a charge so delicate, by a hot and surly temper, always too ready to come to blows and violence; a character void of principle; and a disposition to regard the rabble, who seldom failed to regale him and his soldiers with some marks of their displeasure, as declared enemies, upon whom it was natural and justifiable that he should seek opportunities of vengeance. Being, however, the most active and trustworthy among the captains of the City Guard, he was the person to whom the magistrates confided the command of the soldiers appointed to keep the peace at the time of Wilson's execution. He was ordered to guard the gallows and scaffold, with about eighty men, all the disposable force that could be spared for that duty.

But the magistrates took farther precautions, which affected Porteous's pride very deeply. They requested the assistance of part of a regular infantry regiment, not to attend upon the execution, but to remain drawn up on the principal street of the city, during the time that it went forward, in order to intimidate the multitude, in case they should be disposed to be unruly, with a display of force which could not be resisted without desperation. It may sound ridiculous in our ears, considering the fallen state of this ancient civic corps, that its officer should have felt punctiliously jealous of its honour. Yet so it was. Captain Porteous resented, as an indignity, the introducing the Welsh Fusileers within the city, and drawing them up in the street where no drums but his own were allowed to be sounded, without the special command or permission of the magistrates. As he could not show his ill-humour to his patrons the magistrates, it increased his indignation and his desire to be revenged on the unfortunate criminal Wilson, and all who favoured him. These internal emotions of jealousy and rage wrought a change on the man's mien and bearing, visible to all who saw him on the fatal morning when Wilson was appointed to suffer. Porteous's ordinary appearance was rather favourable. He was about the middle size, stout, and well made, having a military air, and yet rather a gentle and mild countenance. His complexion was brown, his face somewhat fretted with the scars of the smallpox, his eyes rather languid than keen or fierce. On the present occasion, however, it seemed to those who saw him as if he were agitated by some evil demon. His step was irregular, his voice hollow and broken, his countenance pale, his eyes staring and wild, his speech imperfect and confused, and his whole appearance so disordered, that many remarked he seemed to be *fey*, a Scottish expression, meaning the state of those who are driven on to their impending fate by the strong impulse of some irresistible necessity.

One part of his conduct was truly diabolical, if, indeed, it has not been exaggerated by the general prejudice entertained against his memory. When Wilson, the unhappy criminal, was delivered to him by the keeper of the prison, in order that he might be conducted to the place of execution, Porteous, not satisfied with the usual precautions to prevent escape, ordered him to be manacled. This might be justifiable from the character and bodily strength of the malefactor, as well as from the apprehensions so generally entertained of an expected rescue. But the handcuffs which were produced being found too small for the wrists of a man so big-boned as Wilson, Porteous proceeded with his own hands, and by great exertion of strength, to force them till they clasped together, to the exquisite torture of the unhappy criminal. Wilson remonstrated against such barbarous usage, declaring that the pain distracted his thoughts from the subjects of meditation proper to his unhappy condition.

"It signifies little," replied Captain Porteous; "your pain will be soon at an end."

"Your cruelty is great," answered the sufferer. "You know not how soon you yourself may have occasion to ask the mercy, which you are now refusing to a fellow-creature. May God forgive you!"

These words, long afterwards quoted and remembered, were all that passed between Porteous and his prisoner; but as they took air, and became known to the people, they greatly increased the popular compassion for Wilson, and excited a proportionate degree of indignation against Porteous; against whom, as strict, and even violent in the discharge of his unpopular office, the common people had some real, and many imaginary causes of complaint.

When the painful procession was completed, and Wilson, with the escort, had arrived at the scaffold in the Grassmarket, there appeared no signs of that attempt to rescue him which had occasioned such precautions. The multitude, in general, looked on with deeper interest than at ordinary executions; and there might be seen, on the countenances of many, a stern and indignant expression, like that with which the ancient Cameronians might be supposed to witness the execution of their brethren, who glorified the Covenant on the same occasion, and at the same spot. But there was no attempt at violence. Wilson himself seemed disposed to hasten over the space that divided time from eternity. The devotions proper and usual on such occasions were no sooner finished than he submitted to his fate, and the sentence of the law was fulfilled.

He had been suspended on the gibbet so long as to be totally deprived of life, when at once, as if occasioned by some newly-received impulse, there arose a tumult among the multitude. Many stones were thrown at Porteous and his guards; some mischief was done; and the mob continued to press forward with whoops, shrieks, howls, and exclamations. A young fellow, with a sailor's cap slouched over his face, sprung on the scaffold, and cut the rope by which the criminal was suspended. Others approached to carry off the body, either to secure for it a decent grave, or to try, perhaps, some means of resuscitation. Captain Porteous was wrought, by this appearance of insurrection against his authority, into a rage so headlong as made him forget, that, the sentence having been fully executed, it was his duty not to engage in hostilities with the misguided multitude, but to draw off his men as fast as possible. He sprung from the scaffold, snatched a musket from one of his soldiers, commanded the party to give fire, and, as several eye-witnesses concurred in swearing, set them the example, by discharging his piece, and shooting a man dead on the spot. Several soldiers obeyed his command or followed his example; six or seven persons were slain, and a great many were hurt and wounded.

After this act of violence, the Captain proceeded to withdraw his men towards their guard-house in the High Street. The mob were not so much intimidated as incensed by what had been done. They pursued the soldiers with execrations, accompanied by volleys of stones. As they pressed on them, the rearmost soldiers turned, and again fired with fatal aim and execution. It is not accurately known whether Porteous commanded this second act of violence; but of course the odium of the whole transactions of the fatal day attached to him, and to him alone. He arrived at the guard-house, dismissed his soldiers, and went to make his report to the magistrates concerning the unfortunate events of the day.

Apparently by this time Captain Porteous had begun to doubt the propriety of his own conduct, and the reception he met with from the magistrates was such as to make him still more anxious to gloss it over. He denied that he had given orders to fire; he denied he had fired with his own hand; he even produced the fusee which he carried as an officer for examination; it was found still loaded. Of three cartridges which he was seen to put in his pouch that morning, two were still there; a white handkerchief was thrust into the muzzle of the piece, and returned unsoiled or blackened. To the defence founded on these circumstances it was answered, that Porteous had not used his own piece, but had been seen to take one from a soldier. Among the many who had been killed and wounded by the unhappy fire, there were several of better rank; for even the humanity of such soldiers as fired over the heads of the mere rabble around the scaffold, proved in some instances fatal to persons who were stationed in windows, or observed the melancholy scene from a distance. The voice of public indignation was loud and general; and, ere men's tempers had time to cool, the trial of Captain Porteous took place before the High Court of Justiciary. After a long and patient hearing, the jury had the difficult duty of balancing the positive evidence of many persons, and those of respectability, who deposed positively to the prisoner's commanding his soldiers to fire, and himself firing his piece, of which some swore that they saw the smoke and flash, and beheld a man drop at whom it was pointed, with the negative testimony of others, who, though well stationed for seeing what had passed, neither heard Porteous give orders to fire nor saw him fire himself; but, on the contrary, averred that the first shot was fired by a soldier who stood close by him. A great part of his defence was also founded on the turbulence of the mob, which witnesses, according to their feelings, their predilections, and their opportunities of observation, represented differently; some describing as a formidable riot, what others represented as a trifling disturbance, such as always used to take place on the like occasions, when the executioner of the law, and the men commissioned to protect him in his task, were generally exposed to some indignities. The verdict of the jury sufficiently shows how the evidence preponderated in their minds. It declared that John Porteous fired a gun among the people assembled at the execution; that he gave orders to his soldiers to fire, by which many persons were killed and wounded; but, at the same time, that the prisoner and his guard had been wounded and beaten, by stones thrown at them by the multitude. Upon this verdict, the Lords of Justiciary passed sentence of death against Captain John Porteous, adjudging him, in the common form, to be hanged on a gibbet at the common place of execution, on Wednesday, 8th September, 1736, and all his movable property to be forfeited to the king's use, according to the Scottish law in cases of wilful murder.

CHAPTER IV

The hour's come, but not the man.[1]
Kelpie.

ON the day when the unhappy Porteous was expected to suffer the sentence of the law, the place of execution, extensive as it is, was crowded almost to suffocation. There was not a window in all the lofty tenements around it, or in the steep and crooked street called the Bow, by which the fatal procession was to descend from the High Street, that was not absolutely filled with spectators. The uncommon height and antique appearance of these houses, some of which were formerly the property of the Knights Templars, and the Knights of St. John, and still exhibit on their fronts and gables the iron cross of these orders, gave additional effect to a scene in itself so striking. The area of the Grassmarket resembled a huge dark lake or sea of human heads, in the centre of which arose the fatal tree, tall, black, and ominous, from which dangled the deadly halter. Every object takes interest from its uses and associations, and the erect beam and empty noose, things so simple in themselves, became, on such an occasion, objects of terror and of solemn interest.

Amid so numerous an assembly there was scarcely a word spoken, save in whispers. The thirst of vengeance was in some degree allayed by its supposed certainty; and even the populace, with deeper feeling than they are wont to entertain, suppressed all clamorous exultation, and prepared to enjoy the scene of retaliation in triumph, silent and decent, though stern and relentless. It seemed as if the depth of their hatred to the unfortunate criminal scorned to display itself in anything resembling the more noisy current of their ordinary feelings. Had a stranger consulted only the evidence of his ears, he might have supposed that so vast a multitude were assembled for some purpose which affected them with the deepest sorrow, and stilled those noises which, on all ordinary occasions, arise from such a concourse; but if he gazed upon their faces he

[1] There is a tradition, that while a little stream was swollen into a torrent by recent showers, the discontented voice of the Water Spirit was heard to pronounce these words. At the same moment, a man, urged on by his fate, or, in Scottish language, *fey*, arrived at a gallop, and prepared to cross the water. No remonstrance from the bystanders was of power to stop him—he plunged into the stream, and perished.

would have been instantly undeceived. The compressed lip, the bent brow, the stern and flashing eye of almost every one on whom he looked, conveyed the expression of men come to glut their sight with triumphant revenge. It is probable that the appearance of the criminal might have somewhat changed the temper of the populace in his favour, and that they might in the moment of death have forgiven the man against whom their resentment had been so fiercely heated. It had, however, been destined, that the mutability of their sentiments was not to be exposed to this trial.

The usual hour for producing the criminal had been past for many minutes, yet the spectators observed no symptom of his appearance. "Would they venture to defraud public justice?" was the question which men began anxiously to ask at each other. The first answer in every case was bold and positive,—"They dare not." But when the point was further canvassed, other opinions were entertained, and various causes of doubt were suggested. Porteous had been a favourite officer of the magistracy of the city, which, being a numerous and fluctuating body, requires for its support a degree of energy in its functionaries, which the individuals who compose it cannot at all times alike be supposed to possess in their own persons. It was remembered, that in the Information for Porteous (the paper, namely, in which his case was stated to the Judges of the criminal court), he had been described by his counsel as the person on whom the magistrates chiefly relied in all emergencies of uncommon difficulty. It was argued, too, that his conduct, on the unhappy occasion of Wilson's execution, was capable of being attributed to an imprudent excess of zeal in the execution of his duty, a motive for which those under whose authority he acted might be supposed to have great sympathy. And as these considerations might move the magistrates to make a favourable representation of Porteous's case, there were not wanting others in the higher departments of government, which would make such suggestions favourably listened to.

The mob of Edinburgh, when thoroughly excited, had been at all times one of the fiercest which could be found in Europe; and of late years they had risen repeatedly against the government, and sometimes not without temporary success. They were conscious, therefore, that they were no favourites with the rulers of the period, and that, if Captain Porteous's violence was not altogether regarded as good service, it might certainly be thought, that to visit it with a capital punishment would render it both delicate and dangerous for future officers, in the same circumstances, to act with effect in repressing tumults. There is also a natural feeling, on the part of all members of government, for the general maintenance of authority ; and it seemed not unlikely, that what to the relatives of the sufferers appeared a wanton and unprovoked massacre, should be otherwise viewed in the cabinet of St. James's. It might be there supposed, that, upon the whole matter, Captain Porteous was in the exercise of a trust delegated to him by the lawful civil authority ; that he had been assaulted by the populace, and several of his men hurt ; and that, in finally repelling force by force, his conduct could be fairly imputed to no other motive than self-defence in the discharge of his duty.

These considerations, of themselves very powerful, induced the spectators to apprehend the possibility of a reprieve ; and to the various causes which might interest the rulers in his favour, the lower part of the rabble added one which was peculiarly well adapted to their comprehension. It was averred, in order to increase the odium against Porteous, that while he repressed with the utmost severity the slightest excesses of the poor, he not only overlooked the license of the young nobles and gentry, but was very willing to lend them the countenance of his official authority, in execution of such loose pranks as it was chiefly his duty to have restrained. This suspicion, which was perhaps much exaggerated, made a deep impression on the minds of the populace ; and when several of the higher rank joined in a petition, recommending Porteous to the mercy of the crown, it was generally supposed he owed their favour not to any conviction of the hardship of his case, but to the fear of losing a convenient accomplice in their debaucheries. It is scarcely necessary to say how much this suspicion augmented the people's detestation of this obnoxious criminal, as well as their fear of his escaping the sentence pronounced against him.

While these arguments were stated and replied to, and canvassed and supported, the hitherto silent expectation of the people became changed into that deep and agitating murmur, which is sent forth by the ocean before the tempest begins to howl. The crowded populace, as if their motions had corresponded with the unsettled state of their minds, fluctuated to and fro without any visible cause of impulse, like the agitation of the waters, called by sailors the groundswell. The news, which the magistrates had almost hesitated to communicate to them, were at length announced, and spread among the spectators with a rapidity like lightning. A reprieve from the Secretary of State's office, under the hand of his Grace the Duke of Newcastle, had arrived, intimating the pleasure of Queen Caroline (regent of the kingdom during the absence of George II. on the Continent), that the execution of the sentence of death pronounced against John Porteous, late Captain-Lieutenant of the City-Guard of Edinburgh, present prisoner in the Tolbooth of that city, be respited for six weeks from the time appointed for his execution.

The assembled spectators of almost all degrees, whose minds had been wound up to the pitch which we have described, uttered a groan, or rather a roar of indignation and disappointed revenge, similar to that of a tiger from whom his meal has been rent by his keeper when he was just about to devour it. This fierce exclamation seemed to forebode some immediate explosion of popular resentment, and, in fact, such had been expected by the magistrates, and the necessary measures had been taken to repress it. But the shout was not repeated, nor did any sudden tumult ensue, such as it appeared to announce. The populace seemed to be ashamed of having expressed their disappointment in a vain clamour, and the sound changed, not into the silence which had preceded the arrival of these stunning news, but into stifled mutterings, which each group maintained among themselves, and which were blended into one deep and hoarse murmur which floated above the assembly.

Yet still, though all expectation of the execution was over, the mob remained assembled, stationary, as it were, through very resentment, gazing on the preparations for death, which had now been made in vain, and stimulating their feelings, by recalling the various claims which Wilson might have had on royal mercy, from the mistaken motives on which he acted, as well as from the generosity he had displayed towards his accomplice. "This man," they said,—"the brave, the resolute, the generous, was executed to death without mercy for stealing a purse of gold, which in some sense he might consider as a fair reprisal; while the profligate satellite, who took advantage of a trifling tumult, inseparable from such occasions, to shed the blood of twenty of his fellow-citizens, is deemed a fitting object for the exercise of the royal prerogative of mercy. Is this to be borne?—would our fathers have borne it? Are not we, like them, Scotsmen and burghers of Edinburgh?"

The officers of justice began now to remove the scaffold, and other preparations which had been made for the execution, in hopes, by doing so, to accelerate the dispersion of the multitude. The measure had the desired effect; for no sooner had the fatal tree been unfixed from the large stone pedestal or socket in which it was secured, and sunk slowly down upon the wain intended to remove it to the place where it was usually deposited, than the populace, after giving vent to their feelings in a second shout of rage and mortification, began slowly to disperse to their usual abodes and occupations.

The windows were in like manner gradually deserted, and groups of the more decent class of citizens formed themselves, as if waiting to return homewards when the streets should be cleared of the rabble. Contrary to what is frequently the case, this description of persons agreed in general with the sentiments of their inferiors, and considered the cause as common to all ranks. Indeed, as we have already noticed, it was by no means amongst the lowest class of the spectators, or those most likely to be engaged in the riot at Wilson's execution, that the fatal fire of Porteous's soldiers had taken effect. Several persons were killed who were looking out at windows at the scene, who could not of course belong to the rioters, and were persons of decent rank and condition. The burghers, therefore, resenting the loss which had fallen on their own body, and proud and tenacious of their rights, as the citizens of Edinburgh have at all times been, were greatly exasperated at the unexpected respite of Captain Porteous.

It was noticed at the time, and afterwards more particularly remembered, that, while the mob were in the act of dispersing, several individuals were seen busily passing from one place and one group of people to another, remaining long with none, but whispering for a little time with those who appeared to be declaiming most violently against the conduct of government. These active agents had the appearance of men from the country, and were generally supposed t be old friends and confederates of Wilson, whose minds were of course highly excited against Porteous.

If, however, it was the intention of these men to stir the

multitude to any sudden act of mutiny, it seemed for the time to be fruitless. The rabble, as well as the more decent part of the assembly, dispersed, and went home peaceably; and it was only by observing the moody discontent on their brows, or catching the tenor of the conversation they held with each other, that a stranger could estimate the state of their minds. We will give the reader this advantage, by associating ourselves with one of the numerous groups who were painfully ascending the steep declivity of the West Bow, to return to their dwellings in the Lawnmarket.

"An unco thing this, Mrs. Howden," said old Peter Plumdamas to his neighbour the rouping-wife, or saleswoman, as he offered her his arm to assist her in the toilsome ascent, "to see the grit folk at Lunnon set their face against law and gospel, and let loose sic a reprobate as Porteous upon a peaceable town!"

"And to think o' the weary walk they hae gien us," answered Mrs. Howden, with a groan; "and sic a comfortable window as I had gotten, too, just within a penny-stane-cast of the scaffold—I could hae heard every word the minister said—and to pay twalpennies for my stand, and a' for naething!"

"I am judging," said Mr. Plumdamas, "that this reprieve wadna stand gude in the auld Scots law, when the kingdom *was* a kingdom."

"I dinna ken muckle about the law," answered Mrs. Howden; "but I ken, when we had a king, and a chancellor, and parliament-men o' our ain, we could aye peeble them wi' stanes when they werena gude bairns—But naebody's nails can reach the length o' Lunnon."

"Weary on Lunnon, and a' that e'er came out o't!" said Miss Grizel Damahoy, an ancient seamstress; "they hae taen awa our parliament, and they hae oppressed our trade. Our gentles will hardly allow that a Scots needle can sew ruffles on a sark, or lace on an owerlay."

"Ye may say that, Miss Damahoy, and I ken o' them that hae gotten raisins frae Lunnon by forpits at ance," responded Plumdamas; "and then sic an host of idle English gaugers and excisemen as hae come down to vex and torment us, that an honest man canna fetch sae muckle as a bit anker o' brandy frae Leith to the Lawnmarket, but he's like to be rubbit o' the very gudes he's bought and paid for.—Weel, I winna justify Andrew Wilson for pitting hands on what wasna his; but if he took nae mair than his ain, there's an awfu' difference between that and the fact this man stands for."

"If ye speak about the law," said Mrs. Howden, "here comes Mr. Saddletree, that can settle it as weel as ony on the bench."

The party she mentioned, a grave elderly person, with a superb periwig, dressed in a decent suit of sad-coloured clothes, came up as she spoke, and courteously gave his arm to Miss Grizel Damahoy.

It may be necessary to mention, that Mr. Bartoline Saddletree kept an excellent and highly esteemed shop for harness, saddles, &c. &c. at the sign of the Golden Nag, at the head of Bess Wynd. His genius, however (as he himself and most of his neighbours conceived), lay towards the weightier matters of the law, and he failed not to give frequent attendance upon the pleadings and arguments of the lawyers and judges in the neighbouring square, where, to say the truth, he was oftener to be found than would have consisted with his own emolument; but that his wife, an active painstaking person, could, in his absence, make an admirable shift to please the customers and scold the journeymen. This good lady was in the habit of letting her husband take his way, and go on improving his stock of legal knowledge without interruption; but, as if in requital, she insisted upon having her own will in the domestic and commercial departments which he abandoned to her. Now, as Bartoline Saddletree had a considerable gift of words, which he mistook for eloquence, and conferred more liberally upon the society in which he lived than was at all times gracious and acceptable, there went forth a saying, with which wags used sometimes to interrupt his rhetoric, that, as he had a golden nag at his door, so he had a grey mare in his shop. This reproach induced Mr. Saddletree, on all occasions, to assume rather a haughty and stately tone towards his good woman, a circumstance by which she seemed very little affected, unless he attempted to exercise any real authority, when she never failed to fly into open rebellion. But such extremes Bartoline seldom provoked; for, like the gentle King Jamie, he was fonder of talking of authority than really exercising it. This turn of mind was, on the whole, lucky for him; since his substance was increased without any trouble on his part, or any interruption of his favourite studies.

This word in explanation has been thrown in to the reader,

while Saddletree was laying down, with great precision, the law upon Porteous's case, by which he arrived at this conclusion, that, if Porteous had fired five minutes sooner, before Wilson was cut down, he would have been *versans in licito;* engaged, that is, in a lawful act, and only liable to be punished *propter excessum*, or for lack of discretion, which might have mitigated the punishment to *pœna ordinaria*.

"Discretion!" echoed Mrs. Howden, on whom, it may well be supposed, the fineness of this distinction was entirely thrown away,—" whan had Jock Porteous either grace, discretion, or gude manners?—I mind when his father——"

"But, Mrs. Howden——" said Saddletree.

"And I," said Miss Damahoy, "mind when his mother——"

"Miss Damahoy——" entreated the interrupted orator.

"And I," said Plumdamas, "mind when his wife——"

"Mr. Plumdamas—Mrs. Howden—Miss Damahoy," again implored the orator,—"mind the distinction, as Counsellor Crossmyloof says—'I,' says he, 'take a distinction.' Now, the body of the criminal being cut down, and the execution ended, Porteous was no longer official; the act which he came to protect and guard, being done and ended, he was no better than *cuivis ex populo*."

"*Quivis—quivis*, Mr. Saddletree, craving your pardon," said (with a prolonged emphasis on the first syllable) Mr. Butler, the deputy schoolmaster of a parish near Edinburgh, who at that moment came up behind them as the false Latin was uttered.

"What signifies interrupting me, Mr. Butler?—but I am glad to see you notwithstanding—I speak after Counsellor Crossmyloof, and he said *cuivis*."

"If Counsellor Crossmyloof used the dative for the nominative, I would have crossed *his* loof with a tight leathern strap, Mr. Saddletree; there is not a boy on the booby form but should have been scourged for such a solecism in grammar."

"I speak Latin like a lawyer, Mr. Butler, and not like a schoolmaster," retorted Saddletree.

"Scarce like a schoolboy, I think," rejoined Butler.

"It matters little," said Bartoline; "all I mean to say is, that Porteous has become liable to the *pœna extra ordinem*, or capital punishment; which is to say, in plain Scotch, the gallows, simply because he did not fire when he was in office, but waited till the body was cut down, the execution whilk he had in charge to guard implemented, and he himself exonered of the public trust imposed on him."

"But, Mr. Saddletree," said Plumdamas, "do ye really think John Porteous's case wad hae been better if he had begun firing before ony stanes were flung at a'?"

"Indeed do I, neighbour Plumdamas," replied Bartoline, confidently, "he being then in point of trust and in point of power, the execution being but inchoat, or, at least, not implemented, or finally ended; but after Wilson was cut down, it was a' ower—he was clean exauctorate, and had nae mair ado but to get awa wi' his guard up this West Bow as fast as if there had been a caption after him—And this is law, for I heard it laid down by Lord Vincovincentem."

"Vincovincentem?—Is he a lord of state, or a lord of seat?" enquired Mrs. Howden.[1]

"A lord of seat—a lord of session.—I fash mysell little wi' lords o' state; they vex me wi' a wheen idle questions about their saddles, and curpels, and holsters, and horse-furniture, and what they'll cost, and whan they'll be ready—a wheen galloping geese—my wife may serve the like o' them."

"And so might she, in her day, hae served the best lord in the land, for as little as ye think o' her, Mr. Saddletree," said Mrs. Howden, somewhat indignant at the contemptuous way in which her gossip was mentioned; "when she and I were twa gilpies, we little thought to hae sitten doun wi' the like o' my auld Davie Howden, or you either, Mr. Saddletree."

While Saddletree, who was not bright at a reply, was cudgelling his brains for an answer to this home-thrust, Miss Damahoy broke in on him.

"And as for the lords of state," said Miss Damahoy, "ye suld mind the riding o' the parliament, Mr. Saddletree, in the gude auld time before the Union,—a year's rent o' mony a gude estate gaed for horse-graith and harnessing, forby broidered robes and foot-mantles, that wad hae stude by their lane wi' gold brocade, and that were muckle in my ain line."

"Ay, and then the lusty banqueting, with sweetmeats and comfits wet and dry, and dried fruits of divers sorts," said Plumdamas. "But Scotland was Scotland in these days."

"I'll tell ye what it is, neighbours," said Mrs. Howden, "I'll ne'er believe Scotland is Scotland ony mair, if our

---

[1] A nobleman was called a Lord of State. The Senators of the College of Justice were termed Lords of Seat, or of the Session.

kindly Scots sit doun with the affront they hae gien us this day. It's not only the blude that *is* shed, but the blude that might hae been shed, that's required at our hands; there was my daughter's wean, little Eppie Daidle—my oe, ye ken, Miss Grizel—had played the truant frae the school, as bairns will do, ye ken, Mr. Butler——"

"And for which," interjected Mr. Butler, "they should be soundly scourged by their well-wishers."

"And had just cruppen to the gallows' foot to see the hanging, as was natural for a wean; and what for mightna she hae been shot as weel as the rest o' them, and where wad we a' hae been then? I wonder how Queen Carline (if her name be Carline) wad hae liked to hae had ane o' her ain bairns in sic a venture?"

"Report says," answered Butler, "that such a circumstance would not have distressed her majesty beyond endurance."

"Aweel," said Mrs. Howden, "the sum o' the matter is, that, were I a man, I wad hae amends o' Jock Porteous, be the upshot what like o't, if a' the carles and carlines in England had sworn to the nay-say."

"I would claw down the Tolbooth door wi' my nails," said Miss Grizel, "but I wad be at him."

"Ye may be very right, ladies," said Butler, "but I would not advise you to speak so loud."

"Speak!" exclaimed both the ladies together, "there will be naething else spoken about frae the Weigh-house to the Water-gate, till this is either ended or mended."

The females now departed to their respective places of abode. Plumdamas joined the other two gentlemen in drinking their *meridian* (a bumper-dram of brandy), as they passed the well-known low-browed shop in the Lawnmarket, where they were wont to take that refreshment. Mr. Plumdamas then departed towards his shop, and Mr. Butler, who happened to have some particular occasion for the rein of an old bridle (the truants of that busy day could have anticipated its application), walked down the Lawnmarket with Mr. Saddletree, each talking as he could get a word thrust in, the one on the laws of Scotland, the other on those of Syntax, and neither listening to a word which his companion uttered.

CHAPTER V

Elswhair he colde right weel lay down the law,
But in his house was meek as is a daw.

DAVIE LINDSAY.

"THERE has been Jock Driver the carrier here, speering about his new graith," said Mrs. Saddletree to her husband, as he crossed the threshold, not with the purpose, by any means, of consulting him upon his own affairs, but merely to intimate, by a gentle recapitulation, how much duty she had gone through in his absence.

"Weel," replied Bartoline, and deigned not a word more.

"And the Laird of Girdingburst has had his running footman here, and ca'd himsell (he's a civil pleasant young gentleman) to see when the broidered saddle-cloth for his sorrel horse will be ready, for he wants it agane the Kelso races."

"Weel, aweel," replied Bartoline, as laconically as before.

"And his lordship, the Earl of Blazonbury, Lord Flash and Flame, is like to be clean daft, that the harness for the six Flanders mears, wi' the crests, coronets, housings, and mountings conform, are no sent hame according to promise gien."

"Weel, weel, weel—weel, weel, gudewife," said Saddletree, "if he gangs daft, we'll hae him cognosced—it's a' very weel."

"It's weel that ye think sae, Mr. Saddletree," answered his helpmate, rather nettled at the indifference with which her report was received; "there's mony ane wad hae thought themselves affronted, if sae mony customers had ca'd and naebody to answer them but women-folk; for a' the lads were aff, as soon as your back was turned, to see Porteous hanged, that might be counted upon; and sae, you no being at hame——"

"Houts, Mrs. Saddletree," said Bartoline, with an air of consequence, "dinna 'deave me wi' your nonsense; I was under the necessity of being elsewhere—*non omnia*—as Mr. Crossmyloof said, when he was called by two macers at once, *non omnia possumus—pessimus—possimis*—I ken our law-latin offends Mr. Butler's ears, but it means naebody, an it were the Lord President himsell, can do twa turns at ance."

"Very right, Mr. Saddletree," answered his careful help-mate, with a sarcastic smile; "and nae doubt it's a decent thing to leave your wife to look after young gentlemen's saddles and bridles, when ye gang to see a man, that never did ye nae ill, raxing a halter."

"Woman," said Saddletree, assuming an elevated tone, to which the *meridian* had somewhat contributed, "desist,—I say forbear, from intromitting with affairs thou canst not understand. D'ye think I was born to sit here broggin an elshin through bend-leather, when sic men as Duncan Forbes, and that other Arniston chield there, without muckle greater parts, if the close-head speak true, than mysell, maun be presidents and king's advocates, nae doubt, and wha but they? Whereas, were favour equally distribute, as in the days of the wight Wallace——"

"I ken naething we wad hae gotten by the wight Wallace," said Mrs. Saddletree, "unless, as I hae heard the auld folk tell, they fought in thae days wi' bend-leather guns, and then it's a chance but what, if he had bought them, he might have forgot to pay for them. And as for the greatness of your parts, Bartley, the folk in the close-head maun ken mair about them than I do, if they make sic a report of them."

"I tell ye, woman," said Saddletree, in high dudgeon, "that ye ken naething about these matters. In Sir William Wallace's days, there was nae man pinned down to sic a slavish wark as a saddler's, for they got ony leather graith that they had use for ready-made out of Holland."

"Well," said Butler, who was, like many of his profession, something of a humorist and dry joker, "if that be the case, Mr. Saddletree, I think we have changed for the better; since we make our own harness, and only import our lawyers from Holland."

"It's ower true, Mr. Butler," answered Bartoline, with a sigh; "if I had had the luck—or rather, if my father had had the sense to send me to Leyden and Utrecht to learn the Substitutes and Pandex——"

"You mean the Institutes — Justinian's Institutes, Mr. Saddletree?" said Butler.

"Institutes and substitutes are synonymous words, Mr. Butler, and used indifferently as such in deeds of tailzie, as you may see in Balfour's Practiques, or Dallas of St. Martin's Styles. I understand these things pretty weel, I thank God; but I own I should have studied in Holland."

"To comfort you, you might not have been farther forward than you are now, Mr. Saddletree," replied Mr. Butler, "for our Scottish advocates are an aristocratic race. Their brass is of the right Corinthian quality, and *Non cuivis contigit adire Corinthum*—Aha, Mr. Saddletree?"

"And aha, Mr. Butler," rejoined Bartoline, upon whom, as may be well supposed, the jest was lost, and all but the sound of the words, "ye said a gliff syne it was a *quivis*, and now I heard ye say *cuivis* with my ain ears, as plain as ever I heard a word at the fore-bar."

"Give me your patience, Mr. Saddletree, and I'll explain the discrepancy in three words," said Butler, as pedantic in his own department, though with infinitely more judgment and learning, as Bartoline was in his self-assumed profession of the law—"Give me your patience for a moment—You'll grant that the nominative case is that by which a person or thing is nominated or designed, and which may be called the primary case, all others being formed from it by alterations of the termination in the learned languages, and by preposi- tions in our modern Babylonian jargons—You'll grant me that, I suppose, Mr. Saddletree?"

"I dinna ken whether I will or no—*ad avisandum*, ye ken—naebody should be in a hurry to make admissions, either in point of law, or in point of fact," said Saddletree, looking, or endeavouring to look, as if he understood what was said.

"And the dative case——" continued Butler.

"I ken what a tutor dative is," said Saddletree, "readily enough."

"The dative case," resumed the grammarian, "is that in which anything is given or assigned as properly belonging to a person, or thing—You cannot deny that, I am sure."

"I am sure I'll no grant it though," said Saddletree.

"Then, what the *deevil* d'ye take the nominative and the dative cases to be?" said Butler, hastily, and surprised at once out of his decency of expression and accuracy of pronunciation.

"I'll tell you that at leisure, Mr. Butler," said Saddletree, with a very knowing look; "I'll take a day to see and answer every article of your condescendence, and then I'll hold you to confess or deny, as accords."

"Come, come, Mr. Saddletree," said his wife, "we'll hae nae confessions and condescendences here, let them deal in thae sort o' wares that are paid for them—they suit the like o' us as ill as a demipique saddle would set a draught ox."

"Aha!" said Mr. Butler, "*Optat ephippia bos piger*, nothing

new under the sun—But it was a fair hit of Mrs. Saddletree,
however."

"And it wad far better become ye, Mr. Saddletree," continued his helpmate, "since ye say ye hae skeel o' the law, to
try if ye can do onything for Effie Deans, puir thing, that's
lying up in the Tolbooth yonder, cauld, and hungry, and com-
fortless—A servant lass of ours, Mr. Butler, and as innocent a
lass, to my thinking, and as usefu' in the chop—When Mr.
Saddletree gangs out,—and ye're aware he's seldom at hame
when there's ony o' the plea-houses open,—puir Effie used to
help me to tumble the bundles o' barkened leather up and
down, and range out the gudes, and suit a'body's humours—
And troth, she could aye please the customers wi' her answers,
for she was aye civil, and a bonnier lass wasna in Auld
Reekie. And when folk were hasty and unreasonable, she
could serve them better than me, that am no sae young as
I hae been, Mr. Butler, and a wee bit short in the temper into
the bargain. For when there's ower mony folks crying on me
at anes, and nane but ae tongue to answer them, folk maun
speak hastily, or they'll ne'er get through their wark—Sae I
miss Effie daily."

"*De die in diem*," added Saddletree.

"I think," said Butler, after a good deal of hesitation, "I have
seen the girl in the shop—a modest-looking, fair-haired girl?"

"Ay, ay, that's just puir Effie," said her mistress. "How
she was abandoned to hersell, or whether she was sackless
o' the sinfu' deed, God in Heaven knows; but if she's been
guilty, she's been sair tempted, and I wad amaist take my
Bible-aith she hasna been hersell at the time."

Butler had by this time become much agitated; he fidgeted
up and down the shop, and showed the greatest agitation that
a person of such strict decorum could be supposed to give
way to. "Was not this girl," he said, "the daughter of David
Deans, that had the parks at St. Leonard's taken? and has
she not a sister?"

"In troth has she—puir Jeanie Deans, ten years aulder
than hersell; she was here greeting a wee while syne about
her tittie. And what could I say to her, but that she behoved
to come and speak to Mr. Saddletree when he was at hame?
It wasna that I thought Mr. Saddletree could do her or ony
other body muckle good or ill, but it wad aye serve to keep
the puir thing's heart up for a wee while; and let sorrow come
when sorrow maun."

"Ye're mistaen though, gudewife," said Saddletree scornfully, "for I could hae gien her great satisfaction; I could hae proved to her that her sister was indicted upon the statute saxteen hundred and ninety, chapter one—For the mair ready prevention of child-murder—for concealing her pregnancy, and giving no account of the child which she had borne."

"I hope," said Butler,—"I trust in a gracious God, that she can clear herself."

"And sae do I, Mr. Butler," replied Mrs. Saddletree. "I am sure I wad hae answered for her as my ain daughter; but, wae's my heart, I had been tender a' the simmer, and scarce ower the door o' my room for twal weeks. And as for Mr. Saddletree, he might be in a lying-in hospital, and ne'er find out what the women cam there for. Sae I could see little or naething o' her, or I wad hae had the truth o' her situation out o' her, I'se warrant ye—But we a' think her sister maun be able to speak something to clear her."

"The haill Parliament House," said Saddletree, "was speaking o' naething else, till this job o' Porteous's put it out o' head—It's a beautiful point of presumptive murder, and there's been nane like it in the Justiciar Court since the case of Luckie Smith the howdie, that suffered in the year saxteen hundred and seventy-nine."

"But what's the matter wi' you, Mr. Butler?" said the good woman; "ye are looking as white as a sheet; will ye take a dram?"

"By no means," said Butler, compelling himself to speak. "I walked in from Dumfries yesterday, and this is a warm day."

"Sit down," said Mrs. Saddletree, laying hands on him kindly, "and rest ye—ye'll kill yoursell, man, at that rate—And are we to wish you joy o' getting the scule, Mr. Butler?"

"Yes—no—I do not know," answered the young man vaguely. But Mrs. Saddletree kept him to the point, partly out of real interest, partly from curiosity.

"Ye dinna ken whether ye are to get the free scule o' Dumfries or no, after hinging on and teaching it a' the simmer?"

"No, Mrs. Saddletree—I am not to have it," replied Butler, more collectedly. "The Laird of Black-at-the-bane had a natural son bred to the kirk, that the presbytery could not be prevailed upon to license; and so——"

"Ay, ye need say nae mair about it; if there was a laird

that had a puir kinsman or a bastard that it wad suit, there's
eneugh said.—And ye're e'en come back to Libberton to wait
for dead men's shoon?—and, for as frail as Mr. Whackbairn
is, he may live as lang as you, that are his assistant and
successor."

"Very like," replied Butler with a sigh; "I do not know if
I should wish it otherwise."

"Nae doubt it's a very vexing thing," continued the good
lady, "to be in that dependent station; and you that hae
right and title to sae muckle better, I wonder how ye bear
these crosses."

"*Quos diligit castigat*," answered Butler; "even the pagan
Seneca could see an advantage in affliction. The Heathens
had their philosophy, and the Jews their revelation, Mrs.
Saddletree, and they endured their distresses in their day.
Christians have a better dispensation than either—but doubt-
less——"

He stopped and sighed.

"I ken what ye mean," said Mrs. Saddletree, looking
toward her husband; "there's whiles we lose patience in
spite of baith book and Bible—But ye are no gaun awa, and
looking sae poorly—ye'll stay and take some kail wi' us?"

Mr. Saddletree laid aside Balfour's Practiques (his favourite
study, and much good may it do him), to join in his wife's
hospitable importunity. But the teacher declined all entreaty,
and took his leave upon the spot.

"There's something in a' this," said Mrs. Saddletree, looking after him as he walked up the street; "I wonder what
makes Mr. Butler sae distressed about Effie's misfortune—
there was nae acquaintance atween them that ever I saw or
heard of; but they were neighbours when David Deans was
on the Laird o' Dumbiedikes' land. Mr. Butler wad ken her
father, or some o' her folk.—Get up, Mr. Saddletree—ye have
set yoursell down on the very brecham that wants stitching—
and here's little Willie, the prentice.—Ye little rin-there-out
deil that ye are, what takes you raking through the gutters to
see folk hangit?—how wad ye like when it comes to be your
ain chance, as I winna ensure ye, if ye dinna mend your
manners?—And what are ye maundering and greeting for,
as if a word were breaking your banes?—Gang in by, and be
a better bairn another time, and tell Peggy to gie ye a bicker
o' broth, for ye'll be as gleg as a gled, I'se warrant ye.—It's
a fatherless bairn, Mr. Saddletree, and motherless, whilk in

some cases may be waur, and ane would take care o' him if they could—it's a Christian duty."

"Very true, gudewife," said Saddletree, in reply, "we are *in loco parentis* to him during his years of pupillarity, and I hae had thoughts of applying to the Court for a commission as factor *loco tutoris*, seeing there is nae tutor nominate, and the tutor-at-law declines to act; but only I fear the expense of the procedure wad not be *in rem versam*, for I am not aware if Willie has ony effects whereof to assume the administration."

He concluded this sentence with a self-important cough, as one who has laid down the law in an indisputable manner.

"Effects!" said Mrs. Saddletree, "what effects has the puir wean?—he was in rags when his mother died; and the blue polonie that Effie made for him out of an auld mantle of my ain, was the first decent dress the bairn ever had on. Puir Effie! can ye tell me now really, wi' a' your law, will her life be in danger, Mr. Saddletree, when they arena able to prove that ever there was a bairn ava?"

"Whoy," said Mr. Saddletree, delighted at having for once in his life seen his wife's attention arrested by a topic of legal discussion—"Whoy, there are two sorts of *murdrum*, or *murdragium*, or what you *populariter et vulgariter* call murther. I mean there are many sorts; for there's your *murthrum per vigilias et insidias*, and your *murthrum* under trust."

"I am sure," replied his moiety, "that murther by trust is the way that the gentry murther us merchants, and whiles make us shut the booth up—but that has naething to do wi' Effie's misfortune."

"The case of Effie (or Euphemia) Deans," resumed Saddletree, "is one of those cases of murder presumptive, that is, a murder of the law's inferring or construction, being derived from certain *indicia* or grounds of suspicion."

"So that," said the good woman, "unless puir Effie has communicated her situation, she'll be hanged by the neck, if the bairn was still-born, or if it be alive at this moment?"

"Assuredly," said Saddletree, "it being a statute made by our Sovereign Lord and Lady, to prevent the horrid delict of bringing forth children in secret—The crime is rather a favourite of the law, this species of murther being one of its ain creation."

"Then, if the law makes murders," said Mrs. Saddletree, "the law should be hanged for them; or if they wad hang a lawyer instead, the country wad find nae faut."

A summons to their frugal dinner interrupted the further

progress of the conversation, which was otherwise like to take a turn much less favourable to the science of jurisprudence and its professors, than Mr. Bartoline Saddletree, the fond admirer of both, had at its opening anticipated.

CHAPTER VI

But up then raise all Edinburgh,
They all rose up by thousands three.
Johnnie Armstrang's Goodnight.

BUTLER, on his departure from the sign of the Golden Nag, went in quest of a friend of his connected with the law, of whom he wished to make particular enquiries concerning the circumstances in which the unfortunate young woman mentioned in the last chapter was placed, having, as the reader has probably already conjectured, reasons much deeper than those dictated by mere humanity, for interesting himself in her fate. He found the person he sought absent from home, and was equally unfortunate in one or two other calls which he made upon acquaintances whom he hoped to interest in her story. But everybody was, for the moment, stark-mad on the subject of Porteous, and engaged busily in attacking or defending the measures of government in reprieving him ; and the ardour of dispute had excited such universal thirst, that half the young lawyers and writers, together with their very clerks, the class whom Butler was looking after, had adjourned the debate to some favourite tavern. It was computed by an experienced arithmetician, that there was as much twopenny ale consumed on the discussion as would have floated a first-rate man-of-war.

Butler wandered about until it was dusk, resolving to take that opportunity of visiting the unfortunate young woman, when his doing so might be least observed ; for he had his own reasons for avoiding the remarks of Mrs. Saddletree, whose shop-door opened at no great distance from that of the jail, though on the opposite or south side of the street, and a little higher up. He passed, therefore, through the narrow and partly covered passage leading from the north-west end of the Parliament Square.

He stood now before the Gothic entrance of the ancient prison, which, as is well known to all men, rears its ancient front in the very middle of the High Street, forming, as it were, the termination to a huge pile of buildings called the Luckenbooths, which, for some inconceivable reason, our ancestors had jammed into the midst of the principal street of the town, leaving for passage a narrow street on the north, and on the south, into which the prison opens, a narrow crooked lane, winding betwixt the high and sombre walls of the Tolbooth and the adjacent houses on the one side, and the buttresses and projections of the old Cathedral upon the other.   To give some gaiety to this sombre passage (well known by the name of the Krames), a number of little booths, or shops, after the fashion of cobblers' stalls, are plastered, as it were, against the Gothic projections and abutments, so that it seemed as if the traders had occupied with nests, bearing the same proportion to the building, every buttress and coign of vantage, as the martlet did in Macbeth's Castle. Of later years these booths have degenerated into mere toy-shops, where the little loiterers chiefly interested in such wares are tempted to linger, enchanted by the rich display of hobby-horses, babies, and Dutch toys, arranged in artful and gay confusion ; yet half-scared by the cross looks of the withered pantaloon, or spectacled old lady, by whom these tempting stores are watched and superintended. But, in the times we write of, the hosiers, the glovers, the hatters, the mercers, the milliners, and all who dealt in the miscellaneous wares now termed haberdasher's goods, were to be found in this narrow alley.

To return from our digression. Butler found the outer turnkey, a tall, thin, old man, with long silver hair, in the act of locking the outward door of the jail. He addressed himself to this person, and asked admittance to Effie Deans, confined upon accusation of child-murder. The turnkey looked at him earnestly, and, civilly touching his hat out of respect to Butler's black coat and clerical appearance, replied, " It was impossible any one could be admitted at present."

"You shut up earlier than usual, probably on account of Captain Porteous's affair ? " said Butler.

The turnkey, with the true mystery of a person in office, gave two grave nods, and withdrawing from the wards a ponderous key of about two feet in length, he proceeded to shut a strong plate of steel, which folded down above the keyhole, and was secured by a steel spring and catch. Butler stood still instinctively while the door was made fast, and then looking at his watch, walked briskly up the street, muttering to himself almost unconsciously—

> Porta adversa, ingens, solidoque adamante columnæ;
> Vis ut nulla virûm, non ipsi exscindere ferro
> Cœlicolæ valeant—Stat ferrea turris ad auras—&c.[1]

Having wasted half-an-hour more in a second fruitless attempt to find his legal friend and adviser, he thought it time to leave the city and return to his place of residence, in a small village about two miles and a half to the southward of Edinburgh.   The metropolis was at this time surrounded by a high wall, with battlements and flanking projections at some intervals, and the access was through gates, called in the Scottish language *ports*, which were regularly shut at night. A small fee to the keepers would indeed procure egress and ingress at any time, through a wicket left for that purpose in the large gate, but it was of some importance, to a man so poor as Butler, to avoid even this slight pecuniary mulct; and fearing the hour of shutting the gates might be near, he made for that to which he found himself nearest, although, by doing so, he somewhat lengthened his walk homewards. Bristo Port was that by which his direct road lay, but the West Port, which leads out of the Grassmarket, was the nearest of the city gates to the place where he found himself, and to that, therefore, he directed his course.   He reached the port in ample time to pass the circuit of the walls, and enter a suburb called Portsburgh, chiefly inhabited by the lower order of citizens and mechanics.   Here he was unexpectedly interrupted.

He had not gone far from the gate before he heard the sound of a drum, and, to his great surprise, met a number of persons, sufficient to occupy the whole front of the street, and form a considerable mass behind, moving with great speed towards the gate he had just come from, and having in front of them a drum beating to arms.   While he considered how he should escape a party, assembled, as it might be presumed, for no lawful purpose, they came full on him and stopped him.

---

[1] Wide is the fronting gate, and, raised on high,
With adamantine columns threats the sky;
Vain is the force of man, and Heaven's as vain,
To crush the pillars which the pile sustain,
Sublime on these a tower of steel is rear'd.
DRYDEN'S *Virgil*, Book **vi.**

" Are you a clergyman?" one questioned him.

Butler replied, that "he was in orders, but was not a placed minister."

"It's Mr. Butler from Libberton," said a voice from behind; "he'll discharge the duty as weel as ony man."

"You must turn back with us, sir," said the first speaker, in a tone civil but peremptory.

"For what purpose, gentlemen?" said Mr. Butler. "I live at some distance from town—the roads are unsafe by night—you will do me a serious injury by stopping me."

"You shall be sent safely home — no man shall touch a hair of your head – but you must and shall come along with us."

"But to what purpose or end, gentlemen?" said Butler. "I hope you will be so civil as to explain that to me?"

"You shall know that in good time. Come along—for come you must, by force or fair means; and I warn you to look neither to the right hand nor the left, and to take no notice of any man's face, but consider all that is passing before you as a dream."

"I would it were a dream I could awaken from," said Butler to himself; but having no means to oppose the violence with which he was threatened, he was compelled to turn round and march in front of the rioters, two men partly supporting and partly holding him. During this parley the insurgents had made themselves masters of the West Port, rushing upon the Waiters (so the people were called who had the charge of the gates), and possessing themselves of the keys. They bolted and barred the folding doors, and commanded the person, whose duty it usually was, to secure the wicket, of which they did not understand the fastenings. The man, terrified at an incident so totally unexpected, was unable to perform his usual office, and gave the matter up, after several attempts. The rioters, who seemed to have come prepared for every emergency, called for torches, by the light of which they nailed up the wicket with long nails, which, it appeared probable, they had provided on purpose.

While this was going on, Butler could not, even if he had been willing, avoid making remarks on the individuals who seemed to lead this singular mob. The torchlight, while it fell on their forms, and left him in the shade, gave him an opportunity to do so without their observing him. Several of those who appeared most active were dressed in sailors' jackets, trousers, and sea caps; others in large loose-bodied great-coats, and slouched hats; and there were several who, judging from their dress, should have been called women, whose rough deep voices, uncommon size, and masculine deportment and mode of walking, forbade them being so interpreted. They moved as if by some well-concerted plan of arrangement. They had signals by which they knew, and nicknames by which they distinguished each other. Butler remarked, that the name of Wildfire was used among them, to which one stout Amazon seemed to reply.

The rioters left a small party to observe the West Port, and directed the Waiters, as they valued their lives, to remain within their lodge, and make no attempt for that night to repossess themselves of the gate. They then moved with rapidity along the low street called the Cowgate, the mob of the city everywhere rising at the sound of their drum, and joining them. When the multitude arrived at the Cowgate Port, they secured it with as little opposition as the former, made it fast, and left a small party to observe it. It was afterwards remarked, as a striking instance of prudence and precaution, singularly combined with audacity, that the parties left to guard those gates did not remain stationary on their posts, but flitted to and fro, keeping so near the gates as to see that no efforts were made to open them, yet not remaining so long as to have their persons closely observed. The mob, at first only about one hundred strong, now amounted to thousands, and were increasing every moment. They divided themselves so as to ascend with more speed the various narrow lanes which lead up from the Cowgate to the High Street; and still beating to arms as they went, and calling on all true Scotsmen to join them, they now filled the principal street of the city.

The Netherbow Port might be called the Temple Bar of Edinburgh; as, intersecting the High Street at its termination, it divided Edinburgh, properly so called, from the suburb named the Canongate, as Temple Bar separates London from Westminster. It was of the utmost importance to the rioters to possess themselves of this pass, because there was quartered in the Canongate at that time a regiment of infantry, com-manded by Colonel Moyle, which might have occupied the city by advancing through this gate, and would possess the power of totally defeating their purpose. The leaders therefore hastened to the Netherbow Port, which they secured in the same manner, and with as little trouble, as the other gates,

leaving a party to watch it, strong in proportion to the importance of the post.

The next object of these hardy insurgents was at once to
disarm the City Guard, and to procure arms for themselves;
for scarce any weapons but staves and bludgeons had been yet
seen among them. The guard-house was a long, low, ugly
building (removed in 1787), which to a fanciful imagination
might have suggested the idea of a long black snail crawling
up the middle of the High Street, and deforming its beautiful
esplanade. This formidable insurrection had been so unexpected, that there were no more than the ordinary sergeant's
guard of the city corps upon duty; even these were without any
supply of powder and ball; and sensible enough what had
raised the storm, and which way it was rolling, could hardly
be supposed very desirous to expose themselves by a valiant
defence to the animosity of so numerous and desperate a mob,
to whom they were on the present occasion much more than
usually obnoxious.

There was a sentinel upon guard, who (that one town-guard
soldier might do his duty on that eventful evening) presented
his piece, and desired the foremost of the rioters to stand off.
The young amazon, whom Butler had observed particularly
active, sprung upon the soldier, seized his musket, and after
a struggle succeeded in wrenching it from him, and throwing
him down on the causeway. One or two soldiers, who endeavoured to turn out to the support of their sentinel, were in
the same manner seized and disarmed, and the mob without
difficulty possessed themselves of the guard-house, disarming
and turning out of doors the rest of the men on duty. It
was remarked, that, notwithstanding the city soldiers had been
the instruments of the slaughter which this riot was designed
to revenge, no ill usage or even insult was offered to them.
It seemed as if the vengeance of the people disdained to
stoop at any head meaner than that which they considered
as the source and origin of their injuries.

On possessing themselves of the guard, the first act of the
multitude was to destroy the drums, by which they supposed
an alarm might be conveyed to the garrison in the castle;
for the same reason they now silenced their own, which was
beaten by a young fellow, son to the drummer of Portsburgh,
whom they had forced upon that service. Their next business was to distribute among the boldest of the rioters the
guns, bayonets, partisans, halberds, and battle or Lochaber

axes. Until this period the principal rioters had preserved silence on the ultimate object of their rising, as being that which all knew, but none expressed. Now, however, having accomplished all the preliminary parts of their design, they raised a tremendous shout of "Porteous! Porteous! To the Tolbooth! To the Tolbooth!"

They proceeded with the same prudence when the object seemed to be nearly in their grasp, as they had done hitherto when success was more dubious. A strong party of the rioters, drawn up in front of the Luckenbooths, and facing down the street, prevented all access from the eastward, and the west end of the defile formed by the Luckenbooths was secured in the same manner; so that the Tolbooth was completely surrounded, and those who undertook the task of breaking it open effectually secured against the risk of interruption.

The magistrates, in the meanwhile, had taken the alarm, and assembled in a tavern, with the purpose of raising some strength to subdue the rioters. The deacons, or presidents of the trades, were applied to, but declared there was little chance of their authority being respected by the craftsmen, where it was the object to save a man so obnoxious. Mr. Lindsay, member of parliament for the city, volunteered the perilous task of carrying a verbal message from the Lord Provost to Colonel Moyle, the commander of the regiment lying in the Canongate, requesting him to force the Netherbow Port, and enter the city to put down the tumult. But Mr. Lindsay declined to charge himself with any written order, which, if found on his person by an enraged mob, might have cost him his life; and the issue of the application was, that Colonel Moyle, having no written requisition from the civil authorities, and having the fate of Porteous before his eyes as an example of the severe construction put by a jury on the proceedings of military men acting on their own responsibility, declined to encounter the risk to which the Provost's verbal communication invited him.

More than one messenger was despatched by different ways to the Castle, to require the commanding officer to march down his troops, to fire a few cannon-shot, or even to throw a shell among the mob, for the purpose of clearing the streets. But so strict and watchful were the various patrols whom the rioters had established in different parts of the street, that none of the emissaries of the magistrates could reach the gate of the Castle. They were, however, turned back without either injury or insult, and with nothing more of menace than was necessary to deter them from again attempting to accomplish their errand.

The same vigilance was used to prevent everybody of the higher, and those which, in this case, might be deemed the more suspicious orders of society, from appearing in the street, and observing the movements, or distinguishing the persons, of the rioters. Every person in the garb of a gentleman was stopped by small parties of two or three of the mob, who partly exhorted, partly required of them, that they should return to the place from whence they came. Many a quadrille table was spoiled that memorable evening; for the sedan-chairs of ladies, even of the highest rank, were interrupted in their passage from one point to another, in despite of the laced footmen and blazing flambeaux. This was uniformly done with a deference and attention to the feelings of the terrified females, which could hardly have been expected from the videttes of a mob so desperate. Those who stopped the chair usually made the excuse, that there was much disturbance on the streets, and that it was absolutely necessary for the lady's safety that the chair should turn back. They offered themselves to escort the vehicles which they had thus interrupted in their progress, from the apprehension, probably, that some of those who had casually united themselves to the riot might disgrace their systematic and determined plan of vengeance, by those acts of general insult and licence which are common on similar occasions.

Persons are yet living who remember to have heard from the mouths of ladies thus interrupted on their journey in the manner we have described, that they were escorted to their lodgings by the young men who stopped them, and even handed out of their chairs, with a polite attention far beyond what was consistent with their dress, which was apparently that of journeymen mechanics.[1] It seemed as if the conspirators, like those who assassinated the Cardinal Beatoun in former days, had entertained the opinion, that the work about which they went was a judgment of Heaven, which, though

[1] A near relation of the author's used to tell of having been stopped by the rioters, and escorted home in the manner described. On reaching her own home, one of her attendants, in appearance a *baxter*, *i.e.* a baker's lad, handed her out of her chair, and took leave wi. a bow, which, in the lady's opinion, argued breeding that could hardly be learned beside the oven.

unsanctioned by the usual authorities, ought to be proceeded in with order and gravity.

While their outposts continued thus vigilant, and suffered themselves neither from fear nor curiosity to neglect that part of the duty assigned to them, and while the main guards to the east and west secured them against interruption, a select body of the rioters thundered at the door of the jail, and demanded instant admission. No one answered, for the outer keeper had prudently made his escape with the keys at the commencement of the riot, and was nowhere to be found. The door was instantly assailed with sledge-hammers, iron crows, and the coulters of ploughs, ready provided for the purpose, with which they prized, heaved, and battered for some time with little effect; for, being of double oak planks, clenched, both end-long and athwart, with broad-headed nails, the door was so secured as to yield to no means of forcing, without the expenditure of much time. The rioters, however, appeared determined to gain admittance. Gang after gang relieved each other at the exercise, for, of course, only a few could work at a time; but gang after gang retired, exhausted with their violent exertions, without making much progress in forcing the prison-door. Butler had been led up near to this the principal scene of action; so near, indeed, that he was almost deafened by the unceasing clang of the heavy fore-hammers against the iron-bound portals of the prison. He began to entertain hopes, as the task seemed protracted, that the populace might give it over in despair, or that some rescue might arrive to disperse them. There was a moment at which the latter seemed probable.

The magistrates having assembled their officers, and some of the citizens who were able to hazard themselves for the public tranquillity, now sallied forth from the tavern where they held their sitting, and approached the point of danger. Their officers went before them with links and torches, with a herald to read the Riot Act, if necessary. They easily drove before them the outposts and videttes of the rioters; but when they approached the line of guard which the mob, or rather, we should say, the conspirators, had drawn across the street in the front of the Luckenbooths, they were received with an unintermitted volley of stones, and, on their nearer approach, the pikes, bayonets, and Lochaber-axes, of which the populace had possessed themselves, were presented against them. One of their ordinary officers, a strong resolute fellow, went forward, seized a rioter, and took from him a musket; but, being unsupported, he was instantly thrown on his back in the street, and disarmed in his turn. The officer was too happy to be permitted to rise and run away without receiving any farther injury; which afforded another remarkable instance of the mode in which these men had united a sort of moderation towards all others, with the most inflexible inveteracy against the object of their resentment. The magistrates, after vain attempts to make themselves heard and obeyed, possessing no means of enforcing their authority, were constrained to abandon the fields to the rioters, and retreat in all speed from the showers of missiles that whistled around their ears.

The passive resistance of the Tolbooth gate promised to do more to baffle the purpose of the mob than the active interference of the magistrates. The heavy sledge-hammers continued to din against it without intermission, and with a noise which, echoed from the lofty buildings around the spot, seemed enough to have alarmed the garrison in the Castle. It was circulated among the rioters, that the troops would march down to disperse them, unless they could execute their purpose without loss of time; or that, even without quitting the fortress, the garrison might obtain the same end by throwing a bomb or two upon the street.

Urged by such motives for apprehension, they eagerly relieved each other at the labour of assailing the Tolbooth door: yet such was its strength, that it still defied their efforts. At length, a voice was heard to pronounce the words, "Try it with fire." The rioters, with an unanimous shout, called for combustibles, and as all their wishes seemed to be instantly supplied, they were soon in possession of two or three empty tar-barrels. A huge red glaring bonfire speedily arose close to the door of the prison, sending up a tall column of smoke and flame against its antique turrets and strongly grated windows, and illuminating the ferocious and wild gestures of the rioters who surrounded the place, as well as the pale and anxious groups of those, who, from windows in the vicinage, watched the progress of this alarming scene. The mob fed the fire with whatever they could find fit for the purpose. The flames roared and crackled among the heaps of nourishment piled on the fire, and a terrible shout soon announced that the door had kindled, and was in the act of being destroyed. The fire was suffered to decay; but, long

ere it was quite extinguished, the most forward of the rioters
rushed, in their impatience, one after another, over its yet
smouldering remains. Thick showers of sparkles rose high
in the air, as man after man bounded over the glowing
embers, and disturbed them in their passage. It was now
obvious to Butler, and all others who were present, that the
rioters would be instantly in possession of their victim, and
have it in their power to work their pleasure upon him,
whatever that might be.[1]

CHAPTER VII

*The evil you teach us, we will execute; and it shall go hard
but we will better the instruction.*

Merchant of Venice.

THE unhappy object of this remarkable disturbance had been
that day delivered from the apprehension of a public execution,
and his joy was the greater, as he had some reason to question whether government would have run the risk of un-
popularity by interfering in his favour, after he had been
legally convicted by the verdict of a jury, of a crime so very
obnoxious. Relieved from this doubtful state of mind, his
heart was merry within him, and he thought, in the emphatic
words of Scripture on a similar occasion, that surely the
bitterness of death was past. Some of his friends, however,
who had watched the manner and behaviour of the crowd
when they were made acquainted with the reprieve, were of a
different opinion. They augured, from the unusual sternness
and silence with which they bore their disappointment, that
the populace nourished some scheme of sudden and desperate
vengeance; and they advised Porteous to lose no time in
petitioning the proper authorities, that he might be conveyed
to the Castle under a sufficient guard, to remain there in
security until his ultimate fate should be determined.
Habituated, however, by his office, to overawe the rabble
of the city, Porteous could not suspect them of an attempt so
audacious as to storm a strong and defensible prison; and,
despising the advice by which he might have been saved, he
spent the afternoon of the eventful day in giving an entertainment to some friends who visited him in jail, several of

---

[1] Note I.—The Old Tolbooth.

whom, by the indulgence of the Captain of the Tolbooth, with whom he had an old intimacy, arising from their official connection, were even permitted to remain to supper with him, though contrary to the rules of the jail.

It was, therefore, in the hour of unalloyed mirth, when this unfortunate wretch was "full of bread," hot with wine, and high in mistimed and ill-grounded confidence, and alas! with all his sins full-blown, when the first distant shouts of the rioters mingled with the song of merriment and intemperance. The hurried call of the jailor to the guests, requiring them instantly to depart, and his yet more hasty intimation that a dreadful and determined mob had possessed themselves of the city gates and guard-house, were the first explanations of these fearful clamours.

Porteous might, however, have eluded the fury from which the force of authority could not protect him, had he thought of slipping on some disguise, and leaving the prison along with his guests. It is probable that the jailor might have connived at his escape, or even that, in the hurry of this alarming contingency, he might not have observed it. But Porteous and his friends alike wanted presence of mind to suggest or execute such a plan of escape. The former hastily fled from a place where their own safety seemed compromised, and the latter, in a state resembling stupefaction, awaited in his apartment the termination of the enterprise of the rioters. The cessation of the clang of the instruments with which they had at first attempted to force the door, gave him momentary relief. The flattering hopes, that the military had marched into the city, either from the Castle or from the suburbs, and that the rioters were intimidated and dispersing, were soon destroyed by the broad and glaring light of the flames, which, illuminating through the grated window every corner of his apartment, plainly showed that the mob, determined on their fatal purpose, had adopted a means of forcing entrance equally desperate and certain.

The sudden glare of light suggested to the stupefied and astonished object of popular hatred the possibility of concealment or escape. To rush to the chimney, to ascend it at the risk of suffocation, were the only means which seemed to have occurred to him; but his progress was speedily stopped by one of those iron gratings, which are, for the sake of security, usually placed across the vents of buildings designed for imprisonment. The bars, however, which impeded his farther progress, served to support him in the situation which he had gained, and he seized them with the tenacious grasp of one who esteemed himself clinging to his last hope of existence. The lurid light, which had filled the apartment, lowered and died away; the sound of shouts was heard within the walls, and on the narrow and winding stair, which, cased within one of the turrets, gave access to the upper apartments of the prison. The huzza of the rioters was answered by a shout wild and desperate as their own, the cry, namely, of the imprisoned felons, who, expecting to be liberated in the general confusion, welcomed the mob as their deliverers. By some of these the apartment of Porteous was pointed out to his enemies. The obstacle of the lock and bolts was soon overcome, and from his hiding-place the unfortunate man heard his enemies search every corner of the apartment, with oaths and maledictions, which would but shock the reader if we recorded them, but which served to prove, could it have admitted of doubt, the settled purpose of soul with which they sought his destruction.

A place of concealment so obvious to suspicion and scrutiny as that which Porteous had chosen, could not long screen him from detection. He was dragged from his lurking-place, with a violence which seemed to argue an intention to put him to death on the spot. More than one weapon was directed towards him, when one of the rioters, the same whose female disguise had been particularly noticed by Butler, interfered in an authoritative tone. "Are ye mad?" he said, "or would ye execute an act of justice as if it were a crime and a cruelty? This sacrifice will lose half its savour if we do not offer it at the very horns of the altar. We will have him die where a murderer should die, on the common gibbet—We will have him die where he spilled the blood of so many innocents!"

A loud shout of applause followed the proposal, and the cry, "To the gallows with the murderer!—To the Grass-market with him!" echoed on all hands.

"Let no man hurt him," continued the speaker; "let him make his peace with God, if he can; we will not kill both his soul and body."

"What time did he give better folk for preparing their account?" answered several voices. "Let us mete to him with the same measure he measured to them."

But the opinion of the spokesman better suited the temper of those he addressed, a temper rather stubborn than im-

petuous, sedate though ferocious, and desirous of colouring
their cruel and revengeful action with a show of justice and
moderation.

For an instant this man quitted the prisoner, whom he
consigned to a selected guard, with instructions to permit him
to give his money and property to whomsoever he pleased.
A person confined in the jail for debt received this last deposit
from the trembling hand of the victim, who was at the same
time permitted to make some other brief arrangements to
meet his approaching fate. The felons, and all others who
wished to leave the jail, were now at full liberty to do so; not
that their liberation made any part of the settled purpose of
the rioters, but it followed as almost a necessary consequence
of forcing the jail doors. With wild cries of jubilee they
joined the mob, or disappeared among the narrow lanes to
seek out the hidden receptacles of vice and infamy, where they
were accustomed to lurk and conceal themselves from justice.

Two persons, a man about fifty years old, and a girl about
eighteen, were all who continued within the fatal walls,
excepting two or three debtors, who probably saw no advantage in attempting their escape. The persons we have
mentioned remained in the strong-room of the prison, now
deserted by all others. One of their late companions in
misfortune called out to the man to make his escape, in the
tone of an acquaintance. "Rin for it, Ratcliffe—the road's
clear."

"It may be sae, Willie," answered Ratcliffe composedly,
"but I have taen a fancy to leave aff trade, and set up for an
honest man."

"Stay there, and be hanged, then, for a donnard auld
deevil!" said the other, and ran down the prison-stair.

The person in female attire whom we have distinguished as
one of the most active rioters, was about the same time at the
ear of the young woman. "Flee, Effie, flee!" was all he had
time to whisper. She turned towards him an eye of mingled
fear, affection, and upbraiding, all contending with a sort of
stupefied surprise. He again repeated, "Flee, Effie, flee, for
the sake of all that's good and dear to you!" Again she
gazed on him, but was unable to answer. A loud noise was
now heard, and the name of Madge Wildfire was repeatedly
called from the bottom of the staircase.

"I am coming,—I am coming," said the person who
answered to that appellative; and then reiterating hastily,

"For God's sake—for your own sake—for my sake, flee, or they'll take your life!" he left the strong-room.

The girl gazed after him for a moment, and then, faintly muttering, "Better tyne life, since tint is gude fame," she sunk her head upon her hand, and remained, seemingly, unconscious as a statue, of the noise and tumult which passed around her.

That tumult was now transferred from the inside to the outside of the Tolbooth. The mob had brought their destined victim forth, and were about to conduct him to the common place of execution, which they had fixed as the scene of his death. The leader, whom they distinguished by the name of Madge Wildfire, had been summoned to assist at the procession by the impatient shouts of his confederates.

"I will ensure you five hundred pounds," said the unhappy man, grasping Wildfire's hand,—"five hundred pounds for to save my life."

The other answered in the same undertone, and returning his grasp with one equally convulsive, "Five hundred-weight of coined gold should not save you.—Remember Wilson!"

A deep pause of a minute ensued, when Wildfire added, in a more composed tone, "Make your peace with Heaven.— Where is the clergyman?"

Butler, who, in great terror and anxiety, had been detained within a few yards of the Tolbooth door, to wait the event of the search after Porteous, was now brought forward, and commanded to walk by the prisoner's side, and to prepare him for immediate death. His answer was a supplication that the rioters would consider what they did. "You are neither judges nor jury," said he. "You cannot have, by the laws of God or man, power to take away the life of a human creature, however deserving he may be of death. If it is murder even in a lawful magistrate to execute an offender otherwise than in the place, time, and manner which the judges' sentence prescribes, what must it be in you, who have no warrant for interference but your own wills? In the name of Him who is all mercy, show mercy to this unhappy man, and do not dip your hands in his blood, nor rush into the very crime which you are desirous of avenging!"

"Cut your sermon short—you are not in your pulpit," answered one of the rioters.

"If we hear more of your clavers," said another, "we are like to hang you up beside him."

" Peace—hush ! " said Wildfire. " Do the good man no harm —he discharges his conscience, and I like him the better."

He then addressed Butler. " Now, sir, we have patiently heard you, and we just wish you to understand, in the way of answer, that you may as well argue to the ashlar-work and iron stanchels of the Tolbooth as think to change our purpose —Blood must have blood. We have sworn to each other by the deepest oaths ever were pledged, that Porteous shall die the death he deserves so richly ; therefore, speak no more to us, but prepare him for death as well as the briefness of his change will permit."

They had suffered the unfortunate Porteous to put on his night-gown and slippers, as he had thrown off his coat and shoes, in order to facilitate his attempted escape up the chimney. In this garb he was now mounted on the hands of two of the rioters, clasped together, so as to form what is called in Scotland, " The King's Cushion." Butler was placed close to his side, and repeatedly urged to perform a duty always the most painful which can be imposed on a clergyman deserving of the name, and now rendered more so by the peculiar and horrid circumstances of the criminal's case. Porteous at first uttered some supplications for mercy, but when he found there was no chance that these would be attended to, his military education, and the natural stubbornness of his disposition, combined to support his spirits.

" Are you prepared for this dreadful end ? " said Butler in a faltering voice. " Oh turn to Him, in whose eyes time and space have no existence, and to whom a few minutes are as a lifetime, and a lifetime as a minute."

" I believe I know what you would say," answered Porteous sullenly. " I was bred a soldier ; if they will murder we without time, let my sins as well as my blood lie at their door."

" Who was it," said the stern voice of Wildfire, " that said to Wilson, at this very spot, when he could not pray, owing to the galling agony of his fetters, that his pains would soon be over ?—I say to you to take your own tale home ; and if you cannot profit by the good man's lessons, blame not them that are still more merciful to you than you were to others."

The procession now moved forward with a slow and determined pace. It was enlightened by many blazing links and torches ; for the actors of this work were so far from affecting any secrecy on the occasion, that they seemed even to court observation. Their principal leaders kept close to the person of the prisoner, whose pallid yet stubborn features were seen distinctly by the torchlight, as his person was raised considerably above the concourse which thronged around him. Those who bore swords, muskets, and battle-axes, marched on each side, as if forming a regular guard to the procession. The windows, as they went along, were filled with the inhabitants, whose slumbers had been broken by this unusual disturbance. Some of the spectators muttered accents of encouragement; but in general they were so much appalled by a sight so strange and audacious, that they looked on with a sort of stupefied astonishment. No one offered, by act or word, the slightest interruption.

The rioters, on their part, continued to act with the same air of deliberate confidence and security which had marked all their proceedings. When the object of their resentment dropped one of his slippers, they stopped, sought for it, and replaced it upon his foot with great deliberation.[1] As they descended the Bow towards the fatal spot where they designed to complete their purpose, it was suggested that there should be a rope kept in readiness. For this purpose the booth of a man who dealt in cordage was forced open, a coil of rope fit for their purpose was selected to serve as a halter, and the dealer next morning found that a guinea had been left on his counter in exchange; so anxious were the perpetrators of this daring action to show that they meditated not the slightest wrong or infraction of law, excepting so far as Porteous was himself concerned.

Leading, or carrying along with them, in this determined and regular manner, the object of their vengeance, they at length reached the place of common execution, the scene of his crime, and destined spot of his sufferings. Several of the rioters (if they should not rather be described as conspirators) endeavoured to remove the stone which filled up the socket in which the end of the fatal tree was sunk when it was erected for its fatal purpose; others sought for the means of constructing a temporary gibbet, the place in which the gallows itself was deposited being reported too secure to be forced, without much loss of time. Butler endeavoured to avail himself of the delay afforded by these circumstances, to turn the

---

[1] This little incident, characteristic of the extreme composure of this extraordinary mob, was witnessed by a lady, who, disturbed, like others, from her slumbers, had gone to the window. It was told to the author by the lady's daughter.

people from their desperate design. "For God's sake," he exclaimed, "remember it is the image of your Creator which you are about to deface in the person of this unfortunate man! Wretched as he is, and wicked as he may be, he has a share in every promise of Scripture, and you cannot destroy him in impenitence without blotting his name from the Book of Life—Do not destroy soul and body; give time for preparation."

"What time had they," returned a stern voice, "whom he murdered on this very spot?—The laws both of God and man call for his death."

"But what, my friends," insisted Butler, with a generous disregard to his own safety—"what hath constituted you his judges?"

"We are not his judges," replied the same person; "he has been already judged and condemned by lawful authority. We are those whom Heaven, and our righteous anger, have stirred up to execute judgment, when a corrupt government would have protected a murderer."

"I am none," said the unfortunate Porteous; "that which you charge upon me fell out in self-defence, in the lawful exercise of my duty."

"Away with him—away with him!" was the general cry. "Why do you trifle away time in making a gallows?—that dyester's pole is good enough for the homicide."

The unhappy man was forced to his fate with remorseless rapidity. Butler, separated from him by the press, escaped the last horrors of his struggles. Unnoticed by those who had hitherto detained him as a prisoner, he fled from the fatal spot, without much caring in what direction his c urse lay. A loud shout proclaimed the stern delight with which the agents of this deed regarded its completion. Butler, then, at the opening into the low street called the Cowgate, cast back a terrified glance, and, by the red and dusky light of the torches, he could discern a figure wavering and struggling as it hung suspended above the heads of the multitude, and could even observe men striking at it with their Lochaber-axes and partisans. The sight was of a nature to double his horror, and to add wings to his flight.

The street down which the fugitive ran opens to one of the eastern ports or gates of the city. Butler did not stop till he reached it, but found it still shut. He waited nearly an hour, walking up and down in inexpressible perturbation of mind.

At length he ventured to call out, and rouse the attention of the terrified keepers of the gate, who now found themselves at liberty to resume their office without interruption. Butler requested them to open the gate. They hesitated. He told them his name and occupation.

"He is a preacher," said one; "I have heard him preach in Haddo's Hole."

"A fine preaching has he been at the night," said another; "but maybe least said is sunest mended."

Opening then the wicket of the main gate, the keepers suffered Butler to depart, who hastened to carry his horror and fear beyond the walls of Edinburgh. His first purpose was, instantly to take the road homeward; but other fears and cares, connected with the news he had learned in that remarkable day, induced him to linger in the neighbourhood of Edinburgh until daybreak. More than one group of persons passed him as he was whileing away the hours of darkness that yet remained, whom, from the stifled tones of their discourse, the unwonted hour when they travelled, and the hasty pace at which they walked, he conjectured to have been engaged in the late fatal transaction.

Certain it was, that the sudden and total dispersion of the rioters, when their vindictive purpose was accomplished, seemed not the least remarkable feature of this singular affair. In general, whatever may be the impelling motive by which a mob is at first raised, the attainment of their object has usually been only found to lead the way to further excesses. But not so in the present case. They seemed completely satiated with the vengeance they had prosecuted with such staunch and sagacious activity. When they were fully satisfied that life had abandoned their victim, they dispersed in every direction, throwing down the weapons which they had only assumed to enable them to carry through their purpose. At daybreak there remained not the least token of the events of the night, excepting the corpse of Porteous, which still hung suspended in the place where he had suffered, and the arms of various kinds which the rioters had taken from the city guard-house, which were found scattered about the streets as they had thrown them from their hands, when the purpose for which they had seized them was accomplished.

The ordinary magistrates of the city resumed their power, not without trembling at the late experience of the fragility of its tenure. To march troops into the city, and commence a severe inquiry into the transactions of the preceding night, were the first marks of returning energy which they displayed. But these events had been conducted on so secure and well-calculated a plan of safety and secrecy, that there was little or nothing learned to throw light upon the authors or principal actors in a scheme so audacious. An express was despatched to London with the tidings, where they excited great indignation and surprise in the council of regency, and particularly in the bosom of Queen Caroline, who considered her own authority as exposed to contempt by the success of this singular conspiracy. Nothing was spoke of for some time save the measure of vengeance which should be taken, not only on the actors of this tragedy, so soon as they should be discovered, but upon the magistrates who had suffered it to take place, and upon the city which had been the scene where it was exhibited. On this occasion, it is still recorded in popular tradition, that her Majesty, in the height of her displeasure, told the celebrated John, Duke of Argyle, that, sooner than submit to such an insult, she would make Scotland a hunting-field. "In that case, Madam," answered that high-spirited nobleman, with a profound bow, "I will take leave of your Majesty, and go down to my own country to get my hounds ready."

The import of the reply had more than met the ear; and as most of the Scottish nobility and gentry seemed actuated by the same national spirit, the royal displeasure was necessarily checked in mid-volley, and milder courses were recommended and adopted, to some of which we may hereafter have occasion to advert.

NOTE

MEMORIAL CONCERNING THE MURDER OF CAPTAIN PORTEOUS

The following interesting and authentic account of the inquiries made by Crown Counsel into the affair of the Porteous Mob, seems to have been drawn up by the Solicitor-General. The office was held in 1737 by Charles Erskine, Esq.

I owe this curious illustration to the kindness of a professional friend. It throws, indeed, little light on the origin of the tumult; but shows how profound the darkness must have been, which so much investigation could not dispel.

"Upon the 7th of September last, when the unhappy wicked murder of Captain Porteous was committed, His Majesty's Advocate and Solicitor were out of town; the first beyond Inverness, and the other in Annandale, not far from Carlyle; neither of them knew any thing of the reprieve, nor did they in the least suspect that any disorder was to happen.

who really did not appear to be a witness of the greatest weight, and that his life was in danger from the imprisonment, he was admitted to baill by the Lord Justice-Generall, by whose warrand he was committed.

"Braidwood's friends applyed in the same manner; but as he stood charged by more than one witness, he was not released—tho', indeed, the witnesses adduced for him say somewhat in his exculpation—that he does not seem to have been upon any original concert; and one of the witnesses says he was along with him at the Tolbooth door, and refuses what is said against him, with regard to his having advised the burning of the Tolbooth door. But he remains still in prison.

"As to Traill, the journeyman wright, he is charged by the same witness who declared against Stirling, and there is none concurrs with him; and to say the truth concerning him, he seemed to be the most ingenuous of any of them whom the Solicitor examined, and pointed out a witness by whom one of the first accomplices was discovered, and who escaped when the warrand was to be putt in execution against them. He positively denys his having shutt the gate, and 'tis thought Traill ought to be admitted to baill.

"As to Birnie, he is charged only by one witness, who had never seen him before, nor knew his name; so, tho' I dare say, the witness honestly mentioned him, 'tis possible he may be mistaken; and in the examination of above 200 witnesses, there is no body concurrs with him, and he is ane insignificant little creature.

"With regard to M'Lauchlan, the proof is strong against him by one witness, that he acted as a serjeant or sort of commander, for some time, of a Guard, that stood cross between the upper end of the Luckenbooths and the north side of the street, to stop all but friends from going towards the Tolbooth; and by other witnesses, that he was at the Tolbooth door with a link in his hand, while the operation of beating and burning it was going on : that he went along with the mob with a halbert in his hand, untill he came to the gallows stone in the Grassmarket, and that he stuck the halbert into the hole of the gallows stone : that afterwards he went in amongst the mob when Captain Porteus was carried to the dyer's tree; so that the proof seems very heavy against him.

"To sum up this matter with regard to the prisoners in the Castle, 'tis believed there is strong proof against M'Lauchlan; there is also proof against Braidwood. But as it consists only in emission of words said to have been had by him while at the Tolbooth door, and that he is ane insignificant pitifull creature, and will find people to swear heartily in his favours, 'tis at best doubtfull whether a jury will be got to condemn him.

"As to those in the Tolbooth of Edinburgh, John Crawford, who had for some time been employed to ring the bells in the steeple of the new Church of Edinburgh, being in company with a soldier accidentally, the discourse falling in concerning Captain Porteus and his murder, as he appears to be a light-headed fellow, he said, that he knew people that were more guilty than any that were putt in prison. Upon this information, Crawford was seized, and being examined, it appeared, that when the mob begun, as he was come-ing down from the steeple, the mob took the keys from him ; that he was that night in several corners, and did indeed delate severall persons whom he saw there, and immediately warrands were dispatched, and it was found they had absconded and fled. But there was no evidence against him of any kind. Nay, on the contrary, it appeared, that he had been with the Magistrates in Clerk's the vintner's, relating to them what he had seen in the streets. Therefore, after haveing detained him in prison ffor a very considerable time, his Majesties Advocate and Sollicitor signed a warrand for his liberation.

"There was also one James Wilson incarcerated in the said Tolbooth, upon the declaration of one witness, who said he saw him on the streets with a gun; and there he remained for some time, in order to try if a concurring witness could be found, or that he acted any part in the tragedy and wickedness. But nothing further appeared against him ; and being seized with a severe sickness, he is, by a warrand signed by his Majestie's Advocate and Sollicitor, liberated upon giveing sufficient baill.

"As to King, enquiry was made, and the ffact comes out beyond all exception, that he was in the lodge at the Nether-Bow with Lindsay the waiter, and several other people, not at all concerned in the mob. But after the affair was over, he went up towards the guard, and having met with Sandie the Turk and his wife, who escaped out of prison, they returned to his house at the Abbey, and then, 'tis very possible he may have thought fitt in his beer to boast of villany, in which he could not possibly have any share ; for that reason he was desired to find baill and he should be set at liberty. But he is a stranger and a fellow of very indifferent character, and 'tis believed it won't be easy for him to find baill. Wherefore, it's thought he must be sett at liberty without it. Because he is a burden upon the Government while kept in confinement, not being able to maintain himself.

"What is above is all that relates to persons in custody. But there are warrands out against a great many other persons who had fled, particularly against one William White, a journeyman baxter, who, by the evidence, appears to have been at the beginning of the mob, and to have gone along with the drum, from the West-Port to the Nether-Bow, and is said to have been one of those who attacked the guard, and probably was as deep as any one there.

"Information was given that he was lurking at Falkirk, where he was born. Whereupon directions were sent to the Sheriff of the County, and a warrand from his Excellency Generall Wade, to the commanding officers at Stirling and Linlithgow, to assist, and all possible endeavours were used to catch hold of him, and 'tis said he escaped very narrowly, having been concealed in some outhouse ; and the misfortune was, that those who were employed in the search did not know him personally. Nor, indeed, was it easy to trust any of the acquaintances of so low obscure a fellow with the secret of the warrand to be putt in execution.

"There was also strong evidence found against Robert Taylor, servant to William and Charles Thomsons, periwig-makers, that he acted as ane officer among the mob, and he was traced from the guard to the well at the head of Forrester's Wynd, where he stood and had the appellation of Captain from the mob, and from that walking down the Bow before Captain Porteus, with his Lochaber-axe ; and by the description given of one who hawl'd the rope by which Captain Porteus was pulled up, 'tis believed Taylor was the person ; and 'tis further probable, that the witness who delated Stirling had mistaken Taylor for him, their stature and age (so far as can be gathered from the description) being much the same.

"A great deal of pains were taken, and no charge was saved, in order to have catched hold of this Taylor, and warrands were sent to the country where he was born ; but it appears he had shipt himself off for Holland, where it is said he now is.

"There is strong evidence also against Thomas Burns, butcher, that he was ane active person from the beginning of the mob to the end of it. He lurkt for some time amongst those of his trade ; and artfully enough a train was laid to catch him, under pretence of a message that had come from his father in Ireland, so that he came to a blind alehouse in the Flesh-market closs, and a party being ready, was by Webster the soldier, who was upon this exploit, advertised to come down. However, Burns escaped out at a back window, and hid himself in some of the houses which are heaped together upon one another in that place, so that it was not possible to catch him. 'Tis now said he is gone to Ireland to his father, who lives there.

"There is evidence also against one Robert Anderson, journeyman and servant to Colin Alison, wright ; and against Thomas Linnen and James Maxwell, both servants also to the said Colin Alison, who all seem to have been deeply concerned in the matter. Anderson is one of those who putt the rope upon Captain Porteus's neck. Linnen seems also to have been very active; and Maxwell (which is pretty remarkable) is proven to have come to a shop upon the Friday before, and charged the journeymen and prentices there to attend in the Parliament close on Tuesday night, to assist to hang Captain Porteus. These three did early abscond, and though warrands had been issued out against them, and all endeavours used to apprehend them, could not be found.

"One Waldie, a servant to George Campbell, wright, has also absconded, and many others, and 'tis informed that numbers of them have shipt themselves off ffor the Plantations; and upon an information that a ship was going off ffrom Glasgow, in which severall of the rogues were to transport themselves beyond seas, proper warrands were obtained, and persons dispatched to search the said ship, and seize any that can be found.

"The like warrands had been issued with regard to ships from Leith. But whether they had been scard, or whether the information had been groundless, they had no effect.

"This is a summary of the enquiry, ffrom which it appears there is no prooff on which one can rely, but against M'Lauchlan. There is a prooff also against Braidwood, but more exceptionable. His Majesties Advocate, since he came to town, has join'd with the Sollicitor, and has done his utmost to gett at the bottom of this matter, but hitherto it stands, as is above represented. They are resolved to have their eyes and their ears open, and to do what they can. But they labour'd exceedingly against the stream; and it may truly be said, that nothing was wanting on their part. Nor have they declined any labour to answer the commands laid upon them to search the matter to the bottom."

THE PORTEOUS MOB

In the preceding chapters, the circumstances of that extraordinary riot and conspiracy, call'ed the Porteous Mob, are given with as much accuracy as the author was able to collect them. The order, regularity, and determined resolution with which such a violent action was devised and executed, were only equalled by the secrecy which was observed concerning the principal actors.

Although the fact was performed by torchlight, and in presence of a great multitude, to some of whom, at least, the individual actors must have been known, yet no discovery was ever made concerning any of the perpetrators of the slaughter.

Two men only were brought to trial for an offence which the government were so anxious to detect and punish. William M'Lauchlan, footman to the Countess of Wemyss, who is mentioned in the report of the Solicitor-General, (page 275), against whom strong evidence had been obtained, was brought to trial in March 1737, charged as having been accessory to the riot, armed with a Lochaber-axe. But this man (who was at all times a silly creature) proved that he was in a state of mortal intoxication during the time he was present with the rabble, incapable of giving them either advice or assistance, or, indeed, of knowing what he or they were doing. He was also able to prove that he was forced into the riot, and upheld while there by two bakers, who put a Lochaber-axe into his hand. The jury, wisely judging this poor creature could be no proper subject of punishment, found the panel not guilty. The same verdict was given in the case of Thomas Linning, also mentioned in the Solicitor's memorial, who was tried in 1738. In short, neither then, nor for a long period afterwards, was anything discovered relating to the organisation of the Porteous Plot.

The imagination of the people of Edinburgh was long irritated, and their curiosity kept awake, by the mystery attending this extraordinary conspiracy. It was generally reported of such natives of Edinburgh as, having left the city in youth, returned with a fortune amassed in foreign countries, that they had originally fled on account of their share in the Porteous Mob. But little credit can be attached to these surmises, as in most of the cases they are contradicted by dates, and in none supported by anything but vague rumours, grounded on the ordinary wish of the vulgar, to impute the success of prosperous men to some unpleasant source. The secret history of the Porteous Mob has been till this day unravelled ; and it has always been quoted as a close, daring, and calculated act of violence, of a nature peculiarly characteristic of the Scottish people.

Nevertheless, the author, for a considerable time, nourished hopes to have found himself enabled to throw some light on this mysterious story. An old man, who died about twenty years ago, at the advanced age of ninety-three, was said to have made a communication to the clergyman who attended upon his deathbed, respecting the origin of the Porteous Mob. This person followed the trade of a carpenter, and had been employed as such on the estate of a family of opulence and condition. His character, in his line of life and amongst his neighbours, was excellent, and never underwent the slightest suspicion. His confession was said to have been to the following purpose : That he was one of twelve young men belonging to the village of Pathhead, whose animosity against Porteous, on account of the execution of Wilson, was so extreme, that they resolved to execute vengeance on him with their own hands, rather than he should escape punishment. With this resolution they crossed the Forth at different ferries, and rendezvoused at the suburb called Portsburgh, where their appearance in a body soon called numbers around them. The public mind was in such a state of irritation, that it only wanted a single spark to create an explosion ; and this was afforded by the exertions of the small and determined band of associates. The appearance of premeditation and order which distinguished the riot, according to his account, had its origin, not in any previous plan or conspiracy, but in the character of those who were engaged in it. The story also serves to show why nothing of the origin of the riot has ever been discovered, since, though in itself a great conflagration, its source, according to this account, was from an obscure and apparently inadequate cause.

I have been disappointed, however, in obtaining the evidence on which this story rests. The present proprietor of the estate on which the old man died (a particular friend of the author) undertook to question the son of the deceased on the subject. This person follows his father's trade, and holds the employment of carpenter to the same family. He admits that his father's going abroad at the time of the Porteous Mob was popularly attributed to his having been concerned in that affair ; but adds that, so far as is known to him, the old man had never made any confession to that effect ; and, on the contrary, had uniformly denied being present. My kind friend, therefore, had recourse to a person from whom he had formerly heard the story ; but who, either from respect to an old friend's memory, or from failure of his own, happened to have forgotten that ever such a communication was made. So my obliging correspondent (who is a fox-hunter) wrote to me that he was completely *planted ;* and all that can be said with respect to the tradition is, that it certainly once existed, and was generally believed.

CHAPTER VIII

Arthur's Seat shall be my bed,
  The sheets shall ne'er be pressed by me;
St Anton's well shall be my drink,
  Sin' my true-love's forsaken me.
                              Old Song.

IF I were to choose a spot from which the rising or setting
sun could be seen to the greatest possible advantage, it would
be that wild path winding around the foot of the high belt
of semicircular rocks, called Salisbury Crags, and marking
the verge of the steep descent which slopes down into the
glen on the south-eastern side of the city of Edinburgh.
The prospect, in its general outline, commands a close-built,
high-piled city, stretching itself out beneath in a form, which,
to a romantic imagination, may be supposed to represent that
of a dragon; now, a noble arm of the sea, with its rocks,
isles, distant shores, and boundary of mountains; and now,
a fair and fertile champaign country, varied with hill, dale,
and rock, and skirted by the picturesque ridge of the Pentland
mountains.   But as the path gently circles around the base
of the cliffs, the prospect, composed as it is of these enchanting and sublime objects, changes at every step, and presents
them blended with, or divided from, each other, in every
possible variety which can gratify the eye and the imagination.
When a piece of scenery so beautiful, yet so varied,—so
exciting by its intricacy, and yet so sublime,—is lighted up
by the tints of morning or of evening, and displays all that
variety of shadowy depth, exchanged with partial brilliancy,
which gives character even to the tamest of landscapes, the
effect approaches near to enchantment.   This path used to
be my favourite evening and morning resort, when engaged
with a favourite author, or new subject of study.   It is, I am
informed, now become totally impassable; a circumstance
which, if true, reflects little credit on the taste of the Good
Town or its leaders.[1]

It was from this fascinating path—the scene to me of so
much delicious musing, when life was young and promised to
be happy, that I have been unable to pass it over without an

[1] A beautiful and solid pathway has, within a few years, been formed around
these romantic rocks; and the author has the pleasure to think that the
passage in the text gave rise to the undertaking.

episodical description—it was, I say, from this romantic path that Butler saw the morning arise the day after the murder of Porteous. It was possible for him with ease to have found a much shorter road to the house to which he was directing his course, and, in fact, that which he chose was extremely circuitous. But to compose his own spirits, as well as to while away the time, until a proper hour for visiting the family without surprise or disturbance, he was induced to extend his circuit by the foot of the rocks, and to linger upon his way until the morning should be considerably advanced. While, now standing with his arms across, and waiting the slow progress of the sun above the horizon, now sitting upon one of the numerous fragments which storms had detached from the rocks above him, he is meditating, alternately upon the horrible catastrophe which he had witnessed, and upon the melancholy, and to him most interesting, news which he had learned at Saddletree's, we will give the reader to understand who Butler was, and how his fate was connected with that of Effie Deans, the unfortunate handmaiden of the careful Mrs. Saddletree.

Reuben Butler was of English extraction, though born in Scotland. His grandfather was a trooper in Monk's army, and one of the party of dismounted dragoons which formed the forlorn hope at the storming of Dundee in 1651. Stephen Butler (called, from his talents in reading and expounding, Scripture Stephen, and Bible Butler) was a staunch Independent, and received in its fullest comprehension the promise that the saints should inherit the earth. As hard knocks were what had chiefly fallen to his share hitherto in the division of this common property, he lost not the opportunity which the storm and plunder of a commercial place afforded him, to appropriate as large a share of the better things of this world as he could possibly compass. It would seem that he had succeeded indifferently well, for his exterior circumstances appeared, in consequence of this event, to have been much mended.

The troop to which he belonged was quartered at the village of Dalkeith, as forming the bodyguard of Monk, who, in the capacity of general for the Commonwealth, resided in the neighbouring castle. When, on the eve of the Restoration, the general commenced his march from Scotland, a measure pregnant with such important consequences, he new-modelled his troops, and more especially those immediately about his

person, in order that they might consist entirely of individuals
devoted to himself. On this occasion Scripture Stephen was
weighed in the balance and found wanting. It was supposed
he felt no call to any expedition which might endanger the
reign of the military sainthood, and that he did not consider
himself as free in conscience to join with any party which
might be likely ultimately to acknowledge the interest of
Charles Stewart, the son of " the last man," as Charles I. was
familiarly and irreverently termed by them in their common
discourse, as well as in their more elaborate predications and
harangues. As the time did not admit of cashiering such
dissidents, Stephen Butler was only advised in a friendly way
to give up his horse and accoutrements to one of Middleton's
old troopers, who possessed an accommodating conscience of
a military stamp, and which squared itself chiefly upon those
of the Colonel and paymaster. As this hint came recommended by a certain sum of arrears presently payable, Stephen
had carnal wisdom enough to embrace the proposal, and with
great indifference saw his old corps depart for Coldstream
on their route for the south, to establish the tottering government of England on a new basis.

The *zone* of the ex-trooper, to use Horace's phrase, was
weighty enough to purchase a cottage and two or three fields
(still known by the name of Beersheba), within about a Scottish mile of Dalkeith ; and there did Stephen establish himself
with a youthful helpmate, chosen out of the said village, whose
disposition to a comfortable settlement on this side of the
grave reconciled her to the gruff manners, serious temper, and
weather-beaten features of the martial enthusiast. Stephen
did not long survive the falling on " evil days and evil
tongues," of which Milton, in the same predicament, so
mournfully complains. At his death his consort remained an
early widow, with a male child of three years old, which, in
the sobriety wherewith it demeaned itself, in the old-fashioned
and even grim cast of its features, and in its sententious mode
of expressing itself, would sufficiently have vindicated the honour
of the widow of Beersheba, had any one thought proper to
challenge the babe's descent from Bible Butler.

Butler's principles had not descended to his family, or
extended themselves among his neighbours. The air of
Scotland was alien to the growth of independency, however
favourable to fanaticism under other colours. But, nevertheless, they were not forgotten ; and a certain neighbouring

Laird, who piqued himself upon the loyalty of his principles "in the worst of times" (though I never heard they exposed him to more peril than that of a broken head, or a night's lodging in the main guard, when wine and cavalierism predominated in his upper storey), had found it a convenient thing to rake up all matter of accusation against the deceased Stephen. In this enumeration his religious principles made no small figure, as, indeed, they must have seemed of the most exaggerated enormity to one whose own were so small and so faintly traced, as to be well-nigh imperceptible. In these circumstances, poor widow Butler was supplied with her full proportion of fines for non-conformity, and all the other oppressions of the time, until Beersheba was fairly wrenched out of her hands, and became the property of the Laird who had so wantonly, as it had hitherto appeared, persecuted this poor, forlorn woman. When his purpose was fairly achieved, he showed some remorse, or moderation, or whatever the reader may please to term it, in permitting her to occupy her husband's cottage, and cultivate, on no very heavy terms, a croft of land adjacent. Her son Benjamin, in the meanwhile, grew up to man's estate, and, moved by that impulse which makes men seek marriage, even when its end can only be the perpetuation of misery, he wedded and brought a wife, and eventually a son, Reuben, to share the poverty of Beersheba.

The Laird of Dumbiedikes [1] had hitherto been moderate in his exactions, perhaps because he was ashamed to tax too highly the miserable means of support which remained to the widow Butler. But when a stout active young fellow appeared as the labourer of the croft in question, Dumbiedikes began to think so broad a pair of shoulders might bear an additional burden. He regulated, indeed, his management of his dependants (who fortunately were but few in number) much upon the principle of the carters whom he observed loading their carts at a neighbouring coal-hill, and who never failed to clap an additional brace of hundredweights on their burden, so soon as by any means they had compassed a new horse of somewhat superior strength to that which had broken down the day before. However reasonable this practice appeared

---

[1] Dumbiedikes, selected as descriptive of the taciturn character of the imaginary owner, is really the name of a house bordering on the King's Park, so called because the late Mr. Braidwood, an instructor of the deaf and dumb, resided there with his pupils. The situation of the real house is different from that assigned to the ideal mansion.

to the Laird of Dumbiedikes, he ought to have observed, that
it may be overdone, and that it infers, as a matter of course,
the destruction of both horse, cart, and loading. Even so it
befell when the additional "prestations" came to be demanded of Benjamin Butler. A man of few words, and few
ideas, but attached to Beersheba with a feeling like that which
a vegetable entertains to the spot in which it chances to be
planted, he neither remonstrated with the Laird, nor endeavoured to escape from him, but toiling night and day to
accomplish the terms of his task-master, fell into a burning
fever and died. His wife did not long survive him ; and, as
if it had been the fate of this family to be left orphans, our
Reuben Butler was, about the year 1704–5, left in the same
circumstances in which his father had been placed, and under
the same guardianship, being that of his grandmother, the
widow of Monk's old trooper.

The same prospect of misery hung over the head of another
tenant of this hard-hearted lord of the soil. This was a tough
true-blue Presbyterian, called Deans, who, though most obnoxious to the Laird on account of principles in Church and
State, contrived to maintain his ground upon the estate by
regular payment of mail-duties, kain, arriage, carriage, dry
multure, lock, gowpen, and knaveship, and all the various
exactions now commuted for money, and summed up in the
emphatic word RENT. But the years 1700 and 1701, long
remembered in Scotland for dearth and general distress, subdued the stout heart of the agricultural Whig. Citations by
the ground officer, decreets of the Baron Court, sequestrations,
poindings of outside and inside plenishing, flew about his
ears as fast as ever the Tory bullets whistled around those of
the Covenanters at Pentland, Bothwell Brigg, or Airsmoss.
Struggle as he might, and he struggled gallantly, "Douce
David Deans" was routed horse and foot, and lay at the
mercy of his grasping landlord just at the time that Benjamin
Butler died. The fate of each family was anticipated ; but
they who prophesied their expulsion to beggary and ruin, were
disappointed by an accidental circumstance.

On the very term-day when their ejection should have taken
place, when all their neighbours were prepared to pity, and not
one to assist them, the minister of the parish, as well as a
doctor from Edinburgh, received a hasty summons to attend
the Laird of Dumbiedikes. Both were surprised, for his contempt for both faculties had been pretty commonly his theme

over an extra bottle, that is to say, at least once every day. The leech for the soul, and he for the body, alighted in the court of the little old manor-house at almost the same time; and when they had gazed a moment at each other with some surprise, they in the same breath expressed their conviction that Dumbiedikes must needs be very ill indeed, since he summoned them both to his presence at once. Ere the servant could usher them to his apartment the party was augmented by a man of law, Nichil Novit, writing himself procurator before the sheriff-court, for in those days there were no solicitors. This latter personage was first summoned to the apartment of the Laird, where, after some short space, the soul-curer and the body-curer were invited to join him.

Dumbiedikes had been by this time transported into the best bedroom, used only upon occasions of death and marriage, and called, from the former of these occupations, the Dead-Room. There were in this apartment, besides the sick person himself and Mr. Novit, the son and heir of the patient, a tall, gawky, silly-looking boy of fourteen or fifteen, and a house-keeper, a good buxom figure of a woman, betwixt forty and fifty, who had kept the keys and managed matters at Dumbie-dikes since the lady's death. It was to these attendants that Dumbiedikes addressed himself pretty nearly in the following words; temporal and spiritual matters, the care of his health and his affairs, being strangely jumbled in a head which was never one of the clearest:—

"These are sair times wi' me, gentlemen and neighbours! amaist as ill as at the aughty-nine, when I was rabbled by the collegeaners.[1]—They mistook me muckle—they ca'd me a papist, but there was never a papist bit about me, minister.—Jock, ye'll take warning—it's a debt we maun a' pay, and there stands Nichil Novit that will tell ye I was never gude at paying debts in my life.—Mr. Novit, ye'll no forget to draw the annual rent that's due on the yerl's band—if I pay debt to other folk, I think they suld pay it to me—that equals aquals.—Jock, when ye hae naething else to do, ye may be aye sticking in a tree; it will be growing, Jock, when ye're sleeping.[2]   My

[1] Immediately previous to the Revolution, the students at the Edinburgh College were violent anti-Catholics. They were strongly suspected of burning the house of Priestfield, belonging to the Lord Provost; and certainly were guilty of creating considerable riots in 1688-89.

[2] The author has been flattered by the assurance that this *naïve* mode of recommending arboriculture (which was actually delivered in these very words by a Highland laird, while on his deathbed, to his son) had so much weight with a Scottish earl, as to lead to his planting a large tract of country.

father tauld me sae forty years sin', but I ne'er fand time
to mind him—Jock, ne'er drink brandy in the morning, it files
the stamach sair; gin ye take a morning's draught, let it be
aqua mirabilis; Jenny there makes it weel.—Doctor, my breath
is growing as scant as a broken-winded piper's, when he has
played for four-and-twenty hours at a penny wedding—Jenny,
pit the cod aneath my head—but it's a' needless!—Mass John,
could ye think o' rattling ower some bit short prayer, it wad
do me gude maybe, and keep some queer thoughts out o' my
head. Say something, man."

"I cannot use a prayer like a rat-rhyme," answered the
honest clergyman; "and if you would have your soul redeemed
like a prey from the fowler, Laird, you must needs show me
your state of mind."

"And shouldna ye ken that without my telling you?"
answered the patient. "What have I been paying stipend
and teind parsonage and vicarage for, ever sin' the aughty-
nine, an I canna get a spell of a prayer for't, the only time I
ever asked for ane in my life?—Gang awa wi' your whiggery,
if that's a' ye can do; auld Curate Kilstoup wad hae read
half the Prayer-book to me by this time—Awa wi' ye!—
Doctor, let's see if ye can do onything better for me."

The Doctor, who had obtained some information in the
meanwhile from the housekeeper on the state of his complaints, assured him the medical art could not prolong his
life many hours.

"Then damn Mass John and you baith!" cried the furious
and intractable patient. "Did ye come here for naething but
to tell me that ye canna help me at the pinch? Out wi' them,
Jenny—out o' the house! and, Jock, my curse, and the curse
of Cromwell, go wi' ye, if ye gie them either fee or bountith,
or sae muckle as a black pair o' cheverons!"[1]

The clergyman and doctor made a speedy retreat out of the
apartment, while Dumbiedikes fell into one of those transports
of violent and profane language, which had procured him the
surname of Damn-me-dikes.—"Bring me the brandy bottle,
Jenny, ye b——," he cried, with a voice in which passion contended with pain. "I can die as I have lived, without fashing
ony o' them. But there's ae thing," he said, sinking his voice
—"there's ae fearful thing hings about my heart, and an anker
of brandy winna wash it away.—The Deanses at Woodend!—
I sequestrated them in the dear years, and now they are to flit,

---

[1] *Cheverons*—gloves.

they'll starve—and that Beersheba, and that auld trooper's wife and her oe, they'll starve—they'll starve!—Look out, Jock; what kind o' night is't?"

"On-ding o' snaw, father," answered Jock, after having opened the window, and looked out with great composure.

"They'll perish in the drifts!" said the expiring sinner— "they'll perish wi' cauld!—but I'll be het eneugh, gin a' tales be true."

This last observation was made under breath, and in a tone which made the very attorney shudder. He tried his hand at ghostly advice, probably for the first time in his life, and recommended, as an opiate for the agonised conscience of the Laird, reparation of the injuries he had done to these distressed families, which, he observed by the way, the civil law called *restitutio in integrum*. But Mammon was struggling with Remorse for retaining his place in a bosom he had so long possessed; and he partly succeeded, as an old tyrant proves often too strong for his insurgent rebels.

"I canna do't," he answered with a voice of despair. "It would kill me to do't—how can ye bid me pay back siller, when ye ken how I want it? or dispone Beersheba, when it lies sae weel into my ain plaid-nuik? Nature made Dumbie-dikes and Beersheba to be ae man's land—She did, by—— Nichil, it wad kill me to part them."

"But ye maun die whether or no, Laird," said Mr. Novit; "and maybe ye wad die easier—it's but trying. I'll scroll the disposition in nae time."

"Dinna speak o't, sir," replied Dumbiedikes, "or I'll fling the stoup at your head.—But, Jock, lad, ye see how the warld warstles wi' me on my deathbed—be kind to the puir creatures the Deanses and the Butlers—be kind to them, Jock. Dinna let the warld get a grip o' ye, Jock—but keep the gear thegither! and whate'er ye do, dispone Beersheba at no rate. Let the creatures stay at a moderate mailing, and hae bite and soup; it will maybe be the better wi' your father whare he's gaun, lad."

After these contradictory instructions, the Laird felt his mind so much at ease, that he drank three bumpers of brandy continuously, and "soughed awa," as Jenny expressed it, in an attempt to sing "Deil stick the minister."

His death made a revolution in favour of the distressed families. John Dumbie, now of Dumbiedikes in his own right, seemed to be close and selfish enough; but wanted the grasping spirit and active mind of his father; and his guardian happened to agree with him in opinion, that his father's dying recommendation should be attended to. The tenants, therefore, were not actually turned out of doors among the snow-wreaths, and were allowed wherewith to procure butter-milk, and peas-bannocks, which they eat under the full force of the original malediction. The cottage of Deans, called Woodend, was n t very distant from that at Beersheba. Formerly there had been little intercourse between the families. Deans was a sturdy Scotchman, with all sort of prejudices against the southern, and the spawn of the southern. Moreover, Deans was, as we have said, a staunch Presbyterian, of the most rigid and unbending adherence to what he conceived to be the only possible straight line, as he was wont to express himself, between right-hand heats and extremes, and left-hand defections; and, therefore, he held in high dread and horror all Independents, and whomsoever he supposed allied to them.

But, notwithstanding these national prejudices and religious professions, Deans and the widow Butler were placed in such a situation, as naturally and at length created some intimacy between the families. They had shared a common danger and a mutual deliverance. They needed each other's assistance, like a company, who, crossing a mountain stream, are compelled to cling close together, lest the current should be too powerful for any who are not thus supported.

On nearer acquaintance, too, Deans abated some of his prejudices. He found old Mrs. Butler, though not thoroughly grounded in the extent and bearing of the real testimony against the defections of the times, had no opinions in favour of the Independent party; neither was she an Englishwoman. Therefore, it was to be hoped, that, though she was the widow of an enthusiastic corporal of Cromwell's dragoons, her grandson might be neither schismatic nor anti-national, two qualities concerning which Goodman Deans had as wholesome a terror as against papists and malignants. Above all (for Douce Davie Deans had his weak side), he perceived that widow Butler looked up to him with reverence, listened to his advice, and compounded for an occasional fling at the doctrines of her deceased husband, to which, as we have seen, she was by no means warmly attached, in consideration of the valuable counsels which the Presbyterian afforded her for the management of her little farm. These usually concluded with, "They may do otherwise in England, neighbour

Butler, for aught I ken;" or, "It may be different in foreign parts;" or, "They wha think differently on the great foundation of our covenanted reformation, overturning and mishguggling the government and discipline of the kirk, and breaking down the carved work of our Zion, might be for sawing the craft wi' aits; but I say pease, pease." And as his advice was shrewd and sensible, though conceitedly given, it was received with gratitude, and followed with respect.

The intercourse which took place betwixt the families at Beersheba and Woodend, became strict and intimate, at a very early period, betwixt Reuben Butler, with whom the reader is already in some degree acquainted, and Jeanie Deans, the only child of Douce Davie Deans by his first wife, "that singular Christian woman," as he was wont to express himself, "whose name was savoury to all that knew her for a desirable professor, Christian Menzies in Hochmagirdle." The manner of which intimacy, and the consequences thereof, we now proceed to relate.

CHAPTER IX

> Reuben and Rachel, though as fond as doves,
> Were yet discreet and cautious in their loves,
> Nor would attend to Cupid's wild commands,
> Till cool reflection bade them join their hands.
> When both were poor, they thought it argued ill
> Of hasty love to make them poorer still.
>   CRABBE's *Parish Register*.

WHILE widow Butler and widower Deans struggled with poverty, and the hard and sterile soil of those "parts and portions" of the lands of Dumbiedikes which it was their lot to occupy, it became gradually apparent that Deans was to gain the strife, and his ally in the conflict was to lose it. The former was a man, and not much past the prime of life—Mrs. Butler a woman, and declined into the vale of years. This, indeed, ought in time to have been balanced by the circumstance, that Reuben was growing up to assist his grandmother's labours, and that Jeanie Deans, as a girl, could be only supposed to add to her father's burdens. But Douce Davie Deans knew better things, and so schooled and trained the young minion, as he called her, that from the time she could walk, upwards, she was daily employed in some task or other suitable to her age and capacity; a circumstance which, added to her father's daily instructions and lectures, tended to give her mind, even when a child, a grave, serious, firm, and reflecting cast. An uncommonly strong and healthy temperament, free from all nervous affection and every other irregularity, which, attacking the body in its more noble functions, so often influences the mind, tended greatly to establish this fortitude, simplicity, and decision of character.

On the other hand, Reuben was weak in constitution, and, though not timid in temper, might be safely pronounced anxious, doubtful, and apprehensive. He partook of the temperament of his mother, who had died of a consumption in early age. He was a pale, thin, feeble, sickly boy, and somewhat lame, from an accident in early youth. He was, besides, the child of a doting grandmother, whose too solicitous attention to him soon taught him a sort of diffidence in himself, with a disposition to overrate his own importance, which is one of the very worst consequences that children deduce from over-indulgence.

Still, however, the two children clung to each other's society, not more from habit than from taste. They herded together the handful of sheep, with the two or three cows, which their parents turned out rather to seek food than actually to feed upon the unenclosed common of Dumbiedikes. It was there that the two urchins might be seen seated beneath a blooming bush of whin, their little faces laid close together under the shadow of the same plaid drawn over both their heads, while the landscape around was embrowned by an overshadowing cloud, big with the shower which had driven the children to shelter. On other occasions they went together to school, the boy receiving that encouragement and example from his companion, in crossing the little brooks which intersected their path, and encountering cattle, dogs, and other perils, upon their journey, which the male sex in such cases usually consider it as their prerogative to extend to the weaker. But when, seated on the benches of the school-house, they began to con their lessons together, Reuben, who was as much superior to Jeanie Deans in acuteness of intellect, as inferior to her in firmness of constitution, and in that insensibility to fatigue and danger which depends on the conformation of the nerves, was able fully to requite the kindness and countenance with which, in other circumstances, she used to regard him. He was decidedly the best scholar at the little parish school; and so gentle was his temper and disposition, that he was rather admired than envied by the little mob who occupied the noisy mansion, although he was the declared favourite of the master. Several girls, in particular (for in Scotland they are taught with the boys), longed to be kind to, and comfort the sickly lad, who was so much cleverer than his companions. The character of Reuben Butler was so calculated as to offer scope both for their sympathy and their admiration, the feelings, perhaps, through which the female sex (the more deserving part of them at least) is more easily attached.

But Reuben, naturally reserved and distant, improved none of these advantages; and only became more attached to Jeanie Deans, as the enthusiastic approbation of his master assured him of fair prospects in future life, and awakened his ambition. In the meantime, every advance that Reuben made in learning (and, considering his opportunities, they were uncommonly great) rendered him less capable of attending to the domestic duties of his grandmother's farm. While studying the *pons asinorum* in Euclid, he suffered every *cuddie* upon the common to trespass upon a large field of pease belonging to the Laird, and nothing but the active exertions of Jeanie Deans, with her little dog Dustiefoot, could have saved great loss and consequent punishment. Similar miscarriages marked his progress in his classical studies. He read Virgil's Georgics till he did not know bear from barley ; and had nearly destroyed the crofts of Beersheba, while attempting to cultivate them according to the practice of Columella and Cato the Censor.

These blunders occasioned grief to his grand-dame, and disconcerted the good opinion which her neighbour, Davie Deans, had for some time entertained of Reuben.

" I see naething ye can make of that silly callant, neighbour Butler," said he to the old lady, "unless ye train him to the wark o' the ministry. And ne'er was there mair need of poorfu' preachers than e'en now in these cauld Gallio days, when men's hearts are hardened like the nether millstone, till they come to regard none of these things. It's evident this puir callant of yours will never be able to do an usefu' day's wark, unless it be as an ambassador from our Master ; and I will make it my business to procure a license when he is fit for the same, trusting he will be a shaft cleanly polished, and meet to be used in the body of the kirk ; and that he shall not turn again, like the sow, to wallow in the mire of heretical extremes and defections, but shall have the wings of a dove, though he hath lain among the pots."

The poor widow gulped down the affront to her husband's

principles, implied in this caution, and hastened to take Butler from the High School, and encourage him in the pursuit of mathematics and divinity, the only physics and ethics that chanced to be in fashion at the time.

Jeanie Deans was now compelled to part from the companion of her labour, her study, and her pastime, and it was with more than childish feeling that both children regarded the separation. But they were young, and hope was high, and they separated like those who hope to meet again at a more auspicious hour.

While Reuben Butler was acquiring at the University of St. Andrews the knowledge necessary for a clergyman, and macerating his body with the privations which were necessary in seeking food for his mind, his grand-dame became daily less able to struggle with her little farm, and was at length obliged to throw it up to the new Laird of Dumbiedikes. That great personage was no absolute Jew, and did not cheat her in making the bargain more than was tolerable. He even gave her permission to tenant the house in which she had lived with her husband, as long as it should be " tenantable " ; only he protested against paying for a farthing of repairs, any benevolence which he possessed being of the passive, but by no means of the active mood.

In the meanwhile, from superior shrewdness, skill, and other circumstances, some of them purely accidental, Davie Deans gained a footing in the world, the possession of some wealth, the reputation of more, and a growing disposition to preserve and increase his store ; for which, when he thought upon it seriously, he was inclined to blame himself. From his knowledge in agriculture, as it was then practised, he became a sort of favourite with the Laird, who had no pleasure either in active sports or in society, and was wont to end his daily saunter by calling at the cottage of Woodend.

Being himself a man of slow ideas and confused utterance, Dumbiedikes used to sit or stand for half-an-hour with an old laced hat of his father's upon his head, and an empty tobacco-pipe in his mouth, with his eyes following Jeanie Deans, or " the lassie," as he called her, through the course of her daily domestic labour; while her father, after exhausting the subject of bestial, of ploughs, and of harrows, often took an opportunity of going full sail into controversial subjects, to which discussions the dignitary listened with much seeming patience, but without making any reply, or, indeed, as most people thought, without understanding a single word of what the orator was saying. Deans, indeed, denied this stoutly, as an insult at once to his own talents for expounding hidden truths, of which he was a little vain, and to the Laird's capacity of understanding them. He said, "Dumbiedikes was nane of these flashy gentles, wi' lace on their skirts and swords at their tails, that were rather for riding on horseback to hell than ganging barefooted to heaven. He wasna like his father—nae profane company-keeper—nae swearer—nae drinker—nae frequenter of play-house, or music-house, or dancing-house — nae Sabbath-breaker—nae imposer of aiths, or bonds, or denier of liberty to the flock.—He clave to the warld, and the warld's gear, a wee ower muckle, but then there was some breathing of a gale upon his spirit," &c. &c. All this honest Davie said and believed.

It is not to be supposed, that, by a father and a man of sense and observation, the constant direction of the Laird's eyes towards Jeanie was altogether unnoticed. This circumstance, however, made a much greater impression upon another member of his family, a second helpmate, to wit, whom he had chosen to take to his bosom ten years after the death of his first. Some people were of opinion, that Douce Davie had been rather surprised into this step, for in general he was no friend to marriages or giving in marriage, and seemed rather to regard that state of society as a necessary evil,—a thing lawful, and to be tolerated in the imperfect state of our nature, but which clipped the wings with which we ought to soar upwards, and tethered the soul to its mansion of clay, and the creature-comforts of wife and bairns. His own practice, however, had in this material point varied from his principles, since, as we have seen, he twice knitted for himself this dangerous and ensnaring entanglement.

Rebecca, his spouse, had by no means the same horror of matrimony, and as she made marriages in imagination for every neighbour round, she failed not to indicate a match betwixt Dumbiedikes and her step-daughter Jeanie. The goodman used regularly to frown and pshaw whenever this topic was touched upon, but usually ended by taking his bonnet and walking out of the house to conceal a certain gleam of satisfaction, which, at such a suggestion, involuntarily diffused itself over his austere features.

The more youthful part of my readers may naturally ask, whether Jeanie Deans was deserving of this mute attention of the Laird of Dumbiedikes; and the historian, with due regard to veracity, is compelled to answer, that her personal attractions were of no uncommon description. She was short, and rather too stoutly made for her size, had grey eyes, light-coloured hair, a round good-humoured face, much tanned with the sun, and her only peculiar charm was an air of inexpressible serenity, which a good conscience, kind feelings, contented temper, and the regular discharge of all her duties, spread over her features. There was nothing, it may be supposed, very appalling in the form or manners of this rustic heroine; yet, whether from sheepish bashfulness, or from want of decision and imperfect knowledge of his own mind on the subject, the Laird of Dumbiedikes, with his old laced hat and empty tobacco-pipe, came and enjoyed the beatific vision of Jeanie Deans day after day, week after week, year after year, without proposing to accomplish any of the prophecies of the step-mother.

This good lady began to grow doubly impatient on the subject, when, after having been some years married, she herself presented Douce Davie with another daughter, who was named Euphemia, by corruption, Effie. It was then that Rebecca began to turn impatient with the slow pace at which the Laird's wooing proceeded, judiciously arguing, that, as Lady Dumbiedikes would have but little occasion for tocher, the principal part of her gudeman's substance would naturally descend to the child by the second marriage. Other step-dames have tried less laudable means for clearing the way to the succession of their own children; but Rebecca, to do her justice, only sought little Effie's advantage through the promotion, or which must have generally been accounted such, of her elder sister. She therefore tried every female art within the compass of her simple skill, to bring the Laird to a point; but had the mortification to perceive that her efforts, like those of an unskilful angler, only scared the trout she meant to catch. Upon one occasion, in particular, when she joked with the Laird on the propriety of giving a mistress to the house of Dumbiedikes, he was so effectually startled, that neither laced hat, tobacco-pipe, nor the intelligent proprietor of these movables, visited Woodend for a fortnight. Rebecca was therefore compelled to leave the Laird to proceed at his own snail's pace, convinced, by experience, of the grave-digger's aphorism, that your dull ass will not mend his pace for beating.

Reuben, in the meantime, pursued his studies at the university, supplying his wants by teaching the younger lads the knowledge he himself acquired, and thus at once gaining the means of maintaining himself at the seat of learning, and fixing in his mind the elements of what he had already obtained. In this manner, as is usual among the poorer students of divinity at Scottish universities, he contrived not only to maintain himself according to his simple wants, but even to send considerable assistance to his sole remaining parent, a sacred duty, of which the Scotch are seldom negligent. His progress in knowledge of a general kind, as well as in the studies proper to his profession, was very considerable, but was little remarked, owing to the retired modesty of his disposition, which in no respect qualified him to set off his learning to the best advantage. And thus, had Butler been a man given to make complaints, he had his tale to tell, like others, of unjust preferences, bad luck, and hard usage. On these subjects, however, he was habitually silent, perhaps from modesty, perhaps from a touch of pride, or perhaps from a conjunction of both.

He obtained his license as a preacher of the gospel, with some compliments from the presbytery by whom it was bestowed; but this did not lead to any preferment, and he found it necessary to make the cottage at Beersheba his residence for some months, with no other income than was afforded by the precarious occupation of teaching in one or other of the neighbouring families. After having greeted his aged grandmother, his first visit was to Woodend, where he was received by Jeanie with warm cordiality, arising from recollections which had never been dismissed from her mind, by Rebecca with good-humoured hospitality, and by old Deans in a mode peculiar to himself.

Highly as Douce Davie honoured the clergy, it was not upon each individual of the cloth that he bestowed his approbation; and, a little jealous, perhaps, at seeing his youthful acquaintance erected into the dignity of a teacher and preacher, he instantly attacked him upon various points of controversy, in order to discover whether he might not have fallen into some of the snares, defections, and desertions of the time. Butler was not only a man of staunch Presbyterian principles, but was also willing to avoid giving pain to his old friend by

disputing upon points of little importance; and therefore he
might have hoped to have come like refined gold out of the
furnace of Davie's interrogatories. But the result on the mind
of that strict investigator was not altogether so favourable as
might have been hoped and anticipated. Old Judith Butler,
who had hobbled that evening as far as Woodend, in order to
enjoy the congratulations of her neighbours upon Reuben's
return, and upon his high attainments, of which she was
herself not a little proud, was somewhat mortified to find
that her old friend Deans did not enter into the subject
with the warmth she expected. At first, indeed, he seemed
rather silent than dissatisfied; and it was not till Judith had
essayed the subject more than once that it led to the following
dialogue:—

"Aweel, neibor Deans, I thought ye wad hae been glad to
see Reuben amang us again, poor fellow."

"I *am* glad, Mrs. Butler," was the neighbour's concise
answer.

"Since he has lost his grandfather and his father (praised
be Him that giveth and taketh!) I ken nae friend he has in
the world that's been sae like a father to him as the sell o' ye,
neibor Deans."

"God is the only father of the fatherless," said Deans, touching his bonnet and looking upwards. "Give honour where
it is due, gudewife, and not to an unworthy instrument."

"Aweel, that's your way o' turning it, and nae doubt ye ken
best; but I hae kend ye, Davie, send a forpit o' meal to Beersheba when there wasna a bow left in the meal-ark at Woodend; ay, and I hae kend ye——"

"Gudewife," said Davie, interrupting her, "these are but
idle tales to tell me; fit for naething but to puff up our inward
man wi' our ain vain acts. I stude beside blessed Alexander
Peden, when I heard him call the death and testimony of our
happy martyrs but draps of blude and scarts of ink in respect
of fitting discharge of our duty; and what suld I think of onything the like of me can do?"

"Weel, neibor Deans, ye ken best; but I maun say that, I
am sure you are glad to see my bairn again—the halt's gane
now, unless he has to walk ower mony miles at a stretch; and
he has a wee bit colour in his cheek, that glads my auld een
to see it; and he has as decent a black coat as the minister;
and——"

"I am very heartily glad he is weel and thriving," said Mr.

Deans, with a gravity that seemed intended to cut short the subject; but a woman who is bent upon a point is not easily pushed aside from it.

"And," continued Mrs. Butler, "he can wag his head in a pulpit now, neibor Deans, think but of that—my ain oe—and a'body maun sit still and listen to him, as if he were the Paip of Rome."

"The what?—the who?—woman?" said Deans, with a sternness far beyond his usual gravity, as soon as these offensive words had struck upon the tympanum of his ear.

"Eh, guide us!" said the woman; "I had forgot what an ill-will ye had aye at the Paip, and sae had my puir gudeman, Stephen Butler. Mony an afternoon he wad sit and take up his testimony again the Paip, and again baptizing of bairns, and the like."

"Woman!" reiterated Deans, "either speak about what ye ken something o', or be silent; I say that independency is a foul heresy, and anabaptism a damnable and deceiving error, whilk suld be rooted out of the land wi' the fire o' the spiritual, and the sword o' the civil magistrate."

"Weel, weel, neibor, I'll no say that ye mayna be right," answered the submissive Judith. "I am sure ye are right about the sawing and the mawing, the shearing and the leading, and what for suld ye no be right about kirk wark, too? —But concerning my oe, Reuben Butler——"

"Reuben Butler, gudewife," said David, with solemnity, "is a lad I wish heartily weel to, even as if he were mine ain son—but I doubt there will be outs and ins in the track of his walk. I muckle fear his gifts will get the heels of his grace. He has ower muckle human wit and learning, and thinks as muckle about the form of the bicker as he does about the healsomeness of the food—he maun broider the marriage-garment with lace and passments, or it's no gude eneugh for him. And it's like he's something proud o' his human gifts and learning, whilk enables him to dress up his doctrine in that fine airy dress. But," added he, at seeing the old woman's uneasiness at his discourse, "affliction may gie him a jagg, and let the wind out o' him, as out o' a cow that's eaten wet clover, and the lad may do weel, and be a burning and a shining light; and I trust it will be yours to see, and his to feel it, and that soon."

Widow Butler was obliged to retire, unable to make anything more of her neighbour, whose discourse, though she did not comprehend it, filled her with undefined apprehensions on her grandson's account, and greatly depressed the joy with which she had welcomed him on his return. And it must not be concealed, in justice to Mr. Deans's discernment, that Butler, in their conference, had made a greater display of his learning than the occasion called for, or than was likely to be acceptable to the old man, who, accustomed to consider himself as a person pre-eminently entitled to dictate upon theological subjects of controversy, felt rather humbled and mortified when learned authorities were placed in array against him. In fact, Butler had not escaped the tinge of pedantry which naturally flowed from his education, and was apt, on many occasions, to make parade of his knowledge, when there was no need of such vanity.

Jeanie Deans, however, found no fault with this display of learning, but, on the contrary, admired it; perhaps on the same score that her sex are said to admire men of courage, on account of their own deficiency in that qualification. The circumstances of their families threw the young people constantly together; their old intimacy was renewed, though upon a footing better adapted to their age; and it became at length understood betwixt them, that their union should be deferred no longer than until Butler should obtain some steady means of support, however humble. This, however, was not a matter speedily to be accomplished. Plan after plan was formed, and plan after plan failed. The good-humoured cheek of Jeanie lost the first flush of juvenile freshness; Reuben's brow assumed the gravity of manhood, yet the means of obtaining a settlement seemed remote as ever. Fortunately for the lovers, their passion was of no ardent or enthusiastic cast; and a sense of duty on both sides induced them to bear, with patient fortitude, the protracted interval which divided them from each other.

In the meanwhile, time did not roll on without effecting his usual changes. The widow of Stephen Butler, so long the prop of the family of Beersheba, was gathered to her fathers; and Rebecca, the careful spouse of our friend Davie Deans, was also summoned from her plans of matrimonial and domestic economy. The morning after her death, Reuben Butler went to offer his mite of consolation to his old friend and benefactor. He witnessed, on this occasion, a remarkable struggle betwixt the force of natural affection, and the religious stoicism which the sufferer thought it was incumbent upon him to maintain under each earthly dispensation, whether of weal or woe.

On his arrival at the cottage, Jeanie, with her eyes overflowing with tears, pointed to the little orchard, "in which," she whispered with broken accents, "my poor father has been since his misfortune." Somewhat alarmed at this account, Butler entered the orchard, and advanced slowly towards his old friend, who, seated in a small rude arbour, appeared to be sunk in the extremity of his affliction. He lifted his eyes somewhat sternly as Butler approached, as if offended at the interruption; but as the young man hesitated whether he ought to retreat or advance, he arose, and came forward to meet him, with a self-possessed, and even dignified air.

"Young man," said the sufferer, "lay it not to heart, though the righteous perish and the merciful are removed, seeing it may well be said, that they are taken away from the evils to come. Woe to me, were I to shed a tear for the wife of my bosom, when I might weep rivers of water for this afflicted Church, cursed as it is with carnal seekers, and with the dead of heart."

"I am happy," said Butler, "that you can forget your private affliction in your regard for public duty."

"Forget, Reuben?" said poor Deans, putting his handkerchief to his eyes,—"She's not to be forgotten on this side of time; but He that gives the wound can send the ointment. I declare there have been times during this night when my meditation has been so wrapt, that I knew not of my heavy loss. It has been with me as with the worthy John Semple, called Carspharn John,[1] upon a like trial,—I have been this night on the banks of Ulai, plucking an apple here and there."

Notwithstanding the assumed fortitude of Deans, which he conceived to be the discharge of a great Christian duty, he had too good a heart not to suffer deeply under this heavy loss. Woodend became altogether distasteful to him; and as he had obtained both substance and experience by his management of that little farm, he resolved to employ them as a dairy-farmer, or cowfeeder, as they are called in Scotland. The situation he chose for his new settlement was at a place called Saint Leonard's Crags, lying betwixt Edinburgh and the mountain called Arthur's Seat, and adjoining to the extensive sheep pasture still named the King's Park, from its having been formerly dedicated to the preservation of the

[1] Note II.—Carspharn John.

royal game. Here he rented a small lonely house, about half a mile distant from the nearest point of the city, but the site of which, with all the adjacent ground, is now occupied by the buildings which form the south-eastern suburb. An extensive pasture-ground adjoining, which Deans rented from the keeper of the Royal Park, enabled him to feed his milk-cows; and the unceasing industry and activity of Jeanie, his eldest daughter, was exerted in making the most of their produce.

She had now less frequent opportunities of seeing Reuben, who had been obliged, after various disappointments, to accept the subordinate situation of assistant in a parochial school of some eminence, at three or four miles' distance from the city. Here he distinguished himself, and became acquainted with several respectable burgesses, who, on account of health, or other reasons, chose that their children should commence their education in this little village. His prospects were thus gradually brightening, and upon each visit which he paid at Saint Leonard's he had an opportunity of gliding a hint to this purpose into Jeanie's ear. These visits were necessarily very rare, on account of the demands which the duties of the school made upon Butler's time. Nor did he dare to make them even altogether so frequent as these avocations would permit. Deans received him with civility indeed, and even with kindness; but Reuben, as is usual in such cases, imagined that he read his purpose in his eyes, and was afraid too premature an explanation on the subject would draw down his positive disapproval. Upon the whole, therefore, he judged it prudent to call at Saint Leonard's just so frequently as old acquaintance and neighbourhood seemed to authorise, and no oftener. There was another person who was more regular in his visits.

When Davie Deans intimated to the Laird of Dumbiedikes his purpose of "quitting wi' the land and house at Woodend," the Laird stared and said nothing. He made his usual visits at the usual hour without remark, until the day before the term, when, observing the bustle of moving furniture already commenced, the great east-country *awmrie* dragged out of its nook, and standing with its shoulder to the company, like an awkward booby about to leave the room, the Laird again stared mightily, and was heard to ejaculate, "Hegh, sirs!" Even after the day of departure was past and gone, the Laird of Dumbiedikes, at his usual hour, which was that at which David Deans was wont to "loose the pleugh," presented himself before the closed door of the cottage at Woodend, and seemed as much astonished at finding it shut against his approach as if it was not exactly what he had to expect. On this occasion he was heard to ejaculate, "Gude guide us!" which, by those who knew him, was considered as a very unusual mark of emotion. From that moment forward, Dumbiedikes became an altered man, and the regularity of his movements, hitherto so exemplary, was as totally disconcerted as those of a boy's watch when he has broken the main-spring. Like the index of the said watch, did Dumbiedikes spin round the whole bounds of his little property, which may be likened unto the dial of the time-piece, with unwonted velocity. There was not a cottage into which he did not enter, nor scarce a maiden on whom he did not stare. But so it was, that although there were better farm-houses on the land than Woodend, and certainly much prettier girls than Jeanie Deans, yet it did somehow befall that the blank in the Laird's time was not so pleasantly filled up as it had been. There was no seat accommodated him so well as the "bunker" at Woodend, and no face he loved so much to gaze on as Jeanie Deans's. So, after spinning round and round his little orbit, and then remaining stationary for a week, it seems to have occurred to him, that he was not pinned down to circulate on a pivot, like the hands of the watch, but possessed the power of shifting his central point, and extending his circle if he thought proper. To realise which privilege of change of place, he bought a pony from a Highland drover, and with its assistance and company stepped, or rather stumbled, as far as Saint Leonard's Crags.

Jeanie Deans, though so much accustomed to the Laird's staring that she was sometimes scarce conscious of his presence, had nevertheless some occasional fears lest he should call in the organ of speech to back those expressions of admiration which he bestowed on her through his eyes. Should this happen, farewell, she thought, to all chance of a union with Butler. For her father, however stout-hearted and independent in civil and religious principles, was not without that respect for the laird of the land, so deeply imprinted on the Scottish tenantry of the period. Moreover, if he did not positively dislike Butler, yet his fund of carnal learning was often the object of sarcasms on David's part, which were perhaps founded in jealousy, and which certainly indicated no partiality for the party against whom they were launched. And, lastly, the match with Dumbiedikes would have presented irresistible charms to one who used to complain that he felt himself apt to take "ower grit an armfu' o' the warld." So that, upon the whole, the Laird's diurnal visits were disagreeable to Jeanie from apprehension of future consequences, and it served much to console her, upon removing from the spot where she was bred and born, that she had seen the last of Dumbiedikes, his laced hat, and tobacco-pipe. The poor girl no more expected he could muster courage to follow her to Saint Leonard's Crags than that any of her apple-trees or cabbages which she had left rooted in the "yard" at Woodend, would spontaneously, and unaided, have undertaken the same journey. It was, therefore, with much more surprise than pleasure that, on the sixth day after their removal to Saint Leonard's, she beheld Dumbiedikes arrive, laced hat, tobacco-pipe, and all, and, with the self-same greeting of "How's a' wi' ye, Jeanie?—Whare's the gudeman?" assume as nearly as he could the same position in the cottage at Saint Leonard's which he had so long and so regularly occupied at Woodend. He was no sooner, however, seated, than with an unusual exertion of his powers of conversation, he added, "Jeanie—I say, Jeanie, woman"—here he extended his hand towards her shoulder with all the fingers spread out as if to clutch it, but in so bashful and awkward a manner, that when she whisked herself beyond its reach, the paw remained suspended in the air with the palm open, like the claw of a heraldic griffin— "Jeanie," continued the swain, in this moment of inspiration, —"I say, Jeanie, it's a braw day out-by, and the roads are no that ill for boot-hose."

"The deil's in the daidling body," muttered Jeanie between her teeth; "wha wad hae thought o' his daikering out this length?" And she afterwards confessed that she threw a little of this ungracious sentiment into her accent and manner; for her father being abroad, and the "body," as she irreverently termed the landed proprietor, "looking unco gleg and canty, she didna ken what he might be coming out wi' next."

Her frowns, however, acted as a complete sedative, and the Laird relapsed from that day into his former taciturn habits, visiting the cowfeeder's cottage three or four times every week, when the weather permitted, with apparently no other purpose than to stare at Jeanie Deans, while Douce Davie poured forth his eloquence upon the controversies and testimonies of the day.

CHAPTER X

Her airs, her manners, all who saw admired,
Courteous, though coy, and gentle, though retired;
The joy of youth and health her eyes display'd;
And ease of heart her every look convey'd.
—CRABBE.

THE visits of the Laird thus again sunk into matters of ordinary course, from which nothing was to be expected or apprehended. If a lover could have gained a fair one as a snake is said to fascinate a bird, by pertinaciously gazing on her with great stupid greenish eyes, which began now to be occasionally aided by spectacles, unquestionably Dumbie-dikes would have been the person to perform the feat. But the art of fascination seems among the *artes perditæ*, and I cannot learn that this most pertinacious of starers produced any effect by his attentions beyond an occasional yawn.

In the meanwhile, the object of his gaze was gradually attaining the verge of youth, and approaching to what is called in females the middle age, which is impolitely held to begin a few years earlier with their more fragile sex than with men. Many people would have been of opinion, that the Laird would have done better to have transferred his glances to an object possessed of far superior charms to Jeanie's even when Jeanie's were in their bloom, who began now to be distinguished by all who visited the cottage at Saint Leonard's Crags.

Effie Deans, under the tender and affectionate care of her sister, had now shot up into a beautiful and blooming girl. Her Grecian-shaped head was profusely rich in waving ringlets of brown hair, which, confined by a blue snood of silk, and shading a laughing Hebe countenance, seemed the picture of health, pleasure, and contentment. Her brown russet short-gown set off a shape, which time, perhaps, might be expected to render too robust, the frequent objection to Scottish beauty, but which, in her present early age, was slender and taper, with that graceful and easy sweep of outline which at once indicates health and beautiful proportion of parts

These growing charms, in all their juvenile profusion, had no power to shake the steadfast mind, or divert the fixed gaze, of the constant Laird of Dumbiedikes. But there was scarce another eye that could behold this living picture of health and beauty, without pausing on it with pleasure. The traveller stopped his weary horse on the eve of entering the city which was the end of his journey, to gaze at the sylph-like form that tripped by him, with her milk-pail poised on her head, bearing herself so erect, and stepping so light and free under her burden, that it seemed rather an ornament than an encumbrance. The lads of the neighbouring suburb, who held their evening rendezvous for putting the stone, casting the hammer, playing at long bowls, and other athletic exercises, watched the motions of Effie Deans, and contended with each other which should have the good fortune to attract her attention. Even the rigid Presbyterians of her father's persuasion, who held each indulgence of the eye and sense to be a snare at least, if not a crime, were surprised into a moment's delight while gazing on a creature so exquisite,—instantly checked by a sigh, reproaching at once their own weakness, and mourning that a creature so fair should share in the common and hereditary guilt and imperfection of our nature. She was currently entitled the Lily of St. Leonard's, a name which she deserved as much by her guileless purity of thought, speech, and action, as by her uncommon loveliness of face and person.

Yet there were points in Effie's character which gave rise not only to strange doubt and anxiety on the part of Douce David Deans, whose ideas were rigid, as may easily be supposed, upon the subject of youthful amusements, but even of serious apprehension to her more indulgent sister. The children of the Scotch of the inferior classes are usually spoiled by the early indulgence of their parents; how, wherefore, and to what degree, the lively and instructive narrative of the amiable and accomplished authoress of "Glenburnie"[1] has saved me and all future scribblers the trouble of recording. Effie had had a double share of this inconsiderate and misjudged kindness. Even the strictness of her father's principles could not condemn the sports of infancy and childhood; and to the good old man, his younger daughter, the child of his old age, seemed a child for some years after she attained the years of womanhood, was still called the "bit lassie" and

---

[1] Mrs. Elizabeth Hamilton, now no more.—*Editor.*

"little Effie," and was permitted to run up and down uncontrolled, unless upon the Sabbath, or at the times of family worship. Her sister, with all the love and care of a mother, could not be supposed to possess the same authoritative influence; and that which she had hitherto exercised became gradually limited and diminished as Effie's advancing years entitled her, in her own conceit at least, to the right of independence and free agency. With all the innocence and goodness of disposition, therefore, which we have described, the Lily of St. Leonard's possessed a little fund of self-conceit and obstinacy, and some warmth and irritability of temper, partly natural perhaps, but certainly much increased by the unrestrained freedom of her childhood. Her character will be best illustrated by a cottage evening scene.

The careful father was absent in his well-stocked byre, foddering those useful and patient animals on whose produce his living depended, and the summer evening was beginning to close in, when Jeanie Deans began to be very anxious for the appearance of her sister, and to fear that she would not reach home before her father returned from the labour of the evening, when it was his custom to have "family exercise," and when she knew that Effie's absence would give him the most serious displeasure. These apprehensions hung heavier upon her mind, because, for several preceding evenings, Effie had disappeared about the same time, and her stay, at first so brief as scarce to be noticed, had been gradually protracted to half-an-hour, and an hour, and on the present occasion had considerably exceeded even this last limit. And now, Jeanie stood at the door, with her hand before her eyes to avoid the rays of the level sun, and looked alternately along the various tracks which led towards their dwelling, to see if she could descry the nymph-like form of her sister. There was a wall and a stile which separated the royal domain, or King's Park, as it is called, from the public road; to this pass she frequently directed her attention, when she saw two persons appear there somewhat suddenly, as if they had walked close by the side of the wall to screen themselves from observation. One of them, a man, drew back hastily; the other, a female, crossed the stile, and advanced towards her—it was Effie. She met her sister with that affected liveliness of manner, which, in her rank, and sometimes in those above it, females occasionally assume to hide surprise or confusion; and she carolled as she came—

" The elfin knight sate on the brae,
    The broom grows bonny, the broom grows fair;
And by there came lilting a lady so gay,
    And we daurna gang down to the broom nae mair."

" Whisht, Effie," said her sister; " our father's coming out o' the byre."—The damsel stinted in her song.—" Whare hae ye been sae late at e'en? "

" It's no late, lass," answered Effie.

" It's chappit eight on every clock o' the town, and the sun's gaun down ahint the Corstorphine hills—Whare can ye hae been sae late? "

" Nae gate," answered Effie.

" And wha was that parted wi' you at the stile? "

" Naebody," replied Effie, once more.

" Nae gate?—Naebody?—I wish it may be a right gate, and a right body, that keeps folk out sae late at e'en, Effie."

" What needs ye be aye speering then at folk? " retorted Effie. " I'm sure, if ye'll ask nae questions, I'll tell ye nae lees. I never ask what brings the Laird of Dumbiedikes glowering here like a wull-cat (only his een's greener, and no sae gleg), day after day, till we are a' like to gaunt our chafts aff."

" Because ye ken very weel he comes to see our father," said Jeanie, in answer to this pert remark.

" And Dominie Butler—Does he come to see our father, that's sae taen wi' his Latin words? " said Effie, delighted to find that, by carrying the war into the enemy's country, she could divert the threatened attack upon herself, and with the petulance of youth she pursued her triumph over her prudent elder sister. She looked at her with a sly air, in which there was something like irony, as she chanted, in a low but marked tone, a scrap of an old Scotch song—

" Through the kirkyard
    I met wi' the Laird,
The silly puir body he said me nae harm;
    But just ere 'twas dark,
    I met wi' the clerk——"

Here the songstress stopped, looked full at her sister, and, observing the tear gather in her eyes, she suddenly flung her arms round her neck, and kissed them away. Jeanie, though hurt and displeased, was unable to resist the caresses of this untaught child of nature, whose good and evil seemed to flow rather from impulse than from reflection. But as she returned the sisterly kiss, in token of perfect reconciliation, she could not suppress the gentle reproof—" Effie, if ye will learn fule sangs, ye might make a kinder use of them."

"And so I might, Jeanie," continued the girl, clinging to her sister's neck; "and I wish I had never learned ane o' them—and I wish we had never come here—and I wish my tongue had been blistered or I had vexed ye."

"Never mind that, Effie," replied the affectionate sister; "I canna be muckle vexed wi' onything ye say to me—but oh, dinna vex our father!"

"I will not—I will not," replied Effie; "and if there were as mony dances the morn's night as there are merry dancers in the north firmament on a frosty e'en, I winna budge an inch to gang near ane o' them."

"Dance?" echoed Jeanie Deans in astonishment. "O Effie, what could take ye to a dance?"

It is very possible, that, in the communicative mood into which the Lily of St. Leonard's was now surprised, she might have given her sister her unreserved confidence, and saved me the pain of telling a melancholy tale; but at the moment the word dance was uttered, it reached the ear of old David Deans, who had turned the corner of the house, and came upon his daughters ere they were aware of his presence. The word *prelate*, or even the word *pope*, could hardly have produced so appalling an effect upon David's ear; for, of all exercises, that of dancing, which he termed a voluntary and regular fit of distraction, he deemed most destructive of serious thoughts, and the readiest inlet to all sort of licentiousness; and he accounted the encouraging, and even permitting, assemblies or meetings, whether among those of high or low degree, for this fantastic and absurd purpose, or for that of dramatic representations, as one of the most flagrant proofs of defection and causes of wrath. The pronouncing of the word *dance* by his own daughters, and at his own door, now drove him beyond the verge of patience. "Dance!" he exclaimed. "Dance!—dance, said ye? I daur ye, limmers that ye are, to name sic a word at my door-cheek! It's a dissolute profane pastime, practised by the Israelites only at their base and brutal worship of the Golden Calf at Bethel, and by the unhappy lass wha danced aff the head of John the Baptist, upon whilk chapter I will exercise this night for your farther instruction, since ye need it sae muckle, nothing doubting that she has cause to rue the day, lang or this time,

that e'er she suld hae shook a limb on sic an errand. Better
for her to hae been born a cripple, and carried frae door to
door, like auld Bessie Bowie, begging bawbees, than to be a
king's daughter, fiddling and flinging the gate she did. I hae
often wondered that ony ane that ever bent a knee for the
right purpose, should ever daur to crook a hough to fyke and
fling at piper's wind and fiddler's squealing. And I bless
God (with that singular worthy, Peter Walker the packman
at Bristo Port[1]), that ordered my lot in my dancing days, so
that fear of my head and throat, dread of bloody rope and
swift bullet, and trenchant swords and pain of boots and
thumbkins, cauld and hunger, wetness and weariness, stopped
the lightness of my head, and the wantonness of my feet.
And now, if I hear ye, quean lassies, sae muckle as name
dancing, or think there's sic a thing in this warld as flinging
to fiddler's sounds and piper's springs, as sure as my father's
spirit is with the just, ye shall be no more either charge or
concern of mine! Gang in, then—gang in, then, hinnies," he
added, in a softer tone, for the tears of both daughters, but
especially those of Effie, began to flow very fast,—"Gang in,
dears, and we'll seek grace to preserve us frae all manner of
profane folly, whilk causeth to sin, and promoteth the kingdom
of darkness, warring with the kingdom of light."

The objurgation of David Deans, however well meant, was
unhappily timed. It created a division of feelings in Effie's
bosom, and deterred her from her intended confidence in her
sister. "She wad haud me nae better than the dirt below her
feet," said Effie to herself, "were I to confess I hae danced wi'
him four times on the green down by, and ance at Maggie Mac-
queen's; and she'll maybe hing it ower my head that she'll
tell my father, and then she wad be mistress and mair. But
I'll no gang back there again. I'm resolved I'll no gang back.
I'll lay in a leaf of my Bible,[2] and that's very near as if I had
made an aith, that I winna gang back." And she kept her
vow for a week, during which she was unusually cross and
fretful, blemishes which had never before been observed in
her temper, except during a moment of contradiction.

There was something in all this so mysterious as considerably
to alarm the prudent and affectionate Jeanie, the more so as she

---

[1] Note III.—Peter Walker.
[2] This custom, of making a mark by folding a leaf in the party's Bible when
a solemn resolution is formed, is still held to be, in some sense, an appeal to
Heaven for his or her sincerity.

judged it unkind to her sister to mention to their father grounds of anxiety which might arise from her own imagination. Besides, her respect for the good old man did not prevent her from being aware that he was both hot-tempered and positive, and she sometimes suspected that he carried his dislike to youthful amusements beyond the verge that religion and reason demanded. Jeanie had sense enough to see that a sudden and severe curb upon her sister's hitherto unrestrained freedom might be rather productive of harm than good, and that Effie, in the headstrong wilfulness of youth, was likely to make what might be overstrained in her father's precepts an excuse to herself for neglecting them altogether. In the higher classes, a damsel, however giddy, is still under the dominion of etiquette, and subject to the surveillance of mammas and chaperons; but the country girl, who snatches her moment of gaiety during the intervals of labour, is under no such guardianship or restraint, and her amusement becomes so much the more hazardous. Jeanie saw all this with much distress of mind, when a circumstance occurred which appeared calculated to relieve her anxiety.

Mrs. Saddletree, with whom our readers have already been made acquainted, chanced to be a distant relation of Douce David Deans, and as she was a woman orderly in her life and conversation, and, moreover, of good substance, a sort of acquaintance was formally kept up between the families. Now, this careful dame, about a year and a half before our story commences, chanced to need, in the line of her profession, a better sort of servant, or rather shop-woman. "Mr. Saddletree," she said, "was never in the shop when he could get his nose within the Parliament House, and it was an awkward thing for a woman-body to be standing among bundles o' barkened leather her lane, selling saddles and bridles; and she had cast her eyes upon her far-awa cousin Effie Deans, as just the very sort of lassie she would want to keep her in countenance on such occasions."

In this proposal there was much that pleased old David,—there was bed, board, and bountith—it was a decent situation—the lassie would be under Mrs. Saddletree's eye, who had an upright walk, and lived close by the Tolbooth Kirk, in which might still be heard the comforting doctrines of one of those few ministers of the Kirk of Scotland who had not bent the knee unto Baal, according to David's expression, or become accessory to the course of natural defections,—union, toleration, patronages, and a bundle of prelatical Erastian oaths which had been imposed on the Church since the Revolution, and particularly in the reign of "the late woman" (as he called Queen Anne), the last of that unhappy race of Stuarts. In the good man's security concerning the soundness of the theological doctrine which his daughter was to hear, he was nothing disturbed on account of the snares of a different kind, to which a creature so beautiful, young, and wilful, might be exposed in the centre of a populous and corrupted city. The fact is, that he thought with so much horror on all approaches to irregularities of the nature most to be dreaded in such cases, that he would as soon have suspected and guarded against Effie's being induced to become guilty of the crime of murder. He only regretted that she should live under the same roof with such a worldly-wise man as Bartoline Saddletree, whom David never suspected of being an ass as he was, but considered as one really endowed with all the legal knowledge to which he made pretension, and only liked him the worse for possessing it. The lawyers, especially those amongst them who sate as ruling elders in the General Assembly of the Kirk, had been forward in promoting the measures of patronage, of the abjuration oath, and others, which, in the opinion of David Deans, were a breaking down of the carved work of the sanctuary, and an intrusion upon the liberties of the kirk. Upon the dangers of listening to the doctrines of a legalised formalist, such as Saddletree, David gave his daughter many lectures; so much so, that he had time to touch but slightly on the dangers of chambering, company-keeping, and promiscuous dancing, to which, at her time of life, most people would have thought Effie more exposed, than to the risk of theoretical error in her religious faith.

Jeanie parted from her sister, with a mixed feeling of regret, and apprehension, and hope. She could not be so confident concerning Effie's prudence as her father, for she had observed her more narrowly, had more sympathy with her feelings, and could better estimate the temptations to which she was exposed. On the other hand, Mrs. Saddletree was an observing, shrewd, notable woman, entitled to exercise over Effie the full authority of a mistress, and likely to do so strictly, yet with kindness. Her removal to Saddletree's, it was most probable, would also serve to break off some idle acquaintances, which Jeanie suspected her sister to have formed in the neighbouring suburb. Upon the whole, then, she viewed her departure from Saint Leonard's with pleasure, and it was not until the very moment of their parting for the first time in their lives, that she felt the full force of sisterly sorrow. While they repeatedly kissed each other's cheeks, and wrung each other's hands, Jeanie took that moment of affectionate sympathy, to press upon her sister the necessity of the utmost caution in her conduct while residing in Edinburgh. Effie listened, without once raising her large dark eyelashes, from which the drops fell so fast as almost to resemble a fountain. At the conclusion she sobbed again, kissed her sister, promised to recollect all the good counsel she had given her, and they parted.

During the first few weeks, Effie was all that her kinswoman expected, and even more. But with time there came a relaxation of that early zeal which she manifested in Mrs. Saddletree's service. To borrow once again from the poet, who so correctly and beautifully describes living manners,—

> " Something there was,—what, none presumed to say,—
> Clouds lightly passing on a summer's day;
> Whispers and hints, which went from ear to ear,
> And mix'd reports no judge on earth could clear."

During this interval, Mrs. Saddletree was sometimes displeased by Effie's lingering when she was sent upon errands about the shop business, and sometimes by a little degree of impatience which she manifested at being rebuked on such occasions. But she good-naturedly allowed, that the first was very natural to a girl to whom everything in Edinburgh was new, and the other was only the petulance of a spoiled child, when subjected to the yoke of domestic discipline for the first time. Attention and submission could not be learned at once—Holyrood was not built in a day—use would make perfect.

It seemed as if the considerate old lady had presaged truly. Ere many months had passed, Effie became almost wedded to her duties, though she no longer discharged them with the laughing cheek and light step, which at first had attracted every customer. Her mistress sometimes observed her in tears, but they were signs of secret sorrow, which she concealed as often as she saw them attract notice. Time wore on, her cheek grew pale, and her step heavy. The cause of these changes could not have escaped the matronly eye of Mrs. Saddletree, but she was chiefly confined by indisposition to her bedroom for a considerable time during the latter part of Effie's service. This interval was marked by symptoms of anguish almost amounting to despair. The utmost efforts of the poor girl to command her fits of hysterical agony were often totally unavailing, and the mistakes which she made in the shop the while were so numerous and so provoking, that Bartoline Saddletree, who, during his wife's illness, was obliged to take closer charge of the business than consisted with his study of the weightier matters of the law, lost all patience with the girl, who, in his law Latin, and without much respect to gender, he declared ought to be cognosced by inquest of a jury, as *fatuus, furiosus*, and *naturaliter idiota*. Neighbours, also, and fellow-servants, remarked, with malicious curiosity or degrading pity, the disfigured shape, loose dress, and pale cheeks, of the once beautiful and still interesting girl. But to no one would she grant her confidence, answering all taunts with bitter sarcasm, and all serious expostulation with sullen denial, or with floods of tears.

At length, when Mrs. Saddletree's recovery was likely to permit her wonted attention to the regulation of her household, Effie Deans, as if unwilling to face an investigation made by the authority of her mistress, asked permission of Bartoline to go home for a week or two, assigning indisposition, and the wish of trying the benefit of repose and the change of air, as the motives of her request. Sharp-eyed as a lynx (or conceiving himself to be so) in the nice sharp quillits of legal discussion, Bartoline was as dull at drawing inferences from the occurrences of common life as any Dutch professor of mathematics. He suffered Effie to depart without much suspicion, and without any inquiry.

It was afterwards found that a period of a week intervened betwixt her leaving her master's house and arriving at St. Leonard's. She made her appearance before her sister in a state rather resembling the spectre than the living substance of the gay and beautiful girl, who had left her father's cottage for the first time scarce seventeen months before. The lingering illness of her mistress had, for the last few months, given her a plea for confining herself entirely to the dusky precincts of the shop in the Lawnmarket, and Jeanie was so much occupied, during the same period, with the concerns of her father's household, that she had rarely found leisure for a walk into the city, and a brief and hurried visit to her sister. The young women, therefore, had scarcely seen each other for several months, nor had a single scandalous surmise reached the ears of the secluded inhabitants of the cottage at St. Leonard's. Jeanie, therefore, terrified to death at her sister's appearance, at first overwhelmed her with inquiries, to which the unfortunate young woman returned for a time incoherent and rambling answers, and finally fell into a hysterical fit. Rendered too certain of her sister's misfortune, Jeanie had now the dreadful alternative of communicating her ruin to her father, or of endeavouring to conceal it from him. To all questions concerning the name or rank of her seducer, and the fate of the being to whom her fall had given birth, Effie remained mute as the grave, to which she seemed hastening; and indeed the least allusion to either seemed to drive her to distraction. Her sister, in distress and in despair, was about to repair to Mrs. Saddletree to consult her experience, and at the same time to obtain what lights she could upon this most unhappy affair, when she was saved that trouble by a new stroke of fate, which seemed to carry misfortune to the uttermost.

David Deans had been alarmed at the state of health in which his daughter had returned to her paternal residence; but Jeanie had contrived to divert him from particular and specific inquiry. It was, therefore, like a clap of thunder to the poor old man, when, just as the hour of noon had brought the visit of the Laird of Dumbiedikes as usual, other and sterner, as well as most unexpected guests, arrived at the cottage of St. Leonard's. These were the officers of justice, with a warrant of justiciary to search for and apprehend Euphemia, or Effie, Deans, accused of the crime of child-murder. The stunning weight of a blow so totally unexpected bore down the old man, who had in his early youth resisted the brow of military and civil tyranny, though backed with swords and guns, tortures and gibbets. He fell extended and senseless upon his own hearth; and the men, happy to escape from the scene of his awakening, raised, with rude humanity, the object of their warrant from her bed, and placed her in a coach, which they had brought with them. The hasty remedies which Jeanie had applied to bring back her father's senses were scarce begun to operate, when the noise of the wheels in motion recalled her attention to her miserable sister. To run shrieking after the carriage was the first vain effort of her distraction, but she was stopped by one or two female neighbours, assembled by the extraordinary appearance of a coach in that sequestered place, who almost forced her back to her father's house. The deep and sympathetic affliction of these poor people, by whom the little family at St. Leonard's were held in high regard, filled the house with lamentation. Even Dumbiedikes was moved from his wonted apathy, and, groping for his purse as he spoke, ejaculated, " Jeanie, woman!— Jeanie, woman! dinna greet—it's sad wark, but siller will help it ;" and he drew out his purse as he spoke.

The old man had now raised himself from the ground, and, looking about him as if he missed something, seemed gradually to recover the sense of his wretchedness. "Where," he said, with a voice that made the roof ring, "where is the vile harlot, that has disgraced the blood of an honest man?—Where is she, that has no place among us, but has come foul with her sins, like the Evil One, among the children of God?—Where is she, Jeanie?—Bring her before me, that I may kill her with a word and a look!"

All hastened around him with their appropriate sources of consolation — the Laird with his purse, Jeanie with burnt feathers and strong waters, and the women with their exhortations. "O neighbour—O Mr. Deans, it's a sair trial, doubtless—but think of the Rock of Ages, neighbour—think of the promise!"

"And I do think of it, neighbours—and I bless God that I can think of it, even in the wrack and ruin of a' that's nearest and dearest to me.—But to be the father of a castaway—a proffligate—a bloody Zipporah—a mere murderess!—Oh, how will the wicked exult in the high places of their wickedness!—the prelatists, and the latitudinarians, and the hand-waled murderers, whose hands are hard as horn wi' hauding the slaughter-weapons—they will push out the lip, and say that we are even such as themselves. Sair, sair I am grieved, neighbours, for the poor castaway—for the child of mine old age—but sairer for the stumbling-block and scandal it will be to all tender and honest souls!"

"Davie—winna siller do't?" insinuated the Laird, still proffering his green purse, which was full of guineas.

"I tell ye, Dumbiedikes," said Deans, "that if telling down my haill substance could hae saved her frae this black snare, I wad hae walked out wi' naething but my bonnet and my staff to beg an awmous for God's sake, and ca'd mysell an happy man—But if a dollar, or a plack, or the nineteenth part of a boddle, wad save her open guilt and open shame frae open punishment, that purchase wad David Deans never make!— Na, na; an eye for an eye, a tooth for a tooth, life for life, blood for blood—it's the law of man, and it's the law of God. —Leave me, sirs—leave me—I maun warstle wi' this trial in privacy and on my knees."

Jeanie, now in some degree restored to the power of thought, joined in the same request. The next day found the father and daughter still in the depth of affliction, but the father sternly supporting his load of ill through a proud sense of religious duty, and the daughter anxiously suppressing her own feelings to avoid again awakening his. Thus was it with the afflicted family until the morning after Porteous's death, a period at which we are now arrived.

CHAPTER XI

> Is all the counsel that we two have shared,
> The sisters' vows, the hours that we have spent
> When we have chid the hasty-footed time
> For parting us—Oh! and is all forgot?
> *Midsummer Night's Dream.*

WE have been a long while in conducting Butler to the door of the cottage at St. Leonard's; yet the space which we have occupied in the preceding narrative does not exceed in length that which he actually spent on Salisbury Crags on the morning which succeeded the execution done upon Porteous by the rioters. For this delay he had his own motives. He wished to collect his thoughts, strangely agitated as they were, first by the melancholy news of Effie Deans's situation, and afterwards by the frightful scene which he had witnessed. In the situation also in which he stood with respect to Jeanie and her father, some ceremony, at least some choice of fitting time and season, was necessary to wait upon them. Eight in the morning was then the ordinary hour for breakfast, and he resolved that it should arrive before he made his appearance in their cottage.

Never did hours pass so heavily. Butler shifted his place and enlarged his circle to while away the time, and heard the huge bell of St. Giles's toll each successive hour in swelling tones, which were instantly attested by those of the other steeples in succession. He had heard seven struck in this manner, when he began to think he might venture to approach nearer to St. Leonard's, from which he was still a mile distant. Accordingly he descended from his lofty station as low as the bottom of the valley which divides Salisbury Crags from those small rocks which take their name from Saint Leonard. It is, as many of my readers may know, a deep, wild, grassy valley, scattered with huge rocks and fragments which have descended from the cliffs and steep ascent to the east.

This sequestered dell, as well as other places of the open pasturage of the King's Park, was, about this time, often the resort of the gallants of the time who had affairs of honour to discuss with the sword. Duels were then very common in Scotland, for the gentry were at once idle, haughty, fierce, divided by faction, and addicted to intemperance, so that there lacked neither provocation, nor inclination to resent it when given; and the sword, which was part of every gentleman's dress, was the only weapon used for the decision of such differences. When, therefore, Butler observed a young man, skulking, apparently to avoid observation, among the scattered rocks at some distance from the footpath, he was naturally led to suppose that he had sought this lonely spot upon that evil errand. He was so strongly impressed with this, that, notwithstanding his own distress of mind, he could not, according to his sense of duty as a clergyman, pass this person without speaking to him. There are times, thought he to himself, when the slightest interference may avert a great calamity—when a word spoken in season may do more for prevention than the eloquence of Tully could do for remedying evil—And for my own griefs, be they as they may, I shall feel them the lighter, if they divert me not from the prosecution of my duty.

Thus thinking and feeling, he quitted the ordinary path, and advanced nearer the object he had noticed. The man at first directed his course towards the hill, in order, as it appeared, to avoid him; but when he saw that Butler seemed disposed to follow him, he adjusted his hat fiercely, turned round, and came forward, as if to meet and defy scrutiny.

Butler had an opportunity of accurately studying his features as they advanced slowly to meet each other. The stranger seemed about twenty-five years old. His dress was of a kind which could hardly be said to indicate his rank with certainty, for it was such as young gentlemen sometimes wore while on active exercise in the morning, and which, therefore, was imitated by those of the inferior ranks, as young clerks and tradesmen, because its cheapness rendered it attainable, while it approached more nearly to the apparel of youths of fashion than any other which the manners of the times permitted them to wear. If his air and manner could be trusted, however, this person seemed rather to be dressed under than above his rank; for his carriage was bold and somewhat supercilious, his step easy and free, his manner daring and unconstrained. His stature was of the middle size, or rather above it, his limbs well-proportioned, yet not so strong as to infer the reproach of clumsiness. His features were uncommonly handsome, and all about him would have been interesting and prepossessing, but for that indescribable expression which habitual dissipation gives to the countenance, joined with a certain audacity in look and manner of that kind which is often assumed as a mask for confusion and apprehension.

Butler and the stranger met—surveyed each other—when, as the latter, slightly touching his hat, was about to pass by him, Butler, while he returned the salutation, observed, " A fine morning, sir—You are on the hill early."

"I have business here," said the young man, in a tone meant to repress farther inquiry.

"I do not doubt it, sir," said Butler. "I trust you will forgive my hoping that it is of a lawful kind?"

"Sir," said the other, with marked surprise, "I never forgive impertinence, nor can I conceive what title you have to hope anything about what no way concerns you."

"I am a soldier, sir," said Butler, "and have a charge to arrest evil-doers in the name of my Master."

"A soldier?" said the young man, stepping back, and fiercely laying his hand on his sword—" A soldier, and arrest me? Did you reckon what your life was worth, before you took the commission upon you?"

"You mistake me, sir," said Butler gravely; "neither my warfare nor my warrant are of this world. I am a preacher of the gospel, and have power, in my Master's name, to command the peace upon earth and good-will towards men, which was proclaimed with the gospel."

"A minister!" said the stranger carelessly, and with an expression approaching to scorn. "I know the gentlemen of your cloth in Scotland claim a strange right of intermeddling with men's private affairs. But I have been abroad, and know better than to be priest-ridden."

"Sir, if it be true that any of my cloth, or, it might be more decently said, of my calling, interfere with men's private affairs, for the gratification either of idle curiosity, or for worse motives, you cannot have learned a better lesson abroad that to contemn such practices. But, in my Master's work, I am called to be busy in season and out of season; and, conscious as I am of a pure motive, it were better for me to incur your contempt for speaking, than the correction of my own conscience for being silent."

"In the name of the devil!" said the young man impatiently, "say what you have to say, then; though whom you take me for, or what earthly concern you can have with me, a stranger to you, or with my actions and motives, of which you can know nothing, I cannot conjecture for an instant."

"You are about," said Butler, "to violate one of your country's wisest laws—you are about, which is much more dreadful, to violate a law, which God Himself has implanted within our nature, and written, as it were, in the table of our hearts, to which every thrill of our nerves is responsive."

"And what is the law you speak of?" said the stranger, in a hollow and somewhat disturbed accent.

"Thou shalt do no MURDER," said Butler, with a deep and solemn voice.

The young man visibly started, and looked considerably appalled. Butler perceived he had made a favourable impression, and resolved to follow it up. "Think," he said, "young man," laying his hand kindly upon the stranger's shoulder, "what an awful alternative you voluntarily choose for yourself, to kill or be killed. Think what it is to rush uncalled into the presence of an offended Deity, your heart fermenting with evil passions, your hand hot from the steel you had been urging, with your best skill and malice, against the breast of a fellow-creature. Or, suppose yourself the scarce less wretched survivor, with the guilt of Cain, the first murderer, in your heart, with his stamp upon your brow—that stamp, which struck all who gazed on him with unutterable horror, and by which the murderer is made manifest to all who look upon him. Think——"

The stranger gradually withdrew himself from under the hand of his monitor; and, pulling his hat over his brows, thus interrupted him. "Your meaning, sir, I dare say, is excellent, but you are throwing your advice away. I am not in this place with violent intentions against any one. I may be bad enough—you priests say all men are so—but I am here for the purpose of saving life, not of taking it away. If you wish to spend your time rather in doing a good action than in talking about you know not what, I will give you an opportunity. Do you see yonder crag to the right, over which appears the chimney of a lone house? Go thither, inquire for one Jeanie Deans, the daughter of the goodman; let her know that he she wots of remained here from daybreak till this hour, expecting to see her, and that he can abide no longer. Tell her, she *must* meet me at the Hunter's Bog to-night, as the moon rises behind St. Anthony's Hill, or that she will make a desperate man of me."

"Who, or what are you," replied Butler, exceedingly and most unpleasantly surprised, "who charge me with such an errand?"

"I am the devil!——" answered the young man hastily.

Butler stepped instinctively back, and commended himself internally to Heaven; for, though a wise and strong-minded man, he was neither wiser nor more strong-minded than those of his age and education, with whom, to disbelieve witchcraft or spectres, was held an undeniable proof of atheism.

The stranger went on without observing his emotion. "Yes! call me Apollyon, Abaddon, whatever name you shall choose, as a clergyman acquainted with the upper and lower circles of spiritual denomination, to call me by, you shall not find an appellation more odious to him that bears it, than is mine own."

This sentence was spoken with the bitterness of self-up-braiding, and a contortion of visage absolutely demoniacal. Butler, though a man brave by principle, if not by constitution, was overawed; for intensity of mental distress has in it a sort of sublimity which repels and overawes all men, but especially those of kind and sympathetic dispositions. The stranger turned abruptly from Butler as he spoke, but instantly returned, and, coming up to him closely and boldly, said, in a fierce, determined tone, "I have told you who and what I am—who, and what are you? What is your name?"

"Butler," answered the person to whom this abrupt question was addressed, surprised into answering it by the sudden and fierce manner of the querist—"Reuben Butler, a preacher of the gospel."

At this answer, the stranger again plucked more deep over

his brows the hat which he had thrown back in his former agitation. "Butler!" he repeated,—"the assistant of the schoolmaster at Liberton?"

"The same," answered Butler composedly.

The stranger covered his face with his hand, as if on sudden reflection, and then turned away, but stopped when he had walked a few paces; and seeing Butler follow him with his eyes, called out in a stern yet suppressed tone, just as if he had exactly calculated that his accents should not be heard a yard beyond the spot on which Butler stood. "Go your way, and do mine errand. Do not look after me. I will neither descend through the bowels of these rocks, nor vanish in a flash of fire; and yet the eye that seeks to trace my motions shall have reason to curse it was ever shrouded by eyelid or eyelash. Begone, and look not behind you. Tell Jeanie Deans, that when the moon rises I shall expect to meet her at Nicol Muschat's Cairn, beneath Saint Anthony's Chapel."

As he uttered these words, he turned and took the road against the hill, with a haste that seemed as peremptory as his tone of authority.

Dreading he knew not what of additional misery to a lot which seemed little capable of receiving augmentation, and desperate at the idea that any living man should dare to send so extraordinary a request, couched in terms so imperious, to the half-betrothed object of his early and only affection, Butler strode hastily towards the cottage, in order to ascertain how far this daring and rude gallant was actually entitled to press on Jeanie Deans a request, which no prudent, and scarce any modest young woman, was likely to comply with.

Butler was by nature, neither jealous nor superstitious; yet the feelings which lead to those moods of the mind were rooted in his heart, as a portion derived from the common stock of humanity. It was maddening to think that a profligate gallant, such as the manner and tone of the stranger evinced him to be, should have it in his power to command forth his future bride and plighted true love, at a place so improper, and an hour so unseasonable. Yet the tone in which the stranger spoke had nothing of the soft half-breathed voice proper to the seducer who solicits an assignation; it was bold, fierce, and imperative, and had less of love in it than of menace and intimidation.

The suggestions of superstition seemed more plausible, had Butler's mind been very accessible to them. Was this indeed the Roaring Lion, who goeth about seeking whom he may devour? This was a question which pressed itself on Butler's mind with an earnestness that cannot be conceived by those who live in the present day. The fiery eye, the abrupt demeanour, the occasionally harsh, yet studiously subdued tone of voice,—the features, handsome, but now clouded with pride, now disturbed by suspicion, now inflamed with passion —those dark hazel eyes which he sometimes shaded with his cap, as if he were averse to have them seen while they were occupied with keenly observing the motions and bearing of others—those eyes that were now turbid with melancholy, now gleaming with scorn, and now sparkling with fury—was it the passions of a mere mortal they expressed, or the emotions of a fiend who seeks, and seeks in vain, to conceal his fiendish designs under the borrowed mask of manly beauty? The whole partook of the mien, language, and port of the ruined archangel; and, imperfectly as we have been able to describe it, the effect of the interview upon Butler's nerves, shaken as they were at the time by the horrors of the preceding night, were greater than his understanding warranted, or his pride cared to submit to. The very place where he had met this singular person was desecrated, as it were, and unhallowed, owing to many violent deaths, both in duels and by suicide, which had in former times taken place there; and the place which he had named as a rendezvous at so late an hour, was held in general to be accursed, from a frightful and cruel murder which had been there committed by the wretch from whom the place took its name, upon the person of his own wife.[1] It was in such places, according to the belief of that period (when the laws against witchcraft were still in fresh observance, and had even lately been acted upon), that evil spirits had power to make themselves visible to human eyes, and to practise upon the feelings and senses of mankind. Suspicions, founded on such circumstances, rushed on Butler's mind, unprepared as it was, by any previous course of reasoning, to deny that which all of his time, country, and profession, believed; but common sense rejected these vain ideas as inconsistent. if not with possibility, at least with the general rules by which the universe is governed —a deviation from which, as Butler well argued with himself, ought not to be admitted as probable, upon any but the plainest and most incontrovertible evidence. An earthly

[1] Note IV.—Muschat's Cairn.

lover, however, or a young man, who, from whatever cause, had the right of exercising such summary and unceremonious authority over the object of his long-settled, and apparently sincerely returned affection, was an object scarce less appalling to his mind, than those which superstition suggested.

His limbs exhausted with fatigue, his mind harassed with anxiety, and with painful doubts and recollections, Butler dragged himself up the ascent from the valley to Saint Leonard's Crags, and presented himself at the door of Deans's habitation, with feelings much akin to the miserable reflections and fears of its inhabitants.

CHAPTER XII

Then she stretch'd out her lily hand,
  And for to do her best;
"Hae back thy faith and troth, Willie,
  God gie thy soul good rest!"
               Old Ballad.

"COME in," answered the low and sweet-toned voice he loved best to hear, as Butler tapped at the door of the cottage. He lifted the latch, and found himself under the roof of affliction. Jeanie was unable to trust herself with more than one glance towards her lover, whom she now met under circumstances so agonising to her feelings, and at the same time so humbling to her honest pride. It is well known, that much, both of what is good and bad in the Scottish national character, arises out of the intimacy of their family connections. "To be come of honest folk," that is, of people who have borne a fair and unstained reputation, is an advantage as highly prized among the lower Scotch, as the emphatic counterpart, "to be of a good family," is valued among their gentry. The worth and respectability of one member of a peasant's family is always accounted by themselves and others, not only a matter of honest pride, but a guarantee for the good conduct of the whole. On the contrary, such a melancholy stain as was now flung on one of the children of Deans, extended its disgrace to all connected with him, and Jeanie felt herself lowered at once, in her own eyes, and in those of her lover. It was in vain that she repressed this feeling, as far subordinate and too selfish to be mingled with her sorrow for her sister's calamity. Nature prevailed; and while she shed tears for her sister's distress and danger, there mingled with them bitter drops of grief for her own degradation.

As Butler entered, the old man was seated by the fire with his well-worn pocket Bible in his hands, the companion of the wanderings and dangers of his youth, and bequeathed to him on the scaffold by one of those, who, in the year 1686, sealed their enthusiastic principles with their blood. The sun sent its rays through a small window at the old man's back, and, "shining motty through the reek," to use the expression of a bard of that time and country, illumined the grey hairs of the old man, and the sacred page which he studied. His features, far from handsome, and rather harsh and severe, had yet, from their expression of habitual gravity, and contempt for earthly things, an expression of stoical dignity amidst their sternness. He boasted, in no small degree, the attributes which Southey ascribes to the ancient Scandinavians, whom he terms "firm to inflict, and stubborn to endure." The whole formed a picture, of which the lights might have been given by Rembrandt, but the outline would have required the force and vigour of Michael Angelo.

Deans lifted his eye as Butler entered, and instantly withdrew it, as from an object which gave him at once surprise and sudden pain. He had assumed such high ground with this carnal-witted scholar, as he had in his pride termed Butler, that to meet him of all men, under feelings of humiliation, aggravated his misfortune, and was a consummation like that of the dying chief in the old ballad—"Earl Percy sees my fall!"

Deans raised the Bible with his left hand, so as partly to screen his face, and putting back his right as far as he could, held it towards Butler in that position, at the same time turning his body from him, as if to prevent his seeing the working of his countenance. Butler clasped the extended hand which had supported his orphan infancy, wept over it, and in vain endeavoured to say more than the words—"God comfort you —God comfort you!"

"He will—He doth, my friend," said Deans, assuming firmness as he discovered the agitation of his guest; "He doth now, and He will yet more, in His own gude time. I have been ower proud of my sufferings in a gude cause, Reuben, and now I am to be tried with those whilk will turn my pride and glory into a reproach and a hissing. How muckle better I hae thought mysell than them that lay saft, fed sweet, and

drank deep, when I was in the moss-haggs and moors, wi'
precious Donald Cameron, and worthy Mr. Blackadder, called
Guess-again ; and how proud I was o' being made a spectacle
to men and angels, having stood on their pillory at the
Canongate afore I was fifteen years old, for the cause of a
National Covenant ! To think, Reuben, that I, wha hae been
sae honoured and exalted in my youth, nay, when I was
but a hafflins callant, and that hae borne testimony again'
the defections o' the times yearly, monthly, daily, hourly,
minutely, striving and testifying with uplifted hand and voice,
crying aloud, and sparing not, against all great national
snares, as the nation-wasting and church-sinking abomination
of union, toleration, and patronage, imposed by the last
woman of that unhappy race of Stuarts ; also against the
infringements and invasions of the just powers of eldership,
whereanent I uttered my paper, called, a 'Cry of an Howl in
the Desert,' printed at the Bow-head, and sold by all flying
stationers in town and country—and *now*——"

Here he paused. It may well be supposed that Butler,
though not absolutely coinciding in all the good old man's
ideas about church government, had too much consideration
and humanity to interrupt him, while he reckoned up with
conscious pride his sufferings, and the constancy of his
testimony. On the contrary, when he paused under the
influence of the bitter recollections of the moment, Butler
instantly threw in his mite of encouragement.

"You have been well known, my old and revered friend, a
true and tried follower of the Cross ; one who, as Saint
Jerome hath it, '*per infamiam et bonam famam grassari ad
immortalitatem*,' which may be freely rendered, 'who rusheth
on to immortal life, through bad report and good report.'
You have been one of those to whom the tender and fearful
souls cry during the midnight solitude,—'Watchman, what of
the night?—Watchman, what of the night?'—And, assuredly,
this heavy dispensation, as it comes not without Divine
permission, so it comes not without its special commission
and use."

"I do receive it as such," said poor Deans, returning the
grasp of Butler's hand ; "and, if I have not been taught to read
the Scripture in any other tongue but my native Scottish"
(even in his distress Butler's Latin quotation had not escaped
his notice), "I have, nevertheless, so learned them, that I
trust to bear even this crook in my lot with submission. But,

oh! Reuben Butler, the kirk, of whilk, though unworthy, I have yet been thought a polished shaft, and meet to be a pillar, holding, from my youth upward, the place of ruling elder—what will the lightsome and profane think of the guide that cannot keep his own family from stumbling? How will they take up their song and their reproach, when they see that the children of professors are liable to as foul backsliding as the offspring of Belial! But I will bear my cross with the comfort, that whatever showed like goodness in me or mine, was but like the light that shines frae creeping insects, on the brae-side, in a dark night—it kythes bright to the ee, because all is dark around it; but when the morn comes on the mountains, it is but a puir crawling kail-worm after a'. And sae it shows, wi' ony rag of human righteousness, or formal law-work, that we may pit round us to cover our shame."

As he pronounced these words, the door again opened, and Mr. Bartoline Saddletree entered, his three-pointed hat set far back on his head, with a silk handkerchief beneath it, to keep it in that cool position, his gold-headed cane in his hand, and his whole deportment that of a wealthy burgher, who might one day look to have a share in the magistracy, if not actually to hold the curule chair itself.

Rochefoucault, who has torn the veil from so many foul gangrenes of the human heart, says, we find something not altogether unpleasant to us in the misfortunes of our best friends. Mr. Saddletree would have been very angry had any one told him that he felt pleasure in the disaster of poor Effie Deans, and the disgrace of her family; and yet there is great question whether the gratification of playing the person of importance, inquiring, investigating, and laying down the law on the whole affair, did not offer, to say the least, full consolation for the pain which pure sympathy gave him on account of his wife's kinswoman. He had now got a piece of real judicial business by the end, instead of being obliged, as was his common case, to intrude his opinion where it was neither wished nor wanted; and felt as happy in the exchange as a boy when he gets his first new watch, which actually goes when wound up, and has real hands and a true dial-plate. But besides this subject for legal disquisition, Bartoline's brains were also overloaded with the affair of Porteous, his violent death, and all its probable consequences to the city and community. It was what the French call *l'embarras des richesses*, the confusion arising from too much mental wealth.

He walked in with a consciousness of double importance, full fraught with the superiority of one who possesses more information than the company into which he enters, and who feels a right to discharge his learning on them without mercy. "Good-morning, Mr. Deans,—good-morrow to you, Mr. Butler,—I was not aware that you were acquainted with Mr. Deans."

Butler made some slight answer; his reasons may be readily imagined for not making his connection with the family, which, in his eyes, had something of tender mystery, a frequent subject of conversation with indifferent persons, such as Saddletree.

The worthy burgher, in the plenitude of self-importance, now sate down upon a chair, wiped his brow, collected his breath, and made the first experiment of the resolved pith of his lungs, in a deep and dignified sigh, resembling a groan in sound and intonation—"Awfu' times these, neighbour Deans, awfu' times!"

"Sinfu', shamefu', heaven-daring times," answered Deans, in a lower and more subdued tone.

"For my part," continued Saddletree, swelling with importance, "what between the distress of my friends, and my poor auld country, ony wit that ever I had may be said to have abandoned me, sae that I sometimes think myself as ignorant as if I were *inter rusticos*. Here when I arise in the morning, wi' my mind just arranged touching what's to be done in puir Effie's misfortune, and hae gotten the haill statute at my finger-ends, the mob maun get up and string Jock Porteous to a dyester's beam, and ding a' thing out of my head again."

Deeply as he was distressed with his own domestic calamity, Deans could not help expressing some interest in the news. Saddletree immediately entered on details of the insurrection and its consequences, while Butler took the occasion to seek some private conversation with Jeanie Deans. She gave him the opportunity he sought, by leaving the room, as if in prosecution of some part of her morning labour. Butler followed her in a few minutes, leaving Deans so closely engaged by his busy visitor, that there was little chance of his observing their absence.

The scene of their interview was an outer apartment, where Jeanie was used to busy herself in arranging the productions of her dairy. When Butler found an opportunity of stealing after her into this place, he found her silent, dejected, and ready to burst into tears. Instead of the active industry with which she had been accustomed, even while in the act of speaking, to employ her hands in some useful branch of household business, she was seated listless in a corner, sinking apparently under the weight of her own thoughts. Yet the instant he entered, she dried her eyes, and, with the simplicity and openness of her character, immediately entered on conversation.

"I am glad you have come in, Mr. Butler," said she, "for —for—for I wished to tell ye, that all maun be ended between you and me—it's best for baith our sakes."

"Ended!" said Butler, in surprise; "and for what should it be ended?—I grant this is a heavy dispensation, but it lies neither at your door nor mine—it's an evil of God's sending, and it must be borne; but it cannot break plighted troth, Jeanie, while they that plighted their word wish to keep it."

"But, Reuben," said the young woman, looking at him affectionately, "I ken weel that ye think mair of me than yourself; and, Reuben, I can only in requital think mair of your weal than of my ain. Ye are a man of spotless name, bred to God's ministry, and a' men say that ye will some day rise high in the kirk, though poverty keep ye down e'en now. Poverty is a bad back-friend, Reuben, and that ye ken ower weel; but ill-fame is a waur ane, and that is a truth ye sall never learn through my means."

"What do you mean?" said Butler, eagerly and impatiently; "or how do you connect your sister's guilt, if guilt there be, which, I trust in God, may yet be disproved, with our engagement?—how can that affect you or me?"

"How can you ask me that, Mr. Butler? Will this stain, d'ye think, ever be forgotten, as lang as our heads are abune the grund? Will it not stick to us, and to our bairns, and to their very bairns' bairns? To hae been the child of an honest man, might hae been saying something for me and mine; but to be the sister of a——O my God!"—With this exclamation her resolution failed, and she burst into a passionate fit of tears.

The lover used every effort to induce her to compose herself, and at length succeeded; but she only resumed her composure to express herself with the same positiveness as before. "No, Reuben, I'll bring disgrace hame to nae man's hearth; my ain distresses I can bear, and I maun bear, but there is nae occasion for buckling them on other folk's shouthers. I will bear my load alone — the back is made for the burden."

A lover is by charter wayward and suspicious; and Jeanie's readiness to renounce their engagement, under pretence of zeal for his peace of mind and respectability of character, seemed to poor Butler to form a portentous combination with the commission of the stranger he had met with that morning. His voice faltered as he asked, "Whether nothing but a sense of her sister's present distress occasioned her to talk in that manner?"

"And what else can do sae?" she replied with simplicity. "Is it not ten long years since we spoke together in this way?"

"Ten years?" said Butler "It's a long time—sufficient perhaps for a woman to weary——"

"To weary of her auld gown," said Jeanie, "and to wish for a new ane, if she likes to be brave, but not long enough to weary of a friend—The eye may wish change, but the heart never."

"Never?" said Reuben,—"that's a bold promise."

"But not more bauld than true," said Jeanie, with the same quiet simplicity which attended her manner in joy and grief, in ordinary affairs, and in those which most interested her feelings.

Butler paused, and looking at her fixedly—"I am charged," he said, "with a message to you, Jeanie."

"Indeed! From whom? Or what can ony ane have to say to me?"

"It is from a stranger," said Butler, affecting to speak with an indifference which his voice belied—"A young man whom I met this morning in the Park."

"Mercy!" said Jeanie eagerly; "and what did he say?"

"That he did not see you at the hour he expected, but required you should meet him alone at Muschat's Cairn this night, so soon as the moon rises."

"Tell him," said Jeanie hastily, "I shall certainly come."

"May I ask" said Butler, his suspicions increasing at the ready alacrity of the answer, "who this man is to whom you are so willing to give the meeting at a place and hour so uncommon?"

"Folk maun do muckle they have little will to do, in this world," replied Jeanie.

"Granted," said her lover; "but what compels you to this? —who is this person? What I saw of him was not very favourable—who, or what is he?"

"I do not know!" replied Jeanie composedly.

"You do not know!" said Butler, stepping impatiently through the apartment—"You purpose to meet a young man whom you do not know, at such a time, and in a place so lonely—you say you are compelled to do this—and yet you say you do not know the person who exercises such an influence over you!—Jeanie, what am I to think of this?"

"Think only, Reuben, that I speak truth, as if I were to answer at the last day.—I do not ken this man—I do not even ken that I ever saw him; and yet I must give him the meeting he asks—there's life and death upon it."

"Will you not tell your father, or take him with you?" said Butler.

"I cannot," said Jeanie; "I have no permission."

"Will you let *me* go with you? I will wait in the Park till nightfall, and join you when you set out."

"It is impossible," said Jeanie; "there maunna be mortal creature within hearing of our conference."

"Have you considered well the nature of what you are going to do?—the time—the place—an unknown and suspicious character?—Why, if he had asked to see you in this house, your father sitting in the next room, and within call, at such an hour, you should have refused to see him."

"My weird maun be fulfilled, Mr. Butler; my life and my safety are in God's hands, but I'll not spare to risk either of them on the errand I am gaun to do."

"Then, Jeanie," said Butler, much displeased, "we must indeed break short off, and bid farewell. When there can be no confidence betwixt a man and his plighted wife on such a momentous topic, it is a sign that she has no longer the regard for him that makes their engagement safe and suitable."

Jeanie looked at him and sighed. "I thought," she said, "that I had brought myself to bear this parting—but—but— I did not ken that we were to part in unkindness. But I am a woman and you are a man—it may be different wi' you—if your mind is made easier by thinking sae hardly of me, I would not ask you to think otherwise."

"You are," said Butler, "what you have always been— wiser, better, and less selfish in your native feelings, than I can be, with all the helps philosophy can give to a Christian.

—But why—why will you persevere in an undertaking so
desperate? Why will you not let me be your assistant—your
protector, or at least your adviser?"

"Just because I cannot, and I dare not," answered Jeanie.
—"But hark, what's that? Surely my father is no weel?"

In fact, the voices in the next room became obstreperously
loud of a sudden, the cause of which vociferation it is necessary
to explain before we go farther.

When Jeanie and Butler retired, Mr. Saddletree entered
upon the business which chiefly interested the family. In the
commencement of their conversation he found old Deans, who,
in his usual state of mind, was no granter of propositions, so
much subdued by a deep sense of his daughter's danger and
disgrace, that he heard without replying to, or perhaps without
understanding, one or two learned disquisitions on the nature
of the crime imputed to her charge, and on the steps which
ought to be taken in consequence. His only answer at each
pause was, "I am no misdoubting that you wuss us weel—
your wife's our far-awa cousin."

Encouraged by these symptoms of acquiescence, Saddletree,
who, as an amateur of the law, had a supreme deference for
all constituted authorities, again recurred to his other topic of
interest, the murder, namely, of Porteous, and pronounced a
severe censure on the parties concerned.

"These are kittle times—kittle times, Mr. Deans, when the
people take the power of life and death out of the hands of
the rightful magistrate into their ain rough grip. I am of
opinion, and so I believe will Mr. Crossmyloof and the Privy
Council, that this rising in effeir of war, to take away the life
of a reprieved man, will prove little better than perduellion."

"If I hadna that on my mind whilk is ill to bear, Mr.
Saddletree," said Deans, "I wad make bold to dispute that
point wi' you."

"How could you dispute what's plain law, man?" said
Saddletree, somewhat contemptuously; "there's no a callant
that e'er carried a pock wi' a process in't, but will tell you that
perduellion is the warst and maist virulent kind of treason,
being an open convocating of the king's lieges against his
authority (mair especially in arms, and by touk of drum, to
baith whilk accessories my een and lugs bore witness), and
muckle warse than lese-majesty, or the concealment of a
treasonable purpose—It winna bear a dispute, neighbour."

"But it will, though," retorted Douce Davie Deans; "I tell

ye it will bear a dispute—I never like your cauld, legal, formal doctrines, neighbour Saddletree. I had unco little by the Parliament House, since the awfu' downfall of the hopes of honest folk that followed the Revolution."

" But what wad ye hae had, Mr. Deans ? " said Saddletree impatiently ; " didna ye get baith liberty and conscience made fast, and settled by tailzie on you and your heirs for ever ? "

" Mr. Saddletree," retorted Deans, " I ken ye are one of those that are wise after the manner of this world, and that ye haud your part, and cast in your portion, wi' the lang-heads and lang-gowns, and keep with the smart witty-pated lawyers of this our land—Weary on the dark and dolefu' cast that they hae gien this unhappy kingdom, when their black hands of defection were clasped in the red hands of our sworn murtherers: when those who had numbered the towers of our Zion, and marked the bulwarks of our Reformation, saw their hope turn into a snare, and their rejoicing into weeping."

" I canna understand this, neighbour," answered Saddletree. " I am an honest Presbyterian of the Kirk of Scotland, and stand by her and the General Assembly, and the due administration of justice by the fifteen Lords o' Session and the five Lords o' Justiciary."

" Out upon ye, Mr. Saddletree ! " exclaimed David, who, in an opportunity of giving his testimony on the offences and backslidings of the land, forgot for a moment his own domestic calamity—" out upon your General Assembly, and the back of my hand to your Court o' Session !—What is the tane but a waefu' bunch o' cauldrife professors and ministers, that sate bien and warm when the persecuted remnant were warstling wi' hunger, and cauld, and fear of death, and danger of fire and sword, upon wet brae-sides, peat-haggs, and flow-mosses, and that now creep out of their holes, like blue-bottle flees in a blink of sunshine, to take the pu'pits and places of better folk—of them that witnessed, and testified, and fought, and endured pit, prison-house, and transportation beyond seas ?—A bonny bike there's o' them !—And for your Court o' Session——"

" Ye may say what ye will o' the General Assembly," said Saddletree, interrupting him, " and let them clear them that kens them ; but as for the Lords o' Session, forby that they are my next-door neighbours, I would have ye ken, for your ain regulation, that to raise scandal anent them, whilk is termed, to *murmur* again them, is a crime *sui generis—sui generis*, Mr. Deans—ken ye what that amounts to ? "

" I ken little o' the language of Antichrist," said Deans ;
"and I care less than little what carnal courts may call
the speeches of honest men. And as to murmur again
them, it's what a' the folk that loses their pleas, and nine-
tenths o' them that win them, will be gay sure to be guilty
in. Sae I wad hae ye ken that I haud a' your gleg-tongued
advocates, that sell their knowledge for pieces of silver, and
your worldly-wise judges, that will gie three days of hearing in
presence to a debate about the peeling of an ingan, and no ae
half-hour to the gospel testimony, as legalists and formalists,
countenancing, by sentences, and quirks, and cunning terms
of law, the late begun courses of national defections—union,
toleration, patronages, and Yerastian prelatic oaths. As for
the soul and body-killing Court o' Justiciary——"

The habit of considering his life as dedicated to bear
testimony in behalf of what he deemed the suffering and
deserted cause of true religion, had swept honest David along
with it thus far ; but with the mention of the criminal court,
the recollection of the disastrous condition of his daughter
rushed at once on his mind ; he stopped short in the midst of
his triumphant declamation, pressed his hands against his
forehead, and remained silent.

Saddletree was somewhat moved, but apparently not so
much so as to induce him to relinquish the privilege of prosing
in his turn, afforded him by David's sudden silence. " Nae
doubt, neighbour," he said, " it's a sair thing to hae to do
wi' courts of law, unless it be to improve ane's knowledge and
practique, by waiting on as a hearer ; and touching this unhappy affair of Effie—ye'll hae seen the dittay, doubtless ? "
He dragged out of his pocket a bundle of papers, and began
to turn them over. " This is no it—this is the information of
Mungo Marsport, of that ilk, against Captain Lackland, for
coming on his lands of Marsport with hawks, hounds, lying-
dogs, nets, guns, cross-bows, hagbuts of found, or other
engines more or less for destruction of game, sic as red-deer,
fallow-deer, cappercailzies, grey-fowl, moor fowl, paitricks,
herons, and sic like; he the said defender not being ane
qualified person, in terms of the statute sixteen hundred and
twenty-ane; that is, not having ane plough-gate of land.
Now, the defences proponed say, that *non constat* at this
present what is a plough-gate of land, whilk uncertainty is
sufficient to elide the conclusions of the libel. But then the
answers to the defences (they are signed by Mr. Crossmyloof,

but Mr. Younglad drew them), they propone, that it signifies naething, *in hoc statu*, what or how muckle a plough-gate of land may be, in respect the defender has nae lands whatsoe'er, less or mair. ' Sae grant a plough-gate '" (here Saddletree read from the paper in his hand) " ' to be less than the nineteenth part of a guse's grass '—(I trow Mr. Crossmyloof put in that—I ken his style),—' of a guse's grass, what the better will the defender be, seeing he hasna a divot-cast of land in Scotland ?—*Advocatus* for Lackland duplies, that *nihil interest de possessione*, the pursuer must put his case under the statute '—(now, this is worth your notice, neighbour),—' and must show, *formaliter et specialiter*, as well as *generaliter*, what is the qualification that defender Lackland does *not* possess— let him tell me what a plough-gate of land is, and I'll tell him if I have one or no. Surely the pursuer is bound to understand his own libel, and his own statute that he founds upon. *Titius* pursues *Mævius* for recovery of ane *black* horse lent to Mævius—surely he shall have judgment ; but if Titius pursue Mævius for ane *scarlet* or *crimson* horse, doubtless he shall be bound to show that there is sic ane animal *in rerum natura*. No man can be bound to plead nonsense—that is to say, to a charge which cannot be explained or understood '— (he's wrang there—the better the pleadings the fewer understand them),—' and so the reference unto this undefined and unintelligible measure of land is, as if a penalty was inflicted by statute for any man who suld hunt or hawk, or use lying-dogs, and wearing a sky-blue pair of breeches, without having '
——But I am wearying you, Mr. Deans, we'll pass to your ain business,—though this case of Marsport against Lackland has made an unco din in the Outer House. Weel, here's the dittay against puir Effie : ' Whereas it is humbly meant and shown to us,' &c. (they are words of mere style), ' that where, by the laws of this and every other well-regulated realm, the murder of any one, more especially of an infant child, is a crime of ane high nature, and severely punishable : And whereas, without prejudice to the foresaid generality, it was, by ane act made in the second session of the First Parliament of our Most High and Dread Sovereigns William and Mary, especially enacted, that ane woman who shall have concealed her condition, and shall not be able to show that she hath called for help at the birth, in case that the child shall be found dead or amissing, shall be deemed and held guilty of the murder thereof ; and the said facts of concealment and pregnancy

being found proven or confessed, shall sustain the pains of law accordingly; yet, nevertheless, you Effie, or Euphemia Deans——' "

"Read no farther!" said Deans, raising his head up; "I would rather ye thrust a sword into my heart than read a word farther!"

" Weel, neighbour," said Saddletree, " I thought it wad hae comforted ye to ken the best and the warst o't. But the question is, what's to be dune?"

"Nothing," answered Deans firmly, "but to abide the dispensation that the Lord sees meet to send us. Oh, if it had been His will to take the grey head to rest before this awful visitation on my house and name! But His will be done. I can say that yet, though I can say little mair."

" But, neighbour," said Saddletree, " ye'll retain advocates for the puir lassie? it's a thing maun needs be thought of."

"If there was ae man of them," answered Deans, " that held fast his integrity—but I ken them weel, they are a' carnal, crafty, and warld-hunting self-seekers, Yerastians, and Arminians, every ane o' them."

" Hout tout, neighbour, ye maunna take the warld at its word," said Saddletree ; " the very deil is no sae ill as he's ca'd; and I ken mair than ae advocate that may be said to hae some integrity as weel as their neighbours; that is, after a sort o' fashion o' their ain."

" It is indeed but a fashion of integrity that ye will find amang them," replied David Deans, " and a fashion of wisdom, and fashion of carnal learning—gazing, glancing-glasses they are, fit only to fling the glaiks in folk's een, wi' their pawky policy, and earthly ingine, their flights and refinements, and periods of eloquence, frae heathen emperors and popish canons. They canna, in that daft trash ye were reading to me, sae muckle as ca' men that are sae ill-starred as to be amang their hands, by ony name o' the dispensation o' grace, but maun new baptize them by the names of the accursed Titus, wha was made the instrument of burning the holy Temple, and other sic like heathens."

" It's Tishius," interrupted Saddletree, " and no Titus. Mr. Crossmyloof cares as little about Titus or the Latin learning as ye do.—But it's a case of necessity—she maun hae counsel. Now, I could speak to Mr. Crossmyloof—he's weel kend for a round-spun Presbyterian, and a ruling elder to boot."

"He's a rank Yerastian," replied Deans; "one of the

public and polititious warldly-wise men that stude up to prevent ane general owning of the cause in the day of power."

"What say ye to the auld Laird of Cuffabout?" said Saddletree; "he whiles thumps the dust out of a case gay and weel."

"He? the fause loon!" answered Deans—"he was in his bandaliers to hae joined the ungracious Highlanders in 1715, an they had ever had the luck to cross the Firth."

"Weel, Arniston? there's a clever chield for ye!" said Bartoline triumphantly.

"Ay, to bring popish medals in till their very library from that schismatic woman in the north, the Duchess of Gordon."

"Weel, weel, but somebody ye maun hae—What think ye o' Kittlepunt?"

"He's an Arminian."

"Woodsetter?"

"He's, I doubt, a Cocceian."

"Auld Whilliewhaw?"

"He's onything ye like."

"Young Næmmo?"

"He's naething at a'."

"Ye're ill to please, neighbour," said Saddletree; "I hae run ower the pick o' them for you, ye maun e'en choose for yoursell; but bethink ye that in the multitude of counsellors there's safety.—What say ye to try young Mackenyie? he has a' his uncle's Practiques at the tongue's end."

"What, sir, wad ye speak to me," exclaimed the sturdy Presbyterian in excessive wrath, "about a man that has the blood of the saints at his fingers' ends? Didna his eme die and gang to his place wi' the name of the Bluidy Mackenyie? and winna he be kend by that name sae lang as there's a Scots tongue to speak the word? If the life of the dear bairn that's under a suffering dispensation, and Jeanie's, and my ain, and a' mankind's, depended on my asking sic a slave o' Satan to speak a word for me or them, they should a' gae down the water thegither for Davie Deans!"

It was the exalted tone in which he spoke this last sentence that broke up the conversation between Butler and Jeanie, and brought them both "ben the house," to use the language of the country. Here they found the poor old man half frantic between grief, and zealous ire against Saddletree's proposed measures, his cheek inflamed, his hand clenched, and his voice raised, while the tear in his eye, and the occasional quiver of

his accents, showed that his utmost efforts were inadequate to
shaking off the consciousness of his misery. Butler, apprehensive of the consequences of his agitation to an aged and
feeble frame, ventured to utter to him a recommendation to
patience.

"I *am* patient," returned the old man sternly,—"more
patient than any one who is alive to the woful backslidings of
a miserable time can be patient; and in so much, that I need
neither sectarians, nor sons, nor grandsons of sectarians, to
instruct my grey hairs how to bear my cross."

"But, sir," continued Butler, taking no offence at the slur
cast on his grandfather's faith, "we must use human means.
When you call in a physician, you would not, I suppose,
question him on the nature of his religious principles?"

"Wad I *no*?" answered David—"But I wad, though; and
if he didna satisfy me that he had a right sense of the right-
hand and left-hand defections of the day, not a goutte of his
physic should gang through my father's son."

It is a dangerous thing to trust to an illustration. Butler
had done so and miscarried; but, like a gallant soldier when
his musket misses fire, he stood his ground, and charged with
the bayonet.—"This is too rigid an interpretation of your
duty, sir. The sun shines, and the rain descends, on the just
and unjust, and they are placed together in life in circumstances which frequently render intercourse between them
indispensable, perhaps that the evil may have an opportunity
of being converted by the good, and perhaps, also, that the
righteous might, among other trials, be subjected to that of
occasional converse with the profane."

"Ye're a silly callant, Reuben," answered Deans, "with
your bits of argument. Can a man touch pitch and not be
defiled? Or what think ye of the brave and worthy champions
of the Covenant, that wadna sae muckle as hear a minister
speak, be his gifts and graces as they would, that hadna
witnessed against the enormities of the day? Nae lawyer
shall ever speak for me and mine that hasna concurred in the
testimony of the scattered, yet lovely remnant, which abode
in the cliffs of the rocks."

So saying, and as if fatigued, both with the arguments and
presence of his guests, the old man arose, and seeming to bid
them adieu with a motion of his head and hand, went to shut
himself up in his sleeping apartment.

"It's thrawing his daughter's life awa," said Saddletree to

Butler, "to hear him speak in that daft gate. Where will he ever get a Cameronian advocate? Or wha ever heard of a lawyer's suffering either for ae religion or another? The lassie's life is clean flung awa."

During the latter part of this debate, Dumbiedikes had arrived at the door, dismounted, hung the pony's bridle on the usual hook, and sunk down on his ordinary settle. His eyes, with more than their usual animation, followed first one speaker, then another, till he caught the melancholy sense of the whole from Saddletree's last words. He rose from his seat, stumped slowly across the room, and, coming close up to Saddletree's ear, said, in a tremulous, anxious voice, "Will—will siller do naething for them, Mr. Saddletree?"

"Umph!" said Saddletree, looking grave,—"siller will certainly do it in the Parliament House, if onything *can* do it; but whare's the siller to come frae? Mr. Deans, ye see, will do naething; and though Mrs. Saddletree's their far-awa friend, and right good weel-wisher, and is weel disposed to assist, yet she wadna like to stand to be bound *singuli in solidum* to such an expensive wark. An ilka friend wad bear a share o' the burden, something might be dune—ilka ane to be liable for their ain input—I wadna like to see the case fa' through without being pled—it wadna be creditable, for a' that daft whig body says."

"I'll—I will—yes" (assuming fortitude), "I will be answerable," said Dumbiedikes, "for a score of punds sterling."—And he was silent, staring in astonishment at finding himself capable of such unwonted resolution and excessive generosity.

"God Almighty bless ye, Laird!" said Jeanie, in a transport of gratitude.

"Ye may ca' the twenty punds thretty," said Dumbiedikes, looking bashfully away from her, and towards Saddletree.

"That will do bravely," said Saddletree, rubbing his hands; "and ye sall hae a' my skill and knowledge to gar the siller gang far—I'll tape it out weel—I ken how to gar the birkies tak short fees, and be glad o' them too—it's only garring them trow ye hae twa or three cases of importance coming on, and they'll work cheap to get custom. Let me alane for whilly-whaing an advocate:—it's nae sin to get as muckle frae them for our siller as we can—after a', it's but the wind o' their mouth—it costs them naething; whereas, in my wretched occupation of a saddler, horse-milliner, and harness-maker, we are out unconscionable sums just for barkened hides and leather."

" Can I be of no use ? " said Butler. " My means, alas !
are only worth the black coat I wear ; but I am young—I owe
much to the family—Can I do nothing ? "

" Ye can help to collect evidence, sir," said Saddletree ; " if
we could but find ony ane to say she had gien the least hint o'
her condition, she wad be brought aff wi' a wat finger—Mr.
Crossmyloof tell'd me sae. The crown, says he, canna be
craved to prove a positive—was't a positive or a negative they
couldna be ca'd to prove ?—it was the tane or the tither o'
them, I am sure, and it maksna muckle matter whilk. Wherefore, says he, the libel maun be redargued by the panel proving
her defences. And it canna be done otherwise."

" But the fact, sir," argued Butler, " the fact that this poor
girl has borne a child ; surely the crown lawyers must prove
that ? " said Butler.

Saddletree paused a moment, while the visage of Dumbiedikes, which traversed, as if it had been placed on a pivot,
from the one spokesman to the other, assumed a more blithe
expression.

" Ye—ye—ye—es," said Saddletree, after some grave hesitation ; " unquestionably that is a thing to be proved, as the
court will more fully declare by an interlocutor of relevancy in
common form ; but I fancy that job's done already, for she
has confessed her guilt."

" Confessed the murder ? " exclaimed Jeanie, with a scream
that made them all start.

" No, I dinna say that," replied Bartoline. " But she confessed bearing the babe."

" And what became of it, then ? " said Jeanie ; " for not a
word could I get from her but bitter sighs and tears."

" She says it was taken away from her by the woman in
whose house it was born, and who assisted her at the time."

" And who was that woman ? " said Butler. " Surely by her
means the truth might be discovered.—Who was she ? I will
fly to her directly."

" I wish," said Dumbiedikes, " I were as young and as
supple as you, and had the gift of the gab as weel."

" Who is she ? " again reiterated Butler impatiently.—" Who
could that woman be ? "

" Ay, wha kens that but hersell," said Saddletree ; " she
deponed further, and declined to answer that interrogatory."

" Then to herself will I instantly go," said Butler ; " farewell, Jeanie ; " then coming close up to her.—" Take no *rash*

F 134

steps till you hear from me. Farewell!" and he immediately left the cottage.

" I wad gang too," said the landed proprietor, in an anxious, jealous, and repining tone, " but my powny winna for the life o' me gang ony other road than just frae Dumbiedikes to this house-end, and sae straight back again."

" Ye'll do better for them," said Saddletree, as they left the house together, " by sending me the thretty punds."

" Thretty punds ? " hesitated Dumbiedikes, who was now out of the reach of those eyes which had inflamed his generosity ; " I only said *twenty* pund."

" Ay ; but," said Saddletree, " that was under protestation to add and eik ; and so ye craved leave to amend your libel, and made it thretty."

" Did I ? I dinna mind that I did," answered Dumbiedikes. " But whatever I said I'll stand to." Then bestriding his steed with some difficulty, he added, " Dinna ye think poor Jeanie's een wi' the tears in them glanced like lamour beads, Mr. Saddletree ? "

" I kenna muckel about women's een, Laird," replied the insensible Bartoline ; " and I care just as little. I wuss I were as weel free o' their tongues ; though few wives," he added, recollecting the necessity of keeping up his character for domestic rule, " are under better command than mine, Laird. I allow neither perduellion nor lese-majesty against my sovereign authority."

The Laird saw nothing so important in this observation as to call for a rejoinder, and when they had exchanged a mute salutation, they parted in peace upon their different errands.

CHAPTER XIII

I'll warrant that fellow from drowning, were the ship no stronger
than a nut-shell.   *The Tempest.*

BUTLER felt neither fatigue nor want of refreshment, although from the mode in which he had spent the night, he might well have been overcome with either. But in the earnestness with which he hastened to the assistance of the sister of Jeanie Deans, he forgot both.

In his first progress he walked with so rapid a pace as almost approached to running, when he was surprised to hear behind him a call upon his name, contending with an asthmatic cough, and half-drowned amid the resounding trot of an Highland pony. He looked behind, and saw the Laird of Dumbiedikes making after him with what speed he might, for it happened fortunately for the Laird's purpose of conversing with Butler, that his own road homeward was for about two hundred yards the same with that which led by the nearest way to the city. Butler stopped when he heard himself thus summoned, internally wishing no good to the panting equestrian who thus retarded his journey.

"Uh! uh! uh!" ejaculated Dumbiedikes, as he checked the hobbling pace of the pony by our friend Butler. "Uh! uh! it's a hard-set willyard beast this o' mine." He had in fact just overtaken the object of his chase at the very point beyond which it would have been absolutely impossible for him to have continued the pursuit, since there Butler's road parted from that leading to Dumbiedikes, and no means of influence or compulsion which the rider could possibly have used towards his Bucephalus could have induced the Celtic obstinacy of Rory Bean (such was the pony's name) to have diverged a yard from the path that conducted him to his own paddock.

Even when he had recovered from the shortness of breath occasioned by a trot much more rapid than Rory or he were accustomed to, the high purpose of Dumbiedikes seemed to stick as it were in his throat, and impede his utterance, so that Butler stood for nearly three minutes ere he could utter a syllable; and when he did find voice, it was only to say after one or two efforts, "Uh! uh! uhm! I say, Mr.—Mr. Butler, it's a braw day for the ha'rst."

"Fine day, indeed," said Butler. "I wish you good morning, sir."

"Stay—stay a bit," rejoined Dumbiedikes; "that was no what I had gotten to say."

"Then, pray be quick, and let me have your commands," rejoined Butler; "I crave your pardon but I am in haste, and *Tempus nemini*—you know the proverb."

Dumbiedikes did not know the proverb, nor did he even take the trouble to endeavour to look as if he did, as others in his place might have done. He was concentrating all his intellects for one grand proposition, and could not afford any detachment to defend outposts. "I say, Mr. Butler," said he, "ken ye if Mr. Saddletree's a great lawyer?"

"I have no person's word for it but his own," answered Butler dryly; "but undoubtedly he best understands his own qualities."

"Umph!" replied the taciturn Dumbiedikes, in a tone which seemed to say, "Mr. Butler, I take your meaning." "In that case," he pursued, "I'll employ my ain man o' business, Nichil Novit (auld Nichil's son, and amaist as gleg as his father), to agent Effie's plea."

And having thus displayed more sagacity than Butler expected from him, he courteously touched his gold-laced cocked hat, and by a punch on the ribs, conveyed to Rory Bean, it was his rider's pleasure that he should forthwith proceed homewards; a hint which the quadruped obeyed with that degree of alacrity with which men and animals interpret and obey suggestions which entirely correspond with their own inclinations.

Butler resumed his pace, not without a momentary revival of that jealousy, which the honest Laird's attention to the family of Deans had at different times excited in his bosom. But he was too generous long to nurse any feeling which was allied to selfishness. "He is," said Butler to himself, "rich in what I want; why should I feel vexed that he has the heart to dedicate some of his pelf to render them services, which I can only form the empty wish of executing? In God's name, let us each do what we can. May she be but happy!—saved from the misery and disgrace that seems impending—Let me but find the means of preventing the fearful experiment of this evening, and farewell to other thoughts, though my heart-strings break in parting with them!"

He redoubled his pace, and soon stood before the door of the Tolbooth, or rather before the entrance where the door had formerly been placed. His interview with the mysterious stranger, the message to Jeanie, his agitating conversation with her on the subject of breaking off their mutual engagements, and the interesting scene with old Deans, had so entirely occupied his mind as to drown even recollection of the tragical event which he had witnessed the preceding evening. His attention was not recalled to it by the groups who stood scattered on the street in conversation, which they hushed when strangers approached, or by the bustling search of the agents of the city police, supported by small parties of the military, or by the appearance of the Guard-House, before which were treble sentinels, or, finally, by the subdued and intimidated looks of the lower orders of society, who, conscious that they were liable to suspicion, if they were not guilty of accession to a riot likely to be strictly inquired into, glided about with an humble and dismayed aspect, like men whose spirits being exhausted in the revel and the dangers of a desperate debauch over night, or nerve-shaken, timorous, and unenterprising on the succeeding day.

None of these symptoms of alarm and trepidation struck Butler, whose mind was occupied with a different, and to him still more interesting subject, until he stood before the entrance to the prison, and saw it defended by a double file of grenadiers, instead of bolts and bars. Their "Stand, stand!" the blackened appearance of the doorless gateway, and the winding staircase and apartments of the Tolbooth, now open to the public eye, recalled the whole proceedings of the eventful night. Upon his requesting to speak with Effie Deans, the same tall, thin, silver-haired turnkey, whom he had seen on the preceding evening, made his appearance.

"I think," he replied to Butler's request of admission, with true Scottish indirectness, "ye will be the same lad that was for in to see her yestreen?"

Butler admitted he was the same person.

"And I am thinking," pursued the turnkey, "that ye speered at me when we locked up, and if we locked up earlier on account of Porteous?"

"Very likely I might make some such observation," said Butler; "but the question now is, can I see Effie Deans?"

"I dinna ken—gang in by, and up the turnpike stair, and turn till the ward on the left hand."

The old man followed close behind him, with his keys in his hand, not forgetting even that huge one which had once opened and shut the outward gate of his dominions, though at present it was but an idle and useless burden. No sooner had Butler entered the room to which he was directed, than the experienced hand of the warder selected the proper key, and locked it on the outside. At first Butler conceived this manœuvre was only an effect of the man's habitual and official caution and jealousy. But when he heard the hoarse command, "Turn out the guard!" and immediately afterwards heard the clash of a sentinel's arms, as he was posted at the door of his apartment, he again called out to the turnkey, "My good friend, I have business of some consequence with Effie Deans, and I beg to see her as soon as possible." No answer was returned. " If it be against your rules to admit me," repeated Butler, in a still louder tone, " to see the prisoner, I beg you will tell me so, and let me go about my business.—*Fugit irrevocabile tempus !* " muttered he to himself.

" If ye had business to do, ye suld hae dune it before ye cam here," replied the man of keys from the outside ; " ye'll find it's easier wunnin in than wunnin out here—there's sma' likelihood o' another Porteous-mob coming to rabble us again —the law will haud her ain now, neighbour, and that ye'll find to your cost."

" What do you mean by that, sir ? " retorted Butler. " You must mistake me for some other person.   My name is Reuben Butler, preacher of the gospel."

" I ken that weel eneugh," said the turnkey.

' Well, then, if you know me, I have a right to know from you in return, what warrant you have for detaining me ; that, I know, is the right of every British subject."

" Warrant? " said the jailor,—" the warrant's awa to Lib- berton wi' twa sheriff officers seeking ye. If ye had staid at hame, as honest men should do, ye wad hae seen the warrant; but if ye come to be incarcerated of your ain accord, wha can help it, my jo? "

" So I cannot see Effie Deans, then," said Butler; " and you are determined not to let me out? "

" Troth will I no, neighbour," answered the old man doggedly; " as for Effie Deans, ye'll hae eneugh ado to mind your ain business, and let her mind hers; and for letting you out, that maun be as the magistrate will determine.   And fare ye weel for a bit, for I maun see Deacon Sawyers put on ane or twa o' the doors that your quiet folk broke down yesternight, Mr. Butler."

There was something in this exquisitely provoking, but there was also something darkly alarming.   To be imprisoned, even on a false accusation, has something in it disagreeable and menacing even to men of more constitutional courage than Butler had to boast ; for although he had much of that resolution which arises from a sense of duty and an honour- able desire to discharge it, yet, as his imagination was lively, and his frame of body delicate, he was far from possessing that cool insensibility to danger which is the happy portion of men, stronger of health, more firm nerves, and less acute sensibility.   An indistinct idea of peril, which he could neither understand nor ward off, seemed to float before his eyes. He tried to think over the events of the preceding night, in hopes of discovering some means of explaining or vindicating his conduct for appearing among the mob, since it immediately occurred to him that his detention must be founded on that circumstance. And it was with anxiety that he found he could not recollect to have been under the observation of any disinterested witness in the attempts that he made from time to time to expostulate with the rioters, and to prevail on them to release him. The distress of Deans's family, the dangerous rendezvous which Jeanie had formed, and which he could not now hope to interrupt, had also their share in his unpleasant reflections. Yet impatient as he was to receive an *éclaircissement* upon the cause of his confinement, and if possible to obtain his liberty, he was affected with a trepidation which seemed no good omen, when, after remaining an hour in this solitary apartment, he received a summons to attend the sitting magistrate. He was conducted from prison strongly guarded by a party of soldiers, with a parade of precaution, that, however ill-timed and unnecessary, is generally displayed *after* an event, which such precaution, if used in time, might have prevented.

He was introduced into the Council Chamber, as the place is called where the magistrates hold their sittings, and which was then at a little distance from the prison. One or two of the senators of the city were present, and seemed about to engage in the examination of an individual who was brought forward to the foot of the long green-covered table round which the council usually assembled. " Is that the preacher ? " said one of the magistrates, as the city officer in attendance introduced Butler. The man answered in the affirmative. " Let him sit down there for an instant ; we will finish this man's business very briefly."

' Shall we remove Mr. Butler ? " queried the assistant.

" It is not necessary—Let him remain where he is."

Butler accordingly sate down on a bench at the bottom of the apartment, attended by one of his keepers.

It was a large room, partially and imperfectly lighted ; but by chance, or the skill of the architect, who might happen to remember the advantage which might occasionally be derived from such an arrangement, one window was so placed as to throw a strong light at the foot of the table at which prisoners were usually posted for examination, while the upper end, where the examinants sate, was thrown into shadow. Butler's eyes were instantly fixed on the person whose examination was at present proceeding, in the idea that he might recognise some one of the conspirators of the former night. But though the features of this man were sufficiently marked and striking, he could not recollect that he had ever seen them before.

The complexion of this person was dark, and his age somewhat advanced. He wore his own hair, combed smooth down, and cut very short. It was jet black, slightly curled by nature, and already mottled with grey. The man's face expressed rather knavery than vice, and a disposition to sharpness, cunning and roguery, more than the traces of stormy and indulged passions. His sharp, quick black eyes, acute features, ready sardonic smile, promptitude, and effrontery, gave him altogether what is called among the vulgar a *knowing* look, which generally implies a tendency to knavery. At a fair or market, you could not for a moment have doubted that he was a horse-jockey, intimate with all the tricks of his trade; yet had you met him on a moor, you would not have apprehended any violence from him. His dress was also that of a horse-dealer — a close-buttoned jockey-coat, or wrap-rascal, as it was then termed, with huge metal buttons, coarse blue upper stockings, called boot hose, because supplying the place of boots, and a slouched hat. He only wanted a loaded whip under his arm and a spur upon one heel, to complete the dress of the character he seemed to represent.

"Your name is James Ratcliffe?" said the magistrate.

"Ay—always wi' your honour's leave."

"That is to say, you could find me another name if I did not like that one?"

"Twenty to pick and choose upon, always with your honour's leave," resumed the respondent.

"But James Ratcliffe is your present name?—what is your trade?"

"I canna just say, distinctly, that I have what ye wad ca' preceesely a trade."

"But," repeated the magistrate, "what are your means of living—your occupation?"

"Hout tout—your honour, wi' your leave, kens that as weel as I do," replied the examined.

"No matter, I want to hear you describe it," said the examinant.

"Me describe?—and to your honour?—far be it from Jemmie Ratcliffe," responded the prisoner.

"Come, sir, no trifling—I insist on an answer."

"Weel, sir," replied the declarant, "I maun make a clean breast, for ye see, wi' your leave, I am looking for favour—Describe my occupation, quo ye?—troth it will be ill to do that, in a feasible way, in a place like this—but what is't again that the aught command says?"

"Thou shalt not steal," answered the magistrate.

"Are you sure o' that?" replied the accused.—"Troth, then, my occupation, and that command, are sair at odds, for I read it, thou *shalt* steal; and that makes an unco difference, though there's but a wee bit word left out."

"To cut the matter short, Ratcliffe, you have been a most notorious thief," said the examinant.

I believe Highlands and Lowlands ken that, sir, forby England and Holland," replied Ratcliffe, with the greatest composure and effrontery.

"And what d'ye think the end of your calling will be?" said the magistrate.

"I could have gien a braw guess yesterday—but I dinna ken sae weel the day," answered the prisoner.

"And what would you have said would have been your end, had you been asked the question yesterday?"

"Just the gallows," replied Ratcliffe, with the same composure.

"You are a daring rascal, sir," said the magistrate; "and how dare you hope times are mended with you to-day?"

"Dear, your honour," answered Ratcliffe, "there's muckle difference between lying in prison under sentence of death, and staying there of ane's ain proper accord, when it would have cost a man naething to get up and rin awa—what was to hinder me from stepping out quietly, when the rabble walked awa wi' Jock Porteous yestreen?—and does your honour really think I staid on purpose to be hanged?"

"I do not know what you may have proposed to yourself; but I know," said the magistrate, "what the law proposes for you, and that is to hang you next Wednesday eight days."

"Na, na, your honour," said Ratcliffe firmly, "craving your honour's pardon, I'll ne'er believe that till I see it. I have kend the Law this mony a year, and mony a thrawart job I hae had wi' her first and last; but the auld jaud is no sae ill as that comes to—I aye fand her bark waur than her bite."

*F 154

"And if you do not expect the gallows, to which you are condemned (for the fourth time to my knowledge), may I beg the favour to know," said the magistrate, "what it is that you *do* expect, in consideration of your not having taken your flight with the rest of the jail-birds, which I will admit was a line of conduct little to have been expected?"

"I would never have thought for a moment of staying in that auld gousty toom house," answered Ratcliffe, "but that use and wont had just gien me a fancy to the place, and I'm just expecting a bit post in't."

"A post?" exclaimed the magistrate; "a whipping-post, I suppose, you mean?"

"Na, na, sir, I had nae thoughts o' a whuppin-post. After having been four times doomed to hang by the neck till I was dead, I think I am far beyond being whuppit."

"Then, in Heaven's name, what *did* you expect?"

"Just the post of under-turnkey, for I understand there's a vacancy," said the prisoner; "I wadna think of asking the lockman's [1] place ower his head; it wadna suit me sae weel as ither folk, for I never could put a beast out o' the way, much less deal wi' a man."

"That's something in your favour," said the magistrate, making exactly the inference to which Ratcliffe was desirous to lead him, though he mantled his art with an affectation of oddity. "But," continued the magistrate, "how do you think you can be trusted with a charge in the prison, when you have broken at your own hand half the jails in Scotland?"

"Wi' your honour's leave," said Ratcliffe, "if I kend sae weel how to wun out mysell, it's like I wad be a' the better a hand to keep other folk in. I think they wad ken their business weel that held me in when I wanted to be out, or wan out when I wanted to haud them in."

The remark seemed to strike the magistrate, but he made no farther immediate observation, only desired Ratcliffe to be removed.

When this daring, and yet sly freebooter was out of hearing, the magistrate asked the city-clerk, "what he thought of the fellow's assurance?"

"It's no for me to say, sir," replied the clerk; "but if James Ratcliffe be inclined to turn to good, there is not a man e'er came within the ports of the burgh could be of

---

[1] Note V.—Hangman, or Lockman.

sae muckle use to the Good Town in the thief and lock-up line of business. I'll speak to Mr. Sharpitlaw about him."

Upon Ratcliffe's retreat, Butler was placed at the table for examination. The magistrate conducted his inquiry civilly, but yet in a manner which gave him to understand that he laboured under strong suspicion. With a frankness which at once became his calling and character, Butler avowed his involuntary presence at the murder of Porteous, and, at the request of the magistrate, entered into a minute detail of the circumstances which attended that unhappy affair. All the particulars, such as we have narrated, were taken minutely down by the clerk from Butler's dictation.

When the narrative was concluded, the cross-examination commenced, which it is a painful task even for the most candid witness to undergo, since a story, especially if connected with agitating and alarming incidents, can scarce be so clearly and distinctly told, but that some ambiguity and doubt may be thrown upon it by a string of successive and minute interrogatories.

The magistrate commenced by observing, that Butler had said his object was to return to the village of Libberton, but that he was interrupted by the mob at the West Port, "Is the West Port your usual way of leaving town when you go to Libberton?" said the magistrate with a sneer.

"No, certainly," answered Butler, with the haste of a man anxious to vindicate the accuracy of his evidence; "but I chanced to be nearer that port than any other, and the hour of shutting the gates was on the point of striking."

"That was unlucky," said the magistrate dryly. "Pray, being, as you say, under coercion and fear of the lawless multitude, and compelled to accompany them through scenes disagreeable to all men of humanity, and more especially irreconcilable to the profession of a minister, did you not attempt to struggle, resist, or escape from their violence?"

Butler replied, "that their numbers prevented him from attempting resistance, and their vigilance from effecting his escape."

"That was unlucky," again repeated the magistrate, in the same dry inacquiescent tone of voice and manner. He proceeded with decency and politeness, but with a stiffness which argued his continued suspicion, to ask many questions concerning the behaviour of the mob, the manners and dress of the ringleaders; and when he conceived that the caution of Butler, if he was deceiving him, must be lulled asleep, the magistrate suddenly and artfully returned to former parts of his declaration, and required a new recapitulation of the circumstances, to the minutest and most trivial point, which attended each part of the melancholy scene. No confusion or contradiction, however, occurred, that could countenance the suspicion which he seemed to have adopted against Butler. At length the train of his interrogatories reached Madge Wildfire, at whose name the magistrate and town-clerk exchanged significant glances. If the fate of the Good Town had depended on her careful magistrate's knowing the features and dress of this personage, his inquiries could not have been more particular. But Butler could say almost nothing of this person's features, which were disguised apparently with red paint and soot, like an Indian going to battle, besides the projecting shade of a curch or coif, which muffled the hair of the supposed female. He declared that he thought he could not know this Madge Wildfire, if placed before him in a different dress, but that he believed he might recognise her voice.

The magistrate requested him again to state by what gate he left the city.

" By the Cowgate Port," replied Butler.

" Was that the nearest road to Libberton?"

" No," answered Butler with embarrassment; "but it was the nearest way to extricate myself from the mob."

The clerk and magistrate again exchanged glances.

" Is the Cowgate Port a nearer way to Libberton from the Grassmarket than Bristo Port?"

" No," replied Butler; "but I had to visit a friend."

" Indeed?" said the interrogator,—"You were in a hurry to tell the sight you had witnessed, I suppose?"

" Indeed I was not," replied Butler; "nor did I speak on the subject the whole time I was at Saint Leonard's Crags."

" Which road did you take to Saint Leonard's Crags?"

" By the foot of Salisbury Crags," was the reply.

" Indeed?—you seem partial to circuitous routes," again said the magistrate. " Whom did you see after you left the city?"

One by one he obtained a description of every one of the groups who had passed Butler, as already noticed, their number, demeanour, and appearance; and, at length, came to the circumstance of the mysterious stranger in the King's Park. On this subject Butler would fain have remained silent. But the magistrate had no sooner got a slight hint concerning the incident, than he seemed bent to possess himself of the most minute particulars.

"Look ye, Mr. Butler," said he, "you are a young man, and bear an excellent character; so much I will myself testify in your favour. But we are aware there has been, at times, a sort of bastard and fiery zeal in some of your order, and those, men irreproachable in other points, which has led them into doing and countenancing great irregularities, by which the peace of the country is liable to be shaken.—I will deal plainly with you. I am not at all satisfied with this story, of your setting out again and again to seek your dwelling by two several roads, which were both circuitous. And, to be frank, no one whom we have examined on this unhappy affair, could trace in your appearance anything like your acting under compulsion. Moreover, the waiters at the Cowgate Port observed something like the trepidation of guilt in your conduct, and declare that you were the first to command them to open the gate, in a tone of authority, as if still presiding over the guards and outposts of the rabble, who had besieged them the whole night."

"God forgive them!" said Butler; "I only asked free passage for myself; they must have much misunderstood, if they did not wilfully misrepresent me."

"Well, Mr. Butler," resumed the magistrate, "I am inclined to judge the best and hope the best, as I am sure I wish the best; but you must be frank with me, if you wish to secure my good opinion, and lessen the risk of inconvenience to yourself. You have allowed you saw another individual in your passage through the King's Park to Saint Leonard's Crags— I must know every word which passed betwixt you."

Thus closely pressed, Butler, who had no reason for concealing what passed at that meeting, unless because Jeanie Deans was concerned in it, thought it best to tell the whole truth from beginning to end.

"Do you suppose," said the magistrate, pausing, "that the young woman will accept an invitation so mysterious?"

"I fear she will," replied Butler.

"Why do you use the word *fear* it?" said the magistrate.

"Because I am apprehensive for her safety, in meeting, at such a time and place, one who had something of the manner of a desperado, and whose message was of a character so inexplicable."

" Her safety shall be cared for," said the magistrate.   Mr. Butler, I am concerned I cannot immediately discharge you from confinement, but I hope you will not be long detained. —Remove Mr. Butler, and let him be provided with decent accommodation in all respects."

He was conducted back to the prison accordingly ; but, in the food offered to him, as well as in the apartment in which he was lodged, the recommendation of the magistrate was strictly attended to.

CHAPTER XIV

Dark and eerie was the night,
And lonely was the way,
As Janet, wi' her green mantell,
To Miles' Cross she did gae.
Old Ballad.

LEAVING Butler to all the uncomfortable thoughts attached to his new situation, among which the most predominant was his feeling that he was, by his confinement, deprived of all possibility of assisting the family at St. Leonard's in their greatest need, we return to Jeanie Deans, who had seen him depart, without an opportunity of further explanation, in all that agony of mind with which the female heart bids adieu to the complicated sensations so well described by Coleridge,—

Hopes, and fears that kindle hope,
An undistinguishable throng;
And gentle wishes long subdued—
Subdued and cherish'd long.

It is not the firmest heart (and Jeanie, under her russet rokelay, had one that would not have disgraced Cato's daughter) that can most easily bid adieu to these soft and mingled emotions.   She wept for a few minutes bitterly. and without attempting to refrain from this indulgence of passion. But a moment's recollection induced her to check herself for a grief selfish and proper to her own affections, while her father and sister were plunged into such deep and irretrievable affliction.   She drew from her pocket the letter which had been that morning flung into her apartment through an open window, and the contents of which were as singular as the expression was violent and energetic. "If she would save a human being from the most damning guilt, and all its desperate consequences,—if she desired the life and honour of her sister to be saved from the bloody fangs of an unjust law,—if she desired not to forfeit peace of mind here, and happiness hereafter," such was the frantic style of the conjuration, "she was entreated to give a sure, secret, and solitary meeting to the writer. She alone could rescue him," so ran the letter, "and he only could rescue her." He was in such circumstances, the billet farther informed her, that an attempt to bring any witness of their conference, or even to mention to her father, or any other person whatsoever, the letter which requested it, would inevitably prevent its taking place, and insure the destruction of her sister. The letter concluded with incoherent but violent protestations, that in obeying this summons she had nothing to fear personally.

The message delivered to her by Butler from the stranger in the Park tallied exactly with the contents of the letter, but assigned a later hour and a different place of meeting. Apparently the writer of the letter had been compelled to let Butler so far into his confidence, for the sake of announcing this change to Jeanie. She was more than once on the point of producing the billet, in vindication of herself from her lover's half-hinted suspicions. But there is something in stooping to justification which the pride of innocence does not at all times willingly submit to; besides that the threats contained in the letter, in case of her betraying the secret, hung heavy on her heart. It is probable, however, that, had they remained longer together, she might have taken the resolution to submit the whole matter to Butler, and be guided by him as to the line of conduct which she should adopt. And when, by the sudden interruption of their conference, she lost the opportunity of doing so, she felt as if she had been unjust to a friend, whose advice might have been highly useful, and whose attachment deserved her full and unreserved confidence.

To have recourse to her father upon this occasion, she considered as highly imprudent. There was no possibility of conjecturing in what light the matter might strike old David, whose manner of acting and thinking in extraordinary circumstances depended upon feelings and principles peculiar to himself, the operation of which could not be calculated upon even by those best acquainted with him. To have requested some female friend to have accompanied her to the place of rendezvous, would perhaps have been the most eligible expedient; but the threats of the writer, that betraying his secret would prevent their meeting (on which her sister's safety was said to depend) from taking place at all, would have deterred her from making such a confidence, even had she known a person in whom she thought it could with safety have been reposed. But she knew none such. Their acquaintance with the cottagers in the vicinity had been very slight, and limited to trifling acts of good neighbourhood. Jeanie knew little of them, and what she knew did not greatly incline her to trust any of them. They were of the order of loquacious good-humoured gossips usually found in their situation of life; and their conversation had at all times few charms for a young woman, to whom nature and the circumstance of a solitary life had given a depth of thought and force of character superior to the frivolous part of her sex, whether in high or low degree.

Left alone and separated from all earthly counsel, she had recourse to a friend and adviser, whose ear is open to the cry of the poorest and most afflicted of his people. She knelt, and prayed with fervent sincerity, that God would please to direct her what course to follow in her arduous and distressing situation. It was the belief of the time and sect to which she belonged, that special answers to prayer, differing little in their character from divine inspiration, were, as they expressed it, "borne in upon their minds" in answer to their earnest petitions in a crisis of difficulty. Without entering into an abstruse point of divinity, one thing is plain; namely, that the person who lays open his doubts and distresses in prayer, with feeling and sincerity, must necessarily, in the act of doing so, purify his mind from the dross of worldly passions and interests, and bring it into that state, when the resolutions adopted are likely to be selected rather from a sense of duty, than from any inferior motive. Jeanie arose from her devotions, with her heart fortified to endure afflictions, and encouraged to face difficulties.

"I will meet this unhappy man," she said to herself—"unhappy he must be, since I doubt he has been the cause of poor Effie's misfortune—but I will meet him, be it for good or ill. My mind shall never cast up to me, that, for fear of what might be said or done to myself, I left that undone that might even yet be the rescue of her."

With a mind greatly composed since the adoption of this

resolution, she went to attend her father. The old man, firm in the principles of his youth, did not, in outward appearance at least, permit a thought of his family distress to interfere with the stoical reserve of his countenance and manners. He even chid his daughter for having neglected, in the distress of the morning, some trifling domestic duties which fell under her department.

"Why, what meaneth this, Jeanie?" said the old man— "The brown four-year-auld's milk is not seiled yet, nor the bowies put up on the bink. If you neglect your warldly duties in the day of affliction, what confidence have I that ye mind the greater matters that concern salvation? God knows, our bowies, and our pipkins, and our draps o' milk, and our bits o' bread, are nearer and dearer to us than the bread of life."

Jeanie, not unpleased to hear her father's thoughts thus expand themselves beyond the sphere of his immediate distress, obeyed him, and proceeded to put her household matters in order; while old David moved from place to place about his ordinary employments, scarce showing, unless by a nervous impatience at remaining long stationary, an occasional convulsive sigh, or twinkle of the eyelid, that he was labouring under the yoke of such bitter affliction.

The hour of noon came on, and the father and child sat down to their homely repast. In his petition for a blessing on the meal, the poor old man added to his supplication, a prayer that the bread eaten in sadness of heart, and the bitter waters of Marah, might be made as nourishing as those which had been poured forth from a full cup and a plentiful basket and store; and having concluded his benediction, and resumed the bonnet which he had laid "reverently aside," he proceeded to exhort his daughter to eat, not by example indeed, but at least by precept.

"The man after God's own heart," he said, "washed and anointed himself, and did eat bread, in order to express his submission under a dispensation of suffering, and it did not become a Christian man or woman so to cling to creature-comforts of wife or bairns" (here the words became too great, as it were, for his utterance) "as to forget the first duty— submission to the Divine will."

To add force to his precept, he took a morsel on his plate, but nature proved too strong even for the powerful feelings with which he endeavoured to bridle it. Ashamed of his weakness, he started up, and ran out of the house, with haste very unlike the deliberation of his usual movements. In less than five minutes he returned, having successfully struggled to recover his ordinary composure of mind and countenance, and affected to colour over his late retreat, by muttering that he thought he heard the "young staig loose in the byre."

He did not again trust himself with the subject of his former conversation, and his daughter was glad to see that he seemed to avoid further discourse on that agitating topic. The hours glided on, as on they must and do pass, whether winged with joy or laden with affliction. The sun set beyond the dusky eminence of the Castle, and the screen of western hills, and the close of evening summoned David Deans and his daughter to the family duty of the night. It came bitterly upon Jeanie's recollection, how often, when the hour of worship approached, she used to watch the lengthening shadows, and look out from the door of the house, to see if she could spy her sister's return homeward. Alas! this idle and thoughtless waste of time, to what evils had it not finally led? and was she altogether guiltless, who, noticing Effie's turn to idle and light society, had not called in her father's authority to restrain her?—But I acted for the best, she again reflected, and who could have expected such a growth of evil, from one grain of human leaven, in a disposition so kind, and candid, and generous?

As they sate down to the "exercise," as it is called, a chair happened accidentally to stand in the place which Effie usually occupied. David Deans saw his daughter's eyes swim in tears as they were directed towards this object, and pushed it aside, with a gesture of some impatience, as if desirous to destroy every memorial of earthly interest when about to address the Deity. The portion of Scripture was read, the psalm was sung, the prayer was made; and it was remarkable that, in discharging these duties, the old man avoided all passages and expressions, of which Scripture affords so many, that might be considered as applicable to his own domestic misfortune. In doing so it was perhaps his intention to spare the feelings of his daughter, as well as to maintain, in outward show at least, that stoical appearance of patient endurance of all the evil which earth could bring, which was, in his opinion, essential to the character of one who rated all earthly things at their own just estimate of nothingness. When he had finished the duty of the evening, he came up to his daughter, wished her good-night, and, having done so, continued to hold her by the hands for half a minute; then drawing her towards him, kissed her forehead, and ejaculated, " The God of Israel bless you, even with the blessings of the promise, my dear bairn ! "

It was not either in the nature or habits of David Deans to seem a fond father ; nor was he often observed to experience, or at least to evince, that fulness of the heart which seeks to expand itself in tender expressions or caresses even to those who were dearest to him. On the contrary, he used to censure this as a degree of weakness in several of his neighbours, and particularly in poor widow Butler. It followed, however, from the rarity of such emotions, in this self-denied and reserved man, that his children attached to occasional marks of his affection and approbation a degree of high interest and solemnity ; well considering them as evidences of feelings which were only expressed when they became too intense for suppression or concealment.

With deep emotion, therefore, did he bestow, and his daughter receive, this benediction and paternal caress. " And you, my dear father," exclaimed Jeanie, when the door had closed upon the venerable old man, " may you have purchased and promised blessings multiplied upon you—upon *you*, who walk in this world as though you were not of the world, and hold all that it can give or take away but as the *midges* that the sun-blink brings out, and the evening wind sweeps away ! "

She now made preparation for her night-walk. Her father slept in another part of the dwelling, and, regular in all his habits, seldom or never left his apartment when he had betaken himself to it for the evening. It was therefore easy for her to leave the house unobserved, so soon as the time approached at which she was to keep her appointment. But the step she was about to take had difficulties and terrors in her own eyes, though she had no reason to apprehend her father's interference. Her life had been spent in the quiet, uniform, and regular seclusion of their peaceful and monotonous household. The very hour which some damsels of the present day, as well of her own as of higher degree, would consider as the natural period of commencing an evening of pleasure, brought, in her opinion, awe and solemnity in it ; and the resolution she had taken, had a strange, daring, and adventurous character, to which she could hardly reconcile herself when the moment approached for putting it into execution. Her hands trembled as she snooded her fair hair beneath the ribband, then the only ornament or cover which young unmarried women wore on their head, and as she adjusted the scarlet tartan screen or muffler made of plaid, which the Scottish women wore, much in the fashion of the black silk veils still a part of female dress in the Netherlands. A sense of impropriety as well as of danger pressed upon her, as she lifted the latch of her paternal mansion to leave it on so wild an expedition, and at so late an hour, unprotected, and without the knowledge of her natural guardian.

When she found herself abroad and in the open fields, additional subjects of apprehension crowded upon her. The dim cliffs and scattered rocks, interspersed with green sward, through which she had to pass to the place of appointment, as they glimmered before her in a clear autumn night, recalled to her memory many a deed of violence, which, according to tradition, had been done and suffered among them. In earlier days they had been the haunt of robbers and assassins, the memory of whose crimes are preserved in the various edicts which the council of the city, and even the parliament of Scotland, had passed for dispersing their bands, and ensuring safety to the lieges, so near the precincts of the city. The names of these criminals, and of their atrocities, were still remembered in traditions of the scattered cottages and the neighbouring suburb. In latter times, as we have already noticed, the sequestered and broken character of the ground rendered it a fit theatre for duels and rencontres among the fiery youth of the period. Two or three of these incidents, all sanguinary, and one of them fatal in its termination, had happened since Deans came to live at Saint Leonard's. His daughter's recollections, therefore, were of blood and horror as she pursued the small scarce-tracked solitary path, every step of which conveyed her to a greater distance from help, and deeper into the ominous seclusion of these unhallowed precincts.

As the moon began to peer forth on the scene with a doubtful, flitting, and solemn light, Jeanie's apprehensions took another turn, too peculiar to her rank and country to remain unnoticed. But to trace its origin will require another chapter.

CHAPTER XV

———The spirit I have seen
May be the devil. And the devil has power
To assume a pleasing shape.
Hamlet.[1]

WITCHCRAFT and demonology, as we have had already occasion to remark, were at this period believed in by almost all ranks, but more especially among the stricter classes of presbyterians, whose government, when their party were at the head of the state, had been much sullied by their eagerness to inquire into and persecute these imaginary crimes. Now, in this point of view also, Saint Leonard's Crags, and the adjacent Chase, were a dreaded and ill-reputed district. Not only had witches held their meetings there, but even of very late years the enthusiast, or impostor, mentioned in the Pandæmonium of Richard Bovet, Gentleman,[1] had, among the recesses of these romantic cliffs, found his way into the hidden retreats where the fairies revel in the bowels of the earth.

With all these legends Jeanie Deans was too well acquainted, to escape that strong impression which they usually make on the imagination. Indeed, relations of this ghostly kind had been familiar to her from her infancy, for they were the only relief which her father's conversation afforded from controversial argument, or the gloomy history of the strivings and testimonies, escapes, captures, tortures, and executions of those martyrs of the Covenant, with whom it was his chiefest boast to say he had been acquainted. In the recesses of mountains, in caverns, and in morasses, to which these persecuted enthusiasts were so ruthlessly pursued, they conceived they had often to contend with the visible assaults of the Enemy of mankind, as in the cities, and in the cultivated fields, they were exposed to those of the tyrannical government and their soldiery. Such were the terrors which made one of their gifted seers exclaim, when his companion returned to him, after having left him alone in a haunted cavern in Sorn in Galloway, " It is hard living in this world —incarnate devils above the earth, and devils under the earth ! Satan has been here since ye went away, but I have dismissed him by resistance; we will be no more troubled with him this night." David Deans believed this, and many

[1] Note VI.—The Fairy Boy of Leith.

other such ghostly encounters and victories, on the faith of the Ansars, or auxiliaries of the banished prophets. This event was beyond David's remembrance. But he used to tell with great awe, yet not without a feeling of proud superiority to his auditors, how he himself had been present at a field-meeting at Crochmade, when the duty of the day was interrupted by the apparition of a tall black man, who, in the act of crossing a ford to join the congregation, lost ground, and was carried down apparently by the force of the stream. All were instantly at work to assist him, but with so little success, that ten or twelve stout men, who had hold of the rope which they had cast in to his aid, were rather in danger to be dragged into the stream, and lose their own lives, than likely to save that of the supposed perishing man. "But famous John Semple of Carspharn," David Deans used to say with exultation, "saw the whaup in the rape.—' Quit the rope,' he cried to us (for I that was but a callant had a haud o' the rape mysell), 'it is the Great Enemy! he will burn, but not drown; his design is to disturb the good wark, by raising wonder and confusion in your minds; to put off from your spirits all that ye hae heard and felt.'—Sae we let go the rape," said David, "and he went adown the water screeching and bullering like a Bull of Bashan, as he's ca'd in Scripture." [1]

Trained in these and similar legends, it was no wonder that Jeanie began to feel an ill-defined apprehension, not merely of the phantoms which might beset her way, but of the quality, nature, and purpose of the being who had thus appointed her a meeting, at a place and hour of horror, and at a time when her mind must be necessarily full of those tempting and ensnaring thoughts of grief and despair, which were supposed to lay sufferers particularly open to the temptations of the Evil One. If such an idea had crossed even Butler's well-informed mind, it was calculated to make a much stronger impression upon hers. Yet firmly believing the possibility of an encounter so terrible to flesh and blood, Jeanie, with a degree of resolution of which we cannot sufficiently estimate the merit, because the incredulity of the age has rendered us strangers to the nature and extent of her feelings, persevered in her determination not to omit an opportunity of doing something towards saving her sister, although, in the attempt to avail herself of it, she might be

[1] Note VII.—Intercourse of the Covenanters with the Invisible World.

exposed to dangers so dreadful to her imagination. So, like Christiana in the Pilgrim's Progress, when traversing with a timid yet resolved step the terrors of the Valley of the Shadow of Death, she glided on by rock and stone, "now in glimmer and now in gloom," as her path lay through moonlight or shadow, and endeavoured to overpower the suggestions of fear, sometimes by fixing her mind upon the distressed condition of her sister, and the duty she lay under to afford her aid, should that be in her power; and more frequently by recurring in mental prayer to the protection of that Being to whom night is as noon-day.

Thus drowning at one time her fears by fixing her mind on a subject of overpowering interest, and arguing them down at others by referring herself to the protection of the Deity, she at length approached the place assigned for this mysterious conference.

It was situated in the depth of the valley behind Salisbury Crags, which has for a background the north-western shoulder of the mountain called Arthur's Seat, on whose descent still remain the ruins of what was once a chapel, or hermitage, dedicated to Saint Anthony the Eremite. A better site for such a building could hardly have been selected; for the chapel, situated among the rude and pathless cliffs, lies in a desert, even in the immediate vicinity of a rich, populous, and tumultuous capital: and the hum of the city might mingle with the orisons of the recluses, conveying as little of worldly interest as if it had been the roar of the distant ocean. Beneath the steep ascent on which these ruins are still visible, was, and perhaps is still pointed out, the place where the wretch Nicol Muschat, who has been already mentioned in these pages, had closed a long scene of cruelty towards his unfortunate wife, by murdering her, with circumstances of uncommon barbarity.[1] The execration in which the man's crime was held extended itself to the place where it was perpetrated, which was marked by a small *cairn*, or heap of stones, composed of those which each chance passenger had thrown there in testimony of abhorrence, and on the principle, it would seem, of the ancient British malediction, "May you have a cairn for your burial-place!"

As our heroine approached this ominous and unhallowed spot, she paused and looked to the moon, now rising broad on the north-west, and shedding a more distinct light than it

[1] Note IV.—Muschat's Cairn.

had afforded during her walk thither. Eyeing the planet for a moment, she then slowly and fearfully turned her head towards the cairn, from which it was at first averted. She was at first disappointed. Nothing was visible beside the little pile of stones, which shone grey in the moonlight. A multitude of confused suggestions rushed on her mind. Had her correspondent deceived her, and broken his appointment? —was he too tardy at the appointment he had made?—or had some strange turn of fate prevented him from appearing as he proposed?—or, if he were an unearthly being, as her secret apprehensions suggested, was it his object merely to delude her with false hopes, and put her to unnecessary toil and terror, according to the nature, as she had heard, of those wandering demons?—or did he purpose to blast her with the sudden horrors of his presence when she had come close to the place of rendezvous? These anxious reflections did not prevent her approaching to the cairn with a pace that, though slow, was determined.

When she was within two yards of the heap of stones, a figure rose suddenly up from behind it, and Jeanie scarce forbore to scream aloud at what seemed the realisation of the most frightful of her anticipations. She constrained herself to silence, however, and, making a dead pause, suffered the figure to open the conversation, which he did by asking, in a voice which agitation rendered tremulous and hollow, " Are you the sister of that ill-fated young woman ? "

" I am—I am the sister of Effie Deans ! " exclaimed Jeanie. " And as ever you hope God will hear you at your need, tell me, if you can tell, what can be done to save her ! "

" I do *not* hope God will hear me at my need," was the singular answer. " I do not deserve—I do not expect He will." This desperate language he uttered in a tone calmer than that with which he had at first spoken, probably because the shock of first addressing her was what he felt most difficult to overcome. Jeanie remained mute with horror to hear language expressed so utterly foreign to all which she had ever been acquainted with, that it sounded in her ears rather like that of a fiend than of a human being. The stranger pursued his address to her without seeming to notice her surprise. " You see before you a wretch, predestined to evil here and hereafter."

" For the sake of Heaven, that hears and sees us," said Jeanie, " dinna speak in this desperate fashion ! The gospel is sent to the chief of sinners—to the most miserable among the miserable."

"Then should I have my own share therein," said the stranger, "if you call it sinful to have been the destruction of the mother that bore me—of the friend that loved me—of the woman that trusted me—of the innocent child that was born to me. If to have done all this is to be a sinner, and to survive it is to be miserable, then am I most guilty and most miserable indeed."

"Then you are the wicked cause of my sister's ruin?" said Jeanie, with a natural touch of indignation expressed in her tone of voice.

"Curse me for it, if you will," said the stranger; "I have well deserved it at your hand."

"It is fitter for me," said Jeanie, "to pray to God to forgive you."

"Do as you will, how you will, or what you will," he replied, with vehemence; "only promise to obey my directions, and save your sister's life."

"I must first know," said Jeanie, "the means you would have me use in her behalf."

"No!—you must first swear—solemnly swear, that you will employ them, when I make them known to you."

"Surely, it is needless to swear that I will do all that is lawful to a Christian, to save the life of my sister?"

"I will have no reservation!" thundered the stranger; "lawful or unlawful, Christian or heathen, you shall swear to do my hest, and act by my counsel, or—you little know whose wrath you provoke!"

"I will think on what you have said," said Jeanie, who began to get much alarmed at the frantic vehemence of his manner, and disputed in her own mind, whether she spoke to a maniac, or an apostate spirit incarnate—"I will think on what you say, and let you ken to-morrow."

"To-morrow!" exclaimed the man, with a laugh of scorn —"And where will I be to-morrow?—or, where will you be to-night, unless you swear to walk by my counsel?—There was one accursed deed done at this spot before now; and there shall be another to match it, unless you yield up to my guidance body and soul."

As he spoke, he offered a pistol at the unfortunate young woman. She neither fled nor fainted, but sunk on her knees, and asked him to spare her life.

"Is that all you have to say?" said the unmoved ruffian.

"Do not dip your hands in the blood of a defenceless creature that has trusted to you," said Jeanie, still on her knees.

"Is that all you can say for your life?—Have you no promise to give?—Will you destroy your sister, and compel me to shed more blood?"

"I can promise nothing," said Jeanie, "which is unlawful for a Christian."

He cocked the weapon, and held it towards her.

"May God forgive you!" she said, pressing her hands forcibly against her eyes.

"D——n!" muttered the man; and, turning aside from her, he uncocked the pistol, and replaced it in his pocket. "I am a villain," he said, "steeped in guilt and wretchedness, but not wicked enough to do you any harm! I only wished to terrify you into my measures—She hears me not—she is gone!—Great God! what a wretch am I become!"

As he spoke, she recovered herself from an agony which partook of the bitterness of death; and, in a minute or two, through the strong exertion of her natural sense and courage, collected herself sufficiently to understand he intended her no personal injury.

"No!" he repeated; "I would not add to the murder of your sister, and of her child, that of any one belonging to her!—Mad, frantic, as I am, and unrestrained by either fear or mercy, given up to the possession of an evil being, and forsaken by all that is good, I would not hurt you, were the world offered me for a bribe! But, for the sake of all that is dear to you, swear you will follow my counsel. Take this weapon, shoot me through the head, and with your own hand revenge your sister's wrong, only follow the course—the only course, by which her life can be saved."

"Alas! is she innocent or guilty?"

"She is guiltless—guiltless of everything, but of having trusted a villain!—Yet, had it not been for those that were worse than I am—yes, worse than I am, though I am bad indeed—this misery had not befallen."

"And my sister's child—does it live?" said Jeanie.

"No; it was murdered—the new-born infant was barbarously murdered," he uttered in a low, yet stern and sustained voice;—"but," he added hastily, "not by her knowledge or consent."

" Then, why cannot the guilty be brought to justice, and the innocent freed?"

" Torment me not with questions which can serve no purpose," he sternly replied—"The deed was done by those who are far enough from pursuit, and safe enough from discovery!—No one can save Effie but yourself."

" Woe's me! how is it in my power?" asked Jeanie, in despondency.

" Hearken to me!—You have sense—you can apprehend my meaning—I will trust you. Your sister is innocent of the crime charged against her——"

" Thank God for that!" said Jeanie.

" Be still and hearken!—The person who assisted her in her illness murdered the child; but it was without the mother's knowledge or consent. She is therefore guiltless, as guiltless as the unhappy innocent, that but gasped a few minutes in this unhappy world—the better was its hap to be so soon at rest. She is innocent as that infant, and yet she must die—it is impossible to clear her of the law!"

" Cannot the wretches be discovered, and given up to punishment?" said Jeanie.

" Do you think you will persuade those who are hardened in guilt to die to save another?—Is that the reed you would lean to?"

" But you said there was a remedy," again gasped out the terrified young woman.

" There is," answered the stranger, "and it is in your own hands. The blow which the law aims cannot be broken by directly encountering it, but it may be turned aside. You saw your sister during the period preceding the birth of her child—what is so natural as that she should have mentioned her condition to you? The doing so would, as their cant goes, take the case from under the statute, for it removes the quality of concealment. I know their jargon, and have had sad cause to know it; and the quality of concealment is essential to this statutory offence.[1] Nothing is so natural as that Effie should have mentioned her condition to you—think—reflect—I am positive that she did."

" Woe's me!" said Jeanie, "she never spoke to me on the subject, but grat sorely when I spoke to her about her altered looks, and the change on her spirits."

" You asked her questions on the subject?" he said

[1] Note VIII.—Child Murder.

eagerly. "You *must* remember her answer was, a confession that she had been ruined by a villain—yes, lay a strong emphasis on that—a cruel false villain call it—any other name is unnecessary; and that she bore under her bosom the consequences of his guilt and her folly; and that he had assured her he would provide safely for her approaching illness. Well he kept his word!" These last words he spoke as it were to himself, and with a violent gesture of self-accusation, and then calmly proceeded, "You will remember all this?—That is all that is necessary to be said."

"But I cannot remember," answered Jeanie, with simplicity, "that which Effie never told me."

"Are you so dull—so very dull of apprehension?" he exclaimed, suddenly grasping her arm, and holding it firm in his hand. "I tell you" (speaking between his teeth, and under his breath, but with great energy), "you *must* remember that she told you all this, whether she ever said a syllable of it or no. You must repeat this tale, in which there is no falsehood, except in so far as it was not told to you, before these Justices—Justiciary—whatever they call their bloodthirsty court, and save your sister from being murdered, and them from becoming murderers. Do not hesitate—I pledge life and salvation, that in saying what I have said, you will only speak the simple truth."

"But," replied Jeanie, whose judgment was too accurate not to see the sophistry of this argument, "I shall be mansworn in the very thing in which my testimony is wanted, for it is the concealment for which poor Effie is blamed, and you would make me tell a falsehood anent it."

"I see," he said, "my first suspicions of you were right, and that you will let your sister, innocent, fair, and guiltless, except in trusting a villain, die the death of a murderess, rather than bestow the breath of your mouth and the sound of your voice to save her."

"I wad ware the best blood in my body to keep her skaithless." said Jeanie, weeping in bitter agony, "but I canna change right into wrang, or make that true which is false."

"Foolish, hard-hearted girl," said the stranger, "are you afraid of what they may do to you? I tell you, even the retainers of the law, who course life as greyhounds do hares, will rejoice at the escape of a creature so young—so beautiful; that they will not suspect your tale; that if they did suspect

it, they would consider you as deserving, not only of forgiveness, but of praise for your natural affection."

"It is not man I fear," said Jeanie, looking upward; "the
God, whose name I must call on to witness the truth of what
I say, He will know the falsehood."

"And He will know the motive," said the stranger eagerly;
"He will know that you are doing this—not for lucre of gain,
but to save the life of the innocent, and prevent the commission of a worse crime than that which the law seeks to
avenge."

"He has given us a law," said Jeanie, "for the lamp of our
path; if we stray from it we err against knowledge—I may
not do evil, even that good may come out of it. But you—
you that ken all this to be true, which I must take on your
word—you that, if I understood what you said e'en now,
promised her shelter and protection in her travail, why do not
you step forward, and bear leal and soothfast evidence in her
behalf, as ye may with a clear conscience?"

"To whom do you talk of a clear conscience, woman?"
said he, with a sudden fierceness which renewed her terrors,
—"to *me?*—I have not known one for many a year. Bear
witness in her behalf?—a proper witness, that, even to speak
these few words to a woman of so little consequence as yourself, must choose such an hour and such a place as this.
When you see owls and bats fly abroad, like larks, in the
sunshine, you may expect to see such as I am in the assemblies
of men.—Hush—listen to that."

A voice was heard to sing one of those wild and monotonous strains so common in Scotland, and to which the natives
of that country chant their old ballads. The sound ceased—
then came nearer, and was renewed; the stranger listened
attentively, still holding Jeanie by the arm (as she stood by
him in motionless terror), as if to prevent her interrupting the
strain by speaking or stirring. When the sounds were renewed, the words were distinctly audible:

> "When the glede's in the blue cloud,
>   The lavrock lies still;
> When the hound's in the green-wood,
>   The hind keeps the hill."

The person who sung kept a strained and powerful voice at
its highest pitch, so that it could be heard at a very considerable distance. As the song ceased, they might hear a stifled

sound, as of steps and whispers of persons approaching them. The song was again raised, but the tune was changed:

> "O sleep ye sound, Sir James, she said,
>   When ye suld rise and ride?
> There's twenty men, wi' bow and blade,
>   Are seeking where ye hide."

"I dare stay no longer," said the stranger; "return home, or remain till they come up—you have nothing to fear—but do not tell you saw me—your sister's fate is in your hands." So saying, he turned from her, and with a swift, yet cautiously noiseless step, plunged into the darkness on the side most remote from the sounds which they heard approaching, and was soon lost to her sight. Jeanie remained by the cairn terrified beyond expression, and uncertain whether she ought to fly homeward with all the speed she could exert, or wait the approach of those who were advancing towards her. This uncertainty detained her so long, that she now distinctly saw two or three figures already so near to her, that a precipitate flight would have been equally fruitless and impolitic.

CHAPTER XVI

> ————She speaks things in doubt,
> That carry but half sense: her speech is nothing,
> Yet the unshaped use of it doth move
> The hearers to collection; they aim at it,
> And botch the words up to fit their own thoughts.
>   *Hamlet.*

LIKE the digressive poet Ariosto, I find myself under the necessity of connecting the branches of my story, by taking up the adventures of another of the characters, and bringing them down to the point at which we have left those of Jeanie Deans. It is not, perhaps, the most artificial way of telling a story, but it has the advantage of sparing the necessity of resuming what a knitter (if stocking-looms have left such a person in the land) might call our "dropped stitches"; a labour in which the author generally toils much, without getting credit for his pains.

"I could risk a sma' wad," said the clerk to the magistrate, "that this rascal Ratcliffe, if he were insured of his neck's safety, could do more than ony ten of our police-people and constables, to help us to get out of this scrape of Porteous's.

He is weel acquent wi' a' the smugglers, thieves, and banditti about Edinburgh; and, indeed, he may be called the father of a' the misdoers in Scotland, for he has passed amang them for these twenty years by the name of Daddie Rat."

"A bonny sort of a scoundrel," replied the magistrate, "to expect a place under the city!"

"Begging your honour's pardon," said the city's procurator-fiscal, upon whom the duties of superintendent of police devolved, "Mr. Fairscrieve is perfectly in the right. It is just sic as Ratcliffe that the town needs in my department; an' if sae be that he's disposed to turn his knowledge to the city service, ye'll no find a better man.—Ye'll get nae saints to be searchers for uncustomed goods, or for thieves and sic like;—and your decent sort of men, religious professors, and broken tradesmen, that are put into the like o' sic trust, can do nae gude ava. They are feared for this, and they are scrupulous about that, and they are na free to tell a lie, though it may be for the benefit of the city; and they dinna like to be out at irregular hours, and in a dark cauld night, and they like a clout ower the croun far waur; and sae between the fear o' God, and the fear o' man, and the fear o' getting a sair throat, or sair banes, there's a dozen o' our city folk, baith waiters, and officers, and constables, that can find out naething but a wee bit skulduddery for the benefit of the Kirk-treasurer. Jock Porteous, that's stiff and stark, puir fallow, was worth a dozen o' them; for he never had ony fears, or scruples, or doubts, or conscience, about onything your honours bade him."

"He was a gude servant o' the town," said the Bailie, "though he was an ower free-living man. But if you really think this rascal Ratcliffe could do us ony service in discovering these malefactors, I would insure him life, reward, and promotion. It's an awsome thing this mischance for the city, Mr. Fairscrieve. It will be very ill taen wi' abune stairs. Queen Caroline, God bless her! is a woman—at least I judge sae, and it's nae treason to speak my mind sae far—and ye maybe ken as weel as I do, for ye hae a housekeeper, though ye arena a married man, that women are wilfu', and downa bide a slight. And it will sound ill in her ears, that sic a confused mistake suld come to pass, and naebody sae muckle as to be put into the Tolbooth about it."

"If ye thought that, sir," said the procurator-fiscal, "we could easily clap into the prison a few blackguards upon suspicion. It will have a gude active look, and I hae aye plenty on my list, that wadna be a hair the waur of a week or twa's imprisonment; and if ye thought it no strictly just, ye could be just the easier wi' them the neist time they did onything to deserve it; they arena the sort to be lang o' geeing ye an opportunity to clear scores wi' them on that account."

"I doubt that will hardly do in this case, Mr. Sharpitlaw," returned the town-clerk; "they'll run their letters,[1] and be adrift again, before ye ken where ye are."

"I will speak to the Lord Provost," said the magistrate, "about Ratcliffe's business. Mr. Sharpitlaw, you will go with me and receive instructions—something may be made too out of this story of Butler's and his unknown gentleman—I know no business any man has to swagger about in the King's Park, and call himself the devil, to the terror of honest folks, who dinna care to hear mair about the devil than is said from the pulpit on the Sabbath. I cannot think the preacher himsell wad be heading the mob, though the time has been, they hae been as forward in a bruilzie as their neighbours."

"But these times are lang by," said Mr. Sharpitlaw. "In my father's time, there was mair search for silenced ministers about the Bow-head and the Covenant Close, and all the tents of Kedar, as they ca'd the dwellings o' the godly in those days, than there's now for thieves and vagabonds in the Laigh Calton and the back o' the Canongate. But that time's weel by, an it bide. And if the Bailie will get me directions and authority from the Provost, I'll speak wi' Daddie Rat mysell: for I'm thinking I'll make mair out o' him than ye'll do."

Mr. Sharpitlaw, being necessarily a man of high trust, was accordingly empowered, in the course of the day, to make such arrangements, as might seem in the emergency most advantageous for the Good Town. He went to the jail accordingly, and saw Ratcliffe in private.

The relative positions of a police-officer and a professed thief bear a different complexion, according to circumstances. The most obvious simile of a hawk pouncing upon his prey is often least applicable. Sometimes the guardian of justice has the air of a cat watching a mouse, and, while he suspends his purpose of springing upon the pilferer, takes care so to calculate his motions that he shall not get beyond his power.

[1] A Scottish form of procedure, answering, in some respects, to the English Habeas Corpus.

Sometimes, more passive still, he uses the art of fascination ascribed to the rattlesnake, and contents himself with glaring on the victim, through all his devious flutterings; certain that his terror, confusion, and disorder of ideas, will bring him into his jaws at last. The interview between Ratcliffe and Sharpitlaw had an aspect different from all these. They sate for five minutes silent, on opposite sides of a small table, and looked fixedly at each other, with a sharp, knowing, and alert cast of countenance, not unmingled with an inclination to laugh, and resembled more than anything else, two dogs, who, preparing for a game at romps, are seen to couch down, and remain in that posture for a little time, watching each other's movements, and waiting which shall begin the game.

"So, Mr. Ratcliffe," said the officer, conceiving it suited his dignity to speak first, "you give up business, I find?"

"Yes, sir," replied Ratcliffe; "I shall be on that lay nae mair—and I think that will save your folk some trouble, Mr. Sharpitlaw?"

"Which Jock Dalgleish" (then finisher of the law in the Scottish metropolis) "wad save them as easily," returned the procurator-fiscal.

"Ay; if I waited in the Tolbooth here to have him fit my cravat—but that's an idle way o' speaking, Mr. Sharpitlaw."

"Why, I suppose you know you are under sentence of death, Mr. Ratcliffe?" replied Mr. Sharpitlaw.

"Ay, so are a', as that worthy minister said in the Tolbooth Kirk the day Robertson wan off; but naebody kens when it will be executed. Gude faith, he had better reason to say sae than he dreamed of, before the play was played out that morning!"

"This Robertson," said Sharpitlaw, in a lower and something like a confidential tone, "d'ye ken, Rat—that is, can ye gie us ony inkling where he is to be heard tell o'?"

"Troth, Mr. Sharpitlaw, I'll be frank wi' ye; Robertson is rather a cut abune me—a wild deevil he was, and mony a daft prank he played; but except the Collector's job that Wilson led him into, and some tuilzies about run goods wi' the gaugers and the waiters, he never did onything that came near our line o' business."

"Umph! that's singular, considering the company he kept."

"Fact, upon my honour and credit," said Ratcliffe gravely. "He keepit out o' our little bits of affairs, and that's mair than Wilson did; I hae dune business wi' Wilson afore now. But the lad will come on in time; there's nae fear o' him; naebody will live the life he has led, but what he'll come to sooner or later."

"Who or what is he, Ratcliffe? you know, I suppose?" said Sharpitlaw.

"He's better born, I judge, than he cares to let on; he's been a soldier, and he has been a play-actor, and I watna what he has been or hasna been, for as young as he is, sae that it had daffing and nonsense about it."

"Pretty pranks he has played in his time, I suppose?"

"Ye may say that," said Ratcliffe, with a sardonic smile; "and" (touching his nose), "a deevil amang the lasses."

"Like enough," said Sharpitlaw. "Weel, Ratcliffe, I'll no stand niffering wi' ye; ye ken the way that favour's gotten in my office; ye maun be usefu'."

"Certainly, sir, to the best of my power—naething for naething—I ken the rule of the office," said the ex-depredator.

"Now the principal thing in hand e'en now," said the official person, "is this job of Porteous's; an ye can gie us a lift—why, the inner turnkey's office to begin wi', and the captainship in time—ye understand my meaning?"

"Ay, troth do I, sir; a wink's as gude as a nod to a blind horse; but Jock Porteous' job—Lord help ye!—I was under sentence the haill time. God! but I couldna help laughing when I heard Jock skirling for mercy in the lads' hands! Mony a het skin ye hae gien me, neighbour, thought I, tak ye what's gaun: time about's fair play; ye'll ken now what hanging's gude for."

"Come, come, this is all nonsense, Rat," said the procurator. "Ye canna creep out at that hole, lad; you must speak to the point, you understand me, if you want favour; gif-gaf makes gude friends, ye ken."

"But how can I speak to the point, as your honour ca's it," said Ratcliffe demurely, and with an air of great simplicity, "when ye ken I was under sentence, and in the strong-room a' the while the job was going on?"

"And how can we turn ye loose on the public again, Daddie Rat, unless ye do or say something to deserve it?"

"Well, then, d—n it!" answered the criminal, "since it maun be sae, I saw Geordie Robertson among the boys that brake the jail; I suppose that will do me some gude?"

"That's speaking to the purpose, indeed," said the office-bearer; "and now, Rat, where think ye we'll find him?"

"Deil haet o' me kens," said Ratcliffe; "he'll no likely gang back to ony o' his auld howffs; he'll be off the country by this time. He has gude friends some gate or other, for a' the life he's led; he's been weel educate."

"He'll grace the gallows the better," said Mr. Sharpitlaw; "a desperate dog, to murder an officer of the city for doing his duty! Wha kens wha's turn it might be next?—But you saw him plainly?"

"As plainly as I see you."

"How was he dressed?" said Sharpitlaw.

"I couldna weel see; something of a woman's bit mutch on his head; but ye never saw sic a ca'-throw. Ane couldna hae een to a'thing."

"But did he speak to no one?" said Sharpitlaw.

"They were a' speaking and gabbling through other," said Ratcliffe, who was obviously unwilling to carry his evidence farther than he could possibly help.

"This will not do, Ratcliffe," said the procurator; "you must speak out—out—out," tapping the table emphatically, as he repeated that impressive monosyllable.

"It's very hard, sir," said the prisoner; "and but for the under-turnkey's place——"

"And the reversion of the captaincy—the captaincy of the Tolbooth, man—that is, in case of gude behaviour."

"Ay, ay," said Ratcliffe, "gude behaviour!—there's the deevil. And then it's waiting for dead folk's shoon into the bargain."

"But Robertson's head will weigh something," said Sharpitlaw; "something gay and heavy, Rat; the town maun show cause—that's right and reason—and then ye'll hae freedom to enjoy your gear honestly."

"I dinna ken," said Ratcliffe; "it's a queer way of beginning the trade of honesty—but deil ma care. Weel, then, I heard and saw him speak to the wench Effie Deans, that's up there for child-murder."

"The deil ye did? Rat, this is finding a mare's nest wi' a witness.—And the man that spoke to Butler in the Park, and that was to meet wi' Jeanie Deans at Muschat's Cairn—whew! lay that and that thegither! As sure as I live he's been the father of the lassie's wean."

"There hae been waur guesses than that, I'm thinking," observed Ratcliffe, turning his quid of tobacco in his cheek, and squirting out the juice. "I heard something a while syne about his drawing up wi' a bonny quean about the

Pleasaunts, and that it was a' Wilson could do to keep him frae marrying her."

Here a city officer entered, and told Sharpitlaw that they had the woman in custody whom he had directed them to bring before him.

"It's little matter now," said he, "the thing is taking another turn; however, George, ye may bring her in."

The officer retired, and introduced, upon his return, a tall, strapping wench of eighteen or twenty, dressed fantastically, in a sort of blue riding-jacket, with tarnished lace, her hair clubbed like that of a man, a Highland bonnet, and a bunch of broken feathers, a riding-skirt (or petticoat) of scarlet camlet, embroidered with tarnished flowers. Her features were coarse and masculine, yet at a little distance, by dint of very bright, wild-looking black eyes, an aquiline nose, and a commanding profile, appeared rather handsome. She flourished the switch she held in her hand, dropped a curtsy as low as a lady at a birth-night introduction, recovered herself seemingly according to Touchstone's directions to Audrey, and opened the conversation without waiting till any questions were asked.

"God gie your honour gude e'en, and mony o' them, bonny Mr. Sharpitlaw!—Gude e'en to ye, Daddie Ratton—they tauld me ye were hanged, man; or did ye get out o' John Dalgleish's hands like half-hangit Maggie Dickson?"

"Whisht, ye daft jaud," said Ratcliffe, "and hear what's said to ye."

"Wi' a' my heart, Ratton. Great preferment for poor Madge to be brought up the street wi' a grand man, wi' a coat a' passe-mented wi' worset-lace, to speak wi' provosts, and bailies, and town-clerks, and prokitors, at this time o' day—and the haill town looking at me too—This is honour on earth for anes!"

"Ay, Madge," said Mr. Sharpitlaw, in a coaxing tone; "and ye're dressed out in your braws, I see; these are not your every-days' claiths ye have on."

"Deil be in my fingers, then!" said Madge—"Eh, sirs!" (observing Butler come into the apartment), "there's a minister in the Tolbooth—wha will ca' it a graceless place now?—I'se warrant he's in for the gude auld cause—but it's be nae cause o' mine," and off she went into a song.

> "Hey for cavaliers, ho for cavaliers,
> Dub a dub, dub a dub;
> Have at old Beelzebub,—
> Oliver's squeaking for fear."

"Did ye ever see that mad woman before?" said Sharpitlaw to Butler.

"Not to my knowledge, sir," replied Butler.

"I thought as much," said the procurator-fiscal, looking towards Ratcliffe, who answered his glance with a nod of acquiescence and intelligence.

"But that is Madge Wildfire, as she calls herself," said the man of law to Butler.

"Ay, that I am," said Madge, "and that I have been ever since I was something better—Heigh ho"—(and something like melancholy dwelt on her features for a minute)—"But I canna mind when that was—it was lang syne, at ony rate, and I'll ne'er fash my thumb about it.—

> 'I glance like the wildfire through country and town;
> I'm seen on the causeway—I'm seen on the down;
> The lightning that flashes so bright and so free,
> Is scarcely so blithe or so bonny as me.'"

"Haud your tongue, ye skirling limmer!" said the officer, who had acted as master of the ceremonies to this extraordinary performer, and who was rather scandalised at the freedom of her demeanour before a person of Mr. Sharpitlaw's importance—"haud your tongue, or I'se gie ye something to skirl for!"

"Let her alone, George," said Sharpitlaw, "dinna put her out o' tune; I hae some questions to ask her—But first, Mr. Butler, take another look at her."

"Do sae, minister—do sae," cried Madge: "I am as weel worth looking at as ony book in your aught.—And I can say the single carritch, and the double carritch, and justification, and effectual calling, and the assembly of divines at Westminster, that is" (she added in a low tone), "I could say them anes—but it's lang syne—and ane forgets, ye ken." And poor Madge heaved another deep sigh.

"Weel, sir," said Mr. Sharpitlaw to Butler, "what think ye now?"

"As I did before," said Butler; "that I never saw the poor demented creature in my life before."

"Then she is not the person whom you said the rioters last night described as Madge Wildfire?"

"Certainly not," said Butler. "They may be near the same height, for they are both tall, but I see little other resemblance."

"Their dress, then, is not alike?" said Sharpitlaw.

"Not in the least," said Butler.

" Madge, my bonny woman," said Sharpitlaw, in the same coaxing manner, "what did ye do wi' your ilka-day's claise yesterday ? "

" I dinna mind," said Madge.

" Where was ye yesterday at e'en, Madge ? "

" I dinna mind onything about yesterday," answered Madge ; " ae day is eneugh for onybody to wun ower wi' at a time, and ower muckle sometimes."

" But maybe, Madge, ye wad mind something about it, if I was to gie ye this half-crown ? " said Sharpitlaw, taking out the piece of money.

" That might gar me laugh, but it couldna gar me mind."

" But, Madge," continued Sharpitlaw, " were I to send you to the wark-house in Leith Wynd, and gar Jock Dalgleish lay the tawse on your back——"

" That wad gar me greet," said Madge, sobbing, " but it couldna gar me mind, ye ken."

" She is ower far past reasonable folk's motives, sir," said Ratcliffe, " to mind siller, or John Dalgleish, or the cat and nine tails, either ; but I think I could gar her tell us something."

" Try her then, Ratcliffe," said Sharpitlaw, " for I am tired of her crazy pate, and be d—d to her."

" Madge," said Ratcliffe, " hae ye ony joes now ? "

" An onybody ask ye, say ye dinna ken.—Set him to be speaking of my joes, auld Daddie Ratton ! "

" I dare say, ye hae deil ane ? "

" See if I haena then," said Madge, with the toss of the head of affronted beauty—"there's Rob the Ranter, and Will Fleming, and then there's Geordie Robertson, lad—that's Gentleman Geordie—what think ye o' that ? "

Ratcliffe laughed, and, winking to the procurator-fiscal, pursued the inquiry in his own way. " But, Madge, the lads only like ye when ye hae on your braws—they wadna touch you wi' a pair o' tangs when you are in your auld ilka-day rags."

" Ye're a leeing auld sorrow then," replied the fair one ; " for Gentle Geordie Robertson put my ilka-day's claise on his ain bonny sell yestreen, and gaed a' through the town wi' them ; and gawsie and grand he lookit, like ony queen in the land."

" I dinna believe a word o't," said Ratcliffe, with another wink to the procurator. " Thae duds were a' o' the colour o' moonshine in the water, I'm thinking, Madge—The gown would be a sky-blue scarlet, I'se warrant ye?"

"It was nae sic thing," said Madge, whose unretentive memory let out, in the eagerness of contradiction, all that she would have most wished to keep concealed, had her judgment been equal to her inclination. "It was neither scarlet nor sky-blue, but my ain auld brown threshie-coat of a short-gown, and my mother's auld mutch, and my red rokelay—and he gaed me a croun and a kiss for the use o' them, blessing on his bonny face—though it's been a dear ane to me."

"And where did he change his clothes again, hinnie?" said Sharpitlaw, in his most conciliatory manner.

"The procurator's spoiled a'," observed Ratcliffe dryly.

And it was even so; for the question, put in so direct a shape, immediately awakened Madge to the propriety of being reserved upon those very topics on which Ratcliffe had indirectly seduced her to become communicative.

"What was't ye were speering at us, sir?" she resumed, with an appearance of stolidity so speedily assumed, as showed there was a good deal of knavery mixed with her folly.

"I asked you," said the procurator, "at what hour, and to what place, Robertson brought back your clothes."

"Robertson?—Lord haud a care o' us! what Robertson?"

"Why, the fellow we were speaking of, Gentle Geordie, as you call him."

"Geordie Gentle!" answered Madge, with well-feigned amazement—"I dinna ken naebody they ca' Geordie Gentle."

"Come, my jo," said Sharpitlaw, "this will not do; you must tell us what you did with these clothes of yours."

Madge Wildfire made no answer, unless the question may seem connected with the snatch of a song with which she indulged the embarrassed investigator :—

> "What did ye wi' the bridal ring—bridal ring—bridal ring?
> What did ye wi' your wedding ring, ye little cutty quean, O?
> I gied it till a sodger, a sodger, a sodger,
> I gied it till a sodger, an auld true love o' mine, O."

Of all the madwomen who have sung and said, since the days of Hamlet the Dane, if Ophelia be the most affecting, Madge Wildfire was the most provoking.

The procurator-fiscal was in despair. "I'll take some measures with this d—d Bess of Bedlam," said he, "that shall make her find her tongue."

"Wi' your favour, sir," said Ratcliffe, "better let her mind settle a little—Ye have aye made out something."

"True," said the official person; "a brown short-gown, mutch, red rokelay—that agrees with your Madge Wildfire, Mr. Butler?" Butler agreed that it did so. "Yes, there was a sufficient motive for taking this crazy creature's dress and name, while he was about such a job."

"And I am free to say *now*——" said Ratcliffe.

"When you see it has come out without you," interrupted Sharpitlaw.

"Just sae, sir," reiterated Ratcliffe. "I am free to say now, since it's come out otherwise, that these were the clothes I saw Robertson wearing last night in jail, when he was at the head of the rioters."

"That's direct evidence," said Sharpitlaw; "stick to that Rat—I will report favourably of you to the provost, for I have business for you to-night. It wears late; I must home and get a snack, and I'll be back in the evening. Keep Madge with you, Ratcliffe, and try to get her into a good tune again." So saying, he left the prison.

CHAPTER XVII

And some they whistled—and some they sang,
And some did loudly say,
Whenever Lord Barnard's horn it blew,
"Away, Musgrave, away!"
Ballad of Little Musgrave.

WHEN the man of office returned to the Heart of Mid-Lothian, he resumed his conference with Ratcliffe, of whose experience and assistance he now held himself secure. "You must speak with this wench, Rat—this Effie Deans—you must sift her a wee bit, for as sure as a tether she will ken Robertson's haunts —till her, Rat—till her, without delay."

"Craving your pardon, Mr. Sharpitlaw," said the turnkey elect, "that's what I am not free to do."

"Free to do, man? what the deil ails ye now?—I thought we had settled a' that."

"I dinna ken, sir," said Ratcliffe; "I hae spoken to this Effie—she's strange to this place and to it's ways, and to a' our ways, Mr. Sharpitlaw; and she greets, the silly tawpie, and she's breaking her heart already about this wild chield;

and were she the means o' taking him, she wad break it outright."

" She wunna hae time, lad," said Sharpitlaw; "the woodie will hae it's ain o' her before that—a woman's heart takes a lang time o' breaking."

" That's according to the stuff they are made o', sir," replied Ratcliffe—" But to make a lang tale short, I canna undertake the job. It gangs against my conscience."

Your conscience, Rat?" said Sharpitlaw, with a sneer, which the reader will probably think very natural upon the occasion.

" Ou ay, sir," answered Ratcliffe calmly, "just *my* conscience; a'body has a conscience, though it may be ill wunnin at it. I think mine's as weel out o' the gate as maist folk's are; and yet it's just like the noop of my elbow, it whiles gets a bit dirl on a corner."

" Weel, Rat," replied Sharpitlaw, "since ye are nice, I'll speak to the hussy mysell."

Sharpitlaw, accordingly, caused himself to be introduced into the little dark apartment tenanted by the unfortunate Effie Deans. The poor girl was seated on her little flock-bed, plunged in a deep reverie. Some food stood on the table, of a quality better than is usually supplied to prisoners, but it was untouched. The person under whose care she was more particularly placed said, "that sometimes she tasted naething from the tae end of the four-and-twenty hours to the t'other, except a drink of water."

Sharpitlaw took a chair, and, commanding the turnkey to retire, he opened the conversation, endeavouring to throw into his tone and countenance as much commiseration as they were capable of expressing, for the one was sharp and harsh, the other sly, acute, and selfish.

" How's a' wi' ye, Effie?—How d'ye find yoursell, hinny?"

A deep sigh was the only answer.

" Are the folk civil to ye, Effie?—it's my duty to inquire."

" Very civil, sir," said Effie, compelling herself to answer, yet hardly knowing what she said.

" And your victuals," continued Sharpitlaw, in the same condoling tone—" do you get what you like?—or is there onything you would particularly fancy, as your health seems but silly?"

" It's a' very weel, sir, I thank ye," said the poor prisoner, in a tone how different from the sportive vivacity of those of

the Lily of St. Leonard's !—"it's a' very gude—ower gude
for me."

"He must hae been a great villain, Effie, who brought you
to this pass," said Sharpitlaw.

The remark was dictated partly by a natural feeling, of
which even he could not divest himself, though accustomed to
practise on the passions of others, and keep a most heedful
guard over his own, and partly by his wish to introduce the
sort of conversation which might best serve his immediate
purpose. Indeed, upon the present occasion, these mixed
motives of feeling and cunning harmonised together wonderfully ; for, said Sharpitlaw to himself, the greater rogue
Robertson is, the more will be the merit of bringing him to
justice. "He must have been a great villain, indeed," he
again reiterated ; "and I wish I had the skelping o' him."

"I may blame mysell mair than him," said Effie ; "I
was bred up to ken better ; but he, poor fellow——" (she
stopped).

"Was a thorough blackguard a' his life, I dare say," said
Sharpitlaw. "A stranger he was in this country, and a companion of that lawless vagabond, Wilson, I think, Effie ? "

"It wad hae been dearly telling him that he had ne'er seen
Wilson's face."

"That's very true that you are saying, Effie," said Sharpitlaw. "Where was't that Robertson and you were used to
howff thegither ? Somegate about the Laigh Calton, I am
thinking."

The simple and dispirited girl had thus far followed Mr.
Sharpitlaw's lead, because he had artfully adjusted his observations to the thoughts he was pretty certain must be passing
through her own mind, so that her answers became a kind of
thinking aloud, a mood into which those who are either
constitutionally absent in mind, or are rendered so by the
temporary pressure of misfortune, may be easily led by a
skilful train of suggestions. But the last observation of the
procurator-fiscal was too much of the nature of a direct
interrogatory, and it broke the charm accordingly.

"What was it that I was saying ? " said Effie, starting up
from her reclining posture, seating herself upright, and hastily
shading her dishevelled hair back from her wasted, but still
beautiful countenance. She fixed her eyes boldly and keenly
upon Sharpitlaw ;—" You are too much of a gentleman, sir—
too much of an honest man, to take any notice of what a poor

creature like me says, that can hardly ca' my senses my ain—
God help me!"

"Advantage!—I would be of some advantage to you if I
could," said Sharpitlaw, in a soothing tone; "and I ken
naething sae likely to serve ye, Effie, as gripping this rascal,
Robertson."

"Oh, dinna misca' him, sir, that never misca'd you!—Robertson?—I am sure I had naething to say against ony man o' the
name, and naething will I say."

"But if you do not heed your own misfortune, Effie, you
should mind what distress he has brought on your family,"
said the man of law.

"Oh, Heaven help me!" exclaimed poor Effie—"My poor
father—my dear Jeanie—Oh, that's sairest to bide of a'! Oh,
sir, if you hae ony kindness—if ye hae ony touch of compassion—for a' the folk I see here are as hard as the wa'-
stanes—If ye wad but bid them let my sister Jeanie in the
next time she ca's! for when I hear them put her awa frae the
door, and canna climb up to that high window to see sae
muckle as her gown-tail, it's like to pit me out o' my judgment." And she looked on him with a face of entreaty so
earnest, yet so humble, that she fairly shook the steadfast
purpose of his mind.

"You shall see your sister," he began, "if you'll tell me,"—
then interrupting himself, he added, in a more hurried tone,—
"no, d—n it, you shall see your sister whether you tell me anything or no." So saying, he rose up and left the apartment.

When he had rejoined Ratcliffe, he observed, "You are
right, Ratton; there's no making much of that lassie. But
ae thing I have cleared—that is, that Robertson has been the
father of the bairn, and so I will wager a boddle it will be
he that's to meet wi' Jeanie Deans this night at Muschat's
Cairn, and there we'll nail him, Rat, or my name is not
Gideon Sharpitlaw."

"But," said Ratcliffe, perhaps because he was in no hurry
to say anything which was like to be connected with the
discovery and apprehension of Robertson, "an that were the
case, Mr. Butler wad hae kend the man in the King's Park to
be the same person wi' him in Madge Wildfire's claise, that
headed the mob."

"That makes nae difference, man," replied Sharpitlaw—
"the dress, the light, the confusion, and maybe a touch o' a
blackit cork, or a slake o' paint—hout, Ratton, I have seen ye

dress your ainsell, that the deevil ye belang to durstna hae made oath t'ye."

"And that's true, too," said Ratcliffe.

"And besides, ye donnard carle," continued Sharpitlaw triumphantly, "the minister *did* say that he thought he knew something of the features of the birkie that spoke to him in the Park, though he could not charge his memory where or when he had seen them."

"It's evident, then, your honour will be right," said Ratcliffe.

"Then, Rat, you and I will go with the party oursells this night, and see him in grips, or we are done wi' him."

"I seena muckle use I can be o' to your honour," said Ratcliffe reluctantly.

"Use?" answered Sharpitlaw—"You can guide the party —you ken the ground. Besides, I do not intend to quit sight o' you, my good friend, till I have him in hand."

"Weel, sir," said Ratcliffe, but in no joyful tone of ac- quiescence ; "Ye maun hae it your ain way—but mind he's a desperate man."

"We shall have that with us," answered Sharpitlaw, "that will settle him, if it is necessary."

"But, sir," answered Ratcliffe, "I am sure I couldna under- take to guide you to Muschat's Cairn in the night-time ; I ken the place, as mony does, in fair daylight, but how to find it by moonshine, amang sae mony crags and stanes, as like to each other as the collier to the deil, is mair than I can tell. I might as soon seek moonshine in water."

"What's the meaning o' this, Ratcliffe?" said Sharpitlaw, while he fixed his eye on the recusant, with a fatal and ominous expression,—"Have you forgotten that you are still under sentence of death?"

"No, sir," said Ratcliffe, "that's a thing no easily put out o' memory; and if my presence be judged necessary, nae doubt I maun gang wi' your honour. But I was gaun to tell your honour of ane that has mair skeel o' the gate than me, and that's e'en Madge Wildfire."

"The devil she has!—Do you think me as mad as she is, to trust to her guidance on such an occasion?"

"Your honour is the best judge," answered Ratcliffe; "but I ken I can keep her in tune, and garr her haud the straight path—she aften sleeps out, or rambles about amang thae hills the haill simmer night, the daft limmer."

"Well, Ratcliffe," replied the procurator-fiscal, "if you

think she can guide us the right way—but take heed to what you are about—your life depends on your behaviour."

"It's a sair judgment on a man," said Ratcliffe, "when he has ance gane sae far wrang as I hae done, that deil a bit he can be honest, try't whilk way he will."

Such was the reflection of Ratcliffe, when he was left for a few minutes to himself, while the retainer of justice went to procure a proper warrant, and give the necessary directions.

The rising moon saw the whole party free from the walls of the city, and entering upon the open ground. Arthur's Seat, like a couchant lion of immense size—Salisbury Crags, like a huge belt or girdle of granite, were dimly visible. Holding their path along the southern side of the Canongate, they gained the Abbey of Holyrood-house, and from thence found their way by step and stile into the King's Park. They were at first four in number—an officer of justice and Sharpitlaw, who were well armed with pistols and cutlasses; Ratcliffe, who was not trusted with weapons, lest he might, peradventure, have used them on the wrong side; and the female. But at the last stile, when they entered the Chase, they were joined by other two officers, whom Sharpitlaw, desirous to secure sufficient force for his purpose, and at the same time to avoid observation, had directed to wait for him at this place. Ratcliffe saw this accession of strength with some disquietude, for he had hitherto thought it likely that Robertson, who was a bold, stout, and active young fellow, might have made his escape from Sharpitlaw and the single officer, by force or agility, without his being implicated in the matter. But the present strength of the followers of justice was overpowering, and the only mode of saving Robertson (which the old sinner was well disposed to do, providing always he could accomplish his purpose without compromising his own safety), must be by contriving that he should have some signal of their approach. It was probably with this view that Ratcliffe had requested the addition of Madge to the party, having considerable confidence in her propensity to exert her lungs. Indeed, she had already given them so many specimens of her clamorous loquacity, that Sharpitlaw half determined to send her back with one of the officers, rather than carry forward in his company a person so extremely ill qualified to be a guide in a secret expedition. It seemed, too, as if the open air, the approach to the hills, and the ascent of the moon, supposed to be so portentous over those whose brain is infirm, made her spirits rise in a degree tenfold more loquacious than she had hitherto exhibited. To silence her by fair means seemed impossible; authoritative commands and coaxing entreaties she set alike at defiance, and threats only made her sulky, and altogether intractable.

"Is there no one of you," said Sharpitlaw impatiently, "that knows the way to this accursed place—this Nicol Muschat's Cairn—excepting this mad clavering idiot?"

"Deil ane o' them kens it, except mysell," exclaimed Madge; "how suld they, the poor fule cowards? But I hae sat on the grave frae bat-fleeing time till cock-crow, and had mony a fine crack wi' Nicol Muschat and Ailie Muschat, that are lying sleeping below."

"The devil take your crazy brain," said Sharpitlaw; "will you not allow the men to answer a question?"

The officers, obtaining a moment's audience while Ratcliffe diverted Madge's attention, declared that, though they had a general knowledge of the spot, they could not undertake to guide the party to it by the uncertain light of the moon, with such accuracy as to ensure success to their expedition.

"What shall we do, Ratcliffe?" said Sharpitlaw; "if he sees us before we see him—and that's what he is certain to do, if we go strolling about, without keeping the straight road—we may bid gude day to the job; and I would rather lose one hundred pounds, baith for the credit of the police, and because the Provost says somebody maun be hanged for this job o' Porteous, come o't what likes."

"I think," said Ratcliffe, "we maun just try Madge; and I'll see if I can get her keepit in ony better order. And at ony rate, if he suld hear her skirling her auld ends o' sangs, he's no to ken for that that there's onybody wi' her."

"That's true," said Sharpitlaw; "and if he thinks her alone he's as like to come towards her as to rin frae her. So set forward—we hae lost ower muckle time already—see to get her to keep the right road."

"And what sort o' house does Nicol Muschat and his wife keep now?" said Ratcliffe to the madwoman, by way of humouring her vein of folly; "they were but thrawn folk lang syne, an a' tales be true."

"Ou, ay, ay, ay—but a's forgotten now," replied Madge, in the confidential tone of a gossip giving the history of her next-door neighbour—"Ye see, I spoke to them mysell, and tauld them byganes suld be byganes—her throat's sair misguggled and mashackered though; she wears her corpse-sheet drawn weel up to hide it, but that canna hinder the bluid seiping through, ye ken. I wussed her to wash it in St. Anthony's Well, and that will cleanse if onything can—But they say bluid never bleaches out o' linen claith—Deacon Sanders's new cleansing draps winna do't—I tried them mysell on a bit rag we hae at hame that was mailed wi' the bluid of a bit skirling wean that was hurt some gate, but out it winna come—Weel, ye'll say that's queer; but I will bring it out to St. Anthony's blessed Well some braw night just like this, and I'll cry up Ailie Muschat, and she and I will hae a grand bouking-washing, and bleach our claise in the beams of the bonny Lady Moon, that's far pleasanter to me than the sun—the sun's ower het, and ken ye, cummers, my brains are het enough already. But the moon, and the dew, and the night-wind, they are just like a caller kail-blade laid on my brow; and whiles I think the moon just shines on purpose to pleasure me, when naebody sees her but mysell."

This raving discourse she continued with prodigious volubility, walking on at a great pace, and dragging Ratcliffe along with her, while he endeavoured, in appearance at least, if not in reality, to induce her to moderate her voice.

All at once, she stopped short upon the top of a little hillock, gazed upward fixedly, and said not one word for the space of five minutes. "What the devil is the matter with her now?" said Sharpitlaw to Ratcliffe—"Can you not get her forward?"

"Ye maun just take a grain o' patience wi' her, sir," said Ratcliffe. "She'll no gae a foot faster than she likes hersell."

"D—n her," said Sharpitlaw, "I'll take care she has her time in Bedlam or Bridewell, or both, for she's both mad and mischievous."

In the meanwhile, Madge, who had looked very pensive when she first stopped, suddenly burst into a vehement fit of laughter, then paused and sighed bitterly,—then was seized with a second fit of laughter,—then, fixing her eyes on the moon, lifted up her voice and sung,—

> "Good even, good fair moon, good even to thee;
> I prithee, dear moon, now show to me
> The form and the features, the speech and degree,
> Of the man that true lover of mine shall be.

But I need not ask that of the bonny Lady Moon—I ken that weel eneugh mysell—*true*-love though he wasna—But

naebody shall say that I ever tauld a word about the matter—
But whiles I wish the bairn had lived—Weel, God guide us,
there's a heaven aboon us a'"—(here she sighed bitterly),
"and a bonny moon, and sterns in it forby" (and here she
laughed once more).

"Are we to stand here all night?" said Sharpitlaw, very
impatiently. "Drag her forward."

"Ay, sir," said Ratcliffe, "if we kend whilk way to drag
her, that would settle it at ance.—Come, Madge, hinny,"
addressing her, "we'll no be in time to see Nicol and his
wife, unless ye show us the road."

"In troth and that I will, Ratton," said she, seizing him by
the arm, and resuming her route with huge strides, considering
it was a female who took them. "And I'll tell ye, Ratton,
blithe will Nicol Muschat be to see ye, for he says he kens
weel there isna sic a villain out o' hell as ye are, and he wad
be ravished to hae a crack wi' you—like to like, ye ken—it's
a proverb never fails—and ye are baith a pair o' the deevil's
peats, I trow—hard to ken whilk deserves the hettest corner
o' his ingle-side."

Ratcliffe was conscience-struck, and could not forbear
making an involuntary protest against this classification. "I
never shed blood," he replied.

"But ye hae sauld it, Ratton—ye hae sauld blood mony a
time. Folk kill wi' the tongue as weel as wi' the hand—wi'
the word as weel as wi' the gulley !—

> ' It is the bonny butcher lad,
>   That wears the sleeves of blue,
> He sells the flesh on Saturday,
>   On Friday that he slew.' "

"And what is that I am doing now?" thought Ratcliffe.
"But I'll hae nae wyte of Robertson's young bluid, if I
can help it ;" then speaking apart to Madge, he asked her,
"Whether she did not remember ony o' her auld sangs?"

"Mony a dainty ane," said Madge; "and blithely can I
sing them, for lightsome sangs make merry gate." And she
sang—

> "When the glede's in the blue cloud,
>   The lavrock lies still ;
> When the hound's in the green-wood,
>   The hind keeps the hill."

"Silence her cursed noise, if you should throttle her," said
Sharpitlaw ; "I see somebody yonder.—Keep close, my boys,

and creep round the shoulder of the height.   George Poinder, stay you with Ratcliffe and that mad yelling bitch; and you other two, come with me round under the shadow of the brae."

And he crept forward with the stealthy pace of an Indian savage, who leads his band to surprise an unsuspecting party of some hostile tribe.   Ratcliffe saw them glide off, avoiding the moonlight, and keeping as much in the shade as possible. "Robertson's done up," said he to himself, "thae young lads are aye sae thoughtless.   What deevil could he hae to say to Jeanie Deans, or to ony woman on earth, that he suld gang awa and get his neck raxed for her?   And this mad quean, after cracking like a pen-gun, and skirling like a pea-hen for the haill night, behoves just to hae hadden her tongue when her clavers might have done some gude!   But it's aye the way wi' women; if they ever haud their tongues ava', ye may swear it's for mischief.   I wish I could set her on again without this blood-sucker kenning what I am doing.   But he's as gleg as MacKeachan's elshin, that ran through sax plies of bend-leather and half an inch into the king's heel."

He then began to hum, but in a very low and suppressed tone, the first stanza of a favourite ballad of Wildfire's, the words of which bore some distant analogy with the situation of Robertson, trusting that the power of association would not fail to bring the rest to her mind :

> " There's a bloodhound ranging Tinwald wood,
>   There's harness glancing sheen ;
> There's a maiden sits on Tinwald brae,
>   And she sings loud between."

Madge had no sooner received the catch-word, than she vindicated Ratcliffe's sagacity by setting off at score with the song :

> " O sleep ye sound, Sir James, she said,
>   When ye suld rise and ride ?
> There's twenty men, wi' bow and blade,
>   Are seeking where ye hide."

Though Ratcliffe was at a considerable distance from the spot called Muschat's Cairn, yet his eyes, practised like those of a cat to penetrate darkness, could mark that Robertson had caught the alarm.   George Poinder, less keen of sight, or less attentive, was not aware of his flight any more than Sharpitlaw and his assistants, whose view, though they were considerably nearer to the cairn, was intercepted by the broken nature of the ground under which they were screening themselves. At length, however, after an interval of five or six minutes, they also perceived that Robertson had fled, and rushed hastily towards the place, while Sharpitlaw called out aloud, in the harshest tones of a voice which resembled a saw-mill at work, "Chase, lads—chase—haud the brae—I see him on the edge of the hill!" Then hollowing back to the rear-guard of his detachment, he issued his further orders: "Ratcliffe, come here and detain the woman—George, run and kepp the stile at the Duke's Walk—Ratcliffe, come here directly—but first knock out that mad bitch's brains!"

"Ye had better rin for it, Madge," said Ratcliffe, "for it's ill dealing wi' an angry man."

Madge Wildfire was not so absolutely void of common sense as not to understand this innuendo; and while Ratcliffe, in seemingly anxious haste of obedience, hastened to the spot where Sharpitlaw waited to deliver up Jeanie Deans to his custody, she fled with all the despatch she could exert in an opposite direction. Thus the whole party were separated, and in rapid motion of flight or pursuit, excepting Ratcliffe and Jeanie, whom, although making no attempt to escape, he held fast by the cloak, and who remained standing by Muschat's Cairn.

CHAPTER XVIII

You have paid the heavens your function, and the prisoner the very debt of your calling.   *Measure for Measure.*

JEANIE DEANS,—for here our story unites itself with that part of the narrative which broke off at the end of the fifteenth chapter,—while she waited in terror and amazement the hasty advance of three or four men towards her, was yet more startled at their suddenly breaking asunder, and giving chase in different directions to the late object of her terror, who became at that moment, though she could not well assign a reasonable cause, rather the cause of her interest. One of the party (it was Sharpitlaw) came straight up to her, and saying, "Your name is Jeanie Deans, and you are my prisoner," immediately added, "but if you will tell me which way he ran I will let you go."

"I dinna ken, sir," was all the poor girl could utter; and, indeed, it is the phrase which rises most readily to the lips of any person in her rank, as the readiest reply to any embarrassing question.

"But," said Sharpitlaw, "ye *ken* wha it was ye were speaking wi', my leddy, on the hill side, and midnight sae near; ye surely ken *that*, my bonny woman?"

"I dinna ken, sir," again iterated Jeanie, who really did not comprehend in her terror the nature of the questions which were so hastily put to her in this moment of surprise.

"We will try to mend your memory by-and-by, hinny," said Sharpitlaw, and shouted, as we have already told the reader, to Ratcliffe to come up and take charge of her, while he himself directed the chase after Robertson, which he still hoped might be successful. As Ratcliffe approached, Sharpitlaw pushed the young woman towards him with some rudeness, and betaking himself to the more important object of his quest, began to scale crags and scramble up steep banks, with an agility of which his profession and his general gravity of demeanour would previously have argued him incapable. In a few minutes there was no one within sight, and only a distant halloo from one of the pursuers to the other, faintly heard on the side of the hill, argued that there was any one within hearing. Jeanie Deans was left in the clear moonlight, standing under the guard of a person of whom she knew nothing, and, what was worse, concerning whom, as the reader is well aware, she could have learned nothing that would not have increased her terror.

When all in the distance was silent, Ratcliffe for the first time addressed her, and it was in that cold, sarcastic, indifferent tone familiar to habitual depravity, whose crimes are instigated by custom rather than by passion. "This is a braw night for ye, dearie," he said, attempting to pass his arm across her shoulder, "to be on the green hill wi' your jo." Jeanie extricated herself from his grasp, but did not make any reply. "I think lads and lasses," continued the ruffian, "dinna meet at Muschat's Cairn at midnight to crack nuts and he again attempted to take hold of her.

"If ye are an officer of justice, sir," said Jeanie, again eluding his attempt to seize her, "ye deserve to have your coat stripped from your back."

"Very true, hinny," said he, succeeding forcibly in his

attempt to get hold of her, " but suppose I should strip your cloak off first ? "

" Ye are more a man, I am sure, than to hurt me, sir," said Jeanie ; "for God's sake have pity on a half-distracted creature!"

" Come, come," said Ratcliffe, " you're a good-looking wench, and should not be cross-grained. I was going to be an honest man—but the devil has this very day flung first a lawyer, and then a woman, in my gate. I'll tell you what, Jeanie, they are out on the hill-side—if you'll be guided by me, I'll carry you to a wee bit corner in the Pleasance, that I ken o' in an auld wife's, that a' the prokitors o' Scotland wot naething o', and we'll send Robertson word to meet us in Yorkshire, for there is a set o' braw lads about the midland counties, that I hae dune business wi' before now, and sae we'll leave Mr. Sharpitlaw to whistle on his thumb."

It was fortunate for Jeanie, in an emergency like the present, that she possessed presence of mind and courage, so soon as the first hurry of surprise had enabled her to rally her recollection. She saw the risk she was in from a ruffian, who not only was such by profession, but had that evening been stupefying, by means of strong liquors, the internal aversion which he felt at the business on which Sharpitlaw had resolved to employ him.

" Dinna speak sae loud," said she, in a low voice ; "he's up yonder."

" Who?—Robertson ? " said Ratcliffe, eagerly.

" Ay," replied Jeanie, "up yonder ; " and she pointed to the ruins of the hermitage and chapel.

" By G—d, then," said Ratcliffe, " I'll make my ain of him, either one way or other—wait for me here."

But no sooner had he set off, as fast as he could run, towards the chapel, than Jeanie started in an opposite direction, over high and low, on the nearest path homeward. Her juvenile exercise as a herdswoman had put "life and mettle" in her heels, and never had she followed Dustiefoot, when the cows were in the corn, with half so much speed as she now cleared the distance betwixt Muschat's Cairn and her father's cottage at Saint Leonard's. To lift the latch—to enter—to shut, bolt, and double bolt the door—to draw against it a heavy article of furniture (which she could not have moved in a moment of less energy), so as to make yet further provision against violence, was almost the work of a moment, yet done with such silence as equalled the celerity.

Her next anxiety was upon her father's account, and she drew silently to the door of his apartment, in order to satisfy herself whether he had been disturbed by her return. He was awake—probably had slept but little; but the constant presence of his own sorrows, the distance of his apartment from the outer door of the house, and the precautions which Jeanie had taken to conceal her departure and return, had prevented him from being sensible of either. He was engaged in his devotions, and Jeanie could distinctly hear him use these words : "And for the other child Thou hast given me to be a comfort and stay to my old age, may her days be long in the land, according to the promise Thou hast given to those who shall honour father and mother; may all her purchased and promised blessings be multiplied upon her; keep her in the watches of the night, and in the uprising of the morning, that all in this land may know that Thou hast not utterly hid thy face from those that seek Thee in truth and in sincerity." He was silent, but probably continued his petition in the strong fervency of mental devotion.

His daughter retired to her apartment, comforted, that while she was exposed to danger, her head had been covered by the prayers of the just as by a helmet, and under the strong confidence, that while she walked worthy of the protection of Heaven, she would experience its countenance. It was in that moment that a vague idea first darted across her mind, that something might yet be achieved for her sister's safety, conscious as she now was of her innocence of the unnatural murder with which she stood charged. It came, as she described it, on her mind, like a sun-blink on a stormy sea; and although it instantly vanished, yet she felt a degree of composure which she had not experienced for many days, and could not help being strongly persuaded that, by some means or other, she would be called upon, and directed, to work out her sister's deliverance. She went to bed, not forgetting her usual devotions, the more fervently made on account of her late deliverance, and she slept soundly in spite of her agitation.

We must return to Ratcliffe, who had started, like a greyhound from the slips when the sportsman cries halloo, so soon as Jeanie had pointed to the ruins. Whether he meant to aid Robertson's escape, or to assist his pursuers, may be very doubtful; perhaps he did not himself know, but had resolved to be guided by circumstances. He had no opportunity, however, of doing either; for he had no sooner surmounted the steep ascent, and entered under the broken arches of the ruins, than a pistol was presented at his head, and a harsh voice commanded him, in the king's name, to surrender himself prisoner. " Mr. Sharpitlaw!" said Ratcliffe, surprised, "is this your honour?"

" Is it only you, and be d—d to you?" answered the fiscal, still more disappointed—"what made you leave the woman?"

"She told me she saw Robertson go into the ruins, so I made what haste I could to cleek the callant."

" It's all over now," said Sharpitlaw; "we shall see no more of him to-night; but he shall hide himself in a bean-hool, if he remains on Scottish ground without my finding him. Call back the people, Ratcliffe."

Ratcliffe hollowed to the dispersed officers, who willingly obeyed the signal; for probably there was no individual among them who would have been much desirous of a rencontre hand to hand, and at a distance from his comrades, with such an active and desperate fellow as Robertson.

" And where are the two women?" said Sharpitlaw.

"Both made their heels serve them, I suspect," replied Ratcliffe, and he hummed the end of an old song—

> "Then hey play up the rin-awa bride,
> For she has taen the gee."

" One woman," said Sharpitlaw,—for, like all rogues, he was a great calumniator of the fair sex,[1]—"one woman is enough to dark the fairest ploy that ever was planned; and how could I be such an ass as to expect to carry through a job that had two in it? But we know how to come by them both, if they are wanted, that's one good thing."

Accordingly, like a defeated general, sad and sulky, he led back his discomfited forces to the metropolis, and dismissed them for the night.

The next morning early, he was under the necessity of making his report to the sitting magistrate of the day. The gentleman who occupied the chair of office on this occasion (for the bailies, *Anglicé*, aldermen, take it by rotation) chanced to be the same by whom Butler was committed, a person very generally respected among his fellow-citizens. Something he was of a humorist, and rather deficient in general education; but acute, patient, and upright, possessed of a fortune acquired

---

[1] Note IX.—Calumniator of the Fair Sex.

by honest industry, which made him perfectly independent; and, in short, very happily qualified to support the respectability of the office which he held.

Mr. Middleburgh had just taken his seat, and was debating in an animated manner, with one of his colleagues, the doubtful chances of a game of golf which they had played the day before, when a letter was delivered to him, addressed " For Bailie Middleburgh; These: to be forwarded with speed." It contained these words:—

"SIR,—I know you to be a sensible and a considerate magistrate, and one who, as such, will be content to worship God, though the devil bid you. I therefore expect that, notwithstanding the signature of this letter acknowledges my share in an action, which, in a proper time and place, I would not fear either to avow or to justify, you will not on that account reject what evidence I place before you. The clergyman, Butler, is innocent of all but involuntary presence at an action which he wanted spirit to approve of, and from which he endeavoured, with his best set phrases, to dissuade us. But it was not for him that it is my hint to speak. There is a woman in your jail, fallen under the edge of a law so cruel, that it has hung by the wall, like unscoured armour, for twenty years, and is now brought down and whetted to spill the blood of the most beautiful and most innocent creature whom the walls of a prison ever girdled in. Her sister knows of her innocence, as she communicated to her that she was betrayed by a villain. Oh that high Heaven

'Would put in every honest hand a whip,
To scourge me such a villain through the world!'

"I write distractedly—But this girl—this Jeanie Deans, is a peevish puritan, superstitious and scrupulous after the manner of her sect; and I pray your honour, for so my phrase must go, to press upon her, that her sister's life depends upon her testimony. But though she should remain silent, do not dare to think that the young woman is guilty— far less to permit her execution. Remember the death of Wilson was fearfully avenged; and those yet live who can compel you to drink the dregs of your poisoned chalice.—I say, remember Porteous,—and say that you had good counsel from   ONE OF HIS SLAYERS."

The magistrate read over this extraordinary letter twice or thrice. At first he was tempted to throw it aside as the production of a madman, so little did "the scraps from play-books," as he termed the poetical quotation, resemble the correspondence of a rational being. On a re-perusal, however, he thought that, amid its incoherence, he could discover something like a tone of awakened passion, though expressed in a manner quaint and unusual.

"It is a cruelly severe statute," said the magistrate to his assistant, "and I wish the girl could be taken from under the letter of it. A child may have been born, and it may have been conveyed away while the mother was insensible, or it may have perished for want of that relief which the poor creature herself—helpless, terrified, distracted, despairing, and exhausted—may have been unable to afford to it. And yet it is certain, if the woman is found guilty under the statute, execution will follow. The crime has been too common, and examples are necessary."

"But if this other wench," said the city-clerk, "can speak to her sister communicating her situation, it will take the case from under the statute."

"Very true," replied the Bailie; "and I will walk out one of these days to St. Leonard's, and examine the girl myself. I know something of their father Deans—an old true-blue Cameronian, who would see house and family go to wreck ere he would disgrace his testimony by a sinful complying with the defections of the times; and such he will probably uphold the taking an oath before a civil magistrate. If they are to go on and flourish with their bull-headed obstinacy, the legislature must pass an act to take their affirmations, as in the case of Quakers. But surely neither a father nor a sister will scruple in a case of this kind. As I said before, I will go speak with them myself, when the hurry of this Porteous investigation is somewhat over; their pride and spirit of contradiction will be far less alarmed, than if they were called into a court of justice at once."

"And I suppose Butler is to remain incarcerated?" said the city-clerk.

"For the present, certainly," said the magistrate. "But I hope soon to set him at liberty upon bail."

"Do you rest upon the testimony of that light-headed letter?" asked the clerk.

"Not very much," answered the Bailie; "and yet there is

something striking about it too—it seems the letter of a man beside himself, either from great agitation, or some great sense of guilt."

"Yes," said the town-clerk, "it is very like the letter of a mad strolling play-actor, who deserves to be hanged with all the rest of nis gang, as your honour justly observes."

"I was not quite so bloodthirsty," continued the magistrate. "But to the point. Butler's private character is excellent; and I am given to understand, by some inquiries I have been making this morning, that he did actually arrive in town only the day before yesterday, so that it was impossible he could have been concerned in any previous machinations of these unhappy rioters, and it is not likely that he should have joined them on a suddenty."

"There's no saying anent that—zeal catches fire at a slight spark as fast as a brunstane match," observed the secretary. "I hae kent a minister wad be fair gude day and fair gude e'en wi' ilka man in the parochine, and hing just as quiet as a rocket on a stick, till ye mentioned the word abjuration-oath, or patronage, or siclike, and then, whiz, he was off, and up in the air an hundred miles beyond common manners, common sense, and common comprehension."

"I do not understand," answered the burgher-magistrate, "that the young man Butler's zeal is of so inflammable a character. But I will make farther investigation. What other business is there before us?"

And they proceeded to minute investigations concerning the affair of Porteous's death, and other affairs through which this history has no occasion to trace them.

In the course of their business they were interrupted by an old woman of the lower rank, extremely haggard in look, and wretched in her apparel, who thrust herself into the council-room.

"What do you want, gudewife?—Who are you?" said Bailie Middleburgh.

"What do I want!" replied she, in a sulky tone—"I want my bairn, or I want naething frae nane o' ye, for as grand's ye are." And she went on muttering to herself, with the wayward spitefulness of age—"They maun hae lordships and honours, nae doubt—set them up, the gutter-bloods! and deil a gentleman amang them."—Then again addressing the sitting magistrate, "Will *your honour* gie me back my puir crazy bairn? —*His* honour!—I hae kend the day when less wad ser'd him, the oe of a Campvere skipper."

'Good woman," said the magistrate to this shrewish supplicant,—"tell us what it is you want, and do not interrupt the
court."

"That's as muckle as till say, Bark, Bawtie, and be dune
wi't!—I tell ye," raising her termagant voice, "I want my
bairn! isna that braid Scots?"

"Who *are* you?—who is your bairn?" demanded the
magistrate.

"Wha am I?—wha suld I be, but Meg Murdockson, and
wha suld my bairn be but Magdalen Murdockson?—Your
guard soldiers, and your constables, and your officers, ken us
weel eneugh when they rive the bits o' duds aff our backs, and
take what penny o' siller we hae, and harle us to the Correction-
house in Leith Wynd, and pettle us up wi' bread and water, and
siclike sunkets."

"Who is she?" said the magistrate, looking round to some
of his people.

"Other than a gude ane, sir," said one of the city-officers,
shrugging his shoulders, and smiling.

"Will ye say sae?" said the termagant, her eye gleaming
with impotent fury; "an I had ye among the Frigate-Whins,
wadna I set my ten talents in your wuzzent face for that very
word?" and she suited the word to the action, by spreading
out a set of claws resembling those of St. George's dragon on
a country sign-post.

"What does she want here?" said the impatient magistrate.
"Can she not tell her business, or go away?"

"It's my bairn!—it's Magdalen Murdockson I'm wantin',"
answered the beldame, screaming at the highest pitch of her
cracked and mistuned voice—"havena I been telling ye sae
this half-hour? And if ye are deaf, what needs ye sit cockit
up there, and keep folk scraughin' t'ye this gate?"

"She wants her daughter, sir," said the same officer whose
interference had given the hag such offence before—"her
daughter, who was taken up last night—Madge Wildfire, as
they ca' her."

"Madge HELLFIRE, as they ca' her!" echoed the beldame;
"and what business has a blackguard like you to ca' an honest
woman's bairn out o' her ain name?"

"An *honest* woman's bairn, Maggie?" answered the peace-
officer, smiling and shaking his head with an ironical emphasis
on the adjective, and a calmness calculated to provoke to madness the furious old shrew.

"If I am no honest now I was honest ance," she replied;
"and that's mair than ye can say, ye born and bred thief, that
never kend ither folk's gear frae your ain since the day ye was
cleckit. Honest, say ye?—ye pykit your mother's pouch o'
twalpennies Scotch when ye were five years auld, just as she was
taking leave o' your father at the fit o' the gallows."

"She has you there, George," said the assistants, and there
was a general laugh; for the wit was fitted for the meridian of
the place where it was uttered. This general applause somewhat gratified the passions of the old hag; the "grim feature"
smiled, and even laughed—but it was a laugh of bitter scorn.
She condescended, however, as if appeased by the success
of her sally, to explain her business more distinctly, when
the magistrate, commanding silence, again desired her either
to speak out her errand, or to leave the place.

"Her bairn," she said, "*was* her bairn, and she came to
fetch her out of ill haft and waur guiding. If she wasna sae
wise as ither folk, few ither folk had suffered as muckle as she
had done; forby that she could fend the waur for hersell within
the four wa's of a jail. She could prove by fifty witnesses, and
fifty to that, that her daughter had never seen Jock Porteous,
alive or dead, since he had gien her a loundering wi' his cane,
the neger that he was! for driving a dead cat at the provost's
wig on the Elector of Hanover's birthday."

Notwithstanding the wretched appearance and violent demeanour of this woman, the magistrate felt the justice of her
argument, that her child might be as dear to her as to a more
fortunate and more amiable mother. He proceeded to investi-
gate the circumstances which had led to Madge Murdockson's
(or Wildfire's) arrest, and as it was clearly shown that she had
not been engaged in the riot, he contented himself with directing that an eye should be kept upon her by the police, but that
for the present she should be allowed to return home with her
mother. During the interval of fetching Madge from the jail,
the magistrate endeavoured to discover whether her mother
had been privy to the change of dress betwixt that young
woman and Robertson. But on this point he could obtain
no light. She persisted in declaring, that she had never seen
Robertson since his remarkable escape during service-time;
and that, if her daughter had changed clothes with him, it must
have been during her absence at a hamlet about two miles out
of town, called Duddingstone, where she could prove that she
passed that eventful night. And, in fact, one of the town-

officers, who had been searching for stolen linen at the cottage of a washerwoman in that village, gave his evidence, that he had seen Maggie Murdockson there, whose presence had considerably increased his suspicion of the house in which she was a visitor, in respect that he considered her as a person of no good reputation.

"I tauld ye sae," said the hag; "see now what it is to hae a character, gude or bad!—Now, maybe after a', I could tell ye something about Porteous that you council-chamber bodies never could find out, for as muckle stir as ye mak."

All eyes were turned towards her—all ears were alert. "Speak out!" said the magistrate.

"It will be for your ain gude," insinuated the town-clerk.

"Dinna keep the Bailie waiting," urged the assistants.

She remained doggedly silent for two or three minutes, casting around a malignant and sulky glance, that seemed to enjoy the anxious suspense with which they waited her answer. And then she broke forth at once,—"A' that I ken about him is, that he was neither soldier nor gentleman, but just a thief and a blackguard, like maist o' yoursells, dears— What will ye gie me for that news, now?—He wad hae served the gude town lang or provost or bailie wad hae fund that out, my joe!"

While these matters were in discussion, Madge Wildfire entered, and her first exclamation was, "Eh! see if there isna our auld ne'er-do-weel deevil's buckie o' a mither—Hegh, sirs! but we are a hopefu' family, to be twa o' us in the Guard at ance. But there were better days wi' us ance—were there na, mither?"

Old Maggie's eyes had glistened with something like an expression of pleasure when she saw her daughter set at liberty. But either her natural affection, like that of the tigress, could not be displayed without a strain of ferocity, or there was something in the ideas which Madge's speech awakened, that again stirred her cross and savage temper. "What signifies what we were, ye street-raking limmer!" she exclaimed, pushing her daughter before her to the door, with no gentle degree of violence. "I'se tell thee what thou is now—thou's a crazed hellicat Bess o' Bedlam, that sall taste naething but bread and water for a fortnight, to serve ye for the plague ye hae gien me—and ower gude for ye, ye idle taupie!"

Madge, however, escaped from her mother at the door, ran

back to the foot of the table, dropped a very low and fantastic curtsey to the judge, and said, with a giggling laugh,—" Our minnie's sair mis-set, after her ordinar, sir—She'll hae had some quarrel wi' her auld gudeman—that's Satan, ye ken, sirs." This explanatory note she gave in a low, confidential tone, and the spectators of that credulous generation did not hear it without an involuntary shudder. " The gudeman and her disna aye gree weel, and then I maun pay the piper; but my back's broad eneugh to bear't a'—an' if she hae nae havings, that's nae reason why wiser folk shouldna hae some." Here another deep curtsey, when the ungracious voice of her mother was heard.

" Madge, ye limmer! If I come to fetch ye!"

" Hear till her," said Madge. " But I'll wun out a gliff the night for a' that, to dance in the moonlight, when her and the gudeman will be whirrying through the blue lift on a broom-shank, to see Jean Jap, that they hae putten intill the Kirkcaldy tolbooth—ay, they will hae a merry sail ower Inch-keith, and ower a' the bits o' bonny waves that are poppling and plashing against the rocks in the gowden glimmer o' the moon, ye ken.—I'm coming, mother—I'm coming," she con-cluded, on hearing a scuffle at the door betwixt the beldam and the officers, who were endeavouring to prevent her re-entrance. Madge then waved her hand wildly towards the ceiling, and sung, at the topmost pitch of her voice,—

> " Up in the air,
>   On my bonny grey mare,
>   And I see, and I see, and I see her yet."

And with a hop, skip, and jump, sprung out of the room, as the witcnes of Macbeth used, in less refined days, to seem to fly upwards from the stage.

Some weeks intervened before Mr. Middleburgh, agreeably to his benevolent resolution, found an opportunity of taking a walk towards St. Leonard's, in order to discover whether it might be possible to obtain the evidence hinted at in the anonymous letter respecting Effie Deans.

In fact, the anxious perquisitions made to discover the murderers of Porteous occupied the attention of all concerned with the administration of justice.

In the course of these inquiries, two circumstances happened material to our story. Butler, after a close investigation of his conduct, was declared innocent of accession to the death of Porteous ; but, as having been present during the whole transaction, was obliged to find bail not to quit his usual residence at Libberton, that he might appear as a witness when called upon. The other incident regarded the disappearance of Madge Wildfire and her mother from Edinburgh. When they were sought, with the purpose of subjecting them to some further interrogatories, it was discovered by Mr. Sharpitlaw that they had eluded the observation of the police, and left the city so soon as dismissed from the council-chamber. No efforts could trace the place of their retreat.

In the meanwhile the excessive indignation of the Council of Regency, at the slight put upon their authority by the murder of Porteous, had dictated measures, in which their own extreme desire of detecting the actors in that conspiracy were consulted in preference to the temper of the people, and the character of their churchmen. An act of parliament was hastily passed, offering two hundred pounds reward to those who should inform against any person concerned in the deed, and the penalty of death, by a very unusual and severe enactment, was denounced against those who should harbour the guilty. But what was chiefly accounted exceptionable was a clause, appointing the act to be read in churches by the officiating clergyman, on the first Sunday of every month, for a certain period, immediately before the sermon. The ministers who should refuse to comply with this injunction were declared, for the first offence, incapable of sitting or voting in any church judicature, and for the second, incapable of holding any ecclesiastical preferment in Scotland.

This last order united in a common cause those who might privately rejoice in Porteous's death, though they dared not vindicate the manner of it, with the more scrupulous presbyterians, who held that even the pronouncing the name of the "Lords Spiritual" in a Scottish pulpit was, *quodammodo*, an acknowledgment of prelacy, and that the injunction of the legislature was an interference of the civil government with the *jus divinum* of presbytery, since to the General Assembly alone, as representing the invisible head of the kirk, belonged the sole and exclusive right of regulating whatever pertained to public worship. Very many also, of different political or religious sentiments, and therefore not much moved by these considerations, thought they saw, in so violent an act of parliament, a more vindictive spirit than became the legislature of a great country, and something like an attempt to trample upon the rights and independence of Scotland. The various steps adopted for punishing the city of Edinburgh, by taking away her charter and liberties, for what a violent and over-mastering mob had done within her walls, were resented by many, who thought a pretext was too hastily taken for degrading the ancient metropolis of Scotland. In short, there was much heart-burning, discontent, and disaffection, occasioned by these ill-considered measures.[1]

Amidst these heats and dissensions, the trial of Effie Deans, after she had been many weeks imprisoned, was at length about to be brought forward, and Mr. Middleburgh found leisure to inquire into the evidence concerning her. For this purpose, he chose a fine day for his walk towards her father's house.

The excursion into the country was somewhat distant, in the opinion of a burgess of those days, although many of the present inhabit suburban villas considerably beyond the spot to which we allude. Three-quarters of an hour's walk, however, even at a pace of magisterial gravity, conducted our benevolent office-bearer to the Crags of St. Leonard's, and the humble mansion of David Deans.

The old man was seated on the deas, or turf-seat, at the end of his cottage, busied in mending his cart-harness with his own hands; for in those days any sort of labour which required a little more skill than usual fell to the share of the goodman himself, and that even when he was well to pass in the world. With stern and austere gravity he persevered in his task, after having just raised his head to notice the advance of the stranger. It would have been impossible to have discovered, from his countenance and manner, the internal feelings of agony with which he contended. Mr. Middleburgh waited an instant, expecting Deans would in some measure acknowledge his presence, and lead into conversation; but, as he seemed determined to remain silent, he was himself obliged to speak first.

[1] The Magistrates were closely interrogated before the House of Peers, concerning the particulars of the Mob, and the *patois* in which these functionaries made their answers, sounded strange in the ears of the Southern nobles. The Duke of Newcastle having demanded to know with what kind of shot the guard which Porteous commanded had loaded their muskets, was answered naïvely, "Ow, just sic as ane shoots *dukes* and *fools* with." This reply was considered as a contempt of the House of Lords, and the Provost would have suffered accordingly, but that the Duke of Argyle explained, that the expression, properly rendered into English, meant *ducks and water-fowl.*

"My name is Middleburgh—Mr. James Middleburgh, one of the present magistrates of the city of Edinburgh."

"It may be sae," answered Deans laconically, and without interrupting his labour.

"You must understand," he continued, "that the duty of a magistrate is sometimes an unpleasant one."

"It may be sae," replied David; "I hae naething to say in the contrair;" and he was again doggedly silent.

"You must be aware," pursued the magistrate, "that persons in my situation are often obliged to make painful and disagreeable inquiries of individuals, merely because it is their bounden duty."

"It may be sae," again replied Deans; "I hae naething to say anent it, either the tae way or the t'other. But I do ken there was ance in a day a just and God-fearing magistracy in yon town o' Edinburgh, that did not bear the sword in vain, but were a terror to evil-doers, and a praise to such as kept the path. In the glorious days of auld worthy faithfu' Provost Dick,[1] when there was a true and faithfu' General Assembly of the Kirk, walking hand in hand with the real noble Scottish-hearted barons, and with the magistrates of this and other towns, gentles, burgesses, and commons of all ranks, seeing with one eye, hearing with one ear, and upholding the ark with their united strength—And then folk might see men deliver up their silver to the states' use, as if it had been as muckle sclate stanes. My father saw them toom the sacks of dollars out o' Provost Dick's window intill the carts that carried them to the army at Dunse Law; and if ye winna believe his testimony, there is the window itsell still standing in the Luckenbooths—I think it's a claith-merchant's booth the day[2]—at the airn stanchells, five doors abune Gossford's Close.—But now we haena sic spirit amang us; we think mair about the warst wally-draigle in our ain byre, than about the blessing which the angel of the covenant gave to the Patriarch even at Peniel and Mahanaim, or the binding obligation of our national vows; and we wad rather gie a pund Scots to buy an unguent to clear our auld rannell-trees and our beds o' the English bugs as they ca' them, than we wad gie a plack to rid the land of the swarm of Arminian caterpillars, Socinian pismires, and deistical Miss Katies, that

[1] Note X.—Sir William Dick of Braid.
[2] I think so too.—But if the reader be curious he may consult Mr. Chambers' "Traditions of Edinburgh."

have ascended out of the bottomless pit, to plague this perverse, insidious, and lukewarm generation."

It happened to Davie Deans on this occasion as it has done to many other habitual orators ; when once he became embarked on his favourite subject, the stream of his own enthusiasm carried him forward in spite of his mental distress, while his well-exercised memory supplied him amply with all the types and tropes of rhetoric peculiar to his sect and cause.

Mr. Middleburgh contented himself with answering—" All this may be very true, my friend ; but, as you said just now, I have nothing to say to it at present, either one way or other.—You have two daughters, I think, Mr. Deans ? "

The old man winced, as one whose smarting sore is suddenly galled ; but instantly composed himself, resumed the work which, in the heat of his declamation, he had laid down, and answered with sullen resolution, " Ae daughter, sir— only *ane*."

" I understand you," said Mr. Middleburgh ; " you have only one daughter here at home with you—but this unfortunate girl who is a prisoner—she is, I think, your youngest daughter ? "

The presbyterian sternly raised his eyes. " After the world, and according to the flesh, she *is* my daughter ; but when she became a child of Belial, and a company-keeper, and a trader in guilt and iniquity, she ceased to be a bairn of mine."

" Alas, Mr. Deans," said Middleburgh, sitting down by him, and endeavouring to take his hand, which the old man proudly withdrew, " we are ourselves all sinners ; and the errors of our offspring, as they ought not to surprise us, being the portion which they derive of a common portion of corruption inherited through us, so they do not entitle us to cast them off because they have lost themselves."

" Sir," said Deans impatiently, " I ken a' that as weel as— I mean to say," he resumed, checking the irritation he felt at being schooled,—a discipline of the mind, which those most ready to bestow it on others, do themselves most reluctantly submit to receive—" I mean to say, that what ye observe may be just and reasonable—But I hae nae freedom to enter into my ain private affairs wi' strangers—And now, in this great national emergency, when there's the Porteous Act has come doun frae London, that is a deeper blow to this poor sinfu' kingdom and suffering kirk, than ony that has been heard of since the foul and fatal Test—at a time like this——"

"But, goodman," interrupted Mr. Middleburgh, "you must think of your own household first, or else you are worse even than the infidels."

"I tell ye, Bailie Middleburgh," retorted David Deans, "if ye be a bailie, as there is little honour in being ane in these evil days—I tell ye, I heard the gracious Saunders Peden— I wotna whan it was; but it was in killing time, when the plowers were drawing alang their furrows on the back of the Kirk of Scotland—I heard him tell his hearers, gude and waled Christians they were too, that some o' them wad greet mair for a bit drowned calf or stirk, than for a' the defections and oppressions of the day; and that they were some o' them thinking o' ae thing, some o' anither, and there was Lady Hundleslope thinking o' greeting Jock at the fireside! And the lady confessed in my hearing, that a drow of anxiety had come ower her for her son that she had left at hame weak of a decay [1]—And what wad he hae said of me, if I had ceased to think of the gude cause for a castaway—a—It kills me to think of what she is !——"

"But the life of your child, goodman—think of that—if her life could be saved," said Middleburgh.

"Her life?" exclaimed David—"I wadna gie ane o' my grey hairs for her life, if her gude name be gane—And yet," said he, relenting and retracting as he spoke, "I wad make the niffer, Mr. Middleburgh—I wad gie a' these grey hairs that she has brought to shame and sorrow—I wad gie the auld head they grow on for her life, and that she might hae time to amend and return, for what hae the wicked beyond the breath of their nostrils?—But I'll never see her mair.—No! —that—that I am determined in—I'll never see her mair!" His lips continued to move for a minute after his voice ceased to be heard, as if he were repeating the same vow internally.

"Well, sir," said Mr. Middleburgh, "I speak to you as a man of sense; if you would save your daughter's life, you must use human means."

"I understand what you mean; but Mr. Novit, who is the procurator and doer of an honourable person, the Laird of Dumbiedikes, is to do what carnal wisdom can do for her in the circumstances. Mysell am not clear to trinquet and traffic wi' courts o' justice, as they are now constituted; I have a tenderness and scruple in my mind anent them."

"That is to say," said Middleburgh, "that you are a

---

[1] See "Life of Peden," p. 111.

Cameronian, and do not acknowledge the authority of our courts of judicature, or present government?"

"Sir, under your favour," replied David, who was too proud of his own polemical knowledge, to call himself the follower of any one, "ye take me up before I fall down. I canna see why I suld be termed a Cameronian, especially now that ye hae given the name ot that famous and savoury sufferer, not only until a regimental band of souldiers, whereof I am told many can now curse, swear, and use profane language, as fast as ever Richard Cameron could preach or pray; but also because ye have, in as far as it is in your power, rendered that martyr's name vain and contemptible, by pipes, drums, and fifes, playing the vain carnal spring, called the Cameronian Rant, which too many professors of religion dance to—a practice maist unbecoming a professor to dance to any tune whatsoever, more especially promiscuously, that is, with the female sex.[1] A brutish fashion it is, whilk is the beginning of defection with many, as I may hae as muckle cause as maist folk to testify."

"Well, but, Mr. Deans," replied Mr. Middleburgh, "I only meant to say that you were a Cameronian, or MacMillanite, one of the society people, in short, who think it inconsistent to take oaths under a government where the Covenant is not ratified."

"Sir," replied the controversialist, who forgot even his present distress in such discussions as these, "you cannot fickle me sae easily as you do opine. I am *not* a Mac-Millanite, or a Russelite, or a Hamiltonian, or a Harleyite, or a Howdenite [2]—I will be led by the nose by none—I take my name as a Christian from no vessel of clay. I have my own principles and practice to answer for, and am an humble pleader for the gude auld cause in a legal way."

"That is to say, Mr. Deans," said Middleburgh, "that you are a *Deanite*, and have opinions peculiar to yourself."

"I may please you to say sae," said David Deans; "but I have maintained my testimony before as great folk, and in sharper times; and though I will neither exalt myself nor pull down others, I wish every man and woman in this land had kept the true testimony, and the middle and straight path, as it were, on the ridge of a hill, where wind and water shears, avoiding right-hand snares and extremes, and left-hand way-slidings, as weel as Johnny Dodds of Farthing's Acre, and ae man mair that shall be nameless."

---

[1] See Note III.   [2] All various species of the great genus Cameronian.

"I suppose," replied the magistrate, "that is as much as to say, that Johnny Dodds of Farthing's Acre, and David Deans of St. Leonard's, constitute the only members of the true, real, unsophisticated Kirk of Scotland?"

"God forbid that I suld make sic a vainglorious speech, when there are sae mony professing Christians!" answered David; "but this I maun say, that all men act according to their gifts and their grace, sae that it is nae marvel that——"

"This is all very fine," interrupted Mr. Middleburgh; "but I have no time to spend in hearing it. The matter in hand is this—I have directed a citation to be lodged in your daughter's hands—If she appears on the day of trial and gives evidence, there is reason to hope she may save her sister's life—if, from any constrained scruples about the legality of her performing the office of an affectionate sister and a good subject, by appearing in a court held under the authority of the law and government, you become the means of deterring her from the discharge of this duty, I must say, though the truth may sound harsh in your ears, that you, who gave life to this unhappy girl, will become the means of her losing it by a premature and violent death."

So saying, Mr. Middleburgh turned to leave him.

"Bide awee—bide awee, Mr. Middleburgh," said Deans, in great perplexity and distress of mind; but the Bailie, who was probably sensible that protracted discussion might diminish the effect of his best and most forcible argument, took a hasty leave, and declined entering farther into the controversy.

Deans sunk down upon his seat, stunned with a variety of conflicting emotions. It had been a great source of controversy among those holding his opinions in religious matters, how far the government which succeeded the Revolution could be, without sin, acknowledged by true presbyterians, seeing that it did not recognise the great national testimony of the Solemn League and Covenant? And latterly, those agreeing in this general doctrine, and assuming the sounding title of the anti-popish, anti-prelatic, anti-erastian, anti-sectarian, true presbyterian remnant, were divided into many petty sects among themselves, even as to the extent of submission to the existing laws and rulers, which constituted such an acknowledgment as amounted to sin.

At a very stormy and tumultuous meeting, held in 1682, to discuss these important and delicate points, the testimonies of the faithful few were found utterly inconsistent with each other.[1] The place where this conference took place was remarkably well adapted for such an assembly. It was a wild and very sequestered dell in Tweeddale, surrounded by high hills, and far remote from human habitation. A small river, or rather a mountain torrent, called the Talla, breaks down the glen with great fury, dashing successively over a number of small cascades, which has procured the spot the name of Talla-Linns. Here the leaders among the scattered adherents to the Covenant, men who, in their banishment from human society, and in the recollection of the severities to which they had been exposed, had become at once sullen in their tempers, and fantastic in their religious opinions, met with arms in their hands, and by the side of the torrent discussed, with a turbulence which the noise of the stream could not drown, points of controversy as empty and unsubstantial as its foam.

It was the fixed judgment of most of the meeting, that all payment of cess or tribute to the existing government was utterly unlawful, and a sacrificing to idols. About other impositions and degrees of submission there were various opinions ; and perhaps it is the best illustration of the spirit of those military fathers of the church to say, that while all allowed it was impious to pay the cess employed for maintaining the standing army and militia, there was a fierce controversy on the lawfulness of paying the duties levied at ports and bridges, for maintaining roads and other necessary purposes ; that there were some who, repugnant to these imposts for turnpikes and postages, were nevertheless free in conscience to make payment of the usual freight at public ferries, and that a person of exceeding and punctilious zeal, James Russel, one of the slayers of the Archbishop of St. Andrews, had given his testimony with great warmth even against this last faint shade of subjection to constituted authority. This ardent and enlightened person and his followers had also great scruples about the lawfulness of bestowing the ordinary names upon the days of the week and the months of the year, which savoured in their nostrils so strongly of paganism, that at length they arrived at the conclusion that they who owned such names as Monday, Tuesday, January, February, and so forth, "served themselves heirs to the same, if not greater punishment, than had been denounced against the idolaters of old."

David Deans had been present on this memorable occasion,

[1] Note XI.—Meeting at Talla-Linns.

although too young to be a speaker among the polemical combatants. His brain, however, had been thoroughly heated by the noise, clamour, and metaphysical ingenuity of the discussion, and it was a controversy to which his mind had often returned ; and though he carefully disguised his vacillation from others, and perhaps from himself, he had never been able to come to any precise line of decision on the subject. In fact, his natural sense had acted as a counterpoise to his controversial zeal. He was by no means pleased with the quiet and indifferent manner in which King William's government slurred over the errors of the times, when, far from restoring the presbyterian kirk to its former supremacy, they passed an act of oblivion even to those who had been its persecutors, and bestowed on many of them titles, favours, and employments. When, in the first General Assembly which succeeded the Revolution, an overture was made for the revival of the League and Covenant, it was with horror that Douce David heard the proposal eluded by the men of carnal wit and policy, as he called them, as being inapplicable to the present times, and not falling under the modern model of the church. The reign of Queen Anne had increased his conviction, that the Revolution government was not one of the true presbyterian complexion. But then, more sensible than the bigots of his sect, he did not confound the moderation and tolerance of these two reigns with the active tyranny and oppression exercised in those of Charles II. and James II. The presbyterian form of religion, though deprived of the weight formerly attached to its sentences of excommunication, and compelled to tolerate the co-existence of episcopacy, and of sects of various descriptions, was still the National Church ; and though the glory of the second temple was far inferior to that which had flourished from 1639 till the battle of Dunbar, still it was a structure that, wanting the strength and the terrors, retained at least the form and symmetry, of the original model. Then came the insurrection in 1715, and David Deans's horror for the revival of the popish and prelatical faction reconciled him greatly to the government of King George, although he grieved that that monarch might be suspected of a leaning unto Erastianism. In short, moved by so many different considerations, he had shifted his ground at different times concerning the degree of freedom which he felt in adopting any act of immediate acknowledgment or submission to the present government, which, however mild and paternal, was still uncovenanted; and now he felt himself called upon by the most powerful motive conceivable, to authorise his daughter's giving testimony in the court of justice, which all who have been since called Cameronians accounted a step of lamentable and direct defection. The voice of nature, however, exclaimed loud in his bosom against the dictates of fanaticism; and his imagination, fertile in the solution of polemical difficulties, devised an expedient for extricating himself from the fearful dilemma, in which he saw, on the one side, a falling off from principle, and, on the other, a scene from which a father's thoughts could not but turn in shuddering horror.

"I have been constant and unchanged in my testimony," said David Deans; "but then who has said it to me, that I have judged my neighbour over closely, because he hath had more freedom in his walk than I have found in mine? I never was a separatist, nor for quarrelling with tender souls about mint, cummin, or other the lesser tithes. My daughter Jean may have a light in this subject that is hid frae my auld een—it is laid on her conscience, and not on mine—If she hath freedom to gang before this judicatory, and hold up her hand for this poor castaway, surely I will not say she steppeth over her bounds; and if not——" He paused in his mental argument, while a pang of unutterable anguish convulsed his features, yet, shaking it off, he firmly resumed the strain of his reasoning—"And IF NOT—God forbid that she should go into defection at bidding of mine! I wunna fret the tender conscience of one bairn—no, not to save the life of the other."

A Roman would have devoted his daughter to death from different feelings and motives, but not upon a more heroic principle of duty.

CHAPTER XIX

> To man, in this his trial state,
> The privilege is given,
> When tost by tides of human fate,
> To anchor fast on heaven.
> WATTS' *Hymns.*

IT was with a firm step that Deans sought his daughter's apartment, determined to leave her to the light of her own conscience in the dubious point of casuistry in which he supposed her to be placed.

The little room had been the sleeping apartment of both sisters, and there still stood there a small occasional bed which had been made for Effie's accommodation, when, complaining of illness, she had declined to share, as in happier times, her sister's pillow. The eyes of Deans rested involuntarily, on entering the room, upon this little couch, with its dark-green coarse curtains, and the ideas connected with it rose so thick upon his soul as almost to incapacitate him from opening his errand to his daughter. Her occupation broke the ice. He found her gazing on a slip of paper, which contained a citation to her to appear as a witness upon her sister's trial in behalf of the accused. For the worthy magistrate, determined to omit no chance of doing Effie justice, and to leave her sister no apology for not giving the evidence which she was supposed to possess, had caused the ordinary citation, or *subpœna*, of the Scottish criminal court, to be served upon her by an officer during his conference with David.

This precaution was so far favourable to Deans, that it saved him the pain of entering upon a formal explanation with his daughter ; he only said, with a hollow and tremulous voice, " I perceive ye are aware of the matter."

"O father, we are cruelly sted between God's laws and man's laws—What shall we do ?—What can we do ? "

Jeanie, it must be observed, had no hesitation whatever about the mere act of appearing in a court of justice. She might have heard the point discussed by her father more than once ; but we have already noticed, that she was accustomed to listen with reverence to much which she was incapable of understanding, and that subtle arguments of casuistry found her a patient, but unedified hearer. Upon receiving the citation, therefore, her thoughts did not turn upon the chimerical scruples which alarmed her father's mind, but to the language which had been held to her by the stranger at Muschat's Cairn. In a word, she never doubted but she was to be dragged forward into the court of justice, in order to place her in the cruel position of either sacrificing her sister by telling the truth, or committing perjury in order to save her life. And so strongly did her thoughts run in this channel, that she applied her father's words, " Ye are aware of the matter," to his acquaintance with the advice that had been so fearfully enforced upon her. She looked up with anxious surprise, not unmingled with a cast of horror, which his next words, as she interpreted and applied them, were not qualified to remove.

"Daughter," said David, "it has ever been my mind, that in things of ane doubtful and controversial nature, ilk Christian's conscience suld be his ain guide—Wherefore descend into yourself, try your ain mind with sufficiency of soul exercise, and as you sall finally find yourself clear to do in this matter—even so be it."

"But, father," said Jeanie, whose mind revolted at the construction which she naturally put upon his language, "can this—THIS be a doubtful or controversial matter?—Mind, father, the ninth command—'Thou shalt not bear false witness against thy neighbour.'"

David Deans paused; for, still applying her speech to his preconceived difficulties, it seemed to him, as if *she*, a woman, and a sister, was scarce entitled to be scrupulous upon this occasion, where *he*, a man, exercised in the testimonies of that testifying period, had given indirect countenance to her following what must have been the natural dictates of her own feelings. But he kept firm his purpose, until his eyes involuntarily rested upon the little settle-bed, and recalled the form of the child of his old age, as she sate upon it, pale, emaciated, and broken-hearted. His mind, as the picture arose before him, involuntarily conceived, and his tongue involuntarily uttered—but in a tone how different from his usual dogmatical precision!—arguments for the course of conduct likely to ensure his child's safety.

"Daughter," he said, "I did not say that your path was free from stumbling—and, questionless, this act may be in the opinion of some a transgression, since he who beareth witness unlawfully, and against his conscience, doth in some sort bear false witness against his neighbour. Yet in matters of compliance, the guilt lieth not in the compliance sae muckle, as in the mind and conscience of him that doth comply; and, therefore, although my testimony hath not been spared upon public defections, I haena felt freedom to separate mysell from the communion of many who have been clear to hear those ministers who have taken the fatal indulgence, because they might get good of them, though I could not."

When David had proceeded thus far, his conscience reproved him, that he might be indirectly undermining the purity of his daughter's faith, and smoothing the way for her falling off from strictness of principle. He, therefore, suddenly stopped, and changed his tone:—"Jeanie, I perceive that our vile affections,—so I call them in respect of doing the will of our Father,—cling too heavily to me in this hour of trying sorrow, to permit me to keep sight of my ain duty, or to airt you to yours. I will speak nae mair anent this over-trying matter.—Jeanie, if you can, wi' God and gude conscience, speak in favour of this puir unhappy"—(here his voice faltered)—"She is your sister in the flesh—worthless and castaway as she is, she is the daughter of a saint in heaven, that was a mother to you, Jeanie, in place of your ain —but if ye arena free in conscience to speak for her in the court of judicature, follow your conscience, Jeanie, and let God's will be done." After this adjuration he left the apartment, and his daughter remained in a state of great distress and perplexity.

It would have been no small addition to the sorrows of David Deans, even in this extremity of suffering, had he known that his daughter was applying the casuistical arguments which he had been using, not in the sense of a permission to follow her own opinion on a dubious and disputed point of controversy, but rather as an encouragement to transgress one of those divine commandments which Christians of all sects and denominations unite in holding most sacred.

"Can this be?" said Jeanie, as the door closed on her father—"Can these be his words that I have heard, or has the Enemy taken his voice and features to give weight unto the counsel which causeth to perish?—A sister's life, and a father pointing out how to save it!—O God deliver me! —this is a fearfu' temptation."

Roaming from thought to thought, she at one time imagined her father understood the ninth commandment literally, as prohibiting false witness *against* our neighbour, without extending the denunciation against falsehood uttered *in favour* of the criminal. But her clear and unsophisticated power of discriminating between good and evil, instantly rejected an interpretation so limited, and so unworthy of the Author of the law. She remained in a state of the most agitating terror and uncertainty—afraid to communicate her thoughts freely to her father, lest she should draw forth an opinion with which she could not comply,—wrung with distress on her sister's account, rendered the more acute by reflecting that the means of saving her were in her power, but were such as her conscience prohibited her from using,—tossed, in short, like a vessel in an open roadstead, during a storm, and, like that vessel, resting on one only sure cable and anchor, —faith in Providence, and a resolution to discharge her duty.

Butler's affection and strong sense of religion would have been her principal support in these distressing circumstances, but he was still under restraint, which did not permit him to come to St. Leonard's Crags; and her distresses were of a nature, which, with her indifferent habits of scholarship, she found it impossible to express in writing. She was therefore compelled to trust for guidance to her own unassisted sense of what was right or wrong.

It was not the least of Jeanie's distresses, that, although she hoped and believed her sister to be innocent, she had not the means of receiving that assurance from her own mouth.

The double-dealing of Ratcliffe in the matter of Robertson, had not prevented his being rewarded, as double-dealers frequently have been, with favour and preferment. Sharpitlaw, who found in him something of a kindred genius, had been intercessor in his behalf with the magistrates, and the circumstance of his having voluntarily remained in the prison, when the doors were forced by the mob, would have made it a hard measure to take the life which he had such easy means of saving. He received a full pardon; and soon afterwards, James Ratcliffe, the greatest thief and housebreaker in Scotland, was, upon the faith, perhaps, of an ancient proverb, selected as a person to be entrusted with the custody of other delinquents.

When Ratcliffe was thus placed in a confidential situation, he was repeatedly applied to by the sapient Saddletree and others, who took some interest in the Deans family, to procure an interview between the sisters : but the magistrates, who were extremely anxious for the apprehension of Robertson, had given strict orders to the contrary, hoping that, by keeping them separate, they might, from the one or the other, extract some information respecting that fugitive. On this subject Jeanie had nothing to tell them : she informed Mr. Middleburgh, that she knew nothing of Robertson. except having met him that night by appointment to give her some advice respecting her sister's concern, the purport of which, she said, was betwixt God and her conscience. Of his motions, purposes, or plans, past, present, or future, she knew nothing, and so had nothing to communicate.

Effie was equally silent, though from a different cause. It

was in vain that they offered a commutation and alleviation of her punishment, and even a free pardon, if she would confess what she knew of her lover. She answered only with tears; unless, when at times driven into pettish sulkiness by the persecution of the interrogators, she made them abrupt and disrespectful answers.

At length, after her trial had been delayed for many weeks, in hopes she might be induced to speak out on a subject infinitely more interesting to the magistracy than her own guilt or innocence, their patience was worn out, and even Mr. Middleburgh finding no ear lent to further intercession in her behalf, the day was fixed for the trial to proceed.

It was now, and not sooner, that Sharpitlaw, recollecting his promise to Effie Deans, or rather being dinned into compliance by the unceasing remonstrances of Mrs. Saddletree, who was his next-door neighbour, and who declared it was heathen cruelty to keep the twa broken-hearted creatures separate, issued the important mandate, permitting them to see each other.

On the evening which preceded the eventful day of trial, Jeanie was permitted to see her sister—an awful interview, and occurring at a most distressing crisis. This, however, formed a part of the bitter cup which she was doomed to drink, to atone for crimes and follies to which she had no accession; and at twelve o'clock noon, being the time appointed for admission to the jail, she went to meet, for the first time for several months, her guilty, erring, and most miserable sister, in that abode of guilt, error, and utter misery.

CHAPTER XX

————Sweet sister, let me live!
What sin you do to save a brother's life,
Nature dispenses with the deed so far,
That it becomes a virtue
Measure for Measure.

JEANIE DEANS was admitted into the jail by Ratcliffe. This fellow, as void of shame as of honesty, as he opened the now trebly secured door, asked her, with a leer which made her shudder, "whether she remembered him?"

A half-pronounced and timid "No," was her answer.

"What! not remember moonlight, and Muschat's Cairn,

and Rob and Rat?" said he, with the same sneer;—"Your memory needs redding up, my jo."

If Jeanie's distresses had admitted of aggravation, it must have been to find her sister under the charge of such a profligate as this man. He was not, indeed, without something of good to balance so much that was evil in his character and habits. In his misdemeanours he had never been blood-thirsty or cruel; and in his present occupation, he had shown himself, in a certain degree, accessible to touches of humanity. But these good qualities were unknown to Jeanie, who, re-membering the scene at Muschat's Cairn, could scarce find voice to acquaint him, that she had an order from Bailie Middleburgh, permitting her to see her sister.

"I ken that fu' weel, my bonny doo; mair by token, I have a special charge to stay in the ward with you a' the time ye are thegither."

"Must that be sae?" asked Jeanie, with an imploring voice.

"Hout, ay, hinny," replied the turnkey, "and what the waur will you and your titty be of Jim Ratcliffe hearing what ye hae to say to ilk other?—Deil a word ye'll say that will gar him ken your kittle sex better than he kens them already; and another thing is, that if ye dinna speak o' breaking the Tolbooth, deil a word will I tell ower, either to do ye good or ill."

Thus saying, Ratcliffe marshalled her the way to the apart-ment where Effie was confined.

Shame, fear, and grief had contended for mastery in the poor prisoner's bosom during the whole morning, while she had looked forward to this meeting; but when the door opened, all gave way to a confused and strange feeling that had a tinge of joy in it, as, throwing herself on her sister's neck, she ejaculated, "My dear Jeanie!—my dear Jeanie! it's lang since I hae seen ye." Jeanie returned the embrace with an earnestness that partook almost of rapture, but it was only a flitting emotion, like a sunbeam unexpectedly penetrat-ing betwixt the clouds of a tempest, and obscured almost as soon as visible. The sisters walked together to the side of the pallet bed, and sate down side by side, took hold of each other's hands, and looked each other in the face, but without speaking a word. In this posture they remained for a minute, while the gleam of joy gradually faded from their features, and gave way to the most intense expression, first of melancholy, and then of agony, till, throwing themselves again into each other's arms, they, to use the language of Scripture, lifted up their voices and wept bitterly.

Even the hard-hearted turnkey, who had spent his life in scenes calculated to stifle both conscience and feeling, could not witness this scene without a touch of human sympathy. It was shown in a trifling action, but which had more delicacy in it than seemed to belong to Ratcliffe's character and station. The unglazed window of the miserable chamber was open, and the beams of a bright sun fell right upon the bed where the sufferers were seated. With a gentleness that had something of reverence in it, Ratcliffe partly closed the shutter, and seemed thus to throw a veil over a scene so sorrowful.

" Ye are ill, Effie," were the first words Jeanie could utter ; " ye are very ill."

" Oh, what wad I gie to be ten times waur, Jeanie ! " was the reply—" what wad I gie to be cauld dead afore the ten o'clock bell the morn ! And our father—but I am his bairn nae langer now—Oh, I hae nae friend left in the warld !— Oh, that I were lying dead at my mother's side, in Newbattle kirkyard ! "

" Hout, lassie," said Ratcliffe, willing to show the interest which he absolutely felt, " dinna be sae dooms down-hearted as a' that ; there's mony a tod hunted that's no killed. Advocate Langtale has brought mony a folk through waur snappers than a' this, and there's no a cleverer agent than Nichil Novit e'er drew a bill of suspension. Hanged or unhanged, they are weel aff has sic an agent and counsel ; ane's sure o' fair play. Ye are a bonny lass, too, an ye wad busk up your cockernonie a bit ; and a bonny lass will find favour wi' judge and jury, when they would strap up a grewsome carle like me for the fifteenth part of a flea's hide and tallow, d—n them."

To this homely strain of consolation the mourners returned no answer ; indeed, they were so much lost in their own sorrows as to have become insensible of Ratcliffe's presence. " O Effie," said her elder sister, " how could you conceal your situation from me ? O woman, had I deserved this at your hand ?—had ye spoke but ae word—sorry we might hae been, and shamed we might hae been, but this awfu' dispensation had never come ower us."

" And what gude wad that hae done ? " answered the prisoner. " Na, na, Jeanie, a' was ower when ance I forgot what I promised when I faulded down the leaf of my Bible. See," she said, producing the sacred volume, " the book opens aye at the place o' itsell. Oh see, Jeanie, what a fearfu' scripture."

Jeanie took her sister's Bible, and found that the fatal mark was made at this impressive text in the book of Job: " He hath stripped me of my glory, and taken the crown from my head. He hath destroyed me on every side, and I am gone. And mine hope hath He removed like a tree."

" Isna that ower true a doctrine?" said the prisoner— " Isna my crown, my honour removed?   And what am I but a poor wasted, wan-thriven tree, dug up by the roots, and flung out to waste in the highway, that man and beast may tread it under foot?   I thought o' the bonny bit thorn that our father rooted out o' the yard last May, when it had a' the flush o' blossoms on it; and then it lay in the court till the beasts had trod them a' to pieces wi' their feet.   I little thought, when I was wae for the bit silly green bush and its flowers, that I was to gang the same gate mysell."

" Oh, if ye had spoken a word," again sobbed Jeanie,—" if I were free to swear that ye had said but ae word of how it stude wi' ye, they couldna hae touched your life this day."

" Could they na?" said Effie, with something like awakened interest—for life is dear even to those who feel it as a burden— " Wha tauld ye that, Jeanie?"

" It was ane that kend what he was saying weel eneugh," replied Jeanie, who had a natural reluctance at mentioning even the name of her sister's seducer.

" Wha was it?—I conjure ye to tell me," said Effie, seating herself upright.—" Wha could tak interest in sic a cast-by as I am now?—Was it—was it *him*?"

" Hout," said Ratcliffe, " what signifies keeping the poor lassie in a swither?   I'se uphaud it's been Robertson that learned ye that doctrine when ye saw him at Muschat's Cairn."

" Was it him?" said Effie, catching eagerly at his words— " was it him, Jeanie, indeed?—Oh, I see it was him—poor lad, and I was thinking his heart was as hard as the nether millstane—and him in sic danger on his ain part—poor George!"

Somewhat indignant at this burst of tender feeling towards the author of her misery, Jeanie could not help exclaiming— " O Effie, how can ye speak that gate of sic a man as that?"

" We maun forgie our enemies, ye ken," said poor Effie, with a timid look and a subdued voice; for her conscience told her what a different character the feelings with which she still regarded her seducer bore, compared with the Christian charity under which she attempted to veil it.

"And ye hae suffered a' this for him, and ye can think of loving him still?" said her sister, in a voice betwixt pity and blame.

"Love him?" answered Effie—"If I hadna loved as woman seldom loves, I hadna been within these wa's this day; and trow ye, that love sic as mine is lightly forgotten?—Na, na—ye may hew down the tree, but ye canna change its bend—And O Jeanie, if ye wad do good to me at this moment, tell me every word that he said, and whether he was sorry for poor Effie or no!"

"What needs I tell ye onything about it," said Jeanie. "Ye may be sure he had ower muckle to do to save himsell, to speak lang or muckle about onybody beside."

"That's no true, Jeanie, though a saunt had said it," replied Effie, with a sparkle of her former lively and irritable temper. But ye dinna ken, though I do, how far he pat his life in venture to save mine." And looking at Ratcliffe, she checked herself and was silent.

"I fancy," said Ratcliffe, with one of his familiar sneers, "the lassie thinks that naebody has een but hersell—Didna I see when Gentle Geordie was seeking to get other folk out of the Tolbooth forby Jock Porteous? but ye are of my mind, hinny—better sit and rue, than flit and rue—Ye needna look in my face sae amazed. I ken mair things than that, maybe."

"O my God! my God!" said Effie, springing up and throwing herself down on her knees before him—"D'ye ken where they hae putten my bairn?—O my bairn! my bairn! the poor sackless innocent new-born wee ane—bone of my bone, and flesh of my flesh!—O man, if ye wad e'er deserve a portion in heaven, or a broken-hearted creature's blessing upon earth, tell me where they hae put my bairn—the sign of my shame, and the partner of my suffering! tell me wha has taen't away, or what they hae dune wi't!"

"Hout tout," said the turnkey, endeavouring to extricate himself from the firm grasp with which she held him, "that's taking me at my word wi' a witness—Bairn, quo' she? How the deil suld I ken onything of your bairn, huzzy? Ye maun ask that of auld Meg Murdockson, if ye dinna ken ower muckle about it yoursell."

As his answer destroyed the wild and vague hope which had suddenly gleamed upon her, the unhappy prisoner let go her hold of his coat, and fell with her face on the pavement of the apartment in a strong convulsion fit.

Jeanie Deans possessed, with her excellently clear understanding, the concomitant advantage of promptitude of spirit, even in the extremity of distress.

She did not suffer herself to be overcome by her own feelings of exquisite sorrow, but instantly applied herself to her sister's relief, with the readiest remedies which circumstances afforded; and which, to do Ratcliffe justice, he showed himself anxious to suggest, and alert in procuring. He had even the delicacy to withdraw to the farthest corner of the room, so as to render his official attendance upon them as little intrusive as possible, when Effie was composed enough again to resume her conference with her sister.

The prisoner once more, in the most earnest and broken tones, conjured Jeanie to tell her the particulars of the conference with Robertson, and Jeanie felt it was impossible to refuse her this gratification.

"Do ye mind," she said, "Effie, when ye were in the fever before we left Woodend, and how angry your mother, that's now in a better place, was wi' me for gieing ye milk and water to drink, because ye grat for it? Ye were a bairn then, and ye are a woman now, and should ken better than ask what canna but hurt you—But come weal or woe, I canna refuse ye onything that ye ask me wi' the tear in your ee."

Again Effie threw herself into her arms, and kissed her cheek and forehead, murmuring, "Oh, if you kend how lang it is since I heard his name mentioned!—if ye but kend how muckle good it does me but to ken onything o' him, that's like goodness or kindness, ye wadna wonder that I wish to hear o' him!"

Jeanie sighed, and commenced her narrative of all that had passed betwixt Robertson and her, making it as brief as possible. Effie listened in breathless anxiety, holding her sister's hand in hers, and keeping her eye fixed upon her face, as if devouring every word she uttered. The interjections of "Poor fellow,"—"Poor George," which escaped in whispers, and betwixt sighs, were the only sounds with which she interrupted the story. When it was finished she made a long pause.

"And this was his advice?" were the first words she uttered.

"Just sic as I hae tell'd ye," replied her sister.

"And he wanted you to say something to yon folks, that wad save my young life?"

"He wanted," answered Jeanie, "that I suld be man-sworn."

"And you tauld him," said Effie, "that ye wadna hear o' coming between me and the death that I am to die, and me no aughteen year auld yet?"

"I told him," replied Jeanie, who now trembled at the turn which her sister's reflections seemed about to take, "that I daured na swear to an untruth."

"And what d'ye ca' an untruth?" said Effie, again showing a touch of her former spirit—"Ye are muckle to blame, lass, if ye think a mother would, or could, murder her ain bairn—Murder?—I wad hae laid down my life just to see a blink o' its ee!"

"I do believe," said Jeanie, "that ye are as innocent of sic a purpose as the new-born babe itsell."

"I am glad ye do me that justice," said Effie haughtily; "it's whiles the faut of very good folk like you, Jeanie, that they think a' the rest of the warld are as bad as the warst temptations can make them."

"I dinna deserve this frae ye, Effie," said her sister, sobbing, and feeling at once the injustice of the reproach, and compassion for the state of mind which dictated it.

"Maybe no, sister," said Effie. "But ye are angry because I love Robertson—How can I help loving him, that loves me better than body and soul baith?—Here he put his life in a niffer, to break the prison to let me out; and sure am I, had it stood wi' him as it stands wi' you"—Here she paused and was silent.

"Oh, if it stude wi' me to save ye wi' risk of *my* life!" said Jeanie.

"Ay, lass," said her sister, "that's lightly said, but no sae lightly credited, frae ane that winna ware a word for me; and if it be a wrang word, ye'll hae time eneugh to repent o't."

"But that word is a grievous sin, and it's a deeper offence when it's a sin wilfully and presumptuously committed."

"Weel, weel, Jeanie," said Effie, "I mind a' about the sins o' presumption in the questions—we'll speak nae mair about this matter, and ye may save your breath to say your carritch; and for me, I'll soon hae nae breath to waste on onybody."

"I must needs say," interposed Ratcliffe, "that it's d—d

hard, when three words of your mouth would give the girl the chance to nick Moll Blood,[1] that you make such scrupling about rapping to them. D—n me, if they would take me, if I would not rap to all Whatd'yecallum's—Hyssop's Fables, for her life—I am us'd to't, b—t me, for less matters. Why, I have smacked calf-skin fifty times in England for a keg of brandy."

"Never speak mair o't," said the prisoner. "It's just as weel as it is—and gude day, sister; ye keep Mr. Ratcliffe waiting on—Ye'll come back and see me, I reckon, before——" here she stopped, and became deadly pale.

"And are we to part in this way," said Jeanie, "and you in sic deadly peril? O Effie, look but up, and say what ye wad hae me do, and I could find in my heart amaist to say that I would do't."

"No, Jeanie," replied her sister, after an effort, "I am better minded now. At my best, I was never half sae gude as ye were, and what for suld you begin to mak yoursell waur to save me, now that I am no worth saving? God knows, that in my sober mind, I wadna wuss ony living creature to do a wrong thing to save my life. I might have fled frae this tolbooth on that awfu' night wi' ane wad hae carried me through the warld, and friended me, and fended for me. But I said to them, let life gang when gude fame is gane before it. But this lang imprisonment has broken my spirit, and I am whiles sair left to mysell, and then I wad gie the Indian mines of gold and diamonds, just for life and breath—for I think, Jeanie, I have such roving fits as I used to hae in the fever; but, instead of the fiery een, and wolves, and Widow Butler's bullseg, that I used to see spieling up on my bed, I am thinking now about a high, black gibbet, and me standing up, and such seas of faces all looking up at poor Effie Deans, and asking if it be her that George Robertson used to call the Lily of St. Leonard's. And then they stretch out their faces, and make mouths, and girn at me, and which ever way I look, I see a face laughing like Meg Murdockson, when she tauld me I had seen the last of my wean. God preserve us, Jeanie, that carline has a fearsome face!" She clapped her hands before her eyes as she uttered this exclamation, as if to secure herself against seeing the fearful object she had alluded to.

Jeanie Deans remained with her sister for two hours, during which she endeavoured, if possible, to extract something from

[1] The gallows.

her that might be serviceable in her exculpation. But she
had nothing to say beyond what she had declared on her first
examination, with the purport of which the reader will be
made acquainted in proper time and place. "They wadna
believe her," she said, "and she had naething mair to tell
them."

At length Ratcliffe, though reluctantly, informed the sisters
that there was a necessity that they should part. " Mr. Novit,"
he said, "was to see the prisoner, and maybe Mr. Langtale
too. Langtale likes to look at a bonny lass, whether in prison
or out o' prison."

Reluctantly, therefore, and slowly, after many a tear, and
many an embrace, Jeanie retired from the apartment, and
heard its jarring bolts turned upon the dear being from whom
she was separated. Somewhat familiarised now even with her
rude conductor, she offered him a small present in money,
with a request he would do what he could for her sister's
accommodation. To her surprise, Ratcliffe declined the fee.
"I wasna bloody when I was on the pad," he said, "and I
winna be greedy—that is, beyond what's right and reasonable
—now that I am in the lock.—Keep the siller; and for
civility, your sister shall hae sic as I can bestow; but I hope
you'll think better on it, and rap an oath for her—deil a hair
ill there is in it, if ye are rapping again the crown. I kend a
worthy minister, as gude a man, bating the deed they deposed
him for, as ever ye heard claver in a pu'pit, that rapped to a
hogshead of pigtail tobacco, just for as muckle as filled his
spleuchan. But maybe ye are keeping your ain counsel—
weel, weel, there's nae harm in that. As for your sister, I'se
see that she gets her meat clean and warm, and I'll try to
gar her lie down and take a sleep after dinner, for deil a ee
she'll close the night. I hae gude experience of these matters.
The first night is aye the warst o't. I hae never heard o' ane
that sleepit the night afore trial, but of mony a ane that
sleepit as sound as a tap the night before their necks were
straughted. And it's nae wonder—the warst may be tholed
when it's kend—Better a finger aff as aye wagging."

CHAPTER XXI

Yet though thou mayst be dragg'd in scorn
To yonder ignominious tree,
Thou shalt not want one faithful friend
To share the cruel fates' decree.
Jemmy Dawson.

AFTER spending the greater part of the morning in his devotions (for his benevolent neighbours had kindly insisted upon discharging his task of ordinary labour), David Deans entered the apartment when the breakfast meal was prepared. His eyes were involuntarily cast down, for he was afraid to look at Jeanie, uncertain as he was whether she might feel herself at liberty, with a good conscience, to attend the Court of Justiciary that day, to give the evidence which he understood that she possessed, in order to her sister's exculpation. At length, after a minute of apprehensive hesitation, he looked at her dress to discover whether it seemed to be in her contemplation to go abroad that morning. Her apparel was neat and plain, but such as conveyed no exact intimation of her intentions to go abroad. She had exchanged her usual garb for morning labour, for one something inferior to that with which, as her best, she was wont to dress herself for church, or any more rare occasion of going into society. Her sense taught her, that it was respectful to be decent in her apparel on such an occasion, while her feelings induced her to lay aside the use of the very few and simple personal ornaments, which, on other occasions, she permitted herself to wear. So that there occurred nothing in her external appearance which could mark out to her father, with anything like certainty, her intentions on this occasion.

The preparations for their humble meal were that morning made in vain. The father and daughter sat, each assuming the appearance of eating, when the other's eyes were turned to them, and desisting from the effort with disgust, when the affectionate imposture seemed no longer necessary.

At length these moments of constraint were removed. The sound of St. Giles's heavy toll announced the hour previous to the commencement of the trial; Jeanie arose, and, with a degree of composure for which she herself could not account, assumed her plaid, and made her other preparations for a distant walking. It was a strange contrast between the firmness of her demeanour, and the vacillation and cruel uncertainty of purpose indicated in all her father's motions; and one unacquainted with both could scarcely have supposed that the former was, in her ordinary habits of life, a docile, quiet, gentle, and even timid country maiden, while her father, with a mind naturally proud and strong, and supported by religious opinions, of a stern, stoical, and unyielding character, had in his time undergone and withstood the most severe hardships, and the most imminent peril, without depression of spirit, or subjugation of his constancy. The secret of this difference was, that Jeanie's mind had already anticipated the line of conduct which she must adopt, with all its natural and necessary consequences; while her father, ignorant of every other circumstance, tormented himself with imagining what the one sister might say or swear, or what effect her testimony might have upon the awful event of the trial.

He watched his daughter with a faltering and indecisive look, until she looked back upon him, with a look of unutterable anguish, as she was about to leave the apartment.

"My dear lassie," said he, "I will"—His action, hastily and confusedly searching for his worsted mittans[1] and staff, showed his purpose of accompanying her, though his tongue failed distinctly to announce it.

"Father," said Jeanie, replying rather to his action than his words "ye had better not."

"In the strength of my God," answered Deans, assuming firmness, "I will go forth."

And, taking his daughter's arm under his, he began to walk from the door with a step so hasty, that she was almost unable to keep up with him. A trifling circumstance, but which marked the perturbed state of his mind, checked his course.— "Your bonnet, father?" said Jeanie, who observed he had come out with his grey hairs uncovered. He turned back with a slight blush on his cheek, being ashamed to have been detected in an omission which indicated so much mental confusion, assumed his large blue Scottish bonnet, and with a step slower, but more composed, as if the circumstance had obliged him to summon up his resolution, and collect his scattered ideas, again placed his daughter's arm under his, and resumed the way to Edinburgh.

[1] A kind of worsted gloves used by the lower orders.

The courts of justice were then, and are still held in what is called the Parliament Close, or, according to modern phrase, the Parliament Square, and occupied the buildings intended for the accommodation of the Scottish Estates. This edifice, though in an imperfect and corrupted style of architecture, had then a grave, decent, and, as it were, a judicial aspect, which was at least entitled to respect from its antiquity. For which venerable front, I observed, on my last occasional visit to the metropolis, that modern taste had substituted, at great apparent expense, a pile so utterly inconsistent with every monument of antiquity around, and in itself so clumsy at the same time and fantastic, that it may be likened to the decorations of Tom Errand the porter, in the Trip to the Jubilee, when he appears bedizened with the tawdry finery of Beau Clincher. *Sed transeat cum cæteris erroribus.*

The small quadrangle, or Close, if we may presume still to give it that appropriate, though antiquated title, which at Lichfield, Salisbury, and elsewhere, is properly applied to designate the enclosure adjacent to a cathedral, already evinced tokens of the fatal scene which was that day to be acted. The soldiers of the City Guard were on their posts, now enduring, and now rudely repelling with the buts of their muskets, the motley crew who thrust each other forward, to catch a glance at the unfortunate object of trial, as she should pass from the adjacent prison to the Court in which her fate was to be determined. All must have occasionally observed, with disgust, the apathy with which the vulgar gaze on scenes of this nature, and how seldom, unless when their sympathies are called forth by some striking and extraordinary circumstance, the crowd evince any interest deeper than that of callous, unthinking bustle, and brutal curiosity. They laugh, jest, quarrel, and push each other to and fro, with the same unfeeling indifference as if they were assembled for some holiday sport, or to see an idle procession. Occasionally, however, this demeanour, so natural to the degraded populace of a large town, is exchanged for a temporary touch of human affections; and so it chanced on the present occasion.

When Deans and his daughter presented themselves in the Close, and endeavoured to make their way forward to the door of the Court-house, they became involved in the mob, and subject, of course, to their insolence. As Deans repelled with some force the rude pushes which he received on all sides, his figure and antiquated dress caught the attention of

the rabble, who often show an intuitive sharpness in ascribing
the proper character from external appearance.—

> " Ye're welcome, whigs,
>   Frae Bothwell briggs,"

sung one fellow (for the mob of Edinburgh were at that time
jacobitically disposed, probably because that was the line of
sentiment most diametrically opposite to existing authority).

> " Mess David Williamson,
>   Chosen of twenty,
>   Ran up the pu'pit stair,
>   And sang Killiecrankie,"

chanted a siren, whose profession might be guessed by her
appearance. A tattered cadie, or errand porter, whom David
Deans had jostled in his attempt to extricate himself from the
vicinity of these scorners, exclaimed in a strong north-country
tone, " Ta deil ding out her Cameronian een—what gies her
titles to dunch gentlemans about ? "

"Make room for the ruling elder," said yet another ;
"he comes to see a precious sister glorify God in the
Grassmarket ! "

"Whisht ; shame's in ye, sirs," said the voice of a man
very loudly, which, as quickly sinking, said in a low, but
distinct tone, " It's her father and sister."

All fell back to make way for the sufferers ; and all, even
the very rudest and most profligate, were struck with shame
and silence. In the space thus abandoned to them by the
mob, Deans stood, holding his daughter by the hand, and
said to her, with a countenance strongly and sternly expressive
of his internal emotion, " Ye hear with your ears, and ye see
with your eyes, where and to whom the backslidings and
defections of professors are ascribed by the scoffers. Not to
themselves alone, but to the kirk of which they are members,
and to its blessed and invisible Head. Then, weel may we
take wi' patience our share and portion of this outspreading
reproach."

The man who had spoken, no other than our old friend
Dumbiedikes, whose mouth, like that of the prophet's ass,
had been opened by the emergency of the case, now joined
them, and, with his usual taciturnity, escorted them into the
Court-house. No opposition was offered to their entrance,
either by the guards or door-keepers ; and it is even said, that
one of the latter refused a shilling of civility-money, tendered

him by the Laird of Dumbiedikes, who was of opinion that "siller wad mak a' easy." But this last incident wants confirmation.

Admitted within the precincts of the Court-house, they found the usual number of busy office-bearers, and idle loiterers, who attend on these scenes by choice, or from duty. Burghers gaped and stared; young lawyers sauntered, sneered, and laughed, as in the pit of the theatre; while others apart sat on a bench retired, and reasoned highly, *inter apices juris*, on the doctrines of constructive crime, and the true import of the statute. The bench was prepared for the arrival of the judges: the jurors were in attendance. The crown counsel, employed in looking over their briefs and notes of evidence, looked grave, and whispered with each other. They occupied one side of a large table placed beneath the bench; on the other sat the advocates, whom the humanity of the Scottish law (in this particular more liberal than that of the sister country) not only permits, but enjoins, to appear and assist with their advice and skill all persons under trial. Mr. Nichil Novit was seen actively instructing the counsel for the panel (so the prisoner is called in Scottish law-phraseology), busy, bustling, and important. When they entered the Court-room, Deans asked the Laird, in a tremulous whisper, "Where will *she* sit?"

Dumbiedikes whispered Novit, who pointed to a vacant space at the bar, fronting the judges, and was about to conduct Deans towards it.

"No!" he said; "I cannot sit by her—I cannot own her—not as yet, at least—I will keep out of her sight, and turn mine own eyes elsewhere—better for us baith."

Saddletree, whose repeated interference with the counsel had procured him one or two rebuffs, and a special request that he would concern himself with his own matters, now saw with pleasure an opportunity of playing the person of importance. He bustled up to the poor old man, and proceeded to exhibit his consequence, by securing, through his interest with the bar-keepers and macers, a seat for Deans, in a situation where he was hidden from the general eye by the projecting corner of the bench.

"It's gude to have a friend at court," he said, continuing his heartless harangues to the passive auditor, who neither heard nor replied to them; "few folk but mysell could hae sorted ye out a seat like this—the Lords will be here incontinent, and proceed *instanter* to trial. They wunna fence the court as they do at the circuit—The High Court of Justiciary is aye fenced. But, Lord's sake, what's this o't?—Jeanie, ye are a cited witness—Macer, this lass is a witness —she maun be enclosed—she maun on nae account be at large.—Mr. Novit, suldna Jeanie Deans be enclosed?"

Novit answered in the affirmative, and offered to conduct Jeanie to the apartment, where, according to the scrupulous practice of the Scottish Court, the witnesses remain in readiness to be called into court to give evidence; and separated, at the same time, from all who might influence their testimony, or give them information concerning that which was passing upon the trial.

"Is this necessary?" said Jeanie, still reluctant to quit her father's hand.

"A matter of absolute needcessity," said Saddletree; "wha ever heard of witnesses no being enclosed?"

"It is really a matter of necessity," said the younger counsellor, retained for her sister; and Jeanie reluctantly followed the macer of the court to the place appointed.

"This, Mr. Deans," said Saddletree, "is ca'd sequestering a witness; but it's clean different (whilk maybe ye wadna fund out o' yoursell) frae sequestering ane's estate or effects, as in cases of bankruptcy. I hae aften been sequestered as a witness, for the Sheriff is in the use whiles to cry me in to witness the declarations at precognitions, and so is Mr. Sharpitlaw; but I was ne'er like to be sequestered o' land and gudes but ance, and that was lang syne, afore I was married. But whisht, whisht! here's the Court coming."

As he spoke, the five Lords of Justiciary, in their long robes of scarlet, faced with white, and preceded by their mace-bearer, entered with the usual formalities, and took their places upon the bench of judgment.

The audience rose to receive them; and the bustle occasioned by their entrance was hardly composed, when a great noise and confusion of persons struggling, and forcibly endeavouring to enter at the doors of the Court-room and of the galleries, announced that the prisoner was about to be placed at the bar. This tumult takes place when the doors, at first only opened to those either having right to be present, or to the better and more qualified ranks, are at length laid open to all whose curiosity induces them to be present on the occasion. With inflamed countenances and dishevelled dresses, struggling with, and sometimes tumbling over each other, in rushed the rude multitude, while a few soldiers, forming, as it were, the centre of the tide, could scarce, with all their efforts, clear a passage for the prisoner to the place which she was to occupy.   By the authority of the Court, and the exertions of its officers, the tumult among the spectators was at length appeased, and the unhappy girl brought forward, and placed betwixt two sentinels with drawn bayonets, as a prisoner at the bar, where she was to abide her deliverance for good or evil, according to the issue of her trial.

CHAPTER XXII

We have strict statutes, and most biting laws—
The needful bits, and curbs for headstrong steeds—
Which, for these fourteen years, we have let sleep,
Like to an o'ergrown lion in a cave,
That goes not out to prey.
                              Measure for Measure.

" EUPHEMIA DEANS," said the presiding Judge, in an accent in which pity was blended with dignity, "stand up, and listen to the criminal indictment now to be preferred against you."

The unhappy girl, who had been stupefied by the confusion through which the guards had forced a passage, cast a bewildered look on the multitude of faces around her, which seemed to tapestry, as it were, the walls, in one broad slope from the ceiling to the floor, with human countenances, and instinctively obeyed a command, which rung in her ears like the trumpet of the judgment-day.

" Put back your hair, Effie," said one of the macers.   For her beautiful and abundant tresses of long fair hair, which, according to the costume of the country, unmarried women were not allowed to cover with any sort of cap, and which, alas ! Effie dared no longer confine with the snood or ribband, which implied purity of maiden-fame, now hung unbound and dishevelled over her face, and almost concealed her features. On receiving this hint from the attendant, the unfortunate young woman, with a hasty, trembling, and apparently mechanical compliance, shaded back from her face her luxuriant locks, and showed to the whole court, excepting one individual, a countenance, which, though pale and emaciated, was so lovely amid its agony, that it called forth an universal murmur of compassion and sympathy. Apparently the expressive sound of human feeling recalled the poor girl from the stupor of fear, which predominated at first over every other sensation, and awakened her to the no less painful sense of shame and exposure attached to her present situation. Her eye, which had at first glanced wildly around, was turned on the ground; her cheek, at first so deadly pale, began gradually to be overspread with a faint blush, which increased so fast, that, when in agony of shame she strove to conceal her face, her temples, her brow, her neck, and all that her slender fingers and small palms could not cover, became of the deepest crimson.

All marked and were moved by these changes, excepting one. It was old Deans, who, motionless in his seat, and concealed, as we have said, by the corner of the bench, from seeing or being seen, did nevertheless keep his eyes firmly fixed on the ground, as if determined that, by no possibility whatever, would he be an ocular witness of the shame of his house.

"Ichabod!" he said to himself—"Ichabod! my glory is departed!"

While these reflections were passing through his mind, the indictment, which set forth in technical form the crime of which the panel stood accused, was read as usual, and the prisoner was asked if she was Guilty, or Not Guilty.

"Not guilty of my poor bairn's death," said Effie Deans, in an accent corresponding in plaintive softness of tone to the beauty of her features, and which was not heard by the audience without emotion.

The presiding Judge next directed the counsel to plead to the relevancy; that is, to state on either part the arguments in point of law, and evidence in point of fact, against and in favour of the criminal; after which it is the form of the Court to pronounce a preliminary judgment, sending the cause to the cognisance of the jury or assize.

The counsel for the crown briefly stated the frequency of the crime of infanticide, which had given rise to the special statute under which the panel stood indicted. He mentioned the various instances, many of them marked with circumstances of atrocity, which had at length induced the King's Advocate, though with great reluctance, to make the experiment, whether by strictly enforcing the Act of Parliament which had been made to prevent such enormities, their occurrence might be prevented. "He expected," he said, "to be able to establish by witnesses, as well as by the declaration of the panel herself, that she was in the state described by the statute. According to his information, the panel had communicated her pregnancy to no one, nor did she allege in her own declaration that she had done so. This secrecy was the first requisite in support of the indictment. The same declaration admitted, that she had borne a male child, in circumstances which gave but too much reason to believe it had died by the hands, or at least with the knowledge or consent, of the un-happy mother. It was not, however, necessary for him to bring positive proof that the panel was accessory to the murder, nay, nor even to prove that the child was murdered at all. It was sufficient to support the indictment, that it could not be found. According to the stern, but necessary severity of this statute, she who should conceal her pregnancy, who should omit to call that assistance which is most necessary on such occasions, was held already to have meditated the death of her offspring, as an event most likely to be the consequence of her culpable and cruel concealment. And if, under such circum-stances, she could not alternatively show by proof that the infant had died a natural death, or produce it still in life, she must, under the construction of the law, be held to have murdered it, and suffer death accordingly."

The counsel for the prisoner, Mr. Fairbrother, a man of considerable fame in his profession, did not pretend directly to combat the arguments of the King's Advocate. He began by lamenting that his senior at the bar, Mr. Langtale, had been suddenly called to the county of which he was Sheriff, and that he had been applied to, on short warning, to give the panel his assistance in this interesting case. He had had little time, he said, to make up for his inferiority to his learned brother by long and minute research; and he was afraid he might give a specimen of his incapacity, by being compelled to admit the accuracy of the indictment under the statute. "It was enough for their Lordships," he observed, "to know, that such was the law, and he admitted the Advocate had a right to call for the usual interlocutor of relevancy." But he stated, "that when he came to establish his case by proof, he trusted to make out circumstances which would satisfactorily elide the charge in the libel. His client's story was a short, but most melancholy one. She was bred up in the strictest tenets of religion and virtue, the daughter of a worthy and conscientious person, who, in evil times, had established a character for courage and religion, by becoming a sufferer for conscience' sake.

David Deans gave a convulsive start at hearing himself thus mentioned, and then resumed the situation, in which, with his face stooped against his hands, and both resting against the corner of the elevated bench on which the Judges sate, he had hitherto listened to the procedure in the trial. The Whig lawyers seemed to be interested; the Tories put up their lip.

"Whatever may be our difference of opinion," resumed the lawyer, whose business it was to carry his whole audience with him if possible, "concerning the peculiar tenets of these people" (here Deans groaned deeply), "it is impossible to deny them the praise of sound, and even rigid morals, or the merit of training up their children in the fear of God; and yet it was the daughter of such a person whom a jury would shortly be called upon, in the absence of evidence, and upon mere presumptions, to convict of a crime, more properly belonging to an heathen, or a savage, than to a Christian and civilised country. It was true," he admitted, "that the excellent nurture and early instruction which the poor girl had received, had not been sufficient to preserve her from guilt and error. She had fallen a sacrifice to an inconsiderate affection for a young man of prepossessing manners, as he had been informed, but of a very dangerous and desperate character. She was seduced under promise of marriage—a promise, which the fellow might have, perhaps, done her justice by keeping, had he not at that time been called upon by the law to atone for a crime, violent and desperate in itself, but which became the preface to another eventful history, every step of which was marked by blood and guilt, and the final termination of which had not even yet arrived. He believed that no one would hear him without surprise, when he stated that the father of this infant now amissing, and said by the learned Advocate to have been murdered, was no other than the notorious George Robertson, the accomplice of Wilson, the hero of the memorable escape from the Tolbooth Church, and, as no one knew better than his learned friend the Advocate, the principal actor in the Porteous conspiracy."

"I am sorry to interrupt a counsel in such a case as the present," said the presiding Judge; "but I must remind the learned gentleman, that he is travelling out of the case before us."

The counsel bowed, and resumed. "He only judged it necessary," he said, "to mention the name and situation of Robertson, because the circumstance in which that character was placed, went a great way in accounting for the silence on which his Majesty's counsel had laid so much weight, as affording proof that his client proposed to allow no fair play for its life, to the helpless being whom she was about to bring into the world. She had not announced to her friends that she had been seduced from the path of honour—and why had she not done so?—Because she expected daily to be restored to character, by her seducer doing her that justice which she knew to be in his power, and believed to be in his inclination. Was it natural—was it reasonable—was it fair, to expect that she should, in the interim, become *felo de se* of her own character, and proclaim her frailty to the world, when she had every reason to expect, that, by concealing it for a season, it might be veiled for ever? Was it not, on the contrary, pardonable, that, in such an emergency, a young woman, in such a situation, should be found far from disposed to make a confidant of every prying gossip, who, with sharp eyes, and eager ears, pressed upon her for an explanation of suspicious circumstances, which females in the lower—he might say which females of all ranks are so alert in noticing, that they sometimes discover them where they do not exist? Was it strange, or was it criminal, that she should have repelled their inquisitive impertinence, with petulant denials? The sense and feeling of all who heard him would answer directly in the negative. But although his client had thus remained silent towards those to whom she was not called upon to communicate her situation,—to whom," said the learned gentleman, "I will add, it would have been unadvised and improper in her to have done so; yet, I trust, I shall remove this case most triumphantly from under the statute, and obtain the unfortunate young woman an honourable dismission from your Lordships' bar, by showing that she did, in due time and place, and to a person most fit for such confidence, mention the calamitous circumstances in which she found herself. This occurred after Robertson's conviction, and when he was lying in prison in expectation of the fate which his comrade Wilson afterwards suffered, and from which he himself so strangely escaped. It was then, when all hopes of having her honour repaired by wedlock vanished from her eyes,—when an union with one in Robertson's situation, if still practicable, might, perhaps, have been regarded rather as an addition to her disgrace,—it was *then*, that I trust to be able to prove that the prisoner communicated and consulted with her sister, a young woman several years older than herself, the daughter of her father, if I mistake not, by a former marriage, upon the perils and distress of her unhappy situation."

"If, indeed, you are able to instruct *that* point, Mr. Fairbrother——" said the presiding Judge.

"If I am indeed able to instruct that point, my Lord," resumed Mr. Fairbrother, "I trust not only to serve my client, but to relieve your Lordships from that which I know you feel the most painful duty of your high office; and to give all who now hear me the exquisite pleasure of beholding a creature so young, so ingenuous, and so beautiful, as she that is now at the bar of your Lordships' Court, dismissed from thence in safety and in honour."

This address seemed to affect many of the audience, and was followed by a slight murmur of applause. Deans, as he heard his daughter's beauty and innocence appealed to, was involuntarily about to turn his eyes towards her; but, recollecting himself, he bent them again on the ground with stubborn resolution.

"Will not my learned brother, on the other side of the bar," continued the advocate, after a short pause, "share in this general joy, since I know, while he discharges his duty in bringing an accused person here, no one rejoices more in their being freely and honourably sent hence? My learned brother shakes his head doubtfully, and lays his hand on the panel's declaration. I understand him perfectly—he would insinuate that the facts now stated to your Lordships are inconsistent with the confession of Euphemia Deans herself. I need not remind your Lordships, that her present defence is no whit to be narrowed within the bounds of her former confession; and that it is not by any account which she may formerly have given of herself, but by what is now to be proved for or against her, that she must ultimately stand or fall. I am not under the necessity of accounting for her choosing to drop out of her declaration the circumstances of her confession to her sister. She might not be aware of its importance, she might be afraid of implicating her sister; she might even have forgotten the circumstance entirely, in the terror and distress of mind incidental to the arrest of so young a creature on a charge so heinous. Any of these reasons are sufficient to account for her having suppressed the truth in this instance, at whatever risk to herself; and I incline most to her erroneous fear of criminating her sister, because I observe she has had a similar tenderness towards her lover (however undeserved on his part), and has never once mentioned Robertson's name from beginning to end of her declaration.

"But, my Lords," continued Fairbrother, "I am aware the King's Advocate will expect me to show, that the proof I offer is consistent with other circumstances of the case, which I do not and cannot deny. He will demand of me how Effie Deans's confession to her sister, previous to her delivery, is reconcilable with the mystery of the birth, with the disappearance, perhaps the murder (for I will not deny a possibility which I cannot disprove) of the infant. My Lords, the explanation of this is to be found in the placability, perchance, I may say, in the facility and pliability, of the female sex. The *dulcis Amaryllidis irae*, as your Lordships well know, are easily appeased; nor is it possible to conceive a woman so atrociously offended by the man whom she has loved, but what she will retain a fund of forgiveness, upon which his penitence, whether real or affected, may draw largely, with a certainty that his bills will be answered. We can prove, by a letter produced in evidence, that this villain Robertson, from the bottom of the dungeon whence he already probably meditated the escape, which he afterwards accomplished by the assistance of his comrade, contrived to exercise authority over the mind, and to direct the motions, of this unhappy girl. It was in compliance with his injunctions, expressed in that letter, that the panel was prevailed upon to alter the line of conduct which her own better thoughts had suggested; and, instead of resorting, when her time of travail approached, to the protection of her own family, was induced to confide herself to the charge of some vile agent of this nefarious seducer, and by her conducted to one of those solitary and secret purlieus of villainy, which, to the shame of our police, still are suffered to exist in the suburbs of this city, where, with the assistance, and under the charge, of a person of her own sex, she bore a male-child, under circumstances which added treble bitterness to the woe denounced against our original mother. What purpose Robertson had in all this, it is hard to tell or even to guess. He may have meant to marry the girl, for her father is a man of substance. But, for the termination of the story, and the conduct of the woman whom he had placed about the person of

Euphemia Deans, it is still more difficult to account. The unfortunate young woman was visited by the fever incidental to her situation. In this fever she appears to have been deceived by the person that waited on her, and, on recovering her senses, she found that she was childless in that abode of misery. Her infant had been carried off, perhaps for the worst purposes, by the wretch that waited on her. It may have been murdered for what I can tell."

He was here interrupted by a piercing shriek, uttered by the unfortunate prisoner. She was with difficulty brought to compose herself. Her counsel availed himself of the tragical interruption, to close his pleading with effect.

"My Lords," said he, "in that piteous cry you heard the eloquence of maternal affection, far surpassing the force of my poor words—Rachel weeping for her children! Nature herself bears testimony in favour of the tenderness and acuteness of the prisoner's parental feelings. I will not dishonour her plea by adding a word more."

"Heard ye ever the like o' that, Laird?" said Saddletree to Dumbiedikes, when the Counsel had ended his speech. "There's a chield can spin a muckle pirn out of a wee tait of tow! Deil haet he kens mair about it than what's in the declaration, and a surmise that Jeanie Deans suld hae been able to say something about her sister's situation, whilk surmise, Mr. Crossmyloof says, rests on sma' authority. And he's cleckit this great muckle bird out o' this wee egg! He could wile the very flounders out o' the Firth.—What garr'd my father no send me to Utrecht?—But whisht, the Court is gaun to pronounce the interlocutor of relevancy."

And accordingly the Judges, after a few words, recorded their judgment, which bore, that the indictment, if proved, was relevant to infer the pains of law: And that the defence, that the panel had communicated her situation to her sister, was a relevant defence: And, finally, appointed the said indictment and defence to be submitted to the judgment of an assize.

CHAPTER XXIII

Most righteous judge! a sentence.—Come, prepare.
Merchant of Venice.

It is by no means my intention to describe minutely the forms of a Scottish criminal trial, nor am I sure that I could draw up an account so intelligible and accurate as to abide the criticism of the gentlemen of the long robe. It is enough to say that the jury was impanelled, and the case proceeded. The prisoner was again required to plead to the charge, and she again replied, "Not Guilty," in the same heart-thrilling tone as before.

The crown counsel then called two or three female witnesses, by whose testimony it was established, that Effie's situation had been remarked by them, that they had taxed her with the fact, and that her answers had amounted to an angry and petulant denial of what they charged her with. But, as very frequently happens, the declaration of the panel or accused party herself was the evidence which bore hardest upon her case.

In the event of these Tales ever finding their way across the Border, it may be proper to apprise the southern reader that it is the practice in Scotland, on apprehending a suspected person, to subject him to a judicial examination before a magistrate. He is not compelled to answer any of the questions asked of him, but may remain silent if he sees it his interest to do so. But whatever answers he chooses to give are formally written down, and being subscribed by himself and the magistrate, are produced against the accused in case of his being brought to trial. It is true, that these declarations are not produced as being in themselves evidence properly so called, but only as *adminicles* of testimony, tending to corroborate what is considered as legal and proper evidence. Notwithstanding this nice distinction, however, introduced by lawyers to reconcile this procedure to their own general rule, that a man cannot be required to bear witness against himself, it nevertheless usually happens that these declarations become the means of condemning the accused, as it were, out of their own mouths. The prisoner, upon these previous examinations, has indeed the privilege of remaining silent if he pleases; but every man necessarily feels that a refusal to answer natural and pertinent interrogatories, put by judicial authority, is in itself a strong proof of guilt, and will certainly lead to his being committed to prison; and few can renounce the hope of obtaining liberty, by giving some specious account of themselves, and showing apparent frankness in explaining their motives and accounting for their conduct. It, therefore, seldom happens that the prisoner refuses to give a judicial declaration, in which, nevertheless, either by letting out too much of the truth, or by endeavouring to substitute a fictitious story, he almost always exposes himself to suspicion and to contradictions, which weigh heavily in the minds of the jury.

The declaration of Effie Deans was uttered on other principles, and the following is a sketch of its contents, given in the judicial form, in which they may still be found in the Books of Adjournal.

The declarant admitted a criminal intrigue with an individual whose name she desired to conceal. "Being interrogated, what her reason was for secrecy on this point? She declared, that she had no right to blame that person's conduct more than she did her own, and that she was willing to confess her own faults, but not to say anything which might criminate the absent. Interrogated, if she confessed her situation to any one, or made any preparation for her confinement? Declares, she did not. And being interrogated, why she forbore to take steps which her situation so peremptorily required? Declares, she was ashamed to tell her friends, and she trusted the person she has mentioned would provide for her and the infant. Interrogated, if he did so? Declares, that he did not do so personally; but that it was not his fault, for that the declarant is convinced he would have laid down his life sooner than the bairn or she had come to harm. Interrogated, what prevented him from keeping his promise? Declares, that it was impossible for him to do so, he being under trouble at the time, and declines farther answer to this question. Interrogated, where she was from the period she left her master, Mr. Saddletree's family, until her appearance at her father's at St. Leonard's, the day before she was apprehended? Declares, she does not remember. And, on the interrogatory being repeated, declares, she does not mind muckle about it, for she was very ill. On the question being again repeated, she declares, she will tell the truth, if it should be the undoing of her, so long as she is not asked to tell on other folk; and admits, that she passed that interval of time in the lodging of a woman, an acquaintance of that person who had wished her to that place to be delivered, and that she was there delivered accordingly of a male child. Interrogated, what was the name of that person? Declares and refuses to answer this question. Interrogated, where she lives? Declares, she has no certainty, for that she was taken to the lodging aforesaid under cloud of night. Interrogated, if the lodging was in the city or suburbs? Declares and refuses to answer that question. Interrogated, whether, when she left the house of Mr. Saddletree, she went up or down the street? Declares and refuses to answer the question. Interrogated, whether she had ever seen the woman before she was wished to her, as she termed it, by the person whose name she refuses to answer? Declares and replies, not to her knowledge. Interrogated, whether this woman was introduced to her by the said person verbally, or by word of mouth? Declares, she has no freedom to answer this question. Interrogated, if the child was alive when it was born? Declares, that—God help her and it!—it certainly was alive. Interrogated, if it died a natural death after birth? Declares, not to her knowledge. Interrogated, where it now is? Declares, she would give her right hand to ken, but that she never hopes to see mair than the banes of it. And being interrogated, why she supposes it is now dead? the declarant wept bitterly, and made no answer. Interrogated, if the woman, in whose lodging she was, seemed to be a fit person to be with her in that situation? Declares, she might be fit enough for skill, but that she was an hard-hearted bad woman. Interrogated, if there was any other person in the lodging excepting themselves two? Declares, that she thinks there was another woman; but her head was so carried with pain of body and trouble of mind, that she minded her very little. Interrogated, when the child was taken away from her? Declared, that she fell in a fever, and was light-headed, and when she came to her own mind, the woman told her the bairn was dead; and that the declarant answered, if it was dead it had had foul play. That, thereupon, the woman was very sair on her, and gave her much ill-language; and that the deponent was frightened, and crawled out of the house when her back was turned, and went home to Saint Leonard's Crags, as well as a woman in her condition dought. Interrogated, why she did not tell her story to her sister and father, and get force to search the house for her child, dead or alive? Declares, it was her purpose to do so, but she had not time. Interrogated, why she now conceals the name of the woman, and the place of her abode? The declarant remained silent for a time, and then said, that to do so could not repair the skaith that was done, but might be the occasion of more. Interrogated, whether she had herself, at any time, had any purpose of putting away the child by violence? Declares, never; so might God be merciful to her—and then again declares, never when she was in her perfect senses; but what bad thoughts the Enemy might put into her brain when she was out of herself, she cannot answer. And again solemnly interrogated, declares, that she would have been drawn with wild horses, rather than have touched the bairn with an unmotherly hand. Interrogated, declares, that among the ill-language the woman gave her, she did say sure enough that the declarant had hurt the bairn when she was in the brain-fever; but that the declarant does not believe that she said this from any other cause than to frighten her, and make her be silent. Interrogated, what else the woman said to her? Declares, that when the declarant cried loud for her bairn, and was like to raise the neighbours, the woman threatened her, that they that could stop the wean's skirling would stop hers, if she did not keep a' the lounder. And that this threat, with the manner of the woman, made the declarant conclude, that the bairn's life was gone, and her own in danger, for that the woman was a desperate bad woman, as the declarant judged, from the language she used. Interrogated, declares, that the fever and delirium were brought on her by hearing bad news, suddenly told to her, but refuses to say what the said news related to. Interrogated, why she does not now communicate these particulars, which might, perhaps, enable the magistrate to ascertain whether the child is living or dead; and requested to observe, that her refusing to do so exposes her own life, and leaves the child in bad hands; as also, that her present refusal to answer on such points, is inconsistent with her alleged intention to make a clean breast to her sister? Declares, that she kens the bairn is now dead, or, if living, there is one that will look after it; that for her own living or dying, she is in God's hands, who knows her innocence of harming her bairn with her will or knowledge; and that she has altered her resolution of speaking out, which she entertained when she left the woman's lodging, on account of a matter which she has since learned. And declares, in general, that she is wearied, and will answer no more questions at this time."

Upon a subsequent examination, Euphemia Deans adhered to the declaration she had formerly made, with this addition, that a paper found in her trunk being shown to her, she admitted that it contained the credentials, in consequence of which she resigned herself to the conduct of the woman at whose lodgings she was delivered of the child. Its tenor ran thus :—

" DEAREST EFFIE,—I have gotten the means to send to you by a woman who is well-qualified to assist you in y ur approaching streight ; she is not what I could wish her, but I cannot do better for you in my present condition. I am obliged to trust to her in this present calamity, for myself and you too. I hope for the best, though I am now in a sore pinch ; yet thought is free—I think Handie Dandie and I may queer the stifler for all that is come and gone. You will be angry for me writing this, to my little Cameronian Lily ; but if I can but live to be a comfort to you, and a father to your babie, you will have plenty of time to scold.— Once more let none know your counsel—my life depends on this hag, d—n her—she is both deep and dangerous, but she has more wiles and wit than ever were in a beldam's head, and has cause to be true to me. Farewell, my Lily—Do not droop on my account—in a week I will be y urs, or no more my own."

Then followed a postscript. " If they must truss me, I will repent of nothing so much, even at the last hard pinch, as of the injury I have done my Lily."

Effie refused to say from whom she had received this letter, but enough of the story was now known, to ascertain that it came from Robertson ; and from the date, it appeared to have been written about the time when Andrew Wilson (called for a nickname Handie Dandie) and he were meditating their first abortive attempt to escape, which miscarried in the manner mentioned in the beginning of this history.

The evidence of the Crown being concluded, the counsel for the prisoner began to lead a proof in her defence. The first witnesses were examined upon the girl's character. All gave her an excellent one, but none with more feeling than worthy Mrs. Saddletree, who, with the tears on her cheeks, declared, that she could not have had a higher opinion of Effie Deans, nor a more sincere regard for her, if she had been her own daughter. All present gave the honest woman credit for her goodness of heart, excepting her husband, who whispered to Dumbiedikes, " That Nichil Novit of yours is but a raw hand at leading evidence, I'm thinking. What signified his bringing a woman here to snotter and snivel, and bather their Lordships ? He should hae ceeted me, sir, and I should hae gien him sic a screed o' testimony, they shouldna hae touched a hair o' her head."

" Hadna ye better get up and try't yet ? " said the Laird. " I'll mak a sign to Novit."

" Na, na," said Saddletree, " thank ye for naething, neighbour—that would be ultroneous evidence, and I ken what belangs to that ; but Nichil Novit suld hae had me ceeted *debito tempore*." And wiping his mouth with his silk handkerchief with great importance, he resumed the port and manner of an edified and intelligent auditor.

Mr. Fairbrother now premised, in a few words, " that he meant to bring forward his most important witness, upon whose evidence the cause must in a great measure depend. What his client was, they had learned from the preceding witnesses ; and so far as general character, given in the most forcible terms, and even with tears, could interest every one in her fate, she had already gained that advantage. It was necessary, he admitted, that he should produce more positive testimony of her innocence than what arose out of general character, and this he undertook to do by the mouth of the person to whom she had communicated her situation—by the mouth of her natural counsellor and guardian—her sister. —Macer, call into court, Jean, or Jeanie Deans, daughter of David Deans, cow-feeder, at Saint Leonard's Crags."

When he uttered these words, the poor prisoner instantly started up, and stretched herself half-way over the bar, towards the side at which her sister was to enter. And when, slowly following the officer, the witness advanced to the foot of the table, Effie, with the whole expression of her countenance altered, from that of confused shame and dismay, to an eager, imploring, and almost ecstatic earnestness of entreaty, with outstretched hands, hair streaming back, eyes raised eagerly to her sister's face, and glistening through tears, exclaimed, in a tone which went through the heart of all who heard her —" O Jeanie, Jeanie, save me, save me ! "

With a different feeling, yet equally appropriated to his

proud and self-dependent character, old Deans drew himself back still farther under the cover of the bench; so that when Jeanie, as she entered the court, cast a timid glance towards the place at which she had left him seated, his venerable figure was no longer visible. He sate down on the other side of Dumbiedikes, wrung his hand hard, and whispered, "Ah, Laird, this is warst of a'—if I can but win ower this part—I feel my head unca dizzy; but my Master is strong in His servant's weakness." After a moment's mental prayer, he again started up, as if impatient of continuing in any one posture, and gradually edged himself forward towards the place he had just quitted.

Jeanie in the meantime had advanced to the bottom of the table, when, unable to resist the impulse of affection, she suddenly extended her hand to her sister. Effie was just within the distance that she could seize it with both hers, press it to her mouth, cover it with kisses, and bathe it in tears, with the fond devotion that a Catholic would pay to a guardian saint descended for his safety; while Jeanie, hiding her own face with her other hand, wept bitterly. The sight would have moved a heart of stone, much more of flesh and blood. Many of the spectators shed tears, and it was some time before the presiding Judge himself could so far subdue his emotion, as to request the witness to compose herself, and the prisoner to forbear those marks of eager affection, which, however natural, could not be permitted at that time, and in that presence.

The solemn oath,—"the truth to tell, and no truth to conceal, as far as she knew or should be asked," was then administered by the Judge "in the name of God, and as the witness should answer to God at the great day of judgment;" an awful adjuration, which seldom fails to make impression even on the most hardened characters, and to strike with fear even the most upright. Jeanie, educated in deep and devout reverence for the name and attributes of the Deity, was, by the solemnity of a direct appeal to his person and justice, awed, but at the same time elevated above all considerations, save those which she could, with a clear conscience, call HIM to witness. She repeated the form in a low and reverent, but distinct tone of voice, after the Judge, to whom, and not to any inferior officer of the court, the task is assigned in Scotland of directing the witness in that solemn appeal, which is the sanction of his testimony.

When the Judge had finished the established form, he added in a feeling, but yet in a monitory tone, an advice, which the circumstances appeared to him to call for.

"Young woman," these were his words, "you come before this Court in circumstances, which it would be worse than cruel not to pity and to sympathise with. Yet it is my duty to tell you, that the truth, whatever its consequences may be, the truth is what you owe to your country, and to that God whose word is truth, and whose name you have now invoked. Use your own time in answering the questions that gentleman" (pointing to the counsel) "shall put to you—But remember, that what you may be tempted to say beyond what is the actual truth, you must answer both here and hereafter."

The usual questions were then put to her:—Whether any one had instructed her what evidence she had to deliver? Whether any one had given or promised her any good deed, hire, or reward, for her testimony? Whether she had any malice or ill-will at his Majesty's Advocate, being the party against whom she was cited as a witness? To which question she successively answered by a quiet negative. But their tenor gave great scandal and offence to her father, who was not aware that they are put to every witness as a matter of form.

"Na, na," he exclaimed, loud enough to be heard, "my bairn is no like the widow of Tekoah—nae man has putten words into her mouth."

One of the Judges, better acquainted, perhaps, with the Books of Adjournal than with the Book of Samuel, was disposed to make some instant inquiry after this Widow of Tekoah, who, as he construed the matter, had been tampering with the evidence. But the presiding Judge, better versed in Scripture history, whispered to his learned brother the necessary explanation; and the pause occasioned by this mistake, had the good effect of giving Jeanie Deans time to collect her spirits for the painful task she had to perform.

Fairbrother, whose practice and intelligence were considerable, saw the necessity of letting the witness compose herself. In his heart he suspected that she came to bear false witness in her sister's cause.

"But that is her own affair," thought Fairbrother; "and it is my business to see that she has plenty of time to regain composure, and to deliver her evidence, be it true, or be it false—*valeat quantum.*"

Accordingly, he commenced his interrogatories with uninteresting questions, which admitted of instant reply.

"You are, I think, the sister of the prisoner?"

"Yes, sir."

"Not the full sister, however?"

"No, sir—we are by different mothers."

"True; and you are, I think, several years older than your
sister?"

"Yes, sir," &c.

After the advocate had conceived that, by these preliminary
and unimportant questions, he had familiarised the witness
with the situation in which she stood, he asked, "whether she
had not remarked her sister's state of health to be altered,
during the latter part of the term when she had lived with Mrs.
Saddletree?"

Jeanie answered in the affirmative.

"And she told you the cause of it, my dear, I suppose?"
said Fairbrother, in an easy, and, as one may say, an inductive
sort of tone.

"I am sorry to interrupt my brother," said the Crown
Counsel, rising, "but I am in your Lordships' judgment,
whether this be not a leading question?"

"If this point is to be debated," said the presiding Judge,
"the witness must be removed."

For the Scottish lawyers regard with a sacred and scrupulous
horror, every question so shaped by the counsel examining, as
to convey to a witness the least intimation of the nature of the
answer which is desired from him. These scruples, though
founded on an excellent principle, are sometimes carried to an
absurd pitch of nicety, especially as it is generally easy for a
lawyer who has his wits about him to elude the objection.
Fairbrother did so in the present case.

"It is not necessary to waste the time of the Court, my
Lord; since the King's Counsel thinks it worth while to
object to the form of my question, I will shape it otherwise.
—Pray, young woman, did you ask your sister any question
when you observed her looking unwell?—take courage—
speak out."

"I asked her," replied Jeanie, "what ailed her."

"Very well—take your own time—and what was the answer
she made?" continued Mr. Fairbrother.

Jeanie was silent, and looked deadly pale. It was not that
she at any one instant entertained an idea of the possibility of

prevarication—it was the natural hesitation to extinguish the last spark of hope that remained for her sister.

"Take courage, young woman," said Fairbrother.—"I asked what your sister said ailed her when you inquired?"

"Nothing," answered Jeanie, with a faint voice, which was yet heard distinctly in the most distant corner of the Court-room,—such an awful and profound silence had been preserved during the anxious interval, which had interposed betwixt the lawyer's question and the answer of the witness.

Fairbrother's countenance fell; but with that ready presence of mind, which is as useful in civil as in military emergencies, he immediately rallied.—"Nothing? True; you mean nothing at *first*—but when you asked her again, did she not tell you what ailed her?"

The question was put in a tone meant to make her comprehend the importance of her answer, had she not been already aware of it. The ice was broken, however, and, with less pause than at first, she now replied,—"Alack! alack! she never breathed word to me about it."

A deep groan passed through the Court. It was echoed by one deeper and more agonised from the unfortunate father. The hope, to which unconsciously, and in spite of himself, he had still secretly clung, had now dissolved, and the venerable old man fell forward senseless on the floor of the Court-house, with his head at the foot of his terrified daughter. The unfortunate prisoner, with impotent passion, strove with the guards, betwixt whom she was placed. "Let me gang to my father! —I *will* gang to him—I *will* gang to him—he is dead—he is killed—I hae killed him!"—she repeated in frenzied tones of grief, which those who heard them did not speedily forget.

Even in this moment of agony and general confusion, Jeanie did not lose that superiority, which a deep and firm mind assures to its possessor, under the most trying circumstances.

"He is my father—he is our father," she mildly repeated to those who endeavoured to separate them, as she stooped,— shaded aside his grey hairs, and began assiduously to chafe his temples.

The Judge, after repeatedly wiping his eyes, gave directions that they should be conducted into a neighbouring apartment, and carefully attended. The prisoner, as her father was borne from the Court, and her sister slowly followed, pursued them with her eyes so earnestly fixed, as if they would have started from their socket. But when they were no longer visible, she seemed to find, in her despairing and deserted state, a courage which she had not yet exhibited.

"The bitterness of it is now past," she said, and then boldly addressed the Court. "My Lords, if it is your pleasure to gang on wi' this matter, the weariest day will hae its end at last."

The Judge, who, much to his honour, had shared deeply in the general sympathy, was surprised at being recalled to his duty by the prisoner. He collected himself, and requested to know if the panel's counsel had more evidence to produce. Fairbrother replied, with an air of dejection, that his proof was concluded.

The King's Counsel addressed the jury for the crown. He said in few words, that no one could be more concerned than he was for the distressing scene which they had just witnessed. But it was the necessary consequence of great crimes to bring distress and ruin upon all connected with the perpetrators. He briefly reviewed the proof, in which he showed that all the circumstances of the case concurred with those required by the Act under which the unfortunate prisoner was tried : That the counsel for the panel had totally failed in proving, that Euphemia Deans had communicated her situation to her sister : That, respecting her previous good character, he was sorry to observe, that it was females who possessed the world's good report, and to whom it was justly valuable, who were most strongly tempted, by shame and fear of the world's censure, to the crime of infanticide : That the child was murdered, he professed to entertain no doubt. The vacillating and inconsistent declaration of the prisoner herself, marked as it was by numerous refusals to speak the truth on subjects, when, according to her own story, it would have been natural, as well as advantageous, to have been candid ; even this imperfect declaration left no doubt in his mind as to the fate of the unhappy infant. Neither could he doubt that the panel was a partner in this guilt. Who else had an interest in a deed so inhuman ? Surely neither Robertson, nor Robertson's agent, in whose house she was delivered, had the least temptation to commit such a crime, unless upon her account, with her connivance, and for the sake of saving her reputation. But it was not required of him, by the law, that he should bring precise proof of the murder, or of the prisoner's accession to it. It was the very purpose of the statute to substitute a certain chain of presumptive evidence in place of a probation, which, in such cases, it was peculiarly difficult to obtain. The jury might peruse the statute itself, and they had also the libel and inter-locutor of relevancy to direct them in point of law. He put it to the conscience of the jury, that under both he was entitled to a verdict of Guilty.

The charge of Fairbrother was much cramped by his having failed in the proof which he expected to lead. But he fought his losing cause with courage and constancy. He ventured to arraign the severity of the statute under which the young woman was tried. "In all other cases," he said, "the first thing required of the criminal prosecutor was, to prove unequi-vocally that the crime libelled had actually been committed, which lawyers called proving the *corpus delicti*. But this statute, made doubtless with the best intentions, and under the im-pulse of a just horror for the unnatural crime of infanticide, ran the risk of itself occasioning the worst of murders, the death of an innocent person, to atone for a supposed crime which may never have been committed by any one. He was so far from acknowledging the alleged probability of the child's violent death that he could not even allow that there was evidence of its having ever lived."

The King's Counsel pointed to the woman's declaration; to which the counsel replied—"A production concocted in a moment of terror and agony, and which approached to in-sanity," he said, "his learned brother well knew was no sound evidence against the party who emitted it. It was true, that a judicial confession, in presence of the Justices themselves, was the strongest of all proof, in so much that it is said in law, that '*in confitentem nullæ sunt partes judicis.*' But this was true of judicial confession only, by which law meant that which is made in presence of the justices, and the sworn inquest. Of extrajudicial confession, all authorities held with the illustrious Farinaceus, and Matheus, '*confessio extra-judicialis in se nulla est; et quod nullum est, non potest adminiculari.*' It was totally inept, and void of all strength and effect from the beginning; incapable, therefore, of being bolstered up or supported, or, according to the law-phrase, adminiculated, by other presumptive circumstances. In the present case, therefore, letting the extrajudicial confession go, as it ought to go, for nothing," he contended, "the prosecutor had not made out the second quality of the statute, that a live child had been born; and *that*, at least, ought to be estab-lished before presumptions were received that it had been murdered. If any of the assize," he said, "should be of opinion that this was dealing rather narrowly with the statute, they ought to consider that it was in its nature highly penal, and therefore entitled to no favourable construction."

He concluded a learned speech, with an eloquent peroration on the scene they had just witnessed, during which Saddletree fell fast asleep.

It was now the presiding Judge's turn to address the jury. He did so briefly and distinctly.

"It was for the jury," he said, "to consider whether the prosecutor had made out his plea. For himself, he sincerely grieved to say, that a shadow of doubt remained not upon his mind concerning the verdict which the inquest had to bring in. He would not follow the prisoner's counsel through the impeachment which he had brought against the statute of King William and Queen Mary. He and the jury were sworn to judge according to the laws as they stood, not to criticise, or to evade, or even to justify them. In no civil case would a counsel have been permitted to plead his client's case in the teeth of the law; but in the hard situation in which counsel were often placed in the Criminal Court, as well as out of favour to all presumptions of innocence, he had not inclined to interrupt the learned gentleman, or narrow his plea. The present law, as it now stood, had been instituted by the wisdom of their fathers, to check the alarming progress of a dreadful crime; when it was found too severe for its purpose, it would doubtless be altered by the wisdom of the legislature; at present it was the law of the land, the rule of the court, and, according to the oath which they had taken, it must be that of the jury. This unhappy girl's situation could not be doubted; that she had borne a child, and that the child had disappeared, were certain facts. The learned counsel had failed to show that she had communicated her situation. All the requisites of the case required by the statute were therefore before the jury. The learned gentleman had, indeed, desired them to throw out of consideration the panel's own confession, which was the plea usually urged, in penury of all others, by counsel in his situation, who usually felt that the declarations of their clients bore hard on them. But that the Scottish law designed that a certain weight should be laid on these declarations, which, he admitted, were *quodammodo* extrajudicial, was evident from the universal practice by which they were always produced and read, as part of the prosecutor's probation. In the present case, no person, who had heard the witnesses describe the appearance of the young woman before she left Saddletree's house, and contrasted it with that of her state and condition at her return to her father's, could have any doubt that the fact of delivery had taken place, as set forth in her own declaration, which was, therefore, not a solitary piece of testimony, but adminiculated and supported by the strongest circumstantial proof.

"He did not," he said, "state the impression upon his own mind with the purpose of biassing theirs. He had felt no less than they had done from the scene of domestic misery which had been exhibited before them; and if they, having God and a good conscience, the sanctity of their oath, and the regard due to the law of the country, before their eyes, could come to a conclusion favourable to this unhappy prisoner, he should rejoice as much as any one in Court; for never had he found his duty more distressing than in discharging it that day, and glad he would be to be relieved from the still more painful task, which would otherwise remain for him."

The jury, having heard the Judge's address, bowed and retired, preceded by a macer of Court, to the apartment destined for their deliberation.

CHAPTER XXIV

Law, take thy victim—May she find the mercy
In yon mild heaven, which this hard world denies her!

IT was an hour ere the jurors returned, and as they traversed the crowd with slow steps, as men about to discharge themselves of a heavy and painful responsibility, the audience was hushed into profound, earnest, and awful silence.

"Have you agreed on your chancellor, gentlemen?" was the first question of the Judge.

The foreman, called in Scotland the chancellor of the jury, usually the man of best rank and estimation among the assizers, stepped forward, and, with a low reverence, delivered to the Court a sealed paper, containing the verdict, which, until of late years, that verbal returns are in some instances permitted, was always couched in writing. The jury remained standing while the Judge broke the seals, and, having perused the paper, handed it, with an air of mournful gravity, down to the Clerk of Court, who proceeded to engross in the record the yet unknown verdict, of which, however, all omened the tragical contents. A form still remained, trifling and unimportant in itself, but to which imagination adds a sort of solemnity, from the awful occasion upon which it is used. A lighted candle was placed on the table, the original paper containing the verdict was enclosed in a sheet of paper, and, sealed with the Judge's own signet, was transmitted to the Crown Office, to be preserved among other records of the same kind. As all this is transacted in profound silence, the producing and extinguishing the candle seems a type of the human spark which is shortly afterwards doomed to be quenched, and excites in the spectators something of the same effect which in England is obtained by the Judge assuming the fatal cap of judgment. When these preliminary forms had been gone through, the Judge required Euphemia Deans to attend to the verdict to be read.

After the usual words of style, the verdict set forth, that the Jury having made choice of John Kirk, Esq., to be their chancellor, and Thomas Moore, merchant, to be their clerk, did, by a plurality of voices, find the said Euphemia Deans GUILTY of the crime libelled; but, in consideration of her extreme youth, and the cruel circumstances of her case, did earnestly entreat that the Judge would recommend her to the mercy of the Crown.

"Gentlemen," said the Judge, "you have done your duty—and a painful one it must have been to men of humanity like you. I will, undoubtedly, transmit your recommendation to the throne. But it is my duty to tell all who now hear me, but especially to inform that unhappy young woman, in order that her mind may be settled accordingly, that I have not the least hope of a pardon being granted in the present case. You know the crime has been increasing in this land, and I know farther, that this has been ascribed to the lenity in which the laws have been exercised, and that there is therefore no hope whatever of obtaining a remission for this offence." The jury bowed again, and, released from their painful office, dispersed themselves among the mass of bystanders.

The Court then asked Mr. Fairbrother, whether he had anything to say, why judgment should not follow on the verdict? The counsel had spent some time in perusing and reperusing the verdict, counting the letters in each juror's name, and weighing every phrase, nay, every syllable in the nicest scales of legal criticism. But the clerk of the jury had understood his business too well. No flaw was to be found, and Fairbrother mournfully intimated, that he had nothing to say in arrest of judgment.

The presiding Judge then addressed the unhappy prisoner : —"Euphemia Deans, attend to the sentence of the Court now to be pronounced against you."

She rose from her seat, and, with a composure far greater than could have been augured from her demeanour during some parts of the trial, abode the conclusion of the awful scene. So nearly does the mental portion of our feelings resemble those which are corporal, that the first severe blows which we receive bring with them a stunning apathy, which renders us indifferent to those that follow them. Thus said Mandrin, when he was undergoing the punishment of the wheel ; and so have all felt, upon whom successive inflictions have descended with continuous and reiterated violence.

"Young woman," said the Judge, "it is my painful duty to tell you, that your life is forfeited under a law, which, if it may seem in some degree severe, is yet wisely so, to render those of your unhappy situation aware what risk they run, by concealing, out of pride or false shame, their lapse from virtue, and making no preparation to save the lives of the unfortunate infants whom they are to bring into the world. When you concealed your situation from your mistress, your sister, and other worthy and compassionate persons of your own sex, in whose favour your former conduct had given you a fair place, you seem to me to have had in your contemplation, at least, the death of the helpless creature, for whose life you neglected to provide. How the child was disposed of—whether it was dealt upon by another, or by yourself—whether the extraordinary story you have told is partly false, or altogether so, is between God and your own conscience. I will not aggravate your distress by pressing on that topic, but I do most solemnly adjure you to employ the remaining space of your time in making your peace with God, for which purpose such reverend clergyman, as you yourself may name, shall have access to you. Notwithstanding the humane recommendation of the jury, I cannot afford to you, in the present circumstances of the country, the slightest hope that your life will be prolonged beyond the period assigned for the execution of your sentence. Forsaking, therefore, the thoughts of this world, let your mind be prepared by repentance for those of more awful moments—for death, judgment, and eternity.— Doomster, read the sentence."[1]

When the Doomster showed himself, a tall haggard figure, arrayed in a fantastic garment of black and grey, passmented with silver lace, all fell back with a sort of instinctive horror, and made wide way for him to approach the foot of the table. As this office was held by the common executioner, men shouldered each other backward to avoid even the touch of his garment, and some were seen to brush their own clothes, which had accidentally become subject to such contamination. A sound went through the court, produced by each person drawing in their breath hard, as men do when they expect or witness what is frightful, and at the same time affecting. The caitiff villain yet seemed, amid his hardened brutality, to have some sense of his being the object of public detestation, which made him impatient of being in public, as birds of evil omen are anxious to escape from daylight, and from pure air.

Repeating after the Clerk of Court, he gabbled over the words of the sentence, which condemned Euphemia Deans to be conducted back to the Tolbooth of Edinburgh, and detained there until Wednesday the —— day of ——; and upon that day, betwixt the hours of two and four o'clock afternoon, to be conveyed to the common place of execution, and there hanged by the neck upon a gibbet. "And this," said the Doomster, aggravating his harsh voice, "I pronounce for *doom*."

He vanished when he had spoken the last emphatic word, like a foul fiend after the purpose of his visitation has been accomplished; but the impression of horror, excited by his presence and his errand, remained upon the crowd of spectators.

The unfortunate criminal,—for so she must now be termed,— with more susceptibility, and more irritable feelings than her father and sister, was found, in this emergence, to possess a considerable share of their courage. She had remained standing motionless at the bar while the sentence was pronounced, and was observed to shut her eyes when the Doomster appeared. But she was the first to break silence when that evil form had left his place.

"God forgive ye, my Lords," she said, "and dinna be angry wi' me for wishing it—we a' need forgiveness.—As for myself

[1] Note XII.—Doomster, or Dempster, of Court.

I canna blame ye, for ye act up to your lights; and if I havena killed my poor infant, ye may witness a' that hae seen it this day, that I hae been the means of killing my grey-headed father—I deserve the warst frae man, and frae God too—But God is mair mercifu' to us than we are to each other."

With these words the trial concluded. The crowd rushed, bearing forward and shouldering each other, out of the court, in the same tumultuary mode in which they had entered; and, in the excitation of animal motion and animal spirits, soon forgot whatever they had felt as impressive in the scene which they had witnessed. The professional spectators, whom habit and theory had rendered as callous to the distress of the scene as medical men are to those of a surgical operation, walked homeward in groups, discussing the general principle of the statute under which the young woman was condemned, the nature of the evidence, and the arguments of the counsel, without considering even that of the Judge as exempt from their criticism.

The female spectators, more compassionate, were loud in exclamation against that part of the Judge's speech which seemed to cut off the hope of pardon.

"Set him up, indeed," said Mrs. Howden, "to tell us that the poor lassie behoved to die, when Mr. John Kirk, as civil a gentleman as is within the ports of the town, took the pains to prigg for her himsell."

"Ay, but, neighbour," said Miss Damahoy, drawing up her thin maidenly form to its full height of prim dignity—"I really think this unnatural business of having bastard-bairns should be putten a stop to—There isna a hussy now on this side of thirty that you can bring within your doors, but there will be chields—writer-lads, prentice-lads, and what not—coming traiking after them for their destruction, and discrediting ane's honest house into the bargain—I hae nae patience wi' them."

"Hout, neighbour," said Mrs. Howden, "we suld live and let live—we hae been young oursells, and we are no aye to judge the worst when lads and lasses forgather."

"Young oursells? and judge the warst?" said Miss Damahoy. "I am no sae auld as that comes to, Mrs. Howden; and as for what ye ca' the warst, I ken neither good nor bad about the matter, I thank my stars!"

"Ye are thankfu' for sma' mercies, then," said Mrs. Howden, with a toss of her head; "and as for *you* and *young*—I trow ye were doing for yoursell at the last riding of the Scots

Parliament, and that was in the gracious year seven, sae ye can be nae sic chicken at ony rate."

Plumdamas, who acted as squire of the body to the two contending dames, instantly saw the hazard of entering into such delicate points of chronology, and being a lover of peace and good neighbourhood, lost no time in bringing back the conversation to its original subject.

"The Judge didna tell us a' he could hae tell'd us, if he had liked, about the application for pardon, neighbours," said he; "there is aye a wimple in a lawyer's clew; but it's a wee bit of a secret."

"And what is't?—what is't, neighbour Plumdamas?" said Mrs. Howden and Miss Damahoy at once, the acid fermentation of their dispute being at once neutralised by the powerful alkali implied in the word secret.

"Here's Mr. Saddletree can tell ye that better than me, for it was him that tauld me," said Plumdamas as Saddletree came up, with his wife hanging on his arm, and looking very disconsolate.

When the question was put to Saddletree, he looked very scornful. "They speak about stopping the frequency of child-murder," said he, in a contemptuous tone; "do ye think our auld enemies of England, as Glendook aye ca's them in his printed Statute-book, care a boddle whether we didna kill ane anither, skin and birn, horse and foot, man, woman, and bairns, all and sindry, *omnes et singulos*, as Mr. Crossmyloof says? Na, na, it's no *that* hinders them frae pardoning the bit lassie. But here is the pinch of the plea. The king and queen are sae ill pleased wi' that mistak about Porteous, that deil a kindly Scot will they pardon again, either by reprieve or remission, if the haill town o' Edinburgh should be a' hanged on ae tow."

"Deil that they were back at their German kailyard then, as my neighbour MacCroskie ca's it," said Mrs. Howden, "an that's the way they're gaun to guide us!"

"They say for certain," said Miss Damahoy, "that King George flang his periwig in the fire when he heard o' the Porteous mob."

"He has done that, they say," replied Saddletree, "for less thing."

"Aweel," said Miss Damahoy, "he might keep mair wit in his anger—but it's a' the better for his wigmaker, I'se warrant."

"The queen tore her biggonets for perfect anger,—ye'll hae heard o' that too?" said Plumdamas. "And the king, they say, kickit Sir Robert Walpole for no keeping down the mob of Edinburgh; but I dinna believe he wad behave sae ungenteel."

"It's dooms truth, though," said Saddletree; "and he was for kickin the Duke of Argyle [1] too."

"Kickin the Duke of Argyle!" exclaimed the hearers at once, in all the various combined keys of utter astonishment.

"Ay, but MacCallummore's blood wadna sit down wi' that; there was risk of Andro Ferrara coming in thirdsman."

"The duke is a real Scotsman — a true friend to the country," answered Saddletree's hearers.

"Ay, troth is he, to king and country baith, as ye sall hear," continued the orator, "if ye will come in bye to our house, for it's safest speaking of sic things *inter parietes*."

When they entered his shop he thrust his prentice boy out of it, and, unlocking his desk, took out, with an air of grave and complacent importance, a dirty and crumpled piece of printed paper; he observed, "This is new corn—it's no everybody could show ye the like o' this. It's the duke's speech about the Porteous mob, just promulgated by the hawkers. Ye shall hear what Ian Roy Cean [2] says for himsell. My correspondent bought it in the Palace yard, that's like just under the king's nose—I think he claws up their mittans!— It came in a letter about a foolish bill of exchange that the man wanted me to renew for him. I wish ye wad see about it, Mrs. Saddletree."

Honest Mrs. Saddletree had hitherto been so sincerely distressed about the situation of her unfortunate protégée, that she had suffered her husband to proceed in his own way, without attending to what he was saying. The words *bill* and *renew* had, however, an awakening sound in them; and she snatched the letter which her husband held towards her, and wiping her eyes, and putting on her spectacles, endeavoured, as fast as the dew which collected on her glasses would permit, to get at the meaning of the needful part of the epistle; while her husband, with pompous elevation, read an extract from the speech.

[1] Note XIII.—John Duke of Argyle and Greenwich.
[2] Red John the Warrior, a name personal and proper in the Highlands to John Duke of Argyle and Greenwich, as MacCummin was that of his race or dignity.

"I am no minister, I never was a minister, and I never will be one——"

"I didna ken his grace was ever designed for the ministry," interrupted Mrs. Howden.

"He disna mean a minister of the gospel, Mrs. Howden, but a minister of state," said Saddletree, with condescending goodness, and then proceeded : "The time was when I might have been a piece of a minister, but I was too sensible of my own incapacity to engage in any state affair. And I thank God that I had always too great a value for those few abilities which nature has given me, to employ them in doing any drudgery, or any job of what kind soever. I have, ever since I set out in the world (and I believe few have set out more early), served my prince with my tongue ; I have served him with any little interest I had, and I have served him with my sword, and in my profession of arms. I have held employments which I have lost, and were I to be to-morrow deprived of those which still remain to me, and which I have endeavoured honestly to deserve, I would still serve him to the last acre of my inheritance, and to the last drop of my blood——"

Mrs. Saddletree here broke in upon the orator.—"Mr. Saddletree, what *is* the meaning of a' this? Here are ye clavering about the Duke of Argyle, and this man Martingale gaun to break on our hands, and lose us gude sixty pounds—I wonder what duke will pay that, quotha—I wish the Duke of Argyle would pay his ain accounts—He is in a thousand punds Scots on thae very books when he was last at Roystoun—I'm no saying but he's a just nobleman, and that it's gude siller—but it wad drive ane daft to be confused wi' deukes and drakes, and thae distressed folk upstairs, that's Jeanie Deans and her father. And then, putting the very callant that was sewing the curpel out o' the shop, to play wi' blackguards in the close—Sit still, neighbours, it's no that I mean to disturb *you* ; but what between courts o' law and courts o' state, and upper and under parliaments, and parliament houses, here and in London, the gudeman's gane clean gyte, I think."

The gossips understood civility, and the rule of doing as they would be done by, too well, to tarry upon the slight invitation implied in the conclusion of this speech, and therefore made their farewells and departure as fast as possible, Saddletree whispering to Plumdamas that he would "meet him at MacCroskie's" (the low-browed shop in the Luckenbooths, already mentioned), " in the hour of cause, and put MacCallummore's speech in his pocket, for a' the gudewife's din."

When Mrs. Saddletree saw the house freed of her importunate visitors, and the little boy reclaimed from the pastimes of the wynd to the exercise of the awl, she went to visit her unhappy relative, David Deans, and his elder daughter, who had found in her house the nearest place of friendly refuge.

CHAPTER XXV

Isab. Alas! what poor ability's in me
   To do him good?
Lucio. Assay the power you have.
                          Measure for Measure.

When Mrs. Saddletree entered the apartment in which her guests had shrouded their misery, she found the window darkened. The feebleness which followed his long swoon had rendered it necessary to lay the old man in bed. The curtains were drawn around him, and Jeanie sat motionless by the side of the bed. Mrs. Saddletree was a woman of kindness, nay, of feeling, but not of delicacy. She opened the half-shut window, drew aside the curtain, and taking her kinsman by the hand, exhorted him to sit up, and bear his sorrow like a good man, and a Christian man, as he was. But when she quitted his hand, it fell powerless by his side, nor did he attempt the least reply.

" Is all over? " asked Jeanie, with lips and cheeks as pale as ashes—" and is there nae hope for her ? "

" Nane, or next to nane," said Mrs. Saddletree ; " I heard the Judge-carle say it with my ain ears—It was a burning shame to see sae mony o' them set up yonder in their red gowns and black gowns, and a' to take the life o' a bit senseless lassie. I had never muckle broo o' my gudeman's gossips, and now I like them waur than ever. The only wiselike thing I heard onybody say, was decent Mr. John Kirk of Kirk-knowe, and he wussed them just to get the king's mercy, and nae mair about it. But he spake to unreasonable folk—he might just hae keepit his breath to hae blown on his porridge."

" But *can* the king gie her mercy ? " said Jeanie earnestly.

"Some folk tell me he canna gie mercy in cases of mur——— in cases like hers."

"*Can* he gie mercy, hinny?—I weel I wot he *can*, when he likes. There was young Single-sword, that stickit the Laird of Ballencleuch, and Captain Hackum, the Englishman, that killed Lady Colgrain's gudeman, and the Master of Saint Clair, that shot the twa Shaws, and mony mair in my time—to be sure they were gentle blude, and had their kin to speak for them—And there was Jock Porteous the other day—I'se warrant there's mercy, an folk could win at it."

"Porteous?" said Jeanie; "very true—I forget a' that I suld maist mind.—Fare ye weel, Mrs. Saddletree; and may ye never want a friend in the hour o' distress!"

"Will ye no stay wi' your father, Jeanie, bairn?—Ye had better," said Mrs. Saddletree.

"I will be wanted ower yonder," indicating the Tolbooth with her hand, "and I maun leave him now, or I will never be able to leave him. I fearna for his life—I ken how strong-hearted he is—I ken it," she said, laying her hand on her bosom, "by my ain heart at this minute."

"Weel, hinny, if ye think it's for the best, better he stay here and rest him, than gang back to St. Leonard's."

"Muckle better—muckle better—God bless you—God bless you!—At no rate let him gang till ye hear frae me," said Jeanie.

"But ye'll be back belive?" said Mrs. Saddletree, detaining her; "they wunna let ye stay yonder, hinny."

"But I maun gang to St. Leonard's—there's muckle to be dune, and little time to do it in—And I have friends to speak to—God bless you—take care of my father."

She had reached the door of the apartment, when, suddenly turning, she came back, and knelt down by the bedside.— "O father, gie me your blessing—I dare not go till ye bless me. Say but God bless ye, and prosper ye, Jeanie—try but to say that!"

Instinctively, rather than by an exertion of intellect, the old man murmured a prayer, that "purchased and promised blessings might be multiplied upon her."

"He has blessed mine errand," said his daughter, rising from her knees, "and it is borne in upon my mind that I shall prosper."

So saying, she left the room.

Mrs. Saddletree looked after her, and shook her head. "I

wish she binna roving, poor thing—There's something queer about a' thae Deanses. I dinna like folk to be sae muckle better than other folk—seldom comes gude o't. But if she's gaun to look after the kye at St. Leonard's, that's another story; to be sure they maun be sorted.—Grizzie, come up here, and take tent to the honest auld man, and, see he wants naething.—Ye silly tawpie" (addressing the maid-servant as she entered), "what garr'd ye busk up your cockernony that gate?—I think there's been eneugh the day to gie an awfu' warning about your cockups and your fallal duds—see what they a' come to," &c. &c. &c.

Leaving the good lady to her lecture upon worldly vanities, we must transport our reader to the cell in which the unfortunate Effie Deans was now immured, being restricted of several liberties which she had enjoyed before the sentence was pronounced.

When she had remained about an hour in the state of stupefied horror so natural in her situation, she was disturbed by the opening of the jarring bolts of her place of confinement, and Ratcliffe showed himself. "It's your sister," he said, "wants to speak t'ye, Effie."

" I canna see naebody," said Effie, with the hasty irritability which misery had rendered more acute—" I canna see naebody, and least of a' her—Bid her take care of the auld man—I am naething to ony o' them now, nor them to me."

"She says she maun see ye, though," said Ratcliffe; and Jeanie, rushing into the apartment, threw her arms round her sister's neck, who writhed to extricate herself from her embrace.

" What signifies coming to greet ower me," said poor Effie, "when you have killed me?—killed me, when a word of your mouth would have saved me—killed me, when I am an innocent creature—innocent of that guilt at least—and me that wad hae wared body and soul to save your finger from being hurt!"

"You shall not die," said Jeanie, with enthusiastic firmness; "say what ye like o' me—think what ye like o' me—only promise—for I doubt your proud heart—that ye wunna harm yourself, and you shall not die this shameful death."

"A *shameful* death I will not die, Jeanie, lass. I have that in my heart—though it has been ower kind a ane—that wunna bide shame. Gae hame to our father, and think nae mair on me—I have eat my last earthly meal."

"Oh, this was what I feared!" said Jeanie.

"Hout, tout, hinnie," said Ratcliffe; "it's but little ye ken o' thae things. Ane aye thinks at the first dinnle o' the sentence, they hae heart eneugh to die rather than bide out the sax weeks; but they aye bide the sax weeks out for a' that. I ken the gate o't weel; I hae fronted the doomster three times, and here I stand, Jim Ratcliffe, for a' that. Had I tied my napkin strait the first time, as I had a great mind till't—and it was a' about a bit grey cowt, wasna worth ten punds sterling—where would I have been now?"

"And how *did* you escape?" said Jeanie, the fates of this man, at first so odious to her, having acquired a sudden interest in her eyes from their correspondence with those of her sister.

"*How* did I escape?" said Ratcliffe, with a knowing wink, —"I tell ye I 'scapit in a way that naebody will escape from this Tolbooth while I keep the keys."

"My sister shall come out in the face of the sun," said Jeanie; "I will go to London, and beg her pardon from the king and queen. If they pardoned Porteous, they may pardon her; if a sister asks a sister's life on her bended knees, they *will* pardon her—they *shall* pardon her—and they will win a thousand hearts by it."

Effie listened in bewildered astonishment, and so earnest was her sister's enthusiastic assurance, that she almost involuntarily caught a gleam of hope; but it instantly faded away.

"Ah, Jeanie! the king and queen live in London, a thousand miles from this—far ayont the saut sea; I'll be gane before ye win there!"

"You are mistaen," said Jeanie; "it is no sae far, and they go to it by land; I learned something about thae things from Reuben Butler."

"Ah, Jeanie! ye never learned onything but what was gude frae the folk ye keepit company wi'; but I—but I"—she wrung her hands, and wept bitterly.

"Dinna think on that now," said Jeanie; "there will be time for that if the present space be redeemed. Fare ye weel! Unless I die by the road, I will see the king's face that gies grace.—O sir" (to Ratcliffe), "be kind to her—She ne'er kend what it was to need stranger's kindness till now.—Fareweel— fareweel, Effie!—Dinna speak to me—I maunna greet now— my head's ower dizzy already."

She tore herself from her sister's arms, and left the cell.

Ratcliffe followed her, and beckoned her into a small room. She obeyed his signal, but not without trembling.

"What's the fule thing shaking for?" said he; "I mean nothing but civility to you. D—n me, I respect you. and I can't help it. You have so much spunk, that, d—n me, but I think there's some chance of your carrying the day. But you must not go to the king till you have made some friend ; try the duke—try MacCallummore; he's Scotland's friend—I ken that the great folks dinna muckle like him—but they fear him, and that will serve your purpose as weel. D'ye ken naebody wad gie ye a letter to him?"

"Duke of Argyle?" said Jeanie, recollecting herself suddenly —"what was he to that Argyle that suffered in my father's time —in the persecution?"

"His son or grandson, I'm thinking," said Ratcliffe, "but what o' that?"

"Thank God!" said Jeanie, devoutly clasping her hands.

"You whigs are aye thanking God for something," said the ruffian. "But hark ye, hinny, I'll tell ye a secret. Ye may meet wi' rough customers on the Border, or in the Midland, afore ye get to Lunnon. Now, deil ane o' them will touch an acquaintance o' Daddie Ratton's ; for though I am retired frae public practice, yet they ken I can do a gude or an ill turn yet —and deil a gude fellow that has been but a twelvemonth on the lay, be he ruffler or padder, but he knows my gybe as well as the jark of e'er a queer cuffin in England—and there's rogue's Latin for you."

It was, indeed, totally unintelligible to Jeanie Deans, who was only impatient to escape from him. He hastily scrawled a line or two on a dirty piece of paper, and said to her, as she drew back when he offered it, "Hey! what the deil—it wunna bite you, my lass—if it does nae gude, it can do nae ill. But I wish you to show it, if you have ony fasherie wi' ony o' St. Nicholas's clerks."

"Alas!" said she, "I do not understand what you mean."

"I mean, if ye fall among thieves, my precious,—that is a Scripture phrase, if ye will hae ane—the bauldest of them will ken a scart o' my guse feather. And now awa wi' ye—and stick to Argyle; if onybody can do the job, it maun be him."

After casting an anxious look at the grated windows and blackened walls of the old Tolbooth, and another scarce less anxious at the hospitable lodging of Mrs. Saddletree, Jeanie turned her back on that quarter, and soon after on the city itself. She reached St. Leonard's Crags without meeting any one whom she knew, which, in the state of her mind, she considered as a great blessing. "I must do naething," she thought, as she went along, "that can soften or weaken my heart—it's ower weak already for what I hae to do. I will think and act as firmly as I can, and speak as little."

There was an ancient servant, or rather cottar, of her father's, who had lived under him for many years, and whose fidelity was worthy of full confidence. She sent for this woman, and explaining to her that the circumstances of her family required that she should undertake a journey, which would detain her for some weeks from home, she gave her full instructions concerning the management of the domestic affairs in her absence. With a precision, which, upon reflection, she herself could not help wondering at, she described and detailed the most minute steps which were to be taken, and especially such as were necessary for her father's comfort. "It was probable," she said, "that he would return to St. Leonard's to-morrow; certain that he would return very soon—all must be in order for him. He had eneugh to distress him, without being fashed about warldly matters."

In the meanwhile she toiled busily, along with May Hettly, to leave nothing unarranged.

It was deep in the night when all these matters were settled; and when they had partaken of some food, the first which Jeanie had tasted on that eventful day, May Hettly, whose usual residence was a cottage at a little distance from Deans's house, asked her young mistress, whether she would not permit her to remain in the house all night? "Ye hae had an awfu' day," she said, "and sorrow and fear are but bad companions in the watches of the night, as I hae heard the gudeman say himsell."

"They are ill companions indeed," said Jeanie; "but I maun learn to abide their presence, and better begin in the house than in the field "

She dismissed her aged assistant accordingly,—for so slight was the gradation in their rank of life, that we can hardly term May a servant,—and proceeded to make a few preparations for her journey.

The simplicity of her education and country made these preparations very brief and easy. Her tartan screen served all the purposes of a riding-habit, and of an umbrella; a small bundle contained such changes of linen as were absolutely necessary. Barefooted, as Sancho says, she had come into the world, and barefooted she proposed to perform her pilgrimage; and her clean shoes and change of snow-white thread stockings were to be reserved for special occasions of ceremony. She was not aware, that the English habits of *comfort* attach an idea of abject misery to the idea of a barefooted traveller; and if the objection of cleanliness had been made to the practice, she would have been apt to vindicate herself upon the very frequent ablutions to which, with Mahometan scrupulosity, a Scottish damsel of some condition usually subjects herself. Thus far, therefore, all was well.

From an oaken press or cabinet, in which her father kept a few old books, and two or three bundles of papers, besides his ordinary accounts and receipts, she sought out and extracted from a parcel of notes and sermons, calculations of interest, records of dying speeches of the martyrs, and the like, one or two documents which she thought might be of some use to her upon her mission. But the most important difficulty remained behind, and it had not occurred to her until that very evening. It was the want of money, without which it was impossible she could undertake so distant a journey as she now meditated.

David Deans, as we have said, was easy, and even opulent in his circumstances. But his wealth, like that of the patriarchs of old, consisted in his kine and herds, and in two or three sums lent out at interest to neighbours or relatives, who, far from being in circumstances to pay anything to account of the principal sums, thought they did all that was incumbent on them when, with considerable difficulty, they discharged the "annual rent." To these debtors it would be in vain, therefore, to apply, even with her father's concurrence; nor could she hope to obtain such concurrence, or assistance in any mode, without such a series of explanations and debates as she felt might deprive her totally of the power of taking the step, which, however daring and hazardous, she knew was absolutely necessary for trying the last chance in favour of her sister. Without departing from filial reverence, Jeanie had an inward conviction that the feelings of her father, however just, and upright, and honourable, were too little in unison with the spirit of the time to admit of his being a good judge of the measures to be adopted in this crisis. Herself more flexible in manner, though no less upright in principle, she felt that to ask his consent to her pilgrimage would be to encounter the risk of drawing down his positive prohibition, and under that she believed her journey could not be blessed in its progress and event. Accordingly, she had determined upon the means by which she might communicate to him her undertaking and its purpose, shortly after her actual departure. But it was impossible to apply to him for money without altering this arrangement, and discussing fully the propriety of her journey; pecuniary assistance from that quarter, therefore, was laid out of the question.

It now occurred to Jeanie that she should have consulted with Mrs. Saddletree on this subject. But, besides the time that must now necessarily be lost in recurring to her assistance, Jeanie internally revolted from it. Her heart acknowledged the goodness of Mrs. Saddletree's general character, and the kind interest she took in their family misfortunes; but still she felt that Mrs. Saddletree was a woman of an ordinary and worldly way of thinking, incapable, from habit and temperament, of taking a keen or enthusiastic view of such a resolution as she had formed; and to debate the point with her, and to rely upon her conviction of its propriety for the means of carrying it into execution, would have been gall and wormwood.

Butler, whose assistance she might have been assured of, was greatly poorer than herself. In these circumstances, she formed a singular resolution for the purpose of surmounting this difficulty, the execution of which will form the subject of the next chapter.

CHAPTER XXVI

'Tis the voice of the sluggard, I've heard him complain
" You have waked me too soon, I must slumber again; "
As the door on its hinges, so he on his bed,
Turns his side, and his shoulders, and his heavy head.
                                        DR. WATTS.

THE mansion-house of Dumbiedikes, to which we are now to introduce our readers, lay three or four miles—no matter for the exact topography—to the southward of St. Leonard's. It had once borne the appearance of some little celebrity; for the " auld laird," whose humours and pranks were often mentioned in the alehouses for about a mile round it, wore a sword, kept a good horse, and a brace of greyhounds; brawled, swore, and betted at cock-fights and horse-matches; followed Somerville of Drum's hawks, and the Lord Ross's hounds, and called himself *point devise* a gentleman. But the line had been veiled of its splendour in the present proprietor, who cared for no rustic amusements, and was as saving, timid, and retired, as his father had been at once grasping and selfishly extravagant, —daring, wild, and intrusive.

Dumbiedikes was what is called in Scotland a *single* house; that is, having only one room occupying its whole depth from back to front, each of which single apartments was illuminated by six or eight cross lights, whose diminutive panes and heavy frames permitted scarce so much light to enter as shines through one well-constructed modern window. This inartificial edifice, exactly such as a child would build with cards, had a steep roof flagged with coarse grey stones instead of slates; a half-circular turret, battlemented, or, to use the appropriate phrase, bartizan'd on the top, served as a case for a narrow turnpike-stair, by which an ascent was gained from storey to storey; and at the bottom of the said turret was a door studded with large-headed nails. There was no lobby at the bottom of the tower, and scarce a landing-place, opposite to the doors which gave access to the apartments. One or two low and dilapidated out-houses, connected by a courtyard wall equally ruinous, surrounded the mansion. The court had been paved, but the flags being partly displaced, and partly renewed, a gallant crop of docks and thistles sprung up between them, and the small garden, which opened by a postern through the wall, seemed not to be in a much more orderly condition. Over the low-arched gateway which led into the yard, there was a carved stone, exhibiting some attempt at armorial bearings; and above the inner entrance hung, and had hung for many years, the mouldering hatchment, which announced that umquhile Laurence Dumbie, of Dumbiedikes, had been gathered to his fathers in Newbattle kirkyard. The approach to this palace of pleasure was by a road formed by the rude fragments of stone gathered from the fields, and it was surrounded by ploughed but unenclosed land. Upon a baulk, that is, an unploughed ridge of land interposed among the corn, the laird's trusty palfrey was tethered by the head, and picking a meal of grass. The whole argued neglect and discomfort; the consequence, however, of idleness and indifference, not of poverty.

In this inner court, not without a sense of bashfulness and

dimidity, stood Jeanie Deans, at an early hour in a fine spring morning. She was no heroine of romance, and therefore looked with some curiosity and interest on the mansion-house and domains, of which, it might at that moment occur to her, a little encouragement, such as women of all ranks know by instinct how to apply, might have made her mistress. Moreover, she was no person of taste beyond her time, rank, and country, and certainly thought the house of Dumbiedikes, though inferior to Holyrood House, or the palace at Dalkeith, was still a stately structure in its way, and the land a "very bonnie bit, if it were better seen to and done to." But Jeanie Deans was a plain, true-hearted, honest girl, who, while she acknowledged all the splendour of her old admirer's habitation, and the value of his property, never for a moment harboured a thought of doing the Laird, Butler, or herself, the injustice, which many ladies of higher rank would not have hesitated to do to all three, on much less temptation.

Her present errand being with the Laird, she looked round the offices to see if she could find any domestic to announce that she wished to see him. As all was silence, she ventured to open one door;—it was the old Laird's dog-kennel, now deserted, unless when occupied, as one or two tubs seemed to testify, as a washing-house. She tried another—it was the roofless shed where the hawks had been once kept, as appeared from a perch or two not yet completely rotten, and a lure and jesses which were mouldering on the wall. A third door led to the coal-house, which was well stocked. To keep a very good fire, was one of the few points of domestic management in which Dumbiedikes was positively active; in all other matters of domestic economy he was completely passive, and at the mercy of his housekeeper, the same buxom dame whom his father had long since bequeathed to his charge, and who, if fame did her no injustice, had feathered her nest pretty well at his expense.

Jeanie went on opening doors, like the second Calender wanting an eye, in the castle of the hundred obliging damsels, until, like the said prince errant, she came to a stable. The Highland Pegasus, Rory Bean, to which belonged the single entire stall, was her old acquaintance, whom she had seen grazing on the baulk, as she failed not to recognise by the well-known ancient riding furniture and demi-pique saddle, which half hung on the walls, half trailed on the litter. Beyond the "treviss," which formed one side of the stall, stood a cow, who turned her head and lowed when Jeanie came into the stable, an appeal which her habitual occupations enabled her perfectly to understand, and with which she could not refuse complying, by shaking down some fodder to the animal, which had been neglected like most things else in this castle of the sluggard.

While she was accommodating "the milky mother" with the food which she should have received two hours sooner, a slipshod wench peeped into the stable, and perceiving that a stranger was employed in discharging the task which she, at length, and reluctantly, had quitted her slumbers to perform, ejaculated, "Eh, sirs! the Brownie! the Brownie!" and fled, yelling as if she had seen the devil.

To explain her terror, it may be necessary to notice, that the old house of Dumbiedikes had, according to report, been long haunted by a Brownie, one of those familiar spirits, who were believed in ancient times to supply the deficiencies of the ordinary labourer—

"Whirl the long mop, and ply the airy flail.'

Certes, the convenience of such a supernatural assistant could have been nowhere more sensibly felt, than in a family where the domestics were so little disposed to personal activity; yet this serving maiden was so far from rejoicing in seeing a supposed aerial substitute discharging a task which she should have long since performed herself, that she proceeded to raise the family by her screams of horror, uttered as thick as if the Brownie had been flaying her. Jeanie, who had immediately resigned her temporary occupation, and followed the yelling damsel into the courtyard, in order to undeceive and appease her, was there met by Mrs. Janet Balchristie, the favourite sultana of the last Laird, as scandal went—the housekeeper of the present. The good-looking buxom woman, betwixt forty and fifty (for such we described her at the death of the last Laird), was now a fat, red-faced, old dame of seventy, or thereabouts, fond of her place, and jealous of her authority. Conscious that her administration did not rest on so sure a basis as in the time of the old proprietor, this considerate lady had introduced into the family the screamer aforesaid, who added good features and bright eyes to the powers of her lungs. She made no conquest of the Laird, however, who seemed to live as if there was not another woman in the world but Jeanie Deans, and to bear no very

ardent or overbearing affection even to her. Mrs. Janet Balchristie, notwithstanding, had her own uneasy thoughts upon
the almost daily visits to St. Leonard's Crags, and often,
when the Laird looked at her wistfully and paused, according
to his custom before utterance, she expected him to say,
"Jenny, I am gaun to change my condition;" but she was
relieved by "Jenny, I am gaun to change my shoon."

Still, however, Mrs. Balchristie regarded Jeanie Deans with
no small portion of malevolence, the customary feeling of such
persons towards any one who they think has the means of
doing them an injury. But she had also a general aversion to
any female, tolerably young, and decently well-looking, who
showed a wish to approach the house of Dumbiedikes and
the proprietor thereof. And as she had raised her mass of
mortality out of bed two hours earlier than usual, to come
to the rescue of her clamorous niece, she was in such extreme
bad humour against all and sundry, that Saddletree would
have pronounced, that she harboured *inimicitiam contra omnes
mortales.*

"Wha the deil are ye?" said the fat dame to poor Jeanie,
whom she did not immediately recognise, "scouping about a
decent house at sic an hour in the morning?"

"It was ane wanting to speak to the Laird," said Jeanie,
who felt something of the intuitive terror which she had
formerly entertained for this termagant, when she was occasionally at Dumbiedikes on business of her father's.

"Ane?—And what sort of ane are ye?—hae ye nae name?
—D'ye think his honour has naething else to do than to speak
wi' ilka idle tramper that comes about the town, and him in
his bed yet, honest man?"

"Dear Mrs. Balchristie," replied Jeanie, in a submissive
tone, "d'ye no mind me?—d'ye no mind Jeanie Deans?"

"Jeanie Deans!!" said the termagant, in accents affecting
the utmost astonishment; then, taking two strides nearer to
her, she peered into her face with a stare of curiosity, equally
scornful and malignant—"I say Jeanie Deans, indeed—Jeanie
Deevil, they had better hae ca'd ye!—A bonny spot o' wark
your tittie and you hae made out, murdering ae puir wean,
and your light limmer of a sister's to be hanged for't, as weel
she deserves!—And the like o' you to come to ony honest
man's house, and want to be into a decent bachelor gentleman's room at this time in the morning, and him in his bed?
—Gae wa', gae wa'!"

Jeanie was struck mute with shame at the unfeeling brutality of this accusation, and could not even find words to justify herself from the vile construction put upon her visit, when Mrs. Balchristie, seeing her advantage, continued in the same tone, "Come, come, bundle up your pipes and tramp awa wi' ye!—ye may be seeking a father to another wean for onything I ken. If it warna that your father, auld David Deans, had been a tenant on our land, I would cry up the men-folk, and hae ye dookit in the burn for your impudence."

Jeanie had already turned her back, and was walking towards the door of the courtyard, so that Mrs. Balchristie, to make her last threat impressively audible to her, had raised her stentorian voice to its utmost pitch. But, like many a general, she lost the engagement by pressing her advantage too far.

The Laird had been disturbed in his morning slumbers by the tones of Mrs. Balchristie's objurgation, sounds in themselves by no means uncommon, but very remarkable in respect to the early hour at which they were now heard. He turned himself on the other side, however, in hopes the squall would blow by, when, in the course of Mrs. Balchristie's second explosion of wrath, the name of Deans distinctly struck the tympanum of his ear. As he was, in some degree, aware of the small portion of benevolence with which his housekeeper regarded the family at St. Leonard's, he instantly conceived that some message from thence was the cause of this untimely ire, and getting out of his bed, he slipt as speedily as possible into an old brocaded nightgown, and some other necessary integuments, clapped on his head his father's gold-laced hat (for though he was seldom seen without it, yet it is proper to contradict the popular report, that he slept in it, as Don Quixote did in his helmet), and opening the window of his bedroom, beheld, to his great astonishment, the well-known figure of Jeanie Deans herself retreating from his gate ; while his housekeeper, with arms a-kimbo, fist clenched and extended, body erect, and head shaking with rage, sent after her a volley of Billingsgate oaths. His choler rose in proportion to the surprise, and, perhaps, to the disturbance of his repose. "Hark ye," he exclaimed from the window, "ye auld limb of Satan—wha the deil gies you commission to guide an honest man's daughter that gate ? "

Mrs. Balchristie was completely caught in the manner. She was aware, from the unusual warmth with which the

Laird expressed himself, that he was quite serious in this matter, and she knew that, with all his indolence of nature, there were points on which he might be provoked, and that, being provoked, he had in him something dangerous, which her wisdom taught her to fear accordingly. She began, therefore, to retract her false step as fast as she could. "She was but speaking for the house's credit, and she couldna think of disturbing his honour in the morning sae early, when the young woman might as weel wait or call again; and to be sure, she might make a mistake between the twa sisters, for ane o' them wasna sae creditable an acquaintance."

"Haud your peace, ye auld jade," said Dumbiedikes; "the warst quean e'er stude in their shoon may ca' you cousin, an a' be true that I have heard.—Jeanie, my woman, gang into the parlour—but stay, that winna be redd up yet—wait there a minute till I come doun to let ye in—Dinna mind what Jenny says to ye."

"Na, na," said Jenny, with a laugh of affected heartiness, "never mind me, lass—a' the warld kens my bark's waur than my bite—if ye had had an appointment wi' the Laird, ye might hae tauld me—I am nae uncivil person—gang your ways in by, hinny." And she opened the door of the house with a master-key.

"But I had no appointment wi' the Laird," said Jeanie, drawing back; "I want just to speak twa words to him, and I wad rather do it standing here, Mrs. Balchristie."

"In the open courtyard?—Na, na, that wad never do, lass; we maunna guide ye that gate neither—And how's that douce honest man, your father?"

Jeanie was saved the pain of answering this hypocritical question by the appearance of the Laird himself.

"Gang in and get breakfast ready," said he to his house-keeper—"and, d'ye hear, breakfast wi' us yoursell—ye ken how to manage thae porringers of tea-water—and, hear ye, see abune a' that there's a gude fire.—Weel, Jeanie, my woman, gang in by—gang in by, and rest ye."

"Na, Laird," Jeanie replied, endeavouring as much as she could to express herself with composure, notwithstanding she still trembled, "I canna gang in—I have a lang day's darg afore me—I maun be twenty mile o' gate the night yet, if feet will carry me."

"Guide and deliver us!—twenty mile—twenty mile on your feet!" ejaculated Dumbiedikes, whose walks were of

a very circumscribed diameter,—"Ye maun never think o'
that—come in by."

"I canna do that, Laird," replied Jeanie; "the twa words
I hae to say to ye I can say here; forby that Mrs. Balchristie——"

"The deil flee awa wi' Mrs. Balchristie," said Dumbiedikes,
"and he'll hae a heavy lading o' her! I tell ye, Jeanie
Deans, I am a man of few words, but I am laird at hame, as
weel as in the field; deil a brute or body about my house but
I can manage when I like, except Rory Bean, my powny;
but I can seldom be at the plague, an it binna when my
bluid's up."

"I was wanting to say to ye, Laird," said Jeanie, who felt
the necessity of entering upon her business, "that I was gaun
a lang journey, outby of my father's knowledge."

"Outby his knowledge, Jeanie!—Is that right? Ye maun
think o't again—it's no right," said Dumbiedikes, with a
countenance of great concern.

"If I were anes at Lunnon," said Jeanie, in exculpation,
"I am amaist sure I could get means to speak to the queen
about my sister's life."

"Lunnon—and the queen—and her sister's life!" said
Dumbiedikes, whistling for very amazement—"the lassie's
demented."

"I am no out o' my mind," said she, "and, sink or swim,
I am determined to gang to Lunnon, if I suld beg my way
frae door to door—and so I maun, unless ye wad lend me
a small sum to pay my expenses—little thing will do it; and
ye ken my father's a man of substance, and wad see nae man,
far less you, Laird, come to loss by me."

Dumbiedikes, on comprehending the nature of this application, could scarce trust his ears—he made no answer whatever,
but stood with his eyes riveted on the ground.

"I see ye are no for assisting me, Laird," said Jeanie;
"sae fare ye weel—and gang and see my poor father as aften
as ye can—he will be lonely eneugh now."

"Where is the silly bairn gaun?" said Dumbiedikes; and,
laying hold of her hand, he led her into the house. "It's no
that I didna think o't before," he said, "but it stack in my
throat."

Thus speaking to himself, he led her into an old-fashioned
parlour, shut the door behind them, and fastened it with a
bolt. While Jeanie, surprised at this manœuvre, remained as

near the door as possible, the Laird quitted her hand, and pressed upon a spring lock fixed in an oak panel in the wainscot, which instantly slipped aside. An iron strong-box was discovered in a recess of the wall; he opened this also, and, pulling out two or three drawers, showed that they were filled with leathern-bags, full of gold and silver coin.

"This is my bank, Jeanie lass," he said, looking first at her, and then at the treasure, with an air of great complacency,— "nane o' your goldsmith's bills for me,—they bring folk to ruin."

Then suddenly changing his tone, he resolutely said— "Jeanie, I will make ye Leddy Dumbiedikes afore the sun sets, and ye may ride to Lunnon in your ain coach, if ye like."

"Na, Laird," said Jeanie, "that can never be—my father's grief—my sister's situation—the discredit to you——"

"That's *my* business," said Dumbiedikes; "ye wad say naething about that if ye werena a fule—and yet I like ye the better for't—ae wise body's eneugh in the married state. But if your heart's ower fu', take what siller will serve ye, and let it be when ye come back again—as gude syne as sune."

"But, Laird," said Jeanie, who felt the necessity of being explicit with so extraordinary a lover, "I like another man better than you, and I canna marry ye."

"Another man better than me, Jeanie?" said Dumbiedikes —"how is that possible?—It's no possible, woman—ye hae kend me sae lang."

"Ay but, Laird," said Jeanie, with persevering simplicity, "I hae kend him langer."

"Langer?—It's no possible!" exclaimed the poor Laird. "It canna be; ye were born on the land. O Jeanie, woman, ye haena lookit—ye haena seen the half o' the gear." He drew out another drawer—"A' gowd, Jeanie, and there's bands for siller lent—And the rental book, Jeanie—clear three hunder sterling—deil a wadset, heritable band, or burden —Ye haena lookit at them, woman—And then my mother's wardrobe, and my grandmother's forby—silk gowns wad stand on their ends, pearlin-lace as fine as spiders' webs, and rings and ear-rings to the boot of a' that—they are a' in the chamber of deas—Oh, Jeanie, gang up the stair and look at them!"

But Jeanie held fast her integrity, though beset with temptations, which perhaps the Laird of Dumbiedikes did not greatly err in supposing were those most affecting to her sex.

"It canna be, Laird—I have said it—and I canna break my word till him, if ye wad gie me the haill barony of Dalkeith, and Lugton into the bargain."

"Your word to *him*," said the Laird, somewhat pettishly; "but wha is he, Jeanie?—wha is he?—I haena heard his name yet—Come now, Jeanie, ye are but queering us—I am no trowing that there is sic a ane in the warld—ye are but making fashion—What is he?—wha is he?"

"Just Reuben Butler, that's schulemaster at Libberton," said Jeanie.

"Reuben Butler! Reuben Butler!" echoed the Laird of Dumbiedikes, pacing the apartment in high disdain,—"Reuben Butler, the dominie at Libberton—and a dominie depute too! —Reuben, the son of my cottar!—Very weel, Jeanie lass, wilfu' woman will hae her way—Reuben Butler! he hasna in his pouch the value o' the auld black coat he wears—but it disna signify." And, as he spoke, he shut successively, and with vehemence, the drawers of his treasury. "A fair offer, Jeanie, is nae cause of feud—Ae man may bring a horse to the water, but twenty wunna gar him drink—And as for wasting my substance on other folk's joes——"

There was something in the last hint that nettled Jeanie's honest pride. "I was begging nane frae your honour," she said; "least of a' on sic a score as ye pit it on.—Gude morning to ye, sir; ye hae been kind to my father, and it isna in my heart to think otherwise than kindly of you."

So saying, she left the room, without listening to a faint "But, Jeanie—Jeanie—stay, woman!" and traversing the courtyard with a quick step, she set out on her forward journey, her bosom glowing with that natural indignation and shame, which an honest mind feels at having subjected itself to ask a favour, which had been unexpectedly refused. When out of the Laird's ground, and once more upon the public road, her pace slackened, her anger cooled, and anxious anticipations of the consequence of this unexpected disappointment began to influence her with other feelings. Must she then actually beg her way to London? for such seemed the alternative; or must she turn back, and solicit her father for money; and by doing so lose time, which was precious, besides the risk of encountering his positive prohibition respecting her journey? Yet she saw no medium between these alternatives; and, while she walked slowly on, was still meditating whether it were not better to return.

While she was thus in an uncertainty, she heard the clatter of a horse's hoofs, and a well-known voice calling her name. She looked round, and saw advancing towards her on a pony, whose bare back and halter assorted ill with the nightgown, slippers, and laced cocked-hat of the rider, a cavalier of no less importance than Dumbiedikes himself. In the energy of his pursuit, he had overcome even the Highland obstinacy of Rory Bean, and compelled that self-willed palfrey to canter the way his rider chose; which Rory, however, performed with all the symptoms of reluctance, turning his head, and accompanying every bound he made in advance with a side-long motion, which indicated his extreme wish to turn round, —a manœuvre which nothing but the constant exercise of the Laird's heels and cudgel could possibly have counteracted.

When the Laird came up with Jeanie, the first words he uttered were,—"Jeanie, they say ane shouldna aye take a woman at her first word?"

"Ay, but ye maun take me at mine, Laird," said Jeanie, looking on the ground, and walking on without a pause. "I hae but ae word to bestow on onybody, and that's aye a true ane."

"Then," said Dumbiedikes, "at least ye suldna aye take a man at *his* first word. Ye maunna gang this wilfu' gate siller-less, come o't what like."—He put a purse into her hand. "I wad gie you Rory too, but he's as wilfu' as yoursell and he's ower weel used to a gate that maybe he and I hae gaen ower often, and he'll gang nae road else."

"But, Laird," said Jeanie, "though I ken my father will satisfy every penny of this siller, whatever there's o't, yet I wadna like to borrow it frae ane that maybe thinks of something mair than the paying o't back again."

"There's just twenty-five guineas o't," said Dumbiedikes, with a gentle sigh, "and whether your father pays or disna pay, I make ye free till't without another word. Gang where ye like—do what ye like—and marry a' the Butlers in the country, gin ye like—And sae, gude morning to you, Jeanie."

"And God bless you, Laird, wi' mony a gude morning," said Jeanie, her heart more softened by the unwonted gene-rosity of this uncouth character, than perhaps Butler might have approved, had he known her feelings at that moment; "and comfort, and the Lord's peace, and the peace of the world, be with you, if we suld never meet again!"

Dumbiedikes turned and waved his hand; and his pony,

*K 134

much more willing to return than he had been to set out, hurried him homewards so fast, that, wanting the aid of a regular bridle, as well as of saddle and stirrups, he was too much puzzled to keep his seat to permit of his looking behind, even to give the parting glance of a forlorn swain. I am ashamed to say, that the sight of a lover, run away with in nightgown and slippers and a laced hat, by a bare-backed Highland pony, had something in it of a sedative, even to a grateful and deserved burst of affectionate esteem. The figure of Dumbiedikes was too ludicrous not to confirm Jeanie in the original sentiments she entertained towards him.

"He's a gude creature," said she, "and a kind—it's a pity he has sae willyard a powny." And she immediately turned her thoughts to the important journey which she had commenced, reflecting with pleasure, that, according to her habits of life and of undergoing fatigue, she was now amply or even superfluously provided with the means of encountering the expenses of the road, up and down from London, and all other expenses whatever.

CHAPTER XXVII

What strange and wayward thoughts will slide
    Into a lover's head;
"O mercy!" to myself I cried,
    "If Lucy should be dead!"
                    WORDSWORTH.

IN pursuing her solitary journey, our heroine, soon after passing the house of Dumbiedikes, gained a little eminence, from which, on looking to the eastward down a prattling brook, whose meanders were shaded with straggling willows and alder trees, she could see the cottages of Woodend and Beersheba, the haunts and habitation of her early life, and could distinguish the common on which she had so often herded sheep, and the recesses of the rivulet where she had pulled rushes with Butler, to plait crowns and sceptres for her sister Effie, then a beautiful but spoiled child, of about three years old. The recollections which the scene brought with them were so bitter, that, had she indulged them, she would have sate down and relieved her heart with tears.

"But I kend," said Jeanie, when she gave an account of her pilgrimage, "that greeting would do but little good, and that it was mair beseeming to thank the Lord, that had showed me kindness and countenance by means of a man, that mony ca'd a Nabal and churl, but wha was free of his gudes to me as ever the fountain was free of the stream. And I minded the Scripture about the sin of Israel at Meribah, when the people murmured, although Moses had brought water from the dry rock that the congregation might drink and live. Sae, I wad not trust mysell with another look at puir Woodend, for the very blue reek that came out of the lum-head pat me in mind of the change of market days with us."

In this resigned and Christian temper she pursued her journey, until she was beyond this place of melancholy recollections, and not distant from the village where Butler dwelt, which, with its old-fashioned church and steeple, rises among a tuft of trees, occupying the ridge of an eminence to the south of Edinburgh. At a quarter of a mile's distance is a clumsy square tower, the residence of the Laird of Libberton, who, in former times, with the habits of the predatory chivalry of Germany, is said frequently to have annoyed the city of Edinburgh, by intercepting the supplies and merchandise which came to the town from the southward.

This village, its tower, and its church, did not lie precisely in Jeanie's road towards England; but they were not much aside from it, and the village was the abode of Butler. She had resolved to see him in the beginning of her journey, because she conceived him the most proper person to write to her father concerning her resolution and her hopes. There was probably another reason latent in her affectionate bosom. She wished once more to see the object of so early and so sincere an attachment, before commencing a pilgrimage, the perils of which she did not disguise from herself, although she did not allow them so to press upon her mind as to diminish the strength and energy of her resolution. A visit to a lover from a young person in a higher rank of life than Jeanie's, would have had something forward and improper in its character. But the simplicity of her rural habits was unacquainted with these punctilious ideas of decorum, and no notion, therefore, of impropriety crossed her imagination, as, setting out upon a long journey, she went to bid adieu to an early friend.

There was still another motive that pressed upon her mind with additional force as she approached the village. She had looked anxiously for Butler in the court-house, and had expected that certainly, in some part of that eventful day, he would have appeared to bring such countenance and support as he could give to his old friend, and the protector of his youth, even if her own claims were laid aside. She knew, indeed, that he was under a certain degree of restraint; but she still had hoped that he would have found means to emancipate himself from it, at least for one day. In short, the wild and wayward thoughts which Wordsworth has described as rising in an absent lover's imagination suggested, as the only explanation of his absence, that Butler must be very ill. And so much had this wrought on her imagination, that when she approached the cottage in which her lover occupied a small apartment, and which had been pointed out to her by a maiden with a milk-pail on her head, she trembled at anticipating the answer she might receive on inquiring for him.

Her fears in this case had, indeed, only hit upon the truth. Butler, whose constitution was naturally feeble, did not soon recover the fatigue of body and distress of mind which he had suffered, in consequence of the tragical events with which our narrative commenced. The painful idea that his character was breathed on by suspicion, was an aggravation to his distress.

But the most cruel addition was the absolute prohibition laid by the magistrates on his holding any communication with Deans or his family. It had unfortunately appeared likely to them, that some intercourse might be again attempted with that family by Robertson, through the medium of Butler, and this they were anxious to intercept, or prevent, if possible. The measure was not meant as a harsh or injurious severity on the part of the magistrates; but, in Butler's circumstances, it pressed cruelly hard. He felt he must be suffering under the bad opinion of the person who was dearest to him, from an imputation of unkind desertion, the most alien to his nature.

This painful thought, pressing on a frame already injured, brought on a succession of slow and lingering feverish attacks, which greatly impaired his health, and at length rendered him incapable even of the sedentary duties of the school, on which his bread depended. Fortunately, old Mr. Whackbairn, who was the principal teacher of the little parochial establishment, was sincerely attached to Butler. Besides that he was sensible of his merits and value as an assistant, which had greatly raised the credit of his little school, the ancient pedagogue, who had himself been tolerably educated, retained some taste for classical lore, and would gladly relax, after the drudgery of the school was past, by conning over a few pages of Horace or Juvenal with his usher. A similarity of taste begot kindness, and he accordingly saw Butler's increasing debility with great compassion, roused up his own energies to teaching the school in the morning hours, insisted upon his assistant's reposing himself at that period, and, besides, supplied him with such comforts as the patient's situation required, and his means were inadequate to compass.

Such was Butler's situation, scarce able to drag himself to the place where his daily drudgery must gain his daily bread, and racked with a thousand fearful anticipations concerning the fate of those who were dearest to him in the world, when the trial and condemnation of Effie Deans put the copestone upon his mental misery.

He had a particular account of these events from a fellow-student who resided in the same village, and who, having been present on the melancholy occasion, was able to place it in all its agony of horrors before his excruciated imagination. That sleep should have visited his eyes, after such a curfew-note, was impossible. A thousand dreadful visions haunted his imagination all night, and in the morning he was awaked from a feverish slumber, by the only circumstance which could have added to his distress—the visit of an intrusive ass.

This unwelcome visitant was no other than Bartoline Saddletree. The worthy and sapient burgher had kept his appointment at MacCroskie's, with Plumdamas and some other neighbours, to discuss the Duke of Argyle's speech, the justice of Effie Deans's condemnation, and the improbability of her obtaining a reprieve. This sage conclave disputed high and drank deep, and on the next morning Bartoline felt, as he expressed it, as if his head was like a " confused progress of writs."

To bring his reflective powers to their usual serenity, Saddletree resolved to take a morning's ride upon a certain hackney, which he, Plumdamas, and another honest shop-keeper, combined to maintain by joint subscription, for occasional jaunts for the purpose of business or exercise. As Saddletree had two children boarded with Whackbairn, and was, as we have seen, rather fond of Butler's society, he turned his palfrey's head towards Libberton, and came, as we have already said, to give the unfortunate usher that additional vexation, of which Imogen complains so feelingly, when she says,

> "I'm sprighted with a fool—
> Sprighted and anger'd worse."

If anything could have added gall to bitterness, it was the choice which Saddletree made of a subject for his prosing harangues, being the trial of Effie Deans, and the probability of her being executed. Every word fell on Butler's ear like the knell of a death-bell, or the note of a screech-owl.

Jeanie paused at the door of her lover's humble abode upon hearing the loud and pompous tones of Saddletree sounding from the inner apartment, "Credit me, it will be sae, Mr. Butler. Brandy cannot save her. She maun gang down the Bow wi' the lad in the pioted coat[1] at her heels.— I am sorry for the lassie, but the law, sir, maun hae its course—

> ' Vivat Rex,
> Currat Lex,'

as the poet has it, in whilk of Horace's odes I know not."

Here Butler groaned, in utter impatience of the brutality and ignorance which Bartoline had contrived to amalgamate into one sentence. But Saddletree, like other prosers, was blessed with a happy obtuseness of perception concerning the unfavourable impression which he generally made on his auditors. He proceeded to deal forth his scraps of legal knowledge without mercy, and concluded by asking Butler with great self-complacency, "Was it na a pity my father didna send me to Utrecht? Havena I missed the chance to turn out as *clarissimus* an *ictus*, as auld Grunwiggin himsell?—Whatfor dinna ye speak, Mr. Butler? Wad I no hae been a *clarissimus ictus?*—Eh, man?

"I really do not understand you, Mr. Saddletree," said Butler, thus pushed hard for an answer. His faint and exhausted tone of voice was instantly drowned in the sonorous bray of Bartoline.

"No understand me, man?—*Ictus* is Latin for a lawyer, is it not?"

"Not that ever I heard of," answered Butler, in the same dejected tone.

---

[1] The executioner, in a livery of black or dark grey and silver, likened by low wit to a magpie.

"The deil ye didna!—See, man, I got the word but this morning out of a memorial of Mr. Crossmyloof's—see, there it is, *ictus clarissimus et perti—peritissimus*—it's a' Latin, for it's printed in the Italian types."

"Oh, you mean *juris-consultus*—*Ictus* is an abbreviation for *juris-consultus*."

"Dinna tell me, man," persevered Saddletree, "there's nae abbreviates except in adjudications; and this is a' about a servitude of water-drap—that is to say, *tillicidian*[1] (maybe ye'll says that's no Latin neither), in Mary King's Close in the High Street."

"Very likely," said poor Butler, overwhelmed by the noisy perseverance of his visitor. "I am not able to dispute with you."

"Few folk are—few folk are, Mr. Butler, though I say it, that shouldna say it," returned Bartoline, with great delight. "Now, it will be twa hours yet or ye're wanted in the schule, and as ye are no weel, I'll sit wi' you to divert ye, and explain t'ye the nature of a *tillicidian*. Ye maun ken, the petitioner, Mrs. Crombie, a very decent woman, is a friend of mine, and I hae stude her friend in this case, and brought her wi' credit into the court, and I doubtna that in due time she will win out o't wi' credit, win she or lose she. Ye see, being an inferior tenement or laigh house, we grant ourselves to be burdened wi' the *tillicide*, that is, that we are obliged to receive the natural water-drap of the superior tenement, sae far as the same fa's frae the heavens, or the roof of our neighbour's house, and from thence by the gutters or eaves upon our laigh tenement. But the other night comes a Highland quean of a lass, and she flashes, God kens what, out at the eastmost window of Mrs. MacPhail's house, that's the superior tenement. I believe the auld women wad hae greed, for Luckie MacPhail sent down the lass to tell my friend Mrs. Crombie that she had made the gardyloo out of the wrang window, out of respect for twa Highlandmen that were speaking Gaelic in the close below the right ane. But luckily for Mrs. Crombie, I just chanced to come in in time to break aff the communing, for it's a pity the point suldna be tried. We had Mrs. MacPhail into the Ten-Mark Court—The Hieland limmer of a lass wanted to swear herself free—but haud ye there, says I——"

The detailed account of this important suit might have

[1] He meant, probably, *stillicidium*.

lasted until poor Butler's hour of rest was completely exhausted, had not Saddletree been interrupted by the noise of voices at the door. The woman of the house where Butler lodged, on returning with her pitcher from the well, whence she had been fetching water for the family, found our heroine Jeanie Deans standing at the door, impatient of the prolix harangue of Saddletree, yet unwilling to enter until he should have taken his leave.

The good woman abridged the period of hesitation by inquiring, "Was ye wanting the gudeman or me, lass?"

" I wanted to speak with Mr. Butler, if he's at leisure," replied Jeanie.

"Gang in by then, my woman," answered the goodwife; and opening the door of a room, she announced the additional visitor with, " Mr. Butler, here's a lass wants to speak t'ye."

The surprise of Butler was extreme, when Jeanie, who seldom stirred half a mile from home, entered his apartment upon this annunciation.

" Good God!" he said, starting from his chair, while alarm restored to his cheek the colour of which sickness had deprived it ; "some new misfortune must have happened!"

"None, Mr. Reuben, but what you must hae heard of—but oh, ye are looking ill yoursell!"—for "the hectic of a moment" had not concealed from her affectionate eye the ravages which lingering disease and anxiety of mind had made in her lover's person.

"No; I am well—quite well," said Butler, with eagerness; "if I can do anything to assist you, Jeanie—or your father."

" Ay, to be sure," said Saddletree; "the family may be considered as limited to them twa now, just as if Effie had never been in the tailzie, puir thing. But, Jeanie lass, what brings you out to Libberton sae air in the morning, and your father lying ill in the Luckenbooths?"

" I had a message frae my father to Mr. Butler," said Jeanie, with embarrassment; but instantly feeling ashamed of the fiction to which she had resorted, for her love of and veneration for truth was almost quaker-like, she corrected herself— " That is to say, I wanted to speak with Mr. Butler about some business of my father's and puir Effie's."

" Is it law business?" said Bartoline; "because if it be, ye had better take my opinion on the subject than his."

" It is not just law business," said Jeanie, who saw considerable inconvenience might arise from letting Mr. Saddletree into the secret purpose of her journey; "but I want Mr. Butler to write a letter for me."

"Very right," said Mr. Saddletree; "and if ye'll tell me what it is about, I'll dictate to Mr. Butler as Mr. Crossmyloof does to his clerk.—Get your pen and ink *in initialibus*, Mr. Butler."

Jeanie looked at Butler, and wrung her hands with vexation and impatience.

"I believe, Mr. Saddletree," said Butler, who saw the necessity of getting rid of him at all events, "that Mr. Whackbairn will be somewhat affronted, if you do not hear your boys called up to their lessons."

"Indeed, Mr. Butler, and that's as true; and I promised to ask a half play-day to the schule, so that the bairns might gang and see the hanging, which canna but have a pleasing effect on their young minds, seeing there is no knowing what they may come to themselves.—Odd so, I didna mind ye were here, Jeanie Deans; but ye maun use yoursell to hear the matter spoken o'.—Keep Jeanie here till I come back, Mr. Butler; I wunna bide ten minutes."

And with this unwelcome assurance of an immediate return, he relieved them of the embarrassment of his presence.

"Reuben," said Jeanie, who saw the necessity of using the interval of his absence in discussing what had brought her there, "I am bound on a lang journey—I am gaun to Lunnon to ask Effie's life of the king and of the queen."

"Jeanie! you are surely not yourself," answered Butler, in the utmost surprise; "*you* go to London—*you* address the king and queen!"

"And what for no, Reuben?" said Jeanie, with all the composed simplicity of her character; "it's but speaking to a mortal man and woman when a' is done. And their hearts maun be made o' flesh and blood like other folk's, and Effie's story wad melt them were they stane. Forby, I hae heard that they are no sic bad folk as what the Jacobites ca' them."

"Yes, Jeanie," said Butler; "but their magnificence—their retinue—the difficulty of getting audience?"

"I have thought of a' that, Reuben, and it shall not break my spirit. Nae doubt their claiths will be very grand, wi' their crowns on their heads, and their sceptres in their hands, like the great King Ahasuerus when he sate upon his royal throne foranent the gate of his house, as we are told in Scripture. But I have that within me that will keep my heart from failing, and I am amaist sure that I will be strengthened to speak the errand I came for."

"Alas! alas!" said Butler, "the kings nowadays do not sit in the gate to administer justice, as in patriarchal times. I know as little of courts as you do, Jeanie, by experience; but by reading and report I know, that the King of Britain does everything by means of his ministers."

"And if they be upright, God-fearing ministers," said Jeanie, "it's sae muckle the better chance for Effie and me."

"But you do not even understand the most ordinary words relating to a court," said Butler; "by the ministry is meant not clergymen, but the king's official servants."

"Nae doubt," returned Jeanie, "he maun hae a great number mair, I daur to say, than the Duchess has at Dalkeith, and great folk's servants are aye mair saucy than themselves. But I'll be decently put on, and I'll offer them a trifle o' siller, as if I came to see the palace. Or, if they scruple that, I'll tell them I'm come on a business of life and death, and then they will surely bring me to speech of the king and queen?"

Butler shook his head. "O Jeanie, this is entirely a wild dream. You can never see them but through some great lord's intercession, and I think it is scarce possible even then."

"Weel, but maybe I can get that too," said Jeanie, "with a little helping from you."

"From me, Jeanie! this is the wildest imagination of all."

"Ay, but it is not, Reuben. Havena I heard you say, that your grandfather (that my father never likes to hear about) did some gude langsyne to the forbear of this MacCallummore, when he was Lord of Lorn?"

"He did so," said Butler eagerly, "and I can prove it. —I will write to the Duke of Argyle—report speaks him a good kindly man, as he is known for a brave soldier and true patriot—I will conjure him to stand between your sister and this cruel fate. There is but a poor chance of success, but we will try all means."

"We *must* try all means," replied Jeanie; "but writing winna do it—a letter canna look, and pray, and beg, and beseech, as the human voice can do to the human heart. A letter's like the music that the ladies have for their spinets —naething but black scores, compared to the same tune played or sung. It's word of mouth maun do it, or naething, Reuben."

"You are right," said Reuben, recollecting his firmness, "and I will hope that Heaven has suggested to your kind heart and firm courage the only possible means of saving the life of this unfortunate girl. But, Jeanie, you must not take this most perilous journey alone; I have an interest in you, and I will not agree that my Jeanie throws herself away. You must even, in the present circumstances, give me a husband's right to protect you, and I will go with you myself on this journey, and assist you to do your duty by your family."

"Alas, Reuben!" said Jeanie in her turn, "this must not be; a pardon will not gie my sister her fair fame again, or make me a bride fitting for an honest man and an usefu' minister. Wha wad mind what he said in the pu'pit, that had to wife the sister of a woman that was condemned for sic wickedness!"

"But, Jeanie," pleaded her lover, "I do not believe, and I cannot believe, that Effie has done this deed."

"Heaven bless you for saying sae, Reuben!" answered Jeanie; "but she maun bear the blame o't, after all."

"But that blame, were it even justly laid on her, does not fall on you?"

"Ah, Reuben, Reuben," replied the young woman, "ye ken it is a blot that spreads to kith and kin.—Ichabod—as my poor father says—the glory is departed from our house; for the poorest man's house has a glory, where there are true hands, a divine heart, and an honest fame—And the last has gane frae us a'."

"But, Jeanie, consider your word and plighted faith to me; and would ye undertake such a journey without a man to protect you?—and who should that protector be but your husband?"

"You are kind and good, Reuben, and wad tak me wi' a' my shame, I doubtna. But ye canna but own that this is no time to marry or be given in marriage. Na, if that suld ever be, it maun be in another and a better season.—And, dear Reuben, ye speak of protecting me on my journey —Alas! who will protect and take care of you?—your very limbs tremble with standing for ten minutes on the floor; how could you undertake a journey as far as Lunnon?"

"But I am strong—I am well," continued Butler, sinking in his seat totally exhausted, " at least I shall be quite well to-morrow."

"Ye see, and ye ken, ye maun just let me depart," said Jeanie, after a pause ; and then taking his extended hand, and gazing kindly in his face, she added, "It's e'en a grief the mair to me to see you in this way. But ye maun keep up your heart for Jeanie's sake, for if she isna your wife, she will never be the wife of living man. And now gie me the paper for MacCallummore, and bid God speed me on my way."

There was something of romance in Jeanie's venturous resolution ; yet, on consideration, as it seemed impossible to alter it by persuasion, or to give her assistance but by advice, Butler, after some farther debate, put into her hands the paper she desired, which, with the muster-roll in which it was folded up, were the sole memorials of the stout and enthusiastic Bible Butler, his grandfather. While Butler sought this document, Jeanie had time to take up his pocket Bible. " I have marked a scripture," she said, as she again laid it down, " with your kylevine pen, that will be useful to us baith. And ye maun tak the trouble, Reuben, to write a' this to my father, for, God help me, I have neither head nor hand for lang letters at ony time, forby now ; and I trust him entirely to you, and I trust you will soon be permitted to see him. And, Reuben, when ye do win to the speech o' him, mind a' the auld man's bits o' ways, for Jeanie's sake ; and dinna speak o' Latin or English terms to him, for he's o' the auld warld, and downa bide to be fashed wi' them, though I dare say he may be wrang. And dinna ye say muckle to him, but set him on speaking himsell, for he'll bring himsell mair comfort that way. And oh, Reuben, the poor lassie in yon dungeon !—but I needna bid your kind heart—gie her what comfort ye can as soon as they will let ye see her—tell her—But I maunna speak mair about her, for I maunna take leave o' ye wi' the tear in my ee, for that wadna be canny.—God bless ye, Reuben ! "

To avoid so ill an omen she left the room hastily, while her features yet retained the mournful and affectionate smile which she had compelled them to wear, in order to support Butler's spirits.

It seemed as if the power of sight, of speech, and of reflection, had left him as she disappeared from the room, which she had entered and retired from so like an apparition. Saddletree, who entered immediately afterwards, overwhelmed him with questions, which he answered without understanding them, and with legal disquisitions, which conveyed to him no iota of meaning. At length the learned burgess recollected that there was a Baron Court to be held at Loanhead that day, and though it was hardly worth while, "he might as weel go to see if there was onything doing, as he was acquainted with the baron-bailie, who was a decent man, and would be glad of a word of legal advice."

As soon as he departed, Butler flew to the Bible, the last book which Jeanie had touched. To his extreme surprise, a paper, containing two or three pieces of gold, dropped from the book. With a black-lead pencil, she had marked the sixteenth and twenty-fifth verses of the thirty-seventh Psalm,— "A little that a righteous man hath, is better than the riches of the wicked."—"I have been young and am now old, yet have I not seen the righteous forsaken, nor his seed begging their bread."

Deeply impressed with the affectionate delicacy which shrouded its own generosity under the cover of a providential supply to his wants, he pressed the gold to his lips with more ardour than ever the metal was greeted with by a miser. To emulate her devout firmness and confidence seemed now the pitch of his ambition, and his first task was to write an account to David Deans of his daughter's resolution and journey south-ward. He studied every sentiment, and even every phrase, which he thought could reconcile the old man to her extra-ordinary resolution. The effect which this epistle produced will be hereafter adverted to. Butler committed it to the charge of an honest clown, who had frequent dealings with Deans in the sale of his dairy produce, and who readily undertook a journey to Edinburgh, to put the letter into his own hands.[1]

CHAPTER XXVIII

"My native land, good night.
                    LORD BYRON.

IN the present day, a journey from Edinburgh to London is a matter at once safe, brief, and simple, however inexperienced or unprotected the traveller. Numerous coaches of different

[1] By dint of assiduous research I am enabled to certiorate the reader, that the name of this person was Saunders Broadfoot, and that he dealt in the wholesome commodity called kirn-milk (*Anglicè*, butter-milk).—J. C.

rates of charge, and as many packets, are perpetually passing
and repassing betwixt the capital of Britain and her northern
sister, so that the most timid or indolent may execute such a
journey upon a few hours' notice. But it was different in
1737. So slight and infrequent was then the intercourse
betwixt London and Edinburgh, that men still alive remember
that upon one occasion the mail from the former city arrived
at the General Post-Office in Scotland, with only one letter in
it.[1] The usual mode of travelling was by means of post-
horses, the traveller occupying one and his guide another, in
which manner, by relays of horses from stage to stage, the
journey might be accomplished in a wonderfully short time by
those who could endure fatigue. To have the bones shaken
to pieces by a constant change of those hacks was a luxury for
the rich—the poor were under the necessity of using the mode
of conveyance with which nature had provided them.

With a strong heart, and a frame patient of fatigue, Jeanie
Deans, travelling at the rate of twenty miles a day, and sometimes farther, traversed the southern part of Scotland, and
advanced as far as Durham.

Hitherto she had been either among her own country-folk,
or those to whom her bare feet and tartan screen were objects
too familiar to attract much attention. But as she advanced,
she perceived that both circumstances exposed her to sarcasm
and taunts, which she might otherwise have escaped; and
although in her heart she thought it unkind, and inhospitable,
to sneer at a passing stranger on account of the fashion of her
attire, yet she had the good sense to alter those parts of her
dress which attracted ill-natured observation. Her checked
screen was deposited carefully in her bundle, and she conformed to the national extravagance of wearing shoes and
stockings for the whole day. She confessed afterwards, that,
"besides the wastrife, it was lang or she could walk sae comfortably with the shoes as without them; but there was often a
bit saft heather by the road-side, and that helped her weel on."
The want of the screen, which was drawn over the head like a
veil, she supplied by a *bon-grace*, as she called it; a large
straw bonnet, like those worn by the English maidens when
labouring in the fields. "But I thought unco shame o'
mysell," she said, "the first time I put on a married woman's
bon-grace, and me a single maiden."

[1] The fact is certain. The single epistle was addressed to the principal
director of the British Linen Company.

the wind—strange to behold. Ane miller asked me to gang in and see it work, but I wad not, for I am not come to the south to make acquaintance with strangers. I keep the straight road, and just beck if onybody speaks to me ceevily, and answers naebody with the tong but women of mine ain sect. I wish, Mr. Butler, I kend onything that wad make ye weel, for they hae mair medicines in this town of York than wad cure a' Scotland, and surely some of them wad be gude for your complaints. If ye had a kindly motherly body to nurse ye, and no to let ye waste yoursell wi' reading—whilk ye read mair than eneugh with the bairns in the schule—and to gie ye warm milk in the morning, I wad be mair easy for ye. Dear Mr. Butler, keep a good heart, for we are in the hands of Ane that kens better what is gude for us than we ken what is for oursells. I hae nae doubt to do that for which I am come—I canna doubt it—I winna think to doubt it—because, If I haena full assurance, how shall I bear myself with earnest entreaties in the great folk's presence? But to ken that ane's purpose is right, and to make their heart strong, is the way to get through the warst day's darg. The bairns' rime says, the warst blast of the borrowing days[1] couldna kill the three silly poor hog-lambs. And if it be God's pleasure, we that are sindered in sorrow may meet again in joy, even on this hither side of Jordan. I dinna bid ye mind what I said at our partin' anent my poor father and that misfortunate lassie, for I ken ye will do sae for the sake of Christian charity, whilk is mair than the entreaties of her that is your servant to command,   JEANIE DEANS."

This letter also had a postscript.—"Dear Reuben, If ye think that it wad hae been right for me to have said mair and kinder things to ye, just think that I hae written sae, since I am sure that I wish a' that is kind and right to ye and by ye. Ye will think that I am turned waster, for I wear clean hose and shoon every day; but it's the fashion here for decent bodies, and ilka land has its ain land-law. Ower and aboon a', if laughing days were e'er to come back again till us, ye wad laugh weel to see my round face at the far end of a strae *bon-grace*, that looks as muckle and round as the middell aisle

---

[1] The three last days of March, old style, are called the Borrowing Days; for as they are remarked to be unusually stormy, it is feigned that March had borrowed them from April, to extend the sphere of his rougher sway. The rhyme on the subject is quoted in Leyden's edition of the Complaynt of Scotland.

in Libberton Kirk. But it sheds the sun weel aff, and keeps unceevil folk frae staring as if ane were a worrycow. I sall tell ye by writ how I come on wi' the Duke of Argyle, when I won up to Lunnon. Direct a line, to say how ye are. to me, to the charge of Mrs. Margaret Glass, tobacconist, at the sign of the Thistle, Lunnon, whilk, if it assures me of your health, will make my mind sae muckle easier. Excuse bad spelling and writing, as I have ane ill pen."

The orthography of these epistles may seem to the southron to require a better apology than the letter expresses, though a bad pen was the excuse of a certain Galwegian laird for bad spelling; but, on behalf of the heroine, I would have them to know, that, thanks to the care of Butler, Jeanie Deans wrote and spelled fifty times better than half the women of rank in Scotland at that period, whose strange orthography and singular diction form the strongest contrast to the good sense which their correspondence usually intimates.

For the rest, in the tenor of these epistles, Jeanie expressed, perhaps, more hopes, a firmer courage, and better spirits, than she actually felt. But this was with the amiable idea of relieving her father and lover from apprehensions on her account, which she was sensible must greatly add to their other troubles. "If they think me weel, and like to do weel," said the poor pilgrim to herself, "my father will be kinder to Effie, and Butler will be kinder to himself. For I ken weel that they will think mair o' me than I do o' mysell."

Accordingly, she sealed her letters carefully, and put them into the post-office with her own hand, after many inquiries concerning the time in which they were likely to reach Edinburgh. When this duty was performed, she readily accepted her landlady's pressing invitation to dine with her, and remain till the next morning. The hostess, as we have said, was her countrywoman, and the eagerness with which Scottish people meet, communicate, and, to the extent of their power, assist each other, although it is often objected to us as a prejudice and narrowness of sentiment, seems, on the contrary, to arise from a most justifiable and honourable feeling of patriotism, combined with a conviction, which, if undeserved, would long since have been confuted by experience, that the habits and principles of the nation are a sort of guarantee for the character of the individual. At any rate, if the extensive influence of this national partiality be considered as an additional tie, binding man to man, and calling forth the good offices of such as can render them to the countryman who happens to need them, we think it must be found to exceed, as an active and efficient motive to generosity, that more impartial and wider principle of general benevolence, which we have sometimes seen pleaded as an excuse for assisting no individual whatever.

Mrs. Bickerton, lady of the ascendant of the Seven Stars, in the Castle-gate, York, was deeply infected with the unfortunate prejudices of her country. Indeed, she displayed so much kindness to Jeanie Deans (because she herself, being a Merse woman, *marched* with Mid-Lothian, in which Jeanie was born), showed such motherly regard to her, and such anxiety for her farther progress, that Jeanie thought herself safe, though by temper sufficiently cautious, in communicating her whole story to her.

Mrs. Bickerton raised her hands and eyes at the recital, and exhibited much wonder and pity. But she also gave some effectual good advice.

She required to know the strength of Jeanie's purse, reduced by her deposit at Libberton, and the necessary expense of her journey, to about fifteen pounds. "This," she said, "would do very well, providing she could carry it a' safe to London."

"Safe?" answered Jeanie; "I'se warrant my carrying it safe, bating the needful expenses."

"Ay, but highwaymen, lassie," said Mrs. Bickerton; "for ye are come into a more civilised, that is to say, a more roguish country than the north, and how ye are to get forward, I do not profess to know. If ye could wait here eight days, our waggons would go up, and I would recommend you to Joe Broadwheel, who would see you safe to the Swan and two Necks. And dinna sneeze at Joe, if he should be for drawing up wi' you" (continued Mrs. Bickerton, her acquired English mingling with her national or original dialect), "he's a handy boy, and a wanter, and no lad better thought o' on the road; and the English make good husbands enough, witness my poor man, Moses Bickerton, as is i' the kirkyard."

Jeanie hastened to say that she could not possibly wait for the setting forth of Joe Broadwheel; being internally by no means gratified with the idea of becoming the object of his attention during the journey.

"Aweel, lass," answered the good landlady, "then thou must pickle in thine ain poke-nook, and buckle thy girdle thine ain gate. But take my advice, and hide thy gold in thy stays, and keep a piece or two and some silver, in case thou be'st spoke withal; for there's as wud lads haunt within a day's walk from hence, as on the Braes o' Doun in Perthshire. And, lass, thou maunna gang staring through Lunnon, asking wha kens Mrs. Glass at the sign o' the Thistle; marry, they would laugh thee to scorn. But gang thou to this honest man," and she put a direction into Jeanie's hand, "he kens maist part of the sponsible Scottish folk in the city, and he will find out your friend for thee."

Jeanie took the little introductory letter with sincere thanks; but, something alarmed on the subject of the highway robbers, her mind recurred to what Ratcliffe had mentioned to her, and briefly relating the circumstances which placed a document so extraordinary in her hands, she put the paper he had given her into the hands of Mrs. Bickerton.

The Lady of the Seven Stars did not, indeed, ring a bell, because such was not the fashion of the time, but she whistled on a silver-call, which was hung by her side, and a tight serving-maiden entered the room.

"Tell Dick Ostler to come here," said Mrs. Bickerton.

Dick Ostler accordingly made his appearance;—a queer, knowing, shambling animal, with a hatchet-face, a squint, a game-arm, and a limp.

"Dick Ostler," said Mrs. Bickerton, in a tone of authority that showed she was (at least by adoption) Yorkshire too, "thou knowest most people and most things o' the road."

"Eye, eye, God help me, mistress," said Dick, shrugging his shoulders betwixt a repentant and a knowing expression— "Eye! I ha' know'd a thing or twa i' ma day, mistress." He looked sharp and laughed—looked grave and sighed, as one who was prepared to take the matter either way.

"Kenst thou this wee bit paper amang the rest, man?" said Mrs. Bickerton, handing him the protection which Ratcliffe had given Jeanie Deans.

When Dick had looked at the paper, he winked with one eye, extended his grotesque mouth from ear to ear, like a navigable canal, scratched his head powerfully, and then said "Ken?—ay—maybe we ken summat, an it werena for harm to him, mistress."

"None in the world," said Mrs. Bickerton; "only a dram of Hollands to thyself, man, an thou will't speak."

"Why, then," said Dick, giving the head-band of his

breeches a knowing hoist with one hand, and kicking out one foot behind him to accommodate the adjustment of that important habiliment, " I dares to say the pass will be kend weel eneugh on the road, an that be all."

" But what sort of a lad was he?" said Mrs. Bickerton, winking to Jeanie, as proud of her knowing ostler.

"Why, what ken I?—Jim the Rat—why, he was Cock o' the North within this twelmonth—he and Scotch Wilson, Handie Dandie, as they called him—but he's been out o' this country a while, as I rackon; but ony gentleman, as keeps the road o' this side Stamford, will respect Jim's pass."

Without asking farther questions, the landlady filled Dick Ostler a bumper of Hollands. He ducked with his head and shoulders, scraped with his more advanced hoof, bolted the alcohol, to use the learned phrase, and withdrew to his own domains.

"I would advise thee, Jeanie," said Mrs. Bickerton, "an thou meetest with ugly customers o' the road, to show them this bit paper, for it will serve thee, assure thyself."

A neat little supper concluded the evening. The exported Scotswoman, Mrs. Bickerton by name, eat heartily of one or two seasoned dishes, drank some sound old ale, and a glass of stiff negus; while she gave Jeanie a history of her gout, admiring how it was possible that she, whose fathers and mothers for many generations had been farmers in Lammer-muir, could have come by a disorder so totally unknown to them. Jeanie did not choose to offend her friendly landlady, by speaking her mind on the probable origin of this complaint; but she thought on the flesh-pots of Egypt, and, in spite of all entreaties to better fare, made her evening meal upon vegetables, with a glass of fair water.

Mrs. Bickerton assured her, that the acceptance of any reckoning was entirely out of the question, furnished her with credentials to her correspondent in London, and to several inns upon the road where she had some influence or interest, reminded her of the precautions she should adopt for conceal-ing her money, and as she was to depart early in the morning, took leave of her very affectionately, taking her word that she would visit her on her return to Scotland, and tell her how she had managed, and that *summum bonum* for a gossip, "all how and about it." This Jeanie faithfully promised.

CHAPTER XXIX

And Need and Misery, Vice and Danger, bind,
In sad alliance, each degraded mind.

As our traveller set out early on the ensuing morning to prosecute her journey, and was in the act of leaving the inn-yard,
Dick Ostler, who either had risen early or neglected to go to
bed, either circumstance being equally incident to his calling,
hollowed out after her,—"The top of the morning to you,
Moggie! Have a care o' Gunnerby Hill, young one. Robin
Hood's dead and gwone, but there be takers yet in the vale of
Bever." Jeanie looked at him as if to request a further explanation, but, with a leer, a shuffle, and a shrug, inimitable
(unless by Emery), Dick turned again to the raw-boned steed
which he was currying, and sung as he employed the comb
and brush,—

> " Robin Hood was a yeoman good,
>   And his bow was of trusty yew;
> And if Robin said stand on the King's lea-land,
>   Pray, why should not we say so too?"

Jeanie pursued her journey without farther inquiry, for there
was nothing in Dick's manner that inclined her to prolong their
conference. A painful day's journey brought her to Ferrybridge, the best inn, then and since, upon the great northern
road; and an introduction from Mrs. Bickerton, added to her
own simple and quiet manners, so propitiated the landlady of
the Swan in her favour, that the good dame procured her the
convenient accommodation of a pillion and post-horse then
returning to Tuxford, so that she accomplished, upon the
second day after leaving York, the longest journey she had
yet made. She was a good deal fatigued by a mode of travelling to which she was less accustomed than to walking, and it
was considerably later than usual on the ensuing morning that
she felt herself able to resume her pilgrimage. At noon the
hundred-armed Trent, and the blackened ruins of Newark
Castle, demolished in the great civil war, lay before her.
It may easily be supposed, that Jeanie had no curiosity to
make antiquarian researches, but, entering the town, went
straight to the inn to which she had been directed at Ferrybridge. While she procured some refreshment, she observed

the girl who brought it to her, looked at her several times with fixed and peculiar interest, and at last, to her infinite surprise, inquired if her name was not Deans, and if she was not a Scotchwoman, going to London upon justice business. Jeanie, with all her simplicity of character, had some of the caution of her country, and, according to Scottish universal custom, she answered the question by another, requesting the girl would tell her why she had asked these questions?

The Maritornes of the Saracen's Head, Newark, replied, "Two women had passed that morning, who had made inquiries after one Jeanie Deans, travelling to London on such an errand, and could scarce be persuaded that she had not passed on."

Much surprised, and somewhat alarmed (for what is inexplicable is usually alarming), Jeanie questioned the wench about the particular appearance of these two women, but could only learn that the one was aged, and the other young; that the latter was the taller, and that the former spoke most, and seemed to maintain an authority over her companion, and that both spoke with the Scottish accent.

This conveyed no information whatever, and with an indescribable presentiment of evil designed towards her, Jeanie adopted the resolution of taking post-horses for the next stage. In this, however, she could not be gratified; some accidental circumstances had occasioned what is called a run upon the road, and the landlord could not accommodate her with a guide and horses. After waiting some time, in hopes that a pair of horses that had gone southward would return in time for her use, she at length, feeling ashamed of her own pusillanimity, resolved to prosecute her journey in her usual manner.

"It was all plain road," she was assured, "except a high mountain, called Gunnerby Hill, about three miles from Grantham, which was her stage for the night."

"I'm glad to hear there's a hill," replied Jeanie, "for baith my sight and my very feet are weary o' sic tracts o' level ground—it looks a' the way between this and York as if a' the land had been trenched and levelled, whilk is very wearisome to my Scotch een. When I lost sight of a muckle blue hill they ca' Ingleboro', I thought I hadna a friend left in this strange land."

"As for the matter of that, young woman," said mine host, "and you be so fond o' hill, I carena an thou couldst carry Gunnerby away with thee in thy lap, for it's a murder to post-horses.   But here's to thy journey, and mayst thou win well through it, for thou is a bold and a canny lass."

So saying, he took a powerful pull at a solemn tankard of home-brewed ale.

"I hope there is nae bad company on the road, sir?" said Jeanie.

"Why, when it's clean without them I'll thatch Groby pool wi' pancakes. But there arena sae mony now; and since they hae lost Jim the Rat, they hold together no better than the men of Marsham when they lost their common.   Take a drop ere thou goest," he concluded, offering her the tankard; "thou wilt get naething at night save Grantham gruel, nine grots and a gallon of water."

Jeanie courteously declined the tankard, and inquired what was her "lawing"?

"Thy lawing?   Heaven help thee, wench!   What ca'st thou that"?

"It is—I was wanting to ken what was to pay," replied Jeanie.

"Pay?   Lord help thee!—why nought, woman—we hae drawn no liquor but a gill o' beer, and the Saracen's Head can spare a mouthful o' meat to a stranger like o' thee, that cannot speak Christian language.   So here's to thee once more.   The same again, quoth Mark of Bellgrave," and he took another profound pull at the tankard.

The travellers who have visited Newark more lately, will not fail to remember the remarkably civil and gentlemanly manners of the person who now keeps the principal inn there, and may find some amusement in contrasting them with those of his more rough predecessor. But we believe it will be found that the polish has worn off none of the real worth of the metal.

Taking leave of her Lincolnshire Gaius, Jeanie resumed her solitary walk, and was somewhat alarmed when evening and twilight overtook her in the open ground which extends to the foot of Gunnerby Hill, and is intersected with patches of copse and with swampy spots. The extensive commons on the north road, most of which are now enclosed, and in general a relaxed state of police, exposed the traveller to a highway robbery in a degree which is now unknown, excepting in the immediate vicinity of the metropolis. Aware of this circumstance, Jeanie mended her pace when she heard the trampling of a horse behind, and instinctively drew to one side of the road, as if to allow as much room for the rider to pass as might be possible. When the animal came up, she found that it was bearing two women, the one placed on a side-saddle, the other on a pillion behind her, as may still occasionally be seen in England.

"A braw gude night to ye, Jeanie Deans," said the foremost female, as the horse passed our heroine; "what think ye o' yon bonny hill yonder, lifting its brow to the moon? Trow ye yon's the gate to heaven, that ye are sae fain of?— maybe we may win there the night yet, God sain us, though our minny here's rather driegh in the upgang."

The speaker kept changing her seat in the saddle, and half-stopping the horse, as she brought her body round, while the woman that sate behind her on the pillion seemed to urge her on, in words which Jeanie heard but imperfectly.

"Haud your tongue, ye moon-raised b——! what is your business with ——, or with heaven or hell either?"

"Troth, mither, no muckle wi' heaven, I doubt, considering wha I carry ahint me—and as for hell, it will fight its ain battle at its ain time, I'se be bound.—Come, naggie, trot awa, man, an as thou wert a broomstick, for a witch rides thee—

> 'With my curtch on my foot, and my shoe on my hand,
> I glance like the wildfire through brugh and through land.'"

The tramp of the horse, and the increasing distance, drowned the rest of her song, but Jeanie heard for some time the inarticulate sounds ring along the waste.

Our pilgrim remained stupefied with undefined apprehensions. The being named by her name in so wild a manner, and in a strange country, without further explanation or communing, by a person who thus strangely flitted forward and disappeared before her, came near to the supernatural sounds in Comus :—

> The airy tongues, which syllable men's names
> On sands, and shores, and desert wildernesses.

And although widely different in features, deportment, and rank, from the Lady of that enchanting masque, the continuation of the passage may be happily applied to Jeanie Deans upon this singular alarm :—

> These thoughts may startle well, but not astound
> The virtuous mind, that ever walks attended
> By a strong siding champion—Conscience.

In fact, it was, with the recollection of the affectionate and dutiful errand on which she was engaged, her right, if such a word could be applicable, to expect protection in a task so meritorious. She had not advanced much farther, with a mind calmed by these reflections, when she was disturbed by a new and more instant subject of terror. Two men, who had been lurking among some copse, started up as she advanced, and met her on the road in a menacing manner. "Stand and deliver," said one of them, a short stout fellow, in a smock-frock, such as are worn by waggoners.

"The woman," said the other, a tall thin figure, "does not understand the words of action.—Your money, my precious, or your life!"

"I have but very little money, gentlemen," said poor Jeanie, tendering that portion which she had separated from her principal stock, and kept apart for such an emergency; "but if you are resolved to have it, to be sure you must have it."

"This won't do, my girl. D—n me, if it shall pass!" said the shorter ruffian; "do ye think gentlemen are to hazard their lives on the road to be cheated in this way? We'll have every farthing you have got, or we will strip you to the skin, curse me."

His companion, who seemed to have something like compassion for the horror which Jeanie's countenance now expressed, said, "No, no, Tom, this is one of the precious sisters, and we'll take her word, for once, without putting her to the stripping proof.—Hark ye, my lass, if you'll look up to heaven, and say, this is the last penny you have about ye, why, hang it, we'll let you pass."

"I am not free," answered Jeanie, "to say what I have about me, gentlemen, for there's life and death depends on my journey; but if you leave me as much as finds me in bread and water, I'll be satisfied, and thank you, and pray for you."

"D—n your prayers!" said the shorter fellow, "that's a coin that won't pass with us;" and at the same time made a motion to seize her.

"Stay, gentlemen," Ratcliffe's pass suddenly occurring to her; "perhaps you know this paper."

"What the devil is she after now, Frank?" said the more savage ruffian—"Do you look at it, for, d—n me if I could read it, if it were for the benefit of my clergy."

"This is a jark from Jim Ratcliffe," said the taller, having looked at the bit of paper. "The wench must pass by our cutter's law."

"I say no," answered his companion; "Rat has left the lay, and turned bloodhound, they say."

"We may need a good turn from him all the same," said the taller ruffian again.

"But what are we to do then?" said the shorter man.— "We promised, you know, to strip the wench, and send her begging back to her own beggarly country, and now you are for letting her go on."

"I did not say that," said the other fellow, and whispered to his companion, who replied, "Be alive about it then, and don't keep chattering till some travellers come up to nab us."

"You must follow us off the road, young woman," said the taller.

"For the love of God!" exclaimed Jeanie, "as you were born of woman, dinna ask me to leave the road! rather take all I have in the world."

"What the devil is the wench afraid of?" said the other fellow. "I tell you you shall come to no harm; but if you will not leave the road and come with us, d—n me, but I'll beat your brains out where you stand."

"Thou art a rough bear, Tom," said his companion.— "An ye touch her, I'll give ye a shake by the collar shall make the Leicester beans rattle in thy guts.—Never mind him, girl; I will not allow him to lay a finger on you, if you walk quietly on with us; but if you keep jabbering there, d—n me, but I'll leave him to settle it with you."

This threat conveyed all that is terrible to the imagination of poor Jeanie, who saw in him that "was of milder mood" her only protection from the most brutal treatment. She, therefore, not only followed him, but even held him by the sleeve, lest he should escape from her; and the fellow, hardened as he was, seemed something touched by these marks of confidence, and repeatedly assured her that he would suffer her to receive no harm.

They conducted their prisoner in a direction leading more and more from the public road, but she observed that they kept a sort of track or by-path, which relieved her from part of her apprehensions, which would have been greatly increased had they not seemed to follow a determined and ascertained route. After about half-an-hour's walking, all three in profound silence, they approached an old barn, which stood on the edge of some cultivated ground, but remote from everything like a habitation. It was itself, however, tenanted, for there was light in the windows.

One of the footpads scratched at the door, which was opened by a female, and they entered with their unhappy prisoner. An old woman, who was preparing food by the assistance of a stifling fire of lighted charcoal, asked them, in the name of the devil, what they brought the wench there for, and why they did not strip her and turn her abroad on the common?

"Come, come, Mother Blood," said the tall man, "we'll do what's right to oblige you, and we'll do no more; we are bad enough, but not such as you would make us—devils incarnate."

"She has got a *jark* from Jim Ratcliffe," said the short fellow, "and Frank here won't hear of our putting her through the mill."

"No, that will I not, by G—d!" answered Frank; "but if old Mother Blood could keep her here for a little while, or send her back to Scotland, without hurting her, why, I see no harm in that—not I."

"I'll tell you what, Frank Levitt," said the old woman, "if you call me Mother Blood again, I'll paint this gully" (and she held a knife up as if about to make good her threat) "in the best blood in your body, my bonny boy."

"The price of ointment must be up in the north," said Frank, "that puts Mother Blood so much out of humour."

Without a moment's hesitation the fury darted her knife at him with the vengeful dexterity of a wild Indian. As he was on his guard, he avoided the missile by a sudden motion of his head, but it whistled past his ear, and stuck deep in the clay wall of a partition behind.

"Come, come, mother," said the robber, seizing her by both wrists, "I shall teach you who's master;" and so saying, he forced the hag backwards by main force, who strove vehemently until she sunk on a bunch of straw, and then letting go her hands, he held up his finger towards her in the menacing posture by which a maniac is intimidated by his keeper. It appeared to produce the desired effect; for she did not attempt to rise from the seat on which he had placed her, or to resume any measures of actual violence, but wrung her withered hands with impotent rage, and brayed and howled like a demoniac.

"I will keep my promise with you, you old devil," said Frank; "the wench shall not go forward on the London road, but I will not have you touch a hair of her head, if it were but for your insolence."

This intimation seemed to compose in some degree the vehement passion of the old hag; and while her exclamations and howls sunk into a low, maundering, growling tone of voice, another personage was added to this singular party.

"Eh, Frank Levitt," said this new-comer, who entered with a hop, step, and jump, which at once conveyed her from the door into the centre of the party, "were ye killing our mother? or were ye cutting the grunter's weasand that Tam brought in this morning? or have ye been reading your prayers backward, to bring up my auld acquaintance the deil amang ye?"

The tone of the speaker was so particular, that Jeanie immediately recognised the woman who had rode foremost of the pair which passed her just before she met the robbers; a circumstance which greatly increased her terror, as it served to show that the mischief designed against her was premeditated, though by whom, or for what cause, she was totally at a loss to conjecture. From the style of her conversation, the reader also may probably acknowledge in this female an old acquaintance in the earlier part of our narrative.

"Out, ye mad devil!" said Tom, whom she had disturbed in the middle of a draught of some liquor with which he had found means of accommodating himself; "betwixt your Bess of Bedlam pranks, and your dam's frenzies, a man might live quieter in the devil's ken than here."—And he again resumed the broken jug out of which he had been drinking.

"And wha's this o't?" said the madwoman, dancing up to Jeanie Deans, who, although in great terror, yet watched the scene with a resolution to let nothing pass unnoticed which might be serviceable in assisting her to escape, or informing her as to the true nature of her situation, and the danger attending it,—"Wha's this o't?" again exclaimed Madge Wildfire. "Douce Davie Deans, the auld doited whig body's daughter, in a gipsy's barn, and the night setting in; this is a sight for sair een!—Eh, sirs, the falling off o' the godly!—and the t'other sister's in the Tolbooth at Edinburgh! I am very sorry for her, for my share—it's my mother wusses ill to her, and no me—though maybe I hae as muckle cause."

"Hark ye, Madge," said the taller ruffian, "you have not such a touch of the devil's blood as the hag your mother, who may be his dam for what I know—take this young woman to your kennel, and do not let the devil enter, though he should ask in God's name."

"Ou ay; that I will, Frank," said Madge, taking hold of Jeanie by the arm, and pulling her along; "for it's no for decent Christian young leddies, like her and me, to be keeping the like o' you and Tyburn Tam company at this time o' night. Sae gude e'en t'ye, sirs, and mony o' them; and may ye a' sleep till the hangman wauken ye, and then it will be weel for the country."

She then, as her wild fancy seemed suddenly to prompt her, walked demurely towards her mother, who, seated by the charcoal fire, with the reflection of the red light on her withered and distorted features marked by every evil passion, seemed the very picture of Hecate at her infernal rites; and suddenly dropping on her knees, said, with the manner of a six years old child, " Mammie, hear me say my prayers before I go to bed, and say God bless my bonny face, as ye used to do lang syne."

"The deil flay the hide o' it to sole his brogues wi'!" said the old lady, aiming a buffet at the supplicant, in answer to her duteous request.

The blow missed Madge, who, being probably acquainted by experience with the mode in which her mother was wont to confer her maternal benedictions, slipt out of arm's length with great dexterity and quickness. The hag then started up, and, seizing a pair of old fire-tongs, would have amended her motion, by beating out the brains either of her daughter or Jeanie (she did not seem greatly to care which), when her hand was once more arrested by the man whom they called Frank Levitt, who, seizing her by the shoulder, flung her from him with great violence, exclaiming, " What, Mother Damnable—again, and in my sovereign presence?—Hark ye, Madge of Bedlam, get to your hole with your playfellow, or we shall have the devil to pay here, and nothing to pay him with."

Madge took Levitt's advice, retreating as fast as she could, and dragging Jeanie along with her into a sort of recess, partitioned off from the rest of the barn, and filled with straw, from which it appeared that it was intended for the purpose of slumber. The moonlight shone, through an open hole, upon a pillion, a pack-saddle, and one or two wallets, the travelling furniture of Madge and her amiable mother.—

"Now, saw ye e'er in your life," said Madge, "sae dainty a chamber of deas? see as the moon shines down sae caller on the fresh strae! There's no a pleasanter cell in Bedlam, for as braw a place as it is on the outside.—Were ye ever in Bedlam?"

"No," answered Jeanie faintly, appalled by the question, and the way in which it was put, yet willing to soothe her insane companion; being in circumstances so unhappily precarious, that even the society of this gibbering madwoman seemed a species of protection.

"Never in Bedlam!" said Madge, as if with some surprise. —"But ye'll hae been in the cells at Edinburgh?"

"Never," repeated Jeanie.

"Weel, I think thae daft carles the magistrates send naebody to Bedlam but me—they maun hae an unco respect for me, for whenever I am brought to them, they aye hae me back to Bedlam. But troth Jeanie" (she said this in a very confidential tone), "to tell ye my private mind about it, I think ye are at nae great loss; for the keeper's a cross patch, and he maun hae it a' his ain gate, to be sure, or he makes the place waur than hell. I often tell him he's the daftest in a' the house.—But what are they making sic a skirling for?— Deil ane o' them's get in here—it wadna be mensefu'! I will sit wi' my back again the door; it winna be that easy stirring me."

"Madge!"—"Madge!"—"Madge Wildfire!"—"Madge devil! what have ye done with the horse?" was repeatedly asked by the men without.

"He's e'en at his supper. puir thing," answered Madge; "deil an ye were at yours too, an it were scauding brimstane, and then we wad hae less o' your din."

"His supper?" answered the more sulky ruffian—"What d'ye mean by that?—Tell me where he is, or I will knock your Bedlam brains out!"

"He's in Gaffer Gabblewood's wheat-close, an ye maun ken."

"His wheat-close, you crazed jilt!" answered the other, with an accent of great indignation.

"Oh, dear Tyburn Tam, man, what ill will the blades of the young wheat do to the puir naig?"

"That is not the question," said the other robber; "but what the country will say to us to-morrow when they see him in such quarters.—Go, Tom, and bring him in; and avoid the soft ground, my lad; leave no hoof-track behind you."

"I think you give me always the fag of it, whatever is to be done," grumbled his companion.

"Leap, Laurence, you're long enough," said the other; and the fellow left the barn accordingly, without farther remonstrance.

In the meanwhile, Madge had arranged herself for repose on the straw; but still in a half-sitting posture, with her back resting against the door of the hovel, which, as it opened inwards, was in this manner kept shut by the weight of her person.

"There's mair shifts by stealing, Jeanie," said Madge Wildfire; "though whiles I can hardly get our mother to think sae. Wha wad hae thought but mysell of making a bolt of my ain back-bane! But it's no sae strong as thae that I hae seen in the Tolbooth at Edinburgh. The hammermen of Edinburgh are to my mind afore the world for making stanchions, ring-bolts, fetter-bolts, bars, and locks. And they arena that bad at girdles for carcakes neither, though the Cu'ross hammermen have the gree for that. My mother had ance a bonny Cu'ross girdle, and I thought to have baked carcakes on it for my puir wean that's dead and gane nae fair way—but we maun a' dee, ye ken, Jeanie—You Cameronian bodies ken that brawlie; and ye're for making a hell upon earth that ye may be less unwillin' to part wi' it. But as touching Bedlam that ye were speaking about, I'se ne'er recommend it muckle the tae gate or the t'other, be it right —be it wrang. But ye ken what the sang says?" And, pursuing the unconnected and floating wanderings of her mind, she sung aloud—

> "In the bonny cells of Bedlam,
>   Ere I was ane and twenty,
> I had hempen bracelets strong,
> And merry whips, ding-dong,
>   And prayer and fasting plenty.

"Weel, Jeanie, I am something herse the night, and I canna sing muckle mair; and troth, I think, I am gaun to sleep."

She dropped her head on her breast, a posture from which Jeanie, who would have given the world for an opportunity of quiet to consider the means and the probability of her escape, was very careful not to disturb her. After nodding, however, for a minute or two, with her eyes half closed, the unquiet and restless spirit of her malady again assailed Madge. She raised her head, and spoke, but with a lowered tone, which was again gradually overcome by drowsiness, to which the fatigue of a day's journey on horseback had probably given unwonted occasion,—" I dinna ken what makes me sae sleepy — I amaist never sleep till my bonny Lady Moon gangs till her bed—mair by token, when she's at the full, ye ken, rowing aboon us yonder in her grand silver coach—I have danced to her my lane sometimes for very joy —and whiles dead folk came and danced wi' me—the like o' Jock Porteous, or onybody I had kend when I was living— for ye maun ken I was ance dead mysell." Here the poor maniac sung in a low and wild tone—

> "My banes are buried in yon kirkyard
> Sae far ayont the sea,
> And it is but my blithesome ghaist
> That's speaking now to thee.

" But, after a', Jeanie, my woman, naebody kens weel wha's living and wha's dead—or wha's gane to Fairyland—there's another question. Whiles I think my puir bairn's dead—ye ken very weel it's buried—but that signifies naething. I have had it on my knee a hundred times, and a hundred till that, since it was buried, and how could that be were it dead, ye ken?—it's merely impossible."—And here, some conviction half-overcoming the reveries of her imagination, she burst into a fit of crying and ejaculation, "Wae's me! wae's me! wae's me!" till at length she moaned and sobbed herself into a deep sleep, which was soon intimated by her breathing hard, leaving Jeanie to her own melancholy reflections and observations.

CHAPTER XXX

> Bind her quickly; or, by this steel,
> I'll tell, although I truss for company.
>
>   FLETCHER.

THE imperfect light which shone into the window enabled Jeanie to see that there was scarcely any chance of making her escape in that direction; for the aperture was high in the wall, and so narrow, that, could she have climbed up to it, she might well doubt whether it would have permitted her to pass her body through it. An unsuccessful attempt to escape would be sure to draw down worse treatment than she now received, and she, therefore, resolved to watch her opportunity carefully ere making such a perilous effort. For this purpose she applied herself to the ruinous clay partition, which divided the hovel in which she now was from the rest of the waste barn. It was decayed and full of cracks and chinks, one of which she enlarged with her fingers, cautiously and without noise, until she could obtain a plain view of the old hag and the taller ruffian, whom they called Levitt, seated together beside the decayed fire of charcoal, and apparently engaged in close conference. She was at first terrified by the sight, for the features of the old woman had a hideous cast of hardened and inveterate malice and ill-humour, and those of the man, though naturally less unfavourable, were such as corresponded well with licentious habits, and a lawless profession.

"But I remembered," said Jeanie, "my worthy father's tales of a winter evening, how he was confined with the blessed martyr, Mr. James Renwick, who lifted up the fallen standard of the true reformed Kirk of Scotland, after the worthy and renowned Daniel Cameron, our last blessed banner-man, had fallen among the swords of the wicked at Airsmoss, and how the very hearts of the wicked malefactors and murderers, whom they were confined withal, were melted like wax at the sound of their doctrine : and I bethought mysell, that the same help that was wi' them in their strait, wad be wi' me in mine, an I could but watch the Lord's time and opportunity for delivering my feet from their snare ; and I minded the Scripture of the blessed Psalmist, whilk he insisteth on, as weel in the forty-second as in the forty-third psalm, 'Why art thou cast down, O my soul, and why art thou disquieted within me? Hope in God, for I shall yet praise Him, who is the health of my countenance, and my God.'"

Strengthened in a mind naturally calm, sedate, and firm, by the influence of religious confidence, this poor captive was enabled to attend to, and comprehend, a great part of an interesting conversation which passed betwixt those into whose hands she had fallen, notwithstanding that their meaning was partly disguised by the occasional use of cant terms, of which Jeanie knew not the import, by the low tone in which they spoke, and by their mode of supplying their broken phrases by shrugs and signs, as is usual amongst those of their disorderly profession.

The man opened the conversation by saying, "Now, dame, you see I am true to my friend. I have not forgot that you *planked a chury*, which helped me through the bars of the

Castle of York, and I came to do your work without asking questions, for one good turn deserves another. But now that Madge, who is as loud as Tom of Lincoln, is somewhat still, and this same Tyburn Neddie is shaking his heels after the old nag, why, you must tell me what all this is about, and what's to be done—for d—n me if I touch the girl, or let her be touched, and she with Jim Rat's pass too."

"Thou art an honest lad, Frank," answered the old woman, "but e'en too kind for thy trade; thy tender heart will get thee into trouble. I will see ye gang up Holborn Hill backward, and a' on the word of some silly loon that could never hae rapped to ye had ye drawn your knife across his weasand."

"You may be baulked there, old one," answered the robber; "I have known many a pretty lad cut short in his first summer upon the road, because he was something hasty with his flats and sharps. Besides, a man would fain live out his two years with a good conscience. So, tell me what all this is about, and what's to be done for you that one can do decently?"

"Why, you must know, Frank—but first taste a snap of right Hollands." She drew a flask from her pocket, and filled the fellow a large bumper, which he pronounced to be the right thing.—"You must know, then, Frank—wunna ye mend your hand?" again offering the flask.

"No, no—when a woman wants mischief from you, she always begins by filling you drunk. D—n all Dutch courage. What I do I will do soberly—I'll last the longer for that too."

"Well, then, you must know," resumed the old woman, without any farther attempts at propitiation, "that this girl is going to London."

Here Jeanie could only distinguish the word "sister."

The robber answered in a louder tone, "Fair enough that; and what the devil is your business with it?"

"Business enough, I think. If the b— queers the noose, that silly cull will marry her."

"And who cares if he does?" said the man.

"Who cares, ye donnard Neddie? *I* care; and I will strangle her with my own hands, rather than she should come to Madge's preferment."

"Madge's preferment? Does your old blind eyes see no farther than that? If he is as you say, d'ye think he'll ever marry a moon-calf like Madge? Ecod, that's a good one— Marry Madge Wildfire!—Ha! ha! ha!"

"Hark ye, ye crack-rope padder, born beggar, and bred

thief!" replied the hag, "suppose he never marries the wench, is that a reason he should marry another, and that other to hold my daughter's place, and she crazed, and I a beggar, and all along of him? But I know that of him will hang him— I know that of him will hang him, if he had a thousand lives— I know that of him will hang—hang—hang him!"

She grinned as she repeated and dwelt upon the fatal monosyllable, with the emphasis of a vindictive fiend.

"Then why don't you hang—hang—hang him?" said Frank, repeating her words contemptuously. "There would be more sense in that, than in wreaking yourself here upon two wenches that have done you and your daughter no ill."

"No ill?" answered the old woman—"and he to marry this jail-bird, if ever she gets her foot loose!"

"But as there is no chance of his marrying a bird of your brood, I cannot, for my soul, see what you have to do with all this," again replied the robber, shrugging his shoulders. "Where there is aught to be got, I'll go as far as my neighbours, but I hate mischief for mischief's sake."

"And would you go nae length for revenge?" said the hag —"for revenge, the sweetest morsel to the mouth that ever was cooked in hell!"

"The devil may keep it for his own eating, then," said the robber; "for hang me if I like the sauce he dresses it with."

"Revenge!" continued the old woman; "why, it is the best reward the devil gives us for our time here and hereafter. I have wrought hard for it—I have suffered for it, and I have sinned for it—and I will have it,—or there is neither justice in heaven nor in hell!"

Levitt had by this time lighted a pipe, and was listening with great composure to the frantic and vindictive ravings of the old hag. He was too much hardened by his course of life to be shocked with them—too indifferent, and probably too stupid, to catch any part of their animation or energy. "But, mother," he said, after a pause, "still I say, that if revenge is your wish, you should take it on the young fellow himself."

"I wish I could," she said, drawing in her breath, with the eagerness of a thirsty person while mimicking the action of drinking—"I wish I could!—but no—I cannot—I cannot."

"And why not?—You would think little of peaching and hanging him for this Scotch affair.—Rat me, one might have milled the Bank of England, and less noise about it."

" I have nursed him at this withered breast," answered the old woman, folding her hands on her bosom, as if pressing an infant to it, " and though he has proved an adder to me —though he has been the destruction of me and mine— though he has made me company for the devil, if there be a devil, and food for hell, if there be such a place, yet I cannot take his life—No, I cannot," she continued, with an appearance of rage against herself; " I have thought of it—I have tried it—but, Francis Levitt, I canna gang through wi't !— Na, na—he was the first bairn I ever nurst—ill I had been— but man can never ken what woman feels for the bairn she has held first to her bosom ! "

" To be sure," said Levitt, " we have no experience. But, mother, they say you ha'n't been so kind to other bairns, as you call them, that have come in your way.—Nay, d—n me, never lay your hand on the whittle, for I am captain and leader here, and I will have no rebellion."

The hag, whose first motion had been, upon hearing the question, to grasp the haft of a large knife, now unclosed her hand, stole it away from the weapon, and suffered it to fall by her side, while she proceeded with a sort of smile—" Bairns ! ye are joking, lad, wha wad touch bairns? Madge, puir thing, had a misfortune wi' ane—and the t'other "—Here her voice sunk so much, that Jeanie, though anxiously upon the watch, could not catch a word she said, until she raised her tone at the conclusion of the sentence—" So Madge, in her daffin', threw it into the Nor'-loch, I trow."

Madge, whose slumbers, like those of most who labour under mental malady, had been short and were easily broken, now made herself heard from her place of repose.

" Indeed, mother, that's a great lee, for I did nae sic thing."

" Hush ! thou hellicat devil," said her mother—" By Heaven ! the other wench will be waking too ! "

" That may be dangerous," said Frank ; and he rose and followed Meg Murdockson across the floor.

" Rise," said the hag to her daughter, " or I sall drive the knife between the planks into the Bedlam back of thee ! "

Apparently she at the same time seconded her threat, by pricking her with the point of a knife, for Madge, with a faint scream, changed her place, and the door opened.

The old woman held a candle in one hand, and a knife in the other. Levitt appeared behind her ; whether with a view of preventing, or assisting her in any violence she might meditate, could not be well guessed. Jeanie's presence of mind stood her friend in this dreadful crisis. She had resolution enough to maintain the attitude and manner of one who sleeps profoundly, and to regulate even her breathing, notwithstanding the agitation of instant terror, so as to correspond with her attitude.

The old woman passed the light across her eyes; and although Jeanie's fears were so powerfully awakened by this movement, that she often declared afterwards, that she thought she saw the figures of her destined murderers through her closed eyelids, she had still the resolution to maintain the feint, on which her safety perhaps depended.

Levitt looked at her with fixed attention; he then turned the old woman out of the place, and followed her himself. Having regained the outer apartment, and seated themselves, Jeanie heard the highwayman say, to her no small relief, "She's as fast as if she were in Bedfordshire.—Now, old Meg, d—n me, if I can understand a glim of this story of yours, or what good it will do you to hang the one wench, and torment the other; but, rat me, I will be true to my friend, and serve ye the way ye like it. I see it will be a bad job; but I do think I could get her down to Surfleet on the Wash, and so on board Tom Moonshine's neat lugger, and keep her out of the way three or four weeks, if that will please ye?—But d—n me if any one shall harm her, unless they have a mind to choke on a brace of blue plums.—It's a cruel bad job, and I wish you and it, Meg, were both at the devil!'

"Never mind, hinny Levitt," said the old woman; "you are a ruffler, and will have a' your ain gate—She shanna gang to heaven an hour sooner for me; I carena whether she live or die—it's her sister—ay, her sister!"

"Well, we'll say no more about it, I hear Tom coming in. We'll couch a hogshead, and so better had you." They retired to repose, accordingly, and all was silent in this asylum of iniquity.

Jeanie lay for a long time awake. At break of day she heard the two ruffians leave the barn, after whispering with the old woman for some time. The sense that she was now guarded only by persons of her own sex gave her some confidence, and irresistible lassitude at length threw her into slumber.

When the captive awakened, the sun was high in heaven, and the morning considerably advanced. Madge Wildfire was still in the hovel which had served them for the night, and immediately bid her good-morning, with her usual air of insane glee. "And d'ye ken, lass," said Madge, "there's queer things chanced since ye hae been in the land of Nod. The constables hae been here, woman, and they met wi' my minnie at the door, and they whirl'd her awa to the Justice's about the man's wheat.—Dear! thae English churls think as muckle about a blade of wheat or grass, as a Scots laird does about his maukins and his muir-poots. Now, lass, if ye like, we'll play them a fine jink; we will awa out and take a walk— they will make unco wark when they miss us, but we can easily be back by dinner-time, or before dark night at ony rate, and it will be some frolic and fresh air.—But maybe ye wad like to take some breakfast, and then lie down again? I ken by mysell, there's whiles I can sit wi' my head on my hand the haill day, and havena a word to cast at a dog—and other whiles that I canna sit still a moment. That's when the folk think me warst, but I am aye canny eneugh—ye needna be feared to walk wi' me."

Had Madge Wildfire been the most raging lunatic, instead of possessing a doubtful, uncertain, and twilight sort of rationality, varying, probably, from the influence of the most trivial causes, Jeanie would hardly have objected to leave a place of captivity where she had so much to apprehend. She eagerly assured Madge that she had no occasion for farther sleep, no desire whatever for eating; and hoping internally that she was not guilty of sin in doing so, she flattered her keeper's crazy humour for walking in the woods.

"It's no a'thegither for that neither," said poor Madge; "but I am judging ye will wun the better out o' thae folk's hands; no that they are a'thegither bad folk neither, but they have queer ways wi' them, and I whiles dinna think it has been ever very weel wi' my mother and me since we kept siclike company."

With the haste, the joy, the fear, and the hope of a liberated captive, Jeanie snatched up her little bundle, followed Madge into the free air, and eagerly looked round her for a human habitation; but none was to be seen. The ground was partly cultivated, and partly left in its natural state, according as the fancy of the slovenly agriculturists had decided. In its natural state it was waste, in some places covered with dwarf trees and bushes, in others swamp, and elsewhere firm and dry downs or pasture grounds.

Jeanie's active mind next led her to conjecture which way the highroad lay, whence she had been forced. If she regained that public road, she imagined she must soon meet some person, or arrive at some house, where she might tell her story, and request protection. But after a glance around her, she saw with regret that she had no means whatever of directing her course with any degree of certainty, and that she was still in dependence upon her crazy companion. "Shall we not walk upon the highroad?" said she to Madge, in such a tone as a nurse uses to coax a child. "It's brawer walking on the road than amang thae wild bushes and whins."

Madge, who was walking very fast, stopped at this question, and looked at Jeanie with a sudden and scrutinising glance, that seemed to indicate complete acquaintance with her purpose. "Aha, lass!" she exclaimed, "are ye gaun to guide us that gate?—Ye'll be for making your heels save your head, I am judging."

Jeanie hesitated for a moment, on hearing her companion thus express herself, whether she had not better take the hint, and try to outstrip and get rid of her. But she knew not in which direction to fly; she was by no means sure that she would prove the swiftest, and perfectly conscious that, in the event of her being pursued and overtaken, she would be inferior to the madwoman in strength. She therefore gave up thoughts for the present of attempting to escape in that manner, and, saying a few words to allay Madge's suspicions, she followed in anxious apprehension the wayward path by which her guide thought proper to lead her. Madge, infirm of purpose, and easily reconciled to the present scene, whatever it was, began soon to talk with her usual diffuseness of ideas.

"It's a dainty thing to be in the woods on a fine morning like this—I like it far better than the town, for there isna a wheen duddie bairns to be crying after ane, as if ane were a warld's wonder, just because ane maybe is a thought bonnier and better put-on than their neighbours—though, Jeanie, ye suld never be proud o' braw claiths, or beauty neither—waes me! they're but a snare. I ance thought better o' them, and what came o't?"

"Are ye sure ye ken the way ye are taking us?" said Jeanie, who began to imagine that she was getting deeper into the woods, and more remote from the highroad.

"Do I ken the road?—Wasna I mony a day living here,

and whatfor shouldna I ken the road?—I might hae forgotten, too, for it was afore my accident; but there are some things ane can never forget, let them try it as muckle as they like."

By this time they had gained the deepest part of a patch of woodland. The trees were a little separated from each other, and at the foot of one of them, a beautiful poplar, was a variegated hillock of wild flowers and moss, such as the poet of Grasmere has described in his verses on the Thorn. So soon as she arrived at this spot, Madge Wildfire, joining her hands above her head, with a loud scream that resembled laughter, flung herself all at once upon the spot, and remained lying there motionless.

Jeanie's first idea was to take the opportunity of flight; but her desire to escape yielded for a moment to apprehension for the poor insane being, who, she thought, might perish for want of relief. With an effort, which, in her circumstances, might be termed heroic, she stooped down, spoke in a soothing tone, and endeavoured to raise up the forlorn creature. She effected this with difficulty, and, as she placed her against the tree in a sitting posture, she observed with surprise, that her complexion, usually florid, was now deadly pale, and that her face was bathed in tears. Notwithstanding her own extreme danger, Jeanie was affected by the situation of her companion; and the rather, that through the whole train of her wavering and inconsistent state of mind and line of conduct, she discerned a general colour of kindness towards herself, for which she felt grateful.

"Let me alane!—let me alane!" said the poor young woman, as her paroxysm of sorrow began to abate—"Let me alane, it does me good to weep. I canna shed tears but maybe anes or twice a year, and I aye come to wet this turf with them, that the flowers may grow fair, and the grass may be green."

"But what is the matter with you?" said Jeanie—"Why do you weep so bitterly?"

"There's matter enow," replied the lunatic,—"mair than ae puir mind can bear, I trow. Stay a bit, and I'll tell you a' about it; for I like ye, Jeanie Deans—a'body spoke weel about ye when we lived in the Pleasaunts—And I mind aye the drink o' milk ye gae me yon day, when I had been on Arthur's Seat for four-and-twenty hours, looking for the ship that somebody was sailing in."

*L 134

These words recalled to Jeanie's recollection, that, in fact, she had been one morning much frightened by meeting a crazy young woman near her father's door at an early hour, and that, as she appeared to be harmless, her apprehension had been changed into pity, and she had relieved the unhappy wanderer with some food, which she devoured with the haste of a famished person. The incident, trifling in itself, was at present of great importance, if it should be found to have made a favourable and permanent impression on the mind of the object of her charity.

"Yes," said Madge, "I'll tell ye all about it, for ye are a decent man's daughter—Douce Davie Deans, ye ken—and maybe ye'll can teach me to find out the narrow way, and the strait path; for I have been burning bricks in Egypt, and walking through the weary wilderness of Sinai, for lang and mony a day. But whenever I think about mine errors, I am like to cover my lips for shame."—Here she looked up and smiled.—"It's a strange thing now—I hae spoke mair gude words to you in ten minutes, than I wad speak to my mother in as mony years. It's no that I dinna think on them—and whiles they are just at my tongue's end; but then comes the Devil, and brushes my lips with his black wing, and lays his broad black loof on my mouth—for a black loof it is, Jeanie—and sweeps away a' my gude thoughts, and dits up my gude words, and pits a wheen fule sangs and idle vanities in their place."

"Try, Madge," said Jeanie,—"try to settle your mind and make your breast clean, and you'll find your heart easier— Just resist the devil, and he will flee from you—and mind that, as my worthy father tells me, there is nae devil sae deceitfu' as our ain wandering thoughts."

"And that's true too, lass," said Madge, starting up; "and I'll gang a gate where the devil daurna follow me; and it's a gate that you will like dearly to gang—but I'll keep a fast haud o' your arm, for fear Apollyon should stride across the path, as he did in the Pilgrim's Progress."

Accordingly she got up, and, taking Jeanie by the arm, began to walk forward at a great pace; and soon, to her companion's no small joy, came into a marked path, with the meanders of which she seemed perfectly acquainted. Jeanie endeavoured to bring her back to the confessional, but the fancy was gone by. In fact, the mind of this deranged being resembled nothing so much as a quantity of dry leaves, which may for a few minutes remain still, but are instantly discomposed and put in motion by the first casual breath of air. She had now got John Bunyan's parable into her head, to the exclusion of everything else, and on she went with great volubility.

"Did ye never read the Pilgrim's Progress? And you shall be the woman Christiana, and I will be the maiden Mercy—for ye ken Mercy was of the fairer countenance, and the more alluring than her companion—and if I had my little messan dog here, it would be Great-heart their guide, ye ken, for he was e'en as bauld, that he wad bark at onything twenty times his size; and that was e'en the death of him, for he bit Corporal MacAlpine's heels ae morning when they were hauling me to the guard-house, and Corporal MacAlpine killed the bit faithfu' thing wi' his Lochaber axe—deil pike the Highland banes o' him!"

"O fie! Madge," said Jeanie, "ye should not speak such words."

"It's very true," said Madge, shaking her head; "but then I maunna think on my puir bit doggie, Snap, when I saw it lying dying in the gutter. But it's just as weel, for it suffered baith cauld and hunger when it was living, and in the grave there is rest for a' things—rest for the doggie, and my puir bairn, and me."

"Your bairn?" said Jeanie, conceiving that by speaking on such a topic, supposing it to be a real one, she could not fail to bring her companion to a more composed temper.

She was mistaken, however, for Madge coloured, and replied with some anger, "*My* bairn? ay, to be sure, *my* bairn. Whatfor shouldna I hae a bairn, and lose a bairn too, as weel as your bonny tittie, the Lily of St. Leonard's?"

The answer struck Jeanie with some alarm, and she was anxious to soothe the irritation she had unwittingly given occasion to. "I am very sorry for your misfortune——"

"Sorry? what wad ye be sorry for?" answered Madge. "The bairn was a blessing—that is, Jeanie, it wad hae been a blessing if it hadna been for my mother; but my mother's a queer woman.—Ye see, there was an auld carle wi' a bit land, and a gude clat o' siller besides, just the very picture of old Mr. Feeblemind or Mr. Ready-to-halt, that Great-heart delivered from Slaygood the giant, when he was rifling him and about to pick his bones, for Slaygood was of the nature of the flesh-eaters—and Great-heart killed Giant Despair too

—but I am doubting Giant Despair's come alive again, for a' the story-book—I find him busy at my heart whiles."

"Weel, and so the auld carle," said Jeanie, for she was painfully interested in getting to the truth of Madge's history, which she could not but suspect was in some extraordinary way linked and entwined with the fate of her sister. She was also desirous, if possible, to engage her companion in some narrative which might be carried on in a lower tone of voice, for she was in great apprehension lest the elevated notes of Madge's conversation should direct her mother or the robbers in search of them.

"And so the auld carle," said Madge, repeating her words —"I wish you had seen him stoiting about, aff ae leg on to the other, wi' a kind o' dot-and-go-one sort o' motion, as if ilk ane o' his twa legs had belonged to sindry folk—But Gentle George could take him aff brawly—Eh, as I used to laugh to see George gang hip-hop like him!—I dinna ken, I think I laughed heartier then than what I do now, though maybe no just sae muckle."

"And who was Gentle George?" said Jeanie, endeavouring to bring her back to her story.

"Oh, he was Geordie Robertson, ye ken, when he was in Edinburgh; but that's no his right name neither—His name is——But what is your business wi' his name?" said she, as if upon sudden recollection. "What have ye to do asking for folk's names?—Have ye a mind I should scour my knife between your ribs, as my mother says?"

As this was spoken with a menacing tone and gesture, Jeanie hastened to protest her total innocence of purpose in the accidental question which she had asked, and Madge Wildfire went on somewhat pacified.

"Never ask folk's names, Jeanie—it's no civil—I hae seen half-a-dozen o' folk in my mother's at anes, and ne'er ane o' them ca'd the ither by his name; and Daddie Ratton says, it is the most uncivil thing may be, because the bailie bodies are aye asking fashious questions, when ye saw sic a man, or sic a man; and if ye dinna ken their names, ye ken there can be nae mair speer'd about it."

In what strange school, thought Jeanie to herself, has this poor creature been bred up, where such remote precautions are taken against the pursuits of justice? What would my father or Reuben Butler think, if I were to tell them there are sic folk in the world? And to abuse the simplicity of this demented creature! Oh, that I were but safe at hame amang mine ain leal and true people! and I'll bless God, while I have breath, that placed me amongst those who live in His fear, and under the shadow of His wing.

She was interrupted by the insane laugh of Madge Wildfire, as she saw a magpie hop across the path.

"See there!—that was the gait my old joe used to cross the country, but no just sae lightly—he hadna wings to help his auld legs, I trow; but I behoved to have married him for a' that, Jeanie, or my mother would have been the dead o' me. But then came in the story of my poor bairn, and my mother thought he wad be deaved wi' its skirling, and she pat it away in below the bit bourock of turf yonder, just to be out o' the gate; and I think she buried my best wits with it, for I have never been just mysell since. And only think, Jeanie, after my mother had been at a' this pains, the auld doited body Johnny Drottle turned up his nose, and wadna hae aught to say to me! But it's little I care for him, for I have led a merry life ever since, and ne'er a braw gentleman looks at me but ye wad think he was gaun to drop off his horse for mere love of me. I have kend some o' them put their hand in their pocket, and gie me as muckle as sixpence at a time, just for my weel-faured face."

This speech gave Jeanie a dark insight into Madge's history. She had been courted by a wealthy suitor, whose addresses her mother had favoured, notwithstanding the objection of old age and deformity. She had been seduced by some profligate, and, to conceal her shame and promote the advantageous match she had planned, her mother had not hesitated to destroy the offspring of their intrigue. That the consequence should be the total derangement of a mind which was constitutionally unsettled by giddiness and vanity, was extremely natural; and such was, in fact, the history of Madge Wildfire's insanity.

CHAPTER XXXI

So free from danger, free from fear,
They cross'd the court—right glad they were
Christabel.

PURSUING the path which Madge had chosen, Jeanie Deans observed, to her no small delight, that marks of more cultivation appeared, and the thatched roofs of houses, with their blue smoke arising in little columns, were seen embosomed in a tuft of trees at some distance. The track led in that direction, and Jeanie therefore resolved, while Madge continued to pursue it, that she would ask her no questions; having had the penetration to observe, that by doing so she ran the risk of irritating her guide, or awakening suspicions, to the impressions of which, persons in Madge's unsettled state of mind are particularly liable.

Madge, therefore, uninterrupted, went on with the wild disjointed chat which her rambling imagination suggested; a mood in which she was much more communicative respecting her own history, and that of others, than when there was any attempt made, by direct queries, or cross-examinations, to extract information on these subjects.

"It's a queer thing," she said, "but whiles I can speak about the bit bairn and the rest of it, just as if it had been another body's, and no my ain; and whiles I am like to break my heart about it—Had you ever a bairn, Jeanie?"

Jeanie replied in the negative.

"Ay; but your sister had, though—and I ken what came o't too."

"In the name of heavenly mercy," said Jeanie, forgetting the line of conduct which she had hitherto adopted, "tell me but what became of that unfortunate babe, and——"

Madge stopped, looked at her gravely and fixedly, and then broke into a great fit of laughing—"Aha, lass,—catch me if you can—I think it's easy to gar you trow onything.—How suld I ken onything o' your sister's wean? Lasses suld hae naething to do wi' weans till they are married—and then a' the gossips and cummers come in and feast as if it were the blithest day in the warld.—They say maidens' bairns are well guided. I wot that wasna true of your tittie's and mine; but these are sad tales to tell—I maun just sing a bit to keep up my heart —It's a sang that gentle George made on me lang syne, when I went with him to Lockington wake, to see him act upon a stage, in fine clothes, with the player folk. He might have dune waur than married me that night as he promised—better wed over the mixen as over the moor,[1] as they say in Yorkshire—he may gang farther and fare waur—but that's a' ane to the sang,—

---

[1] A homely proverb, signifying, better wed a neighbour than one fetched from a distance.

" 'I'm Madge of the country, I'm Madge of the town,
And I'm Madge of the lad I am blithest to own—
The Lady of Beever in diamonds may shine,
But has not a heart half so lightsome as mine.

' I am Queen of the Wake, and I'm Lady of May,
And I lead the blithe ring round the May-pole to-day;
The wild-fire that flashes so fair and so free,
Was never so bright, or so bonny as me.'

"I like that the best o' a' my sangs," continued the maniac,
"because *he* made it. I am often singing it, and that's maybe
the reason folk ca' me Madge Wildfire. I aye answer to the
name, though it's no my ain, for what's the use o' making a
fash?"

"But ye shouldna sing upon the Sabbath at least," said
Jeanie, who, amid all her distress and anxiety, could not help
being scandalised at the deportment of her companion,
especially as they now approached near to the little village.

"Ay! is this Sunday?" said Madge. "My mother leads
sic a life, wi' turning night into day, that ane loses a' count o'
the days o' the week, and disna ken Sunday frae Saturday.
Besides, it's a' your whiggery—in England, folk sing when
they like—And then, ye ken, you are Christiana, and I am
Mercy—and ye ken, as they went on their way, they sang."—
And she immediately raised one of John Bunyan's ditties :—

" He that is down need fear no fall,
    He that is low no pride;
He that is humble ever shall
    Have God to be his guide.

Fulness to such a burthen is
    That go on pilgrimage;
Here little, and hereafter bliss,
    Is best from age to age.

"And do ye ken, Jeanie, I think there's much truth in that
book, the Pilgrim's Progress. The boy that sings that song
was feeding his father's sheep in the Valley of Humiliation,
and Mr. Great-heart says, that he lived a merrier life, and had
more of the herb called heart's-ease in his bosom, than they
that wear silk and velvet like me, and are as bonny as I am."

Jeanie Deans had never read the fanciful and delightful
parable to which Madge alluded. Bunyan was, indeed, a
rigid Calvinist, but then he was also a member of a Baptist
congregation, so that his works had no place on David Deans's
shelf of divinity. Madge, however, at some time of her life,
had been well acquainted, as it appeared, with the most

popular of his performances, which, indeed, rarely fails to make a deep impression upon children, and people of the lower rank.

"I am sure," she continued, "I may weel say I am come out of the city of Destruction, for my mother is Mrs. Bat's-eyes, that dwells at Deadman's Corner; and Frank Levitt, and Tyburn Tam, they may be likened to Mistrust and Guilt, that came galloping up, and struck the poor pilgrim to the ground with a great club, and stole a bag of silver, which was most of his spending money, and so have they done to many, and will do to more. But now we will gang to the Interpreter's house, for I ken a man that will play the Interpreter right weel; for he has eyes lifted up to heaven, the best of books in his hand, the law of truth written on his lips, and he stands as if he pleaded wi' men—Oh, if I had minded what he had said to me, I had never been the castaway creature that I am!—But it is all over now.—But we'll knock at the gate, and then the keeper will admit Christiana, but Mercy will be left out—and then I'll stand at the door trembling and crying, and then Christiana — that's you, Jeanie—will intercede for me; and then Mercy—that's me, ye ken—will faint; and then the Interpreter—yes, the Interpreter, that's Mr. Staunton himself, will come out and take me—that's poor, lost, demented me— by the hand, and give me a pomegranate, and a piece of honeycomb, and a small bottle of spirits, to stay my fainting— and then the good times will come back again, and we'll be the happiest folk you ever saw."

In the midst of the confused assemblage of ideas indicated in this speech, Jeanie thought she saw a serious purpose on the part of Madge, to endeavour to obtain the pardon and countenance of some one whom she had offended; an attempt the most likely of all others to bring them once more into contact with law and legal protection. She, therefore, resolved to be guided by her while she was in so hopeful a disposition, and act for her own safety according to circumstances.

They were now close by the village, one of those beautiful scenes which are so often found in merry England, where the cottages, instead of being built in two direct lines on each side of a dusty highroad, stand in detached groups, interspersed not only with large oaks and elms, but with fruit-trees, so many of which were at this time in flourish, that the grove seemed enamelled with their crimson and white blossoms. In the centre of the hamlet stood the parish church and its little

Gothic tower, from which at present was heard the Sunday chime of bells.

"We will wait here until the folk are a' in the church—they ca' the kirk a church in England, Jeanie, be sure you mind that—for if I was gaun forward amang them, a' the gaitts o' boys and lasses wad be crying at Madge Wildfire's tail, the little hellrakers! and the beadle would be as hard upon us as if it was our fault. I like their skirling as ill as he does, I can tell him ; I'm sure I often wish there was a het peat doun their throats when they set them up that gate."

Conscious of the disorderly appearance of her own dress after the adventure of the preceding night, and of the grotesque habit and demeanour of her guide, and sensible how important it was to secure an attentive and patient audience to her strange story from some one who might have the means to protect her, Jeanie readily acquiesced in Madge's proposal to rest under the trees, by which they were still somewhat screened, until the commencement of service should give them an opportunity of entering the hamlet without attracting a crowd around them. She made the less opposition, that Madge had intimated that this was not the village where her mother was in custody, and that the two squires of the pad were absent in a different direction.

She sate herself down, therefore, at the foot of an oak, and by the assistance of a placid fountain which had been dammed up for the use of the villagers, and which served her as a natural mirror, she began—no uncommon thing with a Scottish maiden of her rank—to arrange her toilette in the open air, and bring her dress, soiled and disordered as it was, into such order as the place and circumstances admitted.

She soon perceived reason, however, to regret that she had set about this task, however decent and necessary, in the present time and society. Madge Wildfire, who, among other indications of insanity, had a most overweening opinion of those charms, to which, in fact, she had owed her misery, and whose mind, like a raft upon a lake, was agitated and driven about at random by each fresh impulse, no sooner beheld Jeanie begin to arrange her hair, place her bonnet in order, rub the dust from her shoes and clothes, adjust her neck-handkerchief and mittens, and so forth, than with imitative zeal she began to bedizen and trick herself out with shreds and remnants of beggarly finery, which she took out of a little bundle, and which, when disposed around her person, made her appearance ten times more fantastic and apish than it had been before.

Jeanie groaned in spirit, but dared not interfere in a matter so delicate. Across the man's cap or riding hat which she wore, Madge placed a broken and soiled white feather, intersected with one which had been shed from the train of a peacock. To her dress, which was a kind of riding-habit, she stitched, pinned, and otherwise secured, a large furbelow of artificial flowers, all crushed, wrinkled, and dirty, which had first bedecked a lady of quality, then descended to her Abigail, and dazzled the inmates of the servants'-hall. A tawdry scarf of yellow silk, trimmed with tinsel and spangles, which had seen as hard service, and boasted as honourable a transmission, was next flung over one shoulder, and fell across her person in the manner of a shoulder-belt, or baldrick. Madge then stripped off the coarse ordinary shoes which she wore, and replaced them by a pair of dirty satin ones, spangled and embroidered to match the scarf, and furnished with very high heels. She had cut a willow switch in her morning's walk, almost as long as a boy's fishing-rod. This she set herself seriously to peel, and when it was transformed into such a wand as the Treasurer or High Steward bears on public occasions, she told Jeanie that she thought they now looked decent, as young women should do upon the Sunday morning, and that as the bells had done ringing, she was willing to conduct her to the Interpreter's house.

Jeanie sighed heavily, to think it should be her lot on the Lord's day, and during kirk-time too, to parade the street of an inhabited village with so very grotesque a comrade; but necessity had no law, since, without a positive quarrel with the madwoman, which, in the circumstances, would have been very unadvisable, she could see no means of shaking herself free of her society.

As for poor Madge, she was completely elated with personal vanity, and the most perfect satisfaction concerning her own dazzling dress, and superior appearance. They entered the hamlet without being observed, except by one old woman, who, being nearly "high-gravel blind," was only conscious that something very fine and glittering was passing by, and dropped as deep a reverence to Madge as she would have done to a Countess. This filled up the measure of Madge's self-approbation. She minced, she ambled, she smiled, she simpered, and waved Jeanie Deans forward with the condescension of a noble *chaperone*, who has undertaken the charge of a country miss on her first journey to the capital.

Jeanie followed in patience, and with her eyes fixed on the ground, that she might save herself the mortification of seeing her companion's absurdities; but she started when, ascending two or three steps, she found herself in the churchyard, and saw that Madge was making straight for the door of the church. As Jeanie had no mind to enter the congregation in such company, she walked aside from the pathway, and said in a decided tone, "Madge, I will wait here till the church comes out—you may go in by yourself if you have a mind."

As she spoke these words, she was about to seat herself upon one of the gravestones.

Madge was a little before Jeanie when she turned aside; but suddenly changing her course, she followed her with long strides, and, with every feature inflamed with passion, over-took and seized her by the arm. "Do ye think, ye ungratefu' wretch, that I am gaun to let you sit doun upon my father's grave? The deil settle ye doun;—if ye dinna rise and come into the Interpreter's house, that's the house of God, wi' me, but I'll rive every dud aff your back!"

She adapted the action to the phrase; for with one clutch she stripped Jeanie of her straw bonnet and a handful of her hair to boot, and threw it up into an old yew tree, where it stuck fast. Jeanie's first impulse was to scream, but con-ceiving she might receive deadly harm before she could obtain the assistance of any one, notwithstanding the vicinity of the church, she thought it wiser to follow the madwoman into the congregation, where she might find some means of escape from her, or at least be secured against her violence. But when she meekly intimated her consent to follow Madge, her guide's uncertain brain had caught another train of ideas. She held Jeanie fast with one hand, and with the other pointed to the inscription on the gravestone, and commanded her to read it. Jeanie obeyed, and read these words :—

"THIS MONUMENT WAS ERECTED TO THE MEMORY OF DONALD MURDOCKSON OF THE KING'S XXVI., OR CAMERONIAN REGIMENT, A SINCERE CHRISTIAN, A BRAVE SOLDIER, AND A FAITHFUL SERVANT, BY HIS GRATEFUL AND SORROWING MASTER, ROBERT STAUNTON."

"It's very weel read, Jeanie; it's just the very words," said

Madge, whose ire had now faded into deep melancholy, and with a step, which, to Jeanie's great joy, was uncommonly quiet and mournful, she led her companion towards the door of the church.

It was one of those old-fashioned Gothic parish churches which are frequent in England, the most cleanly, decent, and reverential places of worship that are, perhaps, anywhere to be found in the Christian world. Yet, notwithstanding the decent solemnity of its exterior, Jeanie was too faithful to the directory of the Presbyterian kirk to have entered a prelatic place of worship, and would, upon any other occasion, have thought that she beheld in the porch the venerable figure of her father waving her back from the entrance, and pronouncing in a solemn tone, "Cease, my child, to hear the instruction which causeth to err from the words of knowledge." But in her present agitating and alarming situation, she looked for safety to this forbidden place of assembly, as the hunted animal will sometimes seek shelter from imminent danger in the human habitation, or in other places of refuge most alien to its nature and habits. Not even the sound of the organ, and of one or two flutes which accompanied the psalmody, prevented her from following her guide into the chancel of the church.

No sooner had Madge put her foot upon the pavement, and become sensible that she was the object of attention to the spectators, than she resumed all the fantastic extravagance of deportment which some transient touch of melancholy had banished for an instant. She swam rather than walked up the centre aisle, dragging Jeanie after her, whom she held fast by the hand. She would, indeed, have fain slipped aside into the pew nearest to the door, and left Madge to ascend in her own manner and alone to the high places of the synagogue; but this was impossible, without a degree of violent resistance, which seemed to her inconsistent with the time and place, and she was accordingly led in captivity up the whole length of the church by her grotesque conductress, who, with half-shut eyes, a prim smile upon her lips, and a mincing motion with her hands, which corresponded with the delicate and affected pace at which she was pleased to move, seemed to take the general stare of the congregation, which such an exhibition necessarily excited, as a high compliment, and which she returned by nods and half-courtesies to individuals amongst the audience, whom she seemed to distinguish as acquaintances.

Her absurdity was enhanced in the eyes of the spectators by the strange contrast which she formed to her companion, who, with dishevelled hair, downcast eyes, and a face glowing with shame, was dragged, as it were, in triumph after her.

Madge's airs were at length fortunately cut short by her encountering in her progress the looks of the clergyman, who fixed upon her a glance, at once steady, compassionate, and admonitory. She hastily opened an empty pew which happened to be near her, and entered, dragging in Jeanie after her. Kicking Jeanie on the shins, by way of hint that she should follow her example, she sunk her head upon her hand for the space of a minute. Jeanie, to whom this posture of mental devotion was entirely new, did not attempt to do the like, but looked round her with a bewildered stare, which her neighbours, judging from the company in which they saw her, very naturally ascribed to insanity. Every person in their immediate vicinity drew back from this extraordinary couple as far as the limits of their pew permitted; but one old man could not get beyond Madge's reach, ere she had snatched the prayer-book from his hand, and ascertained the lesson of the day. She then turned up the ritual, and, with the most overstrained enthusiasm of gesture and manner, showed Jeanie the passages as they were read in the service, making, at the same time, her own responses so loud as to be heard above those of every other person.

Notwithstanding the shame and vexation which Jeanie felt in being thus exposed in a place of worship, she could not and durst not omit rallying her spirits so as to look around her, and consider to whom she ought to appeal for protection so soon as the service should be concluded. Her first ideas naturally fixed upon the clergyman, and she was confirmed in the resolution by observing that he was an aged gentleman, of a dignified appearance and deportment, who read the service with an undisturbed and decent gravity, which brought back to becoming attention those younger members of the congregation who had been disturbed by the extravagant behaviour of Madge Wildfire. To the clergyman, therefore, Jeanie resolved to make her appeal when the service was over.

It is true she felt disposed to be shocked at his surplice, of which she had heard so much, but which she had never seen upon the person of a preacher of the word. Then she was confused by the change of posture adopted in different parts of the ritual, the more so as Madge Wildfire, to whom they seemed familiar, took the opportunity to exercise authority over her, pulling her up and pushing her down with a bustling assiduity, which Jeanie felt must make them both the objects of painful attention. But notwithstanding these prejudices, it was her prudent resolution, in this dilemma, to imitate as nearly as she could what was done around her. The prophet, she thought, permitted Naaman the Syrian to bow even in the house of Rimmon. Surely if I, in this strait, worship the God of my fathers in mine own language, although the manner thereof be strange to me, the Lord will pardon me in this thing.

In this resolution she became so much confirmed, that, withdrawing herself from Madge as far as the pew permitted, she endeavoured to evince, by serious and undeviating attention to what was passing, that her mind was composed to devotion. Her tormentor would not long have permitted her to remain quiet, but fatigue overpowered her, and she fell fast asleep in the other corner of the pew.

Jeanie, though her mind in her own despite sometimes reverted to her situation, compelled herself to give attention to a sensible, energetic, and well-composed discourse, upon the practical doctrines of Christianity, which she could not help approving, although it was every word written down and read by the preacher, and although it was delivered in a tone and gesture very different from those of Boanerges Storm-heaven, who was her father's favourite preacher. The serious and placid attention with which Jeanie listened, did not escape the clergyman. Madge Wildfire's entrance had rendered him apprehensive of some disturbance, to provide against which, as far as possible, he often turned his eyes to the part of the church where Jeanie and she were placed, and became soon aware that, although the loss of her head-gear, and the awkwardness of her situation, had given an uncommon and anxious air to the features of the former, yet she was in a state of mind very different from that of her companion. When he dismissed the congregation, he observed her look around with a wild and terrified look, as if uncertain what course she ought to adopt, and noticed that she approached one or two of the most decent of the congregation, as if to address them, and then shrunk back timidly, on observing that they seemed to shun and to avoid her. The clergyman was satisfied there must be something extraordinary in all this, and as a benevolent man, as well as a good Christian pastor, he resolved to inquire into the matter more minutely.

CHAPTER XXXII

—————There govern'd in that year
A stern, stout churl—an angry overseer.
                                        CRABBE.

WHILE Mr. Staunton, for such was this worthy clergyman's name, was laying aside his gown in the vestry, Jeanie was in the act of coming to an open rupture with Madge.

"We must return to Mummer's barn directly," said Madge; "we'll be ower late, and my mother will be angry."

"I am not going back with you, Madge," said Jeanie, taking out a guinea, and offering it to her; "I am much obliged to you, but I maun gang my ain road."

"And me coming a' this way out o' my gate to pleasure you, ye ungratefu' cutty," answered Madge; "and me to be brained by my mother when I gang hame, and a' for your sake!—But I will gar ye as good——"

"For God's sake," said Jeanie to a man who stood beside them, "keep her off!—she is mad."

"Ey, ey," answered the boor; "I hae some guess of that, and I trow thou be'st a bird of the same feather.—Howsomever, Madge, I redd thee keep hand off her, or I'se lend thee a whisterpoop."

Several of the lower class of the parishioners now gathered round the strangers, and the cry arose among the boys, that "there was a-going to be a fite between mad Madge Murdockson and another Bess of Bedlam." But while the fry assembled with the humane hope of seeing as much of the fun as possible, the laced cocked-hat of the beadle was discerned among the multitude, and all made way for that person of awful authority. His first address was to Madge.

"What's brought thee back again, thou silly donnot, to plague this parish? Has thou brought ony more bastards wi' thee to lay to honest men's doors? or does thou think to burden us with this goose that's as gare-brained as thysell, as if rates were no up enow? Away wi' thee to thy thief of a mother; she's fast in the stocks at Barkston town-end—Away wi' ye out o' the parish, or I'se be at ye with the ratan."

Madge stood sulky for a minute; but she had been too often taught submission to the beadle's authority by ungentle means, to feel courage enough to dispute it.

"And my mother—my puir auld mother, is in the stocks at Barkston!—This is a' your wyte, Miss Jeanie Deans; but I'll be upsides wi' you, as sure as my name's Madge Wildfire— I mean Murdockson—God help me, I forget my very name in this confused waste!"

So saying, she turned upon her heel, and went off, followed by all the mischievous imps of the village, some crying, "Madge, canst thou tell thy name yet?" some pulling the skirts of her dress, and all, to the best of their strength and ingenuity, exercising some new device or other to exasperate her into frenzy.

Jeanie saw her departure with infinite delight, though she wished, that, in some way or other, she could have requited the service Madge had conferred upon her.

In the meantime, she applied to the beadle to know, whether "there was any house in the village, where she could be civilly entertained for her money, and whether she could be permitted to speak to the clergyman?"

"Ay, ay, we'se ha' reverend care on thee; and I think," answered the man of constituted authority, "that, unless thou answer the Rector all the better, we'se spare thy money and gie thee lodging at the parish charge, young woman."

"Where am I to go then?" said Jeanie, in some alarm.

"Why, I am to take thee to his Reverence, in the first place, to gie an account o' thysell, and to see thou comena to be a burden upon the parish."

"I do not wish to burden any one," replied Jeanie; "I have enough for my own wants, and only wish to get on my journey safely."

"Why, that's another matter," replied the beadle, "and if it be true—and I think thou dost not look so polrumptious as thy playfellow yonder;—thou wouldst be a mettle lass enow, an thou wert snog and snod a bit better. Come thou away, then—the Rector is a good man."

"Is that the minister," said Jeanie, "who preached——"

"The minister? Lord help thee! What kind o' Presbyterian art thou?—Why, 'tis the Rector—the Rector's sell, woman, and there isna the like o' him in the county, nor the four next to it. Come away—away with thee—we munna bide here."

"I am sure I am very willing to go to see the minister," said Jeanie; "for, though he read his discourse, and wore that surplice, as they call it here, I cannot but think he must be a very worthy God-fearing man, to preach the root of the matter in the way he did."

The disappointed rabble, finding that there was like to be no farther sport, had by this time dispersed, and Jeanie, with her usual patience, followed her consequential and surly, but not brutal, conductor towards the rectory.

This clerical mansion was large and commodious, for the living was an excellent one, and the advowson belonged to a very wealthy family in the neighbourhood, who had usually bred up a son or nephew to the church, for the sake of inducting him, as opportunity offered, into this very comfortable provision. In this manner the rectory of Willingham had always been considered as a direct and immediate appanage of Willingham Hall; and as the rich baronets to whom the latter belonged had usually a son, or brother, or nephew, settled in the living, the utmost care had been taken to render their habitation not merely respectable and commodious, but even dignified and imposing.

It was situated about four hundred yards from the village, and on a rising ground which sloped gently upward, covered with small enclosures, or closes, laid out irregularly, so that the old oaks and elms, which were planted in hedge-rows, fell into perspective, and were blended together in beautiful irregularity. When they approached nearer to the house, a handsome gate-way admitted them into a lawn, of narrow dimensions, indeed, but which was interspersed with large sweet-chestnut trees and beeches, and kept in handsome order. The front of the house was irregular. Part of it seemed very old, and had, in fact, been the residence of the incumbent in Romish times. Successive occupants had made considerable additions and improvements, each in the taste of his own age, and without much regard to symmetry. But these incongruities of architecture were so graduated and happily mingled, that the eye, far from being displeased with the combinations of various styles, saw nothing but what was interesting in the varied and intricate pile which they exhibited. Fruit-trees displayed on the southern wall, outer staircases, various places of entrance, a combination of roofs and chimneys of different ages, united to render the front, not indeed beautiful or grand, but intricate, perplexed, or, to use Mr. Price's appropriate phrase, picturesque. The most considerable addition was that of the present Rector, who, "being a bookish man," as the beadle was at the pains to inform Jeanie, to augment, perhaps, her reverence for the person before whom she was to appear, had built a handsome library and parlour, and no less than two additional bedrooms.

"Mony men would hae scrupled such expense," continued the parochial officer, "seeing as the living mun go as it pleases Sir Edmund to will it; but his Reverence has a canny bit land of his own, and need not look on two sides of a penny."

Jeanie could not help comparing the irregular yet extensive and commodious pile of building before her, to the "Manses" in her own country, where a set of penurious heritors, professing all the while the devotion of their lives and fortunes to the Presbyterian establishment, strain their inventions to discover what may be nipped, and clipped, and pared from a building which forms but a poor accommodation even for the present incumbent, and, despite the superior advantage of stone-masonry, must, in the course of forty or fifty years, again burden their descendants with an expense, which, once liberally and handsomely employed, ought to have freed their estates from a recurrence of it for more than a century at least.

Behind the Rector's house the ground sloped down to a small river, which, without possessing the romantic vivacity and rapidity of a northern stream, was, nevertheless, by its occasional appearance through the ranges of willows and poplars that crowned its banks, a very pleasing accompaniment to the landscape. "It was the best trouting stream," said the beadle, whom the patience of Jeanie, and especially the assurance that she was not about to become a burden to the parish, had rendered rather communicative, "the best trouting stream in all Lincolnshire; for when you get lower, there was nought to be done wi' fly-fishing."

Turning aside from the principal entrance, he conducted Jeanie towards a sort of portal connected with the older part of the building, which was chiefly occupied by servants, and knocking at the door, it was opened by a servant in grave purple livery, such as befitted a wealthy and dignified clergyman.

"How dost do, Tummas?" said the beadle—"and how's young Measter Staunton?"

"Why, but poorly—but poorly, Measter Stubbs.—Are you wanting to see his Reverence?"

"Ay, ay, Tummas; please to say I ha' brought up the young woman as came to service to-day with mad Madge Murdockson—she seems to be a decentish koind o' body; but I ha' asked her never a question. Only I can tell his Reverence that she is a Scotchwoman, I judge, and as flat as the fens of Holland."

Tummas honoured Jeanie Deans with such a stare, as the pampered domestics of the rich, whether spiritual or temporal, usually esteem it part of their privilege to bestow upon the poor, and then desired Mr. Stu s and his charge to step in till he informed his master of their presence.

The room into which he showed them was a sort of steward's parlour, hung with a county map or two, and three or four prints of eminent persons connected with the county, as Sir William Monson, James York the blacksmith of Lincoln, and the famous Peregrine, Lord Willoughby, in complete armour, looking as when he said, in the words of the legend below the engraving,—

> " Stand to it, noble pikemen,
>   And face ye well about :
> And shoot ye sharp, bold bowman,
>   And we will keep them out.
> Ye musquet and calliver-men,
>   Do you prove true to me,
> I'll be the foremost man in fight,
>   Said brave Lord Willoughbee."

When they had entered this apartment, Tummas as a matter of course offered, and as a matter of course Mr. Stubbs accepted, a " summat " to eat and drink, being the respectable relics of a gammon of bacon, and a *whole whiskin*, or black pot of sufficient double ale. To these eatables Mr. Beadle seriously inclined himself, and (for we must do him justice), not without an invitation to Jeanie, in which Tummas joined, that his prisoner or charge would follow his good example. But although she might have stood in need of refreshment, considering she had tasted no food that day, the anxiety of the moment, her own sparing and abstemious habits, and a bashful aversion to eat in company of the two strangers, induced her to decline their courtesy. So she sate in her chair apart, while Mr. Stubbs and Mr. Tummas, who had chosen to join his friend in consideration that dinner was to be put back till the afternoon service was over, made a hearty luncheon, which lasted for half-an-hour, and might not then have concluded, had not his Reverence rung his bell, so that Tummas was obliged to attend his master. Then, and no sooner, to save himself the labour of a second journey to the other end of the house, he announced to his master the arrival of Mr. Stubbs, with the other madwoman, as he chose to designate Jeanie, as an event which had just taken place. He returned with an order that Mr. Stubbs and the young woman should be instantly ushered up to the library.

The beadle bolted in haste his last mouthful of fat bacon, washed down the greasy morsel with the last rinsings of the pot of ale, and immediately marshalled Jeanie through one or two intricate passages which led from the ancient to the more modern buildings, into a handsome little hall, or anteroom, adjoining to the library, and out of which a glass door opened to the lawn.

"Stay here," said Stubbs, "till I tell his Reverence you are come."

So saying, he opened a door and entered the library.

Without wishing to hear their conversation, Jeanie, as she was circumstanced, could not avoid it; for as Stubbs stood by the door, and his Reverence was at the upper end of a large room, their conversation was necessarily audible in the anteroom.

"So you have brought the young woman here at last, Mr. Stubbs. I expected you some time since. You know I do not wish such persons to remain in custody a moment without some inquiry into their situation."

"Very true, your Reverence," replied the beadle; "but the young woman had eat nought to-day, and soa Measter Tummas did set down a drap of drink and a morsel, to be sure."

"Thomas was very right, Mr. Stubbs; and what has become of the other most unfortunate being?"

"Why," replied Mr. Stubbs, "I did think the sight of her would but vex your Reverence, and soa I did let her go her ways back to her mother, who is in trouble in the next parish."

"In trouble!—that signifies in prison, I suppose?" said Mr. Staunton.

"Ay, truly; something like it, an it like your Reverence."

"Wretched, unhappy, incorrigible woman!" said the clergyman. "And what sort of person is this companion of hers?"

"Why, decent enow, an it like your Reverence," said Stubbs; "for aught I sees of her, there's no harm of her, and she says she has cash enow to carry her out of the county."

"Cash? that is always what you think of, Stubbs.—But, has she sense?—has she her wits?—has she the capacity of taking care of herself?"

"Why, your Reverence," replied Stubbs, "I cannot just say—I will be sworn she was not born at Witt-ham;[1] for Gaffer Gibbs looked at her all the time of service, and he says she could not turn up a single lesson like a Christian, even though she had Madge Murdockson to help her—but then, as to fending for herself, why, she's a bit of a Scotchwoman, your Reverence, and they say the worst donnot of them can look out for their own turn—and she is decently put on enow, and not bechounched like t'other."

"Send her in here, then, and do you remain below, Mr. Stubbs."

This colloquy had engaged Jeanie's attention so deeply, that it was not until it was over that she observed that the sashed door, which, we have said, led from the anteroom into the garden, was opened, and that there entered, or rather was borne in by two assistants, a young man, of a very pale and sickly appearance, whom they lifted to the nearest couch, and placed there, as if to recover from the fatigue of an unusual exertion. Just as they were making this arrangement, Stubbs came out of the library, and summoned Jeanie to enter it. She obeyed him, but not without tremor; for, besides the novelty of the situation to a girl of her secluded habits, she felt also as if the successful prosecution of her journey was to depend upon the impression she should be able to make on Mr. Staunton.

It is true, it was difficult to suppose on what pretext a person travelling on her own business, and at her own charge, could be interrupted upon her route. But the violent detention she had already undergone, was sufficient to show that there existed persons at no great distance, who had the interest, the inclination, and the audacity, forcibly to stop her journey, and she felt the necessity of having some countenance and protection, at least till she should get beyond their reach. While these things passed through her mind, much faster than our pen and ink can record, or even the reader's eye collect the meaning of its traces, Jeanie found herself in a handsome library, and in

---

[1] A proverbial and punning expression in that county, to intimate that a person is not very clever.

the presence of the Rector of Willingham. The well-furnished presses and shelves which surrounded the large and handsome apartment, contained more books than Jeanie imagined existed in the world, being accustomed to consider as an extensive collection two fir shelves, each about three feet long, which contained her father's treasured volumes, the whole pith and marrow, as he used sometimes to boast, of modern divinity. An orrery, globes, a telescope, and some other scientific implements, conveyed to Jeanie an impression of admiration and wonder not unmixed with fear; for, in her ignorant apprehension, they seemed rather adapted for magical purposes than any other; and a few stuffed animals (as the Rector was fond of natural history) added to the impressive character of the apartment.

Mr. Staunton spoke to her with great mildness. He observed that, although her appearance at church had been uncommon, and in strange, and, he must add, discreditable society, and calculated, upon the whole, to disturb the congregation during divine worship, he wished, nevertheless, to hear her own account of herself before taking any steps which his duty might seem to demand. He was a justice of peace, he informed her, as well as a clergyman.

"His honour" (for she would not say his reverence) "was very civil and kind," was all that poor Jeanie could at first bring out.

"Who are you, young woman?" said the clergyman, more peremptorily—"and what do you do in this country, and in such company?—We allow no strollers or vagrants here."

"I am not a vagrant or a stroller, sir," said Jeanie, a little roused by the supposition. "I am a decent Scotch lass, travelling through the land on my own business and my own expenses; and I was so unhappy as to fall in with bad company, and was stopped a' night on my journey. And this puir creature, who is something light-headed, let me out in the morning."

"Bad company," said the clergyman. "I am afraid, young woman, you have not been sufficiently anxious to avoid them."

"Indeed, sir," returned Jeanie, "I have been brought up to shun evil communication. But these wicked people were thieves, and stopped me by violence and mastery."

"Thieves!" said Mr. Staunton; "then you charge them with robbery, I suppose?"

"No, sir; they did not take so much as a boddle from me," answered Jeanie; "nor did they use me ill, otherwise than by confining me."

The clergyman inquired into the particulars of her adventure, which she told him from point to point.

"This is an extraordinary, and not a very probable tale, young woman," resumed Mr. Staunton. "Here has been, according to your account, a great violence committed without any adequate motive. Are you aware of the law of this country—that if you lodge this charge you will be bound over to prosecute this gang?"

Jeanie did not understand him, and he explained that the English law, in addition to the inconvenience sustained by persons who have been robbed or injured, has the goodness to entrust to them the care and the expense of appearing as prosecutors.

Jeanie said, "that her business at London was express; all she wanted was, that any gentleman would, out of Christian charity, protect her to some town where she could hire horses and a guide; and, finally," she thought, "it would be her father's mind that she was not free to give testimony in an English court of justice, as the land was not under a direct gospel dispensation."

Mr. Staunton stared a little, and asked if her father was a Quaker.

"God forbid, sir," said Jeanie—"He is nae schismatic nor sectary, nor ever treated for sic black commodities as theirs, and that's weel kend o' him."

"And what is his name, pray?" said Mr. Staunton.

"David Deans, sir, the cowfeeder at Saint Leonard's Crags, near Edinburgh."

A deep groan from the anteroom prevented the Rector from replying, and, exclaiming, "Good God! that unhappy boy!" he left Jeanie alone, and hastened into the outer apartment.

Some noise and bustle was heard, but no one entered the library for the best part of an hour.

CHAPTER XXXIII

Fantastic passions' maddening brawl!
And shame and terror over all!
Deeds to be hid which were not hid,
Which, all confused, I could not know
Whether I suffer'd or I did,
For all seem'd guilt, remorse, or woe ;
My own, or others, still the same
Life-stifling fear, soul-stifling shame.
                              COLERIDGE.

DURING the interval while she was thus left alone, Jeanie anxiously revolved in her mind what course was best for her to pursue. She was impatient to continue her journey, yet she feared she could not safely adventure to do so while the old hag and her assistants were in the neighbourhood, without risking a repetition of their violence. She thought she could collect from the conversation which she had partly over-heard, and also from the wild confessions of Madge Wildfire, that her mother had a deep and revengeful motive for ob-structing her journey if possible. And from whom could she hope for assistance if not from Mr. Staunton ? His whole appearance and demeanour seemed to encourage her hopes. His features were handsome, though marked with a deep cast of melancholy ; his tone and language were gentle and en-couraging ; and, as he had served in the army for several years during his youth, his air retained that easy frankness which is peculiar to the profession of arms. He was, besides, a minister of the gospel ; and although a worshipper, according to Jeanie's notions, in the court of the Gentiles, and so be-nighted as to wear a surplice ; although he read the Common Prayer, and wrote down every word of his sermon before delivering it ; and although he was, moreover, in strength of lungs, as well as pith and marrow of doctrine, vastly inferior to Boanerges Stormheaven, Jeanie still thought he must be a very different person from Curate Kiltstoup, and other pre-latical divines of her father's earlier days, who used to get drunk in their canonical dress, and hound out the dragoons against the wandering Cameronians. The house seemed to be in some disturbance, but as she could not suppose she was altogether forgotten, she thought it better to remain quiet in the apartment where she had been left, till some one should take notice of her.

The first who entered was, to her no small delight, one of

her own sex, a motherly-looking aged person of a housekeeper. To her Jeanie explained her situation in a few words, and begged her assistance.

The dignity of a housekeeper did not encourage too much familiarity with a person who was at the Rectory on justice-business, and whose character might seem in her eyes somewhat precarious; but she was civil, although distant.

"Her young master," she said, "had had a bad accident by a fall from his horse, which made him liable to fainting fits; he had been taken very ill just now, and it was impossible his Reverence could see Jeanie for some time; but that she need not fear his doing all that was just and proper in her behalf the instant he could get her business attended to."—She concluded by offering to show Jeanie a room, where she might remain till his Reverence was at leisure.

Our heroine took the opportunity to request the means of adjusting and changing her dress.

The housekeeper, in whose estimation order and cleanliness ranked high among personal virtues, gladly complied with a request so reasonable; and the change of dress which Jeanie's bundle furnished made so important an improvement in her appearance, that the old lady hardly knew the soiled and disordered traveller, whose attire showed the violence she had sustained, in the neat, clean, quiet-looking little Scotchwoman, who now stood before her. Encouraged by such a favourable alteration in her appearance, Mrs. Dalton ventured to invite Jeanie to partake of her dinner, and was equally pleased with the decent propriety of her conduct during that meal.

"Thou canst read this book, canst thou, young woman?" said the old lady, when their meal was concluded, laying her hand upon a large Bible.

"I hope sae, madam," said Jeanie, surprised at the question; "my father wad hae wanted mony a thing, ere I had wanted *that* schuling."

"The better sign of him, young woman. There are men here, well to pass in the world, would not want their share of a Leicester plover, and that's a bag-pudding, if fasting for three hours would make all their poor children read the Bible from end to end. Take thou the book, then, for my eyes are something dazed, and read where thou listest—it's the only book thou canst not happen wrong in."

Jeanie was at first tempted to turn up the parable of the good Samaritan, but her conscience checked her, as if it were an use of Scripture, not for her own edification, but to work upon the mind of others for the relief of her worldly afflictions; and under this scrupulous sense of duty, she selected, in preference, a chapter of the prophet Isaiah, and read it, notwithstanding her northern accent and tone, with a devout propriety, which greatly edified Mrs. Dalton.

"Ah," she said, "an all Scotchwomen were sic as thou!— but it was our luck to get born devils of thy country, I think —every one worse than t'other. If thou knowest of any tidy lass like thysell, that wanted a place, and could bring a good character, and would not go laiking about to wakes and fairs, and wore shoes and stockings all the day round—why, I'll not say but we might find room for her at the Rectory. Hast no cousin or sister, lass, that such an offer would suit?"

This was touching upon a sore point, but Jeanie was spared the pain of replying by the entrance of the same man-servant she had seen before.

"Measter wishes to see the young woman from Scotland," was Tummas's address.

"Go to his Reverence, my dear, as fast as you can, and tell him all your story—his Reverence is a kind man," said Mrs. Dalton. "I will fold down the leaf, and make you a cup of tea, with some nice muffin, against you come down, and that's what you seldom see in Scotland, girl."

"Measter's waiting for the young woman," said Tummas impatiently.

"Well, Mr. Jack-Sauce, and what is your business to put in your oar?—And how often must I tell you to call Mr. Staunton his Reverence, seeing as he is a dignified clergyman, and not be meastering, meastering him, as if he were a little petty squire?"

As Jeanie was now at the door, and ready to accompany Tummas, the footman said nothing till he got into the passage, when he muttered, "There are moe masters than one in this house, and I think we shall have a mistress too, an Dame Dalton carries it thus."

Tummas led the way through a more intricate range of passages than Jeanie had yet threaded, and ushered her into an apartment which was darkened by the closing of most of the window-shutters, and in which was a bed with the curtains partly drawn.

"Here is the young woman, sir," said Tummas.

"Very well," said a voice from the bed, but not that of his

Reverence; "be ready to answer the bell, and leave the room."

"There is some mistake," said Jeanie, confounded at finding herself in the apartment of an invalid; "the servant told me that the minister——"

"Don't trouble yourself," said the invalid, "there is no mistake. I know more of your affairs than my father, and I can manage them better.—Leave the room, Tom." The servant obeyed.—"We must not," said the invalid, "lose time, when we have little to lose. Open the shutter of that window."

She did so, and, as he drew aside the curtain of his bed, the light fell on his pale countenance, as, turban'd with bandages, and dressed in a night-gown, he lay, seemingly exhausted, upon the bed.

"Look at me," he said, "Jeanie Deans; can you not recollect me?"

"No, sir," said she, full of surprise. "I was never in this country before."

"But I may have been in yours. Think—recollect. I should faint did I name the name you are most dearly bound to loathe and to detest. Think—remember!"

A terrible recollection flashed on Jeanie, which every tone of the speaker confirmed, and which his next words rendered certainty.

"Be composed—remember Muschat's Cairn, and the moon-light night!"

Jeanie sunk down on a chair, with clasped hands, and gasped in agony.

"Yes, here I lie," he said, "like a crushed snake, writhing with impatience at my incapacity of motion—here I lie, when I ought to have been in Edinburgh, trying every means to save a life that is dearer to me than my own.—How is your sister? —how fares it with her?—condemned to death, I know it, by this time! Oh, the horse that carried me safely on a thousand errands of folly and wickedness, that he should have broke down with me on the only good mission I have undertaken for years! But I must rein in my passion—my frame cannot endure it, and I have much to say. Give me some of the cordial which stands on that table.—Why do you tremble? But you have too good cause.—Let it stand—I need it not."

Jeanie, however reluctant, approached him with the cup into which she had poured the draught, and could not forbear saying, "There is a cordial for the mind, sir, if the wicked will turn from their transgressions, and seek to the Physician of souls."

"Silence!" he said sternly—"and yet I thank you. But tell me, and lose no time in doing so, what you are doing in this country? Remember, though I have been your sister's worst enemy, yet I will serve her with the best of my blood, and I will serve you for her sake; and no one can serve you to such purpose, for no one can know the circumstances so well—so speak without fear."

"I am not afraid, sir," said Jeanie, collecting her spirits. "I trust in God; and if it pleases Him to redeem my sister's captivity, it is all I seek, whosoever be the instrument. But, sir, to be plain with you, I dare not use your counsel, unless I were enabled to see that it accords with the law which I must rely upon."

"The devil take the puritan!" cried George Staunton, for so we must now call him,—"I beg your pardon; but I am naturally impatient, and you drive me mad! What harm can it possibly do you to tell me in what situation your sister stands, and your own expectations of being able to assist her? It is time enough to refuse my advice when I offer any which you may think improper. I speak calmly to you, though 'tis against my nature:—but don't urge me to impatience—it will only render me incapable of serving Effie."

There was in the looks and words of this unhappy young man a sort of restrained eagerness and impetuosity, which seemed to prey upon itself, as the impatience of a fiery steed fatigues itself with churning upon the bit. After a moment's consideration, it occurred to Jeanie that she was not entitled to withhold from him, whether on her sister's account or her own, the account of the fatal consequences of the crime which he had committed, nor to reject such advice, being in itself lawful and innocent, as he might be able to suggest in the way of remedy. Accordingly, in as few words as she could express it, she told the history of her sister's trial and condemnation, and of her own journey as far as Newark. He appeared to listen in the utmost agony of mind, yet repressed every violent symptom of emotion, whether by gesture or sound, which might have interrupted the speaker, and, stretched on his couch like the Mexican monarch on his bed of live coals, only the contortions of his cheek, and the quivering of his limbs, gave indication of his sufferings. To much of what she said he listened with stifled groans, as if he were only hearing those miseries confirmed, whose fatal reality he had known before ; but when she pursued her tale through the circumstances which had interrupted her journey, extreme surprise and earnest attention appeared to succeed to the symptoms of remorse which he had before exhibited. He questioned Jeanie closely concerning the appearance of the two men, and the conversation which she had overheard between the taller of them and the woman.

When Jeanie mentioned the old woman having alluded to her foster-son—"It is too true," he said ; "and the source from which I derived food, when an infant, must have communicated to me the wretched — the fated — propensity to vices that were strangers in my own family.—But go on."

Jeanie passed slightly over her journey in company with Madge, having no inclination to repeat what might be the effect of mere raving on the part of her companion, and therefore her tale was now closed.

Young Staunton lay for a moment in profound meditation, and at length spoke with more composure than he had yet displayed during their interview.—"You are a sensible, as well as a good young woman, Jeanie Deans, and I will tell you more of my story than I have told to any one.—Story did I call it ?—it is a tissue of folly, guilt, and misery.—But take notice—I do it because I desire your confidence in return—that is, that you will act in this dismal matter by my advice and direction. Therefore do I speak."

"I will do what is fitting for a sister, and a daughter, and a Christian woman to do," said Jeanie ; "but do not tell me any of your secrets—It is not good that I should come into your counsel, or listen to the doctrine which causeth to err."

"Simple fool !" said the young man. "Look at me. My head is not horned, my foot is not cloven, my hands are not garnished with talons ; and, since I am not the very devil himself, what interest can any one else have in destroying the hopes with which you comfort or fool yourself? Listen to me patiently, and you will find that, when you have heard my counsel, you may go to the seventh heaven with it in your pocket, if you have a mind, and not feel yourself an ounce heavier in the ascent.

At the risk of being somewhat heavy, as explanations usually prove, we must here endeavour to combine into a distinct narrative, information which the invalid communicated in a manner at once too circumstantial, and too much broken by passion, to admit of our giving his precise words. Part of it, indeed, he read from a manuscript, which he had perhaps drawn up for the information of his relations after his decease.

"To make my tale short—this wretched hag—this Margaret Murdockson, was the wife of a favourite servant of my father; —she had been my nurse;—her husband was dead;—she resided in a cottage near this place;—she had a daughter who grew up, and was then a beautiful but very giddy girl; her mother endeavoured to promote her marriage with an old and wealthy churl in the neighbourhood;—the girl saw me frequently—She was familiar with me, as our connection seemed to permit—and I—in a word, I wronged her cruelly— It was not so bad as your sister's business, but it was sufficiently villainous—her folly should have been her protection. Soon after this I was sent abroad—To do my father justice, if I have turned out a fiend, it is not his fault—he used the best means. When I returned, I found the wretched mother and daughter had fallen into disgrace, and were chased from this country.—My deep share in their shame and misery was discovered—my father used very harsh language—we quarrelled. I left his house, and led a life of strange adventure, resolving never again to see my father or my father's home.

"And now comes the story!—Jeanie, I put my life into your hands, and not only my own life, which, God knows, is not worth saving, but the happiness of a respectable old man, and the honour of a family of consideration. My love of low society, as such propensities as I was cursed with are usually termed, was, I think, of an uncommon kind, and indicated a nature, which, if not depraved by early debauchery, would have been fit for better things. I did not so much delight in the wild revel, the low humour, the unconfined liberty of those with whom I associated, as in the spirit of adventure, presence of mind in peril, and sharpness of intellect which they displayed in prosecuting their maraudings upon the revenue, or similar adventures.——Have you looked round this rectory?—is it not a sweet and pleasant retreat?"

Jeanie, alarmed at this sudden change of subject, replied in the affirmative.

"Well! I wish it had been ten thousand fathoms under ground, with its church-lands, and tithes, and all that belongs to it! Had it not been for this cursed rectory, I should have been permitted to follow the bent of my own inclinations and

the profession of arms, and half the courage and address that
I have displayed among smugglers and deer-stealers would
have secured me an honourable rank among my contem-
poraries. Why did I not go abroad when I left this house!—
Why did I leave it at all!—why—But it came to that point
with me that it is madness to look back, and misery to look
forward."

He paused, and then proceeded with more composure.

"The chances of a wandering life brought me unhappily
to Scotland, to embroil myself in worse and more criminal
actions than I had yet been concerned in. It was now I
became acquainted with Wilson, a remarkable man in his
station of life; quiet, composed, and resolute, firm in mind,
and uncommonly strong in person, gifted with a sort of rough
eloquence which raised him above his companions. Hitherto
I had been

    ' As dissolute as desperate, yet through both
    Were seen some sparkles of a better hope.'

But it was this man's misfortune, as well as mine, that,
notwithstanding the difference of our rank and education, he
acquired an extraordinary and fascinating influence over me,
which I can only account for by the calm determination of his
character being superior to the less sustained impetuosity of
mine. Where he led, I felt myself bound to follow; and
strange was the courage and address which he displayed in
his pursuits. While I was engaged in desperate adventures,
under so strange and dangerous a preceptor, I became
acquainted with your unfortunate sister at some sports of
the young people in the suburbs, which she frequented by
stealth—and her ruin proved an interlude to the tragic scenes
in which I was now deeply engaged. Yet this let me say—
the villainy was not premeditated, and I was firmly resolved
to do her all the justice which marriage could do, so soon
as I should be able to extricate myself from my unhappy
course of life, and embrace some one more suited to my
birth. I had wild visions—visions of conducting her as if
to some poor retreat, and introducing her at once to rank
and fortune she never dreamt of. A friend, at my request,
attempted a negotiation with my father, which was protracted
for some time, and renewed at different intervals. At length,
and just when I expected my father's pardon, he learned by
some means or other of my infamy, painted in even exaggerated

colours, which was, God knows, unnecessary. He wrote me a letter—how it found me out, I know not—enclosing me a sum of money, and disowning me for ever. I became desperate—I became frantic—I readily joined Wilson in a perilous smuggling adventure in which we miscarried, and was willingly blinded by his logic to consider the robbery of the officer of the customs in Fife as a fair and honourable reprisal. Hitherto I had observed a certain line in my criminality, and stood free of assaults upon personal property, but now I felt a wild pleasure in disgracing myself as much as possible.

"The plunder was no object to me. I abandoned that to my comrades, and only asked the post of danger. I remember well, that when I stood with my drawn sword guarding the door while they committed the felony, I had not a thought of my own safety. I was only meditating on my sense of supposed wrong from my family, my impotent thirst of vengeance, and how it would sound in the haughty ears of the family of Willingham, that one of their descendants, and the heir apparent of their honours, should perish by the hands of the hangman for robbing a Scottish gauger of a sum not equal to one-fifth part of the money I had in my pocket-book. We were taken—I expected no less. We were condemned—that also I looked for. But death, as he approached nearer, looked grimly; and the recollection of your sister's destitute condition determined me on an effort to save my life.—I forgot to tell you, that in Edinburgh I again met the woman Murdockson and her daughter. She had followed the camp when young, and had now, under pretence of a trifling traffic, resumed predatory habits, with which she had already been too familiar. Our first meeting was stormy; but I was liberal of what money I had, and she forgot, or seemed to forget, the injury her daughter had received. The unfortunate girl herself seemed hardly even to know her seducer, far less to retain any sense of the injury she had received. Her mind is totally alienated, which, according to her mother's account, is sometimes the consequence of an unfavourable confinement. But it was *my doing*. Here was another stone knitted round my neck to sink me into the pit of perdition. Every look—every word of this poor creature—her false spirits—her imperfect recollections—her allusions to things which she had forgotten, but which were recorded in my conscience, were stabs of a poniard—stabs did I say?—they were tearing with hot pincers, and scalding the raw wound with burning sulphur—they were to be endured, however, and they *were* endured.—I return to my prison thoughts.

"It was not the least miserable of them that your sister's time approached. I knew her dread of you and of her father. She often said she would die a thousand deaths ere you should know her shame—yet her confinement must be provided for. I knew this woman Murdockson was an infernal hag, but I thought she loved me, and that money would make her true. She had procured a file for Wilson, and a spring-saw for me; and she undertook readily to take charge of Effie during her illness, in which she had skill enough to give the necessary assistance. I gave her the money which my father had sent me. It was settled that she should receive Effie into her house in the meantime, and wait for farther directions from me, when I should effect my escape. I communicated this purpose, and recommended the old hag to poor Effie by a letter, in which I recollect that I endeavoured to support the character of Macheath under condemnation—a fine, gay, bold-faced ruffian, who is game to the last. Such, and so wretchedly poor, was my ambition! Yet I had resolved to forsake the courses I had been engaged in, should I be so fortunate as to escape the gibbet. My design was to marry your sister, and go over to the West Indies. I had still a considerable sum of money left, and I trusted to be able, in one way or other, to provide for myself and my wife.

"We made the attempt to escape, and by the obstinacy of Wilson, who insisted upon going first, it totally miscarried. The undaunted and self-denied manner in which he sacrificed himself to redeem his error, and accomplish my escape from the Tolbooth Church, you must have heard of—all Scotland rang with it. It was a gallant and extraordinary deed.—All men spoke of it—all men, even those who most condemned the habits and crimes of this self-devoted man, praised the heroism of his friendship. I have many vices, but cowardice, or want of gratitude, are none of the number. I resolved to requite his generosity, and even your sister's safety became a secondary consideration with me for the time. To effect Wilson's liberation was my principal object, and I doubted not to find the means.

"Yet I did not forget Effie neither. The bloodhounds of the law were so close after me, that I dared not trust myself near any of my old haunts, but old Murdockson met me by appointment, and informed me that your sister had happily been delivered of a boy. I charged the hag to keep her patient's mind easy, and let her want for nothing that money could purchase, and I retreated to Fife, where, among my old associates of Wilson's gang, I hid myself in those places of concealment where the men engaged in that desperate trade are used to find security for themselves and their uncustomed goods. Men who are disobedient both to human and divine laws, are not always insensible to the claims of courage and generosity. We were assured that the mob of Edinburgh, strongly moved with the hardships of Wilson's situation, and the gallantry of his conduct, would back any bold attempt that might be made to rescue him even from the foot of the gibbet. Desperate as the attempt seemed, upon my declaring myself ready to lead the onset on the guard, I found no want of followers who engaged to stand by me, and returned to Lothian, soon joined by some steady associates, prepared to act whenever the occasion might require.

"I have no doubt I should have rescued him from the very noose that dangled over his head," he continued with animation, which seemed a flash of the interest which he had taken in such exploits ; "but amongst other precautions, the magistrates had taken one, suggested, as we afterwards learned, by the unhappy wretch Porteous, which effectually disconcerted my measures. They anticipated, by half-an-hour, the ordinary period for execution ; and, as it had been resolved amongst us, that, for fear of observation from the officers of justice, we should not show ourselves upon the street until the time of action approached, it followed that all was over before our attempt at a rescue commenced. It did commence, however, and I gained the scaffold and cut the rope with my own hand. It was too late ! The bold, stout-hearted, generous criminal was no more—and vengeance was all that remained to us— a vengeance, as I then thought, doubly due from my hand, to whom Wilson had given life and liberty when he could as easily have secured his own."

"O sir," said Jeanie, "did the Scripture never come into your mind, 'Vengeance is mine, and I will repay it'?"

"Scripture? Why, I had not opened a Bible for five years," answered Staunton.

"Wae's me, sirs," said Jeanie—"and a minister's son too !"

"It is natural for you to say so ; yet do not interrupt me, but let me finish my most accursed history. The beast,

Porteous, who kept firing on the people long after it had ceased to be necessary, became the object of their hatred for having overdone his duty, and of mine for having done it too well. We—that is, I and the other determined friends of Wilson—resolved to be avenged; but caution was necessary. I thought I had been marked by one of the officers, and therefore continued to lurk about the vicinity of Edinburgh, but without daring to venture within the walls. At length, I visited, at the hazard of my life, the place where I hoped to find my future wife and my son—they were both gone. Dame Murdockson informed me, that so soon as Effie heard of the miscarriage of the attempt to rescue Wilson, and the hot pursuit after me, she fell into a brain fever; and that being one day obliged to go out on some necessary business and leave her alone, she had taken that opportunity to escape, and she had not seen her since. I loaded her with reproaches, to which she listened with the most provoking and callous composure; for it is one of her attributes, that, violent and fierce as she is upon most occasions, there are some in which she shows the most imperturbable calmness. I threatened her with justice; she said I had more reason to fear justice than she had. I felt she was right, and was silenced. I threatened her with vengeance; she replied in nearly the same words, that, to judge by injuries received, I had more reason to fear her vengeance, than she to dread mine. She was again right, and I was left without an answer. I flung myself from her in indignation, and employed a comrade to make inquiry in the neighbourhood of Saint Leonard's concerning your sister; but ere I received his answer, the opening quest of a well-scented terrier of the law drove me from the vicinity of Edinburgh to a more distant and secluded place of concealment. A secret and trusty emissary at length brought me the account of Porteous's condemnation, and of your sister's imprisonment on a criminal charge; thus astounding one of mine ears, while he gratified the other.

"I again ventured to the Pleasance—again charged Murdockson with treachery to the unfortunate Effie and her child, though I could conceive no reason, save that of appropriating the whole of the money I had lodged with her. Your narrative throws light on this, and shows another motive, not less powerful because less evident—the desire of wreaking vengeance on the seducer of her daughter,—the destroyer at once of her reason and reputation. Great God! how I wish that, instead of the revenge she made choice of, she had delivered me up to the cord!"

"But what account did the wretched woman give of Effie and the bairn?" said Jeanie, who, during this long and agitating narrative, had firmness and discernment enough to keep her eye on such points as might throw light on her sister's misfortunes.

"She would give none," said Staunton; "she said the mother made a moonlight flitting from her house, with the infant in her arms—that she had never seen either of them since—that the lass might have thrown the child into the North Loch or the Quarry Holes, for what she knew, and it was like enough she had done so."

"And how came you to believe that she did not speak the fatal truth?" said Jeanie, trembling.

"Because, on this second occasion, I saw her daughter, and I understood from her, that, in fact, the child had been removed or destroyed during the illness of the mother. But all knowledge to be got from her is so uncertain and indirect, that I could not collect any farther circumstances. Only the diabolical character of Old Murdockson makes me augur the worst."

"The last account agrees with that given by my poor sister," said Jeanie; "but gang on wi' your ain tale, sir."

"Of this I am certain," said Staunton, "that Effie, in her senses, and with her knowledge, never injured living creature —But what could I do in her exculpation?—Nothing—and, therefore, my whole thoughts were turned towards her safety. I was under the cursed necessity of suppressing my feelings towards Murdockson; my life was in the hag's hand—that I cared not for; but on my life hung that of your sister. I spoke the wretch fair; I appeared to confide in her; and to me, so far as I was personally concerned, she gave proofs of extraordinary fidelity. I was at first uncertain what measures I ought to adopt for your sister's liberation, when the general rage excited among the citizens of Edinburgh on account of the reprieve of Porteous, suggested to me the daring idea of forcing the jail, and at once carrying off your sister from the clutches of the law, and bringing to condign punishment a miscreant, who had tormented the unfortunate Wilson even in the hour of death, as if he had been a wild Indian taken captive by an hostile tribe. I flung myself among the multitude in the moment of fermentation—so did others among

Wilson's mates, who had, like me, been disappointed in the hope of glutting their eyes with Porteous's execution. All was organised, and I was chosen for the captain. I felt not— I do not now feel, compunction for what was to be done, and has since been executed."

"Oh, God forgive ye, sir, and bring ye to a better sense of your ways!" exclaimed Jeanie, in horror at the avowal of such violent sentiments.

"Amen," replied Staunton, "if my sentiments are wrong. But I repeat, that, although willing to aid the deed, I could have wished them to have chosen another leader; because I foresaw that the great and general duty of the night would interfere with the assistance which I proposed to render Effie. I gave a commission, however, to a trusty friend to protect her to a place of safety, so soon as the fatal procession had left the jail. But for no persuasions which I could use in the hurry of the moment, or which my comrade employed at more length, after the mob had taken a different direction, could the unfortunate girl be prevailed upon to leave the prison. His arguments were all wasted upon the infatuated victim, and he was obliged to leave her in order to attend to his own safety. Such was his account; but, perhaps, he persevered less steadily in his attempt to persuade her than I would have done."

"Effie was right to remain," said Jeanie; "and I love her the better for it."

"Why will you say so?" said Staunton.

"You cannot understand my reasons, sir, if I should render them," answered Jeanie composedly; "they that thirst for the blood of their enemies have no taste for the well-spring of life."

"My hopes," said Staunton, "were thus a second time disappointed. My next efforts were to bring her through her trial by means of yourself. How I urged it, and where, you cannot have forgotten. I do not blame you for your refusal; it was founded, I am convinced, on principle, and not on indifference to your sister's fate. For me, judge of me as a man frantic; I knew not what hand to turn to, and all my efforts were unavailing. In this condition, and close beset on all sides, I thought of what might be done by means of my family, and their influence. I fled from Scotland—I reached this place—my miserably wasted and unhappy appearance procured me from my father that pardon, which a parent finds it so hard to refuse, even to the most undeserving son. And here I have awaited in anguish of mind, which the condemned criminal might envy, the event of your sister's trial."

"Without taking any steps for her relief?" said Jeanie.

"To the last I hoped her case might terminate more favourably; and it is only two days since that the fatal tidings reached me. My resolution was instantly taken. I mounted my best horse with the purpose of making the utmost haste to London, and there compounding with Sir Robert Walpole for your sister's safety, by surrendering to him, in the person of the heir of the family of Willingham, the notorious George Robertson, the accomplice of Wilson, the breaker of the Tolbooth prison, and the well-known leader of the Porteous mob."

"But would that save my sister?" said Jeanie, in astonishment.

"It would, as I should drive my bargain," said Staunton. "Queens love revenge as well as their subjects—Little as you seem to esteem it, it is a poison which pleases all palates, from the prince to the peasant. Prime ministers love no less the power of pleasing sovereigns by gratifying their passions. The life of an obscure village girl? Why, I might ask the best of the crown-jewels for laying the head of such an insolent conspiracy at the foot of her Majesty, with a certainty of being gratified. All my other plans have failed, but this could not —Heaven is just, however, and would not honour me with making this voluntary atonement for the injury I have done your sister. I had not rode ten miles, when my horse, the best and most sure-footed animal in this country, fell with me on a level piece of road, as if he had been struck by a cannon-shot. I was greatly hurt, and was brought back here in the miserable condition in which you now see me."

As young Staunton had come to the conclusion, the servant opened the door, and, with a voice which seemed intended rather for a signal, than merely the announcing of a visit, said, "His Reverence, sir, is coming upstairs to wait upon you."

"For God's sake, hide yourself, Jeanie," exclaimed Staunton, "in that dressing closet!"

"No, sir," said Jeanie; "as I am here for nae ill, I canna take the shame of hiding mysell frae the master o' the house."

"But, good heavens!" exclaimed George Staunton, "do but consider——"

Ere he could complete the sentence, his father entered the apartment.

CHAPTER XXXIV

And now, will pardon, comfort, kindness, draw
The youth from vice? will honour, duty, law?
                                    CRABBE.

JEANIE arose from her seat, and made her quiet reverence, when the elder Mr. Staunton entered the apartment. His astonishment was extreme at finding his son in such company.

"I perceive, madam," he said, "I have made a mistake respecting you, and ought to have left the task of interrogating you, and of righting your wrongs, to this young man, with whom, doubtless, you have been formerly acquainted."

"It's unwitting on my part that I am here," said Jeanie; "the servant told me his master wished to speak with me."

"There goes the purple coat over my ears," murmured Tummas. "D—n her, why must she needs speak the truth, when she could have as well said anything else she had a mind?"

"George," said Mr. Staunton, "if you are still—as you have ever been—lost to all self-respect, you might at least have spared your father, and your father's house, such a disgraceful scene as this."

"Upon my life—upon my soul, sir!" said George, throwing his feet over the side of the bed, and starting from his recumbent posture.

"Your life, sir!" interrupted his father, with melancholy sternness,—"What sort of life has it been?—Your soul! alas! what regard have you ever paid to it? Take care to reform both ere offering either as pledges of your sincerity."

"On my honour, sir, you do me wrong," answered George Staunton; "I have been all that you can call me that's bad, but in the present instance you do me injustice. By my honour, you do!"

"Your honour!" said his father, and turned from him, with a look of the most upbraiding contempt, to Jeanie. "From you, young woman, I neither ask nor expect any explanation; but, as a father alike and as a clergyman, I request your departure from this house. If your romantic story has been other than a pretext to find admission into it (which, from the society in which you first appeared, I may be permitted to doubt), you will find a justice of peace within two miles, with whom, more properly than with me, you may lodge your complaint."

"This shall not be," said George Staunton, starting up to his feet. "Sir, you are naturally kind and humane—you shall not become cruel and inhospitable on my account. Turn out that eavesdropping rascal," pointing to Thomas, "and get what hartshorn drops, or what better receipt you have against fainting, and I will explain to you in two words the connection betwixt this young woman and me. She shall not lose her fair character through me. I have done too much mischief to her family already, and I know too well what belongs to the loss of fame."

"Leave the room, sir," said the Rector to the servant; and when the man had obeyed, he carefully shut the door behind him. Then addressing his son, he said sternly, "Now, sir, what new proof of your infamy have you to impart to me?"

Young Staunton was about to speak, but it was one of those moments when persons, who, like Jeanie Deans, possess the advantage of a steady courage and unruffled temper, can assume the superiority over more ardent but less determined spirits.

"Sir," she said to the elder Staunton, " 'e have an undoubted right to ask your ain son to render a reason of his conduct. But respecting me, I am but a wayfaring traveller, no ways obligated or indebted to you, unless it be for the meal of meat which, in my ain country, is willingly gien by rich or poor, according to their ability, to those who need it; and for which, forby that, I am willing to make payment, if I didna think it would be an affront to offer siller in a house like this —only I dinna ken the fashions of the country."

"This is all very well, young woman," said the Rector, a good deal surprised, and unable to conjecture whether to impute Jeanie's language to simplicity or impertinence—"this may be all very well—but let me bring it to a point. Why do you stop this young man's mouth, and prevent his communicating to his father, and his best friend, an explanation (since he says he has one) of circumstances which seem in themselves not a little suspicious?"

"He may tell of his ain affairs what he likes," answered Jeanie; "but my family and friends have nae right to hae ony stories told anent them without their express desire; and, as they canna be here to speak for themselves, I entreat ye wadna ask Mr. George Rob—I mean Staunton, or whatever his name is, ony questions anent me or my folk; for I maun be free to tell you, that he will neither have the bearing of a Christian or a gentleman, if he answers you against my express desire."

"This is the most extraordinary thing I ever met with," said the Rector, as, after fixing his eyes keenly on the placid, yet modest countenance of Jeanie, he turned them suddenly upon his son. "What have you to say, sir?"

"That I feel I have been too hasty in my promise, sir," answered George Staunton; "I have no title to make any communications respecting the affairs of this young person's family without her assent."

The elder Mr. Staunton turned his eyes from one to the other with marks of surprise.

"This is more, and worse, I fear," he said, addressing his son, "than one of your frequent and disgraceful connections—I insist upon knowing the mystery."

"I have already said, sir," replied his son rather sullenly, "that I have no title to mention the affairs of this young woman's family without her consent."

"And I hae nae mysteries to explain, sir," said Jeanie, "but only to pray you, as a preacher of the gospel and a gentleman, to permit me to go safe to the next public-house on the Lunnon road."

"I shall take care of your safety," said young Staunton; "you need ask that favour from no one."

"Do you say so before my face?" said the justly incensed father. "Perhaps, sir, you intend to fill up the cup of disobedience and profligacy by forming a low and disgraceful marriage? But let me bid you beware."

"If you were feared for sic a thing happening wi' me, sir," said Jeanie, "I can only say, that not for all the land that lies between the twa ends of the rainbow wad I be the woman that should wed your son."

"There is something very singular in all this," said the elder Staunton; "follow me into the next room, young woman."

"Hear me speak first," said the young man. "I have but one word to say. I confide entirely in your prudence; tell my father as much or as little of these matters as you will, he shall know neither more nor less from me."

His father darted at him a glance of indignation, which softened into sorrow as he saw him sink down on the couch, exhausted with the scene he had undergone. He left the apartment, and Jeanie followed him, George Staunton raising himself as she passed the doorway, and pronouncing the word, " Remember ! " in a tone as monitory as it was uttered by Charles I. upon the scaffold. The elder Staunton led the way into a small parlour, and shut the door.

" Young woman," said he, " there is something in your face and appearance that marks both sense and simplicity, and, if I am not deceived, innocence also—Should it be otherwise, I can only say, you are the most accomplished hypocrite I have ever seen.—I ask to know no secret that you have unwilling-ness to divulge, least of all those which concern my son. His conduct has given me too much unhappiness to permit me to hope comfort or satisfaction from him. If you are such as I suppose you, believe me, that whatever unhappy circumstances may have connected you with George Staunton, the sooner you break them through the better."

" I think I understand your meaning, sir," replied Jeanie ; " and as ye are sae frank as to speak o' the young gentleman in sic a way, I must needs say that it is but the second time of my speaking wi' him in our lives, and what I hae heard frae him on these twa occasions has been such that I never wish to hear the like again."

" Then it is your real intention to leave this part of the country, and proceed to London ? " said the Rector.

" Certainly, sir ; for I may say, in one sense, that the avenger of blood is behind me ; and if I were but assured against mischief by the way——"

" I have made inquiry," said the clergyman, " after the suspicious characters you described. They have left their place of rendezvous ; but as they may be lurking in the neighbourhood, and as you say you have special reason to apprehend violence from them, I will put you under the charge of a steady person, who will protect you as far as Stamford, and see you into a light coach, which goes from thence to London."

" A coach is not for the like of me, sir," said Jeanie ; to whom the idea of a stage-coach was unknown, as, indeed, they were then only used in the neighbourhood of London.

Mr. Staunton briefly explained that she would find that mode of convenience more commodious, cheaper, and more safe, than travelling on horseback. She expressed her gratitude with so much singleness of heart that he was induced to ask her whether she wanted the pecuniary means of prosecuting her journey. She thanked him, but said she had enough for her purpose; and, indeed, she had husbanded her stock with great care. This reply served also to remove some doubts, which naturally enough still floated in Mr. Staunton's mind, respecting her character and real purpose, and satisfied him, at least, that money did not enter into her scheme of deception, if an impostor she should prove. He next requested to know what part of the city she wished to go to.

"To a very decent merchant, a cousin o' my ain, a Mrs. Glass, sir, that sells snuff and tobacco, at the sign o' the Thistle, somegate in the town."

Jeanie communicated this intelligence with a feeling that a connection so respectable ought to give her consequence in the eyes of Mr. Staunton; and she was a good deal surprised when he answered—

"And is this woman your only acquaintance in London, my poor girl? and have you really no better knowledge where she is to be found?"

"I was gaun to see the Duke of Argyle, forby Mrs. Glass," said Jeanie; "and if your honour thinks it would be best to go there first, and get some of his Grace's folk to show me my cousin's shop——"

"Are you acquainted with any of the Duke of Argyle's people?" said the Rector.

"No, sir."

"Her brain must be something touched after all, or it would be impossible for her to rely on such introductions.— Well," said he aloud, "I must not inquire into the cause of your journey, and so I cannot be fit to give you advice how to manage it. But the landlady of the house where the coach stops is a very decent person; and as I use her house sometimes, I will give you a recommendation to her."

Jeanie thanked him for his kindness with her best courtesy, and said, "That with his honour's line, and ane from worthy Mrs. Bickerton, that keeps the Seven Stars at York, she did not doubt to be well taken out in Lunnon."

"And now," said he, "I presume you will be desirous to set out immediately."

"If I had been in an inn, sir, or any suitable resting-place," answered Jeanie, "I wad not have presumed to use the Lord's day for travelling; but as I am on a journey of mercy, I trust my doing so will not be imputed."

"You may, if you choose, remain with Mrs. Dalton for the evening; but I desire you will have no further correspondence with my son, who is not a proper counsellor for a person of your age, whatever your difficulties may be."

"Your honour speaks ower truly in that," said Jeanie; "it was not with my will that I spoke wi' him just now, and—not to wish the gentleman onything but gude—I never wish to see him between the een again."

"If you please," added the Rector, "as you seem to be a seriously disposed young woman, you may attend family worship in the hall this evening."

"I thank your honour," said Jeanie, "but I am doubtful if my attendance would be to edification."

"How," said the Rector; "so young, and already unfortunate enough to have doubts upon the duties of religion!"

"God forbid, sir," replied Jeanie; "it is not for that; but I have been bred in the faith of the suffering remnant of the Presbyterian doctrine in Scotland, and I am doubtful if I can lawfully attend upon your fashion of worship, seeing it has been testified against by many precious souls of our kirk, and specially by my worthy father."

"Well, my good girl," said the Rector, with a good-humoured smile, "far be it from me to put any force upon your conscience; and yet you ought to recollect that the same divine grace dispenses its streams to other kingdoms as well as to Scotland. As it is as essential to our spiritual, as water to our earthly wants, its springs, various in character, yet alike efficacious in virtue, are to be found in abundance throughout the Christian world."

"Ay, but," said Jeanie, "though the waters may be alike, yet, with your worship's leave, the blessing upon them may not be equal. It would have been in vain for Naaman the Syrian leper to have bathed in Pharphar and Abana, rivers of Damascus, when it was only the waters of Jordan that were sanctified for the cure."

"Well," said the Rector, "we will not enter upon the great debate betwixt our national churches at present. We must endeavour to satisfy you, that, at least, amongst our errors, we preserve Christian charity, and a desire to assist our brethren."

He then ordered Mrs. Dalton into his presence, and consigned Jeanie to her particular charge, with directions to be kind to her, and with assurances, that, early in the morning, a trusty guide and a good horse should be ready to conduct her to Stamford. He then took a serious and dignified, yet kind leave of her, wishing her full success in the objects of her journey, which he said he doubted not were laudable, from the soundness of thinking which she had displayed in conversation.

Jeanie was again conducted by the housekeeper to her own apartment. But the evening was not destined to pass over without further torment from young Staunton. A paper was slipped into her hand by the faithful Tummas, which intimated his young master's desire, or rather demand, to see her instantly, and assured her he had provided against interruption.

"Tell your young master," said Jeanie openly, and regardless of all the winks and signs by which Tummas strove to make her comprehend that Mrs. Dalton was not to be admitted into the secret of the correspondence, "that I promised faithfully to his worthy father that I would not see him again."

"Tummas," said Mrs. Dalton, "I think you might be much more creditably employed, considering the coat you wear, and the house you live in, than to be carrying messages between your young master and girls that chance to be in this house."

"Why, Mrs. Dalton, as to that, I was hired to carry messages, and not to ask any questions about them; and it's not for the like of me to refuse the young gentleman's bidding, if he were a little wildish or so. If there was harm meant, there's no harm done, you see."

"However," said Mrs. Dalton, "I gie you fair warning, Tummas Ditton, that an I catch thee at this work again, his Reverence shall make a clear house of you."

Tummas retired, abashed and in dismay. The rest of the evening passed away without anything worthy of notice.

Jeanie enjoyed the comforts of a good bed and a sound sleep with grateful satisfaction, after the perils and hardships of the preceding day: and such was her fatigue, that she slept soundly until six o'clock, when she was awakened by Mrs. Dalton, who acquainted her that her guide and horse were ready, and in attendance. She hastily rose, and, after her morning devotions, was soon ready to resume her travels. The motherly care of the housekeeper had provided an early breakfast, and, after she had partaken of this refreshment, she found herself safe seated on a pillion behind a stout Lincolnshire peasant, who was, besides, armed with pistols, to protect her against any violence which might be offered.

They trudged on in silence for a mile or two along a country road, which conducted them, by hedge and gate-way, into the principal highway, a little beyond Grantham. At length her master of the horse asked her whether her name was not Jean, or Jane, Deans. She answered in the affirmative, with some surprise. "Then here's a bit of a note as concerns you," said the man, handing it over his left shoulder. "It's from young master, as I judge, and every man about Willingham is fain to pleasure him either for love or fear; for he'll come to be landlord at last, let them say what they like."

Jeanie broke the seal of the note, which was addressed to her, and read as follows :—

"You refuse to see me. I suppose you are shocked at my character : but, in painting myself such as I am, you should give me credit for my sincerity. I am, at least, no hypocrite. You refuse, however, to see me, and your conduct may be natural—but is it wise? I have expressed my anxiety to repair your sister's misfortunes at the expense of my honour,—my family's honour—my own life; and you think me too debased to be admitted even to sacrifice what I have remaining of honour, fame, and life, in her cause. Well, if the offerer be despised, the victim is still equally at hand; and perhaps there may be justice in the decree of Heaven, that I shall not have the melancholy credit of appearing to make this sacrifice out of my own free good-will. You, as you have declined my concurrence, must take the whole upon yourself. Go, then, to the Duke of Argyle, and, when other arguments fail you, tell him you have it in your power to bring to condign punishment the most active conspirator in the Porteous mob. He will hear you on this topic, should he be deaf to every other. Make your own terms, for they will be at your own making. You know where I am to be found; and you may be assured I will not give you the dark side of the hill, as at Muschat's Cairn; I have no thoughts of stirring from the house I was born in; like the hare, I shall be worried in the seat I started from. I repeat it—make your own terms. I need not remind you to ask your sister's life, for that you will do of course; but make terms of advantage for yourself—ask wealth and reward —office and income for Butler—ask anything—you will get anything—and all for delivering to the hands of the executioner a man most deserving of his office ;—one who, though young in years, is old in wickedness, and whose most earnest desire is, after the storms of an unquiet life, to sleep and be at rest."

This extraordinary letter was subscribed with the initials G. S.

Jeanie read it over once or twice with great attention, which the slow pace of the horse, as he stalked through a deep lane, enabled her to do with facility.

When she had perused this billet, her first employment was to tear it into as small pieces as possible, and disperse these pieces in the air by a few at a time, so that a document containing so perilous a secret might not fall into any other person's hand.

The question how far, in point of extremity, she was entitled to save her sister's life by sacrificing that of a person who, though guilty towards the state, had done her no injury, formed the next earnest and most painful subject of consideration. In one sense, indeed, it seemed as if denouncing the guilt of Staunton, the cause of her sister's errors and misfortunes, would have been an act of just, and even providential retribution. But Jeanie, in the strict and severe tone of morality in which she was educated, had to consider not only the general aspect of a proposed action, but its justness and fitness in relation to the actor, before she could be, according to her own phrase, free to enter upon it. What right had she to make a barter between the lives of Staunton and of Effie, and to sacrifice the one for the safety of the other? His guilt—that guilt for which he was amenable to the laws—was a crime against the public indeed, but it was not against her.

Neither did it seem to her that his share in the death of Porteous, though her mind revolted at the idea of using violence to any one, was in the relation of a common murder, against the perpetrator of which every one is called to aid the public magistrate. That violent action was blended with many circumstances, which, in the eyes of those of Jeanie's rank in life, if they did not altogether deprive it of the character of guilt, softened, at least, its most atrocious features. The anxiety of the government to obtain conviction of some of the offenders, had but served to increase the public feeling which connected the action, though violent and irregular, with the idea of ancient national independence. The rigorous procedure adopted or proposed against the city of Edinburgh, the ancient metropolis of Scotland—the extremely unpopular and injudicious measure of compelling the Scottish clergy, contrary to their principles and sense of duty, to promulgate from the pulpit the reward offered for the discovery of the perpetrators of this slaughter, had produced on the public mind the opposite consequences from what were intended; and Jeanie felt conscious, that whoever should lodge information concerning that event, and for whatsoever purpose it might be done, it would be considered as an act of treason against the independence of Scotland. With the fanaticism of the Scotch Presbyterians, there was always mingled a glow of national feeling, and Jeanie trembled at the idea of her name being handed down to posterity with that of the "fause Monteath," and one or two others, who, having deserted and betrayed the cause of their country, are damned to perpetual remembrance and execration among its peasantry. Yet, to part with Effie's life once more, when a word spoken might save it, pressed severely on the mind of her affectionate sister.

"The Lord support and direct me!" said Jeanie, "for it seems to be His will to try me with difficulties far beyond my ain strength."

While this thought passed through Jeanie's mind, her guard, tired of silence, began to show some inclination to be communicative. He seemed a sensible, steady peasant, but not having more delicacy or prudence than is common to those in his situation, he, of course, chose the Willingham family as the subject of his conversation. From this man Jeanie learned some particulars of which she had hitherto been ignorant, and which we will briefly recapitulate for the information of the reader.

The father of George Staunton had been bred a soldier, and, during service in the West Indies, had married the heiress of a wealthy planter. By this lady he had an only child, George Staunton, the unhappy young man who has been so often mentioned in this narrative. He passed the first part of his early youth under the charge of a doting mother, and in the society of negro slaves, whose study it was to gratify his every caprice. His father was a man of worth and sense; but as he alone retained tolerable health among the officers of the regiment he belonged to, he was much engaged with his duty. Besides, Mrs. Staunton was beautiful and wilful, and enjoyed but delicate health; so that it was difficult for a man of affection, humanity, and a quiet disposition, to struggle with her on the point of her over-indulgence to an only child. Indeed, what Mr. Staunton did towards counteracting the baneful effects of his wife's system, only tended to render it more pernicious; for every restraint imposed on the boy in his father's presence, was compensated by treble licence during his absence. So that George Staunton acquired, even in childhood, the habit of regarding his father as a rigid censor, from whose severity he was desirous of emancipating himself as soon and absolutely as possible.

When he was about ten years old, and when his mind had received all the seeds of those evil weeds which afterwards grew apace, his mother died, and his father, half heart-broken, returned to England. To sum up her imprudence and unjustifiable indulgence, she had contrived to place a considerable part of her fortune at her son's exclusive control or disposal; in consequence of which management, George Staunton had not been long in England till he learned his independence, and how to abuse it. His father had endeavoured to rectify the defects of his education by placing him in a well-regulated seminary. But although he showed some capacity for learning, his riotous conduct soon became intolerable to his teachers. He found means (too easily afforded to all youths who have certain expectations) of procuring such a command of money as enabled him to anticipate in boyhood the frolics and follies of a more mature age, and, with these accomplishments, he was returned on his father's hands as a profligate boy, whose example might ruin a hundred.

The elder Mr. Staunton, whose mind, since his wife's death, had been tinged with a melancholy, which certainly his son's conduct did not tend to dispel, had taken orders, and was inducted by his brother Sir William Staunton into the family living of Willingham. The revenue was a matter of consequence to him, for he derived little advantage from the estate of his late wife; and his own fortune was that of a younger brother.

He took his son to reside with him at the rectory; but he soon found that his disorders rendered him an intolerable inmate. And as the young men of his own rank would not endure the purse-proud insolence of the Creole, he fell into that taste for low society, which is worse than "pressing to death, whipping, or hanging." His father sent him abroad, but he only returned wilder and more desperate than before. It is true, this unhappy youth was not without his good qualities. He had lively wit, good temper, reckless generosity, and manners which, while he was under restraint, might pass well in society. But all these availed him nothing. He was so well acquainted with the turf, the gaming-table, the cock-pit, and every worse rendezvous of folly and dissipation, that his mother's fortune was spent before he was twenty-one, and he was soon in debt and in distress. His early history may be concluded in the words of our British Juvenal, when describing a similar character :—

> Headstrong, determined in his own career,
> He thought reproof unjust, and truth severe,
> The soul's disease was to its crisis come,
> He first abused and then abjured his home ;
> And when he chose a vagabond to be,
> He made his shame his glory, " I'll be free ! "

" And yet 'tis pity on Measter George, too," continued the honest boor, " for he has an open hand, and winna let a poor body want an he has it."

The virtue of profuse generosity, by which, indeed, they themselves are most directly advantaged, is readily admitted by the vulgar as a cloak for many sins.

At Stamford our heroine was deposited in safety by her communicative guide. She obtained a place in the coach, which, although termed a light one, and accommodated with no fewer than six horses, only reached London on the afternoon of the second day. The recommendation of the elder Mr. Staunton procured Jeanie a civil reception at the inn where the carriage stopped, and, by the aid of Mrs. Bickerton's correspondent, she found out her friend and relative Mrs. Glass, by whom she was kindly received and hospitably entertained.

CHAPTER XXXV

> My name is Argyle, you may well think it strange,
> To live at the court and never to change.
>   *Ballad.*

FEW names deserve more honourable mention in the history of Scotland, during this period, than that of John, Duke of Argyle and Greenwich. His talents as a statesman and a soldier were generally admitted ; he was not without ambition, but " without the illness that attends it "—without that irregularity of thought and aim, which often excites great men, in his peculiar situation (for it was a very peculiar one), to grasp the means of raising themselves to power, at the risk of throwing a kingdom into confusion. Pope has distinguished him as

> Argyle, the state's whole thunder born to wield,
> And shake alike the senate and the field.

He was alike free from the ordinary vices of statesmen, false-hood, namely, and dissimulation; and from those of warriors, inordinate and violent thirst after self-aggrandisement.

Scotland, his native country, stood at this time in a very precarious and doubtful situation. She was indeed united to England, but the cement had not had time to acquire consistence. The irritation of ancient wrongs still subsisted, and betwixt the fretful jealousy of the Scottish, and the supercilious disdain of the English, quarrels repeatedly occurred, in the course of which the national league, so important to the safety of both, was in the utmost danger of being dissolved. Scotland had, besides, the disadvantage of being divided into intestine factions, which hated each other bitterly, and waited but a signal to break forth into action.

In such circumstances, another man, with the talents and rank of Argyle, but without a mind so happily regulated, would have sought to rise from the earth in the whirlwind, and direct its fury. He chose a course more safe and more honourable.

Soaring above the petty distinctions of faction, his voice was raised, whether in office or opposition, for those measures which were at once just and lenient. His high military talents enabled him, during the memorable year 1715, to render such services to the House of Hanover, as, perhaps, were too great to be either acknowledged or repaid. He had employed, too, his utmost influence in softening the consequences of that insurrection to the unfortunate gentlemen, whom a mistaken sense of loyalty had engaged in the affair, and was rewarded by the esteem and affection of his country in an uncommon degree. This popularity with a discontented and warlike people, was supposed to be a subject of jealousy at court, where the power to become dangerous is sometimes of itself obnoxious, though the inclination is not united with it. Besides, the Duke of Argyle's independent and somewhat haughty mode of expressing himself in Parliament, and acting in public, were ill calculated to attract royal favour. He was, therefore, always respected, and often employed; but he was not a favourite of George the Second, his consort, or his ministers. At several different periods in his life, the Duke might be considered as in absolute disgrace at court, although he could hardly be said to be a declared member of opposition. This rendered him the dearer to Scotland, because it was usually in her cause that he incurred the displeasure of his sovereign; and upon this very occasion of the Porteous mob, the animated and eloquent opposition which he had offered to the severe measures which were about to be adopted towards the city of Edinburgh, was the more gratefully received in that metropolis, as it was understood that the Duke's interposition had given personal offence to Queen Caroline.

His conduct upon this occasion, as, indeed, that of all the Scottish members of the legislature, with one or two unworthy exceptions, had been in the highest degree spirited. The popular tradition, concerning his reply to Queen Caroline, has been given already, and some fragments of his speech against the Porteous Bill are still remembered. He retorted upon the Chancellor, Lord Hardwicke, the insinuation that he had stated himself in this case rather as a party than as a judge :— " I appeal," said Argyle, " to the House—to the nation, if I can be justly branded with the infamy of being a jobber or a partisan. Have I been a briber of votes ?—a buyer of boroughs ?—the agent of corruption for any purpose, or on behalf of any party ?—Consider my life ; examine my actions in the field and in the cabinet, and see where there lies a blot that can attach to my honour. I have shown myself the friend of my country—the loyal subject of my king. I am ready to do so again, without an instant's regard to the frowns or smiles of a court. I have experienced both, and am prepared with indifference for either. I have given my reasons for opposing this bill, and have made it appear that it is repugnant to the international treaty of union, to the liberty of Scotland, and, reflectively, to that of England, to common justice, to common sense, and to the public interest. Shall the metropolis of Scotland, the capital of an independent nation, the residence of a long line of monarchs, by whom that noble city was graced and dignified—shall such a city, for the fault of an obscure and unknown body of rioters, be deprived of its honours and its privileges—its gates and its guards ?—and shall a native Scotsman tamely behold the havoc ? I glory, my Lords, in opposing such unjust rigour, and reckon it my dearest pride and honour to stand up in defence of my native country, while thus laid open to undeserved shame, and unjust spoliation."

Other statesmen and orators, both Scottish and English, used the same arguments, the bill was gradually stripped of its most oppressive and obnoxious clauses, and at length ended in a fine upon the city of Edinburgh in favour of Porteous's widow. So that, as somebody observed at the time, the whole of these fierce debates ended in making the fortune of an old cookmaid, such having been the good woman's original capacity.

The court, however, did not forget the baffle they had received in this affair, and the Duke of Argyle, who had contributed so much to it, was thereafter considered as a person in disgrace. It is necessary to place these circumstances under the reader's observation, both because they are connected with the preceding and subsequent part of our narrative.

The Duke was alone in his study, when one of his gentlemen acquainted him, that a country-girl, from Scotland, was desirous of speaking with his Grace.

"A country-girl, and from Scotland!" said the Duke; "what can have brought the silly fool to London?—Some lover pressed and sent to sea, or some stock sunk in the South-Sea funds, or some such hopeful concern, I suppose, and then nobody to manage the matter but MacCallummore.—Well, this same popularity has its inconveniences.—However, show our countrywoman up, Archibald,—it is ill manners to keep her in attendance."

A young woman of rather low stature, and whose countenance might be termed very modest, and pleasing in expression, though sunburnt, somewhat freckled, and not possessing regular features, was ushered into the splendid library. She wore the tartan plaid of her country, adjusted so as partly to cover her head, and partly to fall back over her shoulders. A quantity of fair hair, disposed with great simplicity and neatness, appeared in front of her round and good-humoured face, to which the solemnity of her errand, and her sense of the Duke's rank and importance, gave an appearance of deep awe, but not of slavish fear or fluttered bashfulness. The rest of Jeanie's dress was in the style of Scottish maidens of her own class; but arranged with that scrupulous attention to neatness and cleanliness, which we often find united with that purity of mind, of which it is a natural emblem.

She stopped near the entrance of the room, made her deepest reverence, and crossed her hands upon her bosom, without uttering a syllable. The Duke of Argyle advanced towards her; and, if she admired his graceful deportment and rich dress, decorated with the orders which had been deservedly bestowed on him, his courteous manner, and quick and intelligent cast of countenance, he, on his part, was not less, or less deservedly, struck with the quiet simplicity and .

modesty expressed in the dress, manners, and countenance of his humble countrywoman.

"Did you wish to speak with me, my bonny lass?" said the Duke, using the encouraging epithet which at once acknowledged the connection betwixt them as country-folk; "or did you wish to see the Duchess?"

"My business is with your honour, my Lord—I mean your Lordship's Grace."

"And what is it, my good girl?" said the Duke, in the same mild and encouraging tone of voice. Jeanie looked at the attendant. "Leave us, Archibald," said the Duke, "and wait in the anteroom." The domestic retired. "And now sit down, my good lass," said the Duke; "take your breath—take your time, and tell me what you have got to say. I guess by your dress, you are just come up from poor old Scotland— Did you come through the streets in your tartan plaid?"

"No, sir," said Jeanie; "a friend brought me in ane o' their street coaches—a very decent woman," she added, her courage increasing as she became familiar with the sound of her own voice in such a presence; "your Lordship's Grace kens her—it's Mrs. Glass, at the sign o' the Thistle."

"Oh, my worthy snuff-merchant—I have always a chat with Mrs. Glass when I purchase my Scotch high-dried.—Well, but your business, my bonny woman—time and tide, you know, wait for no one."

"Your honour—I beg your Lordship's pardon—I mean your Grace,"—for it must be noticed, that this matter of addressing the Duke by his appropriate title had been anxiously inculcated upon Jeanie by her friend Mrs. Glass, in whose eyes it was a matter of such importance, that her last words, as Jeanie left the coach, were, "Mind to say your Grace;" and Jeanie, who had scarce ever in her life spoke to a person of higher quality than the Laird of Dumbiedikes, found great difficulty in arranging her language according to the rules of ceremony.

The Duke, who saw her embarrassment, said, with his usual affability, "Never mind my grace, lassie; just speak out a plain tale, and show you have a Scotch tongue in your head."

"Sir, I am muckle obliged—Sir, I am the sister of that poor unfortunate criminal, Effie Deans, who is ordered for execution at Edinburgh."

"Ah!" said the Duke, "I have heard of that unhappy story, I think—a case of child-murder, under a special act of parliament—Duncan Forbes mentioned it at dinner the other day."

"And I was come up frae the north, sir, to see what could be done for her in the way of getting a reprieve or pardon, sir, or the like of that."

"Alas! my poor girl," said the Duke, "you have made a long and a sad journey to very little purpose—Your sister is ordered for execution."

"But I am given to understand that there is law for reprieving her, if it is in the king's pleasure," said Jeanie.

"Certainly there is," said the Duke; "but that is purely in the king's breast. The crime has been but too common— the Scotch crown-lawyers think it is right there should be an example. Then the late disorders in Edinburgh have excited a prejudice in government against the nation at large, which they think can only be managed by measures of intimidation and severity. What argument have you, my poor girl, except the warmth of your sisterly affection, to offer against all this?— What is your interest?—What friends have you at court?"

"None, excepting God and your Grace," said Jeanie, still keeping her ground resolutely, however.

"Alas!" said the Duke, "I could almost say with old Ormond, that there could not be any, whose influence was smaller with kings and ministers. It is a cruel part of our situation, young woman—I mean of the situation of men in my circumstances, that the public ascribe to them influence which they do not possess; and that individuals are led to expect from them assistance which we have no means of rendering. But candour and plain dealing is in the power of every one, and I must not let you imagine you have resources in my influence, which do not exist, to make your distress the heavier—I have no means of averting your sister's fate—She must die."

"We must a' die, sir," said Jeanie; "it is our common doom for our father's transgression; but we shouldna hasten ilk other out o' the world, that's what your honour kens better than me."

"My good young woman," said the Duke mildly, "we are all apt to blame the law under which we immediately suffer; but you seem to have been well educated in your line of life, and you must know that it is alike the law of God and man, that the murderer shall surely die."

"But, sir, Effie—that is, my poor sister, sir—canna be

proved to be a murderer; and if she be not, and the law take her life notwithstanding, wha is it that is the murderer then?"

"I am no lawyer," said the Duke; "and I own I think the statute a very severe one."

"You are a law-maker, sir, with your leave; and, therefore, ye have power over the law," answered Jeanie.

"Not in my individual capacity," said the Duke; "though, as one of a large body, I have a voice in the legislation. But that cannot serve you—nor have I at present, I care not who knows it, so much personal influence with the sovereign, as would entitle me to ask from him the most insignificant favour. What could tempt you, young woman, to address yourself to me?"

"It was yoursell, sir."

"Myself?" he replied—"I am sure you have never seen me before."

"No, sir; but a' the world kens that the Duke of Argyle is his country's friend; and that ye fight for the right, and speak for the right, and that there's nane like yours in our present Israel, and so they that think themselves wranged draw to refuge under your shadow; and if ye wunna stir to save the blood of an innocent countrywoman of your ain, what should we expect frae southrons and strangers? And maybe I had another reason for troubling your honour."

"And what is that?" asked the Duke.

"I hae understood from my father, that your honour's house, and especially your gudesire and his father, laid down their lives on the scaffold in the persecuting time. And my father was honoured to gie his testimony baith in the cage and in the pillory, as is specially mentioned in the books of Peter Walker the packman, that your honour, I dare say, kens, for he uses maist partly the westland of Scotland. And, sir, there's ane that takes concern in me, that wished me to gang to your Grace's presence, for his gudesire had done your gracious gudesire some good turn, as ye will see frae these papers."

With these words, she delivered to the Duke the little parcel which she had received from Butler. He opened it, and, in the envelope, read with some surprise, "Muster-roll of the men serving in the troop of that godly gentleman, Captain Salathiel Bangtext.—Obadiah Muggleton, Sin-Despise Double-knock, Stand-fast-in-faith Gipps, Turn-to-the-right Thwack-away—What the deuce is this? A list of Praise-

God Barebone's Parliament, I think, or of old Noll's evangelical army—that last fellow should understand his wheelings to judge by his name.—But what does all this mean, my girl?"

"It was the other paper, sir," said Jeanie, somewhat abashed at the mistake.

"Oh, this is my unfortunate grandfather's hand sure enough —'To all who may have friendship for the house of Argyle, these are to certify, that Benjamin Butler, of Monk's regiment of dragoons, having been, under God, the means of saving my life from four English troopers who were about to slay me, I, having no other present means of recompense in my power, do give him this acknowledgment, hoping that it may be useful to him or his during these troublesome times; and do conjure my friends, tenants, kinsmen, and whoever will do aught for me, either in the Highlands or Lowlands, to protect and assist the said Benjamin Butler, and his friends or family, on their lawful occasions, giving them such countenance, maintenance, and supply, as may correspond with the benefit he hath bestowed on me; witness my hand—

'LORNE.'

"This is a strong injunction—This Benjamin Butler was your grandfather, I suppose?—You seem too young to have been his daughter."

"He was nae akin to me, sir—he was grandfather to ane— to a neighbour's son—to a sincere weel-wisher of mine, sir," dropping her little courtesy as she spoke.

"Oh, I understand," said the Duke—"a true-love affair. He was the grandsire of one you are engaged to?"

"One I *was* engaged to, sir," said Jeanie, sighing; "but this unhappy business of my poor sister——"

"What!" said the Duke hastily,—"he has not deserted you on that account, has he?"

"No, sir; he wad be the last to leave a friend in difficulties," said Jeanie; "but I maun think for him, as weel as for mysell. He is a clergyman, sir, and it would not beseem him to marry the like of me, wi' this disgrace on my kindred."

"You are a singular young woman," said the Duke. "You seem to me to think of every one before yourself. And have you really come up from Edinburgh on foot, to attempt this hopeless solicitation for your sister's life?"

"It was not a'thegither on foot, sir," answered Jeanie; "for I sometimes got a cast in a waggon, and I had a horse from Ferrybridge, and then the coach——"

"Well, never mind all that," interrupted the Duke.—— "What reason have you for thinking your sister innocent?"

"Because she has not been proved guilty, as will appear from looking at these papers."

She put into his hand a note of the evidence, and copies of her sister's declaration. These papers Butler had procured after her departure, and Saddletree had them forwarded to London, to Mrs. Glass's care; so that Jeanie found the documents, so necessary for supporting her suit, lying in readiness at her arrival.

"Sit down in that chair, my good girl," said the Duke, "until I glance over the papers."

She obeyed, and watched with the utmost anxiety each change in his countenance as he cast his eye through the papers briefly, yet with attention, and making memoranda as he went along. After reading them hastily over, he looked up, and seemed about to speak, yet changed his purpose, as if afraid of committing himself by giving too hasty an opinion, and read over again several passages which he had marked as being most important. All this he did in shorter time than can be supposed by men of ordinary talents; for his mind was of that acute and penetrating character which discovers, with the glance of intuition, what facts bear on the particular point that chances to be subjected to consideration. At length he rose, after a few minutes' deep reflection.—"Young woman," said he, "your sister's case must certainly be termed a hard one."

"God bless you, sir, for that very word!" said Jeanie.

"It seems contrary to the genius of British law," continued the Duke, "to take that for granted which is not proved, or to punish with death for a crime, which, for aught the prosecutor has been able to show, may not have been committed at all."

"God bless you, sir!" again said Jeanie, who had risen from her seat, and, with clasped hands, eyes glittering through tears, and features which trembled with anxiety, drank in every word which the Duke uttered.

"But, alas! my poor girl," he continued, "what good will my opinion do you, unless I could impress it upon those in whose hands your sister's life is placed by the law? Besides,

I am no lawyer; and I must speak with some of our Scottish gentlemen of the gown about the matter."

"Oh but, sir, what seems reasonable to your honour, will certainly be the same to them," answered Jeanie.

"I do not know that," replied the Duke; "ilka man buckles his belt his ain gate—you know our old Scotch proverb?—But you shall not have placed this reliance on me altogether in vain. Leave these papers with me, and you shall hear from me to-morrow or next day. Take care to be at home at Mrs. Glass's, and ready to come to me at a moment's warning. It will be unnecessary for you to give Mrs. Glass the trouble to attend you;—and, by-the-bye, you will please to be dressed just as you are at present."

"I wad hae putten on a cap, sir," said Jeanie, "but your honour kens it isna the fashion of my country for single women; and I judged that being sae mony hundred miles frae hame, your Grace's heart wad warm to the tartan," looking at the corner of her plaid.

"You judged quite right," said the Duke. "I know the full value of the snood; and MacCallummore's heart will be as cold as death can make it, when it does *not* warm to the tartan. Now, go away, and don't be out of the way when I send."

Jeanie replied,—"There is little fear of that, sir, for I have little heart to go to see sights amang this wilderness of black houses. But if I might say to your gracious honour, that if ye ever condescend to speak to ony ane that is of greater degree than yoursell, though maybe it is nae civil in me to say sae, just if you would think there can be nae sic odds between you and them, as between poor Jeanie Deans from Saint Leonard's and the Duke of Argyle; and so dinna be chappit back or cast down wi' the first rough answer."

"I am not apt," said the Duke, laughing, "to mind rough answers much—Do not you hope too much from what I have promised. I will do my best, but God has the hearts of kings in His own hand."

Jeanie courtesied reverently and withdrew, attended by the Duke's gentleman, to her hackney-coach, with a respect which her appearance did not demand, but which was perhaps paid to the length of the interview with which his master had honoured her.

CHAPTER XXXVI

------Ascend,
While radiant summer opens all its pride,
Thy hill, delightful Shene! Here let us sweep,
The boundless landscape.

THOMSON.

FROM her kind and officious, but somewhat gossiping friend, Mrs. Glass, Jeanie underwent a very close catechism on their road to the Strand, where the Thistle of the good lady flourished in full glory, and, with its legend of *Nemo me impune*, distinguished a shop then well known to all Scottish folk of high and low degree.

"And were you sure aye to say *your Grace* to him?" said the good old lady; "for ane should make a distinction between MacCallummore and the bits o' southern bodies that they ca' lords here—there are as mony o' them, Jeanie, as would gar ane think they maun cost but little fash in the making—some of them I wadna trust wi' six pennies-worth of black rappee—some of them I wadna gie mysell the trouble to put up a hapnyworth in brown paper for.—But I hope you showed your breeding to the Duke of Argyle, for what sort of folk would he think your friends in London, if you had been lording him, and him a Duke?"

"He didna seem muckle to mind," said Jeanie; "he kend that I was landward bred."

"Weel, weel," answered the good lady. "His Grace kens me weel; so I am the less anxious about it. I never fill his snuff-box but he says, 'How d'ye do, good Mrs. Glass?—How are all our friends in the North?' or it may be—'Have ye heard from the North lately?' And you may be sure, I make my best courtesy, and answer, 'My Lord Duke, I hope your Grace's noble Duchess, and your Grace's young ladies, are well; and I hope the snuff continues to give your Grace satisfaction.' And then ye will see the people in the shop begin to look about them; and if there's a Scotchman, as there may be three or half-a-dozen, aff go the hats, and mony a look after him, and 'there goes the Prince of Scotland, God bless him!' But ye have not told me yet the very words he said t'ye."

Jeanie had no intention to be quite so communicative. She had, as the reader may have observed, some of the caution and shrewdness, as well as of the simplicity, of her country. She answered generally, that the Duke had received her very compassionately, and had promised to interest himself in her sister's affair, and to let her hear from him in the course of the next day, or the day after. She did not choose to make any mention of his having desired her to be in readiness to attend him, far less of his hint, that she should not bring her landlady. So that honest Mrs. Glass was obliged to remain satisfied with the general intelligence above mentioned, after having done all she could to extract more.

It may easily be conceived, that, on the next day, Jeanie declined all invitations and inducements, whether of exercise or curiosity, to walk abroad, and continued to inhale the close, and somewhat professional atmosphere of Mrs. Glass's small parlour. The latter flavour it owed to a certain cupboard, containing, among other articles, a few canisters of real Havannah, which, whether from respect to the manufacture, or out of a reverent fear of the excisemen, Mrs. Glass did not care to trust in the open shop below, and which communicated to the room a scent, that, however fragrant to the nostrils of the connoisseur, was not very agreeable to those of Jeanie.

"Dear sirs," she said to herself, "I wonder how my cousin's silk manty, and her gowd watch, or onything in the world, can be worth sitting sneezing all her life in this little stifling room, and might walk on green braes if she liked."

Mrs. Glass was equally surprised at her cousin's reluctance to stir abroad, and her indifference to the fine sights of London. "It would always help to pass away the time," she said, "to have something to look at, though ane *was* in distress." But Jeanie was unpersuadable.

The day after her interview with the Duke was spent in that "hope delayed, which maketh the heart sick." Minutes glided after minutes—hours fled after hours—it became too late to have any reasonable expectation of hearing from the Duke that day; yet the hope which she disowned, she could not altogether relinquish, and her heart throbbed, and her ears tingled, with every casual sound in the shop below. It was in vain. The day wore away in the anxiety of protracted and fruitless expectation.

The next morning commenced in the same manner. But before noon, a well-dressed gentleman entered Mrs. Glass's shop, and requested to see a young woman from Scotland.

"That will be my cousin, Jeanie Deans, Mr. Archibald,"

said Mrs. Glass, with a courtesy of recognisance. " Have you any message for her from his Grace the Duke of Argyle, Mr. Archibald? I will carry it to her in a moment."

" I believe I must give her the trouble of stepping down, Mrs. Glass."

" Jeanie—Jeanie Deans! " said Mrs. Glass, screaming at the bottom of the little staircase, which ascended from the corner of the shop to the higher regions. " Jeanie—Jeanie Deans, I say! come downstairs instantly; here is the Duke of Argyle's groom of the chambers desires to see you directly." This was announced in a voice so loud, as to make all who chanced to be within hearing aware of the important communication.

It may easily be supposed, that Jeanie did not tarry long in adjusting herself to attend the summons, yet her feet almost failed her as she came downstairs.

" I must ask the favour of your company a little way," said Archibald, with civility.

" I am quite ready, sir," said Jeanie.

" Is my cousin going out, Mr. Archibald? then I will hae to go wi' her, no doubt.—James Rasper—Look to the shop, James.—Mr. Archibald," pushing a jar towards him, " you take his Grace's mixture, I think. Please to fill your box, for old acquaintance' sake, while I get on my things."

Mr. Archibald transposed a modest parcel of snuff from the jar to his own mull, but said he was obliged to decline the pleasure of Mrs. Glass's company, as his message was particularly to the young person.

" Particularly to the young person? " said Mrs. Glass; "is not that uncommon, Mr. Archibald? But his Grace is the best judge; and you are a steady person, Mr. Archibald. It is not every one that comes from a great man's house I would trust my cousin with.—But, Jeanie, you must not go through the streets with Mr. Archibald with your tartan what d'ye call it there upon your shoulders, as if you had come up with a drove of Highland cattle. Wait till I bring down my silk cloak. Why, we'll have the mob after you! "

" I have a hackney-coach in waiting, madam," said Mr. Archibald, interrupting the officious old lady, from whom Jeanie might otherwise have found it difficult to escape," and, I believe, I must not allow her time for any change of dress."

So saying, he hurried Jeanie into the coach, while she internally praised and wondered at the easy manner in which he shifted off Mrs. Glass's officious offers and inquiries, without mentioning his master's orders, or going into any explanation whatever.

On entering the coach, Mr. Archibald seated himself in the front seat, opposite to our heroine, and they drove on in silence. After they had proceeded nearly half-an-hour, without a word on either side, it occurred to Jeanie, that the distance and time did not correspond with that which had been occupied by her journey on the former occasion, to and from the residence of the Duke of Argyle. At length she could not help asking her taciturn companion, " Whilk way they were going ? "

" My Lord Duke will inform you himself, madam," answered Archibald, with the same solemn courtesy which marked his whole demeanour. Almost as he spoke, the hackney-coach drew up, and the coachman dismounted and opened the door. Archibald got out, and assisted Jeanie to get down. She found herself in a large turnpike road, without the bounds of London, upon the other side of which road was drawn up a plain chariot and four horses, the panels without arms, and the servants without liveries.

" You have been punctual, I see, Jeanie," said the Duke of Argyle, as Archibald opened the carriage door. " You must be my companion for the rest of the way. Archibald will remain here with the hackney-coach till your return."

Ere Jeanie could make answer, she found herself, to her no small astonishment, seated by the side of a duke, in a carriage which rolled forward at a rapid yet smooth rate, very different in both particulars from the lumbering, jolting vehicle which she had just left ; and which, lumbering and jolting as it was, conveyed to one who had seldom been in a coach before, a certain feeling of dignity and importance.

" Young woman," said the Duke, " after thinking as attentively on your sister's case as is in my power, I continue to be impressed with the belief that great injustice may be done by the execution of her sentence. So are one or two liberal and intelligent lawyers of both countries whom I have spoken with. —Nay, pray hear me out before you thank me.—I have already told you my personal conviction is of little consequence, unless I could impress the same upon others. Now I have done for you, what I would certainly not have done to serve any purpose of my own—I have asked an audience of a lady whose interest with the king is deservedly very high. It has been allowed me, and I am desirous that you should see her and speak for yourself. You have no occasion to be abashed; tell your story simply as you did to me."

"I am much obliged to your Grace," said Jeanie, remembering Mrs. Glass's charge; "and I am sure since I have had the courage to speak to your Grace, in poor Effie's cause, I have less reason to be shame-faced in speaking to a leddy. But, sir, I would like to ken what to ca' her, whether your grace, or your honour, or your leddyship, as we say to lairds and leddies in Scotland, and I will take care to mind it; for I ken leddies are full mair particular than gentlemen about their titles of honour."

"You have no occasion to call her anything but Madam. Just say what you think is likely to make the best impression —look at me from time to time—if I put my hand to my cravat so" (showing her the motion), "you will stop; but I shall only do this when you say anything that is not likely to please."

"But, sir, your Grace," said Jeanie, "if it wasna ower muckle trouble, wad it no be better to tell me what I should say, and I could get it by heart?"

"No, Jeanie, that would not have the same effect—that would be like reading a sermon, you know, which we good Presbyterians think has less unction than when spoken without book," replied the Duke. "Just speak as plainly and boldly to this lady, as you did to me the day before yesterday; and if you can gain her consent, I'll wad ye a plack, as we say in the north, that you get the pardon from the king."

As he spoke he took a pamphlet from his pocket, and began to read. Jeanie had good sense and tact, which constitute betwixt them that which is called natural good breeding: She interpreted the Duke's manœuvre as a hint that she was to ask no more questions, and she remained silent accordingly.

The carriage rolled rapidly onwards through fertile meadows, ornamented with splendid old oaks, and catching occasionally a glance of the majestic mirror of a broad and placid river. After passing through a pleasant village, the equipage stopped on a commanding eminence, where the beauty of English landscape was displayed in its utmost luxuriance. Here the Duke alighted, and desired Jeanie to follow him. They paused for a moment on the brow of a hill, to gaze on the unrivalled landscape which it presented. A huge sea of verdure, with crossing and intersecting promontories of massive and tufted groves, was tenanted by numberless flocks and herds, which seemed to wander unrestrained and unbounded through the rich pastures. The Thames, here turreted with villas, and there garlanded with forests, moved on slowly and placidly, like the mighty monarch of the scene, to whom all its other beauties were but accessories, and bore on his bosom an hundred barques and skiffs, whose white sails and gaily fluttering pennons gave life to the whole.

The Duke of Argyle was, of course, familiar with this scene ; but to a man of taste it must be always new. Yet, as he paused and looked on this inimitable landscape, with the feeling of delight which it must give to the bosom of every admirer of nature, his thoughts naturally reverted to his own more grand, and scarce less beautiful, domains of Inverary.— "This is a fine scene," he said to his companion, curious, perhaps, to draw out her sentiments ; "we have nothing like it in Scotland."

"It's braw rich feeding for the cows, and they have a fine breed o' cattle here," replied Jeanie ; "but I like just as weel to look at the craigs of Arthur's Seat, and the sea coming in ayont them, as at a' thae muckle trees."

The Duke smiled at a reply equally professional and national, and made a signal for the carriage to remain where it was. Then adopting an unfrequented footpath, he conducted Jeanie, through several complicated mazes, to a postern-door in a high brick wall. It was shut ; but as the Duke tapped slightly at it, a person in waiting within, after reconnoitring through a small iron grate contrived for the purpose, unlocked the door, and admitted them. They entered, and it was immediately closed and fastened behind them. This was all done quickly, the door so instantly closing, and the person who opened it so suddenly disappearing, that Jeanie could not even catch a glimpse of his exterior.

They found themselves at the extremity of a deep and narrow alley, carpeted with the most verdant and close-shaven turf, which felt like velvet under their feet, and screened from the sun by the branches of the lofty elms which united over the path, and caused it to resemble, in the solemn obscurity of the light which they admitted, as well as from the range of columnar stems, and intricate union of their arched branches, one of the narrow side aisles in an ancient Gothic cathedral.

CHAPTER XXXVII

————I beseech you—
These **tears** beseech you, and these chaste hands woo **you**,
That never yet were heaved but to things holy—
Things like yourself—You are a God above **us**;
Be as a God, then, full of saving mercy !
The Bloody Brother.

ENCOURAGED as she was by the courteous manners of her
noble countryman, it was not without a feeling of something
like terror that Jeanie felt herself in a place apparently so
lonely, with a man of such high rank. That she should have
been permitted to wait on the Duke in his own house, and
have been there received to a private interview, was in itself
an uncommon and distinguished event in the annals of a life
so simple as hers ; but to find herself his travelling companion
in a journey, and then suddenly to be left alone with him in
so secluded a situation, had something in it of awful mystery.
A romantic heroine might have suspected and dreaded the
power of her own charms ; but Jeanie was too wise to let such
a silly thought intrude on her mind. Still, however, she had
a most eager desire to know where she now was, and to whom
she was to be presented.

She remarked that the Duke's dress, though still such as
indicated rank and fashion (for it was not the custom of men
of quality at that time to dress themselves like their own
coachmen or grooms), was nevertheless plainer than that in
which she had seen him upon a former occasion, and was
divested, in particular, of all those badges of external decora-
tion which intimated superior consequence. In short, he was
attired as plainly as any gentleman of fashion could appear in
the streets of London in a morning ; and this circumstance
helped to shake an opinion which Jeanie began to entertain,
that, perhaps, he intended she should plead her cause in the
presence of royalty itself. " But, surely," said she to herself,
" he wad hae putten on his braw star and garter, an he had
thought o' coming before the face of Majesty—and after a',
this is mair like a gentleman's policy than a royal palace."

There was some sense in Jeanie's reasoning ; yet she was
not sufficiently mistress either of the circumstances of etiquette,
or the particular relations which existed betwixt the government and the Duke of Argyle, to form an accurate judgment.

The Duke, as we have said, was at this time in open opposition to the administration of Sir Robert Walpole, and was understood to be out of favour with the royal family, to whom he had rendered such important services. But it was a maxim of Queen Caroline, to bear herself towards her political friends with such caution, as if there was a possibility of their one day being her enemies, and towards political opponents with the same degree of circumspection, as if they might again become friendly to her measures. Since Margaret of Anjou, no queen-consort had exercised such weight in the political affairs of England, and the personal address which she displayed on many occasions, had no small share in reclaiming from their political heresy many of those determined Tories, who, after the reign of the Stuarts had been extinguished in the person of Queen Anne, were disposed rather to transfer their allegiance to her brother the Chevalier de St. George, than to acquiesce in the settlement of the crown on the Hanover family. Her husband, whose most shining quality was courage in the field of battle, and who endured the office of King of England, without ever being able to acquire English habits, or any familiarity with English dispositions, found the utmost assistance from the address of his partner; and while he jealously affected to do everything according to his own will and pleasure, was in secret prudent enough to take and follow the advice of his more adroit consort. He entrusted to her the delicate office of determining the various degrees of favour necessary to attach the wavering, or to confirm such as were already friendly, or to regain those whose good-will had been lost.

With all the winning address of an elegant, and, according to the times, an accomplished woman, Queen Caroline possessed the masculine soul of the other sex. She was proud by nature, and even her policy could not always temper her expressions of displeasure, although few were more ready at repairing any false step of this kind, when her prudence came up to the aid of her passions. She loved the real possession of power, rather than the show of it, and whatever she did herself that was either wise or popular, she always desired that the king should have the full credit as well as the advantage of the measure, conscious that, by adding to his respectability, she was most likely to maintain her own. And so desirous was she to comply with all his tastes, that, when threatened with the gout, she had repeatedly had recourse to checking the fit, by the use of the cold bath, thereby endangering her life, that she might be able to attend the king in his walks.

It was a very consistent part of Queen Caroline's character, to keep up many private correspondences with those to whom in public she seemed unfavourable, or who, for various reasons, stood ill with the court. By this means she kept in her hands the thread of many a political intrigue, and, without pledging herself to anything, could often prevent discontent from becoming hatred, and opposition from exaggerating itself into rebellion. If by any accident her correspondence with such persons chanced to be observed or discovered, which she took all possible pains to prevent, it was represented as a mere intercourse of society, having no reference to politics; an answer with which even the prime minister, Sir Robert Walpole, was compelled to remain satisfied, when he discovered that the Queen had given a private audience to Pulteney, afterwards Earl of Bath, his most formidable and most inveterate enemy.

In thus maintaining occasional intercourse with several persons who seemed most alienated from the crown, it may readily be supposed, that Queen Caroline had taken care not to break entirely with the Duke of Argyle. His high birth, his great talents, the estimation in which he was held in his own country, the great services which he had rendered the house of Brunswick in 1715, placed him high in that rank of persons who were not to be rashly neglected. He had, almost by his single and unassisted talents, stopped the irruption of the banded force of all the Highland chiefs; there was little doubt, that, with the slightest encouragement, he could put them all in motion, and renew the civil war; and it was well known that the most flattering overtures had been transmitted to the Duke from the court of St. Germains. The character and temper of Scotland were still little known, and it was considered as a volcano, which might, indeed, slumber for a series of years but was still liable, at a moment the least expected, to break out into a wasteful eruption. It was, therefore, of the highest importance to retain some hold over so important a personage as the Duke of Argyle, and Caroline preserved the power of doing so by means of a lady, with whom, as wife of George II., she might have been supposed to be on less intimate terms.

It was not the least instance of the Queen's address, that

she had contrived that one of her principal attendants, Lady
Suffolk, should unite in her own person the two apparently
inconsistent characters, of her husband's mistress, and her
own very obsequious and complaisant confidant. By this
dexterous management the Queen secured her power against
the danger which might most have threatened it—the thwart-
ing influence of an ambitious rival; and if she submitted to
the mortification of being obliged to connive at her husband's
infidelity, she was at least guarded against what she might
think its most dangerous effects, and was besides at 'iberty,
now and then, to bestow a few civil insults upon "her good
Howard," whom, however, in general, she treated with great
decorum.[1] Lady Suffolk lay under strong obligations to the
Duke of Argyle, for reasons which may be collected from
Horace Walpole's Reminiscences of that reign, and through
her means the Duke had some occasional correspondence
with Queen Caroline, much interrupted, however, since the
part he had taken in the debate concerning the Porteous
mob, an affair which the Queen, though somewhat unreason-
ably, was disposed to resent, rather as an intended and premeditated insolence to her own person and authority, than as
a sudden ebullition of popular vengeance. Still, however, the
communication remained open betwixt them, though it had
been of late disused on both sides. These remarks will be
found necessary to understand the scene which is about to be
presented to the reader.

From the narrow alley which they had traversed, the Duke
turned into one of the same character, but broader and still
longer. Here, for the first time since they had entered these
gardens, Jeanie saw persons approaching them.

They were two ladies; one of whom walked a little behind
the other, yet not so much as to prevent her from hearing and
replying to whatever observation was addressed to her by the
lady who walked foremost, and that without her having the
trouble to turn her person. As they advanced very slowly,
Jeanie had time to study their features and appearance. The
Duke also slackened his pace, as if to give her time to collect
herself, and repeatedly desired her not to be afraid. The
lady who seemed the principal person had remarkably good
features, though somewhat injured by the small-pox, that
venomous scourge, which each village Esculapius (thanks to
Jenner) can now tame as easily as their tutelary deity subdued

---

[1] See Horace Walpole's Reminiscences.

the Python. The lady's eyes were brilliant, her teeth good, and her countenance formed to express at will either majesty or courtesy. Her form, though rather *embonpoint*, was nevertheless graceful; and the elasticity and firmness of her step gave no room to suspect, what was actually the case, that she suffered occasionally from a disorder the most unfavourable to pedestrian exercise. Her dress was rather rich than gay, and her manner commanding and noble.

Her companion was of lower stature, with light-brown hair and expressive blue eyes. Her features, without being absolutely regular, were perhaps more pleasing than if they had been critically handsome. A melancholy, or at least a pensive expression, for which her lot gave too much cause, predominated when she was silent, but gave way to a pleasing and good-humoured smile when she spoke to any one.

When they were within twelve or fifteen yards of these ladies, the Duke made a sign that Jeanie should stand still, and stepping forward himself, with the grace which was natural to him, made a profound obeisance, which was formally, yet in a dignified manner, returned by the personage whom he approached.

"I hope," she said, with an affable and condescending smile, "that I see so great a stranger at court, as the Duke of Argyle has been of late, in as good health as his friends there and elsewhere could wish him to enjoy."

The Duke replied, "That he had been perfectly well"; and added, "that the necessity of attending to the public business before the House, as well as the time occupied by a late journey to Scotland, had rendered him less assiduous in paying his duty at the levee and drawing-room than he could have desired."

"When your Grace *can* find time for a duty so frivolous," replied the Queen, ": you are aware of your title to be well received. I hope my readiness to comply with the wish which you expressed yesterday to Lady Suffolk, is a sufficient proof that one of the royal family, at least, has not forgotten ancient and important services, in resenting something which resembles recent neglect." This was said apparently with great good-humour, and in a tone which expressed a desire of conciliation.

The Duke replied, 'That he would account himself the most unfortunate of men, if he could be supposed capable of neglecting his duty, in modes and circumstances when it was expected, and would have been agreeable. He was deeply gratified by the honour which her Majesty was now doing to him personally; and he trusted she would soon perceive that it was in a matter essential to his Majesty's interest, that he had the boldness to give her this trouble."

"You cannot oblige me more, my Lord Duke," replied the Queen, "than by giving me the advantage of your lights and experience on any point of the King's service. Your Grace is aware, that I can only be the medium through which the matter is subjected to his Majesty's superior wisdom; but if it is a suit which respects your Grace personally, it shall lose no support by being preferred through me."

"It is no suit of mine, madam," replied the Duke; "nor have I any to prefer for myself personally, although I feel in full force my obligation to your Majesty. It is a business which concerns his Majesty, as a lover of justice and of mercy, and which, I am convinced, may be highly useful in conciliating the unfortunate irritation which at present subsists among his Majesty's good subjects in Scotland."

There were two parts of this speech disagreeable to Caroline. In the first place, it removed the flattering notion she had adopted, that Argyle designed to use her personal intercession in making his peace with the administration, and recovering the employments of which he had been deprived; and next, she was displeased that he should talk of the discontents in Scotland as irritations to be conciliated, rather than suppressed.

Under the influence of these feelings, she answered hastily, "That his Majesty has good subjects in England, my Lord Duke, he is bound to thank God and the laws—that he has subjects in Scotland, I think he may thank God and his sword."

The Duke, though a courtier, coloured slightly, and the Queen, instantly sensible of her error, added, without displaying the least change of countenance, and as if the words had been an original branch of the sentence—"And the swords of those real Scotchmen who are friends to the House of Brunswick, particularly that of His Grace of Argyle."

"My sword, madam," replied the Duke, "like that of my fathers, has been always at the command of my lawful king, and of my native country—I trust it is impossible to separate their real rights and interests. But the present is a matter of more private concern, and respects the person of an obscure individual."

"What is the affair, my lord?" said the Queen. "Let us find out what we are talking about, lest we should misconstrue and misunderstand each other."

"The matter, madam," answered the Duke of Argyle, "regards the fate of an unfortunate young woman in Scotland, now lying under sentence of death, for a crime of which I think it highly probable that she is innocent. And my humble petition to your Majesty is, to obtain your powerful intercession with the King for a pardon."

It was now the Queen's turn to colour, and she did so over cheek and brow—neck and bosom. She paused a moment, as if unwilling to trust her voice with the first expression of her displeasure; and on assuming an air of dignity and an austere regard of control, she at length replied, "My Lord Duke, I will not ask your motives for addressing to me a request which circumstances have rendered such an extraordinary one. Your road to the King's closet, as a peer and a privy-councillor, entitled to request an audience, was open, without giving me the pain of this discussion. *I*, at least, have had enough of Scotch pardons."

The Duke was prepared for this burst of indignation, and he was not shaken by it. He did not attempt a reply while the Queen was in the first heat of displeasure, but remained in the same firm, yet respectful posture, which he had assumed during the interview. The Queen, trained from her situation to self-command, instantly perceived the advantage she might give against herself by yielding to passion; and added, in the same condescending and affable tone in which she had opened the interview, "You must allow me some of the privileges of the sex, my Lord; and do not judge uncharitably of me, though I am a little moved at the recollection of the gross insult and outrage done in your capital city to the royal authority, at the very time when it was vested in my unworthy person. Your Grace cannot be surprised that I should both have felt it at the time, and recollected it now."

"It is certainly a matter not speedily to be forgotten," answered the Duke. "My own poor thoughts of it have been long before your Majesty, and I must have expressed myself very ill if I did not convey my detestation of the murder which was committed under such extraordinary circumstances. I might, indeed, be so unfortunate as to differ with his Majesty's advisers on the degree in which it was either just or politic to punish the innocent instead of the guilty. But I trust your Majesty will permit me to be silent on a topic in which my sentiments have not the good fortune to coincide with those of more able men."

"We will not prosecute a topic on which we may probably differ," said the Queen. "One word, however, I may say in private—You know our good Lady Suffolk is a little deaf—the Duke of Argyle, when disposed to renew his acquaintance with his master and mistress, will hardly find many topics on which we should disagree."

"Let me hope," said the Duke, bowing profoundly to so flattering an intimation, "that I shall not be so unfortunate as to have found one on the present occasion."

"I must first impose on your Grace the duty of confession," said the Queen, "before I grant you absolution. What is your particular interest in this young woman? She does not seem" (and she scanned Jeanie, as she said this, with the eye of a connoisseur) "much qualified to alarm my friend the Duchess's jealousy."

"I think your Majesty," replied the Duke, smiling in his turn, "will allow my taste may be a pledge for me on that score."

"Then, though she has not much the air *d'une grande dame*, I suppose she is some thirtieth cousin in the terrible chapter of Scottish genealogy?"

"No, madam," said the Duke; "but I wish some of my nearer relations had half her worth, honesty, and affection."

"Her name must be Campbell, at least?" said Queen Caroline.

"No, madam; her name is not quite so distinguished, if I may be permitted to say so," answered the Duke.

"Ah! but she comes from Inverary or Argyleshire?" said the sovereign.

"She has never been farther north in her life than Edinburgh, madam."

"Then my conjectures are all ended," said the Queen, "and your Grace must yourself take the trouble to explain the affair of your protégée."

With that precision and easy brevity which is only acquired by habitually conversing in the higher ranks of society, and which is the diametrical opposite of that protracted style of disquisition,

Which squires call potter, and which men call prose,

the Duke explained the singular law under which Effie Deans had received sentence of death, and detailed the affectionate exertions which Jeanie had made in behalf of her sister, for whose sake she was willing to sacrifice all but truth and conscience.

Queen Caroline listened with attention; she was rather fond, it must be remembered, of an argument, and soon found matter in what the Duke told her for raising difficulties to his request.

"It appears to me, my Lord," she replied, "that this is a severe law. But still it is adopted upon good grounds, I am bound to suppose, as the law of the country, and the girl has been convicted under it. The very presumptions which the law construes into a positive proof of guilt exist in her case; and all that your Grace has said concerning the possibility of her innocence may be a very good argument for annulling the Act of Parliament, but cannot, while it stands good, be admitted in favour of any individual convicted upon the statute."

The Duke saw and avoided the snare; for he was conscious, that, by replying to the argument, he must have been inevitably led to a discussion, in the course of which the Queen was likely to be hardened in her own opinion, until she became obliged, out of mere respect to consistency, to let the criminal suffer. "If your Majesty," he said, "would condescend to hear my poor countrywoman herself, perhaps she may find an advocate in your own heart, more able than I am, to combat the doubts suggested by your understanding."

The Queen seemed to acquiesce, and the Duke made a signal for Jeanie to advance from the spot where she had hitherto remained watching countenances, which were too long accustomed to suppress all apparent signs of emotion, to convey to her any interesting intelligence. Her Majesty could not help smiling at the awe-struck manner in which the quiet demure figure of the little Scotchwoman advanced towards her, and yet more at the first sound of her broad northern accent. But Jeanie had a voice low and sweetly toned, an admirable thing in woman, and eke besought "her Leddyship to have pity on a poor misguided young creature," in tones so affecting, that, like the notes of some of her native songs, provincial vulgarity was lost in pathos.

"Stand up, young woman," said the Queen, but in a kind tone, "and tell me what sort of a barbarous people your countryfolk are, where child-murder is become so common as to require the restraint of laws like yours?"

"If your Leddyship pleases," answered Jeanie, "there are mony places beside Scotland where mothers are unkind to their ain flesh and blood."

It must be observed, that the disputes between George the Second, and Frederick, Prince of Wales, were then at the highest, and that the good-natured part of the public laid the blame on the Queen. She coloured highly, and darted a glance of a most penetrating character first at Jeanie, and then at the Duke. Both sustained it unmoved; Jeanie from total unconsciousness of the offence she had given, and the Duke from his habitual composure. But in his heart he thought, My unlucky protégée has, with this luckless answer, shot dead, by a kind of chance medley, her only hope of success.

Lady Suffolk, good-humouredly and skilfully, interposed in this awkward crisis. "You should tell this lady," she said to Jeanie, "the particular causes which render this crime common in your country."

"Some thinks it's the Kirk-Session—that is—it's the—it's the cutty-stool, if your Leddyship pleases," said Jeanie, looking down, and courtesying.

"The what?" said Lady Suffolk, to whom the phrase was new, and who besides was rather deaf.

"That's the stool of repentance, madam, if it please your Leddyship," answered Jeanie, "for light life and conversation, and for breaking the seventh command." Here she raised her eyes to the Duke, saw his hand at his chin, and, totally unconscious of what she had said out of joint, gave double effect to the innuendo, by stopping short and looking embarrassed.

As for Lady Suffolk, she retired like a covering party, which, having interposed betwixt their retreating friends and the enemy, have suddenly drawn on themselves a fire unexpectedly severe.

The deuce take the lass, thought the Duke of Argyle to himself: there goes another shot—and she has hit with both barrels right and left!

Indeed the Duke had himself his share of the confusion, for, having acted as master of ceremonies to this innocent offender, he felt much in the circumstances of a country squire, who, having introduced his spaniel into a well-appointed

drawing-room, is doomed to witness the disorder and damage
which arises to china and to dress-gowns, in consequence of
its untimely frolics.   Jeanie's last chance hit, however, obliterated the ill impression which had arisen from the first; for
her Majesty had not so lost the feelings of a wife in those
of a Queen, but that she could enjoy a jest at the expense of
" her good Suffolk." She turned towards the Duke of Argyle
with a smile, which marked that she enjoyed the triumph, and
observed, "the Scotch are a rigidly moral people." Then
again applying herself to Jeanie, she asked, how she travelled
up from Scotland.

"Upon my foot mostly, madam," was the reply.

"What, all that immense way upon foot?—How far can
you walk in a day?"

"Five-and-twenty miles and a bittock."

"And a what?" said the Queen, looking towards the Duke
of Argyle.

"And about five miles more," replied the Duke.

"I thought I was a good walker," said the Queen, "but
this shames me sadly."

"May your Leddyship never hae sae weary a heart, that ye
canna be sensible of the weariness of the limbs!" said Jeanie.

That came better off, thought the Duke; it's the first thing
she has said to the purpose.

"And I didna just a'thegither walk the haill way neither,
for I had whiles the cast of a cart; and I had the cast of a
horse from Ferrybridge—and divers other easements," said
Jeanie, cutting short her story, for she observed the Duke
made the sign he had fixed upon.

"With all these accommodations," answered the Queen, "you
must have had a very fatiguing journey, and, I fear, to little
purpose; since, if the King were to pardon your sister, in all
probability it would do her little good, for I suppose your
people of Edinburgh would hang her out of spite."

She will sink herself now outright, thought the Duke.

But he was wrong.   The shoals on which Jeanie had
touched in this delicate conversation lay underground, and
were unknown to her; this rock was above water, and she
avoided it.

"She was confident," she said, "that baith town and
country wad rejoice to see his Majesty taking compassion on
a poor unfriended creature."

"His Majesty has not found it so in a late instance," said

the Queen; "but, I suppose, my Lord Duke would advise him to be guided by the votes of the rabble themselves, who should be hanged and who spared?"

"No, madam," said the Duke; "but I would advise his Majesty to be guided by his own feelings, and those of his royal consort; and then, I am sure, punishment will only attach itself to guilt, and even then with cautious reluctance."

"Well, my Lord," said her Majesty, "all these fine speeches do not convince me of the propriety of so soon showing any mark of favour to your—I suppose I must not say rebellious? —but, at least, your very disaffected and intractable metropolis. Why, the whole nation is in a league to screen the savage and abominable murderers of that unhappy man; otherwise, how is it possible but that, of so many perpetrators, and engaged in so public an action for such a length of time, one at least must have been recognised? Even this wench, for aught I can tell, may be a depository of the secret.—Hark you, young woman, had you any friends engaged in the Porteous mob?"

"No, madam," answered Jeanie, happy that the question was so framed that she could, with a good conscience, answer it in the negative.

"But I suppose," continued the Queen, "if you were possessed of such a secret, you would hold it matter of conscience to keep it to yourself?"

"I would pray to be directed and guided what was the line of duty, madam," answered Jeanie.

"Yes, and take that which suited your own inclinations," replied her Majesty.

"If it like you, madam," said Jeanie, "I would hae gaen to the end of the earth to save the life of John Porteous, or any other unhappy man in his condition; but I might lawfully doubt how far I am called upon to be the avenger of his blood, though it may become the civil magistrate to do so. He is dead and gane to his place, and they that have slain him must answer for their ain act. But my sister, my puir sister Effie, still lives, though her days and hours are numbered!—She still lives, and a word of the King's mouth might restore her to a broken-hearted auld man, that never, in his daily and nightly exercise, forgot to pray that his Majesty might be blessed with a long and a prosperous reign, and that his throne, and the throne of his posterity, might be established in righteousness. Oh, madam, if ever ye kend what it was to sorrow for and with a sinning and a suffering creature, whose mind is sae tossed that she can be neither ca'd fit to live or die, have some compassion on our misery!—Save an honest house from dishonour, and an unhappy girl, not eighteen years of age, from an early and dreadful death! Alas! it is not when we sleep soft and wake merrily ourselves, that we think on other people's sufferings. Our hearts are waxed light within us then, and we are for righting our ain wrangs and fighting our ain battles. But when the hour of trouble comes to the mind or to the body—and seldom may it visit your Leddyship—and when the hour of death comes, that comes to high and low—lang and late may it be yours—Oh, my Leddy, then it isna what we hae dune for oursells, but what we hae dune for others, that we think on maist pleasantly. And the thoughts that ye hae intervened to spare the puir thing's life will be sweeter in that hour, come when it may, than if a word of your mouth could hang the haill Porteous mob at the tail of ae tow."

Tear followed tear down Jeanie's cheeks, as, her features glowing and quivering with emotion, she pleaded her sister's cause with a pathos which was at once simple and solemn.

"This is eloquence," said her Majesty to the Duke of Argyle. "Young woman," she continued, addressing herself to Jeanie, "*I* cannot grant a pardon to your sister—but you shall not want my warm intercession with his Majesty. Take this housewife case," she continued, putting a small embroidered needle-case into Jeanie's hands; "do not open it now, but at your leisure you will find something in it which will remind you that you have had an interview with Queen Caroline."

Jeanie, having her suspicions thus confirmed, dropped on her knees, and would have expanded herself in gratitude; but the Duke, who was upon thorns lest she should say more or less than just enough, touched his chin once more.

"Our business is, I think, ended for the present, my Lord Duke," said the Queen, "and, I trust, to your satisfaction. Hereafter I hope to see your Grace more frequently, both at Richmond and St. James's.—Come, Lady Suffolk, we must wish his Grace good morning."

They exchanged their parting reverences, and the Duke, so soon as the ladies had turned their backs, assisted Jeanie to rise from the ground, and conducted her back through the avenue, which she trode with the feeling of one who walks in her sleep.

CHAPTER XXXVIII

So soon as I can win the offended King,
I will be known your advocate.
Cymbeline.

THE Duke of Argyle led the way in silence to the small postern by which they had been admitted into Richmond Park, so long the favourite residence of Queen Caroline. It was opened by the same half-seen janitor, and they found themselves beyond the precincts of the royal demesne. Still not a word was spoken on either side. The Duke probably wished to allow his rustic protégée time to recruit her faculties, dazzled and sunk with colloquy sublime; and betwixt what she had guessed, had heard, and had seen, Jeanie Deans's mind was too much agitated to permit her to ask any questions.

They found the carriage of the Duke in the place where they had left it; and when they resumed their places, soon began to advance rapidly on their return to town.

"I think, Jeanie," said the Duke, breaking silence, "you have every reason to congratulate yourself on the issue of your interview with her Majesty."

"And that leddy *was* the Queen hersell?" said Jeanie; "I misdoubted it when I saw that your honour didna put on your hat—And yet I can hardly believe it, even when I heard her speak it hersell."

"It was certainly Queen Caroline," replied the Duke. "Have you no curiosity to see what is in the little pocket-book?"

"Do you think the pardon will be in it, sir?" said Jeanie, with the eager animation of hope.

"Why, no," replied the Duke; "that is unlikely. They seldom carry these things about them, unless they were likely to be wanted; and, besides, her Majesty told you it was the King, not she, who was to grant it."

"That is true, too," said Jeanie; "but I am so confused in my mind—But does your honour think there is a certainty of Effie's pardon then?" continued she, still holding in her hand the unopened pocket-book.

"Why, kings are kittle cattle to shoe behind, as we say in the north," replied the Duke; "but his wife knows his trim, and I have not the least doubt that the matter is quite certain."

"O God be praised! God be praised!" ejaculated Jeanie; "and may the gude leddy never want the heart's-ease she has gien me at this moment—And God bless you too, my Lord! without your help I wad ne'er hae won near her."

The Duke let her dwell upon this subject for a considerable time, curious, perhaps, to see how long the feelings of gratitude would continue to supersede those of curiosity. But so feeble was the latter feeling in Jeanie's mind, that his Grace, with whom, perhaps, it was for the time a little stronger, was obliged once more to bring forward the subject of the Queen's present. It was opened accordingly. In the inside of the case were the usual assortment of silk and needles, with scissors, tweezers, &c.; and in the pocket was a bank-bill for fifty pounds.

The Duke had no sooner informed Jeanie of the value of this last document, for she was unaccustomed to see notes for such sums, than she expressed her regret at the mistake which had taken place. "For the hussy itsell," she said, "was a very valuable thing for a keepsake, with the Queen's name written in the inside with her ain hand doubtless—*Caroline*— as plain as could be, and a crown drawn aboon it."

She therefore tendered the bill to the Duke, requesting him to find some mode of returning it to the royal owner.

"No, no, Jeanie," said the Duke, "there is no mistake in the case. Her Majesty knows you have been put to great expense, and she wishes to make it up to you."

"I am sure she is even ower gude," said Jeanie, "and it glads me muckle that I can pay back Dumbiedikes his siller, without distressing my father, honest man."

"Dumbiedikes? What, a freeholder of Mid-Lothian, is he not?" said his Grace, whose occasional residence in that county made him acquainted with most of the heritors, as landed persons are termed in Scotland—"He has a house not far from Dalkeith, wears a black wig and a laced hat?"

"Yes, sir," answered Jeanie, who had her reasons for being brief in her answers upon this topic.

"Ah! my old friend Dumbie!" said the Duke; "I have thrice seen him fou, and only once heard the sound of his voice—Is he a cousin of yours, Jeanie?"

"No, sir,—my Lord."

"Then he must be a well-wisher, I suspect?"

"Ye—yes,—my Lord, sir," answered Jeanie, blushing, and with hesitation.

"Aha! then, if the Laird starts, I suppose my friend Butler must be in some danger?"

"Oh no, sir," answered Jeanie much more readily, but at the same time blushing much more deeply.

"Well, Jeanie," said the Duke, "you are a girl may be safely trusted with your own matters, and I shall inquire no farther about them. But as to this same pardon, I must see to get it passed through the proper forms; and I have a friend in office who will, for auld lang syne, do me so much favour. And then, Jeanie, as I shall have occasion to send an express down to Scotland, who will travel with it safer and more swiftly than you can do, I will take care to have it put into the proper channel; meanwhile, you may write to your friends, by post, of your good success."

"And does your Honour think," said Jeanie, "that will do as weel as if I were to take my tap in my lap, and slip my ways hame again on my ain errand?"

"Much better, certainly," said the Duke. "You know the roads are not very safe for a single woman to travel."

Jeanie internally acquiesced in this observation.

"And I have a plan for you besides. One of the Duchess's attendants, and one of mine—your acquaintance Archibald—are going down to Inverary in a light calash, with four horses I have bought, and there is room enough in the carriage for you to go with them as far as Glasgow, where Archibald will find means of sending you safely to Edinburgh. And in the way, I beg you will teach the woman as much as you can of the mystery of cheese-making, for she is to have a charge in the dairy, and I dare swear you are as tidy about your milk-pail as about your dress."

"Does your honour like cheese?" said Jeanie, with a gleam of conscious delight as she asked the question.

"Like it?" said the Duke, whose good-nature anticipated what was to follow,—"cakes and cheese are a dinner for an emperor, let alone a Highlandman."

"Because," said Jeanie, with modest confidence, and great and evident self-gratulation, "we have been thought so particular in making cheese, that some folk think it as gude as the real Dunlop; and if your Honour's Grace wad but accept a stane or twa, blithe, and fain, and proud it wad make us! But maybe ye may like the ewe-milk, that is, the Buckholm-side[1] cheese better; or maybe the gait-milk, as ye come frae the Highlands—and I canna pretend just to the same skeel o' them; but my cousin Jean, that lives at Lockermachus in Lammermuir, I could speak to her, and——"

"Quite unnecessary," said the Duke; "the Dunlop is the very cheese of which I am so fond, and I will take it as the greatest favour you can do me to send one to Caroline Park. But remember, be on honour with it, Jeanie, and make it all yourself, for I am a real good judge."

"I am not feared," said Jeanie confidently, "that I may please your Honour; for I am sure you look as if you could hardly find fault wi' onybody that did their best; and weel is it my part, I trow, to do mine."

This discourse introduced a topic upon which the two travellers, though so different in rank and education, found each a good deal to say. The Duke, besides his other patriotic qualities, was a distinguished agriculturist, and proud of his knowledge in that department. He entertained Jeanie with his observations on the different breeds of cattle in Scotland, and their capacity for the dairy, and received so much information from her practical experience in return, that he promised her a couple of Devonshire cows in reward for the lesson. In short, his mind was so transported back to his rural employments and amusements, that he sighed when his carriage stopped opposite to the old hackney-coach, which Archibald had kept in attendance at the place where they had left it. While the coachman again bridled his lean cattle, which had been indulged with a bite of musty hay, the Duke cautioned Jeanie, not to be too communicative to her landlady concerning what had passed. "There is," he said, "no use of speaking of matters till they are actually settled; and you may refer the good lady to Archibald, if she presses you hard with questions. She is his old acquaintance, and he knows how to manage with her."

He then took a cordial farewell of Jeanie, and told her to be ready in the ensuing week to return to Scotland—saw her safely established in her hackney-coach, and rolled off in his own carriage, humming a stanza of the ballad which he is said to have composed :—

---

[1] The hilly pastures of Buckholm, which the author now surveys,

　　　"Not in the frenzy of a dreamer's eye,"

are famed for producing the best ewe-milk cheese in the south of Scotland.

" At the sight of Dumbarton once again,
  I'll cock up my bonnet and march amain,
  With my claymore hanging down to my heel,
  To whang at the bannocks of barley meal."

Perhaps one ought to be actually a Scotchman to conceive how ardently, under all distinctions of rank and situation, they feel their mutual connection with each other as natives of the same country. There are, I believe, more associations common to the inhabitants of a rude and wild, than of a well-cultivated and fertile country; their ancestors have more seldom changed their place of residence; their mutual recollection of remarkable objects is more accurate; the high and the low are more interested in each other's welfare; the feelings of kindred and relationship are more widely extended, and, in a word, the bonds of patriotic affection, always honourable even when a little too exclusively strained, have more influence on men's feelings and actions.

The rumbling hackney-coach which tumbled over the (then) execrable London pavement, at a rate very different from that which had conveyed the ducal carriage to Richmond, at length deposited Jeanie Deans and her attendant at the national sign of the Thistle. Mrs. Glass, who had been in long and anxious expectation, now rushed, full of eager curiosity and open-mouthed interrogation, upon our heroine, who was positively unable to sustain the overwhelming cataract of her questions, which burst forth with the sublimity of a grand gardyloo:—" Had she seen the Duke, God bless him —the Duchess—the young ladies?—Had she seen the King, God bless him—the Queen—the Prince of Wales—the Princess —or any of the rest of the royal family?—Had she got her sister's pardon?—Was it out and out—or was it only a commutation of punishment?—How far had she gone—where had she driven to—whom had she seen—what had been said —what had kept her so long?"

Such were the various questions huddled upon each other by a curiosity so eager, that it could hardly wait for its own gratification. Jeanie would have been more than sufficiently embarrassed by this overbearing tide of interrogations, had not Archibald, who had probably received from his master a hint to that purpose, advanced to her rescue. " Mrs. Glass," said Archibald, " his Grace desired me particularly to say, that he would take it as a great favour if you would ask the young woman no questions, as he wishes to explain to you more distinctly than she can do how her affairs stand, and consult you on some matters which she cannot altogether so well explain. The Duke will call at the Thistle to-morrow or next day for that purpose."

"His Grace is very condescending," said Mrs. Glass, her zeal for inquiry slaked for the present by the dexterous administration of this sugar-plum—"his Grace is sensible that I am in a manner accountable for the conduct of my young kinswoman, and no doubt his Grace is the best judge how far he should entrust her or me with the management of her affairs."

"His Grace is quite sensible of that," answered Archibald with national gravity, "and will certainly trust what he has to say to the most discreet of the two; and therefore, Mrs. Glass, his Grace relies you will speak nothing to Mrs. Jean Deans, either of her own affairs or her sister's, until he sees you himself. He desired me to assure you, in the meanwhile, that all was going on as well as your kindness could wish, Mrs. Glass."

"His Grace is very kind—very considerate, certainly, Mr. Archibald—his Grace's commands shall be obeyed, and—— But you have had a far drive, Mr. Archibald, as I guess by the time of your absence, and I guess" (with an engaging smile) "you winna be the waur o' a glass of the right Rosa Solis."

"I thank you, Mrs. Glass," said the great man's great man, "but I am under the necessity of returning to my Lord directly." And making his adieus civilly to both cousins, he left the shop of the Lady of the Thistle.

"I am glad your affairs have prospered so well, Jeanie, my love," said Mrs. Glass; "though, indeed, there was little fear of them so soon as the Duke of Argyle was so condescending as to take them into hand. I will ask you no questions about them, because his Grace, who is most considerate and prudent in such matters, intends to tell me all that you ken yourself, dear, and doubtless a great deal more; so that anything that may lie heavily on your mind may be imparted to me in the meantime, as you see it is his Grace's pleasure that I should be made acquainted with the whole matter forthwith, and whether you or he tells it, will make no difference in the world, ye ken. If I ken what he is going to say beforehand, I will be much more ready to give my advice, and whether you or he tell me about it, cannot much signify after all, my dear. So you may just say whatever you like, only mind I ask you no questions about it."

Jeanie was a little embarrassed. She thought that the communication she had to make was perhaps the only means she might have in her power to gratify her friendly and hospitable kinswoman. But her prudence instantly suggested that her secret interview with Queen Caroline, which seemed to pass under a certain sort of mystery, was not a proper subject for the gossip of a woman like Mrs. Glass, of whose heart she had a much better opinion than of her prudence. She, therefore, answered in general, that the Duke had had the extraordinary kindness to make very particular inquiries into her sister's bad affair, and that he thought he had found the means of putting it a' straight again, but that he proposed to tell all that he thought about the matter to Mrs. Glass herself.

This did not quite satisfy the penetrating Mistress of the Thistle. Searching as her own small rappee, she, in spite of her promise, urged Jeanie with still further questions. "Had she been a' that time at Argyle House? Was the Duke with her the whole time? and had she seen the Duchess? and had she seen the young ladies—and especially Lady Caroline Campbell?"—To these questions Jeanie gave the general reply, that she knew so little of the town that she could not tell exactly where she had been; that she had not seen the Duchess to her knowledge; that she had seen two ladies, one of whom, she understood, bore the name of Caroline; and more, she said, she could not tell about the matter.

"It would be the Duke's eldest daughter, Lady Caroline Campbell—there is no doubt of that," said Mrs. Glass; "but, doubtless, I shall know more particularly through his Grace.— And so, as the cloth is laid in the little parlour above stairs, and it is past three o'clock, for I have been waiting this hour for you, and I have had a snack myself; and, as they used to say in Scotland in my time—I do not ken if the word be used now—there is ill talking between a full body and a fasting."

CHAPTER XXXIX

Heaven first sent letters to some wretch's aid—
Some banish'd lover, or some captive maid.

POPE.

BY dint of unwonted labour with the pen, Jeanie Deans contrived to indite, and give to the charge of the postman on the ensuing day, no less than three letters, an exertion altogether strange to her habits; insomuch so, that, if milk had been plenty, she would rather have made thrice as many Dunlop cheeses. The first of them was very brief. It was addressed to George Staunton, Esq., at the Rectory, Willingham, by Grantham; the address being part of the information which she had extracted from the communicative peasant who rode before her to Stamford. It was in these words:—

"SIR,—To prevent farder mischieves, whereof there hath been enough, comes these: Sir, I have my sister's pardon from the Queen's Majesty, whereof I do not doubt you will be glad, having had to say naut of matters whereof you know the purport. So, sir, I pray for your better welfare in bodie and soul, and that it will please the fisycian to visit you in His good time. Alwaies, sir, I pray you will never come again to see my sister, whereof there has been too much. And so, wishing you no evil, but even your best good, that you may be turned from your iniquity (for why suld ye die?), I rest your humble servant to command,   *Ye ken wha.*"

The next letter was to her father. It is too long altogether for insertion, so we only give a few extracts. It commenced—

"DEAREST AND TRULY HONOURED FATHER,—This comes with my duty to inform you, that it has pleased God to redeem that captivitie of my poor sister, in respect the Queen's blessed Majesty, for whom we are ever bound to pray, hath redeemed her soul from the slayer, granting the ransom of her, whilk is ane pardon or reprieve. And I spoke with the Queen face to face, and yet live; for she is not muckle differing from other grand leddies, saving that she has a stately presence, and een like a blue huntin' hawk's, whilk gaed throu' and throu' me like a Hieland durk—And all this good was, alway under the Great Giver, to whom all are but instruments, wrought forth

for us by the Duk of Argile, wha is ane native true-hearted
Scotsman, and not pridefu', like other folk we ken of—and
likewise skeely enow in bestial, whereof he has promised to
gie me twa Devonshire kye, of which he is enamoured,
although I do still haud by the real hawkit Airshire breed—
and I have promised him a cheese; and I wad wuss ye, if
Gowans, the brockit cow, has a quey, that she suld suck her
fill of milk, as I am given to understand he has none of that
breed, and is not scornfu', but will take a thing frae a puir
body, that it may lighten their heart of the loading of debt
that they awe him. Also his Honour the Duke will accept
ane of our Dunlop cheeses, and it sall be my faut if a better
was ever yearned in Lowden."—[Here follow some observations respecting the breed of cattle, and the produce of the
dairy, which it is our intention to forward to the Board of
Agriculture.]—" Nevertheless, these are but matters of the
after-harvest, in respect of the great good which Providence
hath gifted us with—and, in especial, poor Effie's life. And
oh, my dear father, since it hath pleased God to be merciful to
her, let her not want your free pardon, whilk will make her
meet to be ane vessel of grace, and also a comfort to your ain
graie hairs. Dear father, will ye let the Laird ken that we
have had friends strangely raised up to us, and that the talent
whilk he lent me will be thankfully repaid. I hae some of it
to the fore; and the rest of it is not knotted up in ane purse
or napkin, but in ane wee bit paper, as is the fashion heir,
whilk I am assured is gude for the siller. And, dear father,
through Mr. Butler's means I hae gude friendship with the
Duke, for their had been kindness between their forbears in
the auld troublesome time bye-past. And Mrs. Glass has
been kind like my very mother. She has a braw house here,
and lives bien and warm, wi' twa servant lasses, and a man
and a callant in the shop. And she is to send you doun a
pound of her hie-dried, and some other tobaka, and we maun
think of some propine for her, since her kindness hath been
great. And the Duk is to send the pardun doun by an
express messenger, in respect that I canna travel sae fast; and
I am to come doun wi' twa of his Honour's servants—that is,
John Archibald, a decent elderly gentleman, that says he has
seen you lang syne, when ye were buying beasts in the west
frae the Laird of Aughtermuggitie—but maybe ye winna mind
him—ony way, he's a civil man—and Mrs. Dolly Dutton, that
is to be dairymaid at Inverara; and they bring me on as far

as Glasgo', whilk will make it nae pinch to win hame, whilk I desire of all things. May the Giver of all good things keep ye in your outgauns and incomings, whereof devoutly prayeth your loving dauter,   JEAN DEANS."

The third letter was to Butler, and its tenor as follows :—

"MASTER BUTLER.—SIR,—It will be pleasure to you to ken, that all I came for is, thanks be to God, weel dune and to the gude end, and that your forbear's letter was right welcome to the Duke of Argile, and that he wrote your name down with a kylevine pen in a leathern book, whereby it seems like he will do for you either wi' a scule or a kirk ; he has enow of baith, as I am assured. And I have seen the Queen, which gave me a hussy-case out of her own hand. She had not her crown and skeptre, but they are laid by for her, like the bairns' best claise, to be worn when she needs them. And they are keepit in a tour, whilk is not like the tour of Libberton, nor yet Craigmillar, but mair like to the castell of Edinburgh, if the buildings were taen and set down in the midst of the Nor'-Loch. Also the Queen was very bounteous, giving me a paper worth fiftie pounds, as I am assured, to pay my expenses here and back agen. Sae, Master Butler, as we were aye neebours' bairns, forby onything else that may hae been spoken between us, I trust you winna skrimp yoursell for what is needfu' for your health, since it signifies not muckle whilk o' us has the siller, if the other wants it. And mind this is no meant to haud ye to onything whilk ye wad rather forget, if ye suld get a charge of a kirk or a scule, as above said. Only I hope it will be a scule, and not a kirk, because of these difficulties anent aiths and patronages, whilk might gang ill doun wi' my honest father. Only if ye could compass a harmonious call frae the parish of Skreegh-me-dead, as ye anes had hope of, I trow it wad please him weel ; since I hae heard him say, that the root of the matter was mair deeply hafted in that wild muirland parish than in the Canongate of Edinburgh. I wish I had whaten books ye wanted, Mr. Butler, for they hae haill houses of them here, and they are obliged to set sum out in the street, whilk are sald cheap, doubtless, to get them out of the weather. It is a muckle place, and I hae seen sae muckle of it, that my poor head turns round. And ye ken langsyne I am nae great penwoman—and it is near eleven o'clock o' the night. I am

cumming down in good company, and safe—and I had
troubles in gaun up, whilk makes me blither of travelling wi'
kend folk.   My cousin, Mrs. Glass, has a braw house here,
but a' thing is sae poisoned wi' snuff, that I am like to be
scomfished whiles.   But what signifies these things, in comparison of the great deliverance whilk has been vouchsafed to
my father's house, in whilk you, as our auld and dear well-
wisher, will, I dout not, rejoice and be exceedingly glad.
And I am, dear Mr. Butler, your sincere well-wisher in temporal and eternal things,   J. D."

After these labours of an unwonted kind, Jeanie retired to
her bed, yet scarce could sleep a few minutes together, so
often was she awakened by the heart-stirring consciousness
of her sister's safety, and so powerfully urged to deposit her
burden of joy, where she had before laid her doubts and
sorrows, in the warm and sincere exercises of devotion.

All the next, and all the succeeding day, Mrs. Glass fidgeted
about her shop in the agony of expectation, like a pea (to use
a vulgar simile which her profession renders appropriate) upon
one of her own tobacco-pipes.   With the third morning came
the expected coach, with four servants clustered behind on
the foot-board, in dark-brown and yellow liveries; the Duke
in person, with laced coat, gold-headed cane, star and garter,
all, as the story-book says, very grand.

He inquired for his little countrywoman of Mrs. Glass, but
without requesting to see her, probably because he was unwilling to give an appearance of personal intercourse betwixt
them, which scandal might have misinterpreted.   "The
Queen," he said to Mrs. Glass, "had taken the case of her
kinswoman into her gracious consideration, and being specially moved by the affectionate and resolute character of the
elder sister, had condescended to use her powerful intercession with his Majesty, in consequence of which a pardon
had been despatched to Scotland to Effie Deans, on condition
of her banishing herself forth of Scotland for fourteen years.
The King's Advocate had insisted," he said, "upon this
qualification of the pardon, having pointed out to his Majesty's
ministers, that, within the course of only seven years, twenty-
one instances of child-murder had occurred in Scotland."

"Weary on him!" said Mrs. Glass, "what for needed he
to have telled that of his ain country, and to the English
folk abune a'?   I used aye to think the Advocate a douce

decent man, but it is an ill bird—begging your Grace's pardon for speaking of such a coorse by-word. And then what is the poor lassie to do in a foreign land?—Why, wae's me, it's just sending her to play the same pranks ower again, out of sight or guidance of her friends."

"Pooh! pooh!" said the Duke, "that need not be anticipated. Why, she may come up to London, or she may go to America, and marry well for all that is come and gone."

"In troth, and so she may, as your Grace is pleased to intimate," replied Mrs. Glass; "and now I think upon it, there is my old correspondent in Virginia, Ephraim Buckskin, that has supplied the Thistle this forty years with tobacco, and it is not a little that serves our turn, and he has been writing to me these ten years to send him out a wife. The carle is not above sixty, and hale and hearty, and well to pass in the world, and a line from my hand would settle the matter, and Effie Deans's misfortune (forby that there is no special occasion to speak about it) would be thought little of there."

"Is she a pretty girl?" said the Duke; "her sister does not get beyond a good comely sonsy lass."

"Oh, far prettier is Effie than Jeanie," said Mrs. Glass; "though it is long since I saw her mysell, but I hear of the Deanses by all my Lowden friends when they come—your Grace kens we Scots are clannish bodies."

"So much the better for us," said the Duke, "and the worse for those who meddle with us, as your good old-fashioned Scots sign says, Mrs. Glass. And now I hope you will approve of the measures I have taken for restoring your kinswoman to her friends." These he detailed at length, and Mrs. Glass gave her unqualified approbation, with a smile and a courtesy at every sentence. "And now, Mrs. Glass, you must tell Jeanie, I hope she will not forget my cheese when she gets down to Scotland. Archibald has my orders to arrange all her expenses."

"Begging your Grace's humble pardon," said Mrs. Glass, "it's a pity to trouble yourself about them; the Deanses are wealthy people in their way, and the lass has money in her pocket."

"That's all very true," said the Duke; "but you know, where MacCallummore travels he pays all; it is our Highland privilege to take from all what *we* want, and to give to all what *they* want."

"Your Grace's better at giving than taking," said Mrs. Glass.

"To show you the contrary," said the Duke, "I will fill my box out of this canister without paying you a bawbee;" and again desiring to be remembered to Jeanie, with his good wishes for her safe journey, he departed, leaving Mrs. Glass uplifted in heart and in countenance, the proudest and happiest of tobacco and snuff dealers.

Reflectively, his Grace's good-humour and affability had a favourable effect upon Jeanie's situation. Her kinswoman, though civil and kind to her, had acquired too much of London breeding to be perfectly satisfied with her cousin's rustic and national dress, and was, besides, something scandalised at the cause of her journey to London. Mrs. Glass might, therefore, have been less sedulous in her attentions towards Jeanie, but for the interest which the foremost of the Scottish nobles (for such, in all men's estimation, was the Duke of Argyle) seemed to take in her fate. Now, however, as a kinswoman whose virtues and domestic affections had attracted the notice and approbation of royalty itself, Jeanie stood to her relative in a light very different and much more favourable, and was not only treated with kindness, but with actual observance and respect.

It depended upon herself alone to have made as many visits, and seen as many sights, as lay within Mrs. Glass's power to compass. But, excepting that she dined abroad with one or two "far-away kinsfolk," and that she paid the same respect, on Mrs. Glass's strong urgency, to Mrs. Deputy Dabby, wife of the Worshipful Mr. Deputy Dabby, of Farringdon Without, she did not avail herself of the opportunity. As Mrs. Dabby was the second lady of great rank whom Jeanie had seen in London, she used sometimes afterwards to draw a parallel betwixt her and the Queen, in which she observed, that "Mrs. Dabby was dressed twice as grand, and was twice as big, and spoke twice as loud, and twice as muckle, as the Queen did, but she hadna the same goss-hawk glance that makes the skin creep, and the knee bend; and though she had very kindly gifted her with a loaf of sugar and twa punds of tea, yet she hadna a'thegither the sweet look that the Queen had when she put the needle-book into her hand."

Jeanie might have enjoyed the sights and novelties of this great city more, had it not been for the qualification added to her sister's pardon, which greatly grieved her affectionate disposition. On this subject, however, her mind was somewhat relieved by a letter which she received in return of post, in answer to that which she had written to her father. With his affectionate blessing, it brought his full approbation of the step which she had taken, as one inspired by the immediate dictates of Heaven, and which she had been thrust upon in order that she might become the means of safety to a perishing household.

"If ever a deliverance was dear and precious, this," said the letter, "is a dear and precious deliverance—and if life saved can be made more sweet and savoury, it is when it cometh by the hands of those whom we hold in the ties of affection. And do not let your heart be disquieted within you, that this victim, who is rescued from the horns of the altar, whereuntil she was fast bound by the chains of human law, is now to be driven beyond the bounds of our land. Scotland is a blessed land to those who love the ordinances of Christianity, and it is a faer land to look upon, and dear to them who have dwelt in it a' their days; and weel said that judicious Christian, worthy John Livingstone, a sailor in Borrowstounness, as the famous Patrick Walker reporteth his words, that howbeit he thought Scotland was a Gehennah of wickedness when he was at home, yet, when he was abroad, he accounted it ane paradise; for the evils of Scotland he found everywhere, and the good of Scotland he found nowhere. But we are to hold in remembrance that Scotland, though it be our native land, and the land of our fathers, is not like Goshen, in Egypt, on whilk the sun of the heavens and of the gospel shineth allenarly, and leaveth the rest of the world in utter darkness. Therefore, and also because this increase of profit at Saint Leonard's Crags may be a cauld waff of wind blawing from the frozen land of earthly self, where never plant of grace took root or grew, and because my concerns make me take something ower muckle a grip of the gear of the warld in mine arms, I receive this dispensation anent Effie as a call to depart out of Haran, as righteous Abraham of old, and leave my father's kindred and my mother's house, and the ashes and mould of them who have gone to sleep before me, and which wait to be mingled with these auld crazed bones of mine own. And my heart is lightened to do this, when I call to mind the decay of active and earnest religion in this land, and survey the height and the depth, the length and the breadth, of national defections, and how the love of many is waxing lukewarm and cold; and I am strengthened in this resolution to change my domicile likewise, as I hear that store-farms are to be set at an easy mail in Northumberland, where there are many precious souls that are of our true, though suffering persuasion. And sic part of the kye or stock as I judge it fit to keep, may be driven thither without incommodity—say about Wooler, or that gate, keeping aye a shouther to the hills —and the rest may be sauld to gude profit and advantage, if we had grace weel to use and guide these gifts of the warld. The Laird has been a true friend on our unhappy occasions, and I have paid him back the siller for Effie's misfortune, whereof Mr. Nichil Novit returned him no balance, as the Laird and I did expect he would hae done. But law licks up a', as the common folk say. I have had the siller to borrow out of sax purses. Mr. Saddletree advised to give the Laird of Lounsbeck a charge on his band for a thousand merks. But I hae nae broo' of charges, since that awfu' morning that a tout of a horn, at the Cross of Edinburgh, blew half the faithfu' ministers of Scotland out of their pulpits. However, I sall raise an adjudication, whilk Mr. Saddletree says comes instead of the auld apprisings, and will not lose weel-won gear with the like of him if it may be helped. As for the Queen, and the credit that she hath done to a poor man's daughter, and the mercy and the grace ye found with her, I can only pray for her weel-being here and hereafter, for the establish-ment of her house now and for ever, upon the throne of these kingdoms. I doubt not but what you told her Majesty, that I was the same David Deans of whom there was a sport at the Revolution when I noited thegither the heads of twa false prophets, these ungracious Graces the prelates, as they stood on the Hie Street, after being expelled from the Convention Parliament. The Duke of Argyle is a noble and true-hearted nobleman, who pleads the cause of the poor, and those who have none to help them ; verily his reward shall not be lacking unto him.—I have been writing of many things, but not of that whilk lies nearest mine heart. I have seen the misguided thing ; she will be at freedom the morn, on enacted caution that she shall leave Scotland in four weeks. Her mind is in an evil frame,—casting her eye backward on Egypt, I doubt, as if the bitter waters of the wilderness were harder to endure than the brick furnaces, by the side of which there were savoury flesh-pots. I need not bid you make haste down, for you are, excepting always my Great Master, my only comfort in these straits. I charge you to withdraw your feet from the delusion of that Vanity Fair in whilk you are a sojourner, and not to go to their worship, which is an ill-mumbled mass, as it was weel termed by James the Sext, though he afterwards, with his unhappy son, strove to bring it ower back and belly into his native kingdom, wherethrough their race have been cut off as foam upon the water, and shall be as wanderers among the nations —see the prophecies of Hosea, ninth and seventeenth, and the same, tenth and seventh. But us and our house, let us say with the same prophet: 'Let us return to the Lord, for He hath torn, and He will heal us—He hath smitten, and He will bind us up.'"

He proceeded to say, that he approved of her proposed mode of returning by Glasgow, and entered into sundry minute particulars not necessary to be quoted. A single line in the letter, but not the least frequently read by the party to whom it was addressed, intimated, that "Reuben Butler had been as a son to him in his sorrows." As David Deans scarce ever mentioned Butler before, without some gibe, more or less direct, either at his carnal gifts and learning, or at his grandfather's heresy, Jeanie drew a good omen from no such qualifying clause being added to this sentence respecting him.

A lover's hope resembles the bean in the nursery tale,—let it once take root, and it will grow so rapidly, that in the course of a few hours the giant Imagination builds a castle on the top, and by-and-by comes Disappointment with the "curtal axe," and hews down both the plant and the superstructure. Jeanie's fancy, though not the most powerful of her faculties, was lively enough to transport her to a wild farm in Northumberland, well stocked with milk-cows, yeald beasts, and sheep; a meeting-house hard by, frequented by serious Presbyterians, who had united in a harmonious call to Reuben Butler to be their spiritual guide; Effie restored, not to gaiety, but to cheerfulness at least;—their father, with his grey hairs smoothed down, and spectacles on his nose;—herself, with the maiden snood exchanged for a matron's curch—all arranged in a pew in the said meeting-house, listening to words of devotion, rendered sweeter and more powerful by the affectionate ties which combined them with the preacher. She cherished such visions from day to day, until her residence in London began to become insupportable and tedious to her; and it was with no ordinary satisfaction that she received a summons from Argyle House, requiring her in two days to be prepared to join their northward party.

CHAPTER XL

One was a female, who had grievous ill
Wrought in revenge, and she enjoy'd it still;
Sullen she was, and threatening; in her eye
Glared the stern triumph that she dared to die.
CRABBE.

THE summons of preparation arrived after Jeanie Deans had resided in the metropolis about three weeks.

On the morning appointed she took a grateful farewell of Mrs. Glass, as that good woman's attention to her particularly required, placed herself and her movable goods, which purchases and presents had greatly increased, in a hackney-coach, and joined her travelling companions in the housekeeper's apartment at Argyle House. While the carriage was getting ready, she was informed that the Duke wished to speak with her; and being ushered into a splendid saloon, she was surprised to find that he wished to present her to his lady and daughters.

"I bring you my little countrywoman, Duchess," these were the words of the introduction. "With an army of young fellows, as gallant and steady as she is, and a good cause, I would not fear two to one."

"Ah, papa!" said a lively young lady, about twelve years old, "remember you were full one to two at Sheriff-muir, and yet" (singing the well-known ballad)—

"'Some say that we wan, and some say that they wan,
        And some say that nane wan at a', man;
    But of ae thing I'm sure, that on Sheriff-muir
        A battle there was that I saw, man.'"

"What, little Mary turned Tory on my hands?—This will be fine news for our countrywoman to carry down to Scotland!"

"We may all turn Tories for the thanks we have got for remaining Whigs," said the second young lady.

"Well, hold your peace, you discontented monkeys, and do dress your babies; and as for the Bob of Dunblane,

'If it wasna weel bobbit, weel bobbit, weel bobbit,
    If it wasna weel bobbit, we'll bob it again.'"

"Papa's wit is running low," said Lady Mary; "the poor gentleman is repeating himself—he sang that on the field of battle, when he was told the Highlanders had cut his left wing to pieces with their claymores."

A pull by the hair was the repartee to this sally.

"Ah! brave Highlanders and bright claymores," said the Duke, "well do I wish them, 'for a' the ill they've done me yet,' as the song goes.—But come, madcaps, say a civil word to your countrywoman—I wish ye had half her canny hamely sense; I think you may be as leal and true-hearted."

The Duchess advanced, and, in few words, in which there was as much kindness as civility, assured Jeanie of the respect which she had for a character so affectionate, and yet so firm, and added, "When you get home, you will perhaps hear from me."

"And from me." "And from me." "And from me, Jeanie," added the young ladies one after the other, "for you are a credit to the land we love so well."

Jeanie, overpowered with these unexpected compliments, and not aware that the Duke's investigation had made him acquainted with her behaviour on her sister's trial, could only answer by blushing, and courtseying round and round, and uttering at intervals, "Mony thanks! mony thanks!"

"Jeanie," said the Duke, "you must have *doch an' dorroch*, or you will be unable to travel."

There was a salver with cake and wine on the table. He took up a glass, drank "to all true hearts that lo'ed Scotland," and offered a glass to his guest.

Jeanie, however, declined it, saying, "that she had never tasted wine in her life."

"How comes that, Jeanie?" said the Duke,—"wine maketh glad the heart, you know."

"Ay, sir, but my father is like Jonadab the son of Rechab, who charged his children that they should drink no wine."

"I thought your father would have had more sense," said the Duke, "unless, indeed, he prefers brandy. But, however, Jeanie, if you will not drink, you must eat, to save the character of my house."

He thrust upon her a large piece of cake, nor would he permit her to break off a fragment, and lay the rest on the salver. "Put it in your pouch, Jeanie," said he; "you will be glad of it before you see St. Giles's steeple. I wish to Heaven I were to see it as soon as you! and so my best service to all my friends at and about Auld Reekie, and a blithe journey to you."

And, mixing the frankness of a soldier with his natural affability, he shook hands with his protégée, and committed her to the charge of Archibald, satisfied that he had provided sufficiently for her being attended to by his domestics, from the unusual attention with which he had himself treated her.

Accordingly, in the course of her journey, she found both her companions disposed to pay her every possible civility, so that her return, in point of comfort and safety, formed a strong contrast to her journey to London.

Her heart also was disburdened of the weight of grief, shame, apprehension, and fear, which had loaded her before her interview with the Queen at Richmond. But the human mind is so strangely capricious, that, when freed from the pressure of real misery, it becomes open and sensitive to the apprehension of ideal calamities. She was now much disturbed in mind, that she had heard nothing from Reuben Butler, to whom the operation of writing was so much more familiar than it was to herself.

"It would have cost him sae little fash," she said to herself; "for I hae seen his pen gang as fast ower the paper, as ever it did ower the water when it was in the grey goose's wing. Wae's me! maybe he may be badly—but then my father wad likely hae said something about it—Or maybe he may hae taen the rue, and kensna how to let me wot of his change of mind. He needna be at muckle fash about it," she went on, drawing herself up, though the tear of honest pride and injured affection gathered in her eye, as she entertained the suspicion,—"Jeanie Deans is no the lass to pu' him by the sleeve, or put him in mind of what he wishes to forget. I shall wish him weel and happy a' the same; and if he has the luck to get a kirk in our country, I sall gang and hear him just the very same, to show that I bear nae malice." And as she imagined the scene, the tear stole over her eye.

In these melancholy reveries, Jeanie had full time to indulge herself; for her travelling companions, servants in a distinguished and fashionable family, had, of course, many topics of conversation, in which it was absolutely impossible she could have either pleasure or portion. She had, therefore, abundant leisure for reflection, and even for self-tormenting, during the several days which, indulging the young horses the Duke was sending down to the North with sufficient ease and short stages, they occupied in reaching the neighbourhood of Carlisle.

In approaching the vicinity of that ancient city, they discerned a considerable crowd upon an eminence at a little distance from the high road, and learned from some passengers who were gathering towards that busy scene from the southward, that the cause of the concourse was, the laudable public desire "to see a domned Scotch witch and thief get half of her due upo' Haribeebroo' yonder, for she was only to be hanged; she should hae been boorned aloive, an' cheap on't."

"Dear Mr. Archibald," said the dame of the dairy elect, "I never seed a woman hanged in a' my life, and only four men, as made a goodly spectacle."

Mr. Archibald, however, was a Scotchman, and promised himself no exuberant pleasure in seeing his countrywoman undergo "the terrible behests of law." Moreover, he was a man of sense and delicacy in his way, and the late circumstances of Jeanie's family, with the cause of her expedition to London, were not unknown to him; so that he answered drily, it was impossible to stop, as he must be early at Carlisle on some business of the Duke's, and he accordingly bid the postilions get on.

The road at that time passed at about a quarter of a mile's distance from the eminence, called Haribee or Harabee Brow, which, though it is very moderate in size and height, is nevertheless seen from a great distance around, owing to the flatness of the country through which the Eden flows. Here many an outlaw, and border-rider of both kingdoms, had wavered in the wind during the wars, and scarce less hostile truces, between the two countries. Upon Harabee, in latter days, other executions had taken place with as little ceremony as compassion; for these frontier provinces remained long unsettled, and, even at the time of which we write, were ruder than those in the centre of England.

The postilions drove on, wheeling, as the Penrith road led them, round the verge of the rising ground. Yet still the eyes of Mrs. Dolly Dutton, which, with the head and substantial person to which they belonged, were all turned towards the scene of action, could discern plainly the outline of the gallows-tree, relieved against the clear sky, the dark shade formed by the persons of the executioner and the criminal upon the light rounds of the tall aerial ladder, until one of the objects, launched into the air, gave unequivocal signs of mortal agony, though appearing in the distance not larger than a spider dependent at the extremity of his invisible thread, while the remaining form descended from its elevated situation, and regained with all speed an undistinguished place among the crowd. This termination of the tragic scene drew forth a squall from Mrs. Dutton, and Jeanie, with instinctive curiosity, turned her head in the same direction.

The sight of a female culprit in the act of undergoing the fatal punishment from which her beloved sister had been so recently rescued, was too much, not perhaps for her nerves, but for her mind and feelings. She turned her head to the other side of the carriage, with a sensation of sickness, of loathing, and of fainting. Her female companion overwhelmed her with questions, with proffers of assistance, with requests that the carriage might be stopped—that a doctor might be fetched—that drops might be gotten—that burnt feathers and assafœtida, fair water, and hartshorn, might be procured, all at once, and without one instant's delay. Archibald, more calm and considerate, only desired the carriage to push forward; and it was not till they had got beyond sight of the fatal spectacle, that, seeing the deadly paleness of Jeanie's countenance, he stopped the carriage, and jumping out himself, went in search of the most obvious and most easily procured of Mrs. Dutton's pharmacopœia—a draught, namely, of fair water.

While Archibald was absent on this good-natured piece of service, damning the ditches which produced nothing but mud, and thinking upon the thousand bubbling springlets of his own mountains, the attendants on the execution began to pass the stationary vehicle in their way back to Carlisle.

From their half-heard and half-understood words, Jeanie, whose attention was involuntarily riveted by them, as that of children is by ghost stories, though they know the pain with which they will afterwards remember them, Jeanie, I say, could discern that the present victim of the law had died *game*, as it is termed by those unfortunates; that is, sullen, reckless, and impenitent, neither fearing God nor regarding man.

"A sture woife, and a dour," said one Cumbrian peasant, as he clattered by in his wooden brogues, with a noise like the trampling of a dray-horse.

"She has gone to ho master, with ho's name in her mouth," said another; "Shame the country should be harried wi' Scotch witches and Scotch bitches this gate—but I say hang and drown."

"Ay, ay, Gaffer Tramp, take awa yealdon, take awa low—nang the witch, and there will be less scathe amang us; mine owsen hae been reckan this towmont."

"And mine bairns hae been crining too, mon," replied his neighbour.

"Silence wi' your fule tongues, ye churls," said an old woman, who hobbled past them, as they stood talking near the carriage; "this was nae witch, but a bluidy-fingered thief and murderess."

"Ay? was it e'en sae, Dame Hinchup?" said one in a civil tone, and stepping out of his place to let the old woman pass along the footpath—"Nay, you know best, sure—but at ony rate, we hae but tint a Scot of her, and that's a thing better lost than found."

The old woman passed on without making any answer.

"Ay, ay, neighbour," said Gaffer Tramp, "seest thou how one witch will speak for t'other—Scots or English, the same to them."

His companion shook his head, and replied in the same subdued tone, "Ay, ay, when a Sark-foot wife gets on her broomstick, the dames of Allonby are ready to mount, just as sure as the by-word gangs o' the hills,

"If Skiddaw hath a cap,
Criffel wot's full weel of that.'

"But," continued Gaffer Tramp, "thinkest thou the daughter o' yon hangit body isna as rank a witch as ho?"

"I kenna clearly," returned the fellow, "but the folk are speaking o' swimming her i' the Eden." And they passed on their several roads, after wishing each other good morning.

Just as the clowns left the place, and as Mr. Archibald returned with some fair water, a crowd of boys and girls, and some of the lower rabble of more mature age, came up from the place of execution, grouping themselves with many a yell of delight around a tall female fantastically dressed, who was dancing, leaping, and bounding in the midst of them. A horrible recollection pressed on Jeanie as she looked on this unfortunate creature; and the reminiscence was mutual, for by a sudden exertion of great strength and agility, Madge Wildfire broke out of the noisy circle of tormentors who surrounded her, and clinging fast to the door of the calash, uttered, in a sound betwixt laughter and screaming, "Eh, d'ye ken, Jeanie Deans, they hae hangit our mother?" Then suddenly changing her tone to that of the most piteous entreaty, she added, "Oh, gar them let me gang to cut her down!—let me but cut her down!—she is my mother, if she was waur than the deil, and she'll be nae mair kenspeckle than half-hangit Maggie Dickson, that cried saut mony a day after she had been hangit; her voice was roupit and hoarse, and her neck was a wee agee, or ye wad hae kend nae odds on her frae ony other saut-wife."

Mr. Archibald, embarrassed by the madwoman's clinging to the carriage, and detaining around them her noisy and mischievous attendants, was all this while looking out for a constable or beadle, to whom he might commit the unfortunate creature. But seeing no such person of authority, he endeavoured to loosen her hold from the carriage, that they might escape from her by driving on. This, however, could hardly be achieved without some degree of violence; Madge held fast, and renewed her frantic entreaties to be permitted to cut down her mother. "It was but a tenpenny tow lost," she said, "and what was that to a woman's life?" There came up, however, a parcel of savage-looking fellows, butchers and graziers chiefly, among whose cattle there had been of late a very general and fatal distemper, which their wisdom imputed to witchcraft. They laid violent hands on Madge, and tore her from the carriage, exclaiming—"What, doest stop folk o' king's highway? Hast no done mischief enow already, wi' thy murders and thy witcherings?"

"O Jeanie Deans—Jeanie Deans!" exclaimed the poor maniac, "save my mother, and I will take ye to the Interpreter's house again,—and I will teach ye a' my bonny sangs,—and I will tell ye what came o' the——" The rest of her entreaties were drowned in the shouts of the rabble.

"Save her, for God's sake!—save her from those people!" exclaimed Jeanie to Archibald.

"She is mad, but quite innocent; she is mad, gentlemen," said Archibald; "do not use her ill, take her before the Mayor."

"Ay, ay, we'se hae care enow on her," answered one of the fellows; "gang thou thy gate, man, and mind thine own matters."

"He's a Scot by his tongue," said another; "and an he will come out o' his whirligig there, I'se gie him his tartan plaid fu' o' broken banes."

It was clear nothing could be done to rescue Madge; and

Archibald, who was a man of humanity, could only bid the postilions hurry on to Carlisle, that he might obtain some assistance to the unfortunate woman. As they drove off, they heard the hoarse roar with which the mob preface acts of riot or cruelty, yet even above that deep and dire note, they could discern the screams of the unfortunate victim. They were soon out of hearing of the cries, but had no sooner entered the streets of Carlisle, than Archibald, at Jeanie's earnest and urgent entreaty, went to a magistrate, to state the cruelty which was likely to be exercised on this unhappy creature.

In about an hour and a half he returned, and reported to Jeanie that the magistrate had very readily gone in person, with some assistants, to the rescue of the unfortunate woman, and that he had himself accompanied him; that when they came to the muddy pool, in which the mob were ducking her, according to their favourite mode of punishment, the magistrate succeeded in rescuing her from their hands, but in a state of insensibility, owing to the cruel treatment which she had received. He added, that he had seen her carried to the workhouse, and understood that she had been brought to herself, and was expected to do well.

This last averment was a slight alteration in point of fact, for Madge Wildfire was not expected to survive the treatment she had received; but Jeanie seemed so much agitated, that Mr. Archibald did not think it prudent to tell her the worst at once. Indeed, she appeared so fluttered and disordered by this alarming accident, that, although it had been their intention to proceed to Longtown that evening, her companions judged it most advisable to pass the night at Carlisle.

This was particularly agreeable to Jeanie, who resolved, if possible, to procure an interview with Madge Wildfire. Connecting some of her wild flights with the narrative of George Staunton, she was unwilling to omit the opportunity of extracting from her, if possible, some information concerning the fate of that unfortunate infant which had cost her sister so dear. Her acquaintance with the disordered state of poor Madge's mind did not permit her to cherish much hope that she could acquire from her any useful intelligence; but then, since Madge's mother had suffered her deserts, and was silent for ever, it was her only chance of obtaining any kind of information, and she was loath to lose the opportunity.

She coloured her wish to Mr. Archibald by saying, that she had seen Madge formerly, and wished to know, as a matter of

Again she changed the tune to one wilder, less monotonous, and less regular. But of the words only a fragment or two could be collected by those who listened to this singular scene:

> " Proud Maisie is in the wood,
>   Walking so early;
> Sweet Robin sits on the bush,
>   Singing so rarely.
>
> ' Tell me, thou bonny bird,
>   When shall I marry me?'—
> ' When six braw gentlemen
>   Kirkward shall carry ye.'
>
> .   .   .   .   .   .
>
> ' Who makes the bridal bed,
>   Birdie, say truly?'—
> ' The grey-headed sexton,
>   That delves the grave duly.'
>
> .   .   .   .   .   .
>
> ' The glow-worm o'er grave and stone
>   Shall light thee steady;
> The owl from the steeple sing,
>   ' Welcome, proud lady.' "

Her voice died away with the last notes, and she fell into a slumber, from which the experienced attendant assured them, that she never would awake at all, or only in the death agony.

The nurse's prophecy proved true. The poor maniac parted with existence, without again uttering a sound of any kind. But our travellers did not witness this catastrophe. They left the hospital as soon as Jeanie had satisfied herself that no elucidation of her sister's misfortunes was to be hoped from the dying person.[1]

CHAPTER XLI

> Wilt thou go on with me?
> The moon is bright, the sea is calm,
> And I know well the ocean paths . . .
> Thou wilt go on with me!
>
> *Thalaba.*

THE fatigue and agitation of these various scenes had agitated Jeanie so much, notwithstanding her robust strength of constitution, that Archibald judged it necessary that she should have a day's repose at the village of Longtown. It was in

[1] Note XIV.—Madge Wildfire.

vain that Jeanie herself protested against any delay. The Duke of Argyle's man of confidence was of course consequential; and as he had been bred to the medical profession in his youth (at least he used this expression to describe his having, thirty years before, pounded for six months in the mortar of old Mungo Mangleman, the surgeon at Greenock), he was obstinate whenever a matter of health was in question.

In this case he discovered febrile symptoms, and having once made a happy application of that learned phrase to Jeanie's case, all farther resistance became in vain; and she was glad to acquiesce, and even to go to bed, and drink water-gruel, in order that she might possess her soul in quiet, and without interruption.

Mr. Archibald was equally attentive in another particular. He observed that the execution of the old woman, and the miserable fate of her daughter, seemed to have had a more powerful effect upon Jeanie's mind, than the usual feelings of humanity might naturally have been expected to occasion. Yet she was obviously a strong-minded, sensible young woman, and in no respect subject to nervous affections; and therefore Archibald, being ignorant of any special connection between his master's protégée and these unfortunate persons, excepting that she had seen Madge formerly in Scotland, naturally imputed the strong impression these events had made upon her, to her associating them with the unhappy circumstances in which her sister had so lately stood.   He became anxious, therefore, to prevent anything occurring which might recall these associations to Jeanie's mind.

Archibald had speedily an opportunity of exercising this precaution.   A pedlar brought to Longtown that evening, amongst other wares, a large broadside sheet, giving an account of the "Last Speech and Execution of Margaret Murdockson, and of the barbarous Murder of her Daughter, Magdalene or Madge Murdockson, called Madge Wildfire; and of her pious Conversation with his Reverence Archdeacon Fleming;" which authentic publication had apparently taken place on the day they left Carlisle, and being an article of a nature peculiarly acceptable to such country-folk as were within hearing of the transaction, the itinerant bibliopolist had forthwith added them to his stock in trade.   He found a merchant sooner than he expected; for Archibald, much applauding his own prudence, purchased the whole lot for two shillings and ninepence; and the pedlar, delighted with

the profit of such a wholesale transaction, instantly returned
to Carlisle to supply himself with more.

The considerate Mr. Archibald was about to commit his
whole purchase to the flames, but it was rescued by the yet
more considerate dairy-damsel, who said, very prudently, it
was a pity to waste so much paper, which might crepe hair,
pin up bonnets, and serve many other useful purposes; and
who promised to put the parcel into her own trunk, and keep
it carefully out of the sight of Mrs. Jeanie Deans: "Though,
by-the-bye, she had no great notion of folk being so very
nice. Mrs. Deans might have had enough to think about
the gallows all this time to endure a sight of it, without all
this to do about it."

Archibald reminded the dame of the dairy of the Duke's
very particular charge, that they should be attentive and civil
to Jeanie; as also that they were to part company soon, and
consequently would not be doomed to observing any one's
health or temper during the rest of the journey. With
which answer Mrs. Dolly Dutton was obliged to hold herself satisfied.

On the morning they resumed their journey, and prosecuted it successfully, travelling through Dumfriesshire and
part of Lanarkshire, until they arrived at the small town of
Rutherglen, within about four miles of Glasgow. Here an
express brought letters to Archibald from the principal agent
of the Duke of Argyle in Edinburgh.

He said nothing of their contents that evening; but when
they were seated in the carriage the next day, the faithful
squire informed Jeanie, that he had received directions from
the Duke's factor, to whom his Grace had recommended him
to carry her, if she had no objection, for a stage or two beyond
Glasgow. Some temporary causes of discontent had occasioned tumults in that city and the neighbourhood, which
would render it unadvisable for Mrs. Jeanie Deans to travel
alone and unprotected betwixt that city and Edinburgh;
whereas, by going forward a little farther, they would meet
one of his Grace's subfactors, who was coming down from
the Highlands to Edinburgh with his wife, and under whose
charge she might journey with comfort and in safety.

Jeanie remonstrated against this arrangement. "She had
been lang," she said, "frae hame—her father and her sister
behoved to be very anxious to see her—there were other
friends she had that werena weel in health. She was willing

to pay for man and horse at Glasgow, and surely naebody wad meddle wi' sae harmless and feckless a creature as she was.— She was muckle obliged by the offer; but never hunted deer langed for its resting-place as I do to find myself at Saint Leonard's."

The groom of the chambers exchanged a look with his female companion, which seemed so full of meaning, that Jeanie screamed aloud—"O Mr. Archibald—Mrs. Dutton, if ye ken of onything that has happened at Saint Leonard's, for God's sake—for pity's sake, tell me, and dinna keep me in suspense!"

"I really know nothing, Mrs. Deans," said the groom of the chamber.

"And I—I—I am sure, I knows as little," said the dame of the dairy, while some communication seemed to tremble on her lips, which, at a glance of Archibald's eye, she appeared to swallow down, and compressed her lips thereafter into a state of extreme and vigilant firmness, as if she had been afraid of its bolting out before she was aware.

Jeanie saw that there was to be something concealed from her, and it was only the repeated assurances of Archibald that her father—her sister—all her friends were, as far as he knew, well and happy, that at all pacified her alarm. From such respectable people as those with whom she travelled she could apprehend no harm, and yet her distress was so obvious, that Archibald, as a last resource, pulled out, and put into her hand, a slip of paper, on which these words were written:—

"JEANIE DEANS—You will do me a favour by going with Archibald and my female domestic a day's journey beyond Glasgow, and asking them no questions, which will greatly oblige your friend,   ARGYLE AND GREENWICH."

Although this laconic epistle, from a nobleman to whom she was bound by such inestimable obligations, silenced all Jeanie's objections to the proposed route, it rather added to than diminished the eagerness of her curiosity. The proceeding to Glasgow seemed now no longer to be an object with her fellow-travellers. On the contrary, they kept the left-hand side of the river Clyde, and travelled through a thousand beautiful and changing views down the side of that noble stream, till, ceasing to hold its inland character, it began to assume that of a navigable river

"You are not for gaun intill Glasgow then?" said Jeanie, as she observed that the drivers made no motion for inclining their horses' heads towards the ancient bridge, which was then the only mode of access to St. Mungo's capital.

"No," replied Archibald; "there is some popular commotion, and as our Duke is in opposition to the court, perhaps we might be too well received; or they might take it in their heads to remember that the Captain of Carrick came down upon them with his Highlandmen in the time of Shawfield's mob in 1725, and then we would be too ill received.[1] And, at any rate, it is best for us, and for me in particular, who may be supposed to possess his Grace's mind upon many particulars, to leave the good people of the Gorbals to act according to their own imaginations, without either provoking or encouraging them by my presence."

To reasoning of such tone and consequence Jeanie had nothing to reply, although it seemed to her to contain fully as much self-importance as truth.

The carriage meantime rolled on; the river expanded itself, and gradually assumed the dignity of an estuary, or arm of the sea. The influence of the advancing and retiring tides became more and more evident, and in the beautiful words of him of the laurel wreath, the river waxed

> "A broader and a broader stream.
> .   .   .   .   .
> The cormorant stands upon its shoals,
> His black and dripping wings
> Half open'd to the wind."

"Which way lies Inverary?" said Jeanie, gazing on the dusky ocean of Highland hills, which now, piled above each other, and intersected by many a lake, stretched away on the opposite side of the river to the northward. "Is yon high castle the Duke's hoose?"

"That, Mrs. Deans?—Lud help thee," replied Archibald, "that's the old Castle of Dumbarton, the strongest place in Europe, be the other what it may. Sir William Wallace was governor of it in the old wars with the English, and his Grace

---

[1] In 1725, there was a great riot in Glasgow on account of the malt-tax. Among the troops brought in to restore order, was one of the independent companies of Highlanders levied in Argyleshire, and distinguished, in a lampoon of the period, as "Campbell of Carrick and his Highland thieves." It was called Shawfield's Mob, because much of the popular violence was directed against Daniel Campbell, Esq., of Shawfield, M.P., Provost of the town.

is governor just now. It is always entrusted to the best man in Scotland."

"And does the Duke live on that high rock, then?" demanded Jeanie.

"No, no, he has his deputy-governor, who commands in his absence; he lives in the white house you see at the bottom of the rock — His Grace does not reside there himself."

"I think not, indeed," said the dairy-woman, upon whose mind the road, since they had left Dumfries, had made no very favourable impression; "for if he did, he might go whistle for a dairy-woman, an he were the only duke in England. I did not leave my place and my friends to come down to see cows starve to death upon hills as they be at that pig-stye of Elfinfoot, as you call it, Mr. Archibald, or to be perched up on the top of a rock, like a squirrel in his cage, hung out of a three pair of stairs window."

Inwardly chuckling that these symptoms of recalcitration had not taken place until the fair malecontent was, as he mentally termed it, under his thumb, Archibald coolly replied, "that the hills were none of his making, nor did he know how to mend them; but as to lodging, they would soon be in a house of the Duke's in a very pleasant island called Rose-neath, where they went to wait for shipping to take them to Inverary, and would meet the company with whom Jeanie was to return to Edinburgh."

"An island?" said Jeanie, who, in the course of her various and adventurous travels, had never quitted terra firma, "then I am doubting we maun gang in ane of these boats; they look unco sma', and the waves are something rough, and——"

"Mr. Archibald," said Mrs. Dutton, "I will not consent to it; I was never engaged to leave the country, and I desire you will bid the boys drive round the other way to the Duke's house."

"There is a safe pinnace belonging to his Grace, ma'am, close by," replied Archibald, "and you need be under no apprehensions whatsoever."

"But I *am* under apprehensions," said the damsel; "and I insist upon going round by land, Mr. Archibald, were it ten miles about."

"I am sorry I cannot oblige you, madam, as Roseneath happens to be an island."

"If it were ten islands," said the incensed dame, "that's no reason why I should be drowned in going over the seas to it."

"No reason why you should be drowned, certainly, ma'am," answered the unmoved groom of the chambers, "but an admirable good one why you cannot proceed to it by land." And, fixed his master's mandates to perform, he pointed with his hand, and the drivers, turning off the high-road, proceeded towards a small hamlet of fishing huts, where a shallop, somewhat more gaily decorated than any which they had yet seen, having a flag which displayed a boar's-head, crested with a ducal coronet, waited with two or three seamen, and as many Highlanders.

The carriage stopped, and the men began to unyoke their horses, while Mr. Archibald gravely superintended the removal of the baggage from the carriage to the little vessel. "Has the *Caroline* been long arrived?" said Archibald to one of the seamen.

"She has been here in five days from Liverpool, and she's lying down at Greenock," answered the fellow.

"Let the horses and carriage go down to Greenock then," said Archibald, "and be embarked there for Inverary when I send notice—they may stand in my cousin's, Duncan Archibald the stabler's.—Ladies," he added, "I hope you will get yourselves ready, we must not loss the tide."

"Mrs. Deans," said the Cowslip of Inverary, "you may do as you please—but I will sit here all night, rather than go into that there painted egg-shell.—Fellow—fellow!" (this was addressed to a Highlander who was lifting a travelling trunk) "that trunk is *mine*, and that there band-box, and that pillion mail, and those seven bundles, and the paper bag; and if you venture to touch one of them, it shall be at your peril."

The Celt kept his eye fixed on the speaker, then turned his head towards Archibald, and receiving no countervailing signal, he shouldered the portmanteau, and without farther notice of the distressed damsel, or paying any attention to remonstrances, which probably he did not understand, and would certainly have equally disregarded whether he understood them or not, moved off with Mrs. Dutton's wearables, and deposited the trunk containing them safely in the boat.

The baggage being stowed in safety, Mr. Archibald handed Jeanie out of the carriage, and, not without some tremor on her part, she was transported through the surf and placed in the boat.   He then offered the same civility to his fellow-servant, but she was resolute in her refusal to quit the carriage, in which she now remained in solitary state, threatening all concerned or unconcerned with actions for wages and board-wages, damages, and expenses, and numbering on her fingers the gowns and other habiliments, from which she seemed in the act of being separated for ever.   Mr. Archibald did not give himself the trouble of making many remonstrances, which, indeed, seemed only to aggravate the damsel's indignation, but spoke two or three words to the Highlanders in Gaelic ; and the wily mountaineers, approaching the carriage cautiously, and without giving the slightest intimation of their intention, at once seized the recusant so effectually fast that she could neither resist no struggle, and hoisting her on their shoulders in nearly a horizontal posture, rushed down with her to the beach, and through the surf, and, with no other inconvenience than ruffling her garments a little, deposited her in the boat ; but in a state of surprise, mortification, and terror, at her sudden transportation, which rendered her absolutely mute for two or three minutes.   The men jumped in themselves ; one tall fellow remained till he had pushed off the boat, and then tumbled in upon his companions.   They took their oars and began to pull from the shore, then spread their sail, and drove merrily across the firth.

"You Scotch villain !" said the infuriated damsel to Archibald, "how dare you use a person like me in this way ?"

"Madam," said Archibald, with infinite composure, "it's high time you should know you are in the Duke's country, and that there is not one of these fellows but would throw you out of the boat as readily as into it, if such were his Grace's pleasure."

"Then the Lord have mercy on me !" said Mrs. Dutton. "If I had had any on myself, I would never have engaged with you."

"It's something of the latest to think of that now, Mrs. Dutton," said Archibald ; "but I assure you, you will find the Highlands have their pleasures.   You will have a dozen of cow-milkers under your own authority at Inverary, and you may throw any of them into the lake, if you have a mind, for the Duke's head people are almost as great as himself."

"This is a strange business, to be sure, Mr. Archibald," said the lady ; "but I suppose I must make the best on't.—

Are you sure the boat will not sink? it leans terribly to one side, in my poor mind."

"Fear nothing," said Mr. Archibald, taking a most important pinch of snuff; "this same ferry on Clyde knows us very well, or we know it, which is all the same; no fear of any of our people meeting with any accident. We should have crossed from the opposite shore, but for the disturbances at Glasgow, which made it improper for his Grace's people to pass through the city."

"Are you not afeard, Mrs. Deans," said the dairy-vestal, addressing Jeanie, who sat, not in the most comfortable state of mind, by the side of Archibald, who himself managed the helm;—"Are you not afeard of these wild men with their naked knees, and of this nut-shell of a thing, that seems bobbing up and down like a skimming-dish in a milk-pail?"

"No—no—madam," answered Jeanie, with some hesitation, "I am not feared; for I hae seen Hielandmen before, though I never was sae near them; and for the danger of the deep waters, I trust there is a Providence by sea as well as by land."

"Well," said Mrs. Dutton, "it is a beautiful thing to have learned to write and read, for one can always say such fine words whatever should befall them."

Archibald, rejoicing in the impression which his vigorous measures had made upon the intractable dairymaid, now applied himself, as a sensible and good-natured man, to secure by fair means the ascendency which he had obtained by some wholesome violence; and he succeeded so well in representing to her the idle nature of her fears, and the impossibility of leaving her upon the beach, enthroned in an empty carriage, that the good understanding of the party was completely revived ere they landed at Roseneath.

CHAPTER XLII

> Did Fortune guide,
> Or rather Destiny, our bark, to which
> We could appoint no port, to this best place?
> FLETCHER.

THE islands in the Firth of Clyde, which the daily passage of so many smoke-pennoned steamboats now renders so easily accessible, were, in our fathers' times, secluded spots, frequented by no travellers, and few visitants of any kind. They are of exquisite, yet varied beauty. Arran, a mountainous region, or Alpine island, abounds with the grandest and most romantic scenery. Bute is of a softer and more woodland character. The Cumrays, as if to exhibit a contrast to both, are green, level, and bare, forming the links of a sort of natural bar, which is drawn along the mouth of the firth, leaving large intervals, however, of ocean. Roseneath, a smaller isle, lies much higher up the firth, and towards its western shore, near the opening of the lake called the Gare-Loch, and not far from Loch Long and Loch Seant, or the Holy Loch, which wind from the mountains of the Western Highlands to join the estuary of the Clyde.

In these isles the severe frost winds, which tyrannise over the vegetable creation during a Scottish spring, are comparatively little felt ; nor, excepting the gigantic strength of Arran, are they much exposed to the Atlantic storms, lying land-locked and protected to the westward by the shores of Ayrshire. Accordingly, the weeping-willow, the weeping-birch, and other trees of early and pendulous shoots, flourish in these favoured recesses in a degree unknown in our eastern districts ; and the air is also said to possess that mildness which is favourable to consumptive cases.

The picturesque beauty of the island of Roseneath, in particular, had such recommendations, that the Earls and Dukes of Argyle, from an early period, made it their occasional residence, and had their temporary accommodation in a fishing or hunting-lodge, which succeeding improvements have since transformed into a palace. It was in its original simplicity, when the little bark, which we left traversing the firth at the end of last chapter, approached the shores of the isle.

When they touched the landing-place, which was partly shrouded by some old low but wide-spreading oak-trees, inter-mixed with hazel-bushes, two or three figures were seen as if awaiting their arrival. To these Jeanie paid little attention, so that it was with a shock of surprise almost electrical, that, upon being carried by the rowers out of the boat to the shore, she was received in the arms of her father !

It was too wonderful to be believed—too much like a happy dream to have the stable feeling of reality—She extricated herself from his close and affectionate embrace, and held him at arm's length, to satisfy her mind that it was no illusion. But the form was indisputable—Douce David Deans himself, in his best light-blue Sunday's coat, with broad metal-buttons, and waistcoat and breeches of the same, his strong gramashes or leggins of thick grey cloth—the very copper buckles— the broad Lowland blue bonnet, thrown back as he lifted his eyes to Heaven in speechless gratitude—the grey locks that straggled from beneath it down his weather-beaten "haffets"— the bald and furrowed forehead—the clear blue eye, that, undimmed by years, gleamed bright and pale from under its shaggy grey pent-house—the features, usually so stern and stoical, now melted into the unwonted expression of rapturous joy, affection, and gratitude—were all those of David Deans ; and so happily did they assort together, that, should I ever again see my friends Wilkie or Allan, I will try to borrow or steal from them a sketch of this very scene.

"Jeanie—my ain Jeanie—my best—my maist dutiful bairn— the Lord of Israel be thy father, for I am hardly worthy of thee ! Thou hast redeemed our captivity—brought back the honour of our house—Bless thee, my bairn, with mercies pro-mised and purchased !—But He *has* blessed thee, in the good of which He has made thee the instrument."

These words broke from him not without tears, though David was of no melting mood. Archibald had, with delicate attention, withdrawn the spectators from the interview, so that the wood and setting sun alone were witnesses of the expansion of their feelings.

"And Effie ?—and Effie, dear father ? " was an eager inter-jectional question which Jeanie repeatedly threw in among her expressions of joyful thankfulness.

"Ye will hear—ye will hear," said David hastily, and ever and anon renewed his grateful acknowledgments to Heaven for sending Jeanie safe down from the land of prelatic dead-ness and schismatic heresy ; and had delivered her from the dangers of the way, and the lions that were in the path.

"And Effie ? " repeated her affectionate sister again and again. "And—and—" (fain would she have said Butler, but she modified the direct inquiry)—"and Mr. and Mrs. Saddle-tree—and Dumbiedikes—and a' friends ? "

"A' weel—a' weel, praise to His name ! "

"And—and Mr. Butler—he wasna weel when I gaed awa ? "

"He is quite mended—quite weel," replied her father.

"Thank God—but oh, dear father, Effie ?—Effie ? "

"You will never see her mair, my bairn," answered Deans

in a solemn tone—" You are the ae and only leaf left now on
the auld tree—heal be your portion ! "

"She is dead !—She is slain !—It has come ower late ! "
exclaimed Jeanie, wringing her hands.

"No, Jeanie," returned Deans, in the same grave, melancholy tone.   "She lives in the flesh, and is at freedom from
earthly restraint, if she were as much alive in faith, and as free
from the bonds of Satan."

"The Lord protect us ! " said Jeanie.—" Can the unhappy
bairn hae left you for that villain ? "

"It is ower truly spoken," said Deans—" She has left her
auld father, that has wept and prayed for her—She has left her
sister, that travailed and toiled for her like a mother—She has
left the bones of her mother, and the land of her people,
and she is ower the march wi' that son of Belial—She has
made a moonlight flitting of it."   He paused, for a feeling
betwixt sorrow and strong resentment choked his utterance.

"And wi' that man ?—that fearfu' man ? " said Jeanie.
"And she has left us to gang aff wi' him ?—O Effie, Effie,
wha could hae thought it, after sic a deliverance as you had
been gifted wi' ! "

"She went out from us, my bairn, because she was not
of us," replied David.   "She is a withered branch will never
bear fruit of grace—a scapegoat gone forth into the wilderness
of the world, to carry wi' her, as I trust, the sins of our
little congregation.   The peace of the warld gang wi' her, and
a better peace when she has the grace to turn to it !   If
she is of His elected, His ain hour will come.   What would
her mother have said, that famous and memorable matron,
Rebecca M'Naught, whose memory is like a flower of sweet
savour in Newbattle, and a pot of frankincense in Lugton ?
But be it sae—let her part—let her gang her gate—let her bite
on her ain bridle—The Lord kens His time—She was the
bairn of prayers, and may not prove an utter castaway.   But
never, Jeanie—never more let her name be spoken between
you and me—She hath passed from us like the brook which
vanisheth when the summer waxeth warm, as patient Job saith
—let her pass, and be forgotten."

There was a melancholy pause which followed these expressions.   Jeanie would fain have asked more circumstances
relating to her sister's departure, but the tone of her father's
prohibition was positive.   She was about to mention her interview with Staunton at his father's rectory ; but, on hastily

running over the particulars in her memory, she thought that, on the whole, they were more likely to aggravate than diminish his distress of mind. She turned, therefore, the discourse from this painful subject, resolving to suspend farther inquiry until she should see Butler, from whom she expected to learn the particulars of her sister's elopement.

But when was she to see Butler? was a question she could not forbear asking herself, especially while her father, as if eager to escape from the subject of his youngest daughter, pointed to the opposite shore of Dumbartonshire, and asking Jeanie " if it werena a pleasant abode? " declared to her his intention of removing his earthly tabernacle to that country, " in respect he was solicited by his Grace the Duke of Argyle, as one well skilled in country labour, and a' that appertained to flocks and herds, to superintend a store-farm, whilk his Grace has taen into his ain hand for the improvement of stock."

Jeanie's heart sunk within her at this declaration. " She allowed it was a goodly and pleasant land, and sloped bonnily to the western sun; and she doubtedna that the pasture might be very gude, for the grass looked green, for as drouthy as the weather had been. But it was far frae hame, and she thought she wad be often thinking on the bonny spots of turf, sae fu' of gowans and yellow king-cups, amang the Crags at St. Leonard's."

" Dinna speak on't, Jeanie," said her father; " I wish never to hear it named mair—that is, after the rouping is ower, and the bills paid. But I brought a' the beasts ower-by that I thought ye wad like best. There is Gowans, and there's your ain brockit cow, and the wee hawkit ane, that ye ca'd—I needna tell ye how ye ca'd it—but I couldna bid them sell the petted creature, though the sight o't may sometimes gie us a sair heart—it's no the poor dumb creature's fault—And ane or twa beasts mair I hae reserved, and I caused them to be driven before the other beasts, that men might say, as when the son of Jesse returned from battle, ' This is David's spoil.' "

Upon more particular inquiry, Jeanie found new occasion to admire the active beneficence of her friend the Duke of Argyle. While establishing a sort of experimental farm on the skirts of his immense Highland estates, he had been somewhat at a loss to find a proper person in whom to vest the charge of it. The conversation his Grace had upon country matters with Jeanie Deans during their return from Richmond, had impressed him with a belief that the father, whose experience and success she so frequently quoted, must be exactly the sort of person whom he wanted.   When the condition annexed to Effie's pardon rendered it highly probable that David Deans would choose to change his place of residence, this idea again occurred to the Duke more strongly, and as he was an enthusiast equally in agriculture and in benevolence, he imagined he was serving the purposes of both, when he wrote to the gentleman in Edinburgh entrusted with his affairs, to inquire into the character of David Deans, cowfeeder, and so forth, at St. Leonard's Crags ; and if he found him such as he had been represented, to engage him without delay, and on the most liberal terms, to superintend his fancy farm in Dumbartonshire.

The proposal was made to old David by the gentleman so commissioned, on the second day after his daughter's pardon had reached Edinburgh. His resolution to leave St. Leonard's had been already formed ; the honour of an express invitation from the Duke of Argyle to superintend a department where so much skill and diligence was required, was in itself extremely flattering ; and the more so, because honest David, who was not without an excellent opinion of his own talents, persuaded himself that, by accepting this charge, he would in some sort repay the great favour he had received at the hands of the Argyle family. The appointments, including the right of sufficient grazing for a small stock of his own, were amply liberal ; and David's keen eye saw that the situation was convenient for trafficking to advantage in Highland cattle. There was risk of "her'ship"[1] from the neighbouring mountains, indeed, but the awful name of the Duke of Argyle would be a great security, and a trifle of *black-mail* would, David was aware, assure his safety.

Still, however, there were two points on which he haggled. The first was the character of the clergyman with whose worship he was to join ; and on this delicate point he received, as we will presently show the reader, perfect satisfaction. The next obstacle was the condition of his youngest daughter, obliged as she was to leave Scotland for so many years.

The gentleman of the law smiled, and said, " There was no occasion to interpret that clause very strictly—that if the young woman left Scotland for a few months, or even weeks,

---

[1] Her'ship, a Scottish word which may be said to be now obsolete ; because, fortunately, the practice of " plundering by armed force," which is its meaning, does not require to be commonly spoken of.

and came to her father's new residence by sea from the western side of England, nobody would know of her arrival, or at least nobody who had either the right or inclination to give her disturbance. The extensive heritable jurisdictions of his Grace excluded the interference of other magistrates with those living on his estates, and they who were in immediate dependence on him would receive orders to give the young woman no disturbance. Living on the verge of the Highlands, she might, indeed, be said to be out of Scotland, that is, beyond the bounds of ordinary law and civilisation."

Old Deans was not quite satisfied with this reasoning; but the elopement of Effie, which took place on the third night after her liberation, rendered his residence at St. Leonard's so detestable to him, that he closed at once with the proposal which had been made him, and entered with pleasure into the idea of surprising Jeanie, as had been proposed by the Duke, to render the change of residence more striking to her. The Duke had apprised Archibald of these circumstances, with orders to act according to the instructions he should receive from Edinburgh, and by which accordingly he was directed to bring Jeanie to Roseneath.

The father and daughter communicated these matters to each other, now stopping, now walking slowly towards the Lodge, which showed itself among the trees, at about half a mile's distance from the little bay in which they had landed.

As they approached the house, David Deans informed his daughter, with somewhat like a grim smile, which was the utmost advance he ever made towards a mirthful expression of visage, that "there was baith a worshipful gentleman, and ane reverend gentleman, residing therein. The worshipful gentleman was his honour the Laird of Knocktarlitie, who was bailie of the Lordship under the Duke of Argyle, ane Hieland gentleman, tarr'd wi' the same stick," David doubted, "as mony of them, namely, a hasty and choleric temper, and a neglect of the higher things that belong to salvation, and also a gripping unto the things of this world, without muckle distinction of property; but, however, ane gude hospitable gentleman, with whom it would be a part of wisdom to live on a gude understanding (for Hielandmen were hasty, ower hasty). As for the reverend person of whom he had spoken, he was candidate by favour of the Duke of Argyle (for David would not for the universe have called him presentee) for the kirk of the parish in which their farm was situated, and he was likely to be highly acceptable unto the Christian souls of the parish, who were hungering for spiritual manna, having been fed but upon sour Hieland sowens by Mr. Duncan MacDonought, the last minister, who began the morning duly, Sunday and Saturday, with a mutchkin of usquebaugh. "But I need say the less about the present lad," said David, again grimly grimacing, "as I think ye may hae seen him afore; and here he is come to meet us."

She had indeed seen him before, for it was no other than Reuben Butler himself.

CHAPTER XLIII

No more shalt thou behold thy sister's face;
Thou hast already had her last embrace.
Elegy on Mrs. Anne Killigrew.

THIS second surprise had been accomplished for Jeanie Deans by the rod of the same benevolent enchanter, whose power had transplanted her father from the Crags of St. Leonard's to the banks of the Gare-Loch. The Duke of Argyle was not a person to forget the hereditary debt of gratitude, which had been bequeathed to him by his grandfather, in favour of the grandson of old Bible Butler. He had internally resolved to provide for Reuben Butler in this kirk of Knocktarlitie, of which the incumbent had just departed this life. Accordingly, his agent received the necessary instructions for that purpose, under the qualifying condition always, that the learning and character of Mr. Butler should be found proper for the charge. Upon inquiry, these were found as highly satisfactory as had been reported in the case of David Deans himself.

By this preferment, the Duke of Argyle more essentially benefited his friend and protégée, Jeanie, than he himself was aware of, since he contributed to remove objections in her father's mind to the match, which he had no idea had been in existence.

We have already noticed that Deans had something of a prejudice against Butler, which was, perhaps, in some degree owing to his possessing a sort of consciousness, that the poor usher looked with eyes of affection upon his eldest daughter. This, in David's eyes, was a sin of presumption, even although it should not be followed by any overt act, or actual proposal.

But the lively interest which Butler had displayed in his distresses, since Jeanie set forth on her London expedition, and which, therefore, he ascribed to personal respect for himself individually, had greatly softened the feelings of irritability with which David had sometimes regarded him. And, while he was in this good disposition towards Butler, another incident took place which had great influence on the old man's mind.

So soon as the shock of Effie's second elopement was over, it was Deans's early care to collect and refund to the Laird of Dumbiedikes the money which he had lent for Effie's trial, and for Jeanie's travelling expenses. The Laird, the pony, the cocked hat, and the tobacco-pipe, had not been seen at St. Leonard's Crags for many a day; so that, in order to pay this debt, David was under the necessity of repairing in person to the mansion of Dumbiedikes.

He found it in a state of unexpected bustle. There were workmen pulling down some of the old hangings, and replacing them with others, altering, repairing, scrubbing, painting, and white-washing. There was no knowing the old house, which had been so long the mansion of sloth and silence. The Laird himself seemed in some confusion, and his reception, though kind, lacked something of the reverential cordiality with which he used to greet David Deans. There was a change also, David did not very well know of what nature, about the exterior of this landed proprietor—an improvement in the shape of his garments, a spruceness in the air with which they were put on, that were both novelties. Even the old hat looked smarter; the cock had been newly pointed, the lace had been refreshed, and instead of slouching backward or forward on the Laird's head, as it happened to be thrown on, it was adjusted with a knowing inclination over one eye.

David Deans opened his business, and told down the cash. Dumbiedikes steadily inclined his ear to the one, and counted the other with great accuracy, interrupting David, while he was talking of the redemption of the captivity of Judah, to ask him whether he did not think one or two of the guineas looked rather light. When he was satisfied on this point, had pocketed his money, and had signed a receipt, he addressed David with some little hesitation—"Jeanie wad be writing ye something, gudeman?"

"About the siller?" replied David—"nae doubt, she did."

"And did she say nae mair about me?" asked the Laird.

*p 134

"Nae mair but kind and Christian wishes—what suld she hae said?" replied David, fully expecting that the Laird's long courtship (if his dangling after Jeanie deserves so active a name) was now coming to a point. And so indeed it was, but not to that point which he wished or expected.

"Aweel, she kens her ain mind best, gudeman. I hae made a clean house o' Jenny Balchristie and her niece. They were a bad pack—steal'd meat and mault, and loot the carters magg the coals—I'm to be married the morn, and kirkit on Sunday."

Whatever David felt, he was too proud and too steady-minded to show any unpleasant surprise in his countenance and manner.

"I wuss ye happy, sir, through Him that gies happiness—marriage is an honourable state."

"And I am wedding into an honourable house, David—the Laird of Lickpelf's youngest daughter—she sits next us in the kirk, and that's the way I came to think on't."

There was no more to be said, but again to wish the Laird joy, to taste a cup of his liquor, and to walk back again to St. Leonard's, musing on the mutability of human affairs and human resolutions. The expectation that one day or other Jeanie would be Lady Dumbiedikes, had, in spite of himself, kept a more absolute possession of David's mind than he himself was aware of. At least, it had hitherto seemed an union at all times within his daughter's reach, whenever she might choose to give her silent lover any degree of encouragement, and now it was vanished for ever. David returned, therefore, in no very gracious humour for so good a man. He was angry with Jeanie for not having encouraged the Laird—he was angry with the Laird for requiring encouragement—and he was angry with himself for being angry at all on the occasion.

On his return he found the gentleman who managed the Duke of Argyle's affairs was desirous of seeing him, with a view to completing the arrangement between them. Thus, after a brief repose, he was obliged to set off anew for Edinburgh, so that old May Hettly declared, "that a' this was to end with the master just walking himself aff his feet."

When the business respecting the farm had been talked over and arranged, the professional gentleman acquainted David Deans, in answer to his inquiries concerning the state of public worship, that it was the pleasure of the Duke to put an excellent young clergyman, called Reuben Butler, into the parish, which was to be his future residence.

"Reuben Butler!" exclaimed David—"Reuben Butler, the usher at Libberton?"

"The very same," said the Duke's commissioner; "his Grace has heard an excellent character of him, and has some hereditary obligations to him besides—few ministers will be so comfortable as I am directed to make Mr. Butler."

"Obligations?—The Duke?—Obligations to Reuben Butler —Reuben Butler a placed minister of the Kirk of Scotland!" exclaimed David, in interminable astonishment, for somehow he had been led by the bad success which Butler had hitherto met with in all his undertakings, to consider him as one of those stepsons of Fortune, whom she treats with unceasing rigour, and ends with disinheriting altogether.

There is, perhaps, no time at which we are disposed to think so highly of a friend, as when we find him standing higher than we expected in the esteem of others. When assured of the reality of Butler's change of prospects, David expressed his great satisfaction at his success in life, which, he observed, was entirely owing to himself (David). "I advised his puir grandmother, who was but a silly woman, to breed him up to the ministry; and I prophesied that, with a blessing on his endeavours, he would become a polished shaft in the temple. He may be something ower proud o' his carnal learning, but a gude lad, and has the root of the matter—as ministers gang now, where ye'll find ane better, ye'll find ten waur, than Reuben Butler."

He took leave of the man of business, and walked homeward, forgetting his weariness in the various speculations to which this wonderful piece of intelligence gave rise. Honest David had now, like other great men, to go to work to reconcile his speculative principles with existing circumstances; and, like other great men, when they set seriously about that task, he was tolerably successful.

"Ought Reuben Butler in conscience to accept of this preferment in the Kirk of Scotland, subject as David at present thought that establishment was to the Erastian encroachments of the civil power?" This was the leading question, and he considered it carefully. "The Kirk of Scotland was shorn of its beams, and deprived of its full artillery and banners of authority; but still it contained zealous and fructifying pastors, attentive congregations, and, with all her spots and blemishes, the like of this Kirk was nowhere else to be seen upon earth."

David's doubts had been too many and too critical to permit him ever unequivocally to unite himself with any of the dissenters, who, upon various accounts, absolutely seceded from the national church. He had often joined in communion with such of the established clergy as approached nearest to the old Presbyterian model and principles of 1640. And although there were many things to be amended in that system, yet he remembered that he, David Deans, had himself ever been a humble pleader for the good old cause in a legal way, but without rushing into right-hand excesses, divisions, and separations. But, as an enemy to separation, he might join the right hand of fellowship with a minister of the Kirk of Scotland in its present model. *Ergo*, Reuben Butler might take possession of the parish of Knocktarlitie, without forfeiting his friendship or favour—Q. E. D. But, secondly, came the trying point of lay-patronage, which David Deans had ever maintained to be a coming in by the window, and over the wall, a cheating and starving the souls of a whole parish, for the purpose of clothing the back and filling the belly of the incumbent.

This presentation, therefore, from the Duke of Argyle, whatever was the worth and high character of that nobleman, was a limb of the brazen image, a portion of the evil thing, and with no kind of consistency could David bend his mind to favour such a transaction. But if the parishioners themselves joined in a general call to Reuben Butler to be their pastor, it did not seem quite so evident that the existence of this unhappy presentation was a reason for his refusing them the comforts of his doctrine. If the Presbytery admitted him to the kirk, in virtue rather of that act of patronage than of the general call of the congregation, that might be their error, and David allowed it was a heavy one. But if Reuben Butler accepted of the care as tendered to him by those whom he was called to teach, and who had expressed themselves desirous to learn, David, after considering and reconsidering the matter, came, through the great virtue of IF, to be of opinion that he might safely so act in that matter.

There remained a third stumbling-block — the oaths to government exacted from the established clergymen, in which they acknowledge an Erastian king and parliament, and homologate the incorporating Union between England and Scotland, through which the latter kingdom had become part and portion of the former, wherein Prelacy, the sister of Popery, had made fast her throne, and elevated the horns of her mitre. These were symptoms of defection which had often made David cry out, "My bowels—my bowels!—I am pained at the very heart!" And he remembered that a godly Bow-head matron had been carried out of the Tolbooth Church in a swoon, beyond the reach of brandy and burnt feathers, merely on hearing these fearful words, "It is enacted by the Lords *spiritual* and temporal," pronounced from a Scottish pulpit, in the proem to the Porteous Proclamation. These oaths were, therefore, a deep compliance and dire abomination—a sin and a snare, and a danger and a defection. But this shibboleth was not always exacted. Ministers had respect to their own tender consciences, and those of their brethren ; and it was not till a later period that the reins of discipline were taken up tight by the General Assemblies and Presbyteries. The peace-making particle came again to David's assistance. *If* an incumbent was not called upon to make such compliances, and *if* he got a right entry into the church without intrusion, and by orderly appointment, why, upon the whole, David Deans came to be of opinion, that the said incumbent might lawfully enjoy the spirituality and temporality of the cure of souls at Knocktarlitie, with stipend, manse, glebe, and all thereunto appertaining.

The best and most upright-minded men are so strongly influenced by existing circumstances, that it would be somewhat cruel to inquire too nearly what weight paternal affection gave to these ingenious trains of reasoning. Let David Deans's situation be considered. He was just deprived of one daughter, and his eldest, to whom he owed so much, was cut off, by the sudden resolution of Dumbiedikes, from the high hope which David had entertained, that she might one day be mistress of that fair lordship. Just while this disappointment was bearing heavy on his spirits, Butler comes before his imagination—no longer the half-starved, threadbare usher, but fat and sleek and fair, the beneficed minister of Knocktarlitie, beloved by his congregation,—exemplary in his life,—powerful in his doctrine, —doing the duty of the kirk as never Highland minister did it before,—turning sinners as a colley dog turns sheep,—a favourite of the Duke of Argyle, and drawing a stipend of eight hundred punds Scots, and four chalders of victual. Here was a match, making up, in David's mind, in a tenfold degree, the disappointment in the case of Dumbiedikes, in so far as the Goodman of St. Leonard's held a powerful minister in much greater admiration than a mere landed proprietor. It did not occur to him, as an additional reason in favour of the match, that Jeanie might herself have some choice in the matter; for the idea of consulting her feelings never once entered the honest man's head, any more than the possibility that her inclination might perhaps differ from his own.

The result of his meditations was, that he was called upon to take the management of the whole affair into his own hand, and give, if it should be found possible without sinful compliance, or back-sliding, or defection of any kind, a worthy pastor to the kirk of Knocktarlitie. Accordingly, by the intervention of the honest dealer in butter-milk who dwelt in Libberton, David summoned to his presence Reuben Butler. Even from this worthy messenger he was unable to conceal certain swelling emotions of dignity, insomuch, that, when the carter had communicated his message to the usher, he added, that "Certainly the Gudeman of St. Leonard's had some grand news to tell him, for he was as uplifted as a midden-cock upon pattens."

Butler, it may readily be conceived, immediately obeyed the summons. His was a plain character, in which worth and good sense and simplicity were the principal ingredients; but love, on this occasion, gave him a certain degree of address. He had received an intimation of the favour designed him by the Duke of Argyle, with what feelings those only can conceive, who have experienced a sudden prospect of being raised to independence and respect, from penury and toil. He resolved, however, that the old man should retain all the consequence of being, in his own opinion, the first to communicate his important intelligence. At the same time, he also determined that in the expected conference he would permit David Deans to expatiate at length upon the proposal, in all its bearings, without irritating him either by interruption or contradiction. This last plan was the most prudent he could have adopted; because, although there were many doubts which David Deans could himself clear up to his own satisfaction, yet he might have been by no means disposed to accept the solution of any other person; and to engage him in an argument would have been certain to confirm him at once and for ever in the opinion which Butler chanced to impugn.

He received his friend with an appearance of important gravity, which real misfortune had long compelled him to lay aside, and which belonged to those days of awful authority in which he predominated over Widow Butler, and dictated the mode of cultivating the crofts at Beersheba. He made known to Reuben with great prolixity the prospect of his changing his present residence for the charge of the Duke of Argyle's stock-farm in Dumbartonshire, and enumerated the various advantages of the situation with obvious self-congratulation; but assured the patient hearer, that nothing had so much moved him to acceptance, as the sense that, by his skill in bestial, he could render the most important services to his Grace the Duke of Argyle, to whom, "in the late unhappy circumstance" (here a tear dimmed the sparkle of pride in the old man's eye), "he had been sae muckle obliged."

"To put a rude Hielandman into sic a charge," he continued, "what could be expected but that he suld be sic a chiefest herdsman, as wicked Doeg the Edomite? whereas, while this grey head is to the fore, not a clute o' them but sall be as weel cared for as if they were the fatted kine of Pharaoh. —And now, Reuben, lad, seeing we maun remove our tent to a strange country, ye will be casting a dolefu' look after us, and thinking with whom ye are to hold council anent your government in thae slippery and backsliding times; and nae doubt remembering, that the auld man, David Deans, was made the instrument to bring you out of the mire of schism and heresy, wherein your father's house delighted to wallow; aften also, nae doubt, when ye are pressed wi' ensnaring trials and tentations and heart-plagues, you, that are like a recruit that is marching for the first time to the took of drum, will miss the auld, bauld, and experienced veteran soldier that has felt the brunt of mony a foul day, and heard the bullets whistle as aften as he has hairs left on his auld pow."

It is very possible that Butler might internally be of opinion, that the reflection on his ancestor's peculiar tenets might have been spared, or that he might be presumptuous enough even to think, that, at his years and with his own lights, he might be able to hold his course without the pilotage of honest David. But he only replied, by expressing his regret, that anything should separate him from an ancient, tried, and affectionate friend.

"But how can it be helped, man?" said David, twisting his features into a sort of smile—"How can we help it?—I trow ye canna tell me that—Ye maun leave that to ither folk—to the Duke of Argyle and me, Reuben. It's a gude thing to hae friends in this warld—how muckle better to hae an interest beyond it!"

And David, whose piety, though not always quite rational, was as sincere as it was habitual and fervent, looked reverentially upward, and paused. Mr. Butler intimated the pleasure with which he would receive his friend's advice on a subject so important, and David resumed.

"What think ye now, Reuben, of a kirk—a regular kirk under the present establishment?—Were sic offered to ye, wad ye be free to accept it, and under whilk provisions?—I am speaking but by way of query."

Butler replied, "That if such a prospect were held out to him, he would probably first consult whether he was likely to be useful to the parish he should be called to; and if there appeared a fair prospect of his proving so, his friend must be aware, that, in every other point of view, it would be highly advantageous for him."

"Right, Reuben, very right, lad," answered the monitor, "your ain conscience is the first thing to be satisfied—for how sall he teach others that has himsell sae ill learned the Scriptures, as to grip for the lucre of foul earthly preferment, sic as gear and manse, money and victual, that which is not his in a spiritual sense—or wha makes his kirk a stalking-horse, from behind which he may tak aim at his stipend? But I look for better things of you—and specially ye maun be minded not to act altogether on your ain judgment, for therethrough comes sair mistakes, backslidings, and defections, on the left and on the right. If there were sic a day of trial put to you, Reuben, you, who are a young lad, although it may be ye are gifted wi' the carnal tongues, and those whilk were spoken at Rome, whilk is now the seat of the scarlet abomination, and by the Greeks, to whom the gospel was as foolishness, yet nae-the-less ye may be entreated by your weel-wisher to take the counsel of those prudent and resolved and weather-withstanding professors, wha hae kend what it was to lurk on banks and in mosses, in bogs and in caverns, and to risk the peril of the head rather than renunce the honesty of the heart."

Butler replied, "That certainly, possessing such a friend as he hoped and trusted he had in the goodman himself, who had seen so many changes in the preceding century, he should be much to blame if he did not avail himself of his experience and friendly counsel."

"Eneugh said—eneugh said, Reuben," said David Deans, with internal exultation; "and say that ye were in the pre-

The Heart of Mid-Lothian 449

dicament whereof I hae spoken, of a surety I would deem it
my duty to gang to the root o' the matter, and lay bare to you
the ulcers and imposthumes, and the sores and the leprosies,
of this our time, crying aloud and sparing not."

David Deans was now in his element. He commenced
his examination of the doctrines and belief of the Christian
Church with the very Culdees, from whom he passed to
John Knox,—from John Knox to the recusants in James the
Sixth's time,—Bruce, Black, Blair, Livingstone,—from them
to the brief, and at length triumphant period of the Presbyterian Church's splendour, until it was overrun by the English
Independents. Then followed the dismal times of prelacy,
the indulgences, seven in number, with all their shades and
bearings, until he arrived at the reign of King James the
Second, in which he himself had been, in his own mind,
neither an obscure actor nor an obscure sufferer. Then was
Butler doomed to hear the most detailed and annotated
edition of what he had so often heard before—David Deans's
confinement, namely, in the iron cage in the Canongate Tolbooth, and the cause thereof.

We should be very unjust to our friend David Deans, if we
should "pretermit," to use his own expression, a narrative
which he held essential to his fame. A drunken trooper of
the Royal Guards, Francis Gordon by name, had chased five
or six of the skulking Whigs, among whom was our friend
David; and after he had compelled them to stand, and was
in the act of brawling with them, one of their number fired a
pocket-pistol, and shot him dead. David used to sneer and
shake his head when any one asked him whether *he* had been
the instrument of removing this wicked persecutor from the
face of the earth. In fact, the merit of the deed lay between
him and his friend, Patrick Walker, the pedlar, whose works
he was so fond of quoting. Neither of them cared directly to
claim the merit of silencing Mr. Francis Gordon of the Life-
Guards, there being some wild cousins of his about Edinburgh,
who might have been even yet addicted to revenge, but yet
neither of them chose to disown or yield to the other the
merit of this active defence of their religious rites. David
said, that if he had fired a pistol then, it was what he never
did after or before. And as for Mr. Patrick Walker, he has
left it upon record, that his great surprise was, that so small a
pistol could kill so big a man. These are the words of that
venerable biographer, whose trade had not taught him by

experience, that an inch was as good as an ell. "He" (Francis Gordon) "got a shot in his head out of a pocket-pistol, rather fit for diverting a boy than killing such a furious, mad, brisk man, which notwithstanding killed him dead!"[1]

Upon the extensive foundation which the history of the kirk afforded, during its short-lived triumph and long tribulation, David, with length of breath and of narrative, which would have astounded any one but a lover of his daughter, proceeded to lay down his own rules for guiding the conscience of his friend, as an aspirant to serve in the ministry. Upon this subject, the good man went through such a variety of nice and casuistical problems, supposed so many extreme cases, made the distinctions so critical and nice betwixt the right hand and the left hand—betwixt compliance and defection—holding back and stepping aside—slipping and stumbling—snares and errors—that at length, after having limited the path of truth to a mathematical line, he was brought to the broad admission, that each man's conscience, after he had gained a certain view of the difficult navigation which he was to encounter, would be the best guide for his pilotage. He stated the examples and arguments for and against the acceptance of a kirk on the present revolution model, with much more impartiality to Butler than he had been able to place them before his own view. And he concluded, that his young friend ought to think upon these things, and be guided by the voice of his own conscience, whether he could take such an awful trust as the charge of souls, without doing injury to his own internal conviction of what is right or wrong.

When David had finished his very long harangue, which was only interrupted by monosyllables, or little more, on the part of Butler, the orator himself was greatly astonished to find that the conclusion, at which he very naturally wished to arrive, seemed much less decisively attained than when he had argued the case in his own mind.

In this particular, David's current of thinking and speaking only illustrated the very important and general proposition, concerning the excellence of the publicity of debate. For, under the influence of any partial feeling, it is certain, that most men can more easily reconcile themselves to any favourite measure, when agitating it in their own mind, than when obliged to expose its merits to a third party, when the

<hr />

[1] Note XV.—Death of Francis Gordon.

necessity of seeming impartial procures for the opposite arguments a much more fair statement than that which he affords it in tacit meditation. Having finished what he had to say, David thought himself obliged to be more explicit in point of fact, and to explain that this was no hypothetical case, but one on which (by his own influence and that of the Duke of Argyle) Reuben Butler would soon be called to decide.

It was even with something like apprehension that David Deans heard Butler announce, in return to this communication, that he would take that night to consider on what he had said with such kind intentions, and return him an answer the next morning. The feelings of the father mastered David on this occasion. He pressed Butler to spend the evening with him—He produced, most unusual at his meals, one, nay, two bottles of aged strong ale.—He spoke of his daughter—of her merits—her housewifery—her thrift—her affection. He led Butler so decidedly up to a declaration of his feelings towards Jeanie, that, before nightfall, it was distinctly understood she was to be the bride of Reuben Butler; and if they thought it indelicate to abridge the period of deliberation which Reuben had stipulated, it seemed to be sufficiently understood betwixt them, that there was a strong probability of his becoming minister of Knocktarlitie, providing the congregation were as willing to accept of him, as the Duke to grant him the presentation. The matter of the oaths, they agreed, it was time enough to dispute about, whenever the shibboleth should be tendered.

Many arrangements were adopted that evening, which were afterwards ripened by correspondence with the Duke of Argyle's man of business, who entrusted Deans and Butler with the benevolent wish of his principal, that they should all meet with Jeanie, on her return from England, at the Duke's hunting-lodge in Roseneath.

This retrospect, so far as the placid loves of Jeanie Deans and Reuben Butler are concerned, forms a full explanation of the preceding narrative up to their meeting on the island as already mentioned.

CHAPTER XLIV

"I come," he said, "my love, my life,
And—nature's dearest name—my wife:
Thy father's house and friends resign.
My home, my friends, my sire, are thine."
                                        LOGAN.

THE meeting of Jeanie and Butler, under circumstances promising to crown an affection so long delayed, was rather affecting from its simple sincerity than from its uncommon vehemence of feeling. David Deans, whose practice was sometimes a little different from his theory, appalled them at first, by giving them the opinion of sundry of the suffering preachers and champions of his younger days, that marriage, though honourable by the laws of Scripture, was yet a state over-rashly coveted by professors, and specially by young ministers, whose desire, he said, was at whiles too inordinate for kirks, stipends, and wives, which had frequently occasioned over-ready compliance with the general defections of the times. He endeavoured to make them aware also, that hasty wedlock had been the bane of many a savoury professor — that the unbelieving wife had too often reversed the text, and perverted the believing husband—that when the famous Donald Cargill, being then hiding in Leewood, in Lanarkshire, it being killing-time, did, upon importunity, marry Robert Marshal of Starry Shaw, he had thus expressed himself: "What hath induced Robert to marry this woman ? her ill will overcome his good— he will not keep the way long—his thriving days are done." To the sad accomplishment of which prophecy David said he was himself a living witness, for Robert Marshal, having fallen into foul compliances with the enemy, went home, and heard the curates, declined into other steps of defection, and became lightly esteemed. Indeed, he observed, that the great up-holders of the standard, Cargill, Peden, Cameron, and Renwick, had less delight in tying the bonds of matrimony than in any other piece of their ministerial work ; and although they would neither dissuade the parties, nor refuse their office, they considered the being called to it as an evidence of indifference, on the part of those between whom it was solemnised, to the many grievous things of the day. Notwithstanding, however, that marriage was a snare unto many, David was of opinion (as, indeed, he had showed in his practice) that it was in itself honourable, especially if times were such that honest men could be secure against being shot, hanged, or banished, and had ane competent livelihood to maintain themselves, and those that might come after them. "And, therefore," as he concluded something abruptly, addressing Jeanie and Butler, who, with faces as high-coloured as crimson, had been listening to this lengthened argument for and against the holy state of matrimony, "I will leave ye to your ain cracks."

As their private conversation, however interesting to themselves, might probably be very little so to the reader, so far as it respected their present feelings and future prospects, we shall pass it over, and only mention the information which Jeanie received from Butler concerning her sister's elopement, which contained many particulars that she had been unable to extract from her father.

Jeanie learned, therefore, that, for three days after her pardon had arrived, Effie had been the inmate of her father's house at St. Leonard's—that the interviews betwixt David and his erring child, which had taken place before she was liberated from prison, had been touching in the extreme; but Butler could not suppress his opinion, that, when he was freed from the apprehension of losing her in a manner so horrible, her father had tightened the bands of discipline, so as, in some degree, to gall the feelings and aggravate the irritability of a spirit naturally impatient and petulant, and now doubly so from the sense of merited disgrace.

On the third night, Effie disappeared from St. Leonard's, leaving no intimation whatever of the route she had taken. Butler, however, set out in pursuit of her, and with much trouble traced her towards a little landing-place, formed by a small brook which enters the sea betwixt Musselburgh and Edinburgh. This place, which has been since made into a small harbour, surrounded by many villas and lodging-houses, is now termed Portobello. At this time it was surrounded by a waste common, covered with furze, and unfrequented, save by fishing-boats, and now and then a smuggling lugger. A vessel of this description had been hovering in the firth at the time of Effie's elopement, and, as Butler ascertained, a boat had come ashore in the evening on which the fugitive had disappeared, and had carried on board a female. As the vessel made sail immediately, and landed no part of their cargo, there seemed little doubt that they were accomplices of the notorious Robertson, and that the vessel had only come into the firth to carry off his paramour.

This was made clear by a letter which Butler himself soon afterwards received by post, signed E. D., but without bearing any date of place or time. It was miserably ill written and spelt; sea-sickness having apparently aided the derangement of Effie's very irregular orthography and mode of expression. In this epistle, however, as in all that that unfortunate girl said or did, there was something to praise as well as to blame. She said in her letter, "That she could not endure that her father and her sister should go into banishment, or be partakers of her shame—that if her burden was a heavy one, it was of her own binding, and she had the more right to bear it alone,—that in future they could not be a comfort to her, or she to them, since every look and word of her father put her in mind of her transgression, and was like to drive her mad,— that she had nearly lost her judgment during the three days she was at St. Leonard's—her father meant weel by her, and all men, but he did not know the dreadful pain he gave her in casting up her sins. If Jeanie had been at hame, it might hae dune better—Jeanie was ane, like the angels in heaven, that rather weep for sinners, than reckon their transgressions. But she should never see Jeanie ony mair, and that was the thought that gave her the sairest heart of a' that had come and gane yet. On her bended knees would she pray for Jeanie, night and day, baith for what she had done, and what she had scorned to do, in her behalf; for what a thought would it have been to her at that moment o' time, if that upright creature had made a fault to save her! She desired her father would give Jeanie a' the gear—her ain (i.e. Effie's) mother's and a'—She had made a deed, giving up her right, and it was in Mr. Novit's hand—Warld's gear was henceforward the least of her care, nor was it likely to be muckle her mister—She hoped this would make it easy for her sister to settle;" and immediately after this expression, she wished Butler himself all good things, in return for his kindness to her. "For herself," she said, "she kend her lot would be a waesome ane, but it was of her own framing, sae she desired the less pity. But, for her friends' satisfaction, she wished them to know that she was gaun nae ill gate —that they who had done her maist wrong were now willing to do her what justice was in their power; and she would, in some warldly respects, be far better off than she deserved. But she desired her family to remain satisfied with this assurance, and give themselves no trouble in making farther inquiries after her."

To David Deans and to Butler this letter gave very little comfort; for what was to be expected from this unfortunate girl's uniting her fate to that of a character so notorious as Robertson, who they readily guessed was alluded to in the last sentence, excepting that she should become the partner and victim of his future crimes. Jeanie, who knew George Staunton's character and real rank, saw her sister's situation under a ray of better hope. She augured well of the haste he had shown to reclaim his interest in Effie, and she trusted he had made her his wife. If so, it seemed improbable that, with his expected fortune, and high connections, he should again resume the life of criminal adventure which he had led, especially since, as matters stood, his life depended upon his keeping his own secret, which could only be done by an entire change of his habits, and particularly by avoiding all those who had known the heir of Willingham under the character of the audacious, criminal, and condemned Robertson.

She thought it most likely that the couple would go abroad for a few years, and not return to England until the affair of Porteous was totally forgotten. Jeanie, therefore, saw more hopes for her sister than Butler or her father had been able to perceive; but she was not at liberty to impart the comfort which she felt in believing that she would be secure from the pressure of poverty, and in little risk of being seduced into the paths of guilt. She could not have explained this without making public what it was essentially necessary for Effie's chance of comfort to conceal, the identity, namely, of George Staunton and George Robertson. After all, it was dreadful to think that Effie had united herself to a man condemned for felony, and liable to trial for murder, whatever might be his rank in life, and the degree of his repentance. Besides, it was melancholy to reflect, that, she herself being in possession of the whole dreadful secret, it was most probable he would, out of regard to his own feelings, and fear for his safety, never again permit her to see poor Effie. After perusing and re-perusing her sister's valedictory letter, she gave ease to her feelings in a flood of tears, which Butler in vain endeavoured to check by every soothing attention in his power. She was obliged, however, at length to look up and wipe her eyes, for her father, thinking he had allowed the lovers time enough for conference, was now advancing towards them from the Lodge, accompanied by the Captain of Knockdunder, or, as his friends called him for brevity's sake, Duncan Knock, a title which some youthful exploits had rendered peculiarly appropriate.

This Duncan of Knockdunder was a person of first-rate importance in the island of Roseneath, and the continental parishes of Knocktarlitie, Kilmun, and so forth; nay, his influence extended as far as Cowal, where, however, it was obscured by that of another factor. The Tower of Knockdunder still occupies, with its remains, a cliff overhanging the Holy Loch. Duncan swore it had been a royal castle; if so, it was one of the smallest, the space within only forming a square of sixteen feet, and bearing therefore a ridiculous proportion to the thickness of the walls, which was ten feet at least. Such as it was, however, it had long given the title of Captain, equivalent to that of Chatellain, to the ancestors of Duncan, who were retainers of the house of Argyle, and held a hereditary jurisdiction under them, of little extent indeed, but which had great consequence in their own eyes, and was usually administered with a vigour somewhat beyond the law.

The present representative of that ancient family was a stout short man about fifty, whose pleasure it was to unite in his own person the dress of the Highlands and Lowlands, wearing on his head a black tie-wig, surmounted by a fierce cocked-hat, deeply guarded with gold lace, while the rest of his dress consisted of the plaid and philabeg. Duncan superintended a district which was partly Highland, partly Lowland, and therefore might be supposed to combine their national habits, in order to show his impartiality to Trojan or Tyrian. The incongruity, however, had a whimsical and ludicrous effect, as it made his head and body look as if belonging to different individuals; or, as some one said who had seen the executions of the insurgent prisoners in 1715, it seemed as if some Jacobite enchanter, having recalled the sufferers to life, had clapped, in his haste, an Englishman's head on a Highlander's body. To finish the portrait, the bearing of the gracious Duncan was brief, bluff, and consequential, and the upward turn of his short copper-coloured nose indicated that he was somewhat addicted to wrath and usquebaugh.

When this dignitary had advanced up to Butler and to Jeanie, "I take the freedom, Mr. Deans," he said, in a very consequential manner, "to salute your daughter, whilk I presume this young lass to be—I kiss every pretty girl that comes to Roseneath, in virtue of my office." Having made this gallant speech, he took out his quid, saluted Jeanie with a hearty smack, and bade her welcome to Argyle's country. Then addressing Butler, he said, "Ye maun gang ower and meet the carle ministers yonder the morn, for they will want to do your job, and synd it down with usquebaugh doubtless —they seldom make dry wark in this kintra."

"And the Laird——" said David Deans, addressing Butler in further explanation.

"The Captain, man," interrupted Duncan; "folk winna ken wha ye are speaking aboot, unless ye gie shentlemens their proper title."

"The Captain, then," said David, "assures me that the call is unanimous on the part of the parishioners—a real harmonious call, Reuben."

"I pelieve," said Duncan, "it was as harmonious as could pe expected, when the tae half o' the bodies were clavering Sassenach, and the t'other skirling Gaelic, like sea-maws and clack-geese before a storm. Ane wad hae needed the gift of tongues to ken preceesely what they said—but I pelieve the best end of it was, 'Long live MacCallummore and Knock-dunder!'—And as to its being an unanimous call, I wad be glad to ken fat business the carles have to call onything or onybody but what the Duke and mysell likes?"

"Nevertheless," said Mr. Butler, "if any of the parishioners have any scruples, which sometimes happen in the mind of sincere professors, I should be happy of an opportunity of trying to remove——"

"Never fash your peard about it, man," interrupted Duncan Knock—"Leave it a' to me.—Scruple! deil ane o' them has been bred up to scruple onything that they're bidden to do. And if sic a thing suld happen as ye speak o', ye sall see the sincere professor, as ye ca' him, towed at the stern of my boat for a few furlongs. I'll try if the water of the Haly Loch winna wash off scruples as weel as fleas—Cot tam!——"

The rest of Duncan's threat was lost in a growling, gurgling sort of sound, which he made in his throat, and which menaced recusants with no gentle means of conversion. David Deans would certainly have given battle in defence of the right of the Christian congregation to be consulted in the choice of their own pastor, which, in his estimation, was one of the choicest and most inalienable of their privileges; but he had again engaged in close conversation with Jeanie, and, with more

interest than he was in use to take in affairs foreign alike to
his occupation and to his religious tenets, was inquiring into
the particulars of her London journey. This was, perhaps,
fortunate for the new-formed friendship betwixt him and the
Captain of Knockdunder, which rested, in David's estimation,
upon the proofs he had given of his skill in managing stock;
but, in reality, upon the special charge transmitted to Duncan
from the Duke and his agent, to behave with the utmost
attention to Deans and his family.

"And now, sirs," said Duncan, in a commanding tone, "I
am to pray ye a' to come into your supper, for yonder is Mr.
Archibald half famished, and a Saxon woman, that looks as if
her een were fleeing out o' her head wi' fear and wonder, as
if she had never seen a shentleman in a philabeg pefore."

"And Reuben Butler," said David, "will doubtless desire
instantly to retire, that he may prepare his mind for the
exercise of to-morrow, that his work may suit the day, and
be an offering of a sweet savour in the nostrils of the reverend
Presbytery."

"Hout tout, man, it's but little ye ken about them," interrupted the Captain. "Teil a ane o' them wad gie the savour
of the hot venison pasty which I smell" (turning his squab
nose up in the air) "a' the way frae the Lodge, for a' that
Mr. Putler, or you either, can say to them."

David groaned; but judging he had to do with a Gallio, as
he said, did not think it worth his while to give battle. They
followed the Captain to the house, and arranged themselves
with great ceremony round a well-loaded supper-table. The
only other circumstance of the evening worthy to be recorded
is, that Butler pronounced the blessing; that Knockdunder
found it too long, and David Deans censured it as too short,
from which the charitable reader may conclude it was exactly
the proper length.

CHAPTER XLV

Now turn the Psalms of David ower,
  And lilt wi' holy clangor;
Of double verse come gie us four,
  And skirl up the Bangor.
                                        BURNS.

THE next was the important day, when, according to the forms
and ritual of the Scottish Kirk, Reuben Butler was to be
ordained minister of Knocktarlitie by the Presbytery of ——.

And so eager were the whole party, that all, excepting Mrs. Dutton, the destined Cowslip of Inverary, were stirring at an early hour.

Their host, whose appetite was as quick and keen as his temper, was not long in summoning them to a substantial breakfast, where there were at least a dozen different preparations of milk, plenty of cold meat, scores boiled and roasted eggs, a huge cag of butter, half a firkin herrings boiled and broiled, fresh and salt, and tea and coffee for them that liked it, which, as their landlord assured them, with a nod and a wink, pointing, at the same time, to a little cutter which seemed dodging under the lee of the island, cost them little beside the fetching ashore.

"Is the contraband trade permitted here so openly?" said Butler. "I should think it very unfavourable to the people's morals."

"The Duke, Mr. Putler, has gien nae orders concerning the putting of it down," said the magistrate, and seemed to think that he had said all that was necessary to justify his connivance.

Butler was a man of prudence, and aware that real good can only be obtained by remonstrance when remonstrance is well-timed; so for the present he said nothing more on the subject.

When breakfast was half over, in flounced Mrs. Dolly, as fine as a blue sacque and cherry-coloured ribbands could make her.

"Good morrow to you, madam," said the master of ceremonies; "I trust your early rising will not skaith ye."

The dame apologised to Captain Knockunder, as she was pleased to term their entertainer; "but, as we say in Cheshire," she added, "I was like the Mayor of Altringham, who lies in bed while his breeches are mending, for the girl did not bring up the right bundle to my room, till she had brought up all the others by mistake one after t'other.—Well, I suppose we are all for church to-day, as I understand—Pray may I be so bold as to ask, if it is the fashion for you North-country gentlemen to go to church in your petticoats, Captain Knockunder?"

"Captain of Knockdunder, madam, if you please, for I knock under to no man; and in respect of my garb, I shall go to church as I am, at your service, madam; for if I were to lie in bed like your Major What-d'ye-callum, till my preeches were mended, I might be there all my life, seeing I never had a pair of them on my person but twice in my life, which I am proud to remember, it peing when the Duke brought his Duchess here, when her Grace pehoved to be pleasured ; so I e'en porrowed the minister's trews for the twa days his Grace was pleased to stay—but I will put myself under sic confinement again for no man on earth, or woman either, but her Grace being always excepted, as in duty pound."

The mistress of the milking-pail stared, but, making no answer to this round declaration, immediately proceeded to show, that the alarm of the preceding evening had in no degree injured her appetite.

When the meal was finished, the Captain proposed to them to take boat, in order that Mistress Jeanie might see her new place of residence, and that he himself might inquire whether the necessary preparations had been made there, and at the Manse, for receiving the future inmates of these mansions.

The morning was delightful, and the huge mountain-shadows slept upon the mirror'd wave of the firth, almost as little disturbed as if it had been an inland lake. Even Mrs. Dutton's fears no longer annoyed her. She had been informed by Archibald, that there was to be some sort of junketting after the sermon, and that was what she loved dearly ; and as for the water, it was so still that it would look quite like a pleasuring on the Thames.

The whole party being embarked, therefore, in a large boat, which the captain called his coach and six, and attended by a smaller one termed his gig, the gallant Duncan steered straight upon the little tower of the old-fashioned church of Knocktarlitie, and the exertions of six stout rowers sped them rapidly on their voyage. As they neared the land, the hills appeared to recede from them, and a little valley, formed by the descent of a small river from the mountains, evolved itself as it were upon their approach. The style of the country on each side was simply pastoral, and resembled, in appearance and character, the description of a forgotten Scottish poet, which runs nearly thus :—

> " The water gently down a level slid,
>   With little din, but couthy what it made ;
>   On ilka side the trees grew thick and lang,
>   And wi' the wild birds' notes were a' in sang ;
>   On either side, a full bow-shot and mair,
>   The green was even, gowany, and fair ;

With easy slope on every hand the braes
To the hills' feet with scattered bushes raise ;
With goats and sheep aboon, and kye below,
The bonny banks all in a swarm did go." [1]

They landed in this Highland Arcadia, at the mouth of the small stream which watered the delightful and peaceable valley. Inhabitants of several descriptions came to pay their respects to the Captain of Knockdunder, a homage which he was very peremptory in exacting, and to see the new settlers. Some of these were men after David Deans's own heart, elders of the kirk-session, zealous professors, from the Lennox, Lanarkshire, and Ayrshire, to whom the preceding Duke of Argyle had given *rooms* in this corner of his estate, because they had suffered for joining his father, the unfortunate Earl, during his ill-fated attempt in 1686. These were cakes of the right leaven for David regaling himself with ; and, had it not been for this circumstance, he has been heard to say, "that the Captain of Knockdunder would have swore him out of the country in twenty-four hours, sae awsome it was to ony thinking soul to hear his imprecations, upon the slightest temptation that crossed his humour."

Besides these, there were a wilder set of parishioners, mountaineers from the upper glen and adjacent hill, who spoke Gaelic, went about armed, and wore the Highland dress. But the strict commands of the Duke had established such good order in this part of his territories, that the Gael and Saxons lived upon the best possible terms of good neighbourhood.

They first visited the Manse, as the parsonage is termed in Scotland. It was old, but in good repair, and stood snugly embosomed in a grove of sycamore, with a well-stocked garden in front, bounded by the small river, which was partly visible from the windows, partly concealed by the bushes, trees, and bounding hedge. Within, the house looked less comfortable than it might have been, for it had been neglected by the late incumbent ; but workmen had been labouring under the directions of the Captain of Knockdunder, and at the expense of the Duke of Argyle, to put it into some order. The old "plenishing" had been removed, and neat, but plain household furniture had been sent down by the Duke in a brig of his own, called the *Caroline*, and was now ready to be placed in order in the apartments.

[1] Ross's Fortunate Shepherdess.   Edit. 1778, p. 23.

The gracious Duncan, finding matters were at a stand among the workmen, summoned before him the delinquents, and impressed all who heard him with a sense of his authority, by the penalties with which he threatened them for their delay. Mulcting them in half their charge, he assured them, would be the least of it; for, if they were to neglect his pleasure and the Duke's, "he would be tamn'd if he paid them the t'other half either, and they might seek law for it where they could get it." The work-people humbled themselves before the offended dignitary, and spake him soft and fair; and at length, upon Mr. Butler recalling to his mind that it was the ordination day, and that the workmen were probably thinking of going to church, Knockdunder agreed to forgive them, out of respect to their new minister.

"But an I catch them neglecking my duty again, Mr. Putler, the teil pe in me if the kirk shall be an excuse; for what has the like o' them rapparees to do at the kirk ony day put Sundays, or then either, if the Duke and I has the necessitous uses for them?"

It may be guessed with what feelings of quiet satisfaction and delight Butler looked forward to spending his days, honoured and useful as he trusted to be, in this sequestered valley, and how often an intelligent glance was exchanged betwixt him and Jeanie, whose good-humoured face looked positively handsome, from the expression of modesty, and, at the same time, of satisfaction, which she wore when visiting the apartments of which she was soon to call herself mistress. She was left at liberty to give more open indulgence to her feelings of delight and admiration, when, leaving the Manse, the company proceeded to examine the destined habitation of David Deans.

Jeanie found with pleasure that it was not above a musket-shot from the Manse; for it had been a bar to her happiness to think she might be obliged to reside at a distance from her father, and she was aware that there were strong objections to his actually living in the same house with Butler. But this brief distance was the very thing which she could have wished.

The farm-house was on the plan of an improved cottage, and contrived with great regard to convenience; an excellent little garden, an orchard, and a set of offices complete, according to the best ideas of the time, combined to render it a most desirable habitation for the practical farmer, and far superior to the hovel at Woodend, and the small house at Saint Leonard's Crags. The situation was considerably higher than that of the Manse, and fronted to the west. The windows commanded an enchanting view of the little vale over which the mansion seemed to preside, the windings of the stream, and the firth, with its associated lakes and romantic islands. The hills of Dumbartonshire, once possessed by the fierce clan of MacFarlanes, formed a crescent behind the valley, and far to the right were seen the dusky and more gigantic mountains of Argyleshire, with a seaward view of the shattered and thunder-splitten peaks of Arran.

But to Jeanie, whose taste for the picturesque, if she had any by nature, had never been awakened or cultivated, the sight of the faithful old May Hettly, as she opened the door to receive them in her clean toy, Sunday's russet-gown, and blue apron, nicely smoothed down before her, was worth the whole varied landscape. The raptures of the faithful old creature at seeing Jeanie were equal to her own, as she hastened to assure her, "that baith the gudeman and the beasts had been as weel seen after as she possibly could contrive." Separating her from the rest of the company, May then hurried her young mistress to the offices, that she might receive the compliments she expected for her care of the cows. Jeanie rejoiced, in the simplicity of her heart, to see her charge once more; and the mute favourites of our heroine, Gowans, and the others, acknowledged her presence by lowing, turning round their broad and decent brows when they heard her well-known "Pruh, my leddy—pruh, my woman," and, by various indications, known only to those who have studied the habits of the milky mothers, showing sensible pleasure as she approached to caress them in their turn.

"The very brute beasts are glad to see ye again," said May; "but nae wonder, Jeanie, for ye were aye kind to beast and body. And I maun learn to ca' ye *mistress* now, Jeanie, since ye hae been up to Lunnon, and seen the Duke, and the King, and a' the braw folk. But wha kens," added the old dame slyly, "what I'll hae to ca' ye forby mistress, for I am thinking it wunna lang be Deans."

"Ca' me your ain Jeanie, May, and then ye can never gang wrang."

In the cow-house which they examined, there was one animal which Jeanie looked at till the tears gushed from her eyes. May, who had watched her with a sympathising expression, immediately observed, in an undertone, " The gudeman aye sorts that beast himsell, and is kinder to it than ony beast in the byre; and I noticed he was that way e'en when he was angriest, and had maist cause to be angry.—Eh, sirs! a parent's heart's a queer thing!—Mony a warsle he has had for that puir lassie—I am thinking he petitions mair for her than for your-sell, hinny; for what can he plead for you but just to wish you the blessing ye deserve? And when I sleepit ayont the hallan, when we came first here, he was often earnest a' night, and I could hear him come ower and ower again wi', ' Effie— puir blinded misguided thing!' it was aye ' Effie! Effie!'— If that puir wandering lamb comena into the sheepfauld in the Shepherd's ain time, it will be an unco wonder, for I wot she has been a child of prayers. Oh, if the puir prodigal wad return, sae blithely as the goodman wad kill the fatted calf! —though Brockie's calf will no be fit for killing this three weeks yet."

And then, with the discursive talent of persons of her description, she got once more afloat in her account of domestic affairs, and left this delicate and affecting topic.

Having looked at everything in the offices and the dairy, and expressed her satisfaction with the manner in which matters had been managed in her absence, Jeanie rejoined the rest of the party, who were surveying the interior of the house, all excepting David Deans and Butler, who had gone down to the church to meet the kirk-session and the clergy-man of the Presbytery, and arrange matters for the duty of the day.

In the interior of the cottage all was clean, neat, and suit-able to the exterior. It had been originally built and furnished by the Duke, as a retreat for a favourite domestic of the higher class, who did not long enjoy it, and had been dead only a few months, so that everything was in excellent taste and good order. But in Jeanie's bedroom was a neat trunk, which had greatly excited Mrs. Dutton's curiosity, for she was sure that the direction, " For Mrs. Jean Deans, at Auchingower, parish of Knocktarlitie," was the writing of Mrs. Semple, the Duchess's own woman. May Hettly produced the key in a sealed parcel, which bore the same address, and attached to the key was a label, intimating that the trunk and its contents were " a token of remembrance to Jeanie Deans, from her friends the Duchess of Argyle and the young ladies." The trunk, hastily opened, as the reader will not doubt, was found to be full of wearing apparel of the best quality, suited to Jeanie's rank in life; and to most of the articles the names of the particular donors were attached, as if to make Jeanie sensible not only of the general, but of the individual interest she had excited in the noble family. To name the various articles by their appropriate names, would be to attempt things unattempted yet in prose or rhyme; besides, that the old-fashioned terms of manteaus, sacques, kissing-strings, and so forth, would convey but little information even to the milliners of the present day. I shall deposit, however, an accurate inventory of the contents of the trunk with my kind friend, Miss Martha Buskbody, who has promised, should the public curiosity seem interested in the subject, to supply me with a professional glossary and commentary. Suffice it to say, that the gift was such as became the donors, and was suited to the situation of the receiver; that everything was handsome and appropriate, and nothing forgotten which belonged to the wardrobe of a young person in Jeanie's situation in life, the destined bride of a respectable clergyman.

Article after article was displayed, commented upon, and admired, to the wonder of May, who declared, " she didna think the Queen had mair or better claise," and somewhat to the envy of the northern Cowslip. This unamiable, but not very unnatural, disposition of mind, broke forth in sundry unfounded criticisms to the disparagement of the articles, as they were severally exhibited. But it assumed a more direct character, when, at the bottom of all, was found a dress of white silk, very plainly made, but still of white silk, and French silk to boot, with a paper pinned to it, bearing, that it was a present from the Duke of Argyle to his travelling companion, to be worn on the day when she should change her name.

Mrs. Dutton could forbear no longer, but whispered into Mr. Archibald's ear, that it was a clever thing to be a Scotch-woman: " She supposed all *her* sisters, and she had half-a-dozen, might have been hanged, without any one sending her a present of a pocket-handkerchief."

" Or without your making any exertion to save them, Mrs. Dolly," answered Archibald drily.—" But I am surprised we do not hear the bell yet," said he, looking at his watch.

" Fat ta deil, Mr. Archibald," answered the Captain of Knockdunder, " wad ye hae them ring the bell before I am ready to gang to kirk?—I wad gar the bedral eat the bell-rope,

if he took ony sic freedom. But if ye want to hear the bell,
I will just show mysell on the knowe-head, and it will begin
jowing forthwith."

Accordingly, so soon as they sallied out, and that the gold-
laced hat of the Captain was seen rising like Hesper above
the dewy verge of the rising ground, the clash (for it was rather
a clash than a clang) of the bell was heard from the old moss-
grown tower, and the clapper continued to thump its cracked
sides all the while they advanced towards the kirk, Duncan
exhorting them to take their own time, "for teil ony sport
wad be till he came." [1]

Accordingly, the bell only changed to the final and impatient
chime when they crossed the stile ; and "rang in," that is,
concluded its mistuned summons, when they had entered the
Duke's seat, in the little kirk, where the whole party arranged
themselves, with Duncan at their head, excepting David Deans,
who already occupied a seat among the elders.

The business of the day, with a particular detail of which
it is unnecessary to trouble the reader, was gone through
according to the established form, and the sermon pronounced
upon the occasion had the good fortune to please even the
critical David Deans, though it was only an hour and a
quarter long, which David termed a short allowance of spiritual provender.

The preacher, who was a divine that held many of David's
opinions, privately apologised for his brevity by saying, "That
he observed the Captain was ganting grievously, that if he had
detained him longer, there was no knowing how long he might
be in paying the next term's victual stipend."

David groaned to find that such carnal motives could have
influence upon the mind of a powerful preacher. He had,
indeed, been scandalised by another circumstance during the
service.

So soon as the congregation were seated after prayers, and
the clergyman had read his text, the gracious Duncan, after
rummaging the leathern purse which hung in front of his
petticoat, produced a short tobacco-pipe made of iron, and
observed, almost aloud, "I hae forgotten my spleuchan—
Lachlan, gang down to the Clachan, and bring me a penny-
worth of twist." Six arms, the nearest within reach, presented,
with an obedient start, as many tobacco-pouches to the man
of office. He made choice of one with a nod of acknowledg-

[1] Note XVI.—Tolling to Service in Scotland.

ment, filled his pipe, lighted it with the assistance of his pistol-flint, and smoked with infinite composure during the whole time of the sermon. When the discourse was finished, he knocked the ashes out of his pipe, replaced it in its sporran, returned the tobacco-pouch or spleuchan to its owner, and joined in the prayer with decency and attention.

At the end of the service, when Butler had been admitted minister of the kirk of Knocktarlitie, with all its spiritual immunities and privileges, David, who had frowned, groaned, and murmured at Knockdunder's irreverent demeanour, communicated his plain thoughts of the matter to Isaac Meiklehose, one of the elders, with whom a reverential aspect and huge grizzle wig had especially disposed him to seek fraternisation. "It didna become a wild Indian," David said, "much less a Christian, and a gentleman, to sit in the kirk puffing tobacco-reek, as if he were in a change-house."

Meiklehose shook his head, and allowed it was "far frae beseeming—But what will ye say? The Captain's a queer hand, and to speak to him about that or onything else that crosses the maggot, wad be to set the kiln a-low. He keeps a high hand ower the country, and we couldna deal wi' the Hielandmen without his protection, sin' a' the keys o' the kintray hings at his belt; and he's no an ill body in the main, and maistry, ye ken, maws the meadows doun."

"That may be very true, neighbour," said David; "but Reuben Butler isna the man I take him to be, if he disna learn the Captain to fuff his pipe some other gate than in God's house, or the quarter be ower."

"Fair and softly gangs far," said Meiklehose; "and if a fule may gie a wise man a counsel, I wad hae him think twice or he mells wi' Knockdunder—He suld hae a lang-shankit spune that wad sup kail wi' the deil. But they are a' away to their dinner to the change-house, and if we dinna mend our pace, we'll come short at meal-time."

David accompanied his friend without answer; but began to feel from experience, that the glen of Knocktarlitie, like the rest of the world, was haunted by its own special subjects of regret and discontent. His mind was so much occupied by considering the best means of converting Duncan of Knock to a sense of reverent decency during public worship, that he altogether forgot to inquire, whether Butler was called upon to subscribe the oaths to government.

Some have insinuated, that his neglect on this head was, in

some degree, intentional ; but I think this explanation inconsistent with the simplicity of my friend David's character. Neither have I ever been able, by the most minute inquiries, to know whether the *formula*, at which he so much scrupled, had been exacted from Butler, aye or no.   The books of the kirk-session might have thrown some light on this matter ; but unfortunately they were destroyed in the year 1746, by one Donacha Dhu na Dunaigh, at the instance, it was said, or at least by the connivance, of the gracious Duncan of Knock, who had a desire to obliterate the recorded foibles of a certain Kate Finlayson.

CHAPTER XLVI

Now butt and ben the change-house fills
Wi' yill-caup commentators,—
Here's crying out for bakes and gills,
And there the pint-stoup clatters,
Wi' thick and thrang, and loud and lang,—
Wi' logic and wi' scripture,
They raise a din that in the end
Is like to breed a rupture,
O' wrath that day.
BURNS.

A PLENTIFUL entertainment, at the Duke of Argyle's cost, regaled the reverend gentlemen who had assisted at the ordination of Reuben Butler, and almost all the respectable part of the parish. The feast was, indeed, such as the country itself furnished ; for plenty of all the requisites for "a rough and round" dinner were always at Duncan of Knock's command. There was the beef and mutton on the braes, the fresh and salt-water fish in the lochs, the brooks, and firth ; game of every kind, from the deer to the leveret, were to be had for the killing, in the Duke's forests, moors, heaths, and mosses ; and for liquor, home-brewed ale flowed as freely as water ; brandy and usquebaugh both were had in those happy times without duty ; even white wine and claret were got for nothing, since the Duke's extensive rights of admiralty gave him a title to all the wine in cask which is drifted ashore on the western coasts and isles of Scotland, when shipping have suffered by severe weather. In short, as Duncan boasted, the entertainment did not cost MacCallummore a plack out of his sporran, and was nevertheless not only liberal, but overflowing.

The Duke's health was solemnised in a *bonâ fide* bumper, and David Deans himself added perhaps the first huzza that his lungs had ever uttered, to swell the shout with which the pledge was received. Nay, so exalted in heart was he upon this memorable occasion, and so much disposed to be indulgent, that he expressed no dissatisfaction when three bagpipers struck up, "The Campbells are coming." The health of the reverend minister of Knocktarlitie was received with similar honours; and there was a roar of laughter, when one of his brethren slyly subjoined the addition of, "A good wife to our brother, to keep the Manse in order." On this occasion David Deans was delivered of his first-born joke; and apparently the parturition was accompanied with many throes, for sorely did he twist about his physiognomy, and much did he stumble in his speech, before he could express his idea, "That the lad being now wedded to his spiritual bride, it was hard to threaten him with ane temporal spouse in the same day." He then laughed a hoarse and brief laugh, and was suddenly grave and silent, as if abashed at his own vivacious effort.

After another toast or two, Jeanie, Mrs. Dolly, and such of the female natives as had honoured the feast with their presence, retired to David's new dwelling at Auchingower, and left the gentlemen to their potations.

The feast proceeded with great glee. The conversation, where Duncan had it under his direction, was not indeed always strictly canonical, but David Deans escaped any risk of being scandalised, by engaging with one of his neighbours in a recapitulation of the sufferings of Ayrshire and Lanarkshire, during what was called the invasion of the Highland Host; the prudent Mr. Meiklehose cautioning them from time to time to lower their voices, for "that Duncan Knock's father had been at that onslaught, and brought back muckle gude plenishing, and that Duncan was no unlikely to hae been there himself, for what he kend."

Meanwhile, as the mirth grew fast and furious, the graver members of the party began to escape as well as they could. David Deans accomplished his retreat, and Butler anxiously watched an opportunity to follow him. Knockdunder, however, desirous, he said, of knowing what stuff was in the new minister, had no intention to part with him so easily, but kept him pinned to his side, watching him sedulously, and with obliging violence filling his glass to the brim, as often as

470 The Heart of Mid-Lothian

he could seize an opportunity of doing so. At length, as the
evening was wearing late, a venerable brother chanced to ask
Mr. Archibald when they might hope to see the Duke, *tam
carum caput*, as he would venture to term him, at the Lodge
of Roseneath. Duncan of Knock, whose ideas were somewhat conglomerated, and who, it may be believed, was no
great scholar, catching up some imperfect sound of the words,
conceived the speaker was drawing a parallel between the
Duke and Sir Donald Gorme of Sleat; and being of opinion
that such comparison was odious, snorted thrice, and prepared himself to be in a passion.

To the explanation of the venerable divine the Captain
answered, "I heard the word Gorme myself, sir, with my
ain ears. D'ye think I do not know Gaelic from Latin?"

"Apparently not, sir;"—so the clergyman, offended in
his turn, and taking a pinch of snuff, answered with great
coolness.

The copper nose of the gracious Duncan now became heated
like the bull of Phalaris, and while Mr. Archibald mediated
betwixt the offended parties, and the attention of the company was engaged by their dispute, Butler took an opportunity to effect his retreat.

He found the females at Auchingower, very anxious for
the breaking up of the convivial party; for it was a part of
the arrangement, that although David Deans was to remain
at Auchingower, and Butler was that night to take possession
of the Manse, yet Jeanie, for whom complete accommodations
were not yet provided in her father's house, was to return for
a day or two to the Lodge at Roseneath, and the boats had
been held in readiness accordingly. They waited, therefore,
for Knockdunder's return, but twilight came, and they still
waited in vain. At length Mr. Archibald, who, as a man of
decorum, had taken care not to exceed in his conviviality,
made his appearance, and advised the females strongly to
return to the island under his escort; observing, that, from
the humour in which he had left the Captain, it was a great
chance whether he budged out of the public-house that night,
and it was absolutely certain that he would not be very fit
company for ladies. The gig was at their disposal, he said,
and there was still pleasant twilight for a party on the water.

Jeanie, who had considerable confidence in Archibald's
prudence, immediately acquiesced in this proposal; but Mrs.
Dolly positively objected to the small boat. If the big boat

could be gotten, she agreed to set out, otherwise she would sleep on the floor, rather than stir a step. Reasoning with Dolly was out of the question, and Archibald did not think the difficulty so pressing as to require compulsion. He observed, it was not using the Captain very politely to deprive him of his coach and six; "but as it was in the ladies' service," he gallantly said, "he would use so much freedom —besides the gig would serve the Captain's purpose better, as it could come off at any hour of the tide; the large boat should, therefore, be at Mrs. Dolly's service."

They walked to the beach accordingly, accompanied by Butler. It was some time before the boatmen could be assembled, and ere they were well embarked, and ready to depart, the pale moon was come over the hill, and flinging a trembling reflection on the broad and glittering waves. But so soft and pleasant was the night, that Butler, in bidding farewell to Jeanie, had no apprehension for her safety; and, what is yet more extraordinary, Mrs. Dolly felt no alarm for her own. The air was soft, and came over the cooling wave with something of summer fragrance. The beautiful scene of headlands, and capes, and bays, around them, with the broad blue chain of mountains, were dimly visible in the moonlight; while every dash of the oars made the waters glance and sparkle with the brilliant phenomenon called the sea fire.

This last circumstance filled Jeanie with wonder, and served to amuse the mind of her companion, until they approached the little bay, which seemed to stretch its dark and wooded arms into the sea as if to welcome them.

The usual landing-place was at a quarter of a mile's distance from the Lodge, and although the tide did not admit of the large boat coming quite close to the jetty of loose stones which served as a pier, Jeanie, who was both bold and active, easily sprung ashore; but Mrs. Dolly positively refusing to commit herself to the same risk, the complaisant Mr. Archibald ordered the boat round to a more regular landing-place, at a considerable distance along the shore. He then prepared to land himself, that he might, in the meanwhile, accompany Jeanie to the Lodge. But as there was no mistaking the woodland lane, which led from thence to the shore, and as the moonlight showed her one of the white chimneys rising out of the wood which embosomed the building, Jeanie declined this favour with thanks, and requested him to proceed with Mrs. Dolly, who, being "in a country where the ways were strange to her, had mair need of countenance."

This, indeed, was a fortunate circumstance, and might even be said to save poor Cowslip's life, if it was true, as she herself used solemnly to aver, that she must positively have expired for fear, if she had been left alone in the boat with six wild Highlanders in kilts.

The night was so exquisitely beautiful, that Jeanie, instead of immediately directing her course towards the Lodge, stood looking after the boat as it again put off from the side, and rowed out into the little bay, the dark figures of her companions growing less and less distinct as they diminished in the distance, and the jorram, or melancholy boat-song of the rowers, coming on the ear with softened and sweeter sound, until the boat rounded the headland, and was lost to her observation.

Still Jeanie remained in the same posture, looking out upon the sea. It would, she was aware, be some time ere her companions could reach the Lodge, as the distance by the more convenient landing-place was considerably greater than from the point where she stood, and she was not sorry to have an opportunity to spend the interval by herself.

The wonderful change which a few weeks had wrought in her situation, from shame and grief, and almost despair, to honour, joy, and a fair prospect of future happiness, passed before her eyes with a sensation which brought the tears into them. Yet they flowed at the same time from another source. As human happiness is never perfect, and as well-constructed minds are never more sensible of the distresses of those whom they love, than when their own situation forms a contrast with them, Jeanie's affectionate regrets turned to the fate of her poor sister—the child of so many hopes—the fondled nursling of so many years—now an exile, and, what was worse, dependent on the will of a man, of whose habits she had every reason to entertain the worst opinion, and who, even in his strongest paroxysms of remorse, had appeared too much a stranger to the feelings of real penitence.

While her thoughts were occupied with these melancholy reflections, a shadowy figure seemed to detach itself from the copsewood on her right hand. Jeanie started, and the stories of apparitions and wraiths, seen by solitary travellers in wild situations, at such times, and in such an hour, suddenly came full upon her imagination. The figure glided on, and as it came betwixt her and the moon, she was aware that it had the appearance of a woman. A soft voice twice repeated, "Jeanie —Jeanie!"—Was it indeed—could it be the voice of her sister?—Was she still among the living, or had the grave given up its tenant?—Ere she could state these questions to her own mind, Effie, alive, and in the body, had clasped her in her arms, and was straining her to her bosom, and devouring her with kisses. "I have wandered here," she said, "like a ghaist, to see you, and nae wonder you take me for ane—I thought but to see you gang by, or to hear the sound of your voice; but to speak to yoursell again, Jeanie, was mair than I deserved, and mair than I durst pray for."

"Oh, Effie! how came ye here alone, and at this hour, and on the wild sea-beach?—Are you sure it's your ain living sell?"

There was something of Effie's former humour in her practically answering the question by a gentle pinch, more beseeming the fingers of a fairy than of a ghost. And again the sisters embraced, and laughed, and wept by turns.

"But ye maun gang up wi' me to the Lodge, Effie," said Jeanie, "and tell me a' your story—I hae gude folk there that will make ye welcome for my sake."

"Na, na, Jeanie," replied her sister sorrowfully,—"ye hae forgotten what I am—a banished outlawed creature, scarce escaped the gallows by your being the bauldest and the best sister that ever lived—I'll gae near nane o' your grand friends, even if there was nae danger to me."

"There is nae danger—there shall be nae danger," said Jeanie eagerly. "Oh, Effie, dinna be wilfu'—be guided for anes—we will be sae happy a' thegither!"

"I have a' the happiness I deserve on this side of the grave, now that I hae seen you," answered Effie; "and whether there were danger to mysell or no, naebody shall ever say that I come with my cheat-the-gallows face to shame my sister amang her grand friends."

"I hae nae grand friends," said Jeanie; "nae friends but what are friends of yours—Reuben Butler and my father.— Oh, unhappy lassie, dinna be dour, and turn your back on your happiness again! We wunna see another acquaintance —Come hame to us, your ain dearest friends—it's better sheltering under an auld hedge than under a new-planted wood."

"It's in vain speaking, Jeanie—I maun drink as I hae brewed—I am married, and I maun follow my husband for better for worse."

*Q 134

" Married, Effie ! " exclaimed Jeanie—" Misfortunate creature ! and to that awfu'———"

" Hush, hush," said Effie, clapping one hand on her mouth,
and pointing to the thicket with the other, " he is yonder."

She said this in a tone which showed that her husband had
found means to inspire her with awe, as well as affection.   At
this moment a man issued from the wood.

It was young Staunton.   Even by the imperfect light of the
moon, Jeanie could observe that he was handsomely dressed,
and had the air of a person of rank.

" Effie," he said, " our time is well-nigh spent—the skiff will
be aground in the creek, and I dare not stay longer.—I hope
your sister will allow me to salute her ? "   But Jeanie shrunk
back from him with a feeling of internal abhorrence.   " Well,"
he said, " it does not much signify ; if you keep up the feeling
of ill-will, at least you do not act upon it, and I thank you for
your respect to my secret, when a word (which in your place
I would have spoken at once) would have cost me my life.
People say, you should keep from the wife of your bosom
the secret that concerns your neck—my wife and her sister
both know mine, and I shall not sleep a wink the less sound."

" But are you really married to my sister, sir ? " asked Jeanie,
in great doubt and anxiety ; for the haughty, careless tone in
which he spoke seemed to justify her worst apprehensions.

" I really am legally married, and by my own name," replied
Staunton, more gravely.

" And your father—and your friends ? "

" And my father and my friends must just reconcile themselves to that which is done and cannot be undone," replied
Staunton.   " However, it is my intention, in order to break
off dangerous connections, and to let my friends come to their
temper, to conceal my marriage for the present, and stay
abroad for some years.   So that you will not hear of us for
some time, if ever you hear of us again at all.   It would
be dangerous, you must be aware, to keep up the correspondence ; for all would guess that the husband of Effie was
the—what shall I call myself ?—the slayer of Porteous."

Hard-hearted light man ! thought Jeanie—to what a
character she has entrusted her happiness !—She has sown
the wind, and maun reap the whirlwind.

" Dinna think ill o' him," said Effie, breaking away from
her husband, and leading Jeanie a step or two out of hearing,
—" dinna think *very* ill o' him—he's gude to me, Jeanie—as

gude as I deserve—And he is determined to gie up his bad courses—Sae, after a', dinna greet for Effie; she is better off than she has wrought for.—But you—oh, you!—how can you be happy eneugh!—never till ye get to Heaven, where a'body is as gude as yoursell.—Jeanie, if I live and thrive, ye shall hear of me—if not, just forget that sic a creature ever lived to vex ye—fare ye weel—fare—fare ye weel!"

She tore herself from her sister's arms—rejoined her husband — they plunged into the copsewood, and she saw them no more. The whole scene had the effect of a vision, and she could almost have believed it such, but that very soon after they quitted her, she heard the sound of oars, and a skiff was seen on the firth, pulling swiftly towards the small smuggling sloop which lay in the offing. It was on board of such a vessel that Effie had embarked at Portobello, and Jeanie had no doubt that the same conveyance was destined, as Staunton had hinted, to transport them to a foreign country.

Although it was impossible to determine whether this interview, while it was passing, gave more pain or pleasure to Jeanie Deans, yet the ultimate impression which remained on her mind was decidedly favourable. Effie was married—made, according to the common phrase, an honest woman—that was one main point; it seemed also as if her husband were about to abandon the path of gross vice, in which he had run so long and so desperately—that was another. For his final and effectual conversion, he did not want understanding, and God knew his own hour.

Such were the thoughts with which Jeanie endeavoured to console her anxiety respecting her sister's future fortune. On her arrival at the Lodge, she found Archibald in some anxiety at her stay, and about to walk out in quest of her. A headache served as an apology for retiring to rest, in order to conceal her visible agitation of mind from her companions.

By this secession also, she escaped another scene of a different sort. For, as if there were danger in all gigs, whether by sea or land, that of Knockdunder had been run down by another boat, an accident owing chiefly to the drunkenness of the captain, his crew, and passengers. Knockdunder, and two or three guests, whom he was bringing along with him to finish the conviviality of the evening at the Lodge, got a sound ducking; but, being rescued by the crew of the boat which endangered them, there was no ultimate loss, excepting that of the Captain's laced hat, which, greatly to the satisfaction of the Highland part of the district, as well as to the improvement of the conformity of his own personal appearance, he replaced by a smart Highland bonnet next day. Many were the vehement threats of vengeance which, on the succeeding morning, the gracious Duncan threw out against the boat which had upset him ; but as neither she, nor the small smuggling vessel to which she belonged, was any longer to be seen in the firth, he was compelled to sit down with the affront. This was the more hard, he said, as he was assured the mischief was done on purpose, these scoundrels having lurked about after they had landed every drop of brandy, and every bag of tea they had on board ; and he understood the coxswain had been on shore, making particular inquiries concerning the time when his boat was to cross over, and to return, and so forth.

"Put the neist time they meet me on the firth," said Duncan, with great majesty, "I will teach the moonlight rapscallions and vagabonds to keep their ain side of the road, and be tamn'd to them !"

CHAPTER XLVII

Lord! who would live turmoiled in a court,
And may enjoy such quiet walks as these ?
                                SHAKESPEARE.

WITHIN a reasonable time after Butler was safely and comfortably settled in his living, and Jeanie had taken up her abode at Auchingower with her father,—the precise extent of which interval we request each reader to settle according to his own sense of what is decent and proper upon the occasion, —and after due proclamation of banns, and all other formalities, the long wooing of this worthy pair was ended by their union in the holy bands of matrimony. On this occasion, David Deans stoutly withstood the iniquities of pipes, fiddles, and promiscuous dancing, to the great wrath of the Captain of Knockdunder, who said, if he "had guessed it was to be sic a tamn'd Quakers' meeting, he wad hae seen them peyont the cairn before he wad hae darkened their doors."

And so much rancour remained on the spirits of the gracious Duncan upon this occasion, that various "picqueer-

ings," as David called them, took place upon the same and
similar topics; and it was only in consequence of an accidental
visit of the Duke to his Lodge at Roseneath, that they were
put a stop to. But upon that occasion his Grace showed such
particular respect to Mr. and Mrs. Butler, and such favour
even to old David, that Knockdunder held it prudent to
change his course towards the latter. He, in future, used to
express himself among friends, concerning the minister and his
wife, as "very worthy decent folk, just a little over strict in
their notions; put it was pest for thae plack cattle to err on
the safe side." And respecting David, he allowed that "he
was an excellent judge of nowte and sheep, and a sensible
enough carle, an it werena for his tamn'd Cameronian nonsense, whilk it is not worth while of a shentleman to knock
out of an auld silly head, either by force of reason, or otherwise." So that, by avoiding topics of dispute, the personages
of our tale lived in great good habits with the gracious
Duncan, only that he still grieved David's soul, and set a
perilous example to the congregation, by sometimes bringing
his pipe to the church during a cold winter day, and almost
always sleeping during sermon in the summer time.

Mrs. Butler, whom we must no longer, if we can help it,
term by the familiar name of Jeanie, brought into the married
state the same firm mind and affectionate disposition,—the
same natural and homely good sense, and spirit of useful
exertion,—in a word, all the domestic good qualities of which
she had given proof during her maiden life. She did not
indeed rival Butler in learning; but then no woman more
devoutly venerated the extent of her husband's erudition.
She did not pretend to understand his expositions of divinity;
but no minister of the Presbytery had his humble dinner so
well arranged, his clothes and linen in equal good order, his
fireside so neatly swept, his parlour so clean, and his books
so well dusted.

If he talked to Jeanie of what she did not understand,—
and (for the man was mortal, and had been a schoolmaster)
he sometimes did ,harangue more scholarly and wisely than
was necessary,—she listened in placid silence; and whenever
the point referred to common life, and was such as came
under the grasp of a strong natural understanding, her views
were more forcible, and her observations more acute, than his
own. In acquired politeness of manners, when it happened
that she mingled a little in society, Mrs. Butler was, of course,

judged deficient.   But then she had that obvious wish to oblige, and that real and natural good-breeding depending on good sense and good-humour, which, joined to a considerable degree of archness and liveliness of manner, rendered her behaviour acceptable to all with whom she was called upon to associate.   Notwithstanding her strict attention to all domestic affairs, she always appeared the clean well-dressed mistress of the house, never the sordid household drudge. When complimented on this occasion by Duncan Knock, who swore, "that he thought the fairies must help her, since her house was always clean, and nobody ever saw anybody sweeping it," she modestly replied, "That much might be dune by timing ane's turns."

Duncan replied, " He heartily wished she could teach that art to the huzzies at the Lodge, for he could never discover that the house was washed at a', except now and then by breaking his shins over the pail—Cot tamn the jauds ! "

Of lesser matters there is not occasion to speak much.   It may easily be believed that the Duke's cheese was carefully made, and so graciously accepted, that the offering became annual.   Remembrances and acknowledgments of past favours were sent to Mrs. Bickerton and Mrs. Glass, and an amicable intercourse maintained from time to time with these two respectable and benevolent persons.

It is especially necessary to mention, that, in the course of five years, Mrs. Butler had three children, two boys and a girl, all stout healthy babes of grace, fair-haired, blue-eyed, and strong-limbed.   The boys were named David and Reuben, an order of nomenclature which was much to the satisfaction of the old hero of the Covenant, and the girl, by her mother's special desire, was christened Euphemia, rather contrary to the wish both of her father and husband, who nevertheless loved Mrs. Butler too well, and were too much indebted to her for their hours of happiness, to withstand any request which she made with earnestness, and as a gratification to herself.   But from some feeling, I know not of what kind, the child was never distinguished by the name of Effie, but by the abbreviation of Femie, which in Scotland is equally commonly applied to persons called Euphemia.

In this state of quiet and unostentatious enjoyment, there were, besides the ordinary rubs and ruffles which disturb even the most uniform life, two things which particularly chequered Mrs. Butler's happiness.   " Without these," she said to our

informer, "her life would have been but too happy ; and perhaps," she added, "she had need of some crosses in this world
to remind her that there was a better to come behind it."

The first of these related to certain polemical skirmishes
betwixt her father and her husband, which, notwithstanding
the mutual respect and affection they entertained for each
other, and their great love for her,—notwithstanding also
their general agreement in strictness, and even severity, of
Presbyterian principle,—often threatened unpleasant weather
between them. David Deans, as our readers must be aware,
was sufficiently opinionative and intractable, and having prevailed on himself to become a member of a kirk-session under
the Established Church, he felt doubly obliged to evince, that,
in so doing, he had not compromised any whit of his former
professions, either in practice or principle. Now, Mr. Butler,
doing all credit to his father-in-law's motives, was frequently
of opinion that it were better to drop out of memory points of
division and separation, and to act in the manner most likely
to attract and unite all parties who were serious in religion.
Moreover, he was not pleased, as a man and a scholar, to be
always dictated to by his unlettered father-in-law ; and as a
clergyman, he did not think it fit to seem for ever under the
thumb of an elder of his own kirk-session. A proud but
honest thought carried his opposition now and then a little
farther than it would otherwise have gone. "My brethren,"
he said, "will suppose I am flattering and conciliating the old
man for the sake of his succession, if I defer and give way to
him on every occasion ; and, besides, there are many on which
I neither can nor will conscientiously yield to his notions. I
cannot be persecuting old women for witches, or ferreting out
matter of scandal among the young ones, which might otherwise have remained concealed."

From this difference of opinion it happened, that, in many
cases of nicety, such as in owning certain defections, and failing to testify against certain backslidings of the time, in not
always severely tracing forth little matters of scandal and *fama
clamosa*, which David called a loosening of the reins of discipline, and in failing to demand clear testimonies in other
points of controversy which had, as it were, drifted to leeward
with the change of times, Butler incurred the censure of his
father-in-law ; and sometimes the disputes betwixt them became
eager and almost unfriendly. In all such cases Mrs. Butler
was a mediating spirit, who endeavoured, by the alkaline

smoothness of her own disposition, to neutralise the acidity of theological controversy. To the complaints of both she lent an unprejudiced and attentive ear, and sought always rather to excuse than absolutely to defend the other party.

She reminded her father that Butler had not "his experience of the auld and wrastling times, when folk were gifted wi' a far look into eternity, to make up for the oppressions whilk they suffered here below in time. She freely allowed that many devout ministers and professors in times past had enjoyed downright revelation, like the blessed Peden, and Lundie, and Cameron, and Renwick, and John Caird the tinkler, wha entered into the secrets, and Elizabeth Melvil, Lady Culross, wha prayed in her bed, surrounded by a great many Christians in a large room, in whilk it was placed on purpose, and that for three hours' time, with wonderful assistance ; and Lady Robertland, whilk got six sure outgates of grace, and mony other in times past ; and of a specialty, Mr. John Scrimgeour, minister of Kinghorn, who, having a beloved child sick to death of the crewels, was free to expostulate with his Maker with such impatience of displeasure, and complaining so bitterly, that at length it was said unto him, that he was heard for this time, but that he was requested to use no such boldness in time coming ; so that, when he returned, he found the child sitting up in the bed hale and fair, with all its wounds closed, and supping its parritch, whilk babe he had left at the time of death. But though these things might be true in these needful times, she contended that those ministers who had not seen such vouchsafed and especial mercies, were to seek their rule in the records of ancient times ; and therefore Reuben was carefu' both to search the Scriptures and the books written by wise and good men of old ; and sometimes in this way it wad happen that twa precious saints might pu' sundry wise, like twa cows riving at the same hayband."

To this David used to reply, with a sigh, " Ah, hinny, thou kenn'st little o't ; but that saam John Scrimgeour, that blew open the gates of heaven as an it had been wi' a sax-pund cannon-ball, used devoutly to wish that most part of books were burnt, except the Bible. Reuben's a gude lad and a kind—I have aye allowed that ; but as to his not allowing inquiry anent the scandal of Margery Kittlesides and Rory MacRand, under pretence that they have southered sin wi' marriage, it's clear agane the Christian discipline o' the kirk.

And then there's Aily MacClure of Deepheugh, that practises her abominations, spaeing folks' fortunes wi' egg-shells, and mutton-banes, and dreams and divinations, whilk is a scandal to ony Christian land to suffer sic a wretch to live; and I'll uphaud that, in a' judicatures, civil or ecclesiastical."

" I dare say ye are very right, father," was the general style of Jeanie's answer; " but ye maun come down to the Manse to your dinner the day. The bits o' bairns, puir things, are wearying to see their luckie-dad; and Reuben never sleeps weel, nor I neither, when you and he hae had ony bit outcast."

" Nae outcast, Jeanie; God forbid I suld cast out wi' thee, or aught that is dear to thee!" And he put on his Sunday's coat, and came to the Manse accordingly.

With her husband, Mrs. Butler had a more direct conciliatory process. Reuben had the utmost respect for the old man's motives, and affection for his person, as well as gratitude for his early friendship. So that, upon any such occasion of accidental irritation, it was only necessary to remind him with delicacy of his father-in-law's age, of his scanty education, strong prejudices, and family distresses. The least of these considerations always inclined Butler to measures of conciliation, in so far as he could accede to them without compromising principle; and thus our simple and unpretending heroine had the merit of those peace-makers, to whom it is pronounced as a benediction, that they shall inherit the earth.

The second crook in Mrs. Butler's lot, to use the language of her father, was the distressing circumstance, that she had never heard of her sister's safety, or of the circumstances in which she found herself, though betwixt four and five years had elapsed since they had parted on the beach of the island of Roseneath. Frequent intercourse was not to be expected —not to be desired, perhaps, in their relative situations; but Effie had promised, that, if she lived and prospered, her sister should hear from her. She must then be no more, or sunk into some abyss of misery, since she had never redeemed her pledge. Her silence seemed strange and portentous, and wrung from Jeanie, who could never forget the early years of their intimacy, the most painful anticipation concerning her fate. At length, however, the veil was drawn aside.

One day, as the Captain of Knockdunder had called in at the Manse, on his return from some business in the Highland part of the parish, and had been accommodated, according to his special request, with a mixture of milk, brandy, honey, and water, which he said Mrs. Butler compounded " petter than ever a woman in Scotland,"—for, in all innocent matters, she studied the taste of every one around her,—he said to Butler, " Py the py, minister, I have a letter here either for your canny pody of a wife or you, which I got when I was last at Glasco ; the postage comes to fourpence, which you may either pay me forthwith, or give me tooble or quits in a hit at packcammon."

The playing at backgammon and draughts had been a frequent amusement of Mr. Whackbairn, Butler's principal, when at Libberton school. The minister, therefore, still piqued himself on his skill at both games, and occasionally practised them, as strictly canonical, although David Deans, whose notions of every kind were more rigorous, used to shake his head, and groan grievously, when he espied the tables lying in the parlour, or the children playing with the dice-boxes or backgammon men. Indeed, Mrs. Butler was sometimes chidden for removing these implements of pastime into some closet or corner out of sight. " Let them be where they are, Jeanie," would Butler say upon such occasions ; " I am not conscious of following this, or any other trifling relaxation, to the interruption of my more serious studies, and still more serious duties. I will not, therefore, have it supposed that I am indulging by stealth, and against my conscience, in an amusement which, using it so little as I do, I may well practise openly, and without any check of mind—*Nil conscire sibi,* Jeanie, that is my motto ; which signifies, my love, the honest and open confidence which a man ought to entertain when he is acting openly, and without any sense of doing wrong."

Such being Butler's humour, he accepted the Captain's defiance to a twopenny hit at backgammon, and handed the letter to his wife, observing the post-mark was York, but, if it came from her friend Mrs. Bickerton, she had considerably improved her handwriting, which was uncommon at her years.

Leaving the gentlemen to their game, Mrs. Butler went to order something for supper, for Captain Duncan had proposed kindly to stay the night with them, and then carelessly broke open her letter. It was not from Mrs. Bickerton, and, after glancing over the first few lines, she soon found it necessary to retire into her own bedroom, to read the document at leisure.

CHAPTER XLVIII

Happy thou art! then happy be.
Nor envy me my lot;
Thy happy state I envy thee,
And peaceful cot.
                                    LADY C— C—L.

THE letter, which Mrs. Butler, when retired into her own apartment, perused with anxious wonder, was certainly from Effie, although it had no other signature than the letter E.; and although the orthography, style, and penmanship, were very far superior not only to anything which Effie could produce, who, though a lively girl, had been a remarkably careless scholar, but even to her more considerate sister's own powers of composition and expression. The manuscript was a fair Italian hand, though something stiff and constrained—the spelling and the diction that of a person who had been accustomed to read good composition, and mix in good society.

The tenor of the letter was as follows :—

"MY DEAREST SISTER,—At many risks I venture to write to you, to inform you that I am still alive, and, as to worldly situation, that I rank higher than I could expect or merit. If wealth, and distinction, and an honourable rank, could make a woman happy, I have them all; but you, Jeanie, whom the world might think placed far beneath me in all these respects, are far happier than I am. I have had means of hearing of your welfare, my dearest Jeanie, from time to time—I think I should have broken my heart otherwise. I have learnt with great pleasure of your increasing family. We have not been worthy of such a blessing; two infants have been successively removed, and we are now childless—God's will be done! But, if we had a child, it would perhaps divert him from the gloomy thoughts which make him terrible to himself and others. Yet do not let me frighten you, Jeanie; he continues to be kind, and I am far better off than I deserve. You will wonder at my better scholarship; but when I was abroad, I had the best teachers, and I worked hard because my progress pleased him. He is kind, Jeanie, only he has much to distress him, especially when he looks backward. When I look backward myself, I have always a ray of comfort; it is in the generous conduct of a sister, who forsook me not when I was forsaken by every one. You have had your reward. You live happy in the esteem and love of all who know you, and I drag on the life of a miserable impostor, indebted for the marks of regard I receive to a tissue of deceit and lies, which the slightest accident may unravel. He has produced me to his friends, since the estate opened to him, as the daughter of a Scotchman of rank, banished on account of the Viscount of Dundee's wars—that is, our Fr's old friend Clavers, you know—and he says I was educated in a Scotch convent; indeed, I lived in such a place long enough to enable me to support the character. But when a countryman approaches me, and begins to talk, as they all do, of the various families engaged in Dundee's affair, and to make inquiries into my connections, and when I see *his* eye bent on mine with such an expression of agony, my terror brings me to the very risk of detection. Good-nature and politeness have hitherto saved me, as they prevented people from pressing on me with distressing questions. But how long—O how long, will this be the case!—And if I bring this disgrace on him, he will hate me—he will kill me, for as much as he loves me; he is as jealous of his family honour now, as ever he was careless about it. I have been in England four months, and have often thought of writing to you; and yet, such are the dangers that might arise from an intercepted letter, that I have hitherto forborne. But now I am obliged to run the risk. Last week I saw your great friend, the D. of A. He came to my box, and sate by me; and something in the play put him in mind of you—Gracious Heaven! he told over your whole London journey to all who were in the box, but particularly to the wretched creature who was the occasion of it all. If he had known—if he could have conceived, beside whom he was sitting, and to whom the story was told!—I suffered with courage, like an Indian at the stake, while they are rending his fibres and boring his eyes, and while he smiles applause at each well-imagined contrivance of his torturers. It was too much for me at last, Jeanie—I fainted; and my agony was imputed partly to the heat of the place, and partly to my extreme sensibility; and, hypocrite all over, I encouraged both opinions—anything but discovery! Luckily *he* was not there. But the incident has led to more alarms. I am obliged to meet your great man often; and he seldom sees me without talking of E. D. and J. D., and R. B. and D. D., as persons in whom my amiable sensibility is interested. My amiable sensibility ! ! !—And then the cruel tone of light

indifference with which persons in the fashionable world speak
together on the most affecting subjects! To hear my guilt,
my folly, my agony, the foibles and weaknesses of my friends
—even your heroic exertions, Jeanie, spoken of in the drolling
style which is the present tone in fashionable life—Scarce all
that I formerly endured is equal to this state of irritation—
then it was blows and stabs—now it is pricking to death with
needles and pins.—He—I mean the D.—goes down next
month to spend the shooting season in Scotland—he says, he
makes a point of always dining one day at the Manse—be on
your guard, and do not betray yourself, should he mention
me—Yourself, alas! *you* have nothing to betray—nothing to
fear; you, the pure, the virtuous, the heroine of unstained
faith, unblemished purity, what can you have to fear from the
world or its proudest minions? It is E. whose life is once
more in your hands—it is E. whom you are to save from being
plucked of her borrowed plumes, discovered, branded, and
trodden down, first by him, perhaps, who has raised her to
this dizzy pinnacle!—The enclosure will reach you twice a
year—do not refuse it—it is out of my own allowance, and
may be twice as much when you want it. With you it may
do good—with me it never can.

"Write to me soon, Jeanie, or I shall remain in the
agonising apprehension that this has fallen into wrong hands
—Address simply to L. S., under cover, to the Reverend
George Whiterose, in the Minster-Close, York. He thinks
I correspond with some of my noble Jacobite relations who
are in Scotland. How high-church and jacobitical zeal would
burn in his cheeks, if he knew he was the agent, not of
Euphemia Setoun, of the honourable house of Winton, but
of E. D., daughter of a Cameronian cowfeeder!—Jeanie, I
can laugh yet sometimes—but God protect you from such
mirth.—My father—I mean your father, would say it was like
the idle crackling of thorns; but the thorns keep their poig-
nancy, they remain unconsumed.—Farewell, my dearest Jeanie
—Do not show this even to Mr. Butler, much less to any one
else—I have every respect for him, but his principles are over
strict, and my case will not endure severe handling.—I rest
your affectionate sister, E."

In this long letter there was much to surprise as well as to
distress Mrs. Butler. That Effie—her sister Effie, should be
mingling freely in society, and apparently on not unequal

terms, with the Duke of Argyle, sounded like something so extraordinary, that she even doubted if she read truly. Nor was it less marvellous, that, in the space of four years, her education should have made such progress. Jeanie's humility readily allowed that Effie had always, when she chose it, been smarter at her book than she herself was, but then she was very idle, and, upon the whole, had made much less proficiency. Love, or fear, or necessity, however, had proved an able school-mistress, and completely supplied all her deficiencies.

What Jeanie least liked in the tone of the letter was a smothered degree of egotism. "We should have heard little about her," said Jeanie to herself, "but that she was feared the Duke might come to learn wha she was, and a' about her puir friends here; but Effie, puir thing, aye looks her ain way, and folk that do that think mair o' themselves than of their neighbours.—I am no clear about keeping her siller," she added, taking up a £50 note which had fallen out of the paper to the floor. "We hae eneugh, and it looks unco like theftboot, or hush-money, as they ca' it; she might hae been sure that I wad say naething wad harm her, for a' the gowd in Lunnon. And I maun tell the minister about it. I dinna see that she suld be sae feared for her ain bonny bargain o' a gudeman, and that I shouldna reverence Mr. Butler just as much; and sae I'll e'en tell him, when that tippling body the Captain has ta'en boat in the morning.——But I wonder at my ain state of mind," she added, turning back, after she had made a step or two to the door to join the gentlemen; "surely I am not sic a fule as to be angry that Effie's a braw lady, while I am only a minister's wife?—and yet I am as petted as a bairn, when I should bless God, that has redeemed her from shame, and poverty, and guilt, as ower likely she might hae been plunged into."

Sitting down upon a stool at the foot of the bed, she folded her arms upon her bosom, saying within herself, "From this place will I not rise till I am in a better frame of mind;" and so placed, by dint of tearing the veil from the motives of her little temporary spleen against her sister, she compelled herself to be ashamed of them, and to view as blessings the advantages of her sister's lot, while its embarrassments were the necessary consequences of errors long since committed. And thus she fairly vanquished the feeling of pique which she naturally enough entertained, at seeing Effie, so long the object of her care and her pity, soar suddenly so high above her in life, as to reckon amongst the chief objects of her apprehension the risk of their relationship being discovered.

When this unwonted burst of *amour propre* was thoroughly subdued, she walked down to the little parlour where the gentlemen were finishing their game, and heard from the Captain a confirmation of the news intimated in her letter, that the Duke of Argyle was shortly expected at Roseneath.

"He'll find plenty of moor-fowls and plack-cock on the moors of Auchingower, and he'll pe nae doubt for taking a late dinner, and a ped at the Manse, as he has done pefore now."

"He has a gude right, Captain," said Jeanie.

"Teil ane petter to ony ped in the kintra," answered the Captain. "And ye had petter tell your father, puir body, to get his beasts a' in order, and put his tamn'd Cameronian nonsense out o' his head for twa or three days, if he can pe so opliging; for fan I speak to him apout prute pestial, he answers me out o' the Pible, whilk is not using a shentleman weel, unless it be a person of your cloth, Mr. Putler."

No one understood better than Jeanie the merit of the soft answer, which turneth away wrath; and she only smiled, and hoped that his Grace would find everything that was under her father's care to his entire satisfaction.

But the Captain, who had lost the whole postage of the letter at backgammon, was in the pouting mood not unusual to losers, and which, says the proverb, must be allowed to them.

"And, Master Putler, though you know I never meddle with the things of your kirk-sessions, yet I must pe allowed to say that I will not pe pleased to allow Ailie MacClure of Deepheugh to pe poonished as a witch, in respect she only spaes fortunes, and does not lame, or plind, or pedevil any persons, or coup cadgers' carts, or ony sort of mischief; put only tells people good fortunes, as anent our poats killing so many seals and doug-fishes, whilk is very pleasant to hear."

"The woman," said Butler, "is, I believe, no witch, but a cheat; and it is only on that head that she is summoned to the kirk-session, to cause her to desist in future from practising her impostures upon ignorant persons."

"I do not know," replied the gracious Duncan, "what her practices or her postures are, but I pelieve that if the poys take hould on her to duck her in the Clachan purn, it will be a very sorry practice—and I pelieve, moreover, that if I come in thirdsman among you at the kirk-sessions, you will be all in a tamn'd pad posture indeed."

Without noticing this threat, Mr. Butler replied, "That he had not attended to the risk of ill usage which the poor woman might undergo at the hands of the rabble, and that he would give her the necessary admonition in private, instead of bringing her before the assembled session."

"This," Duncan said, "was speaking like a reasonable shentleman;" and so the evening passed peaceably off.

Next morning, after the Captain had swallowed his morning draught of Athole brose, and departed in his coach and six, Mrs. Butler anew deliberated upon communicating to her husband her sister's letter. But she was deterred by the recollection, that, in doing so, she would unveil to him the whole of a dreadful secret, of which, perhaps, his public character might render him an unfit depositary. Butler already had reason to believe that Effie had eloped with that same Robertson who had been a leader in the Porteous mob, and who lay under sentence of death for the robbery at Kirkcaldy. But he did not know his identity with George Staunton, a man of birth and fortune, who had now apparently reassumed his natural rank in society. Jeanie had respected Staunton's own confession as sacred, and upon reflection she considered the letter of her sister as equally so, and resolved to mention the contents to no one.

On reperusing the letter, she could not help observing the staggering and unsatisfactory condition of those who have risen to distinction by undue paths, and the outworks and bulwarks of fiction and falsehood, by which they are under the necessity of surrounding and defending their precarious advantages. But she was not called upon, she thought, to unveil her sister's original history—it would restore no right to any one, for she was usurping none—it would only destroy her happiness, and degrade her in the public estimation. Had she been wise, Jeanie thought she would have chosen seclusion and privacy, in place of public life and gaiety; but the power of choice might not be hers. The money, she thought, could not be returned without her seeming haughty and unkind. She resolved, therefore, upon reconsidering this point, to employ it as occasion should serve, either in educating her children better than her own means could compass, or for their future portion. Her sister had enough, was strongly bound to assist Jeanie by any means in her power, and the arrangement was so natural and proper, that it ought not to be declined out of fastidious or romantic delicacy. Jeanie accordingly wrote to her sister, acknowledging her letter, and requesting to hear from her as often as she could. In entering into her own little details of news, chiefly respecting domestic affairs, she experienced a singular vacillation of ideas; for sometimes she apologised for mentioning things unworthy the notice of a lady of rank, and then recollected that everything which concerned her should be interesting to Effie. Her letter, under the cover of Mr. Whiterose, she committed to the post-office at Glasgow, by the intervention of a parishioner who had business at that city.

The next week brought the Duke to Roseneath, and shortly afterwards he intimated his intention of sporting in their neighbourhood, and taking his bed at the Manse; an honour which he had once or twice done to its inmates on former occasions.

Effie proved to be perfectly right in her anticipations. The Duke had hardly set himself down at Mrs. Butler's right hand, and taken upon himself the task of carving the excellent "barn-door chucky," which had been selected as the high dish upon this honourable occasion, before he began to speak of Lady Staunton of Willingham, in Lincolnshire, and the great noise which her wit and beauty made in London. For much of this Jeanie was, in some measure, prepared—but Effie's wit! that would never have entered into her imagination, being ignorant how exactly raillery in the higher rank resembles flippancy among their inferiors.

"She has been the ruling belle—the blazing star—the universal toast of the winter," said the Duke; "and is really the most beautiful creature that was seen at court upon the birthday."

The birthday! and at court!—Jeanie was annihilated, remembering well her own presentation, all its extraordinary circumstances, and particularly the cause of it.

"I mention this lady particularly to you, Mrs. Butler," said the Duke, "because she has something in the sound of her voice, and cast of her countenance, that reminded me of you—not when you look so pale though—you have over-fatigued yourself—you must pledge me in a glass of wine."

She did so, and Butler observed, "It was dangerous flattery in his Grace to tell a poor minister's wife that she was like a court-beauty."

"Oho! Mr. Butler," said the Duke, "I find you are growing jealous; but it's rather too late in the day, for you know how long I have admired your wife. But seriously, there is betwixt them one of those inexplicable likenesses which we see in countenances, that do not otherwise resemble each other."

"The perilous part of the compliment has flown off," thought Mr. Butler.

His wife, feeling the awkwardness of silence, forced herself to say, "That, perhaps, the lady might be her countrywoman, and the language might make some resemblance."

"You are quite right," replied the Duke. "She is a Scotchwoman, and speaks with a Scotch accent, and now and then a provincial word drops out so prettily, that it is quite Doric, Mr. Butler."

"I should have thought," said the clergyman, "that would have sounded vulgar in the great city."

"Not at all," replied the Duke; "you must suppose it is not the broad coarse Scotch that is spoken in the Cowgate of Edinburgh, or in the Gorbals. This lady has been very little in Scotland, in fact—She was educated in a convent abroad, and speaks that pure court-Scotch, which was common in my younger days; but it is so generally disused now, that it sounds like a different dialect, entirely distinct from our modern *patois*."

Notwithstanding her anxiety, Jeanie could not help admiring within herself, how the most correct judges of life and manners can be imposed on by their own preconceptions, while the Duke proceeded thus: "She is of the unfortunate house of Winton, I believe; but, being bred abroad, she had missed the opportunity of learning her own pedigree, and was obliged to me for informing her, that she must certainly come of the Setons of Windygoul. I wish you could have seen how prettily she blushed at her own ignorance. Amidst her noble and elegant manners, there is now and then a little touch of bashfulness and conventual rusticity, if I may call it so, that makes her quite enchanting. You see at once the rose that had bloomed untouched amid the chaste precincts of the cloister, Mr. Butler."

True to the hint, Mr. Butler failed not to start with his

"Ut flos in septis secretus nascitur hortis," &c.

while his wife could hardly persuade herself that all this was spoken of Effie Deans, and by so competent a judge as the Duke of Argyle; and had she been acquainted with Catullus, would have thought the fortunes of her sister had reversed the whole passage.

She was, however, determined to obtain some indemnification for the anxious feelings of the moment, by gaining all the intelligence she could; and therefore ventured to make some inquiry about the husband of the lady his Grace admired so much.

"He is very rich," replied the Duke; "of an ancient family, and has good manners; but he is far from being such a general favourite as his wife. Some people say he can be very pleasant—I never saw him so; but should rather judge him reserved, and gloomy, and capricious. He was very wild in his youth, they say, and has bad health; yet he is a good-looking man enough—a great friend of your Lord High Commissioner of the Kirk, Mr. Butler."

"Then he is the friend of a very worthy and honourable nobleman," said Butler.

"Does he admire his lady as much as other people do?" said Jeanie, in a low voice.

"Who—Sir George? They say he is very fond of her," said the Duke; "but I observe she trembles a little when he fixes his eye on her, and that is no good sign—But it is strange how I am haunted by this resemblance of yours to Lady Staunton, in look and tone of voice. One would almost swear you were sisters."

Jeanie's distress became uncontrollable, and beyond concealment. The Duke of Argyle was much disturbed, good-naturedly ascribing it to his having unwittingly recalled to her remembrance her family misfortunes. He was too well-bred to attempt to apologise; but hastened to change the subject, and arrange certain points of dispute which had occurred betwixt Duncan of Knock and the minister, acknowledging that his worthy substitute was sometimes a little too obstinate, as well as too energetic, in his executive measures.

Mr. Butler admitted his general merits; but said, "He would presume to apply to the worthy gentleman the words of the poet to Marrucinus Asinius,

'Manu——
Non belle uteris in joco atque vino.'"

The discourse being thus turned on parish business, nothing farther occurred that can interest the reader.

CHAPTER XLIX

Upon my head they placed a fruitless crown,
And put a barren sceptre in my gripe,
Thence to be wrench'd by an unlineal hand,
No son of mine succeeding.

Macbeth.

AFTER this period, but under the most strict precautions against discovery, the sisters corresponded occasionally, exchanging letters about twice every year. Those of Lady Staunton spoke of her husband's health and spirits as being deplorably uncertain; her own seemed also to be sinking, and one of the topics on which she most frequently dwelt was their want of family. Sir George Staunton, always violent, had taken some aversion at the next heir, whom he suspected of having irritated his friends against him during his absence; and he declared, he would bequeath Willingham and all its lands to an hospital, ere that fetch-and-carry tell-tale should inherit an acre of it.

" Had he but a child," said the unfortunate wife, " or had that luckless infant survived, it would be some motive for living and for exertion. But Heaven has denied us a blessing which we have not deserved."

Such complaints, in varied form, but turning frequently on the same topic, filled the letters which passed from the spacious but melancholy halls of Willingham, to the quiet and happy parsonage at Knocktarlitie. Years meanwhile rolled on amid these fruitless repinings. John, Duke of Argyle and Greenwich, died in the year 1743, universally lamented, but by none more than by the Butlers, to whom his benevolence had been so distinguished. He was succeeded by his brother Duke Archibald, with whom they had not the same intimacy; but who continued the protection which his brother had extended towards them. This, indeed, became more necessary than ever; for, after the breaking out and suppression of the rebellion in 1745, the peace of the country, adjacent to the Highlands, was considerably disturbed. Marauders, or men that had been driven to that desperate mode of life, quartered themselves in the fastnesses nearest to the Lowlands, which were their scene of plunder; and there is scarce a glen in the romantic and now peaceable Highlands of Perth, Stirling, and Dumbartonshire, where one or more did not take up their residence.

The prime pest of the parish of Knocktarlitie was a certain Donacha dhu na Dunaigh, or Black Duncan the Mischievous, whom we have already casually mentioned. This fellow had been originally a tinkler or *caird*, many of whom stroll about these districts; but when all police was disorganised by the civil war, he threw up his profession, and from half thief became whole robber; and being generally at the head of three or four active young fellows, and he himself artful, bold, and well acquainted with the passes, he plied his new profession with emolument to himself, and infinite plague to the country.

All were convinced that Duncan of Knock could have put down his namesake Donacha any morning he had a mind; for there were in the parish a set of stout young men, who had joined Argyle's banner in the war under his old friend, and behaved very well upon several occasions. And as for their leader, as no one doubted his courage, it was generally supposed that Donacha had found out the mode of conciliating his favour, a thing not very uncommon in that age and country. This was the more readily believed, as David Deans's cattle (being the property of the Duke) were left untouched, when the minister's cows were carried off by the thieves. Another attempt was made to renew the same act of rapine, and the cattle were in the act of being driven off, when Butler, laying his profession aside in a case of such necessity, put himself at the head of some of his neighbours, and rescued the creagh, an exploit at which Deans attended in person, notwithstanding his extreme old age, mounted on a Highland pony, and girded with an old broadsword, likening himself (for he failed not to arrogate the whole merit of the expedition) to David, the son of Jesse, when he recovered the spoil of Ziklag from the Amalekites. This spirited behaviour had so far a good effect, that Donacha dhu na Dunaigh kept his distance for some time to come; and, though his distant exploits were frequently spoken of, he did not exercise any depredations in that part of the country. He continued to flourish, and to be heard of occasionally, until the year 1751, when, if the fear of the second David had kept him in check, fate released him from that restraint, for the venerable patriarch of St. Leonard's was that year gathered to his fathers.

David Deans died full of years and of honour. He is believed, for the exact time of his birth is not known, to have lived upwards of ninety years; for he used to speak of events as falling under his own knowledge, which happened about the time of the battle of Bothwell Bridge. It was said that he even bore arms there; for once, when a drunken Jacobite laird wished for a Bothwell-Brigg whig, that " he might stow the lugs out of his head," David informed him with a peculiar austerity of countenance, that, if he liked to try such a prank, there was one at his elbow; and it required the interference of Butler to preserve the peace.

He expired in the arms of his beloved daughter, thankful for all the blessings which Providence had vouchsafed to him while in this valley of strife and toil—and thankful also for the trials he had been visited with; having found them, he said, needful to mortify that spiritual pride and confidence in his own gifts, which was the side on which the wily Enemy did most sorely beset him. He prayed in the most affecting manner for Jeanie, her husband, and her family, and that her affectionate duty to the puir auld man might purchase her length of days here, and happiness hereafter; then, in a pathetic petition, too well understood by those who knew his family circumstances, he besought the Shepherd of souls, while gathering His flock, not to forget the little one that had strayed from the fold, and even then might be in the hands of the ravening wolf.—He prayed for the national Jerusalem, that peace might be in her land, and prosperity in her palaces —for the welfare of the honourable House of Argyle, and for the conversion of Duncan of Knockdunder. After this he was silent, being exhausted, nor did he again utter anything distinctly. He was heard, indeed, to mutter something about national defections, right-hand extremes, and left-hand fallings off; but, as May Hettly observed, his head was carried at the time: and it is probable that these expressions occurred to him merely out of general habit, and that he died in the full spirit of charity with all men. About an hour afterwards he slept in the Lord.

Notwithstanding her father's advanced age, his death was a severe shock to Mrs. Butler. Much of her time had been dedicated to attending to his health and his wishes, and she felt as if part of her business in the world was ended, when the good old man was no more. His wealth, which came nearly to fifteen hundred pounds, in disposable capital, served to raise the fortunes of the family at the Manse. How to dispose of this sum for the best advantage of his family, was matter of anxious consideration to Butler.

"If we put it on heritable bond we shall maybe lose the interest; for there's that bond over Lounsbeck's land, your father could neither get principal nor interest for it—If we bring it into the funds, we shall maybe lose the principal and all, as many did in the South Sea scheme. The little estate of Craigsture is in the market—it lies within two miles of the Manse, and Knock says his Grace has no thought to buy it. But they ask £2500, and they may, for it is worth the money; and were I to borrow the balance, the creditor might call it up suddenly, or in case of my death my family might be distressed."

"And so, if we had mair siller, we might buy that bonny pasture-ground, where the grass comes so early?" asked Jeanie.

"Certainly, my dear; and Knockdunder, who is a good judge, is strongly advising me to it.—To be sure it is his nephew that is selling it."

"Aweel, Reuben," said Jeanie, "ye maun just look up a text in Scripture, as ye did when ye wanted siller before—just look up a text in the Bible."

"Ah, Jeanie," said Butler, laughing and pressing her hand at the same time, "the best people in these times can only work miracles once."

"We will see," said Jeanie composedly; and going to the closet in which she kept her honey, her sugar, her pots of jelly, her vials of the more ordinary medicines, and which served her, in short, as a sort of store-room, she jangled vials and gallipots, till, from out the darkest nook, well flanked by a triple row of bottles and jars, which she was under the necessity of displacing, she brought a cracked brown cann, with a piece of leather tied over the top. Its contents seemed to be written papers, thrust in disorder into this uncommon *secrétaire*. But from among these Jeanie brought an old clasped Bible, which had been David Deans's companion in his earlier wanderings, and which he had given to his daughter when the failure of his eyes had compelled him to use one of a larger print. This she gave to Butler, who had been looking at her motions with some surprise, and desired him to see what that book could do for him. He opened the clasps, and to his astonishment a parcel of £50 bank-notes dropped out from betwixt the leaves, where they had been separately lodged, and fluttered upon the floor. "I didna think to hae tauld you o' my wealth, Reuben," said his wife, smiling at his surprise, "till on my deathbed, or maybe on some family pinch ; but it wad be better laid out on yon bonny grass-holms, than lying useless here in this auld pigg."

"How on earth came ye by that siller, Jeanie?—Why, here is more than a thousand pounds," said Butler, lifting up and counting the notes.

"If it were ten thousand, it's a' honestly come by," said Jeanie ; "and troth I kenna how muckle there is o't, but it's a' there that ever I got.—And as for how I came by it, Reuben —it's weel come by, and honestly, as I said before—And it's mair folk's secret than mine, or ye wad hae kend about it lang syne ; and as for onything else, I am not free to answer mair questions about it, and ye maun just ask me nane."

"Answer me but one," said Butler. "Is it all freely and indisputably your own property, to dispose of it as you think fit?—Is it possible no one has a claim in so large a sum except you?"

"It *was* mine, free to dispose of it as I like," answered Jeanie ; "and I have disposed of it already, for now it is yours, Reuben—You are Bible Butler now, as weel as your forbear, that my puir father had sic an ill will at. Only, if ye like, I wad wish Femie to get a gude share o't when we are gane."

"Certainly, it shall be as you choose—But who on earth ever pitched on such a hiding-place for temporal treasures?"

"That is just ane o' my auld-fashioned gates, as you ca' them, Reuben. I thought if Donacha Dhu was to make an outbreak upon us, the Bible was the last thing in the house he wad meddle wi'—but an ony mair siller should drap in, as it is not unlikely, I shall e'en pay it ower to you, and ye may lay it out your ain way."

"And I positively must not ask you how you have come by all this money?" said the clergyman.

"Indeed, Reuben, you must not ; for if you were asking me very sair I wad maybe tell you, and then I am sure I would do wrong."

"But tell me," said Butler, "is it anything that distresses your own mind?"

"There is baith weal and woe come aye wi' warld's gear, Reuben ; but ye maun ask me naething mair—This siller binds me to naething, and can never be speered back again."

"Surely," said Mr. Butler, when he had again counted over the money, as if to assure himself that the notes were real,

" there was never man in the world had a wife like mine—a blessing seems to follow her."

"Never," said Jeanie, "since the enchanted princess in the bairns' fairy tale, that kamed gold nobles out o' the tae side of her haffit locks, and Dutch dollars out o' the t'other. But gang away now, minister, and put by the siller, and dinna keep the notes wampishing in your hand that gate, or I shall wish them in the brown pigg again, for fear we get a black cast about them—we're ower near the hills in these times to be thought to hae siller in the house. And, besides, ye maun gree wi' Knockdunder, that has the selling o' the lands ; and dinna you be simple and let him ken o' this windfa', but keep him to the very lowest penny, as if ye had to borrow siller to make the price up."

In the last admonition Jeanie showed distinctly, that, although she did not understand how to secure the money which came into her hands otherwise than by saving and hoarding it, yet she had some part of her father David's shrewdness, even upon worldly subjects. And Reuben Butler was a prudent man, and went and did even as his wife had advised him.

The news quickly went abroad into the parish that the minister had bought Craigsture ; and some wished him joy, and some "were sorry it had gane out of the auld name." However, his clerical brethren, understanding that he was under the necessity of going to Edinburgh about the ensuing Whitsunday, to get together David Deans's cash to make up the purchase-money of his new acquisition, took the opportunity to name him their delegate to the General Assembly, or Convocation of the Scottish Church, which takes place usually in the latter end of the month of May.

CHAPTER L

But who is this ? what thing of sea or land—
Female of sex it seems—
That so bedeck'd, ornate, and gay,
Comes this way sailing ?

                                    MILTON.

NOT long after the incident of the Bible and the bank-notes, Fortune showed that she could surprise Mrs. Butler as well as her husband. The minister, in order to accomplish the various pieces of business, which his unwonted visit to Edinburgh rendered necessary, had been under the necessity of setting out from home in the latter end of the month of February, concluding justly, that he would find the space betwixt his departure and the term of Whitsunday (24th May) short enough for the purpose of bringing forward those various debtors of old David Deans, out of whose purses a considerable part of the price of his new purchase was to be made good.

Jeanie was thus in the unwonted situation of inhabiting a lonely house, and she felt yet more solitary from the death of the good old man, who used to divide her cares with her husband. Her children were her principal resource, and to them she paid constant attention.

It happened, a day or two after Butler's departure, that, while she was engaged in some domestic duties, she heard a dispute among the young folk, which, being maintained with obstinacy, appeared to call for her interference. All came to their natural umpire with their complaints. Femie, not yet ten years old, charged Davie and Reubie with an attempt to take away her book by force; and David and Reuben replied, the elder, "That it was not a book for Femie to read," and Reuben, "That it was about a bad woman."

"Where did you get the book, ye little hempie?" said Mrs. Butler. "How dare ye touch papa's books when he is away?"

But the little lady, holding fast a sheet of crumpled paper, declared, "It was nane o' papa's books, and May Hettly had taken it off the muckle cheese which came from Inverara;" for, as was very natural to suppose, a friendly intercourse, with interchange of mutual civilities, was kept up from time to time between Mrs. Dolly Dutton, now Mrs. MacCorkindale, and her former friends.

Jeanie took the subject of contention out of the child's hand, to satisfy herself of the propriety of her studies; but how much was she struck when she read upon the title of the broadside-sheet, "The Last Speech, Confession, and Dying Words of Margaret MacCraw, or Murdockson, executed on Harabee Hill, near Carlisle, the — day of —— 1737." It was, indeed, one of those papers which Archibald had bought at Longtown, when he monopolised the pedlar's stock, which Dolly had thrust into her trunk out of sheer economy. One or two copies, it seems, had remained in her repositories at Inverary, till she chanced to need them in packing a cheese, which, as a very superior production, was sent, in the way of civil challenge, to the dairy at Knocktarlitie.

The title of this paper, so strangely fallen into the very hands from which, in well-meant respect to her feelings, it had been so long detained, was of itself sufficiently startling; but the narrative itself was so interesting, that Jeanie, shaking herself loose from the children, ran upstairs to her own apartment, and bolted the door, to peruse it without interruption.

The narrative, which appeared to have been drawn up, or at least corrected, by the clergyman who attended this unhappy woman, stated the crime for which she suffered to have been "her active part in that atrocious robbery and murder, committed near two years since near Haltwhistle, for which the notorious Frank Levitt was committed for trial at Lancaster assizes. It was supposed the evidence of the accomplice, Thomas Tuck, commonly called Tyburn Tom, upon which the woman had been convicted, would weigh equally heavy against him; although many were inclined to think it was Tuck himself who had struck the fatal blow, according to the dying statement of Meg Murdockson."

After a circumstantial account of the crime for which she suffered, there was a brief sketch of Margaret's life. It was stated, that she was a Scotchwoman by birth, and married a soldier in the Cameronian regiment—that she long followed the camp, and had doubtless acquired in fields of battle, and similar scenes, that ferocity and love of plunder for which she had been afterwards distinguished—that her husband, having obtained his discharge, became servant to a beneficed clergyman of high situation and character in Lincolnshire, and that she acquired the confidence and esteem of that honourable family. She had lost this many years after her husband's death, it was stated, in consequence of conniving at the irregularities of her daughter with the heir of the family, added to the suspicious circumstances attending the birth of a child, which was strongly suspected to have met with foul play, in order to preserve, if possible, the girl's reputation. After this, she had led a wandering life both in England and Scotland, under colour sometimes of telling fortunes, sometimes of driving a trade in smuggled wares, but, in fact, receiving stolen goods, and occasionally actively joining in the exploits by which they were obtained. Many of her crimes she had boasted of after conviction, and there was one circumstance for which she seemed to feel a mixture of joy and occasional compunction. When she was residing in the suburbs of Edinburgh during the preceding summer, a girl, who had been seduced by one of her confederates, was entrusted to her charge, and in her house delivered of a male infant. Her daughter, whose mind was in a state of derangement ever since she had lost her own child, according to the criminal's account, carried off the poor girl's infant, taking it for her own, of the reality of whose death she at times could not be persuaded.

Margaret Murdockson stated, that she, for some time, believed her daughter had actually destroyed the infant in her mad fits, and that she gave the father to understand so, but afterwards learned that a female stroller had got it from her. She showed some compunction at having separated mother and child, especially as the mother had nearly suffered death, being condemned, on the Scotch law, for the supposed murder of her infant. When it was asked what possible interest she could have had in exposing the unfortunate girl to suffer for a crime she had not committed, she asked, if they thought she was going to put her own daughter into trouble to save another? She did not know what the Scotch law would have done to her for carrying the child away. This answer was by no means satisfactory to the clergyman, and he discovered, by close examination, that she had a deep and revengeful hatred against the young person whom she had thus injured. But the paper intimated, that, whatever besides she had communicated upon this subject, was confided by her in private to the worthy and reverend Archdeacon who had bestowed such particular pains in affording her spiritual assistance. The broadside went on to intimate, that, after her execution, of which the particulars were given, her daughter, the insane person mentioned more than once, and who was generally known by the name of Madge Wildfire, had been very ill-used by the populace, under the belief that she was a sorceress, and an accomplice in her mother's crimes, and had been with difficulty rescued by the prompt interference of the police.

Such (for we omit moral reflections, and all that may seem unnecessary to the explanation of our story) was the tenor of the broadside. To Mrs. Butler it contained intelligence of the highest importance, since it seemed to afford the most unequivocal proof of her sister's innocence respecting the crime for which she had so nearly suffered. It is true, neither she, nor her husband, nor even her father, had ever believed her capable of touching her infant with an unkind hand when in possession of her reason; but there was a darkness on the subject, and what might have happened in a moment of insanity was dreadful to think upon. Besides, whatever was their own conviction, they had no means of establishing Effie's innocence to the world, which, according to the tenor of this fugitive publication, was now at length completely manifested by the dying confession of the person chiefly interested in concealing it.

After thanking God for a discovery so dear to her feelings, Mrs. Butler began to consider what use she should make of it. To have shown it to her husband would have been her first impulse; but, besides that he was absent from home, and the matter too delicate to be the subject of correspondence by an indifferent penwoman, Mrs. Butler recollected that he was not possessed of the information necessary to form a judgment upon the occasion; and that, adhering to the rule which she had considered as most advisable, she had best transmit the information immediately to her sister, and leave her to adjust with her husband the mode in which they should avail themselves of it. Accordingly, she despatched a special messenger to Glasgow, with a packet, enclosing the Confession of Margaret Murdockson, addressed, as usual, under cover, to Mr. Whiterose of York. She expected, with anxiety, an answer, but none arrived in the usual course of post, and she was left to imagine how many various causes might account for Lady Staunton's silence. She began to be half sorry that she had parted with the printed paper, both for fear of its having fallen into bad hands, and from the desire of regaining the document, which might be essential to establish her sister's innocence. She was even doubting whether she had not better commit the whole matter to her husband's consideration, when other incidents occurred to divert her purpose.

Jeanie (she is a favourite, and we beg her pardon for still using the familiar title) had walked down to the sea-side with her children one morning after breakfast, when the boys, whose sight was more discriminating than hers, exclaimed, that "the Captain's coach and six was coming right for the shore, with ladies in it." Jeanie instinctively bent her eyes on the approaching boat, and became soon sensible that there were two females in the stern, seated beside the gracious Duncan, who acted as pilot. It was a point of politeness to walk towards the landing-place, in order to receive them, especially as she saw that the Captain of Knockdunder was upon honour and ceremony. His piper was in the bow of the boat, sending forth music, of which one half sounded the better that the other was drowned by the waves and the breeze. Moreover, he himself had his brigadier wig newly frizzed, his bonnet (he had abjured the cocked-hat) decorated with Saint George's red cross, his uniform mounted as a captain of militia, the Duke's flag with the boar's head displayed—all intimated parade and gala.

As Mrs. Butler approached the landing-place, she observed the Captain hand the ladies ashore with marks of great attention, and the parties advanced towards her, the Captain a few steps before the two ladies, of whom the taller and elder leaned on the shoulder of the other, who seemed to be an attendant or servant.

As they met, Duncan, in his best, most important, and deepest tone of Highland civility, "pegged leave to introduce to Mrs. Putler, Lady—eh—eh—I hae forgotten your leddy-ship's name!"

"Never mind my name, sir," said the lady; "I trust Mrs. Butler will be at no loss. The Duke's letter——" And, as she observed Mrs. Butler look confused, she said again to Duncan something sharply, "Did you not send the letter last night, sir?"

"In troth and I didna, and I crave your leddyship's pardon; but you see, matam, I thought it would do as weel to-tay, pecause Mrs. Putler is never taen out o' sorts—never—and the coach was out fishing—and the gig was gane to Greenock for a cag of prandy—and—— Put here's his Grace's letter."

"Give it me, sir," said the lady, taking it out of his hand; "since you have not found it convenient to do me the favour to send it before me, I will deliver it myself."

Mrs. Butler looked with great attention, and a certain dubious feeling of deep interest, on the lady, who thus expressed herself with authority over the man of authority, and to whose mandates he seemed to submit, resigning the letter with a "Just as your leddyship is pleased to order it."

The lady was rather above the middle size, beautifully made, though something *embonpoint*, with a hand and arm exquisitely formed. Her manner was easy, dignified, and commanding, and seemed to evince high birth and the habits of elevated society. She wore a travelling dress—a grey beaver hat, and a veil of Flanders lace. Two footmen, in rich liveries, who got out of the barge, and lifted out a trunk and portmanteau, appeared to belong to her suite.

"As you did not receive the letter, madam, which should have served for my introduction—for I presume you are Mrs. Butler—I will not present it to you till you are so good as to admit me into your house without it."

' To pe sure, matam," said Knockdunder, " ye canna doubt Mrs. Putler will do that.—Mrs. Putler, this is Lady—Lady—these tamn'd Southern names rin out o' my head like a stane trowling down hill—put I believe she is a Scottish woman porn—the mair our credit—and I presume her leddyship is of the house of——"

"The Duke of Argyle knows my family very well, sir," said the lady, in a tone which seemed designed to silence Duncan, or, at any rate, which had that effect completely.

There was something about the whole of this stranger's address, and tone, and manner, which acted upon Jeanie's feelings like the illusions of a dream, that tease us with a puzzling approach to reality. Something there was of her sister in the gait and manner of the stranger, as well as in the sound of her voice, and something also, when, lifting her veil, she showed features, to which, changed as they were in expression and complexion, she could not but attach many remembrances.

The stranger was turned of thirty certainly ; but so well were her personal charms assisted by the power of dress, and arrangement of ornament, that she might well have passed for one-and-twenty. And her behaviour was so steady and so composed, that, as often as Mrs. Butler perceived anew some point of resemblance to her unfortunate sister, so often the sustained self-command and absolute composure of the stranger destroyed the ideas which began to arise in her imagination. She led the way silently towards the Manse, lost in a confusion of reflections, and trusting the letter with which she was to be there entrusted, would afford her satisfactory explanation of what was a most puzzling and embarrassing scene.

The lady maintained in the meanwhile the manners of a stranger of rank. She admired the various points of view like one who has studied nature, and the best representations of art. At length she took notice of the children.

"These are two fine young mountaineers—Yours, madam, I presume ? "

Jeanie replied in the affirmative. The stranger sighed, and sighed once more as they were presented to her by name.

"Come here, Femie," said Mrs. Butler, "and hold your head up."

"What is your daughter's name, madam?" said the lady.

"Euphemia, madam," answered Mrs. Butler.

"I thought the ordinary Scottish contraction of the name had been Effie," replied the stranger, in a tone which went to Jeanie's heart; for in that single word there was more of her sister—more of *lang syne* ideas—than in all the reminiscences which her own heart had anticipated, or the features and manner of the stranger had suggested.

When they reached the Manse, the lady gave Mrs. Butler the letter which she had taken out of the hands of Knock-dunder; and as she gave it she pressed her hand, adding aloud, "Perhaps, madam, you will have the goodness to get me a little milk."

"And me a drap of the grey-peard, if you please, Mrs. Putler," added Duncan.

Mrs. Butler withdrew; but, deputing to May Hettly and to David the supply of the strangers' wants, she hastened into her own room to read the letter. The envelope was addressed in the Duke of Argyle's hand, and requested Mrs. Butler's attentions and civility to a lady of rank, a particular friend of his late brother, Lady Staunton of Willingham, who, being recommended to drink goats' whey by the physicians, was to honour the Lodge at Roseneath with her residence, while her husband made a short tour in Scotland. But within the same cover, which had been given to Lady Staunton unsealed, was a letter from that lady, intended to prepare her sister for meeting her, and which, but for the Captain's negligence, she ought to have received on the preceding evening. It stated that the news in Jeanie's last letter had been so interesting to her husband, that he was determined to inquire farther into the confession made at Carlisle, and the fate of that poor innocent, and that, as he had been in some degree successful, she had, by the most earnest entreaties, extorted rather than obtained his permission, under promise of observing the most strict incognito, to spend a week or two with her sister, or in her neighbourhood, while he was prosecuting researches, to which (though it appeared to her very vainly) he seemed to attach some hopes of success.

There was a postscript, desiring that Jeanie would trust to Lady S. the management of their intercourse, and be content with assenting to what she should propose. After reading and again reading the letter, Mrs. Butler hurried downstairs, divided betwixt the fear of betraying her secret, and the desire to throw herself upon her sister's neck. Effie received her with a glance at once affectionate and cautionary, and immediately proceeded to speak.

"I have peen telling Mr. —, Captain —, this gentleman, Mrs. Butler, that if you could accommodate me with an apartment in your house, and a place for Ellis to sleep, and for the two men, it would suit me better than the Lodge, which his Grace has so kindly placed at my disposal. I am advised I should reside as near where the goats feed as possible."

"I have peen assuring my Leddy, Mrs. Putler," said Duncan, "that though it could not discommode you to receive any of his Grace's visitors or mine, yet she had mooch petter stay at the Lodge; and for the gaits, the creatures can be fetched there, in respect it is mair fitting they suld wait upon her Leddyship, than she upon the like of them."

"By no means derange the goats for me," said Lady Staunton; "I am certain the milk must be much better here." And this she said with languid negligence, as one whose slightest intimation of humour is to bear down all argument.

Mrs. Butler hastened to intimate, that her house, such as it was, was heartily at the disposal of Lady Staunton; but the Captain continued to remonstrate.

"The Duke," he said, "had written——"

"I will settle all that with his Grace——"

"And there were the things had been sent down frae Glasco——"

"Anything necessary might be sent over to the Parsonage —She would beg the favour of Mrs. Butler to show her an apartment, and of the Captain to have her trunks, &c., sent over from Roseneath."

So she courtesied off poor Duncan, who departed, saying in his secret soul, "Cot tamn her English impudence!—she takes possession of the minister's house as an it were her ain—and speaks to shentlemens as if they were pounden servants, an pe tamn'd to her!—And there's the deer that was shot too—but we will send it ower to the Manse, whilk will pe put civil, seeing I hae prought worthy Mrs. Putler sic a fliskmahoy."— And with these kind intentions, he went to the shore to give his orders accordingly.

In the meantime, the meeting of the sisters was as affectionate as it was extraordinary, and each evinced her feelings in the way proper to her character. Jeanie was so much overcome by wonder, and even by awe, that her feelings were deep, stunning, and almost overpowering. Effie, on the other hand, wept, laughed, sobbed, screamed, and clapped her hands for joy, all in the space of five minutes, giving way at once, and without reserve, to a natural excessive vivacity of temper, which no one, however, knew better how to restrain under the rules of artificial breeding.

After an hour had passed like a moment in their expressions of mutual affection, Lady Staunton observed the Captain walking with impatient steps below the window. "That tiresome Highland fool has returned upon our hands," she said. "I will pray him to grace us with his absence."

"Hout no! hout no!" said Mrs. Butler, in a tone of entreaty; "ye mauna affront the Captain."

"Affront?" said Lady Staunton; "nobody is ever affronted at what I do or say, my dear. However, I will endure him, since you think it proper."

The Captain was accordingly graciously requested by Lady Staunton to remain during dinner. During this visit his studious and punctilious complaisance towards the lady of rank was happily contrasted by the cavalier air of civil familiarity in which he indulged towards the minister's wife.

"I have not been able to persuade Mrs. Butler," said Lady Staunton to the Captain, during the interval when Jeanie had left the parlour, "to let me talk of making any recompense for storming her house, and garrisoning it in the way I have done."

"Doubtless, matam," said the Captain, "it wad ill pecome Mrs. Putler, wha is a very decent pody, to make any such sharge to a lady who comes from my house, or his Grace's, which is the same thing.—And, speaking of garrisons, in the year forty-five, I was poot with a garrison of twenty of my lads in the house of Inver-Garry, whilk had near been unhappily, for——"

"I beg your pardon, sir—But I wish I could think of some way of indemnifying this good lady."

"Oh, no need of intemnifying at all—no trouble for her, nothing at all—So, peing in the house of Inver-Garry, and the people about it being uncanny, I doubted the warst, and——"

"Do you happen to know, sir," said Lady Staunton, "if any of these two lads, these young Butlers, I mean, show any turn for the army?"

"Could not say, indeed, my leddy," replied Knockdunder—

"So, I knowing the people to pe unchancy, and not to lippen to, and hearing a pibroch in the wood, I pegan to pid my lads look to their flints, and then——"

"For," said Lady Staunton, with the most ruthless disregard to the narrative which she mangled by these interruptions, "if that should be the case, it should cost Sir George but the asking a pair of colours for one of them at the War Office, since we have always supported government, and never had occasion to trouble ministers."

"And if you please, my leddy," said Duncan, who began to find some savour in this proposal, "as I hae a braw weel-grown lad of a nevoy, ca'd Duncan MacGilligan, that is as pig as paith the Putler pairns putten thegither, Sir George could ask a pair for him at the same time, and it wad pe put ae asking for a'."

Lady Staunton only answered this hint with a well-bred stare, which gave no sort of encouragement.

Jeanie, who now returned, was lost in amazement at the wonderful difference betwixt the helpless and despairing girl, whom she had seen stretched on a flock-bed in a dungeon, expecting a violent and disgraceful death, and last as a forlorn exile upon the midnight beach, with the elegant, well-bred, beautiful woman before her. The features, now that her sister's veil was laid aside, did not appear so extremely different, as the whole manner, expression, look, and bearing. In outside show, Lady Staunton seemed completely a creature too soft and fair for sorrow to have touched; so much accustomed to have all her whims complied with by those around her, that she seemed to expect she should even be saved the trouble of forming them; and so totally unacquainted with contradiction, that she did not even use the tone of self-will, since to breathe a wish was to have it fulfilled. She made no ceremony of ridding herself of Duncan as soon as the evening approached; but complimented him out of the house under pretext of fatigue, with the utmost *nonchalance*.

When they were alone, her sister could not help expressing her wonder at the self-possession with which Lady Staunton sustained her part.

"I dare say you are suprised at it," said Lady Staunton composedly; "for you, my dear Jeanie, have been truth itself from your cradle upwards; but you must remember that I am a liar of fifteen years' standing, and therefore must by this time be used to my character."

In fact, during the feverish tumult of feelings excited during the two or three first days, Mrs. Butler thought her sister's manner was completely contradictory of the desponding tone which pervaded her correspondence. She was moved to tears, indeed, by the sight of her father's grave, marked by a modest stone, recording his piety and integrity; but lighter impressions and associations had also power over her. She amused herself with visiting the dairy, in which she had so long been assistant, and was so near discovering herself to May Hettly, by betraying her acquaintance with the celebrated receipt for Dunlop cheese, that she compared herself to Bedreddin Hassan, whom the vizier, his father-in-law, discovered by his superlative skill in composing cream-tarts with pepper in them. But when the novelty of such avocations ceased to amuse her, she showed to her sister but too plainly, that the gaudy colouring with which she veiled her unhappiness afforded as little real comfort, as the gay uniform of the soldier when it is drawn over his mortal wound. There were moods and moments, in which her despondence seemed to exceed even that which she herself had described in her letters, and which too well convinced Mrs. Butler how little her sister's lot, which in appearance was so brilliant, was in reality to be envied.

There was one source, however, from which Lady Staunton derived a pure degree of pleasure. Gifted in every particular with a higher degree of imagination than that of her sister, she was an admirer of the beauties of nature, a taste which compensates many evils to those who happen to enjoy it. Here her character of a fine lady stopped short, where she ought to have

> Scream'd at ilk cleugh, and screech'd at ilka how,
> As loud as she had seen the worrie-cow.

On the contrary, with the two boys for her guides, she undertook long and fatiguing walks among the neighbouring mountains to visit glens, lakes, waterfalls, or whatever scenes of natural wonder or beauty lay concealed among their recesses. It is Wordsworth, I think, who, talking of an old man under difficulties, remarks, with a singular attention to nature—

> ——whether it was care that spurred him,
> God only knows; but to the very last,
> He had the lightest foot in Ennerdale.

In the same manner, languid, listless, and unhappy, within doors, at times even indicating something which approached near to contempt of the homely accommodations of her sister's house, although she instantly endeavoured, by a thousand kindnesses, to atone for such ebullitions of spleen, Lady Staunton appeared to feel interest and energy while in the open air, and traversing the mountain landscapes in society with the two boys, whose ears she delighted with stories of what she had seen in other countries, and what she had to show them at Willingham Manor. And they, on the other hand, exerted themselves in doing the honours of Dumbarton-shire to the lady who seemed so kind, insomuch that there was scarce a glen in the neighbouring hills to which they did not introduce her.

Upon one of these excursions, while Reuben was otherwise employed, David alone acted as Lady Staunton's guide, and promised to show her a cascade in the hills, grander and higher than any they had yet visited. It was a walk of five long miles, and over rough ground, varied, however, and cheered, by mountain views, and peeps now of the firth and its islands, now of distant lakes, now of rocks and precipices. The scene itself, too, when they reached it, amply rewarded the labour of the walk. A single shoot carried a considerable stream over the face of a black rock, which contrasted strongly in colour with the white foam of the cascade, and, at the depth of about twenty feet, another rock intercepted the view of the bottom of the fall. The water, wheeling out far beneath, swept round the crag, which thus bounded their view, and tumbled down the rocky glen in a torrent of foam. Those who love nature always desire to penetrate into its utmost recesses, and Lady Staunton asked David whether there was not some mode of gaining a view of the abyss at the foot of the fall. He said that he knew a station on a shelf on the farther side of the intercepting rock, from which the whole waterfall was visible, but that the road to it was steep and slippery and dangerous. Bent, however, on gratifying her curiosity, she desired him to lead the way; and accordingly he did so over crag and stone, anxiously pointing out to her the resting-places where she ought to step, for their mode of advancing soon ceased to be walking, and became scrambling.

In this manner, clinging like sea-birds to the face of the rock, they were enabled at length to turn round it, and came full in front of the fall, which here had a most tremendous aspect, boiling, roaring, and thundering with unceasing din, into a black cauldron, a hundred feet at least below them, which resembled the crater of a volcano. The noise, the dashing of the waters, which gave an unsteady appearance to all around them, the trembling even of the huge crag on which they stood, the precariousness of their footing, for there was scarce room for them to stand on the shelf of rock which they had thus attained, had so powerful an effect on the senses and imagination of Lady Staunton, that she called out to David she was falling, and would in fact have dropped from the crag had he not caught hold of her. The boy was bold and stout of his age—still he was but fourteen years old, and as his assistance gave no confidence to Lady Staunton, she felt her situation become really perilous. The chance was, that, in the appalling novelty of the circumstances, he might have caught the infection of her panic, in which case it is likely that both must have perished. She now screamed with terror, though without hope of calling any one to her assistance. To her amazement, the scream was answered by a whistle from above, of a tone so clear and shrill, that it was heard even amid the noise of the waterfall.

In this moment of terror and perplexity, a human face, black, and having grizzled hair hanging down over the forehead and cheeks, and mixing with mustaches and a beard of the same colour, and as much matted and tangled, looked down on them from a broken part of the rock above.

" It is The Enemy! " said the boy, who had very nearly become incapable of supporting Lady Staunton.

" No, no," she exclaimed, inaccessible to supernatural terrors, and restored to the presence of mind of which she had been deprived by the danger of her situation, " it is a man—For God's sake, my friend, help us! "

The face glared at them, but made no answer; in a second or two afterwards, another, that of a young lad, appeared beside the first, equally swart and begrimed, but having tangled black hair, descending in elf locks, which gave an air of wildness and ferocity to the whole expression of the countenance. Lady Staunton repeated her entreaties, clinging to the rock with more energy, as she found that, from the superstitious terror of her guide, he became incapable of supporting her. Her words were probably drowned in the roar of the falling stream, for, though she observed the lips of the younger being whom she supplicated move as he spoke in reply, not a word reached her ear.

A moment afterwards it appeared he had not mistaken the

nature of her supplication, which, indeed, was easy to be understood from her situation and gestures. The younger apparition
disappeared, and immediately after lowered a ladder of twisted
osiers, about eight feet in length, and made signs to David
to hold it fast while the lady ascended. Despair gives courage,
and finding herself in this fearful predicament, Lady Staunton
did not hesitate to risk the ascent by the precarious means
which this accommodation afforded; and, carefully assisted
by the person who had thus providentially come to her aid,
she reached the summit in safety. She did not, however,
even look around her until she saw her nephew lightly and
actively follow her example, although there was now no one
to hold the ladder fast. When she saw him safe she looked
round, and could not help shuddering at the place and company
in which she found herself.

They were on a sort of platform of rock, surrounded on
every side by precipices, or overhanging cliffs, and which it
would have been scarce possible for any research to have discovered, as it did not seem to be commanded by any accessible
position. It was partly covered by a huge fragment of stone,
which, having fallen from the cliffs above, had been intercepted
by others in its descent, and jammed so as to serve for a
sloping roof to the farther part of the broad shelf or platform
on which they stood. A quantity of withered moss and leaves,
strewed beneath this rude and wretched shelter, showed the
lairs,—they could not be termed the beds,—of those who
dwelt in this eyry, for it deserved no other name. Of these,
two were before Lady Staunton. One, the same who had
afforded such timely assistance, stood upright before them, a
tall, lathy young savage; his dress a tattered plaid and philabeg, no shoes, no stockings, no hat or bonnet, the place of the
last being supplied by his hair, twisted and matted like the
glibbe of the ancient wild Irish, and, like theirs, forming a
natural thick-set, stout enough to bear off the cut of a sword.
Yet the eyes of the lad were keen and sparkling; his gesture
free and noble, like that of all savages. He took little notice
of David Butler, but gazed with wonder on Lady Staunton, as
a being different probably in dress, and superior in beauty,
to anything he had ever beheld. The old man, whose face
they had first seen, remained recumbent in the same posture
as when he had first looked down on them, only his face was
turned towards them as he lay and looked up with a lazy and
listless apathy, which belied the general expression of his dark

and rugged features. He seemed a very tall man, but was scarce better clad than the younger. He had on a loose Lowland greatcoat, and ragged tartan trews or pantaloons.

All around looked singularly wild and unpropitious. Beneath the brow of the incumbent rock was a charcoal fire, on which there was a still working, with bellows, pincers, hammers, a movable anvil, and other smith's tools; three guns, with two or three sacks and barrels, were disposed against the wall of rock, under shelter of the superincumbent crag; a dirk and two swords, and a Lochaber-axe, lay scattered around the fire, of which the red glare cast a ruddy tinge on the precipitous foam and mist of the cascade. The lad, when he had satisfied his curiosity with staring at Lady Staunton, fetched an earthen jar and a horn cup, into which he poured some spirits, apparently hot from the still, and offered them successively to the lady and to the boy. Both declined, and the young savage quaffed off the draught, which could not amount to less than three ordinary glasses. He then fetched another ladder from the corner of the tavern, if it could be termed so, adjusted it against the transverse rock, which served as a roof, and made signs for the lady to ascend it, while he held it fast below. She did so, and found herself on the top of a broad rock, near the brink of the chasm into which the brook precipitates itself. She could see the crest of the torrent flung loose down the rock, like the mane of a wild horse, but without having any view of the lower platform from which she had ascended.

David was not suffered to mount so easily; the lad, from sport or love of mischief, shook the ladder a good deal as he ascended, and seemed to enjoy the terror of young Butler, so that, when they had both come up, they looked on each other with no friendly eyes. Neither, however, spoke. The young caird, or tinker, or gipsy, with a good deal of attention, assisted Lady Staunton up a very perilous ascent which she had still to encounter, and they were followed by David Butler, until all three stood clear of the ravine on the side of a mountain, whose sides were covered with heather and sheets of loose shingle. So narrow was the chasm out of which they ascended, that, unless when they were on the very verge, the eye passed to the other side without perceiving the existence of a rent so fearful, and nothing was seen of the cataract, though its deep hoarse voice was still heard.

Lady Staunton, freed from the danger of rock and river,

had now a new subject of anxiety. Her two guides confronted each other with angry countenances; for David, though younger by two years at least, and much shorter, was a stout, well-set, and very bold boy.

"You are the black-coat's son of Knocktarlitie," said the young caird; "if you come here again, I'll pitch you down the linn like a football."

"Ay, lad, ye are very short to be sae lang," retorted young Butler undauntedly, and measuring his opponent's height with an undismayed eye; "I am thinking you are a gillie of Black Donacha; if you come down the glen, we'll shoot you like a wild buck."

"You may tell your father," said the lad, "that the leaf on the timber is the last he shall see—we will hae amends for the mischief he has done to us."

"I hope he will live to see mony simmers, and do ye muckle mair," answered David.

More might have passed, but Lady Staunton stepped between them with her purse in her hand, and taking out a guinea, of which it contained several, visible through the network, as well as some silver in the opposite end, offered it to the caird.

"The white siller, lady—the white siller," said the young savage, to whom the value of gold was probably unknown.

Lady Staunton poured what silver she had into his hand, and the juvenile savage snatched it greedily, and made a sort of half inclination of acknowledgment and adieu.

"Let us make haste now, Lady Staunton," said David, "for there will be little peace with them since they hae seen your purse."

They hurried on as fast as they could; but they had not descended the hill a hundred yards or two before they heard a halloo behind them, and looking back, saw both the old man and the young one pursuing them with great speed, the former with a gun on his shoulder. Very fortunately, at this moment a sportsman, a gamekeeper of the Duke, who was engaged in stalking deer, appeared on the face of the hill. The bandits stopped on seeing him, and Lady Staunton hastened to put herself under his protection. He readily gave them his escort home, and it required his athletic form and loaded rifle to restore to the lady her usual confidence and courage.

Donald listened with much gravity to the account of their adventure; and answered with great composure to David's repeated inquiries, whether he could have suspected that the cairds had been lurking there,—"Inteed, Master Tavie, I might hae had some guess that they were there, or thereabout, though maybe I had nane. But I am aften on the hill ; and they are like wasps—they stang only them that fashes them ; sae, for my part, I make a point not to see them, unless I were ordered out on the preceese errand by MacCallummore or Knockdunder, whilk is a clean different case."

They reached the Manse late ; and Lady Staunton, who had suffered much both from fright and fatigue, never again permitted her love of the picturesque to carry her so far among the mountains without a stronger escort than David, though she acknowledged he had won the stand of colours by the intrepidity he had displayed, so soon as assured he had to do with an earthly antagonist. " I couldna maybe hae made muckle o' a bargain wi' yon lang callant," said David, when thus complimented on his valour; " but when ye deal wi' thae folk, it's tyne heart tyne a'."

CHAPTER LI

——What see you there,
That hath so cowarded and chased your blood
Out of appearance ?

Henry the Fifth.

WE are under the necessity of returning to Edinburgh, where the General Assembly was now sitting. It is well known, that some Scottish nobleman is usually deputed as High Commissioner, to represent the person of the King in this convocation ; that he has allowances for the purpose of maintaining a certain outward show and solemnity, and supporting the hospitality of the representative of Majesty. Whoever is distinguished by rank, or office, in or near the capital, usually attend the morning levees of the Lord Commissioner, and walk with him in procession to the place where the Assembly meets.

The nobleman who held this office chanced to be particularly connected with Sir George Staunton, and it was in his train that he ventured to tread the High Street of Edinburgh for the first time since the fatal night of Porteous's execution. Walking at the right hand of the representative of Sovereignty, covered with lace and embroidery, and with all the paraphernalia of wealth and rank, the handsome though wasted form of the English stranger attracted all eyes. Who could have recognised in a form so aristocratic the plebeian convict, that, disguised in the rags of Madge Wildfire, had led the formidable rioters to their destined revenge? There was no possibility that this could happen, even if any of his ancient acquaintances, a race of men whose lives are so brief, had happened to survive the span commonly allotted to evil-doers. Besides, the whole affair had long fallen asleep, with the angry passions in which it originated. Nothing is more certain than that persons known to have had a share in that formidable riot, and to have fled from Scotland on that account, had made money abroad, returned to enjoy it in their native country, and lived and died undisturbed by the law.[1] The forbearance of the magistrate was in these instances wise, certainly, and just; for what good impression could be made on the public mind by punishment, when the memory of the offence was obliterated, and all that was remembered was the recent inoffensive, or perhaps exemplary, conduct of the offender?

Sir George Staunton might, therefore, tread the scene of his former audacious exploits, free from the apprehension of the law, or even of discovery or suspicion. But with what feelings his heart that day throbbed, must be left to those of the reader to imagine. It was an object of no common interest which had brought him to encounter so many painful remembrances.

In consequence of Jeanie's letter to Lady Staunton, transmitting the confession, he had visited the town of Carlisle, and had found Archdeacon Fleming still alive, by whom that confession had been received. This reverend gentleman, whose character stood deservedly very high, he so far admitted into his confidence, as to own himself the father of the unfortunate infant which had been spirited away by Madge Wildfire, representing the intrigue as a matter of juvenile extravagance on his own part, for which he was now anxious to atone, by tracing, if possible, what had become of the child. After some recollection of the circumstances, the clergyman was able to call to memory, that the unhappy woman had written a letter to George Staunton, Esq., younger, Rectory, Willingham, by Grantham; that he had forwarded it to the address accordingly, and that it had been returned, with a note from the Reverend Mr. Staunton, Rector of Willingham, saying, he knew no such person as him to whom the letter was addressed. As this had happened just at the time when George had, for the last time, absconded from his father's house to carry off Effie, he was at no loss to account for the cause of the resentment, under the influence of which his father had disowned him. This was another instance in which his ungovernable temper had occasioned his misfortune; had he remained at Willingham but a few days longer, he would have received Margaret Murdockson's letter, in which was exactly described the person and haunts of the woman, Annaple Bailzou, to whom she had parted with the infant. It appeared that Meg Murdockson had been induced to make this confession, less from any feelings of contrition, than from the desire of obtaining, through George Staunton or his father's means, protection and support for her daughter Madge. Her letter to George Staunton said, "That while the writer lived, her daughter would have needed nought from anybody, and that she would never have meddled in these affairs, except to pay back the ill that George had done to her and hers. But she was to die, and her daughter would be destitute, and without reason to guide her. She had lived in the world long enough to know that people did nothing for nothing;—so she had told George Staunton all he could wish to know about his wean, in hopes he would not see the demented young creature he had ruined perish for want. As for her motives for not telling them sooner, she had a long account to reckon for in the next world, and she would reckon for that too."

The clergyman said, that Meg had died in the same desperate state of mind, occasionally expressing some regret about the child which was lost, but oftener sorrow that the mother had not been hanged—her mind at once a chaos of guilt, rage, and apprehension for her daughter's future safety; that instinctive feeling of parental anxiety which she had in common with the she-wolf and lioness, being the last shade of kindly affection that occupied a breast equally savage.

The melancholy catastrophe of Madge Wildfire was occasioned by her taking the confusion of her mother's execution, as affording an opportunity of leaving the workhouse to which the clergyman had sent her, and presenting herself to the mob in their fury, to perish in the way we have already seen. When Dr. Fleming found the convict's letter was returned from Lincolnshire, he wrote to a friend in Edinburgh, to inquire into the fate of the unfortunate girl whose child had been stolen, and was informed by his correspondent, that she had been pardoned, and that, with all her family, she had retired to some distant part of Scotland, or left the kingdom entirely. And here the matter rested, until, at Sir George Staunton's application, the clergyman looked out, and produced Margaret Murdockson's returned letter, and the other memoranda which he had kept concerning the affair.

Whatever might be Sir George Staunton's feelings in ripping up this miserable history, and listening to the tragical fate of the unhappy girl whom he had ruined, he had so much of his ancient wilfulness of disposition left, as to shut his eyes on everything, save the prospect which seemed to open itself of recovering his son. It was true, it would be difficult to produce him, without telling much more of the history of his birth, and the misfortunes of his parents, than it was prudent to make known. But let him once be found, and, being found, let him but prove worthy of his father's protection, and many ways might be fallen upon to avoid such risk. Sir George Staunton was at liberty to adopt him as his heir, if he pleased, without communicating the secret of his birth ; or an Act of Parliament might be obtained, declaring him legitimate, and allowing him the name and arms of his father. He was, indeed, already a legitimate child according to the law of Scotland, by the subsequent marriage of his parents. Wilful in everything, Sir George's sole desire now was to see this son, even should his recovery bring with it a new series of misfortunes, as dreadful as those which followed on his being lost.

But where was the youth who might eventually be called to the honours and estates of this ancient family? On what heath was he wandering, and shrouded by what mean disguise? Did he gain his precarious bread by some petty trade, by menial toil, by violence, or by theft? These were questions on which Sir George's anxious investigations could obtain no light. Many remembered that Annaple Bailzou wandered through the country as a beggar and fortune-teller, or spaewife—some remembered that she had been seen with an infant in 1737 or 1738, but for more than ten years she had not travelled that district; and that she had been heard to say she was going to a distant part of Scotland, of which country she was a native. To Scotland, therefore, came Sir George Staunton, having parted with his lady at Glasgow ;

and his arrival at Edinburgh happening to coincide with the sitting of the General Assembly of the Kirk, his acquaintance with the nobleman who held the office of Lord High Commissioner forced him more into public than suited either his views or inclinations.

At the public table of this nobleman, Sir George Staunton was placed next to a clergyman of respectable appearance, and well-bred, though plain demeanour, whose name he discovered to be Butler. It had been no part of Sir George's plan to take his brother-in-law into his confidence, and he had rejoiced exceedingly in the assurances he received from his wife, that Mrs. Butler, the very soul of integrity and honour, had never suffered the account he had given of himself at Willingham Rectory to transpire, even to her husband. But he was not sorry to have an opportunity to converse with so near a connection, without being known to him, and to form a judgment of his character and understanding. He saw much, and heard more, to raise Butler very high in his opinion. He found he was generally respected by those of his own profession, as well as by the laity who had seats in the Assembly. He had made several public appearances in the Assembly, distinguished by good sense, candour, and ability; and he was followed and admired as a sound, and, at the same time, an eloquent preacher.

This was all very satisfactory to Sir George Staunton's pride, which had revolted at the idea of his wife's sister being obscurely married. He now began, on the contrary, to think the connection so much better than he expected, that, if it should be necessary to acknowledge it, in consequence of the recovery of his son, it would sound well enough that Lady Staunton had a sister, who, in the decayed state of the family, had married a Scottish clergyman, high in the opinion of his countrymen, and a leader in the Church.

It was with these feelings, that, when the Lord High Commissioner's company broke up, Sir George Staunton, under pretence of prolonging some inquiries concerning the constitution of the Church of Scotland, requested Butler to go home to his lodgings in the Lawnmarket, and drink a cup of coffee. Butler agreed to wait upon him, providing Sir George would permit him, in passing, to call at a friend's house where he resided, and make his apology for not coming to partake her tea. They proceeded up the High Street, entered the Krames, and passed the begging-box, placed to remind those at liberty of the distresses of the poor prisoners. Sir George paused there one instant, and next day a £20 note was found in that receptacle for public charity.

When he came up to Butler again, he found him with his eyes fixed on the entrance of the Tolbooth, and apparently in deep thought.

"That seems a very strong door," said Sir George, by way of saying something.

"It is so, sir," said Butler, turning off and beginning to walk forward, " but it was my misfortune at one time to see it prove greatly too weak."

At this moment, looking at his companion, he asked him whether he felt himself ill? and Sir George Staunton admitted, that he had been so foolish as to eat ice, which sometimes disagreed with him. With kind officiousness, that would not be gainsaid, and ere he could find out where he was going, Butler hurried Sir George into the friend's house, near to the prison, in which he himself had lived since he came to town, being, indeed, no other than that of our old friend Bartoline Saddletree, in which Lady Staunton had served a short noviciate as a shop-maid. This recollection rushed on her husband's mind, and the blush of shame which it excited overpowered the sensation of fear which had produced his former paleness. Good Mrs. Saddletree, however, bustled about to receive the rich English baronet as the friend of Mr. Butler, and requested an elderly female in a black gown to sit still, in a way which seemed to imply a wish, that she would clear the way for her betters. In the meanwhile, understanding the state of the case, she ran to get some cordial waters, sovereign, of course, in all cases of faintishness whatsoever. During her absence, her visitor, the female in black, made some progress out of the room, and might have left it altogether without particular observation, had she not stumbled at the threshold, so near Sir George Staunton, that he, in point of civility, raised her and assisted her to the door.

"Mrs. Porteous is turned very doited now, puir body," said Mrs. Saddletree, as she returned with her bottle in her hand —"She is no sae auld, but she got a sair back-cast wi' the slaughter o' her husband—Ye had some trouble about that job, Mr. Butler.—I think, sir," to Sir George, "ye had better drink out the haill glass, for to my een ye look waur than when ye came in."

And, indeed, he grew as pale as a corpse, on recollecting

who it was that his arm had so lately supported—the widow whom he had so large a share in making such.

"It is a prescribed job that case of Porteous now," said old Saddletree, who was confined to his chair by the gout—"clean prescribed and out of date."

"I am not clear of that, neighbour," said Plumdamas, "for I have heard them say twenty years should rin, and this is but the fifty-ane—Porteous's mob was in thretty-seven."

"Ye'll no teach me law, I think, neighbour—me that has four gaun pleas, and might hae had fourteen, an it hadna been the gudewife? I tell ye, if the foremost of the Porteous mob were standing there where that gentleman stands, the King's Advocate wadna meddle wi' him—it fa's under the negative prescription."

"Haud your din, carles," said Mrs. Saddletree, "and let the gentleman sit down and get a dish of comfortable tea."

But Sir George had had quite enough of their conversation; and Butler, at his request, made an apology to Mrs. Saddletree, and accompanied him to his lodgings. Here they found another guest waiting Sir George Staunton's return. This was no other than our reader's old acquaintance, Ratcliffe.

This man had exercised the office of turnkey with so much vigilance, acuteness, and fidelity, that he gradually rose to be governor, or captain of the Tolbooth. And it is yet remembered in tradition, that young men, who rather sought amusing than select society in their merry-meetings, used sometimes to request Ratcliffe's company, in order that he might regale them with legends of his extraordinary feats in the way of robbery and escape.[1] But he lived and died without resuming his original vocation, otherwise than in his narratives over a bottle.

Under these circumstances, he had been recommended to Sir George Staunton by a man of the law in Edinburgh, as a person likely to answer any questions he might have to ask about Annaple Bailzou, who, according to the colour which Sir George Staunton gave to his cause of inquiry, was supposed to have stolen a child in the west of England,

[1] There seems an anachronism in the history of this person. Ratcliffe, among other escapes from justice, was released by the Porteous mob when under sentence of death; and he was again under the same predicament when the Highlanders made a similar jail-delivery in 1745. He was too sincere a Whig to embrace liberation at the hands of the Jacobites, and in reward was made one of the keepers of the Tolbooth. So at least runs a constant tradition.

belonging to a family in which he was interested. The gentleman had not mentioned his name, but only his official title; so that Sir George Staunton, when told that the captain of the Tolbooth was waiting for him in his parlour, had no idea of meeting his former acquaintance, Jem Ratcliffe.

This, therefore, was another new and most unpleasant surprise, for he had no difficulty in recollecting this man's remarkable features. The change, however, from George Robertson to Sir George Staunton, baffled even the penetration of Ratcliffe, and he bowed very low to the baronet and his guest, hoping Mr. Butler would excuse his recollecting that he was an old acquaintance.

"And once rendered my wife a piece of great service," said Mr. Butler, "for which she sent you a token of grateful acknowledgment, which I hope came safe and was welcome."

"Deil a doubt on't," said Ratcliffe, with a knowing nod; "but ye are muckle changed for the better since I saw ye, Maister Butler."

"So much so, that I wonder you knew me."

"Aha, then!—Deil a face I see I ever forget," said Ratcliffe; while Sir George Staunton, tied to the stake, and incapable of escaping, internally cursed the accuracy of his memory. "And yet, sometimes," continued Ratcliffe, "the sharpest hand will be ta'en in. There is a face in this very room, if I might presume to be sae bauld, that if I didna ken the honourable person it belangs to—I might think it had some cast of an auld acquaintance."

"I should not be much flattered," answered the Baronet sternly, and roused by the risk in which he saw himself placed, "if it is to me you mean to apply that compliment."

"By no manner of means, sir," said Ratcliffe, bowing very low; "I am come to receive your honour's commands, and no to trouble your honour wi' my poor observations."

"Well, sir," said Sir George, "I am told you understand police matters—So do I.—To convince you of which, here are ten guineas of retaining fee—I make them fifty when you can find me certain notice of a person, living or dead, whom you will find described in that paper. I shall leave town presently—you may send your written answer to me to the care of Mr. —— " (naming his highly respectable agent), "or of his Grace the Lord High Commissioner." Ratcliffe bowed and withdrew.

"I have angered the proud peat now," he said to himself,

" by finding out a likeness—but if George Robertson's father had lived within a mile of his mother, d—n me if I should not know what to think, for as high as he carries his head."

When he was left alone with Butler, Sir George Staunton ordered tea and coffee, which were brought by his valet, and then, after considering with himself for a minute, asked his guest whether he had lately heard from his wife and family. Butler, with some surprise at the question, replied, " that he had received no letter for some time ; his wife was a poor pen-woman."

"Then," said Sir George Staunton, "I am the first to inform you there has been an invasion of your quiet premises since you left home.   My wife, whom the Duke of Argyle had the goodness to permit to use Roseneath Lodge, while she was spending some weeks in your country, has sallied across and taken up her quarters in the Manse, as she says, to be nearer the goats, whose milk she is using ; but I believe, in reality, because she prefers Mrs. Butler's company to that of the respectable gentleman who acts as seneschal on the Duke's domains."

Mr. Butler said, " He had often heard the late Duke and the present speak with high respect of Lady Staunton, and was happy if his house could accommodate any friend of theirs—it would be but a very slight acknowledgment of the many favours he owed them."

"That does not make Lady Staunton and myself the less obliged to your hospitality, sir," said Sir George.   "May I inquire if you think of returning home soon?"

"In the course of two days," Mr. Butler answered, "his duty in the Assembly would be ended ; and the other matters he had in town being all finished, he was desirous of returning to Dumbartonshire as soon as he could ; but he was under the necessity of transporting a considerable sum in bills and money with him, and therefore wished to travel in company with one or two of his brethren of the clergy."

"My escort will be more safe," said Sir George Staunton, "and I think of setting off to-morrow or next day.   If you will give me the pleasure of your company, I will undertake to deliver you and your charge safe at the Manse, provided you will admit me along with you."

Mr. Butler gratefully accepted of this proposal ; the appointment was made accordingly, and by despatches with one of Sir George's servants, who was sent forward for the purpose, the inhabitants of the manse of Knocktarlitie were made acquainted with the intended journey ; and the news rung through the whole vicinity, "that the minister was coming back wi' a braw English gentleman, and a' the siller that was to pay for the estate of Craigsture."

This sudden resolution of going to Knocktarlitie had been adopted by Sir George Staunton in consequence of the incidents of the evening. In spite of his present consequence, he felt he had presumed too far in venturing so near the scene of his former audacious acts of violence, and he knew too well, from past experience, the acuteness of a man like Ratcliffe, again to encounter him. The next two days he kept his lodgings, under pretence of indisposition, and took leave, by writing, of his noble friend, the High Commissioner, alleging the opportunity of Mr. Butler's company as a reason for leaving Edinburgh sooner than he had proposed. He had a long conference with his agent on the subject of Annaple Bailzou ; and the professional gentleman, who was the agent also of the Argyle family, had directions to collect all the information which Ratcliffe or others might be able to obtain concerning the fate of that woman and the unfortunate child, and, so soon as anything transpired which had the least appearance of being important, that he should send an express with it instantly to Knocktarlitie. These instructions were backed with a deposit of money, and a request that no expense might be spared ; so that Sir George Staunton had little reason to apprehend negligence on the part of the persons entrusted with the commission.

The journey, which the brothers made in company, was attended with more pleasure, even to Sir George Staunton, than he had ventured to expect. His heart lightened in spite of himself when they lost sight of Edinburgh ; and the easy, sensible conversation of Butler was well calculated to withdraw his thoughts from painful reflections. He even began to think whether there could be much difficulty in removing his wife's connections to the Rectory of Willingham ; it was only on his part procuring some still better preferment for the present incumbent, and on Butler's, that he should take orders according to the English church, to which he could not conceive a possibility of his making objection, and then he had them residing under his wing. No doubt, there was pain in seeing Mrs. Butler, acquainted, as he knew her to be, with the full truth of his evil history—But then her silence, though he had no reason to complain of her indiscretion hitherto, was still more absolutely ensured. It would keep his lady, also, both in good temper and in more subjection; for she was sometimes troublesome to him, by insisting on remaining in town when he desired to retire to the country, alleging the total want of society at Willingham. "Madam, your sister is there," would, he thought, be a sufficient answer to this ready argument.

He sounded Butler on this subject, asking what he would think of an English living of twelve hundred pounds yearly, with the burden of affording his company now and then to a neighbour whose health was not strong, or his spirits equal. "He might meet," he said, "occasionally, a very learned and accomplished gentleman, who was in orders as a Catholic priest, but he hoped that would be no insurmountable objection to a man of his liberality of sentiment. What," he said, "would Mr. Butler think of as an answer, if the offer should be made to him?"

"Simply that I could not accept of it," said Mr. Butler. "I have no mind to enter into the various debates between the churches; but I was brought up in mine own, have received her ordination, am satisfied of the truth of her doctrines, and will die under the banner I have enlisted to.'

"What may be the value of your preferment?" said Sir George Staunton, "unless I am asking an indiscreet question."

"Probably one hundred a year, one year with another, besides my glebe and pasture-ground."

"And you scruple to exchange that for twelve hundred a year, without alleging any damning difference of doctrine betwixt the two Churches of England and Scotland?"

"On that, sir, I have reserved my judgment; there may be much good, and there are certainly saving means in both, but every man must act according to his own lights. I hope I have done, and am in the course of doing, my Master's work in this Highland parish; and it would ill become me, for the sake of lucre, to leave my sheep in the wilderness. But, even in the temporal view which you have taken of the matter, Sir George, this hundred pounds a year of stipend hath fed and clothed us, and left us nothing to wish for; my father-in-law's succession, and other circumstances, have added a small estate of about twice as much more, and how we are to dispose of it I do not know—So I leave it to you, sir, to think if I were wise, not having the wish or opportunity of spending three hundred a year, to covet the possession of four times that sum."

"This is philosophy," said Sir George; "I have heard of it, but I never saw it before."

"It is common sense," replied Butler, "which accords with philosophy and religion more frequently than pedants or zealots are apt to admit."

Sir George turned the subject, and did not again resume it. Although they travelled in Sir George's chariot, he seemed so much fatigued with the motion, that it was necessary for him to remain for a day at a small town called Mid-Calder, which was their first stage from Edinburgh. Glasgow occupied another day, so slow were their motions.

They travelled on to Dumbarton, where they had resolved to leave the equipage, and to hire a boat to take them to the shores near the Manse, as the Gare-Loch lay betwixt them and that point, besides the impossibility of travelling in that district with wheel-carriages. Sir George's valet, a man of trust, accompanied them, as also a footman; the grooms were left with the carriage. Just as this arrangement was completed, which was about four o'clock in the afternoon, an express arrived from Sir George's agent in Edinburgh, with a packet, which he opened and read with great attention, appearing much interested and agitated by the contents. The packet had been despatched very soon after their leaving Edinburgh, but the messenger had missed the travellers by passing through Mid-Calder in the night, and overshot his errand by getting to Roseneath before them. He was now on his return, after having waited more than four-and-twenty hours. Sir George Staunton instantly wrote back an answer, and, rewarding the messenger liberally, desired him not to sleep till he placed it in his agent's hands.

At length they embarked in the boat, which had waited for them some time. During their voyage, which was slow, for they were obliged to row the whole way, and often against the tide, Sir George Staunton's inquiries ran chiefly on the subject of the Highland banditti who had infested that country since the year 1745. Butler informed him, that many of them were not native Highlanders, but gipsies, tinkers, and other men of desperate fortunes, who had taken advantage of the confusion introduced by the civil war, the general discontent of the mountaineers, and the unsettled state of police, to practise their plundering trade with more audacity. Sir George next inquired into their lives, their habits, whether the violences which they committed were not sometimes atoned for by acts of generosity, and whether they did not possess the virtues, as well as the vices, of savage tribes?

Butler answered, that certainly they did sometimes show sparks of generosity, of which even the worst class of male-factors are seldom utterly divested; but that their evil pro-pensities were certain and regular principles of action, while any occasional burst of virtuous feeling was only a transient impulse not to be reckoned upon, and excited probably by some singular and unusual concatenation of circumstances. In discussing these inquiries, which Sir George pursued with an apparent eagerness that rather surprised Butler, the latter chanced to mention the name of Donacha Dhu na Dunaigh, with which the reader is already acquainted. Sir George caught the sound up eagerly, and as if it conveyed particular interest to his ear. He made the most minute inquiries con-cerning the man whom he mentioned, the number of his gang, and even the appearance of those who belonged to it. Upon these points Butler could give little answer. The man had a name among the lower class, but his exploits were con-siderably exaggerated; he had always one or two fellows with him, but never aspired to the command of above three or four. In short, he knew little about him, and the small acquaintance he had, had by no means inclined him to desire more.

"Nevertheless, I should like to see him some of these days."

"That would be a dangerous meeting, Sir George, unless you mean we are to see him receive his deserts from the law, and then it were a melancholy one."

"Use every man according to his deserts, Mr. Butler, and who shall escape whipping? But I am talking riddles to you. I will explain them more fully to you when I have spoken over the subject with Lady Staunton.—Pull away, my lads," he added, addressing himself to the rowers; "the clouds threaten us with a storm."

In fact, the dead and heavy closeness of the air, the huge piles of clouds which assembled in the western horizon, and glowed like a furnace under the influence of the setting sun—that awful stillness in which nature seems to expect the thunder-burst, as a condemned soldier waits for the platoon-fire which is to stretch him on the earth, all betokened a speedy storm.

Large broad drops fell from time to time, and induced the gentlemen to assume the boat-cloaks; but the rain again ceased, and the oppressive heat, so unusual in Scotland in the end of May, inclined them to throw them aside. "There is something solemn in this delay of the storm," said Sir George; "it seems as if it suspended its peal till it solemnised some important event in the world below."

"Alas!" replied Butler, "what are we, that the laws of nature should correspond in their march with our ephemeral deeds or sufferings? The clouds will burst when surcharged with the electric fluid, whether a goat is falling at that instant from the cliffs of Arran, or a hero expiring on the field of battle he has won."

"The mind delights to deem it otherwise," said Sir George Staunton; "and to dwell on the fate of humanity as on that which is the prime central movement of the mighty machine. We love not to think that we shall mix with the ages that have gone before us, as these broad black raindrops mingle with the waste of waters, making a trifling and momentary eddy, and are then lost for ever."

"*For ever!*—we are not—we cannot be lost for ever," said Butler, looking upward; "death is to us change, not consummation; and the commencement of a new existence, corresponding in character to the deeds which we have done in the body."

While they agitated these grave subjects, to which the solemnity of the approaching storm naturally led them, their voyage threatened to be more tedious than they expected, for gusts of wind, which rose and fell with sudden impetuosity, swept the bosom of the firth, and impeded the efforts of the rowers. They had now only to double a small headland, in order to get to the proper landing-place in the mouth of the little river; but in the state of the weather, and the boat being heavy, this was like to be a work of time, and in the meanwhile they must necessarily be exposed to the storm.

"Could we not land on this side of the headland," asked Sir George, "and so gain some shelter?"

Butler knew of no landing-place, at least none affording a convenient or even practicable passage up the rocks which surrounded the shore.

"Think again," said Sir George Staunton; "the storm will soon be violent."

"Hout, ay," said one of the boatmen, "there's the Caird's

Cove; but we dinna tell the minister about it, and I am no sure if I can steer the boat to it, the bay is sae fu' o' shoals and sunk rocks."

"Try," said Sir George, "and I will give you half-a-guinea."

The old fellow took the helm, and observed, "that if they could get in, there was a steep path up from the beach, and half-an-hour's walk from thence to the Manse."

"Are you sure you know the way?" said Butler to the old man.

"I maybe kend it a wee better fifteen years syne, when Dandie Wilson was in the firth wi' his clean-ganging lugger. I mind Dandie had a wild young Englisher wi' him, that they ca'd——"

"If you chatter so much," said Sir George Staunton, "you will have the boat on the Grindstone—bring that white rock in a line with the steeple."

"By G——," said the veteran, staring, "I think your honour kens the bay as weel as me.—Your honour's nose has been on the Grindstane ere now, I'm thinking."

As they spoke thus, they approached the little cove, which, concealed behind crags, and defended on every point by shallows and sunken rocks, could scarce be discovered or approached, except by those intimate with the navigation. An old shattered boat was already drawn up on the beach within the cove, close beneath the trees, and with precautions for concealment.

Upon observing this vessel, Butler remarked to his companion, "It is impossible for you to conceive, Sir George, the difficulty I have had with my poor people, in teaching them the guilt and the danger of this contraband trade—yet they have perpetually before their eyes all its dangerous consequences. I do not know anything that more effectually depraves and ruins their moral and religious principles."

Sir George forced himself to say something in a low voice, about the spirit of adventure natural to youth, and that unquestionably many would become wiser as they grew older.

"Too seldom, sir," replied Butler. "If they have been deeply engaged, and especially if they have mingled in the scenes of violence and blood to which their occupation naturally leads, I have observed, that, sooner or later, they come to an evil end. Experience, as well as Scripture, teaches us, Sir George, that mischief shall hunt the violent man, and that the bloodthirsty man shall not live half his days—But take my arm to help you ashore."

Sir George needed assistance, for he was contrasting in his altered thought the different feelings of mind and frame with which he had formerly frequented the same place. As they landed, a low growl of thunder was heard at a distance.

"That is ominous, Mr. Butler," said Sir George.

"*Intonuit lœvum*—it is ominous of good, then," answered Butler, smiling.

The boatmen were ordered to make the best of their way round the headland to the ordinary landing-place; the two gentlemen, followed by their servant, sought their way by a blind and tangled path, through a close copsewood to the Manse of Knocktarlitie, where their arrival was anxiously expected.

The sisters in vain had expected their husbands' return on the preceding day, which was that appointed by Sir George's letter. The delay of the travellers at Calder had occasioned this breach of appointment. The inhabitants of the Manse began even to doubt whether they would arrive on the present day. Lady Staunton felt this hope of delay as a brief reprieve; for she dreaded the pangs which her husband's pride must undergo at meeting with a sister-in-law, to whom the whole of his unhappy and dishonourable history was too well known. She knew, whatever force or constraint he might put upon his feelings in public, that she herself must be doomed to see them display themselves in full vehemence in secret,—consume his health, destroy his temper, and render him at once an object of dread and compassion. Again and again she cautioned Jeanie to display no tokens of recognition, but to receive him as a perfect stranger,—and again and again Jeanie renewed her promise to comply with her wishes.

Jeanie herself could not fail to bestow an anxious thought on the awkwardness of the approaching meeting; but her conscience was ungalled—and then she was cumbered with many household cares of an unusual nature, which, joined to the anxious wish once more to see Butler, after an absence of unusual length, made her extremely desirous that the travellers should arrive as soon as possible. And—why should I disguise the truth?—ever and anon a thought stole across her mind that her gala dinner had now been postponed for two days; and how few of the dishes, after every art of her simple *cuisine* had been exerted to dress them, could with any

credit or propriety appear again upon the third; and what
was she to do with the rest?—Upon this last subject she
was saved the trouble of farther deliberation, by the sudden
appearance of the Captain at the head of half-a-dozen stout
fellows, dressed and armed in the Highland fashion.

"Goot-morrow morning to ye, Leddy Staunton, and I hope
I hae the pleasure to see ye weel—And goot-morrow to you,
goot Mrs. Putler—I do peg you will order some victuals and
ale and prandy for the lads, for we hae peen out on firth and
moor since afore daylight, and a' to no purpose neither—
Cot tam!"

So saying, he sate down, pushed back his brigadier wig,
and wiped his head with an air of easy importance; totally
regardless of the look of well-bred astonishment by which
Lady Staunton endeavoured to make him comprehend that
he was assuming too great a liberty.

"It is some comfort, when one has had a sair tussell," continued the Captain, addressing Lady Staunton, with an air of
gallantry, "that it is in a fair leddy's service, or in the service
of a gentleman whilk has a fair leddy, whilk is the same thing,
since serving the husband is serving the wife, as Mrs. Putler
does very weel know."

"Really, sir," said Lady Staunton, "as you seem to intend
this compliment for me, I am at a loss to know what interest
Sir George or I can have in your movements this morning."

"O Cot tam!—this is too cruel, my leddy—as if it was not
py special express from his Grace's honourable agent and
commissioner at Edinburgh, with a warrant conform, that
I was to seek for and apprehend Donacha dhu na Dunaigh,
and pring him pefore myself and Sir George Staunton, that
he may have his deserts, that is to say, the gallows, whilk he
has doubtless deserved, py peing the means of frightening
your leddyship, as weel as for something of less importance."

"Frightening me?" said her ladyship; "why, I never
wrote to Sir George about my alarm at the waterfall."

"Then he must have heard it otherwise; for what else can
give him sic an earnest tesire to see this rapscallion, that
I maun ripe the haill mosses and muirs in the country for
him, as if I were to get something for finding him, when the
pest o't might pe a pall through my prains?"

"Can it be really true, that it is on Sir George's account
that you have been attempting to apprehend this fellow?"

"Py Cot, it is for no other cause that I know than his

honour's pleasure; for the creature might hae gone on in a decent quiet way for me, sae lang as he respectit the Duke's pounds—put reason goot he suld be taen, and hangit to poot, if it may pleasure ony honourable shentleman that is the Duke's friend—Sae I got the express over night, and I caused warn half a score of pretty lads, and was up in the morning pefore the sun, and I garr'd the lads take their kilts and short coats."

"I wonder you did that, Captain," said Mrs. Butler, "when you know the Act of Parliament against wearing the Highland dress."

"Hout, tout, ne'er fash your thumb, Mrs. Putler. The law is put twa-three years auld yet, and is ower young to hae come our length; and pesides, how is the lads to climb the praes wi' thae tamn'd breekens on them? It makes me sick to see them. Put ony how, I thought I kend Donacha's haunts gey and weel, and I was at the place where he had rested yestreen; for I saw the leaves the limmers had lain on, and the ashes of them; by the same token there was a pit greeshoch purning yet. I am thinking they got some word out o' the island what was intended—I sought every glen and cleuch, as if I had been deer-stalking, but teil a wauff of his coat-tail could I see—Cot tam!"

"He'll be away down the firth to Cowal," said David; and Reuben, who had been out early that morning a-nutting, observed, "That he had seen a boat making for the Caird's Cove;" a place well known to the boys, though their less adventurous father was ignorant of its existence.

"Py Cot," said Duncan, "then I will stay here no longer than to trink this very horn of prandy and water, for it is very possible they will pe in the wood. Donacha's a clever fellow, and maybe thinks it pest to sit next the chimley when the lum reeks. He thought naebody would look for him sae near hand! I peg your leddyship will excuse my aprupt departure, as I will return forthwith, and I will either pring you Donacha in life, or else his head, whilk I dare to say will be as satisfactory. And I hope to pass a pleasant evening with your leddyship; and I hope to have mine revenges on Mr. Putler at packgammon, for the four pennies whilk he won, for he will pe surely at home soon, or else he will have a wet journey, seeing it is apout to pe a scud."

Thus saying, with many scrapes and bows, and apologies for leaving them, which were very readily received, and reiterated assurances of his speedy return (of the sincerity whereof Mrs. Butler entertained no doubt, so long as her best greybeard of brandy was upon duty), Duncan left the Manse, collected his followers, and began to scour the close and entangled wood which lay between the little glen and the Caird's Cove. David, who was a favourite with the Captain, on account of his spirit and courage, took the opportunity of escaping, to attend the investigations of that great man.

CHAPTER LII

———I did send for thee,
That Talbot's name might be in thee revived,
When sapless age, and weak unable limbs,
Should bring thy father to his drooping chair.
But—O malignant and ill-boding stars!—
First Part of Henry the Sixth.

DUNCAN and his party had not proceeded very far in the direction of the Caird's Cove before they heard a shot, which was quickly followed by one or two others. "Some tamn'd villains among the roedeer," said Duncan; "look sharp out, lads."

The clash of swords was next heard, and Duncan and his myrmidons, hastening to the spot, found Butler and Sir George Staunton's servant in the hands of four ruffians. Sir George himself lay stretched on the ground, with his drawn sword in his hand. Duncan, who was as brave as a lion, instantly fired his pistol at the leader of the band, unsheathed his sword, cried out to his men, *Claymore!* and run his weapon through the body of the fellow whom he had previously wounded, who was no other than Donacha dhu na Dunaigh himself. The other banditti were speedily overpowered, excepting one young lad, who made wonderful resistance for his years, and was at length secured with difficulty.

Butler, so soon as he was liberated from the ruffians, ran to raise Sir George Staunton, but life had wholly left him.

"A creat misfortune," said Duncan; "I think it will pe pest that I go forward to intimate it to the coot leddy.— Tavie, my dear, you hae smelled pouther for the first time this day—take my sword and hack off Donacha's head, whilk will pe coot practice for you against the time you may wish to do the same kindness to a living shentleman—or hould, as your father does not approve, you may leave it alone, as he will pe a greater object of satisfaction to Leddy Staunton to see him entire; and I hope she will do me the credit to pelieve that I can afenge a shentleman's plood fery speedily and well."

Such was the observation of a man too much accustomed to the ancient state of manners in the Highlands, to look upon the issue of such a skirmish as anything worthy of wonder or emotion.

We will not attempt to describe the very contrary effect which the unexpected disaster produced upon Lady Staunton, when the bloody corpse of her husband was brought to the house, where she expected to meet him alive and well. All was forgotten, but that he was the lover of her youth; and whatever were his faults to the world, that he had towards her exhibited only those that arose from the inequality of spirits and temper, incident to a situation of unparalleled difficulty. In the vivacity of her grief she gave way to all the natural irritability of her temper; shriek followed shriek, and swoon succeeded swoon. It required all Jeanie's watchful affection to prevent her from making known, in these paroxysms of affliction, much which it was of the highest importance that she should keep secret.

At length silence and exhaustion succeeded to frenzy, and Jeanie stole out to take counsel with her husband, and to exhort him to anticipate the Captain's interference, by taking possession in Lady Staunton's name, of the private papers of her deceased husband. To the utter astonishment of Butler, she now, for the first time, explained the relation betwixt herself and Lady Staunton, which authorised, nay, demanded, that he should prevent any stranger from being unnecessarily made acquainted with her family affairs. It was in such a crisis that Jeanie's active and undaunted habits of virtuous exertion were most conspicuous. While the Captain's attention was still engaged by a prolonged refreshment, and a very tedious examination, in Gaelic and English, of all the prisoners, and every other witness of the fatal transaction, she had the body of her brother-in-law undressed and properly disposed.— It then appeared, from the crucifix, the beads, and the shirt of hair which he wore next his person, that his sense of guilt had induced him to receive the dogmata of a religion, which pretends, by the maceration of the body, to expiate the crimes of the soul. In the packet of papers, which the express had brought to Sir George Staunton from Edinburgh, and which Butler, authorised by his connection with the deceased, did not scruple to examine, he found new and astonishing intelligence, which gave him reason to thank God he had taken that measure.

Ratcliffe, to whom all sorts of misdeeds and misdoers were familiar, instigated by the promised reward, soon found himself in a condition to trace the infant of these unhappy parents. The woman to whom Meg Murdockson had sold that most unfortunate child, had made it the companion of her wanderings and her beggary, until he was about seven or eight years old, when, as Ratcliffe learned from a companion of hers, then in the Correction House of Edinburgh, she sold him in her turn to Donacha dhu na Dunaigh. This man, to whom no act of mischief was unknown, was occasionally an agent in a horrible trade then carried on betwixt Scotland and America, for supplying the plantations with servants, by means of *kidnapping*, as it was termed, both men and women, but especially children under age. Here Ratcliffe lost sight of the boy, but had no doubt but Donacha Dhu could give an account of him. The gentleman of the law, so often mentioned, despatched therefore an express, with a letter to Sir George Staunton, and another covering a warrant for apprehension of Donacha, with instructions to the Captain of Knockdunder to exert his utmost energy for that purpose.

Possessed of this information, and with a mind agitated by the most gloomy apprehensions, Butler now joined the Captain, and obtained from him with some difficulty a sight of the examinations. These, with a few questions to the elder of the prisoners, soon confirmed the most dreadful of Butler's anticipations. We give the heads of the information, without descending into minute details.

Donacha Dhu had indeed purchased Effie's unhappy child, with the purpose of selling it to the American traders, whom he had been in the habit of supplying with human flesh. But no opportunity occurred for some time; and the boy, who was known by the name of "The Whistler," made some impression on the heart and affections even of this rude savage, perhaps because he saw in him flashes of a spirit as fierce and vindictive as his own. When Donacha struck or threatened him—a very common occurrence—he did not answer with complaints and entreaties like other children, but with oaths and efforts at revenge—he had all the wild merit, too, by which Woggarwolfe's arrow-bearing page won the hard heart of his master :

> Like a wild cub, rear'd at the ruffian's feet,
> He could say biting jests, bold ditties sing,
> And quaff his foaming bumper at the board,
> With all the mockery of a little man. [1]

In short, as Donacha Dhu said, the Whistler was a born imp of Satan, and *therefore* he should never leave him. Accordingly, from his eleventh year forward, he was one of the band, and often engaged in acts of violence. The last of these was more immediately occasioned by the researches which the Whistler's real father made after him whom he had been taught to consider as such. Donacha Dhu's fears had been for some time excited by the strength of the means which began now to be employed against persons of his description. He was sensible he existed only by the precarious indulgence of his namesake, Duncan of Knockdunder, who was used to boast that he could put him down or string him up when he had a mind. He resolved to leave the kingdom by means of one of those sloops which were engaged in the traffic of his old kidnapping friends, and which was about to sail for America ; but he was desirous first to strike a bold stroke.

The ruffian's cupidity was excited by the intelligence, that a wealthy Englishman was coming to the Manse—he had neither forgotten the Whistler's report of the gold he had seen in Lady Staunton's purse, nor his old vow of revenge against the minister ; and, to bring the whole to a point, he conceived the hope of appropriating the money, which, according to the general report of the country, the minister was to bring from Edinburgh to pay for his new purchase. While he was considering how he might best accomplish his purpose, he received the intelligence from one quarter, that the vessel in which he proposed to sail was to sail immediately from Greenock ; from another, that the minister and a rich English lord, with a great many thousand pounds, were expected the next evening at the Manse ; and from a third, that he must consult his safety by leaving his ordinary haunts as soon as possible, for that the Captain had ordered out a party to

[1] Ethwald.

scour the glens for him at break of day. Donacha laid his
plans with promptitude and decision. He embarked with the
Whistler and two others of his band (whom, by-the-bye, he
meant to sell to the kidnappers), and set sail for the Caird's
Cove. He intended to lurk till night-fall in the wood adjoining to this place, which he thought was too near the habitation
of men to excite the suspicion of Duncan Knock, then break
into Butler's peaceful habitation, and flesh at once his appetite
for plunder and revenge. When his villainy was accomplished,
his boat was to convey him to the vessel, which, according to
previous agreement with the master, was instantly to set sail.

This desperate design would probably have succeeded, but
for the ruffians being discovered in their lurking-place by Sir
George Staunton and Butler, in their accidental walk from
the Caird's Cove towards the Manse. Finding himself detected, and at the same time observing that the servant carried
a casket, or strong-box, Donacha conceived that both his
prize and his victims were within his power, and attacked the
travellers without hesitation. Shots were fired and swords
drawn on both sides; Sir George Staunton offered the bravest
resistance, till he fell, as there was too much reason to believe,
by the hand of a son, so long sought, and now at length so
unhappily met.

While Butler was half-stunned with this intelligence, the
hoarse voice of Knockdunder added to his consternation.

"I will take the liperty to take down the pell-ropes, Mr.
Putler, as I must pe taking order to hang these idle people
up to-morrow morning, to teach them more consideration in
their doings in future."

Butler entreated him to remember the act abolishing the
heritable jurisdictions, and that he ought to send them to
Glasgow or Inverary, to be tried by the Circuit. Duncan
scorned the proposal.

"The Jurisdiction Act," he said, "had nothing to do put
with the rebels, and specially not with Argyle's country; and
he would hang the men up all three in one row before coot
Leddy Staunton's windows, which would be a creat comfort
to her in the morning to see that the coot gentleman, her
husband, had been suitably afenged."

And the utmost length that Butler's most earnest entreaties
could prevail was, that he would reserve "the twa pig carles
for the Circuit, but as for him they ca'd the Fustler, he should
try how he could fustle in a swinging tow, for it suldna be

said that a shentleman, friend to the Duke, was killed in his country, and his people didna take at least twa lives for ane."

Butler entreated him to spare the victim for his soul's sake. But Knockdunder answered, "that the soul of such a scum had been long the tefil's property, and that, Cot tam! he was determined to gif the tefil his due."

All persuasion was in vain, and Duncan issued his mandate for execution on the succeeding morning. The child of guilt and misery was separated from his companions, strongly pinioned, and committed to a separate room, of which the Captain kept the key.

In the silence of the night, however, Mrs. Butler arose, resolved, if possible, to avert, at least to delay, the fate which hung over her nephew, especially if, upon conversing with him, she should see any hope of his being brought to better temper. She had a master-key that opened every lock in the house; and at midnight, when all was still, she stood before the eyes of the astonished young savage, as, hard bound with cords, he lay, like a sheep designed for slaughter, upon a quantity of the refuse of flax which filled a corner in the apartment. Amid features sunburnt, tawny, grimed with dirt, and obscured by his shaggy hair of a rusted black colour, Jeanie tried in vain to trace the likeness of either of his very handsome parents. Yet how could she refuse compassion to a creature so young and so wretched,—so much more wretched than even he himself could be aware of, since the murder he had too probably committed with his own hand, but in which he had at any rate participated, was in fact a parricide. She placed food on a table near him, raised him, and slacked the cords on his arms, so as to permit him to feed himself. He stretched out his hands, still smeared with blood, perhaps that of his father, and he ate voraciously and in silence.

"What is your first name?" said Jeanie, by way of opening the conversation.

"The Whistler."

"But your Christian name, by which you were baptized?"

"I never was baptized that I know of—I have no other name than the Whistler."

"Poor unhappy abandoned lad!" said Jeanie. "What would ye do if you could escape from this place, and the death you are to die to-morrow morning?"

"Join wi' Rob Roy, or wi' Sergeant More Cameron" (noted

freebooters at that time), "and revenge Donacha's death on all and sundry."

"O ye unhappy boy," said Jeanie, "do ye ken what will come o' ye when ye die?"

"I shall neither feel cauld nor hunger more," said the youth doggedly.

"To let him be execute in this dreadful state of mind would be to destroy baith body and soul—and to let him gang I dare not—what will be done?—But he is my sister's son—my own nephew—our flesh and blood—and his hands and feet are yerked as tight as cords can be drawn.—Whistler, do the cords hurt you?"

"Very much."

"But, if I were to slacken them, you would harm me?"

"No, I would not—you never harmed me or mine."

There may be good in him yet, thought Jeanie; I will try fair play with him.

She cut his bonds—he stood upright, looked round with a laugh of wild exultation, clapped his hands together, and sprung from the ground, as if in transport on finding himself at liberty. He looked so wild, that Jeanie trembled at what she had done.

"Let me out," said the young savage.

"I wunna, unless you promise——"

"Then I'll make you glad to let us both out."

He seized the lighted candle and threw it among the flax, which was instantly in a flame. Jeanie screamed, and ran out of the room; the prisoner rushed past her, threw open a window in the passage, jumped into the garden, sprung over its enclosure, bounded through the woods like a deer, and gained the sea-shore. Meantime, the fire was extinguished, but the prisoner was sought in vain. As Jeanie kept her own secret, the share she had in his escape was not discovered; but they learned his fate some time afterwards—it was as wild as his life had hitherto been.

The anxious inquiries of Butler at length learned, that the youth had gained the ship in which his master, Donacha, had designed to embark. But the avaricious shipmaster, inured by his evil trade to every species of treachery, and disappointed of the rich booty which Donacha had proposed to bring aboard, secured the person of the fugitive, and having transported him to America, sold him as a slave, or indented servant, to a Virginian planter, far up the country. When

these tidings 'reached Butler, he sent over to America a
sufficient sum to redeem the lad from slavery, with instructions that measures should be taken for improving his mind,
restraining his evil propensities, and encouraging whatever
good might appear in his character. But this aid came too
late. The young man had headed a conspiracy in which his
inhuman master was put to death, and had then fled to the
next tribe of wild Indians. He was never more heard of;
and it may therefore be presumed that he lived and died after
the manner of that savage people, with whom his previous
habits had well fitted him to associate.

All hopes of the young man's reformation being now ended,
Mr. and Mrs. Butler thought it could serve no purpose to
explain to Lady Staunton a history so full of horror. She
remained their guest more than a year, during the greater part
of which period her grief was excessive. In the latter months,
it assumed the appearance of listlessness and low spirits,
which the monotony of her sister's quiet establishment
afforded no means of dissipating. Effie, from her earliest
youth, was never formed for a quiet low content. Far
different from her sister, she required the dissipation of
society to divert her sorrow, or enhance her joy. She left
the seclusion of Knocktarlitie with tears of sincere affection,
and after heaping its inmates with all she could think of that
might be valuable in their eyes. But she *did* leave it ; and
when the anguish of the parting was over, her departure was
a relief to both sisters.

The family at the Manse of Knocktarlitie, in their own
quiet happiness, heard of the well-dowered and beautiful
Lady Staunton resuming her place in the fashionable world.
They learned it by more substantial proofs, for David received
a commission ; and as the military spirit of Bible Butler
seemed to have revived in him, his good behaviour qualified
the envy of five hundred young Highland cadets, " come of
good houses," who were astonished at the rapidity of his promotion. Reuben followed the law, and rose more slowly, yet
surely. Euphemia Butler, whose fortune, augmented by her
aunt's generosity, and added to her own beauty, rendered her
no small prize, married a Highland laird, who never asked
the name of her grandfather, and was loaded on the occasion
with presents from Lady Staunton, which made her the envy
of all the beauties in Dumbarton and Argyle-shires.

After blazing nearly ten years in the fashionable world, and hiding, like many of her compeers, an aching heart with a gay demeanour;—after declining repeated offers of the most respectable kind for a second matrimonial engagement, Lady Staunton betrayed the inward wound by retiring to the Continent, and taking up her abode in the convent where she had received her education. She never took the veil, but lived and died in severe seclusion, and in the practice of the Roman Catholic religion, in all its formal observances, vigils, and austerities.

Jeanie had so much of her father's spirit as to sorrow bitterly for this apostacy, and Butler joined in her regret. "Yet any religion, however imperfect," he said, "was better than cold scepticism, or the hurrying din of dissipation, which fills the ears of worldlings, until they care for none of these things."

Meanwhile, happy in each other, in the prosperity of their family, and the love and honour of all who knew them, this simple pair lived beloved, and died lamented.

READER—This tale will not be told in vain, if it shall be found to illustrate the great truth, that guilt, though it may attain temporal splendour, can never confer real happiness; that the evil consequences of our crimes long survive their commission, and, like the ghosts of the murdered, for ever haunt the steps of the malefactor; and that the paths of virtue, though seldom those of worldly greatness, are always those of pleasantness and peace.

L'ENVOY, BY JEDEDIAH CLEISHBOTHAM

THUS concludeth the Tale of "THE HEART OF MID-LOTHIAN," which hath filled more pages than I opined. The Heart of Mid-Lothian is now no more, or rather it is transferred to the extreme side of the city, even as the Sieur Jean Baptiste Poquelin hath it, in his pleasant comedy called *Le Médecin Malgré lui*, where the simulated doctor wittily replieth to a charge, that he had placed the heart on the right side, instead of the left, "*Cela étoit autrefois ainsi, mais nous avons changé tout cela.*" Of which witty speech, if any reader shall demand the purport, I have only to respond, that I teach the French as well as the Classical tongues, at the easy rate of five shillings per quarter, as my advertisements are periodically making known to the public.

AUTHOR'S NOTES

Note I. p. 71.—TOLBOOTH OF EDINBURGH

THE ancient Tolbooth of Edinburgh, situated and described as in the last chapter, was built by the citizens in 1561, and destined for the accommodation of Parliament, as well as of the High Courts of Justice; and at the same time for the confinement of prisoners for debt, or on criminal charges. Since the year 1640, when the present Parliament House was erected, the Tolbooth was occupied as a prison only. Gloomy and dismal as it was, the situation in the centre of the High Street rendered it so particularly well-aired, that when the plague laid waste the city in 1645, it affected none within these melancholy precincts. The Tolbooth was removed, with the mass of buildings in which it was incorporated, in the autumn of the year 1817. At that time the kindness of his old schoolfellow and friend, Robert Johnstone, Esquire, then Dean of Guild of the city, with the liberal acquiescence of the persons who had contracted for the work, procured for the author of Waverley the stones which composed the gateway, together with the door, and its ponderous fastenings, which he employed in decorating the entrance of his kitchen-court at Abbotsford. "To such base offices may we return." The application of these relics of the Heart of Mid-Lothian to serve as the postern gate to a court of modern offices, may be justly ridiculed as whimsical; but yet it is not without interest, that we see the gateway through which so much of the stormy politics of a rude age, and the vice and misery of later times, had found their passage, now occupied in the service of rural economy. Last year, to complete the change, a tom-tit was pleased to build her nest within the lock of the Tolbooth,—a strong temptation to have committed a sonnet, had the author, like Tony Lumpkin, been in a concatenation accordingly.

It is worth mentioning, that an act of beneficence celebrated the demolition of the Heart of Mid-Lothian. A subscription, raised and applied by the worthy Magistrate above mentioned, procured the manumission of most of the unfortunate debtors confined in the old jail, so that there were few or none transferred to the new place of confinement.

Note II. p. 106.—CARSPHARN JOHN

John Semple, called Carspharn John, because minister of the parish in Galloway so called, was a Presbyterian clergyman of singular piety and great zeal, of whom Patrick Walker records the following passage: "That night after his wife died, he spent the whole ensuing night in prayer and meditation in his garden. The next morning, one of his elders coming to see him, and lamenting his great loss and want of rest, he replied,—'I declare I have not, all night, had one thought of the death of my wife, I have been so taken up in meditating on heavenly things. I have been this night on the banks of Ulai, plucking an apple here and there.'"—*Walker's Remarkable Passages of the Life and Death of Mr. John Semple.*

Note III. p. 115.—PETER WALKER

This personage, whom it would be base ingratitude in the author to pass over without some notice, was by far the most zealous and faithful collector and recorder of the actions and opinions of the Cameronians. He resided, while stationary, at the Bristo Port of Edinburgh, but was by trade an itinerant merchant or pedlar, which profession he seems to have exercised in Ireland as well as Britain. He composed biographical notices of Alexander Peden, John Semple, John Welwood, and Richard Cameron, all ministers of the Cameronian persuasion, to which the last-mentioned member gave the name.

It is from such tracts as these, written in the sense, feeling, and spirit of the sect, and not from the sophisticated narratives of a later period, that the real character of the persecuted class is to be gathered. Walker writes with a simplicity which sometimes slides into the burlesque, and sometimes attains a tone of simple pathos, but always expressing the most daring confidence in his own correctness of creed and sentiments, sometimes with narrow-minded and disgusting bigotry. His turn for the marvellous was that of his time and sect ; but there is little room to doubt his veracity concerning whatever he quotes on his own knowledge. His small tracts now bring a very high price, especially the earlier and authentic editions.

The tirade against dancing, pronounced by David Deans, is, as intimated in the text, partly borrowed from Peter Walker. He notices, as a foul reproach upon the name of Richard Cameron, that his memory was vituperated " by pipers and fiddlers playing the Cameronian march—carnal vain springs, which too many professors of religion dance to ; a practice unbecoming the professors of Christianity to dance to any spring, but somewhat more to this. Whatever," he proceeds, " be the many foul blots recorded of the saints in Scripture, none of them is charged with this regular fit of distraction. We find it has been practised by the wicked and profane, as the dancing at that brutish, base action of the calf-making ; and it had been good for that unhappy lass, who danced off the head of John the Baptist, that she had been born a cripple, and never drawn a limb to her. Historians say, that her sin was written upon her judgment, who some time thereafter was dancing upon the ice, and it broke, and snapt the head off her ; her head danced above, and her feet beneath. There is ground to think and conclude, that when the world's wickedness was great, dancing at their marriages was practised ; but when the heavens above, and the earth beneath, were let loose upon them with that overflowing flood, their mirth was soon staid ; and when the Lord in holy justice rained fire and brimstone from heaven upon that wicked people and city Sodom, enjoying fulness of bread and idleness, their fiddle-strings and hands went all in a flame ; and the whole people in thirty miles of length, and ten of breadth, as historians say, were all made to fry in their skins ; and at the end, whoever are giving in marriages and dancing when all will go in a flame, they will quickly change their note.

" I have often wondered thorow my life, how any that ever knew what it was to bow a knee in earnest to pray, durst crook a hough to fyke and fling at a piper's and fiddler's springs. I bless the Lord that ordered my lot so in my dancing days, that made the fear of the bloody rope and bullets to my neck and head, the pain of boots, thumikens, and irons, cold and hunger, wetness and weariness, to stop the lightness of my head, and the wantonness of my feet. What the never-to-be-forgotten Man of God, John Knox, said to Queen Mary, when she gave him that sharp challenge, which would strike our mean-spirited, tongue-tacked ministers dumb, for his giving public faithful warning of the danger of the church and nation, through her marrying the Dauphine of France, when he left her bubbling and greeting, and came to an outer court, where her Lady Maries were fyking and dancing, he said, ' O brave ladies, a brave world, if it would last, and heaven at the hinder end ! But fye upon the knave Death, that will seize upon those bodies of yours ; and where will all your fiddling and flinging be then ?' Dancing being such a common evil, especially amongst young professors, that all the lovers of the Lord should hate, has caused me to insist the more upon it, especially that foolish spring the Cameronian march !"—*Life and Death of three famous Worthies, &c.,* by *Peter Walker*, 12mo, p. 59.

It may here be observed, that some of the milder class of Cameronians

Notes

made a distinction between the two sexes dancing separately, and allowed of it as a healthy and not unlawful exercise ; but when men and women mingled in sport, it was then called *promiscuous dancing*, and considered as a scandalous enormity.

Note IV. p. 128.—MUSCHAT'S CAIRN

Nicol Muschat, a debauched and profligate wretch, having conceived a hatred against his wife, entered into a conspiracy with another brutal libertine and gambler, named Campbell of Burnbank (repeatedly mentioned in Pennycuick's satirical poems of the time) by which Campbell undertook to destroy the woman's character, so as to enable Muschat, on false pretences, to obtain a divorce from her. The brutal devices to which these worthy accomplices resorted for that purpose having failed, they endeavoured to destroy her by administering medicine of a dangerous kind, and in extraordinary quantities.

This purpose also failing, Nicol Muschat, or Muschet, did finally, on the 17th October 1720, carry his wife under cloud of night to the King's Park, adjacent to what is called the Duke's Walk, near Holyrood Palace, and there took her life by cutting her throat almost quite through, and inflicting other wounds. He pleaded guilty to the indictment, for which he suffered death. His associate, Campbell, was sentenced to transportation for his share in the previous conspiracy. See "MacLaurin's Criminal Cases," pp. 64 and 738.

In memory, and at the same time execration, of the deed, a *cairn*, or pile of stones, long marked the spot. It is now almost totally removed, in consequence of an alteration on the road in that place.

Note V. p.154.—HANGMAN, OR LOCKMAN

Lockman, so called from the small quantity of meal (Scottice, *lock*) which he was entitled to take out of every boll exposed to market in the city. In Edinburgh the duty has been very long commuted ; but in Dumfries the finisher of the law still exercises, or did lately exercise, his privilege, the quantity taken being regulated by a small iron ladle, which he uses as the measure of his perquisite. The expression *lock*, for a small quantity of any readily divisible dry substance, as corn, meal, flax, or the like, is still preserved, not only popularly, but in a legal description, as the *lock* and *gowpen*, or small quantity and handful, payable in thirlage cases, as in-town multure.

Note VI. p. 165.—THE FAIRY BOY OF LEITH

This legend was in former editions inaccurately said to exist in Baxter's "World of Spirits" ; but is, in fact, to be found in "Pandæmonium, or the Devil's Cloyster ; being a further blow to Modern Sadduceism," by Richard Barton, Gentleman, 12mo, 1684. The work is inscribed to Dr. Henry More. The story is entitled, "A remarkable passage of one named the Fairy Boy of Leith, in Scotland, given me by my worthy friend Captain George Burton, and attested under his hand ; " and is as follows :—

"About fifteen years since, having business that detained me for some time in Leith, which is near Edenborough, in the kingdom of Scotland, I often met some of my acquaintance at a certain house there, where we used to drink a glass of wine for our refection. The woman which kept the house, was of honest reputation amongst the neighbours, which made me give the more attention to what she told me one day about a Fairy Boy (as they called him) who lived about that town. She had given me so strange an account of him, that I desired her I might see him the first opportunity, which she promised ; and not long after, passing that way, she told me there was the Fairy Boy but a little before I came by ; and casting her eye into the street, said, ' Look you, sir, yonder he is at play with those other boys,' and designing him to me, I went, and by smooth words, and a piece of money, got him to come into the house with me; where, in the presence of divers people, I demanded of him several astrological questions, which he answered with great subtility, and through all his discourse carried it with a cunning much beyond his years, which seemed not to exceed ten or eleven. He seemed to make a motion like drumming upon the table with his fingers, upon which I asked him, whether he could beat a drum, to which he replied, ' Yes, sir, as well as any man in Scotland; for every Thursday night I beat all points to a sort of people that use to meet under yonder hill' (pointing to the great hill between Edenborough and Leith). 'How, boy,' quoth I; 'what company have you there?' —'There are, sir,' said he, 'a great company both of men and women, and they are entertained with many sorts of musick besides my drum; they have, besides, plenty variety of meats and wine; and many times we are carried into France or Holland in a night, and return again; and whilst we are there, we enjoy all the pleasures the country doth afford.' I demanded of him, how they got under that hill? To which he replied, 'that there were a great pair of gates that opened to them, though they were invisible to others, and that within there were brave large rooms, as well accommodated as most in Scotland.' I then asked him, how I should know what he said to be true? upon which he told me he would read my fortune, saying I should have two wives, and that he saw the forms of them sitting on my shoulders; that both would be very handsome women.

" As he was thus speaking, a woman of the neighbourhood, coming into the room, demanded of him what her fortune should be? He told her that she had two bastards before she was married; which put her in such a rage, that she desired not to hear the rest. The woman of the house told me that all the people in Scotland could not keep him from the rendezvous on Thursday night; upon which, by promising him some more money, I got a promise of him to meet me at the same place, in the afternoon of the Thursday following, and so dismissed him at that time. The boy came again at the place and time appointed, and I had prevailed with some friends to continue with me, if possible, to prevent his moving that night; he was placed between us, and answered many questions without offering to go from us, until about eleven of the clock, he was got away unperceived of the company; but I suddenly missing him, hasted to the door, and took hold of him, and so returned him into the same room: we all watched him, and on a sudden he was again got out of the doors. I followed him close, and he made a noise in the street as if he had been set upon; but from that time I could never see him.   GEORGE BURTON."

Note VII. p. 166.—INTERCOURSE OF THE COVENANTERS WITH THE INVISIBLE WORLD

The gloomy, dangerous, and constant wanderings of the persecuted sect of Cameronians, naturally led to their entertaining with peculiar credulity the belief, that they were sometimes persecuted, not only by the wrath of men, but by the secret wiles and open terrors of Satan. In fact, a flood could not happen, a horse cast a shoe, or any other the most ordinary interruption thwart a minister's wish to perform service at a particular spot, than the accident was imputed to the immediate agency of fiends. The encounter of Alexander Peden with the Devil in the cave, and that of John Semple with the demon in the ford, are given by Peter Walker, almost in the language of the text.

Note VIII. p. 171.—CHILD MURDER

The Scottish Statute Book, anno 1690, chapter 21, in consequence of the great increase of the crime of child murder, both from the temptations to commit the offence and the difficulty of discovery, enacted a certain set of presumptions, which, in the absence of direct proof, the jury were directed to receive as evidence of the crime having actually been committed. The circumstances selected for this purpose were, that the woman should have concealed her situation during the whole period of pregnancy; that she should not have called for help at her delivery; and that, combined with these grounds of suspicion, the child should be either found dead or be altogether missing. Many persons suffered death during the last century under this severe act. But during the author's memory a more lenient course was followed, and the female accused under the act, and conscious of no competent defence, usually lodged a petition to the Court of Justiciary, denying, for form's sake, the tenor of the indictment, but stating, that as her good name had been destroyed by the charge, she was willing to submit to sentence of banishment, to which the crown counsel usually consented. This lenity in practice, and the comparative infrequency of the crime since the doom of public ecclesiastical penance has been generally dispensed with, have led to the abolition of the statute of William and Mary, which is now replaced by another, imposing banishment in those circumstances in which the crime was formerly capital. This alteration took place in 1803.

Note IX. p. 198.—CALUMNIATOR OF THE FAIR SEX

The journal of Graves, a Bow Street officer, despatched to Holland to obtain the surrender of the unfortunate William Brodie, bears a reflection on the ladies somewhat like that put in the mouth of the police-officer Sharpitlaw. It had been found difficult to identify the unhappy criminal; and, when a Scotch gentleman of respectability had seemed disposed to give evidence on the point required, his son-in-law, a clergyman in Amsterdam, and his daughter, were suspected by Graves to have used arguments with the witness to dissuade him from giving his testimony. On which subject the journal of the Bow Street officer proceeds thus:

"Saw then a manifest reluctance in Mr. ——, and had no doubt the daughter and parson would endeavour to persuade him to decline troubling himself in the matter, but judged he could not go back from what he had said to Mr. Rich. – NOTA BENE. *No mischief but a woman or a priest in it*—here both."

Note X. p. 208.—SIR WILLIAM DICK OF BRAID

This gentleman formed a striking example of the instability of human prosperity. He was once the wealthiest man of his time in Scotland, a merchant in an extensive line of commerce, and a farmer of the public revenue; insomuch that, about 1640, he estimated his fortune at two hundred thousand pounds sterling. Sir William Dick was a zealous Covenanter; and in the memorable year 1641, he lent the Scottish Convention of Estates one hundred thousand merks at once, and thereby enabled them to support and pay their army, which must otherwise have broken to pieces. He afterwards advanced £20,000 for the service of King Charles, during the usurpation; and having, by owning the royal cause, provoked the displeasure of the ruling party, he was fleeced of more money, amounting in all to £65,000 sterling.

Being in this manner reduced to indigence, he went to London to try to recover some part of the sums which had been lent on government security. Instead of receiving any satisfaction, the Scottish Crœsus was thrown into prison, in which he died, 19th December 1655. It is said his death was hastened by the want of common necessaries. But this statement is somewhat exaggerated, if it be true, as is commonly said, that though he was not supplied with bread, he had plenty of pie-crust, thence called "Sir William Dick's necessity."

The changes of fortune are commemorated in a folio pamphlet entitled, "The lamentable state of the deceased Sir William Dick." It contains several copper-plates, one representing Sir William on horseback, and attended with guards as Lord Provost of Edinburgh, superintending the unloading of one of his rich argosies. A second exhibiting him as arrested, and in the hands of the bailiffs. A third presents him dead in prison. The tract is esteemed highly valuable by collectors of prints. The only copy I ever saw upon sale, was rated at £30.

Note XI. p. 213.—MEETING AT TALLA-LINNS

This remarkable convocation took place upon 15th June 1682, and an account of its confused and divisive proceedings may be found in Michael Shield's Faithful Contendings Displayed, Glasgow, 1780, p. 21. It affords a singular and melancholy example how much a metaphysical and polemical spirit had crept in amongst these unhappy sufferers, since, amid so many real injuries which they had to sustain, they were disposed to add disagreement and disunion concerning the character and extent of such as were only imaginary.

Note XII. p. 259.—DOOMSTER, OR DEMPSTER, OF COURT

The name of this officer is equivalent to the pronouncer of doom or sentence. In this comprehensive sense, the Judges of the Isle of Man were called Dempsters. But in Scotland the word was long restricted to the designation of an official person, whose duty it was to recite the sentence after it had been pronounced by the Court, and recorded by the clerk; on which occasion the Dempster legalised it by the words of form, "*And this I pronounce for doom.*" For a length of years, the office, as mentioned in the text, was held *in commendam* with that of the executioner; for when this odious but necessary officer of justice received his appointment, he petitioned the Court of Justiciary to be received as their Dempster, which was granted as a matter of course.

The production of the executioner in open court, and in presence of the wretched criminal, had something in it hideous and disgusting to the more refined feelings of later times. But if an old tradition of the Parliament House of Edinburgh may be trusted, it was the following anecdote which occasioned the disuse of the Dempster's office.

It chanced at one time that the office of public executioner was vacant. There was occasion for some one to act as Dempster, and, considering the party who generally held the office, it is not wonderful that a *locum tenens* was hard to be found. At length, one Hume, who had been sentenced to transportation, for an attempt to burn his own house, was induced to consent that he would pronounce the doom on this occasion. But when brought forth to officiate, instead of repeating the doom to the criminal, Mr. Hume addressed himself to their lordships in a bitter complaint of the injustice of his own sentence. It was in vain that he was interrupted, and reminded of the purpose for which he had come hither; " I ken what ye want of me weel eneugh," said the fellow, " ye want me to be your Dempster; but I am come to be none of your Dempster, I am come to you, Lord T—, and you, Lord E—, to answer at the bar of another world for the injustice you have done me in this." In short, Hume had only made a pretext of complying with the proposal, in order to have an opportunity of reviling the Judges to their faces, or giving them, in the phrase of his country, "a sloan." He was hurried off amid the laughter of the audience, but the indecorous scene which had taken place contributed to the abolition of the office of Dempster. The sentence is now read over by the clerk of court, and the formality of pronouncing doom is altogether omitted.

Note XIII. p. 262.—JOHN DUKE OF ARGYLE AND GREENWICH

This nobleman was very dear to his countrymen, who were justly proud of his military and political talents, and grateful for the ready zeal with which he asserted the rights of his native country. This was never more conspicuous than in the matter of the Porteous Mob, when the Ministers brought in a violent and vindictive Bill, for declaring the Lord Provost of Edinburgh incapable of bearing any public office in future, for not foreseeing a disorder which no one foresaw, or interrupting the course of a riot too formidable to endure opposition. The same Bill made provision for pulling down the city gates, and abolishing the city guard,—rather a Hibernian mode of enabling them better to keep the peace within burgh in future.

The Duke of Argyle opposed this Bill as a cruel, unjust, and fanatical proceeding, and an encroachment upon the privileges of the royal burghs of Scotland, secured to them by the treaty of Union. "In all the proceedings of that time," said his Grace, "the nation of Scotland treated with the English as a free and independent people ; and as that treaty, my Lords, had no other guarantee for the due performance of its articles, but the faith and honour of a British Parliament, it would be both unjust and ungenerous, should this House agree to any proceedings that have a tendency to injure it."

Lord Hardwicke, in reply to the Duke of Argyle, seemed to insinuate, that his Grace had taken up the affair in a party point of view, to which the nobleman replied in the spirited language quoted in the text—Lord Hardwicke apologised. The Bill was much modified, and the clauses concerning the dismantling the city, and disbanding the Guard, were departed from. A fine of £2000 was imposed on the city for the benefit of Porteous's widow. She was contented to accept three-fourths of the sum, the payment of which closed the transaction. It is remarkable, that, in our day, the Magistrates of Edinburgh have had recourse to both those measures, held in such horror by their predecessors, as necessary steps for the improvement of the city.

It may be here noticed, in explanation of another circumstance mentioned in the text, that there is a tradition in Scotland, that George II., whose irascible temper is said sometimes to have hurried him into expressing his displeasure *par voie du fait*, offered to the Duke of Argyle, in angry audience, some menace of this nature, on which he left the presence in high disdain, and with little ceremony. Sir Robert Walpole, having met the Duke as he retired, and learning the cause of his resentment and discomposure, endeavoured to reconcile him to what had happened by saying, "Such was his Majesty's way, and that he often took such liberties with himself without meaning any harm." This did not mend matters in M'Callummore's eyes, who replied, in great disdain, "You will please to remember, Sir Robert, the infinite distance there is betwixt you and me." Another frequent expression of passion on the part of the same monarch, is alluded to in the old Jacobite song—

> The fire shall get both hat and wig,
> As oft times they've got a' that.

Note XIV. p. 425.—MADGE WILDFIRE

In taking leave of the poor maniac, the author may here observe, that the first conception of the character, though afterwards greatly altered, was taken from that of a person calling herself, and called by others, Feckless Fannie (weak or feeble Fannie), who always travelled with a small flock of sheep. The following account, furnished by the persevering kindness of Mr. Train, contains probably all that can now be known of her history, though many, among whom is the author, may remember having heard of Feckless Fannie, in the days of their youth.

" My leisure hours," says Mr. Train, " for some time past have been mostly spent in searching for particulars relating to the maniac called Feckless Fannie, who travelled over all Scotland and England, between the years 1767 and 1775, and whose history is altogether so like a romance, that I have been at all possible pains to collect every particular that can be found relative to her in Galloway, or in Ayrshire.

" When Feckless Fannie appeared in Ayrshire, for the first time, in the summer of 1769, she attracted much notice, from being attended by twelve or thirteen sheep, who seemed all endued with faculties so much superior to the ordinary race of animals of the same species, as to excite universal astonishment. She had for each a different name, to which it answered when called by its mistress, and would likewise obey in the most surprising manner any command she thought proper to give. When travelling, she always walked in front of her flock, and they followed her closely behind. When she lay down at night in the fields, for she would never enter into a house, they always disputed who should lie next to her, by which means she was kept warm, while she lay in the midst of them ; when she attempted to rise from the ground, an old ram, whose name was Charlie, always claimed the sole right of assisting her ; pushing any that stood in his way aside, until he arrived right before his mistress ; he then bowed his head nearly to the ground that she might lay her hands on his horns, which were very large ; he then lifted her gently from the ground by raising his head. If she chanced to leave her flock feeding, as soon as they discovered she was gone, they all began to bleat most piteously, and would continue to do so till she returned ; they would then testify their joy by rubbing their sides against her petticoat, and frisking about.

" Feckless Fannie was not, like most other demented creatures, fond of fine dress ; on her head she wore an old slouched hat, over her shoulders an old plaid, and carried always in her hand a shepherd's crook ; with any of these articles, she invariably declared she would not part for any consideration whatever. When she was interrogated why she set so much value on things seemingly so insignificant, she would sometimes relate the history of her misfortune, which was briefly as follows :

" ' I am the only daughter of a wealthy squire in the north of England, but I loved my father's shepherd, and that has been my ruin ; for my father, fearing his family would be disgraced by such an alliance, in a passion mortally wounded my lover with a shot from a pistol. I arrived just in time to receive the last blessing of the dying man, and to close his eyes in death. He bequeathed me his little all, but I only accepted these sheep to be my sole companions through life, and this hat, this plaid, and this crook, all of which I will carry until I descend into the grave.'

" This is the substance of a ballad, eighty-four lines of which I copied down lately from the recitation of an old woman in this place, who says she has seen it in print with a plate on the title-page, representing Fannie with her sheep behind her. As this ballad is said to have been written by Lowe, the author of Mary's Dream, I am surprised that it has not been noticed by Cromek, in his Remains of Nithsdale and Galloway Song ; but he perhaps thought it unworthy of a place in his collection, as there is very little merit in the composition ; which want of room prevents me from transcribing at present. But if I thought you had never seen it, I would take an early opportunity of doing so.

" After having made the tour of Galloway in 1769, as Fannie was wandering in the neighbourhood of Moffat, on her way to Edinburgh, where, I am informed, she was likewise well known, Old Charlie, her favourite ram, chanced to break into a kaleyard, which the proprietor observing, let loose a mastiff that hunted the poor sheep to death. This was a sad misfortune ; it seemed to renew all the pangs which she formerly felt on the death of her lover. She would not part from the side of her old friend for several days, and it was with much difficulty she consented to allow him to be buried ; but, still wishing to pay a tribute to his memory, she covered his grave with moss, and fenced it round with osiers, and annually returned to the same spot, and pulled the weeds from the grave and repaired the fence. This is altogether like a romance ; but I believe it is really true that she did so. The grave of Charlie is still held sacred even by the schoolboys of the present day in that quarter. It is now, perhaps, the only instance of the law of Kenneth being attended to, which says, 'The grave where anie that is slaine lieth buried, leave untilled for seven years. Repute every grave holie so as thou be well advised, that in no wise with thy feet thou tread upon it.'

" Through the storms of winter, as well as in the milder season of the year, she continued her wandering course, nor could she be prevented from doing so, either by entreaty or promise of reward. The late Dr. Fullarton of Rosemount, in the neighbourhood of Ayr, being well acquainted with her father when in England, endeavoured, in a severe season, by every means in his power, to detain her at Rosemount for a few days until the weather should become more mild ; but when she found herself rested a little, and saw her sheep fed, she raised her crook, which was the signal she always gave for the sheep to follow her, and off they all marched together.

" But the hour of poor Fannie's dissolution was now at hand, and she seemed anxious to arrive at the spot where she was to terminate her mortal career. She proceeded to Glasgow, and, while passing through that city, a crowd of idle boys, attracted by her singular appearance, together with the novelty of seeing so many sheep obeying her command, began to torment her with their pranks, till she became so irritated that she pelted them with bricks and stones, which they returned in such a manner, that she was actually stoned to death between Glasgow and Anderston.

" To the real history of this singular individual, credulity has attached several superstitious appendages. It is said, that the farmer who was the cause of Charlie's death, shortly afterwards drowned himself in a peat-hag ; and that the hand, with which a butcher in Kilmarnock struck one of the other sheep, became powerless, and withered to the very bone. In the summer of 1769, when she was passing by New Cumnock, a young man, whose name was William Forsyth, son of a farmer in the same parish, plagued her so much that she wished he might never see the morn ; upon which he went home and hanged himself in his father's barn. And I doubt not many such stories may yet be remembered in other parts where she had been."

So far Mr. Train. The author can only add to his narrative, that Feckless Fannie and her little flock were well known in the pastoral districts.

In attempting to introduce such a character into fiction, the author felt the risk of encountering a comparison with the Maria of Sterne ; and, besides, the mechanism of the story would have been as much retarded by Feckless Fannie's flock, as the night-march of Don Quixote was delayed by Sancho's tale of the sheep that were ferried over the river.

The author has only to add, that notwithstanding the preciseness of his friend Mr. Train's statement, there may be some hopes that the outrage on Feckless Fannie and her little flock was not carried to extremity. There is no mention of any trial on account of it, which, had it occurred in the manner stated, would have certainly taken place ; and the author has understood that it was on the Border she was last seen, about the skirts of the Cheviot hills, but without her little flock.

Note XV. p. 450.—DEATH OF FRANCIS GORDON

This exploit seems to have been one in which Patrick Walker prided himself not a little ; and there is reason to fear, that that excellent person would have highly resented the attempt to associate another with him, in the slaughter of a King's Life-Guardsman. Indeed, he would have had the more right to be offended at losing any share of the glory, since the party against Gordon was already three to one, besides having the advantage of fire-arms. The manner in which he vindicates his claim to the exploit, without committing himself by a direct statement of it, is not a little amusing. It is as follows:—

" I shall give a brief and true account of that man's death, which I did not design to do while I was upon the stage ; I resolve, indeed (if it be the Lord's will), to leave a more full account of that and many other remarkable steps of the Lord's dispensations towards me through my life. It was then commonly said, that Francis Gordon was a volunteer out of wickedness of principles, and could not stay with the troop, but was still raging and ranging to catch hiding suffering people. Meldrum and Airly's troops, lying at Lanark upon the first day of March 1682, Mr. Gordon and another wicked comrade, with their two servants and four horses, came to Kilcaigow, two miles from Lanark, searching for William Caigow and others, under hiding.

" Mr. Gordon, rambling throw the town, offered to abuse the women. At night, they came a mile further to the Easter-Seat, to Robert Muir's, he being also under hiding. Gordon's comrade and the two servants went to bed, but he could sleep none, roaring all night for women. When day came, he took only his sword in his hand, and came to Moss-platt, and some new men (who had been in the fields all night) seeing him, they fled, and he pursued. James Wilson, Thomas Young, and myself, having been in a meeting all night, were lying down in the morning. We were alarmed, thinking there were many more than one; he pursued hard, and overtook us. Thomas Young said, 'Sir, what do ye pursue us for?' he said, 'he was come to send us to hell.' James Wilson said, 'that shall not be, for we will defend ourselves.' He said, 'that either he or we should go to it now.' He run his sword furiously throw James Wilson's coat. James fired upon him, but missed him. All this time he cried, Damn his soul! He got a shot in his head out of a pocket pistol, rather fit for diverting a boy than killing such a furious, mad, brisk man, which, notwithstanding, killed him dead. The foresaid William Caigow and Robert Muir came to us. We searched him for papers, and found a long scroll of sufferers' names, either to kill or take. I tore it all in pieces. He had also some Popish books and bonds of money, with one dollar, which a poor man took off the ground ; all which we put in his pocket again. Thus, he was four miles from Lanark, and near a mile from his comrade, seeking his own death, and got it. And for as much as we have been condemned for this, I could never see how any one could condemn us that allows of self-defence, which the laws both of God and nature allow to every creature. For my own part, my heart never smote me for this. When I saw his blood run, I wished that all the blood of the Lord's stated and avowed enemies in Scotland had been in his veins. Having such a clear call and opportunity, I would have rejoiced to have seen it all gone out with a gush. I have many times wondered at the greater part of the indulged, lukewarm ministers and professors in that time, who made more noise of murder, when one of these enemies had been killed even in our own defence, than of twenty of us being murdered by them. None of these men present was challenged for this but myself. Thomas Young thereafter suffered at Machline, but was not challenged for this ; Robert Muir was banished ; James Wilson outlived the persecution ; William Caigow died in the Canongate Tolbooth, in the beginning of 1685. Mr. Wodrow is misinformed ; who says, that he suffered unto death."

Note XVI. p. 466.—Tolling to Service in Scotland

In the old days of Scotland, when persons of property (unless they happened to be non-jurors) were as regular as their inferiors in attendance on parochial worship, there was a kind of etiquette, in waiting till the patron or

Notes

acknowledged great man of the parish should make his appearance. This ceremonial was so sacred in the eyes of a parish beadle in the Isle of Bute, that the kirk bell being out of order, he is said to have mounted the steeple every Sunday, to imitate with his voice the successive summonses which its mouth of metal used to send forth. The first part of this imitative harmony was simply the repetition of the words *Bell, bell, bell, bell,* two or three times, in a manner as much resembling the sound as throat of flesh could imitate throat of iron. *Bellùm! bellùm!* was sounded forth in a more urgent manner; but he never sent forth the third and conclusive peal, the varied tone of which is called in Scotland the *ringing-in*, until the two principal heritors of the parish approached, when the chime ran thus :—

> *Bellùm Bellèllum*
> *Bernera and Knockdow's coming!*
> *Bellùm Bellèllum,*
> *Bernera and Knockdow's coming!*

Thereby intimating, that service was instantly to proceed.

GLOSSARY

Aboon, abune, above.
Ae, one.
Aff, off.
Afore, before.
Agane, against, before.
Agee, twisted, awry.
Ahint, behind.
Ain, own.
Airt, direction, direct.
Aiths, oaths.
Allenarly, solely, only.
Alow, aflame, in a flame.
Alwaies, also, moreover.
Ance, once.
Aneath, beneath.
Anent, respecting, opposite.
Anes, once.
An it bide, let it remain so.
Anker, a Dutch liquid measure, containing ten wine gallons.
Arriage and carriage, plough and cart service.
Athegither, altogether.
Athole Brose, honey and whisky mixed.
Aught, possession, keeping.
Auld, old.
Ava, at all.
Awa, away.
A wee, a little.
Aweel, well.
Awmous, alms.
Awmrie, cupboard for provisions.
Ayont, beyond.

Back-cast, disaster.
Bailie, magistrate.
Bairn, child.
Baith, both.
Bake, a small cake or biscuit.

Band, a bond.
Bannocks, flat round cakes.
Bauld, bold.
Bauson-faced, having a white spot on the forehead.
Bawbee, halfpenny.
Bean-hool, snug hiding-place.
Bedral, sexton.
Belive, by-and-by.
Ben-leather, thick sole leather.
Ben the house, into the house, or inner apartment.
Bibe, nest.
Bicker, a wooden bowl.
Bide awee, wait a little.
Bide yont, keep clear.
Bien, comfortable, well provided.
Biggonets, linen caps of the style worn by the Beguine sisterhood.
Bink, wooden frame.
Binna, be not.
Birkies, lively young fellows.
Bit mutch, little cap.
Bittock, a diminutive of 'bit.'
Blawn, blown.
Blink, glimpse, glance, twinkling.
Blithe, glad, pleasant, happy.
Bluid, blood.
Bodle, boddle, a copper coin, value the sixth part of an English penny.
Booby form, lowest form.
Boot-hose, knitted gaiters covering the shoe and reaching to the knees.
Bouking-washing, the great annual purification of the linen used in a family.

Glossary

Bountith, the bounty given in addition to stipulated wages.

Bourock, small mound.

Bow, boll or dry measure, containing the sixteenth part of a chalder.

Bowies, milk pails.

Brae, hillside, bank.

Braw, fine.

Brawly, finely.

Braws, best clothes, finery.

Brecham, a working-horse's collar.

Brockit, white-faced.

Brogging, boring.

Brogues, shoes of half-dressed leather.

Broo, inclination.

Brugh, town.

Bruilzie, brawl.

Buckie, imp, mischievous madcap.

Bullseg, gilded bull.

Bunker, chest used as a seat.

Burn, rivulet.

Busk, dress, arrange.

Butt and ben, on both sides of the partition in a house with two compartments.

By, besides.

Byre, cow-house.

By their lane, by themselves, alone.

Ca', call.

Cadgers, pedlars, huxters.

Caird, tinker.

Caitiff, mean, despicable person.

Callant, lad.

Caller, fresh.

Canna, cannot.

Canny, sensible, prudent.

Canty, lively.

Capernoity, crabbed, peevish.

Caption, warrant for arrest.

Carcakes, cakes made with eggs, etc.

Carle, fellow, gruff old man.

Carline, old woman, also a witch.

Carritch, catechism.

Cast, lot, fate.

Cauldrife, chilly.

Caup, a cup, a wooden bowl.

Ceeted, cited.

Chafts, jaws.

Chalder, a dry measure = 16 bolls.

Chamber of deas, best chamber.

Change-house, roadside inn or tavern where horses are changed on a journey.

Chappit, struck, driven.

Chevrons, zigzag ornaments.

Chield, young fellow.

Clachan, a hamlet.

Clack-geese, barnacle geese.

Claes, *claise*, *claiths*, clothes.

Clat, raking together.

Clatter, tattle.

Claver, *clavers*, idle talk.

Claw, scratch.

Cleckit, hooked.

Cleek, seize.

Cleuch, *cleugh*, a ravine.

Clew, winding.

Closehead, entrance to a close or alley.

Clute, hoof.

Cockernonie, *cockernony*, a lady's top-knot.

Cod, pillow.

Cognosced, subjected to a judicial decision.

Collegeaners, the students of Edinburgh College.

Couch a hogshead, lie down to sleep.

Coup, upset.

Couthy, pleasant to the ear.

Cowt, a colt.

Crack, *cracks*, conversation, gossip.

Creagh, the plunder of cattle.

Crewels, scrofula.

Criming, pining.

Croft, an enclosure of pasture or tillage-land.

Crook a hough to fyke, an expression descriptive of the motions of dancing.

Cuddie, donkey.

Cuffin, Justice of the Peace.

Cummers, gossips.

Curch, a woman's cap.

Curpel, crupper.

Cutty, slut, a worthless woman.

Cutty-stool, stool of repentance for fornication.

Daffin', daffing, foolery.

Daft, silly, crack-brained.

Daidling, lazy, careless, worthless.

Daikering, toiling, searching.

Darg, a day's work.

Deave, deafen.

Deevil's buckie, an imp of Satan.

Deuk, a duck.

Ding, strike, beat.

Dinna, do not.

Dinnle, a shivering or tingling blow.

Dirl, a tingling or thrilling stroke.

Dispone, make over.

Dits, closes up.

Dittay, indictment.

Divot-cast, so much as a sod.

Doch an' dorroch, a parting cup.

Doited, stupid.

Donnard, grossly stupid.

Dookit, ducked.

Dooms, very, absolutely.

Door-cheek, side of the door.

Douce, sedate, quiet, modest.

Dought, was able.

Doun, down.

Dour, obstinate.

Downa, do not.

Driegh, slow, tiresome.

Droughty, thirsty.

Drow, fit.

Dry multure, astricted mill-dues paid to one mill for grain ground at another.

Dud, rag.

Duddie bairns, ragged children.

Duds, garments, clothes.

Dyster, dyer.

Een, eyes.

Eik, addition.

Elshin, awl.

Eme, uncle.

Eneuch, eneugh, enough.

Fair, in perfect health.

Fallal duds, gawdy clothes.

Family exercise, family worship.

Fash, fasherie, trouble.

Fashious, troublesome.

Fat-ta-deil, what the devil!

Fause, false.

Faut, fault.

Feckless, feeble.

Fee, wages.

Fend, makeshift.

Fickle, difficult, puzzling.

Files, defiles.

Fleg, a fright.

Fliskmahoys, giddy girls.

Flow-mosses, morasses.

Foranent, directly opposite to.

Forbears, ancestors.

Forby, besides.

Fore-bar, counsel's seat in court.

Forgather, to come together, to become intimate.

Fou, full, drunk.

Found, a kind of fire-arms.

Frae, from.

Fu', full.

Fuff, puff, whiff.

Fule, a fool.

Fustle, whistle.

Fyme, dance a lively measure.

Gade, went.

Gaitts, brats.

Gane, gone.

Gang, go.

Ganting, yawning.

Gar, make, force.

Gardyloo (Fr. garde de l'eau), a cry made when slops were thrown out of a window.

Gate, way, direction, manner.

Gauger, an exciseman.

Gaun, going.

Gaunt, gant, yawn.

Gawsie, plump, jolly.

Gear, property.

Gee, rue.

Gentles, gentlefolk.

Gey sure, pretty sure.

Gie, to give.

Giff-gaff, give and take.

Gillie, Highland manservant.

Gilpies, frolicsome young persons.

Gin, if, suppose.

Girdles, iron plates for firing cakes on.

Girn, to be crabbed or peevish.

Glaiks, deception, delusion.

Glede, a hawk.

Gleg as a gled, hungry as a hawk.

Gliff, a moment, a glimpse.

Gliff-syne, a minute ago.

Glowering, staring.

Got a sair back-cast, met with a sore disaster.

Gousty, desolate.

Goutte, drop.

Gowan, a daisy.

Gowd, gold.

Gowpen, as much as can be contained in both hands held together with the palms upward, and contracted in a circular form.

Graith, harness, horse-furniture.

Grat, wept, cried.

Gree, to agree; pre-eminence, fame.

Greeshoch, peat-fire piled on the hearth.

Greet, weep, cry.

Grewsome, ugly, horrible.

Grips, custody.

Gudeman, the husband, the head of the house.

Gudewife, a familiar term applied to a wife as head of the household.

Guide, save, preserve.

Gully, large knife.

Guse, a goose.

Gutter-bloods, of mean birth.

Gybe, pass.

Gyte, mad, crazy.

Hadden, holden.

Hae, have.

Haena, have not.

Haffet, haffit, side of the head.

Hafflins, half grown.

Haft, dwelling-place.

Hafted, rooted, fixed.

Haill, hale, whole.

Hallan, partition between the door of a cottage and the fire-place.

Hame, home.

Hand-waled, carefully selected.

Hapnyworth, a halfpenny-worth.

Harle, drag.

Har'st, harvest.

Haud, hold.

Havings, behaviour, manners.

Hawkit, white-faced.

Heal, health.

Hellicat, a wicked creature.

Hempie, rogue.

Herse, hoarse.

Hership, plunder.

Het, hot.

Hinny, a term of affection = honey or darling.

Hirple, walk lamely.

Hog, a young unshorn sheep.

Horse-graith, harness.

Houff, a haunt, to resort to a haunt.

How, valley.

How or *howe*, a hollow.

Howdie, midwife.

Howffs, places of resort, haunts.

Hund, a hound.

Hussy-case, needle-case.

Ilk, *ilka*, each, every.

Ingan, onion.

Ingane, ingenuity.

Ingleside, fireside.

Input, contribution.

Instruct, to show evidence for.

Intill, into.

I'se, I shall.

Ither, other.

Jagg, prick.

Jark, seal.

Jaud, jade.

Jink, to dodge, a quick elusory turn.

Jo, Joe, sweetheart.

Jorram, boat-song.

Jowing, the swinging of a large bell.

Kail, broth made of greens, especially of ideworts.

Kail-blade, colewort leaf.

Kail-worm, caterpillar.

Kain, duty paid by a tenant to his landlord in eggs, fowls, etc.

Kamed, combed.

Ken, know.

Kensna, knows not.

Kenspeckle, recognized, noticeable.

Kepp the stile, bar the way, stop the passage.

Killing-time, the time of persecution.

Kintra, the country.

Kirk, church.

Kirkit, led to church.

Kittle, ticklish, uncertain.

Knaveship, mill-dues paid to servants.

Knowehead, the top of a knoll.

Kye, cattle.

Kylevine pen, black lead pencil.

Kythes, seems, appears, shows.

Laigh, low.

Laiking, idling.

Laird, squire.

Lamour, amber.

Landward bred, country bred.

Lane, lone, alone. In Scots frequently conjoined with the pronoun as 'his lane,' by himself.

Langsyne, long ago, long since.

Lawing, *lawin*, tavern reckoning.

Lay, law.

Leal, true.

Learn, to teach.

Lee, a lie.

Leech, physician.

Lese-majesty, treason.

Lift, the sky.

Lilting, singing cheerfully, carolling.

Limmers, loose women.

Lippen, trust.

Lock, handful, small quantity.

Lockman, hangman.

Loof, palm of the hand.

Loon, rascal.

Loose the pleugh, unyoke the plough.

Lounder, to thump.

Loundering, thrashing.

Low, a flame.

Luckie-dad, grandfather.

Lug, an ear.

Lum, chimney.

Lum-head, chimney-pot.

Lunnon, London.

Magg, steal, cheat over.
Maggot, whim, fancy.
Mail, mailing, payable rent.
Mailed, stained.
Mair, more.
Maist, most.
Maistry, authority.
Manse, a Scots parsonage.
Manty, mantle.
Marched, adjoined.
Mashackered, lacerated.
Maukin, mawkin, a hare.
Maun, must.
Maunna, must not.
Maw, to mow.
Meal-ark, meal-chest.
Mells, intermeddles.
Mensfu', mannerly, modest.
Merk, a Scottish coin, value 13s. 4d.
Midden, a heap of ashes, a dunghill.
Midges, gnats.
Mind, to remember.
Minny, mother.
Misca', to miscall, to malign.
Misguggled, mishguggled, mangled, disfigured.
Miss Katies, mosquitoes.
Mister, need, necessity.
Mixen, dunghill.
Mony, many.
Morn, the, to-morrow.
Muckle, much, great.
Muir-ill, cattle plague.
Muir-poots, young grouse.
Mull, a snuff-box.
Mutch, a woman's cap.
Mutchkin, an English pint.

Na, nae, no, not.
Nae-say, contrary.
Naig, a nag.
Natheless, nevertheless.
Neger, negro.
Nevoy, nephew.
Nick Moll Blood, cheat the gallows.
Niffer, exchange, barter.

Noited, struck.
Noop, the point of the elbow.
Nowte, black cattle.

Oe, grandchild.
Onding, a heavy fall of rain or snow.
Oner-by, over the way.
Or, before.
Out-by, without.
Outgate, a way for egress.
Ower, over.
Owerby, over the way.
Owerlay, cravat.
Owsen, oxen.

Pad, king's highway.
Paiks, strokes.
Panel, prisoner at the bar.
Parochine, parish.
Parritch, porridge.
Passemented, adorned.
Passments, external ornamentation.
Pawky, cunning, sly.
Pea-gun, pop-gun.
Peat, pet, favourite.
Peat-haggs, sloughs whence peat has been dug.
Peeble, pelt.
Penny-stane cast, the distance to which a stone quoit can be thrown.
Philabeg, Highland kilt.
Pibroch, Highland war-song adapted to the bagpipes.
Pickle in thine ain Pokenook, supply yourself from your own means.
Pigg, earthen vessel.
Pike, to pick.
Pioted, piebald.
Piqueerings, disputes.
Pirn, reel.
Pismires, ants.
Pit, to put.
Plack, a copper coin, value the third part of an English penny.

Plaid-nuik, corner of the plaid forming a bag or pocket.

Planked a chury, concealed a knife.

Plea-houses, law courts.

Plenishing, household furniture.

Pock, bag.

Poco-curante, one having no care or interest.

Poindings, distrainings.

Policies, the grounds about a gentleman's seat.

Polonie, dress for a child.

Polrumptious, undisciplined.

Poorfu', powerful.

Pouch, a pocket.

Pow, head.

Powny, a pony.

Prestation, payment of money

Prigg, beg, plead.

Propine, a gift, a present.

Pu'pit, a pulpit.

Puir, poor.

Pykit, picked.

Quean, wench, young woman.

Queer the stifler, avoid the gallows.

Quey, heifer.

Quo', quoth.

Rannell-tress, beams across the chimney.

Rap, to swear falsely.

Rapparees, wild Irish plunderers.

Rat-rhyme, poetry repeated by rota.

Raxing, stretching.

Redarged, set aside, disqualified.

Redd, advise.

Redding, clearing up.

Reek, smoke.

Richt, right.

Rin-there-out, vagrant.

Ripe, to search.

Rive, tear.

Rokelay, woman's short cloak.

Rouping, selling by auction.

Roupit, hoarse, cracked.

Ruffler or padder, ruffian or highwayman.

Sackless, innocent.

Sae, so.

Sain, bless.

St Nicholas's clerks, highwaymen.

Sair, sore.

Sall, shall.

Sark, shirt.

Sauld, sold.

Saunt, a saint.

Saut, salt.

Scart, scratch.

Scathe, skaith, harm.

Scauding, scalding.

Schule, a school.

Scomfished, suffocated.

Scouping, scampering.

Scour, to put forward.

Scraughin', shrieking.

Screed, a long tirade.

Seiled, strained.

Seiping, oozing, soaking.

Sell o' ye, yourself.

Shankit, handled.

Shears, divides.

Shed, to protect, to divide, to separate.

Shoon, shoes.

Shouther, shoulder.

Sic, such.

Siller, money.

Silly, tender, weak.

Skaith, see *Scathe*.

Skaithless, uninjured.

Skeel o' the gate, knowledge of the road.

Skeely, skilful.

Skelping, a thrashing with the open hand on the bottom.

Skirling, screaming.

Shrimp, to stint, to save.

Skulduddery, obscenity.

Slake o' paint, splotch of paint.

Glossary 559

Smacked calf-skin, kissed the book.
Sma' wad, small bet.
Snappers, misfortunes.
Snaw, snow.
Snog and snod, snug and neat.
Snotter and snivel, blubber and snuffle.
Sodger, a soldier.
Somegate, somehow, somewhere.
Sonsy, plump, good-humoured, thriving.
Soothfast, honest.
Sorted, arranged, accommodated.
Soup, sup.
Southered, soldered.
Sowens, flummery made from the dust of oatmeal.
Spaeing, foretelling.
Speering, asking.
Spieling, climbing.
Spleuchan, tobacco-pouch.
Sporran, the leather pouch, or large purse, worn by the Highlanders in front of their kilt.
Spring, a quick, merry tune.
Spune, a spoon.
Spunk, a fire, a match; spirit, courage.
Staig, a young horse not broken in.
Stanchells, iron bars for securing windows.
Stang, sting.
Sted, hemmed.
Sterns, stars.
Stinted, paused.
Stirk, a young steer or heifer.
Stoiting, staggering.
Stow, to cut off, to lop.
Straughted, stretched.
Stude, stood.
Sture and dure, stern and impenetrable.

Suld, should.
Sune, soon.
Swither, doubt, hesitation.
Synd, rinse.
Syne as sune, late as well as early.

Tae, the one.
Tailzie, deed of entail.
Tait, a small portion.
Tap, belongings.
Tap in my lap, take up my baggage.
Taupie, tawpie, a slovenly foolish woman.
Teind, tithe.
Tender, delicate.
Tent, care, heed.
Thae, these, those.
Tholed, suffered, borne patiently.
Thrang, throng.
Thrawart, froward, perverse, cross-grained.
Thrawn, perverse.
Threshie-coat, courting-dress.
Thumkins, thumbscrews.
Tint, lost.
Tither, tother, the other.
Tittie, a little pet, a sister.
Tocher, dowry.
Tod, fox.
Tolbooth, jail.
Toom, empty.
Touk, a beat (as of a drum).
Tout, sound (of a horn).
Tow, rope, wool.
Towmont, twelvemonth.
Toy, head-dress hanging down on the shoulders.
Traiking, wandering idly.
Treviss, cross-bar.
Trews, trousers.
Trinquet, equivocate.
Trow, believe, consider.
Truss, hang.
Tuilzies, squabbles.
Twal, twelve.
Tyne, lose.

Umquhile, late, deceased.
Unchancy, dangerous.
Unco, very, unusual, particularly.
Upgang, ascent, the act of ascending.
Uphaud, uphold.
Usquebaugh, whisky.

Victual, grain of any kind.

Wa', wall.
Wad, bet, wager; would.
Wadset, a mortgage.
Wae, sad.
Waesome, woeful.
Waff, a blast.
Wales, selected.
Wallydraigle, a feeble ill-grown creature.
Wampishing, frantically tossing.
Wanter, a bachelor, a widower, one wanting a wife.
Ware, spend.
Warna, were not.
Warsle, *warstle*, to struggle with difficulty.
Warst, worst.
Wastrife, waste.
Wauff, a wave.
Wauken, awaken.
Waup in the rape, flaw in the rope.
Waur, worse.
Wean, child.
Weasand, the windpipe.
Weel, well.
Weel-faurd, well favoured, good-looking.
Weet, wet.

Weird, destiny.
Wha, who.
Whang, to cut, to slice, also leather.
What for, why.
Wheat-close, a courtyard beside a farmhouse.
Wheen, few.
Whiggery, Whig principles.
Whiles, sometimes.
Whilk, which.
Whillywhaing, cajoling.
Whin, furze, gorse.
Whisterpoop, blow.
Whorn, horn.
Wi', with.
Wight, strong, mighty.
Willyard, wild, shy, wilful.
Wimple, a winding, or turn, in the road.
Win, to get.
Wizzent, *wuzzent*, withered.
Woodie, the gallows, gallows-rope.
Worriecow, *worrycow*, a bugbear, a scarecrow, a ghost or goblin.
Wot, to know.
Wud, mad.
Wull-cat, wild cat.
Wunna, will not.
Wussed, wished.
Wyte, blame.

Yard, vegetable garden.
Yearned, curdled.
Yerked, bound tightly.
Yerl, earl.
Yestreen, last night.
Yill, ale.
Yill-caup, ale-cup.
Yont, beyond, away from.

QUESTIONS AND EXERCISES

SERIAL QUESTIONS

(Unless chapters are indicated in parentheses, the number of the chapter on which the question is based corresponds to the number of the question.)

1. To what extent is Scott's introductory chapter (*a*) jocose, (*b*) necessary?

2. Give fully the reasons for the imprisonment of Wilson and Robertson, and show why the latter was able to escape.

3. Describe the incidents which led to the passing of the sentence of death on Captain Porteous.

4. What was the principal reason for the resentment of the mob which had gathered to see the hanging of Captain Porteous?

5. Summarise the respective characteristics of Mr. and Mrs. Saddletree.

6. Describe how the mob executed vengeance on Captain Porteous, and in what way Mr. Butler was involved. (VI, VII.)

7. What do you learn of the old Laird of Dumbiedikes? (VIII.)

8. What humour does Scott infuse into his account of the Laird's last moments?

9. Give an account of the early life of Reuben Butler and his friendship with Jeanie Deans.

10. What do you learn of the antecedents and character of David Deans? (IX, X.)

11. Narrate briefly the story of Effie Deans up to the point where the novel opens. (X.)

12. How were the several offers of help from Mr. Saddletree, Reuben, and the Laird of Dumbiedikes received by David Deans?

13. What was Reuben's special mission to Jeanie, and what was the result? (XI, XII.)

14. For what reasons was Jeanie afraid of attending the rendezvous at Muschat's Cairn? (XIV, XV.)

15. Describe what occurred at the meeting.

16. Show what reason there was in Madge Wildfire's madness. (XVI, XVII.)

17. Discuss whether there is anything worthy of admiration in the character of Ratcliffe. (XVI, XVII.)

18. Explain clearly the tragic conflict in David Deans's mind, and how it was resolved.

19. What did the defence of Effie mainly depend on, and how did Jeanie fail at the crisis? (XXII, XXIII.)

20. What light is thrown during the trial on (a) David Deans, (b) Jeanie? (XXII, XXIII.)

21. Why were the Porteous riots likely to have unfortunate consequences for Effie? (XXIV.)

22. How did they, on the contrary, afford hope to Jeanie? (XXV.)

23. What preparations were made for her visit to London? (XXV, XXVI.)

24. Describe Jeanie's visit to Dumbiedikes. What were the unfortunate results, on this occasion, of her habit of telling the truth? (XXVI.)

25. What are your impressions of the Laird? (XXVI.)

26. Describe Jeanie's visit to Butler. (XXVII.)

27. Describe the events which led to the second meeting of Jeanie and Madge Wildfire. (XXIX.)

28. What were the motives for holding Jeanie captive? (XXX.)

29. What were the causes of Madge Wildfire's insanity? (XXX.)

30. Describe Jeanie's visit to the church in Madge's company. (XXXI.)

31. Describe how Jeanie met Robertson the second time. (XXXIII.)

32. Give an account of George Staunton's life up to the time of his escape from the Tolbooth Church. (XXXIII, XXXIV.)

33. Describe briefly the course of his life after that escape.

34. What features of Jeanie's character are disclosed in her parting conversation with Mr. Staunton?

35. Describe Jeanie's interview with the Duke of Argyle. What grounds of hope had he for thinking he might be able to help?

36. Why was Queen Caroline anxious to retain the Duke's support, and why was she angry at his request? (XXXVII.)

37. How did Jeanie succeed in making a deep impression on the Queen?

38. What are your impressions of Mrs. Glass?

39. What courtesy and generosity did the Duke show towards Jeanie?

40. Describe the last hours of Madge Wildfire.

41. Show how Mrs. Dutton contributes to the humour of the novel.

42. Describe briefly the changed circumstances of the Deans family.

43. What arguments made David Deans more favourably disposed towards Reuben?

44. Describe the humours of the Captain of Knock-dunder. (XLIV, XLV.)

45. Describe how Jeanie met Effie and George Staunton. (XLVI.)

46. Contrast the life of Jeanie in Roseneath and that of Effie in London. (XLVII, XLVIII.)

47. How did Reuben acquire sufficient money to buy Craigsture? (XLIX.)

48. How did Meg Murdockson's confession come into Jeanie's hands? (L.)

49. Describe the plight of Lady Staunton while out with David, and how they were rescued. (L.)

50. Describe the manner in which Sir George Staunton met his death. (LI, LII.)

CONTEXTS

Briefly relate the following passages to the main episodes of the story. Wherever possible, give the speaker and the principal persons present, and explain all allusions and difficulties.

The pages from which they are taken are indicated in parentheses.

1. The edicts of each succeeding set of magistrates have, like those of Goneril and Regan, diminished this venerable band . . . (38.)

2. "I'll ne'er believe Scotland is Scotland ony mair, if our kindly Scots sit doun with the affront they hae gien us this day." (52.)

3. " . . . —how wad ye like when it comes to be your ain chance, as I winna ensure ye, if ye dinna mend your manners?" (59.)

4. "Better tyne life, since tint is gude fame." (75.)

5. "What have I been paying stipend and teind parsonage and vicarage for, ever sin' the aughty-nine, an I canna get a spell of a prayer for't, the only time I ever asked for ane in my life?" (93.)

6. "And ne'er was there mair need of poorfu' preachers than e'en now in these cauld Gallio days, when men's hearts are hardened like the nether millstone . . ." (98.)

7. . . . it seems to have occurred to him, that he was not pinned down to circulate on a pivot, like the hands of the watch . . . (108.)

8. The stunning weight of a blow so totally unexpected bore down the old man, who had in his early youth resisted the brow of military and civil tyranny, though backed with swords and guns, tortures and gibbets. (120.)

9. It was what the French call *l'embarras des richesses*, the confusion arising from too much mental wealth. (132.)

10. So, like Christiana in the Pilgrim's Progress, when traversing with a timid yet resolved step the terrors of the

Valley of the Shadow of Death, she glided on by rock and stone, "now in glimmer and now in gloom," . . . (167).

11. "And this mad quean, after cracking like a pea-gun, and skirling like a pea-hen for the haill night, behoves just to hae hadden her tongue when her clavers might have done some gude!" (193.)

12. . . . as the witches of Macbeth used, in less refined days, to seem to fly upwards from the stage. (205.)

13. A Roman would have devoted his daughter to death from different feelings and motives, but not upon a more heroic principle of duty. (215.)

14. "Ichabod! my glory is departed!" (236.)

15. "My Lords, if it is your pleasure to gang on wi' this matter, the weariest day will hae its end at last." (253.)

16. "But I wish you to show it, if you have ony fasherie wi' ony o' St. Nicholas's clerks." (268.)

17. ". . . but he's as wilfu' as yoursell and he's ower weel used to a gate that maybe he and I hae gaen ower aften, and he'll gang nae road else." (281.)

18. ". . . I carena an thou couldst carry Gunnerby away with thee in thy lap, for it's a murder to post-horses." (303.)

19. ". . . for I have been burning bricks in Egypt, and walking through the weary wilderness of Sinai, for lang and mony a day." (322.)

20. "It would have been in vain for Naaman the Syrian leper to have bathed in Pharphar and Abana, rivers of Damascus, when it was only the waters of Jordan that were sanctified for the cure." (364.)

21. "A list of Praise-God Barebone's Parliament, I think, or of old Noll's evangelical army—that last fellow should understand his wheelings to judge by his name.—But what does all this mean . . .?" (376.)

22. . . . there goes another shot—and she has hit with both barrels right and left! (395.)

23. "To show you the contrary," said the Duke, "I will

fill my box out of this canister without paying you a bawbee." (411.)

24. "I thought your father would have had more sense," said the Duke . . . (416.)

25. ". . . it is a beautiful thing to have learned to write and read, for one can always say such fine words whatever should befall them." (433.)

26. . . . but judging he had to do with a Gallio, as he said, did not think it worth while to give battle. (458.)

27. "Hush, hush," said Effie, clapping one hand on her mouth, and pointing to the thicket with the other, "he is yonder." (474.)

28. . . . not to forget the little one that had strayed from the fold, and even then might be in the hands of the ravening wolf. (494.)

29. "I thought the ordinary Scottish contraction of the name had been Effie." (504.)

30. ". . . but it was my misfortune at one time to see it prove greatly too weak." (519.)

GENERAL QUESTIONS

1. "Jeanie, without youth, beauty, genius, warm passions, or any other novel-perfection, is here our object from beginning to end" (Lady Louisa Stuart). What are Jeanie's limitations, and why is she an attractive heroine from beginning to end?

2. Compare the characters and roles of Madge Wildfire and Ophelia.

3. As one of the True Blue Presbyterians, David Deans is not overdrawn. In what respect does he appear extreme to-day?

4. What incidents of importance happened at the Grassmarket, Muschat's Cairn, Harabee Brow, the Grindstone?

5. What part was played in the story by: Margaret Murdockson, Mr. Fairbrother, Mrs. Balchristie, Mrs. Bickerton, Mrs. Glass, Mrs. Dutton?

6. Outline the part played by (*a*) Ratcliffe, (*b*) the Captain of Knockdunder.

7. Distinguish between the humour afforded by the first Laird of Dumbiedikes, the younger Laird, Saddletree, Mrs. Glass, Mrs. Dutton, and the Captain of Knockdunder.

8. Lady Louisa Stuart thought English readers would not be entertained by Mr. Saddletree. Give your views, and support them with illustrative detail.

9. How and where does Scott (influenced, no doubt, by the novels of Mrs. Radcliffe) succeed in evoking a sense of terror and the supernatural?

10. Show Scott's skill in handling crowd scenes.

11. How much melodrama do you think there is in *The Heart of Midlothian*?

12. Describe two occasions which illustrate the mingling of humour and deep pathos.

13. Scott's wit is frequently heavy or flat. Collect examples to support this view.

14. "Like the digressive poet Ariosto . . ." Read the opening paragraph of Chapter XVI, and show whether it is true of *The Heart of Midlothian*. Give reasons for the view that Scott would have benefited from the writing of a few plays.

15. To what extent is history inextricably mingled with fiction in this novel?

16. "He combines the substance of the realist with the fantasy of the romantic. He had a foot in both worlds and made the best of both of them" (Lord David Cecil). How far is this true of *The Heart of Midlothian*?

17. Show as fully as possible Scott's relentlessness in the pursuit and punishment of the guilty. (In this respect, Scott seems to have inherited some of the traits of the Covenanters.)

18. How much of the story was written "to point a moral"? (See note for the reader on page 540.)

19. ". . . it is a lame, huddled conclusion" (Lady Louisa Stuart). "The final catastrophe is needlessly improbable and startling" (*The Edinburgh Review*). "He is indeed an expert in anticlimax" (Lord David Cecil). Discuss these views.

20. Despite its defects, *The Heart of Midlothian* has been claimed as one of the world's greatest novels. Enumerate the main defects, and consider what claims this novel has to greatness and sublimity.